World Religions

ALL-IN-ONE

by Christopher Kimball Bigelow; David Blatner; Stephan Bodian; Rev. Fr. Kenneth Brighenti, PhD, KGCO; Gudrun Bühnemann; Warren Malcolm Clark; Rabbi Ted Falcon, PhD; Rabbi Marc Gellman; Monsignor Thomas Hartman; Jonathan R. Herman; Jonathan Landaw; William Paul Lazarus; Jana Riess, PhD; Dr. Amrutur Venkatachar Srinivasan; Annie Sullivan; Mark Sullivan; Rev. Fr. John Trigilio, Jr., PhD, ThD, KGCO; and Richard Wagner

World Religions All-in-One For Dummies®

Published by: **John Wiley & Sons, Inc.**, 111 River Street, Hoboken, NJ 07030-5774, www.wiley.com

Published simultaneously in Canada

For general information on our other products and services, please contact our Customer Care Department within the U.S. at 877-762-2974, outside the U.S. at 317-572-3993, or fax 317-572-4002. For technical support, please visit https://hub.wiley.com/community/support/dummies.

Wiley publishes in a variety of print and electronic formats and by print-on-demand. Some material included with standard print versions of this book may not be included in e-books or in print-on-demand. If this book refers to media that is not included in the version you purchased, you may download this material at http://booksupport.wiley.com. For more information about Wiley products, visit www.wiley.com.

Library of Congress Control Number: 2024951148

ISBN 978-1-394-29394-0 (pbk); ISBN 978-1-394-29396-4 (ebk); ISBN 978-1-394-29395-7 (ebk)

SKY10093232_120724

Contents at a Glance

Table of Contents

Introduction

Most people have had some contact with religion. Many of us have grown up as Christians, Jews, Muslims, Hindus, Buddhists, or something else entirely. Our parents or grandparents raised us up in some religion or another. The holidays of some religion were probably our holidays; the beliefs, our beliefs; the foods, our foods. All that raising up makes it easy for us to understand religion because we already know a lot about it from our own lives. Others of us have no religion at all but have run into it, in some form or another, most of our lives.

What makes religion familiar also makes it strange. Many of us grew up doing religious things without really understanding what we were doing. Many of us grew up understanding our own religion but were clueless about the religions of our neighbors. Some of us grew up without any religion and kind of feel left out and maybe even skeptical of the whole religion thing.

Whether you're a believer or not (or want to be or not), religion affects your life. Your religion, your neighbor's religion, the religions within your culture, the religions in other cultures that interact with your culture — they all play an important role in how people view the world, their place in it, and how they interact collectively and individually with other people. *World Religions All-in-One For Dummies* can help you understand what you've been doing all your life and what folks in other religions have been doing all of theirs. It will answer questions about how different religions worship, what they believe, and the rituals they perform.

About This Book

This book covers a lot of stuff about seven different major religions, but you don't need religious training to read it. In fact, you don't need to know anything about religion at all. This book gives you easy-to-understand information about various religions of the world and makes that information easy to find.

Each chapter is divided into sections, and each section contains information that helps you understand some part of religion, including topics such as:

- The basic beliefs of different religions.
- The ideas and values that many religions share.
- The ways that people express their faith.

You also get all sorts of interesting tidbits about the cultures that religions come from, and to make the content more accessible, we've divided it into seven parts, each exploring a single religion. We chose to highlight the seven religions included in this book because they each have a vast following and represent both Eastern and Western religions. (Eastern religions include Hinduism, Taoism, and Buddhism; Western religions include Judaism, Christianity, Islam, and Mormonism.) We've also included a Prelude chapter, examining what religion, faith, spirituality, divinity, salvation, and other religious concepts mean in general terms.

We've done our best to refer to each Divine Being/God/god(s) with the words and pronouns the given religion prefers — and with the capitalization they prefer. The same goes for what we call each religion and how we cite holy texts.

If you see the word *church* with a small letter *c*, it refers to a church building or parish, but *Church* with a capital *C* refers to the broader body of believers of the religion in question.

For dates, we've stuck to a consistent timeline, using BCE and CE in place of BC and AD, even though certain faiths favor the use of BC and AD.

When it comes to translations, nothing is harder than taking an ancient text and trying to convert it into modern English. With ancient documents, particularly those seen as holy, some people even object to the concept of translating. Nevertheless, we relied on the best translations we could find. Other writers may translate the words in a different way, but the gist is the same.

Finally, to help you understand new words and concepts relevant to the religions we discuss, we *italicize* all definitions of new words and important terms. We also use italics for unfamiliar words from languages other than English. And finally, we add shaded boxes of text (called sidebars) to dive deeper into specific subjects relating to a chapter's theme.

Foolish Assumptions

In writing this book, we made some assumptions about you:

- You want to know more about religion, whether you're a member of a religion or not.
- You're curious about religion the way you're curious about how penguins live. You're mildly interested, but it's not a really big thing in your life. On the other hand, you may want to understand your own religion better.
- You know someone who grew up in a religion different from yours and you want to know more about it.
- You may want to find a religion to belong to, and you're not sure which one is right for you or how to get hooked up.
- You have a passing knowledge of some religions. But don't worry, the book will make sense to you even if you don't.

Icons Used in This Book

To help you find information you're interested in or to highlight information that's particularly helpful, we've used the following icons throughout the text:

You find this icon next to important information that you'll want to remember. It highlights the key takeaways within each chapter.

This icon appears next to information that you may find interesting but can skip without impairing your understanding of the topic, such as when we explore the reasoning behind a religious practice or discuss a topic that's good to know about but not essential.

This icon highlights suggestions or comparisons included to help you understand the current topic or an idea that may be unfamiliar to you. Often we use it to share practical advice when exploring religion.

This icon gives you a heads-up about places where the subject could start to get more complicated or controversial. We also use it to share wisdom that helps you avoid causing unintended offense.

Beyond the Book

In addition to the abundance of information and guidance related to religions provided in this book, you get access to even more help and information online at `Dummies.com`. Check out this book's online Cheat Sheet. Just go to `www.dummies.com` and search for "World Religions All-in-One For Dummies Cheat Sheet."

Where to Go from Here

World Religions All-in-One For Dummies is like a spiritual buffet. You can sample faiths from all over the world. Just jump in where you want, read as much (or as little) as you want, and jump back out. This book is designed so that you can use it as a reference, flipping here and there willy-nilly. Of course, if you prefer, you can start at the beginning and read through to the end. We can't promise you much of a plot, but we can promise you a lot of good information.

Just decide what you want to know and head to that place using the Table of Contents and Index as your guide. If you're not sure where to begin — or want a general overview before you delve into specific topics — why not start at the beginning? It's as good a place as any. Thumb your way straight to the Prelude.

IN THIS CHAPTER

- **Looking at a broad definition of religion**
- **Discovering the power and purpose of ritual**
- **Recognizing the universality of religious ethics**
- **Understanding the attraction religion has for so many people**
- **Knowing how religion differs from philosophy and spirituality**
- **Looking at how people of faith prove the existence of God**
- **Divining the nature of God, gods, and goddesses**
- **Searching for answers and maintaining faith**

Prelude

In the Beginning: Religion Basics

If you travel to some remote part of Earth and find a group of people who had never met anyone outside their tribe, you'd discover that these people have some type of food, shelter, and language. The group would also have some kind of religion, which is one of the basic parts of human life.

This chapter helps you understand what defines a religion; what the main components of a religion are; and how religion differs from other approaches to life — such as spirituality and philosophy — that, on the face of it, sound an awful lot like religion. Understanding religion helps you understand what it means to be human.

Defining Religion

You can say that religion is a belief, except not all beliefs are religions. (Your Aunt Martha may believe that her potato salad is the best in the world.) You can narrow that definition and say religion is a belief in God. Well, that definition covers *monotheistic religions* (those that believe in one god), but it doesn't cover the religions that believe in many gods *(polytheistic religions)* or religions that believe in a chief god and other, lesser, gods and goddesses *(henotheistic religions)*. You could say that religion is a way of behaving — being decent to others and caring for your environment; but not all decent, responsible people are religious. You could say that religion is the belief in the *truth*. But what's the truth? Different religions have different understandings of what is "true."

Basically, the definition of religion includes all of these definitions (expect for the potato salad, maybe): A religion is a belief in divine (superhuman or spiritual) being(s) and the practices (rituals) and moral code (ethics) that result from that belief. Beliefs give religion its mind, rituals give religion its shape, and ethics give religion its heart.

REMEMBER

Every religion has a *belief system*. *Beliefs* are the ideas that make any religion what it is. Of the three elements that make something a religion (beliefs, rituals, and ethics), beliefs are the most important because they give rise to and shape the ethics and the rituals of a faith. Each religion teaches or expounds its own truths about the world and humanity and God (or gods) as those truths are seen by that particular faith. These beliefs also explain how a religion's followers achieve salvation or enlightenment and why these are important goals for their spiritual journeys. From these fundamental beliefs flow the beliefs that establish authority and explain how the leaders of organized religions rightfully exercise the power of that authority.

Through these belief systems, religions teach their truths about life and death, suffering and hope, and whatever comes after death. These beliefs give meaning to the lives of the religion's followers and sustain hope in the face of suffering and loss.

REMEMBER

A religion's *theology* (its religious teachings, or *doctrine*) and its stories connect the beliefs. A religion's theology is its handbook of beliefs (although many theologies are not even written down). Theology is important because it puts a religion's beliefs in an order that people can understand. Some religions, such as Christianity (see Book 5) and Islam (see Book 6), have a long tradition of theologies that are complex and sophisticated. Other religions — such as Judaism (see Book 4) and Hinduism (see Book 1) — use stories, not systematic theologies, to convey their beliefs. For this reason, pinning down the essential beliefs of Judaism or Hinduism is much more difficult. Yet, other religions, such as Buddhism (see Book 3), combine both.

Whether or not religions use theology or storytelling as the main way to teach, their beliefs depend on the following:

- **Their history:** Both Judaism and Hinduism are very ancient and developed before contact with the Greeks, who first organized beliefs into a system. In the ancient faiths, stories convey beliefs, and the impulse to yank the beliefs out of the stories and put them down in some systematic order would have been an insult to the sacred texts.
- **How they define membership:** *Tribal religions* define members of the faith not by belief but by blood. Many Native American religions are like Judaism in this respect. You have to be born into the tribe or culture in order to share the faith of the tribe. If you're born into a tribal religion, what you believe doesn't matter very much; you're a member whether you like it or not and whether you believe in the religion or not.

  In contrast, *belief-oriented (open) religions,* like Islam and Christianity, seek converts. These religions need to have clear and easily identifiable theologies because people need to understand the religion's beliefs in order to join up. A good example is the *shahada,* the Islamic profession of faith: "There is no god but God, and Muhammad is his prophet" (which can also be said other ways, like "I bear witness that there is no God but Allah, and I bear witness that Muhammad is his messenger.") This simple and powerful statement of belief is all you have to say to enter Islam and become a Muslim.

Acting It Out: Religion and Rituals

Rituals are important to religions because they provide a tangible way for believers to experience their faith. Beliefs are the province of your mind, but rituals get the rest of your body into the act. Through rituals, religions take physical form. These practices give texture and taste, form and function to a religion.

REMEMBER

Religious rituals

- Establish the sacred calendar and its holy days.
- Set the ways followers celebrate the passages in life.
- Focus the mind in a spiritually disciplined way.

Religious rituals are also often limited to the people who make up a particular religion. In fact, many religions specifically forbid those of other faiths from practicing their traditional rituals:

- When Judaism instructs Jews to light candles on Friday night, it's a ritual meant especially for Jews.
- When some Christian groups, such as Roman Catholics and Greek Orthodox, offer Holy Communion (also known as the Lord's Supper or the Eucharist), only their members can receive it.
- The Muslim pilgrimage to Mecca, the *Hajj*, is only for Muslims. Non-Muslims are not even allowed to visit Mecca.

Happy holidays to you

Holidays are basic religious rituals and one of the main ways that religions define themselves. Whether these days are called festivals, holidays, holy days, or something else, religions celebrate or note a particular event that's important to them and mark it in a specific way. (See the related sidebar titled, "Sacred calendars," later in this chapter.)

Following is a sampling of important religious observances:

- **Easter:** This holy day (which celebrates the resurrection of Jesus after his crucifixion) is the most important holiday for Christians; Christmas (the day celebrating Christ's birth) is another big one, but Christians have a whole slew of other holy days. Learn more in Book 5, Chapter 2.
- **Ramadan:** In addition to other dates of note, Muslims fast during the holy month of Ramadan (see Book 6, Chapter 4 for more on Ramadan) and celebrate the night that the prophet Muhammad ascended to heaven and descended into hell (a trip he made so that he could tell Muslims about the rewards and punishments that awaited moral and immoral people).
- **Passover:** An important holy day for Jewish people, Passover commemorates God's deliverance of the Israelites from Egypt. Another Jewish holiday is Hanukkah, which celebrates the rededication of the Temple of Jerusalem. Learn more in Book 4, Chapter 3.

Rites of passage

The rituals that accompany the rites of passage are another way that religions define themselves. In every religion, rituals surround the milestones of life: birth, adulthood, marriage, childbirth, and death. These rituals recognize (and even enhance) the importance of these events. As such, they serve as rites of passage that help their followers make the transition between what came before and what comes after.

REMEMBER

Rites of passage accomplish the following:

- **Connect the followers to their ancestors,** their traditions, their beliefs, and their duties and reinforce the religion's beliefs about the way life begins, progresses, and ends.
- **Help reinforce the value of the family** as a primary religious value (one of the main tasks and purposes of religion).

So important are these rituals that, many times, people who don't live particularly devout lives (that is, in strict accordance with the tenets of their faith) return to their religions to help them consecrate these special dates.

Prayers from the faithful

All religions include prayer. People pray to express thankfulness for life's blessings, to repent for sins, and to grant forgiveness to other people. They pray to clear and focus their minds. They pray so that they can achieve calmness and wisdom. They pray to express awe and wonder at the mystery of life and at the beauty of the world around them. They pray to find release from suffering. They pray while kneeling, while standing, with eyes downcast or lifted heavenward. They pray alone and they pray as a community. They pray at proscribed times and in proscribed ways, or they pray whenever the mood hits them:

- The Catholic Mass (see Book 5, Chapter 4) is a prayer service that includes the most important Christian ritual, the Eucharist, and defines the community that prays together.
- Many Hindu and Buddhist (see Books 1 and 3, respectively) sects pray for many hours at a time. They find solace and release from stress by looking inside themselves in order to experience the great void or emptiness. This emptiness quiets them and frees them from the constraints of their own lives.
- Five times a day, Muslims (see Book 6) remember Allah and their relationship with him. The content of their prayer includes praise, gratitude, and supplication. The prayer's purpose is to keep life — and their place in it (submissive to God) — in perspective.

» Regular Jewish (see Book 4) prayer must be said three times a day (although afternoon and evening prayers are often combined), with special prayers added for the Sabbath and holidays. A formal Jewish prayer service requires a *minyan,* which is a group of ten Jewish male adults. For more liberal Jews, a minyan consists of ten Jewish adults of any gender.

Regardless of how they do it or when they do it or what they're praying for, people pray to communicate with what their religion considers sacred or holy.

Understanding prayer

Prayer is by far the most important and common form of communal ritual in the religions of the world. For some, prayer is a way of repeating the stories of tradition; for others, it's a way of thanking God for blessings and for asking for divine help in life. Others use it as a way of showing submission to the will of God. Others use it as a way of sharing in communion the mystery of God's gifts to humankind.

The communal form of prayer is necessary in some religions and optional in others. Although the structure and guidelines for prayer vary, the desired result is still the same: When someone prays, they are seeking to make contact with the holy and the sacred. In essence, prayer is a relationship for the person of faith who tries to touch on the transcendent in life while binding themselves to a community.

TECHNICAL STUFF

From the earliest times, people have been preoccupied with understanding the forces behind nature. People found the presence of something supernatural in the wind, rain, sky, and earth. These natural instincts gave way to fear and awe. In time, religionists developed prayers and rituals to respond to their gods or God in many and elementary ways. Prayer became linked to sacrifice. People sacrificed animals, possessions, and time to make their gods happy. They tried to gain the attention and the good will of the deity of supernatural powers. Some chose magic as a way of manipulating the divine favor. They created formulas and rituals that had to be adhered to in a strict sense. Some religions, on the other hand, offered not magic, but rituals that connected the prayer to the force of the supernatural. Literatures explained the stories of creation, destruction, redemption, and faith. Armed with these new stories, people began to build altars, churches, synagogues, mosques, temples, and shrines. People went to these places to give homage to the supernatural. In prayer, people sought not only to connect with the divine but also to transform the human.

REMEMBER

Congregations gather together to pray to God or gods for four reasons:

» **Adoration:** They offer praise to the Divine, surrender to the Divine, while offering a life of love and devotion in return.

- **Penance:** They ask for forgiveness of their sins and the means to overcome their faults, eliminate the evil side of their lives, and make amends to the Divine and to people for their failures.
- **Petition:** They come to ask a divine favor and for healing in times of illness, pain, tragedy, and human need. They ask for food, for a good life, for health, and for courage, amongst others.
- **Thanksgiving:** They acknowledge that the Divine is the source of blessings. They come to thank the Divine for those blessings and ask the Divine to watch over them as a special favor.

Prayers in these four contexts are sometimes vocal and sometimes nonverbal.

Acting Ethically: Religion and Ethics

If beliefs give religions their distinctive wisdom and rituals give religions their distinctive form, then ethics give religions their distinctive virtue. The ethics of a religion are both personal and communal. Some ethical teachings direct followers how to live their own lives, while other ethical teachings of a religion explain how to order society.

Ethics compose the moral code of life — the way people should live with one another and with nature. By following an ethical or moral code (we think ethics and morals refer to the same thing), any person can live a good, decent, compassionate, just, and loving life. Ethics give religion its moral force and universal message. And it all comes down to deciding on the right thing to do.

I've heard that before: Universal ethics

TIP

The beliefs and rituals of the world's religions are very different, so you may be surprised to discover that the ethics of the world's religions are almost identical. This similarity even holds for religions that haven't had much (or any) contact with the rest of the world. For example, in Talmud, a post-biblical commentary on Jewish law and legend (see Book 4), you can find the saying "sticks in a bundle are unbreakable, but sticks alone can be broken by a child." This ethical teaching about the value of community is found in exactly the same language in the Masai tribe of sub-Saharan Africa. The golden rule, "Do unto others what you would have them do unto you," appears in almost the same words in many different and geographically separated faiths. For some reason, religions that don't share a single common belief or ritual may share the same vision of human virtue.

Some theologians explain the common ethical teachings of the world's religions by a concept called *natural law*. The idea is that human life produces common ethical laws for the same reason that physical laws (like the law of gravity) are the same in any part of the universe. Natural law imagines a kind of universal law of human goodness. Somehow, the nature of human existence leads all people to derive the same ethical norms. Perhaps natural law is real; maybe it's some kind of divine revelation to all people; or maybe it's something we don't understand yet. What's important is that many of these teachings don't vary much from religion to religion. That similarity is a mystery to us, but a very wonderful mystery.

Hand in hand in hand: Ethics, beliefs, and rituals

Some folks say that because the ethics of the world's religions are similar, we should just throw out all the different beliefs and rituals and stick with the ethical teachings. A religion called Ethical Culture, founded in 1876, tries to do just that.

One reason this approach probably wouldn't work in the long run is that many religious ethics are part of religious rituals. The Passover meal in Judaism is both a ritual and an ethical commentary on the importance of freedom. The Hindu practice of meditation is part of the ethical teaching of tranquility and patience. The tea ceremony in Zen Buddhism is both ritual and a way to teach the value of hospitality. Rituals that may seem to be nothing more than tribal rites end up containing tribal ethical wisdom when you look more closely.

Another reason that separating religious ethics from religious ritual and belief wouldn't work is because ethics are taught through sacred texts and stories that are particular to a religion — even though the ethic itself is universal. Some of the Jataka legends of the Buddha, for example, teach compassion by linking this particular ethic to a related story in the Buddha's life. Although you can make the same point — be compassionate to others — without the story, you rob it of the power of narrative. The tone of a *parable* (the short religious stories found in the Old and New Testaments), for example, is deliberately intended to be mysterious and suggestive, the better to drive home the moral or spiritual truths.

Figuring Out Why People Flock to Religion

In a world of high-pressure sales and a prove-to-me-I-need-it mentality, it's normal that some people expect religion to sell itself to them with promises of money, problem-free lives, and miracle cures. But for people of faith, religion generally offers something deeper. Some of these things are tangible; most aren't.

For example, one of the main beliefs of religions is hope — the hope that tomorrow will be better than today; the hope that death is not the end of us; the hope that good will win. In essence, think of religion as offering people a way to navigate a broken world full of cruelty and disappointment.

Dealing with problems, big and small

Most religions maintain that one primary hurdle stops people from realizing their potential. By being able to overcome this hurdle, people can achieve whatever the ultimate reward in their religion is.

The hurdle is different for different religions, as is the goal:

- **In Buddhism, the biggest problem is suffering,** and Buddhism solves that problem by offering a path to enlightenment, where suffering is no more.
- **For the Abrahamic faiths, sin is the problem;** and Judaism, Christianity, and Islam offer a path to salvation from sin. The three paths to salvation are different, but the goal is the same.
- **For Hinduism, the problem is being repeatedly reincarnated.** Hinduism offers a solution to the problem of rebirth by offering a way to release, moksha, from the cycle of birth, death, and rebirth.
- **For Taoists (see Book 2), the problem is living in harmony with the universe, with nature, with the *Tao* itself.** But by being in tune with "the way" this balance can be found.

Suffering, sin, and rebirth are cosmic problems affecting all people, and the solutions that a religion offers are solutions that apply to all people.

Religion also provides answers to the big problems that confound people: What is the meaning of life? What happens after death? Why do the innocent suffer? How can we live a decent life in a crummy world? These and other questions have vexed humans from time immemorial. To the faithful, religion provides the answers to questions like these, too.

Religions don't generally promise solutions to daily personal problems. Instead, they help people deal with the problems and accept the suffering the problems cause. Many people use religious faith as a way to maintain (or tap into) courage and patience as they work their way from sorrow or hardship into a time of joy and happiness. For many, living a life of faith is a way to deal with problems, not a way to magically sweep them away.

Finding joy

Many people find joy in religion. Hindus call the ultimate happiness *moksha*, the term that refers to finally having attained perfection and being released from the constant cycle of birth-death-rebirth. Christians call this state *ecstasy*, the time when the believer, through faith, experiences an inner vision or union with God. Jews call it *simha*, the joy they feel when they experience the Torah. This joy comes from immersing oneself in the divine and, from that immersion, being able to appreciate the beauty and wonder of life in all its forms and rejoicing at being alive to share that wonder.

This type of happiness is far different from the happiness that advertisers try to convince people will come if they just buy some new thing. Religious happiness points believers to lasting joy — to the joy of family and friends, the joy of rituals, and the joys of life's passages — by challenging them to examine the happiness that comes from selfishness and replace it with selfless acts of kindness and generosity. Religious people believe that the greatest happiness comes from helping others, seeking wisdom, and doing God's works.

Being responsible

Many people find in religion a guide that leads them to do good works by challenging and goading them to do their part to fix the broken world. This guide reminds people of their duty to the poor, the widowed and orphaned, and the homeless. This source impels them to accept duty as a way of serving the Divine, even when that duty is burdensome or exhausting.

In Islam, the link between a devout life and one of service is particularly notable. Humans, the noblest of God's creatures according to the Qur'an, have a tendency to fall into arrogance. Humans see themselves as self-sufficient, and, in their pride (the gravest sin in Islam), consider themselves God's partners. To help them remember the purpose of their existence (complete submission to God), Muslims must struggle against their pride. One way to do that is to go beyond themselves and serve people who are less fortunate. So important is this obligation to help others that the third of the Five Pillars (or duties) of Islam is to give to charity. (For more on the Five Pillars of Islam, see Book 6, Chapter 4.)

A great nineteenth-century preacher once said, "Happiness is the natural fruit of duty," which suggests that religions can make you happy, but only if doing the right thing makes you happy. For example, if walking out on the people who love you and need you makes you happy, chances are you are going to be miserable in your religion.

Accepting suffering

Suffering is a part of life. The illness of someone we love, the death of a child, and a hundred other defeats we suffer every day are often not caused by our choices and are not within our power to solve. If you didn't cause the suffering and you can't do anything about it, what lesson can you possibly learn from it — except to duck and run?

REMEMBER

Every religious tradition answers the question of suffering differently:

- **Christianity (see Book 5) teaches that the deepest help God gives people** is in suffering with them. Knowing that God is with them during the most difficult times of their lives is an immense comfort, but the lesson goes beyond that. Christians believe that God is compassionate, and Christianity teaches its followers to be compassionate to others. In this way, personal suffering can produce positive outcomes. Although accepting God when things are bad is difficult to do, Christians believe that this acceptance is essential if they are to acquire a mature faith.
- **At the end of a Jewish (see Book 4) funeral service,** the last words spoken at the grave are, *Adonai natan, adonai lakach, y'hi shem adonai m'vorach.* (God has given and God has taken away. Blessed be the name of the Lord.) This simple phrase contains a spiritual truth: It is far easier to bless God when God is giving to us than it is to bless God when God is taking from us, but it is spiritually important to understand that the giving and the taking are both from God — that everything we have is just a gift, just a loan, from God and that it must be surrendered some day.
- **Theravada Buddhism (see Book 3) teaches that suffering is an illusion** that comes from our desires. We make ourselves unhappy because we won't accept the pain that comes from being attached to the things, people, and feelings in our lives. We crave things that make us miserable when we don't get them. We love people whose death causes us pain when they die. According to Theravada Buddhism, the only way we can find peace is to abandon our attachment to our desires, hopes, and dreams. In this release of attachment, we will find the happiness we are looking for in our lives.

  The Buddha once helped solve the problem of grief for a woman who had just buried her child. She came to the Buddha and asked him to comfort her. He put a tiny mustard seed in her hand and told her to go and collect one mustard seed from every one of her neighbors who had never lost a loved one to death. She returned with just the same one mustard seed and with the comforting awareness that every person has been touched by death.

» **Many who practice within the Hindu (see Book 1) faiths** view suffering as having a purpose. The goal of Hindus is to find release from the cycle of birth-death-rebirth that continues until a person can finally free themselves from desires, which keeps the cycle going. The suffering people experience in this life is a result of their actions (karma) in a former life. By acting to relieve suffering (or by having the suffering taken away by someone else), a person cannot escape the birth-death cycle. In addition, many Hindus believe that by taking away the suffering, a person may be reborn in a lower life form. So, although things may be easier in this life, they could be that much worse in the next.

» **For Taoists (see Book 2), they believe that the *Tao* is "the way."** So if you're not following "the way" then that could lead to suffering. But if you live in harmony with the *Tao*, then you could potentially end your suffering.

Comparing Religion with Philosophy and Spirituality

Questions we hear a lot have to do with the differences between philosophy and religion. Many philosophies, for example, wrestle with the question "What is good?" and try to solve what it means to live a "good" life. Other philosophies try to explain the nature and meaning of existence — topics that fall well within the sphere of religion.

Spirituality is another area that ties into (but in some cases is separate from) religion. Religion is about spirituality, so when people say they're spiritual but not religious, what does that mean? What distinction are they making? This section helps you find out.

Philosophy and religion

Many philosophies take up the questions of what is good and how people should act. In providing guidelines on living, philosophies have ethics just as religions do.

REMEMBER

Religions differ from philosophies in several ways:

» **Only a religion has rituals.** Only a religion has holy days. Only a religion has ceremonies to consecrate birth, marriage, and death. Rituals are the clearest way of differentiating religions from philosophies.

Some religions, such as Buddhism or Confucianism, however, have often been termed philosophies because Westerners looked in these religions for an image of a transcendent God and didn't find it. Some Buddhist sects, such as Zen, don't teach a belief in a god or supreme being; their goal is to find enlightenment or happiness within themselves. Other Buddhist sects, such as Pure Land, do believe in a transcendent God, similar to Christianity, which leads to a rebirth in paradise. But because of their rituals, Buddhism and Confucianism are both clearly religions.

- **Philosophies use reason to figure out what is true, and religions use both reason and revelation.** Reason depends solely upon the use of unaided human rational thinking to determine what is true. Reason doesn't appeal to the authority of God or tradition to establish the truth. By contrast, religion often depends on *revelation*, a gift of knowledge given in a holy text or directly by God to a prophet. To accept reason you just have to think, but to accept revelation you have to believe. (See the related sidebar titled, "Natural Law of Theology and other ideas," later in this section.)
- **Religions teach that miracles, which appear to supersede commonly held beliefs about Nature, are actually true.** To the religious mind, miracles actually happen. These events are not simply metaphorical or symbolic tales that represent some divine principle. In Nature, bushes do not burn without being consumed, and people don't rise from the dead. Miracles are examples of God's power and love for people of faith. They're also classic examples of how religions can seem irrational to philosophers, who seek to prove all truth by reason.

TIP

Think of religions and philosophies as two circles that intersect. The part they both share is the search for what is true about life here on earth. The belief that stealing and murder is wrong is in the part where the two circles overlap. The beliefs in Moses' splitting the Red Sea or Jesus' rising from the dead or Buddha's turning rain into a shower of flowers are in the part of a religion circle that does not touch human reason or secular philosophy.

Spirituality and religion

Our opinion is that religion is just organized and ancient spirituality. Nowadays, however, you often hear people say, "I'm spiritual, but I am not really religious." This kind of distinction between religion and spirituality is hard to understand, but it's clear that they are trying to say something even if it's not always clear what that is.

NATURAL LAW OF THEOLOGY AND OTHER IDEAS

In the Middle Ages, some religious thinkers — such as St. Anselm (the archbishop of Canterbury from 1093–1109); St. Thomas Aquinas (1225–1274), Italian theologian and philosopher; and Maimonides (1135–1204), Spanish rabbi and physician — tried to show that both reason and revelation came to the same conclusions. This school of thought is called Natural Law Theology. However, some philosophers such as the German philosopher Immanuel Kant (1724–1804) said that if you do something because God said so, it couldn't be right or moral even if it is the same as the truth of reason. Religious rationalists say that how you come to the same truth doesn't matter, just as long as you get there, and that God would never reveal something to human beings that was irrational.

REMEMBER

In this context, a spiritual life can be different from a religious life in the following ways:

- **Spirituality does not require membership** within an organized religion, nor does it have the authority structure that religions do.
- **Spirituality is the willingness to follow rituals,** ethics, and beliefs of different religions that are personally appealing, and not just the rituals, ethics, and beliefs of one single religion.
- **Spirituality is deeply personal and not systematic,** while religion has all its ideas clearly set out and organized.

Beyond this, the distinctions are primarily ones of perception rather than reality. Both sides weigh in with their ideas on how one is better than the other. For us, religion and spirituality aren't two opposing ideas at all; they're just two ways of speaking about humankind's deepest yearning for the profound gift of hope and healing in a wounded world.

Consider this verse from the prophet Isaiah in the Hebrew Bible:

> You are my witnesses, says the Lord, and my servant whom I have chosen, that you may know and believe me and understand that I am He. Before me no god was formed, nor shall there be any after me (Isaiah 43:10).

This simple statement of the monotheistic faith of Judaism reveals the point of spiritual humanity in the West: We are here to bear witness to one true God. Our faith begins with God, is animated by God, and is informed at every stage by God.

This verse, however, may have little meaning to a Hindu, a Buddhist, a Taoist, or to the faithful of many other Eastern religions. For these people, the spiritual journey isn't to find the God that the Christians, Jews, and Muslims revere, but to seek enlightenment and reunion with the divine essence that imbues everything in the universe.

TIP

No matter how you look at it, all religions — monotheistic and polytheistic — offer a way for you to connect with the Divine. The Divine, of course, is different for different religions. Moreover, because you have to believe in the existence of a god before you can believe in a particular god, the next section shows how people of faith prove the reality of God.

Finding the Proof in the Pudding

The terrible suffering of innocent children. The Holocaust, slavery, and a million wars. Disease, famine, and homelessness. Earthquakes, floods, hurricanes, typhoons, lightning, forest fires, pestilence, and elevator music. All refute the divine . . . or so you would think.

The question is: Does God (or do gods and goddesses) exist? The answer for most people is a resounding yes. A whopping 74 percent of people in the United States believe in the divine, for example. The following sections explain the evidence that, to these believers, proves God's existence.

Cosmological proof: The existence of time proves God

Everything in the world, at this present moment, seems to have been caused to exist by something that came before it. The question arises: Was the series of causes that led up to the present moment infinite or finite? In other words, was there infinite time before this moment, or was there a moment when all time began?

If the sequence of causes leading up to the present moment is infinite, we have a huge problem, because an infinite series can never be completed! You cannot, for example, count from 1 to infinity. So, if there was an infinite series of moments and causes before this present moment, we could never get to the present moment. Nevertheless, we are at the present moment, which is proof that the series of moments that began at the creation and went from that moment to this is not an infinite series, but a finite series.

Consider the following:

- Time and the world of causation must have a beginning, a moment when some force/being/thing began the series of time and chain of events that eventually led to the present.
- The force/being/thing that caused everything to start must have had no cause itself. Nothing created it, and nothing came before it.
- The force/being/thing must be the only thing that had no cause, no creator, and nothing that came before it because if that force/being/thing had a cause, then we are still going backward in time, and the problem of getting to the present comes up again.
- Our certainty that we are here now (pinch yourself if you aren't sure) requires us to be equally certain that there was some force/being/thing that created everything from nothing.

In a nutshell, the cosmological proof is this: Something had to begin the chain of events that led to the present, or we could not have arrived at this moment. Obviously, we are in the present moment, so God must have started everything way back then. It doesn't matter how far back the first moment of time occurred. It just matters that God began it, and nothing began God.

Teleological proof: The existence of the world proves God

Teleology is the study of design or purpose in nature.

TIP

The best way to explain a teleological proof is to imagine that you are walking along a beach when suddenly you see something shiny in the sand. You pick it up and discover that it's a watch. Here's the question: Do you know that the watch is the product of a watchmaker, or do you just suppose that someone made the watch? Obviously, the answer is that you know, with absolute certainty, that somebody made that watch. Things like watches show purposefulness, design, and function, and they don't just *poof!* into existence. Even if you never meet the watchmaker or learn their name, you still know they exist because that watch could not exist without them. Your knowledge of the existence of a watchmaker is not an assumption, and it's not a belief. It's a fact.

So, turn from the watch to the world. The world is like the watch, in that it shows design and purpose. It is complex and intricate. Everything works according to plan. Flowers don't bloom in the winter, and birds don't fly north in the fall. In addition, the human body shows far more complexity, purpose, design brilliance, and structure than any paltry watch.

If we know that a watchmaker exists when we look at the design of a watch (because we are sure that such a thing could not exist without a watchmaker), then all we have to do is look at the designs and patterns of the universe and everything in it to know a world maker, a creator of all that we see, does exist.

The ontological proof: The idea of God proves God

Ontology concerns the nature of being or existing. In the ontological argument, the idea of God proves the existence of God.

Here's how the concept works: What we really mean by "God" is a being greater than anything else that can be conceived. That idea either exists in our mind alone or in the world. If the idea of God exists only in our mind, then it isn't as great as a God that also exists in the world. However, since we have an idea of God as the greatest being we could possibly imagine, God must also exist in the world.

The ontological argument is simple and complex, and, not surprisingly, it attracts the most interest by philosophers. The idea is that when we think about God, we are not thinking nonsense concepts such as a married bachelor or a square circle. When we think about God, we are thinking about the greatest and most perfect being imaginable; and such a being must exist because we can think about it, and we could not think about it if it didn't exist.

TIP

This concept may seem strange and perfectly ridiculous at first. After all, we can, and do. Just think about unicorns and Minotaurs and the Cubs winning the World Series (okay, that one actually happened in 2016 after going 108 years without winning it. But you get the idea.) Thinking about such matters doesn't make them exist, but that misses the point of this abstract proof. According to the ontological proof, the idea of God is the only idea that requires existence of the thing we are thinking about. The idea of God is all about perfection, and perfection requires existence.

The moral proof: The existence of morality proves God

The moral argument begins from a fact about animals on earth: Only people can choose between good and evil. No animals other than human beings, as far as we can tell, have free will and make moral choices. Lions don't choose to kill antelopes; they're driven by instinct to kill antelopes. All other animals obey the laws of nature and the compulsions of nature: They mate with whom they want; they eliminate body waste wherever they want; they eat when and what they want; and they kill when they want. Only people can resist animal urges for the sake of some moral good.

ONE GOD OR MANY?

Not all religions believe in a single God. A monotheistic God is a basic idea in Judaism, Christianity, and Islam, but not in some sects of Buddhism and Confucianism, none of which believe in any God. Other religions, such as Hinduism and Shinto, and many tribal religions around the world believe in many gods.

If you grow up thinking that the Abrahamic faiths (Islam, Christianity, and Judaism) are the only faiths, you may be surprised to realize that many religions get along just fine without the idea of a single creator God who is all powerful and all good.

The question of this proof is simple: Where does the human capacity for moral choice come from? It can't come from nature, because nothing else in nature shows this capacity. So it must come from some force beyond nature, from God who made nature but who isn't a part of nature.

Therefore, God must exist in order to explain the existence of morality in human beings. See the related sidebar titled "One God or many?"

Understanding the Nature of the Divine

In Islam, Judaism, and Christianity (the Abrahamic faiths), God is more than the world in the same way that the potter is more than the pot, the painter more than the painting, and the plumber more than the plumbing. God preexisted the world (and by the *world*, we mean the universe, not just planet Earth) and created the world at some moment in time. God is totally different from the universe but present in it completely. This belief is called classical theism.

Other religions believe that God is the universe and nothing more. God is the spirit of the universe, its purpose, and its deepest meaning, but not its creator. This belief is called *pantheism.* Pantheistic religions can believe in many gods, as in Hinduism, or in just one god, as in Taoism. The advantage of pantheism is that when we see the universe, we see God. We don't have to struggle with the concept that an invisible creator God made the world but isn't the world.

WARNING

These distinctions seem simple enough, but they lead to a lot of confusion and misunderstanding among faiths. For example, the belief about God in the Abrahamic faiths produces a distance between God and the world. God created the world but is not defined by it or dependent on it, and this belief is the reason why Christianity, Judaism, and Islam oppose idolatry. Idolatry is making a god out of something God created. Idolatry confuses the created with the creator.

In Hinduism, the gods are each a part of the world, and no god is beyond the world. Hinduism has no trouble worshiping parts of nature because they are all really gods. To the Abrahamic faiths, Hindu practice looks like idolatry, and to Hinduism, the Western religions look excessively abstract and removed from human existence. For Jews and Muslims, the Christian worship of Jesus looks like idolatry because it seems to be the worshiping of a human being. To Christians, Jesus is a part of the mystery of God, and worshiping Jesus is not idolatry. Some Protestants who have no trouble worshiping Jesus think that the worship of Mary in Catholicism is idolatry; but to Catholics, Mary is also a part of the mystery that is God, although Mary, the mother of Jesus, is not a part of the Trinity. For more on Mary, see Book 5, Chapter 4.

REMEMBER

To help eliminate some of this confusion, this list outlines the current state of belief in God among some of the religions of the world:

- **Buddhism.** Find God in yourself, in community, in everything. Some forms of Buddhism, especially the Mahayana form, have spiritual beings who assist humans.
- **Christianity.** One God represented in three parts (the Father, the Son, and the Holy Spirit).
- **Confucianism.** Humans are essentially good and can be led by the ancient ancestors in making good decisions about life.
- **Hinduism.** Hundreds of gods and goddesses, but one divine essence.
- **Indigenous religions.** The Divine is present in the sky, the water, and the trees. We are all part of this divine essence.
- **Islam.** One God (no ifs, ands, or buts).
- **Jainism.** Various gods, subordinate to 24 perfected souls that have attained liberation from corporeal bodies. Even insects and other animals contain some divine essence.
- **Judaism.** One God (but you can be Jewish and not believe in God).
- **Shinto.** There are doorways in Nature through which you can walk and find the divine *Kami* (deities), which are present in every aspect of existence.
- **Taoism.** The Absolute Tao, an unknowable, transcendent reality that produces all things.
- **Zoroastrianism.** One chief god and many divine entities created by that god.

Searching for Answers

The world has mysteries that we confront and problems that we try to solve. However, mysteries are different from problems. The questions, "Does life have meaning?" "Is evil punished and goodness rewarded?" and "What is the cause of suffering?" are mysteries. No matter how many times philosophers and prophets provide answers to these and other of life's big questions, the questions remain real and pressing in every generation and in every life.

The questions "What causes lightning?" and "How will I spend my evening if the power goes out?" are problems. Of course, not all problems are this easily answered or (to be honest) this irrelevant. "How will we feed the children if I lose my job?" and "Where should we go if the war comes to our front door?" are some of the bigger problems that people face.

For many folks, trying to find answers to life's mysteries is the place where the religious impulse begins. When we understand mystery, we come to understand God more as an ongoing action than as a thing and the religious life more as a quest than a destination. Comprehending such mysteries helps us figure out how to survive life's problems and enjoy life's blessings.

Searching for meaning

Every culture has some kind of religion, and all faiths answer the question "What is the meaning of life?" Humanity's search for an answer to this question is one of the main reasons that people are drawn to religion. The answers, although different from religion to religion, give people's lives purpose, meaning, and hope.

REMEMBER

The different religions have their own views on the meaning of life:

- **Hinduism:** Gain release from the cycle of rebirth and merge with the eternal Divine, thus escaping an inhospitable world. Learn more in Book 1.
- **Taoism:** Achieve inner harmony. Learn more in Book 2.
- **Buddhism:** Gain enlightenment and, in that way, free yourself from the sufferings that come from illusions and attachments to life. Learn more in Book 3.
- **Judaism:** Do God's commandments. Learn more in Book 4.
- **Christianity:** Try to love the way Jesus loved. Learn more in Book 5.
- **Islam:** Submit oneself to the will of Allah. Learn more in Book 6.
- **Mormonism:** Learn, grow, live by faith, and return to live with God. Learn more in Book 7.

Accounting for sin and suffering

"Why is there suffering in the world?" That's another big mystery that religion addresses. For most religions, suffering is the result of human failing or the lack of human understanding. In monotheistic religions, suffering is wrapped up in the concept of sin and human failing. In the Eastern religions, suffering is the result of humankind's lack of understanding, or enlightenment. Whatever the source of suffering and death is — human failure or human "blindness" — religions give their members hope by offering ways to overcome suffering and death. In Western religions, the goal is salvation; in Eastern religions, it's enlightenment.

TECHNICAL STUFF

Eastern religions covered in this book include Hinduism, Taoism, and Buddhism. Western religions include Judaism, Christianity, Islam, and Mormonism.

Sin: The devil made me do it

One of the most powerful reasons people come to religion is to find salvation from sin. Monotheistic religions use the term *sin* to describe the brokenness of human existence. The belief is that humans, in and of themselves, are not whole. Only by living through God's commandments or in accordance with God's will can humans be complete. Sin is a human failing, the result of human rebelliousness and arrogance and the source of evil in the world.

REMEMBER

What makes a sin depends on the religion:

- **An action:** All monotheistic religions agree that sins are actions that violate God's law. By behaving in ways that contradict divine will, a person sins. In Judaism and Islam, sin is always an act, a wrong act, and an immoral or impure act.
- **A thought:** In Judaism, a thought cannot be a sin, but a thought can lead to a sin. In Christianity, a thought can be a sin.
- **A state of being:** In some Christian traditions, sin is not only a thought or an act; it is also a state of being, represented in the concept of *original sin*. Original sin is a condition that humans are born to because of Adam's disobedience (he ate the forbidden fruit) in the Garden of Eden. (See the related sidebar titled, "Paul, Augustine, and original sin," in this section.)

Whether sin is an act, a thought, or a condition, it is, at its heart, distance from God.

Atonement and salvation: Getting right with the Lord

For monotheistic religions, sin and suffering are the results of choosing badly, of allowing selfishness and grasping to overcome what we know to be the will of God. By willfully and deliberately violating the divine will, we distance ourselves from God.

PAUL, AUGUSTINE, AND ORIGINAL SIN

Saint Paul, who interprets the creation story in Genesis (in the book of Romans in the New Testament), makes the first connection between Adam's fall and original sin (see Book 5, Chapter 2 for more). Hundreds of years later, Saint Augustine, a theologian within the Roman Catholic Church, popularized the idea of original sin. According to Saint Augustine, no person can cleanse the original sin that damns us all and blocks our salvation. Only Jesus' atoning death and resurrection saves people from original sin and opens the way to salvation — but only for those who believe in Jesus and his sacrifice.

REMEMBER

By atoning for bad deeds, people can cleanse themselves from the effects of sins and reconcile with God. Also called *reconciliation*, atonement requires repentance (being sorry for what you've done) and a change of behavior to conform to a religiously prescribed one. Through the process of atonement, people can reconstruct their relationships with God and those they have sinned against. By teaching people how to forgive others, religion helps people ask forgiveness themselves. In this way, these faiths address the basic human need to admit moral failings and move forward to a better way of living.

For most religions, salvation is a lifelong process, aided by both the discipline of ritual and the moral teachings of the faith.

Being negative

Buddhism doesn't concern itself much with sin as a separate issue. For Buddhists, the goal isn't to find salvation from sin but to achieve enlightenment and release from all human issues, including sin. Negativity or attachment to material life, Buddhists believe, is the obstacle that holds people back.

Within some Buddhist sects, negativity is expressed in the teaching of *tahna* (craving) and *dukkha* (suffering or imperfection). Our human desires, illusions, and attachments cause our suffering.

The reason people are so unhappy is that they want or crave things: love, adventure, and material possessions, chocolate, whatever. When people don't get what they want, they become sad. The idea is that we are our own source of unhappiness, and we can change how we feel by changing our attitude and desires.

Some Buddhist sects teach that life is a constant process of overcoming this suffering by learning why we suffer and giving up our attachments and our illusions. *Dukkha*, which describes the source of all human suffering, is the first of the Four Noble Truths of Buddhism.

Being born again . . . and again . . . and again . . .

In Hinduism, the nature of human limitation is that we are all trapped in the world of *samsara*, which forces us to die and be reborn endless numbers of times. Hinduism also offers hope that we can stop the process of rebirth and death. With proper practice, a person can attain release (*moksha*) from the suffering of samsara and find freedom and oneness with the infinite, the ultimate goal in most Hindu sects.

Practicing holiness

The word *holy*, which means sacred or hallowed, comes from Judaism and appears in the other monotheistic faiths. The sense of holiness, however, cuts across all religions and even goes beyond them. Many people who reject organized religion describe themselves as spiritual, indicating that they want to find some way to express and connect to holiness in the world.

The term *holiness* means a state of moral and spiritual perfection, but even that doesn't adequately convey the deep sense of mystery that imbues the word. The root meaning of the Hebrew word for holy, *kadosh*, is "something set apart from ordinary things." The objects of the Temple in Jerusalem, the ark that held the tablets of the law, the food of the priests — all these things were set apart and untouchable by non-priests. (See book 4 for more.) These objects somehow communicated the power of absolute holiness that is God.

REMEMBER

Holiness means many different things and is understood differently in different religions.

(Not quite six) degrees of holiness

Holiness is also usually seen as having degrees. Among holy things, some are more holy than others. For example, in the creation account in Genesis (see Book 4, Chapter 5), the order of holiness is as follows (from least to most holy):

- All things in the world are minimally holy because God makes them. This includes rocks, plants, the land, and so on.
- Animals are more holy than the inanimate items because they are alive.
- People are more holy than animals because they are both alive and, according to the belief of the three monotheistic faiths, are "made in the image of God."
- God, of course, is absolutely holy.

TECHNICAL STUFF

For inanimate objects and animals, holiness is a natural expression; they can't be anything other than they are. For people, holiness is a struggle because of our dual natures: part strivers toward God and part strivers against God.

Holiness and the avoidance of impurities

The Eastern faiths don't use the word *holiness*, but the idea of something set apart and closer to absolute purity and perfection is a basic part of the faiths. A Buddha is one example, and a *bodhisattva* is another. (A *bodhisattva* is an average person who reaches nirvana but chooses to fulfill a vow not to enter Buddhahood and instead turns back to help others.) The Buddha and *bodhisattva* have gone beyond the struggles of human existence and have attained the higher realm of the truth.

Holy things

All sorts of things can be holy:

- **Time:** Holy days and holidays are a part of every religion. These days connect followers of the faith to holy events and the turn of the seasons and the cycle of the moon.
- **People (in certain religions):** In Hinduism, for example, probably the most holy or sacred person is the *Sannyasin,* or renouncer. Sannyasins give up everything to search for the Divine and become conveyors of spiritual wisdom to all who would be taught by them. Whole communities adopt *Sannyasins* and take care of their needs. In monotheistic religions, on the other hand, people can't attain absolute holiness. Within some religious communities, ancestors are venerated. In Taiwan, Mexico, and Central American communities, special holidays are set aside to remember the dead. Even in the United States, we do not step on or deface a grave. We consider the space to be sacred ground.
- **Objects:** Consider the sprinkling of holy water at a Roman Catholic or Greek Orthodox service. The Orthodox believe that the hands of the priest become the hands of God during the service.
- **Places:** In India, the city of Banares (or Varanasi) is holy because it is where holy rivers find their homes. For many in India, the river Ganges is a holy goddess.
- **Nature:** Native Americans consider all of life and the earth to be holy. Taoism and Shinto also share this immense respect and awe of Nature.

Hanging On to Faith

When people think of religion as a set of beliefs, they often use the word *faith* to describe what they mean: When someone makes the simple statement "I am of the [fill-in-the-blank] faith," they reveal what religious belief system they consider true. In this definition, faith is the group of ideas that a religion holds to be true. People learn this type of faith because their parents taught them the faith of their ancestors, or because they convert to a religion that they come to believe is true.

Faith is also trust. In Hebrew, the word for faith is *emunah*, which has as its root meaning, trust. The word *amen*, spoken by Jews and Christians after prayer, comes from emunah. This idea of trust is found in the New Testament, for example, "Now faith is the assurance of things hoped for, the conviction of things not seen" (Hebrews 11:1). This type of faith means trust in a God or gods, trust in the truth of a religion's teachings, trust in a teacher, and trust in the traditions of one's ancestors. Although many of the beliefs of the world's religions can be proved true by using reason, the essence of faith is trust.

1 Hinduism

Contents at a Glance

IN THIS CHAPTER

- » Seeing the broad view of life in Hinduism
- » Checking out the sacred texts
- » Getting into Hindu worship
- » Understanding how you can convert to Hinduism
- » Appreciating modes of worship and societal structure

Chapter 1
A Quick Overview of Hinduism

Hinduism, the oldest and perhaps the most complex religion in the world, has its origin in India. It has survived as a faith for thousands of years despite many outside influences, including invasions and occupations of the land. Hinduism has always been interested in — and welcomed — ideas from anywhere. One of its earliest sacred scriptures, known as the Rig Veda, declares "Let noble thoughts come to us from all directions."

While absorbing into its bosom almost all good ideas from outside, Hinduism has been successful at keeping its own good ideas intact. Its focus has always been (and continues to be) inward; it has little interest in convincing others to embrace its values. Therefore, Hindu religious leaders rarely try to convert others. Hinduism firmly believes in both a supreme being and the idea that other belief systems are as valid as its own. This flexibility may be one factor that has led to the religion's survival over the millennia.

This chapter provides a general overview of Hinduism, introducing you to the basic beliefs, ways to worship, and more.

Understanding the Hindu Worldview

Unlike Christianity, Islam, Judaism, and Buddhism, Hinduism has no founder. It has no single religious book, such as the Bible or Koran, as its basis. Nor is it an organized religion. Hinduism has no founding date. It has no hierarchy of priests and no organizational structure that relies on a powerful leader (such as a pope) at its head. There are no standard sacraments or rites of initiation accepted and practiced by all those who profess to be Hindus. With no such anchors, or even an expectation that the followers believe the same things, you won't be surprised to know that scholars have had a field day trying to assess Hinduism in a Western framework. Not only has that task been nearly impossible, but it has led to hundreds of interpretations — some of which portray Hinduism as flexible, broad, and secular and others that treat the religion with ridicule or doubt.

When it comes to ultimate values, Hindu thought has never recognized or accepted any boundaries, be they geographical, racial, or otherwise. According to the Hindu worldview, Truth is unquestionably valid universally. In fact, this belief leads to the universal outlook typical of Hindus.

REMEMBER

Hinduism, the oldest of all religions, has a unique perspective on life. It excludes nothing! Hinduism has as its adherents a broad spectrum of people who span from the extremely orthodox immersed in elaborate ritual worship of the Almighty to those who openly declare that they do not believe in any god. In fact, Hinduism's view of the world is epitomized by this declaration from one of its sacred scriptures, the Mahopanishad (Chapter VI, Verse 72): "Vasudhaiva kutumbakam," which means "The whole world is a family." This fundamental belief helps Hindus feel connected with the world. The belief that there is but One Supreme Soul from which everything — all living entities and inanimate objects — emerged further strengthens the connection with the entire universe.

Devout Hindus worship many gods and goddesses. They worship cows, monkeys, snakes, trees, plants, and even tools. They worship mountains, rivers, and oceans. In the life of a Hindu, every day of the week involves worship of a minor or major god or goddess or the celebration of a festival. Religion is in the air for Hindus no matter where they are. The ideas and practices are at once complex and simple. But fear not, we help unravel some mysteries and still leave you with a sense of awe!

A broad set of key beliefs

Survey after survey reveals that more than 95 percent of Hindus believe in the existence of God. A broad set of beliefs stem from that most basic of beliefs, and they include the following:

- **Belief in the Supreme Soul:** This being is identified as Brahman, universal spirit. Brahman is the One who reveals himself in the minds of the sages and seers as the Supreme Consciousness. Hindus understand Brahman to be the only thing real in the universe. All else is therefore unreal, false, or illusory, and untrue. Brahman sounds like an abstract entity but is entirely real in every sense — the one and only Reality. You can find out about Brahman and the other divine entities in Book 1, Chapter 5.
- **Belief that Truth is the goal of life:** The goal of life, according to Hindus, is to reach back to Brahman, the one Reality, by realizing our true nature. That goal is defined as *moksha:* liberation from repeated cycles of births and deaths. The goal is to realize unity, or oneness, with Brahman. For that reason, the Hindu prays, "Asato ma sat gamaya," which means "Lead me from the unreal to the real."
- **Belief in the authority of the Vedas:** The Vedas are Hindu sacred books of knowledge, written in Sanskrit, the ancient and liturgical language of India. There are four Vedas: Rig Veda, Yajur Veda, Atharva Veda, and Sama Veda. Hindus believe that all four were revealed to Hindu sages. The Vedas contain hymns of praise to various gods, procedures for sacrificial rites and rituals, recommendations of cures for all ills, and musical chants appropriate at rituals. The Vedas are considered so sacred that the very definition of a Hindu is often stated as one who accepts/believes in the authority of the Vedas. Book 1, Chapter 2 covers more on Vedas.
- **Belief in the idea that time is circular and not linear:** According to this concept of time, there are no beginnings and no endings; time is simply a continuum. Hindus define periods of time as cyclical in nature, with each cycle containing four subperiods known as *yugas:* Krita, Treta, Dwapara, and Kali. Added together, the four yugas total about 4.32 million years. At the end of each cycle, gradually declining time spans and human values lead to dissolution. Then another period starts, and the cycle repeats all over again. This view of time has helped in developing the ancient Hindu perspective on life — a perspective that allows for a tolerant view of events and people.
- **Belief in karma and karmic consequences:** *Karma* is action that relates to service, specifically service to society. Hindus believe that what we are today is the result of our actions in the past. It stands to reason that what we will be in the future depends on what we do now, this moment, and onward for the rest of this life.
- **Belief in the concept of dharma:** The root word for dharma is *dhr,* which means "to hold" or "to sustain," specifically within the context of maintaining harmony and balance in nature. Dharma or right conduct is so central to Hindu life that it encompasses everyone, irrespective of age, station in life, or caste. Each being has its own dharma consistent with its nature. A tiger's

dharma, for example, is to kill and eat its prey. Yielding milk to sustain the life of the young is a cow's dharma. The dharma of humans is to serve.

TIP

Understanding the concepts inherent in the words *dharma* and *Veda* is in some ways vital to understanding the Hindu faith.

- **Belief in tolerance as the core value:** Ancient universities and religious centers in India attracted students and visitors from many parts of the settled world. They invited debate and inquiry into religious ideas. With this same spirit, modern Hindus accept all religions to be true and self-contained. A Hindu hymn asserts this view by comparing the various paths to God with hundreds of rivers and streams all mingling finally with the ocean.

These fundamental beliefs have paved the way for Hindus to develop a philosophical outlook on life. This outlook is based firmly on the belief in an intimate connection between the individual soul, called atman (or *Jivatman*), and the Supreme Soul, called *Paramatman*. Broadly speaking, these fundamentals comprise a code of behavior that continues to form the contemporary Hindu view of life.

A brief look at Hindu gods and goddesses

The Chandogya Upanishad — one of the sacred texts of Hindus — contains an eloquent phrase: "ekam eva adwiteeyam." It means, "There is but One without a second." Yet Hinduism ended up embracing a large number of gods and goddesses. This one-size-doesn't-fit-all realization provided an extraordinary variety of choice for individuals to worship. The One without a second doctrine, however, which holds that God and the universe are one and the same, remains fundamental and is still preserved. The simple prayer offered by Hindus at the conclusion of any worship, irrespective of the god or goddess being worshipped, sums it all up:

> You alone are our mother and father
>
> You alone are our sibling and friend
>
> You alone are our knowledge and prosperity
>
> You alone are everything to us
>
> My Lord, my Lord

Hindu mythology identifies three gods at the head of a hierarchy of gods. These three are

- Brahma, whose main function is to create
- Vishnu, who sustains the created universe

» Shiva, who is in charge of dissolution prior to the next time cycle of creation in an endless cycle

In simplistic terms, these three are sometimes referred to as Creator, Sustainer, and Destroyer, respectively. Each of these major gods has a female consort also playing a major role:

» Saraswati, consort of Brahma, is the goddess of learning.

» Lakshmi, consort of Vishnu, is the goddess of wealth and well-being.

» Devi, Shiva's consort, represents the creative power known as Shakti.

Below these primary gods are a variety of forms of gods including the avatars of Vishnu (who you can learn more about in Book 1, Chapter 5). Many temples exist and continue to be built for Shiva, his sons (Ganapati and Murugan), the previous goddesses named, and the various forms of Vishnu. The concept and presence of Brahma is enshrined in the heart of every sanctified Hindu temple.

During the early Vedic period, nature gods such as sun, wind, fire, and dawn were objects of Hindu worship. (When was the early Vedic period? Different scholars offer widely differing dates, but probably between 1500 and 1000 BCE.) These Vedic gods are invoked and worshipped in household rituals, weddings, and temple rituals to this day. Except for the sun god, no temples exist for other Vedic gods. However, hymns of praise for these gods fill the revealed sacred scriptures.

The Vedic gods fall into several general categories:

» Nature gods, especially gods connected with weather and climate

» Planetary gods who feature in destiny and the composition of horoscopes

» Gods who rule over household health and wealth and community values

In addition, other gods and goddesses, who are regional and local, preside over small villages and towns; their patronage is sought during natural disasters such as floods, epidemics, and the like.

You can read much more on the subject of gods and goddesses in Book 1, Chapter 5.

Hindu religious leaders

Hinduism is a more than 5,000-year-old culture, philosophy, and faith, so you can imagine how many religious leaders have contributed to it! The number is very large — perhaps thousands — and covers a broad spectrum of people. For now, we briefly describe what the various Hindu religious titles mean:

- **Sages:** In Hindu parlance, a *sage* (or *rishi* in Sanskrit) is an extraordinary spiritual person who is totally devoted to seeking Reality and practicing austerities in remote environments such as caves and deep forests. Sages first "heard" the revelations that formed the basis of Hinduism.

  A long list of such sages exists, and all Hindus who belong to the first three castes (see the upcoming section "Looking at Societal Structure") trace their origins to one of these sages of the ancient past. While performing rituals, Hindus cite their lineage (called *gotra*) by referring to a set of sages (generally three, but sometimes five or seven) from whom they claim spiritual descent. You occasionally read about the Seven Sages called *Saptarshis* who are represented in the seven stars in the constellation Ursa Major.

  Some names of ancient sages often cited in the scriptures are Vasishta, Vishwamitra, Atri, Jamadagni, Bharadwaja, Narada, Agastya, Markandeya, Garga, Kanva, Bhrigu, and Kaushika.

- **Gurus:** The word *guru* means teacher. Hinduism accords a special place for teachers in general but in particular for religious teachers. Each family has a revered teacher, and more often than not, that teacher is also the founder of a particular Hindu sect and referred to as an *acharya*. For example, in the Srivaishnava denomination (more on denominations in Book 1, Chapter 3), the most revered teacher is Ramanujacharya. Families belonging to this denomination would cite this guru in reverence at the conclusion of rituals and offer their allegiance to him.

  A very well-known prayer is addressed to such gurus during daily prayers:

  - I salute that guru who is Brahma, Vishnu and
  - Shiva and who is verily the Brahman.

- **Swamis:** *Swamis* are religious leaders who belong to an order, such as the Ramakrishna Order. When such a leader is ordained, his name is prefixed with the title *Swami* and ends with *ananda* (meaning "bliss"). The ordained name replaces the given and family names. Swami Vivekananda and Swami Satchidananda are examples. Swamis set up missions and accept, train, and ordain disciples in order to continue their particular tradition.

- **Monks and preachers:** To this general category may belong any and all persons who have a religious interest, talent, and perhaps some following. Monks and preachers may travel around, offer advice, preach, tell stories from the great epics, sing, chant, bless, and be a part of a community in general. Monks may also belong to an *ashram* (a place of religious retreat) as a celibate community, or they may live alone.

» **Priests:** Priests (also known as *purohits*) conduct worships regularly at temples and when devotees visit. They also go to private homes, upon request, to help families perform rituals and ceremonies. Hindu priests may marry.

» **Reformers:** Hinduism has had important reformers who have introduced various approaches to salvation over the past several thousand years. The most famous reformers are Shankaracharya (who introduced a philosophy of Nondualism known as *Advaita*), Ramanujacharya (who introduced the philosophy of qualified Nondualism known as *Vishishtadvaita*), and Madhvacharya (who introduced Dualism, known as *Dvaita*).

WHY DATES AND OTHER DETAILS IN HINDU HISTORY MAY NOT BE SPECIFIC

The history of the Hindu religion can get a bit hazy simply because it's so very old. Here are some factors that make it difficult to pin down exact dates and other details about the religion's history:

- **The oral tradition:** The Hindu religion began with revelations "heard" by several sages over several centuries and then preserved through oral tradition — that is, a system of memorization. Much later, again at unknown dates, these revelations were compiled and put in writing. Does it surprise you that controversy exists about who did what and when?
- **Uncertain dates:** Scholars cannot agree about the period in which certain significant events in Hindu history took place — especially when the focus is events occurring more than several thousand years ago. For example, there is still no agreement on the period in which the most sacred scriptures of Hindus, the Vedas, were compiled.

  Here's another example: Hindus believe that the end of the era known as Dwapara Yuga occurred when the Kurukshetra battle (which almost wiped out a whole royal race that ruled ancient India) ended. Some scholars claim that the sole surviving prince (known as Parikshit) ascended the throne at Hastinavati (present-day Delhi) around 3500 BCE. Other scholars place the date of the battle as anywhere between 500 BCE and 200 CE. The discrepancy here isn't a squabble about 100 or 200 years; we're talking about disagreements in the order of *thousands* of years.
- **Lack of hard evidence:** Some scholars have made extraordinary efforts to carefully note events recorded in Hindu epic histories and correlate them with the

(continued)

(continued)

corresponding astronomical events mentioned, such as the position and phase of the moon, alignment of planets, and the like. But some of these astronomical events recur each century or two, so the scholars' conclusions may still be in some doubt.

- **Identical names and alternate names:** We're not talking about identity theft here, but sometimes the name of a sage is taken by another sage centuries later. When that happens, it raises the question of which sage is being referred to. In addition, some sages are referred to by alternate names. For example, a well-recognized sage known as Veda Vyasa (whom some call "the Homer of India") is claimed, by some scholars, to be the same as sage Badarayana. Other scholars deny that identity entirely.

Keep these factors in mind as you read about the extraordinary saints, sages, scholars, and leaders whose contributions have molded the lives of billions of Hindus over the millennia.

Studying Hinduism's Sacred Texts

Hinduism is not a faith that is based on one book. Very many sacred texts serve as the basis for the philosophy, rituals, and practices of Hinduism. These texts are mainly written in Sanskrit, but several major contributions are also to be found in other vernacular languages. The following sections provide a brief overview of these texts.

Revealed texts: The Vedas

REMEMBER

A basic Hindu belief is that the Vedas were inspired by what is known as *shruti*, meaning they were directly revealed by God and heard by sages performing intense penance. Accumulated over millennia, the Vedas form the basis of Hindu faith. The Sanskrit word *Veda* has its root in *vid* (to know), so the Vedas are the sacred knowledge of the ancient Hindus. They are recognized as *apaurusheya*, meaning that their origin is not traced to any individual and is, therefore, divine.

There are four Vedas, or Vedic traditions: Rig Veda, Yajur Veda, Sama Veda, and Atharva Veda. Each Veda is divided into three or four major sections, referred to as Saṃhitas, Brahmanas, and Upanishads. The word *Upanishads* literally means "something below the surface;" the Upanishads comprise the intellectual content of the Vedas and serve as the very foundation of Hindu philosophy.

Remembered texts: The Shastras, the epics, and the puranas

An equally voluminous literature known as *smrti*, which means "remembered" (as opposed to revealed), emerged, undoubtedly inspired by the rich shruti literature. The dates of these scriptures are equally uncertain. The remembered texts include Dharma Shastras (rules of right conduct), the two major Hindu epics (the *Ramayana* and the *Mahabharata*), and puranas (stories of gods); they consist of thousands of exciting tales to drive home the basic principles and values of Hindu thought. Their influence on the psyche of Hindus remains intact to this day.

The Hindu value system is embedded in the epics, puranas, and many other stories. In these texts, you find emperors, empresses, kings, queens, gods, goddesses, demons, festivities, holy rivers and mountains, prayers, devotional songs, weddings, births and deaths, successes and failures, the heights to which humans can rise, and the depths to which they can sink — all summed up in one word: life!

The Bhagavad Gita

The Bhagavad Gita ("Song of the Lord"), or simply *the Gita*, is considered very sacred by all Hindus and many Western scholars and devotees of Hinduism. The Gita is, in some sense, a Hindu manual for a spiritual life. Its story occurs just before the great Mahabharata War is about to commence, when the hero Arjuna decides to quit the battlefield. He suddenly realizes that a battle that pits brothers against brothers, students against teachers, and the young against the old makes no sense. He throws down his powerful bow and becomes silent and dejected. In a timeless moment, the Lord teaches Arjuna the meaning of duty and charges him that he has no choice but to fulfill his duty as a warrior to restore dharma.

The 18 chapters of the Gita have inspired millions of Hindus over the centuries. Not a day goes by in India when some aspect of the Gita is not evoked among the Hindu populace in the form of recitation, discussions, or enactment.

Exploring the Key Components of Hindu Worship

Hindus worship in myriad ways, from simply closing their eyes and offering a short prayer to conducting elaborate ceremonies at home or in temples that last the whole day. We touch upon components of worship briefly here, and you can find the details in Book 1, Chapter 4.

Devotions

For most Hindus, prayer is a daily event. Home altars are common in devout Hindu households. The orthodox may pray at least three times a day, first in the morning after *ablutions* (ritual washings), at midday before a meal, and in the late evening around sunset before supper. These prayers are known as *sandhya vandanam* and are a prescribed daily routine for young men who have been initiated into *brahmacharya* (meaning they are students of the Vedas) and their elders. We cite a few prayers here.

Upon waking up, this prayer is addressed to Bhudevi (earth goddess):

> I salute you, whose bosom is represented by a range of mountains and whose clothing is the cosmic ocean, and beg your forgiveness for stepping on you.

Immediately after, looking at open palms, this prayer is recited:

> At the tip of my fingers resides Lakshmi
>
> At the center of the palms is Saraswati
>
> At the base of the palms is Govinda (Vishnu)
>
> So we should look at the palms in the morning

During bathing, this prayer invokes the sacred rivers:

> O Ganga, Yamuna, Godavari, Saraswati
>
> Narmada, Sindhu and Kaveri,
>
> May you manifest yourselves here and now.

To wish for a good day, Hindus say this prayer:

> May Brahma, Vishnu and Shiva along with the planets
>
> Sun, Moon, Mars, Mercury, Jupiter, Venus, Saturn,
>
> Rahu and Ketu grant this day to be a good day for me.

Before undertaking an important task during the day or before any religious function, this prayer is offered to Ganapati — an elephant-headed god who is Hinduism's lord of obstacles:

> O Lord of the curved tusk, immense being, blazing with the brilliance of a million suns, please help remove all obstacles to this undertaking.

One of the most well-known prayers to Vishnu declares that a mere remembrance of the almighty is enough to absolve one of all the shackles of life. So mere remembrance it is, and off we go! Thus prayers can be very brief.

Festivals

Festivals for Hindus are like a 365-day Thanksgiving! Pick up a Hindu calendar and pick a day, any day — you're bound to find a reason for a celebration somewhere in the Hindu world. Some festivals are celebrated at home, and some are out in the community. Some may be low-key and serious, and some may be grand and lively. But most involve community gatherings in the open or at temples, and all involve prayers, special foods, excitement, and fun.

The festivals are seasonal. Tied in with a lunar calendar, they land on different days but in essentially the same month of the common calendar each year. In the month of January, Hindus celebrate Makara Sankranti, which is devoted to the sun god. In February is a night of Shiva called Shivaratri. Spring festivals include Rama Navami: celebrations over a nine-day period of Lord Rama's birth and life. Krishna Janmashtami is a worldwide celebration of the birthday of Lord Krishna in August. Ganesha Chaturthi honors Lord Ganapati in September. In the fall, Hindus worship goddesses Lakshmi, Saraswati, and Durga with festivals including grand processions, musical performances, and feasting. The well-known festival of lights (Diwali) celebrated all over India and the rest of the Hindu world in late fall is a celebration of the triumph of good over evil.

In addition, colorful festivals are conducted regionally that exploit regional legends and flora and fauna. We cover a wide variety of festivals in Book 1, Chapter 4.

Worship in temples and shrines

Any excuse will do for Hindus to show up at a temple to have *darshan*, which is "seeing" God. A new baby, a new job, a promotion, an approaching examination at school or college, or visiting family . . . you name it. Hindu families offer a plate of fruits and coconut and light incense sticks, and the priest goes through some rituals. Then the family prostrates in front of the deity, the priest blesses the family, and all is well.

In addition to the millions of such visits that take place every day, devout Hindus also observe the days and nights of special worship when the family must find its way to a nearby temple. The intent is the same (to "see" God), the routine is the same, and the effect is the same: a feeling of satisfaction and gratitude.

Rituals to mark the stages of life

Hindu scriptures have prescribed rituals and ceremonies to mark 16 defined stages of life. These 16 cradle-to-cremation rituals are known as *samskaras*. They begin with conception and continue with rituals performed before the baby is born. After the birth, the childhood rituals continue, marking the naming of the child, the first feeding, the first haircut, and the piercing of the ears. The childhood rituals are followed by ceremonies that initiate the young into adulthood, followed by householder-related rituals that include the wedding. The final stages of life bring rituals that prepare the individual for retirement, followed by the rituals to bury or cremate the dead.

Converting to Hinduism

You can convert to Hinduism if you so desire and if you find a guru who is willing to initiate you. Fundamentally, Hindus are not set up to convert others. If and when it does occur, the initiation is at a spiritual or philosophical level. If you want to practice Hinduism, you can do everything Hindus do and still remain in your faith, if you don't see any conflict. Hindus most certainly do not see any conflict.

Looking at Societal Structure

Hindu society of the distant past was organized on the basis of societal functions that included

- Providing for the society's intellectual and spiritual interests
- Protecting the land against domestic and foreign enemies
- Conducting trade and commerce
- Tilling the land and performing manual labor

Creating a systematic way to provide for all these needs and functions — at both the individual and community level — makes logical sense. The fact that this system went awry with the stigma of caste and hereditary ownership is an unfortunate matter of history that Hinduism is stuck with. A *caste* is a social hierarchy based on family lineage.

Following are the four major castes as they are understood and practiced:

- **Brahmin:** Spiritual and intellectual services
- **Kshatriya:** Defense-related services
- **Vaishya:** Trade and commerce-related services
- **Shudra:** Manual labor services

Note the word "major" carefully. Many, many minor castes and subcastes exist.

A lower caste, known as *untouchables*, also exists and includes people who undertake to do society's dirty work such as cleaning latrines, tanning leather, and so on. The existence of this lowest caste — the poverty, ill treatment, and prejudice against it — infuriated Mahatma Gandhi (the political and social leader who led the Indian independence movement and is considered the father of the nation) to the extent that he named the very lowest level *Harijans*, or "God's people."

REMEMBER

In general, the sharp divisions among castes no longer exist in practice in India and the rest of the Hindu world. Except that sometimes they *do* still exist, especially in respecting family traditions.

Is the caste system still alive? The proper answer is a resounding *yes* — and *no!* Today, the system exists from one extreme (where the idea and practice are condemned with obvious disgust) to the other (strict observation, within reason — that is, not violating state and federal laws) and a whole lot in between. Hindus of all castes now sit together side by side in classrooms, buses, restaurants, and workplaces, and they can live in the same neighborhoods thanks largely to modern education and the laws of the land.

IN THIS CHAPTER

- **Emphasizing the importance of Truth**
- **Learning about Hinduism's three core beliefs**
- **Finding out what Hindus believe about the soul**
- **Exploring karma and moksha**
- **Recognizing key Hindu values**

Chapter 2

Hinduism's Core Beliefs and Values

A belief system defines the bedrock of a religion whose followers go about their daily lives working, raising families, and interacting with neighbors. Even though individuals may not be aware of it, every action they perform is based on a set of beliefs they learned from parents, teachers, and the community. Hindu children learn their codes of behavior by observing elders around them, listening to stories from their epics, attending traditional ceremonies at home and in the community, and participating in worship services at temples.

REMEMBER

Unlike other organized religions, Hinduism does not have a single systematic, Sunday school-type of approach to teach its value system. Nor is there a simple set of rules like the Ten Commandments. Local, regional, caste, and community-driven practices influence the interpretation and practice of beliefs throughout the Hindu world. Yet a common thread among all these variations may be found in Hindus' belief in a Supreme Being and a feel for certain basic concepts such as Truth, dharma, and karma, irrespective of an individual's caste, knowledge base, and educational background. Of course, belief in the authority of the Vedas serves, to a large extent, as the very definition of a Hindu, even though how the Vedas are interpreted may vary greatly.

This chapter explains the core beliefs of Hinduism, including the Hindu concept of Truth/Reality; the nature of the soul and the Supreme Being, Brahman; and the spiritual goal of *moksha*, which means liberation within the context of attaining release from the cycle of deaths and rebirths.

Exploring Truth: The Foundation of Hindu Belief

The concept of Truth is at the intersection of philosophy and religion. Hindus, however, have traditionally made no sharp distinctions among Truth, religion, and Reality. They see these three concepts as deeply related and overlapping.

TECHNICAL STUFF

Hindu scriptures, epic stories, folktales, proverbs, and even ordinary conversations are full of subtle and not-so-subtle references to the concept of Truth and Reality. Consider these quotes from a variety of Hindu sources:

> From the Taittiriya Upanishad: "I shall speak the truth."
>
> From A Hindu Primer: Yaksha Prashna: "It is the truth of the good that causes the brilliance in the sun," and "What in one word is heaven? Truth."
>
> From the Rig Veda: "Truth is the base that bears the earth," and "Truth is One, but the wise express it in different ways."
>
> From the Brihadaranyaka Upanisad: "Lead me from the unreal to the Real."
>
> The Republic of India's national motto, taken from the Mundakopanishad: "Truth alone triumphs."

Each one of these statements emphasizes the high honor Hindus bestow on the concept of Truth. Yet to fully grasp this idea, you need to understand the Hindu concepts of Truth and Reality.

REMEMBER

Truth is a multilayered concept. It is more than just being "right" or factual. It is even more than being ethical and moral. In fact, Truth is more than all those attributes combined. In Hinduism, Truth comprehends the natural laws of the universe. Truth is absolute and eternal. For Hindus, Truth is, in a word, God. Realization of the Truth is a Hindu's goal, and that means realization of the self, God, and Brahman.

Because Truth isn't a particular path or answer but the very essence of the universe, it is, therefore, the only *real* thing. It is Reality. In Hinduism, Reality is eternal; it doesn't change with time. Instead, it remains forever as is and as it always has been. As an example, consider this book you are reading. Is the book real? Of course it is — but only in a physical sense. Otherwise, it is not real because over time, the book will be gone! But the concepts such as dharma discussed in this book will remain eternal and therefore real.

Understanding Hinduism's Three Core Beliefs

Hindus are brought up to believe in God — in whatever form (Fire, Sun, Krishna, Rama, Linga . . .) the individual's family and community perceive God to be. At the practical level, a family's or community's godhead may be Vishnu, Shiva, or Devi (goddess) in one or more of their forms. (See Book 1, Chapter 1 for an introduction to these primary Hindu gods.) But Hindus also hear and are aware of something deeper, the One.

Although educated Hindus and intellectuals undoubtedly know that the origin of their faith is rooted in the Vedas, all other Hindus, irrespective of their sectarian affiliations, are also aware of this fact. Many of them may not be able to recite even a single hymn from any of the Vedas, but the very word *Veda* generates an immediate reverence.

The concept of dharma is likewise held in great esteem. The word is used in common parlance in casual conversations to point out right from wrong.

The three core beliefs — belief in the Supreme Being, the authority of the Vedas, and a commitment to the concept of dharma — serve as a firm foundation on which all other beliefs and values that guide Hindus are built. We explain all three in this section.

Brahman: The one true (real) entity

That there is an entity that defies description, which excludes nothing, that can be seen and not seen, that can be conceived or not by Hindus in their quest for something beyond material well-being is ingrained in Hindu thinking. This Being is identified as Brahman, a universal spirit. Brahman is the One that reveals Itself in the minds of the sages and seers as the Supreme Consciousness.

Brahman is all-inclusive, encompassing everything in the universe. It has no form. (Don't mistake Brahman for the god Brahma or the caste of brahmin.) Brahman, the pure and formless One, limitless and all-pervading, is everywhere. It is the divine essence and substratum of the universe containing being and nonbeing. It is the timeless entity from which all else issues and into which all else returns.

Brahman is the only thing real in the universe. All else is unreal, false, illusory, untrue, or has (at best) a dependent and relative reality in relation to Brahman. Although Brahman sounds like an abstract entity, it is entirely real in every sense. It is the Supreme Soul, Supreme Being, Creator, the One and Only Reality. This is the *pantheistic* doctrine — the doctrine that equates God with forces and laws of the universe — leading to the firm declaration *ekameva advitiyam*: "There is but one without a second." These attributes of Brahman are complex concepts and are less known and talked about by Hindus in general.

REMEMBER

The root word for Brahman is *brh*, which means "to grow" and indicates infinite growth and expansion of the Being from barely visible living and nonliving objects at the lowest level (atomic) to the highest forms of life.

Belief in the authority of the Vedas

Ancient Hindus received their religion through revelation: the Vedas. There are four Vedas known as Rig Veda, Yajur Veda, Sama Veda, and Atharva Veda. Hindus believe that the Vedas are without beginning and without end. You may be wondering how a book can be described in that way. But the Vedas, in the eternal sense, aren't actual books. In 1893, Swami Vivekananda explained that the Vedas are "the accumulated treasure of spiritual laws discovered by different persons at different times." Being eternal, the Vedas existed before they were revealed to (or discovered by) the sages. (We introduce you to the sages in Book 1, Chapter 1.)

Once revealed, the Vedas have been passed on from generation to generation for more than 5,000 years through the process of oral transmission.

TECHNICAL STUFF

On the basis of star positions and calendars used in the Vedas, some scholars are of the opinion that the Rig Veda (1,028 fairly short hymns of praise) in its oral form was composed around 6000 to 4000 BCE. (Most scholars trace them in their current, written form to around 1500 to 1000 BCE.)

A true test of a Hindu is their acceptance of the authority of the Vedas. Throughout this book you can see the extraordinary influence of the Vedas on every aspect of Hindu life.

Committing to the concept of dharma

In Hinduism, there are four personal aims to be realized or striven for during the course of a lifetime. These aims are known as *chaturvidha phala purushartha.*

The first of these is dharma. The other three are *artha* (wealth, prosperity, reputation, fame), *kama* (sensory and aesthetic fulfillment), and *moksha* (liberation and salvation, covered later in this chapter). Hindus are obligated to practice artha and kama with dharma as the foundation in order to attain salvation and release from cycles of birth.

WARNING

Happiness, prosperity, and the good life are legitimate human experiences for Hindus as long as they are within the framework of dharma. Hindus have no problem tolerating atheism, but when it comes to those who violate dharma, they will not look the other way!

Understanding dharma

Dharma is the first of four personal aims to be realized or striven for during the course of one's lifetime. It is central to Hindu life and encompasses everyone, irrespective of age, station in life, or caste. In a nutshell, dharma insists on each person performing their duty. This aspect is the key component of the Bhagavad Gita when Lord Krishna charges the hero Arjuna to perform his duty. Winning or losing is not the issue, but doing one's duty is.

So just what is that duty? It depends. At different stages in life, each person has a different role, which means different duties. Your duty as a child is very different from your duty as a young adult, which in turn is different from the duties that fall on the shoulders of a householder. Your duties continue to change until the end of your life.

How does a Hindu determine what their duties are at any given time? An individual may be able to define the boundaries of dharma through interacting and talking with others; reading Hindu sacred texts (the scriptures, the epics, legends, and mythologies); studying history and drama; and paying attention to the wide variety of stories heard throughout the formative years. These various experiences help constitute personal measures and yardsticks that a Hindu may use in making decisions throughout their life. In a sense, dharma forms the individual's conscience, and it is perhaps the only available light that guides individual actions.

Avoiding the six temptations

Hindus learn early in their lives that there are six temptations they should try hard to avoid in order to stay on the path of dharma leading to moksha. The temptations are the following:

- **Kama:** Lust and desire for material possessions (Caution: The word *kama* in this context differs from *kama* in the context of the personal aims we introduce in Book 1, Chapter 1. There it means love, beauty, aesthetic aspects, and so on. Here it is the opposite. Welcome to the world of Sanskrit, where context is paramount!)

» **Krodha:** Anger

» **Lobha:** Greed

» **Moha:** Delusion through unrealistic attachment to things, people, and power

» **Mada:** Egotistic pride

» **Matsarya:** Jealousy

These undesirable qualities play a major role in the daily life of human beings; thus the cautionary warning to remain alert to avoid these pitfalls.

Following your conscience

Although dharma is a key component of Hinduism, other cultures and people have also defined what it means to be a good citizen and a good person — and what to do when those two roles are in conflict. Aristotle, for example, said:

A good citizen is one who acts in accordance with the laws of the state. A good man is one who acts in accordance with the principles of virtue . . . . In the best state, however, laws will be in accordance with the principles of virtue and so there would be no distinction between a good man and a good citizen.

But what does one do when there is, in fact, a clear difference between the laws of the state and the demands of conscience — which in Hinduism are dharmic laws? Such cases result in an internal conflict. Such was the case when Mahatma Gandhi was asked to vacate his seat on a train in South Africa because he was not a white man, when Rosa Parks was asked to vacate a seat on a bus merely because she was black, and when Abraham Lincoln agonized over the need to go to war to preserve the Union.

REMEMBER

When a Hindu faces a conflict that pits their conscience against prevailing laws or accepted standards of conduct, the conscience alone is the true guide that helps the individual choose what to do. That is precisely the reason Hindus train their conscience in dharma so that they may, when called on, have the benefit of guidance at crucial times.

Believing in the Existence of an Immortal Soul

A Hindu believes that the soul (or *atman*) is pure, perfect, and holy. It is neither created nor destroyed. It is simply there. The soul has been, it is, and it will be. It is unbounded and free. Actions of the soul while residing in a body require that it reap the consequences of those actions in the next life — the same soul in a different body. A body is a mere medium. Depending upon the experiences and tendencies during one life, the soul finds itself next in a body most appropriate to those tendencies, and a new life begins. The process of movement of the atman from one body to another is known as *transmigration*. The kind of body the soul inhabits next is determined by karma. This is what Hindus (and others) mean by karma and karmic consequences; the concept refers to the "pre-history" of the soul.

REMEMBER

The philosophical outlook of Hinduism is based firmly on the belief that there is an intimate connection between the *jivatman*, the individual soul, and the *Paramatman*, the Supreme Soul.

Transmigration, death, and rebirth

The human experience is like a coin; it has two sides. Life is one side, and the other is what we call death. The two come as a package. Birth and death are two aspects of life on this earth which no one, neither a pauper nor a monarch, has any control over. The born must die. That is inevitable.

The Bhagavad Gita (Chapter II, Verse 27) puts it this way: *jaatasyahi dhruvo mrtyu: dhruvam janma mrtasya cha*, which means "Death is certain to the one that is born and birth is certain to the one who dies."

Upon death of the body, the soul needs a residence in another body being born in order to experience the results of karma carried out in the previous body — unless, that is, it is ready for the final step of being absorbed in the Supreme Self.

REMEMBER

In Hinduism, death refers only to the body: Only the body dies, never the soul.

Final release from the cycle of death and rebirth

The Hindu's goal is to live a dharmic life in order to avoid rebirths so that the individual soul merges with the Supreme Soul. Merging with the Supreme Soul is liberation or salvation *(moksha)*; see the later section "Understanding the Goal of Life: Moksha." Upon release from the cycles of time, the soul merges with the essence of the Supreme Soul and becomes unbounded, pure spirit.

Contemplating Karma and Its Consequences

Karma is more than the title of a Taylor Swift song. Most people, Hindu or not, have heard of karma; you may even use the word in your daily conversations. But most people don't have a complete understanding of the concept of karma. In this section, we illuminate it for you.

Linking karma to character and willpower

Karma is action. Writing this sentence, that is action. You are reading this sentence; that is action. You are thinking; that is also action. All such actions, 24/7 throughout a person's life, help build that person's character. The nature of such character depends upon the nature of the actions. The strength of this character translates into willpower. That willpower determines our actions as well as their effects on us, our families, and our society at large.

TECHNICAL STUFF

Swami Vivekananda reasons that heredity alone does not define our character and the resulting willpower. He illustrates this fact by pointing to a great man with a giant will: the Buddha. Without strength of character generated through the nature of action, how can one explain that the Buddha, son of a petty king, had half the world worship him? His giant will, accumulated from his own actions, helped him burst on society like a giant wave and change the world forever.

Can such giant willpower have been accumulated in a single lifetime, or even two? Hindus believe the answer is "No!" It must have taken ages and several lifetimes for this willpower to accumulate to such a degree.

Good karma versus bad karma

The soul moves on and on, carrying the consequences of its karma in one body on to the next. The body dies, but the soul does not; it continues on forever or until it reaches perfection, upon which it merges with the Supreme Soul and achieves salvation.

What we are today is the result of our actions in the past. It stands to reason that what we will be in the future depends on what we do now, at this very moment and onward for the rest of our life.

Although Hindus do not refer specifically to good and bad karma, they understand that actions during a lifetime influence what happens in later lives. Hundreds of stories from the Hindu epics are used to impress upon the young the need to pay attention to their actions. In practical terms, this view serves as a trigger to motivate service to themselves, to their families, and to society at large. Knowledge and understanding of another crucial Hindu concept, dharma, help serve as a torchlight to guide actions. Good action may be the result — an accumulated treasure that influences the next life.

In that context, one can similarly view bad karma and its consequences. The story of stealing Vasishta's cow, which we tell in the sidebar "Prabhasa, Vasishta, and Nandini the Cow," serves as an example. This simple fable also shows that even gods and demigods are not immune to consequences of their actions.

PRABHASA, VASISHTA, AND NANDINI THE COW

This interesting story is found at the very beginning of the epic *Mahabharata*.

Once a group of higher celestial beings known as Vasus, all eight of them brothers, along with their wives went on a holiday. They were close to the *ashram* (monastery) of sage Vasishta. This ashram was an idyllic setting, indeed, with luscious grass and fruit and flowering trees. There the kings and their wives observed one of Vasishta's cows named Nandini (yes, they gave names to cows!), an extraordinarily healthy and handsome animal. One of the ladies wanted to have the cow, but the men, wondering why they, who were already immortals, needed a cow at all, resisted her pleas. Still, the lady insisted. She had a friend on the earth, she said, and she wanted to give the cow as a gift. Persuaded by this story, one of the Vasus, Prabhasa, stole the cow and its calf, and the entire party fled the scene. When the sage Vasishta rose after his austerities, he noticed Nandini's absence and through his Yogic powers understood what had happened. He cursed all the Vasus to be born on earth as a consequence of their action. The Vasus fell at Vasishta's feet and begged forgiveness. The sage reduced the sentence to all but Prabhasa. Seven of the kings would leave the earth right after birth, but Prabhasa would have a long life and pay in full for the crime.

Breaking free of karma

A Hindu's ultimate goal is to end the suffering and bondage of karma and its consequences, no matter how many lives it takes. Successive lives led according to the principles of dharma elevate each next life, leading to higher and higher planes of existence until the individual's life is totally absorbed in realizing the self. Under such conditions, the soul breaks free of the bondage of life as we know it and is absorbed by the Supreme Soul. That is true freedom, known as *moksha* — the subject of the next section.

Understanding the Goal of Life: Moksha

The goal of life, according to Hindus, is to reach back to Brahman by realizing our true nature. Upon attaining this awareness, we achieve liberation (salvation, or *moksha*).

Brahman is *the* common element in each living being. Our differences come through the individualized body and mind each of us inherits. That feature — the inherited body and mind, which is far less important than the commonality (the Brahman in each of us) — makes us think, act, and feel different and makes us forget that we are the same.

The goal is to realize our unity, our oneness; it's the reason Hindus pray *asato ma sat gamaya* ("Lead me from the Unreal to the Real"). Hindus are urged to give up the unreal, realize the real, and experience freedom from bondage to the body. That freedom is bliss, and as the great sage Swami Sivananda (1887–1963) declared, "Bliss is your birthright."

What is the path toward this goal? The Bhagavad Gita reveals many paths.

REMEMBER

Each person has their own qualities, likes, dislikes, and preferences. Therefore, each person should be able to choose a path toward liberation that suits their own taste, mindset, persona, and interest. Hindus firmly believe that *any* path, however different, peculiar, crooked, or straight, leads to the same goal of reaching the One. Such freedom leads not only to the choice of a philosophy that works for the individual but also to the rejection of any philosophy that doesn't work for that person. The result may seem chaotic (and sometimes it really is!), but the underlying spirit of this approach cannot be denied. After all, the effort to achieve liberation is a personal affair, and no one else — including those who are near and dear to the individual — has any right to impose any restraint or constraint on that effort.

The path of duty

The Yoga of Karma is selfless service to society. *Yoga* means union — with God. Yoga of Karma is the approach, which in this case involves action — in other words, reaching that union through selfless action. Each of us inherits a role in society. Whatever that role may be, our successful performance in that role is essential to a successful society. The path of duty insists that we fulfill our roles with enthusiasm, with objectivity, and with passion — fully absorbed even while remaining detached. This concept, which we call *detached dynamism*, is truly Hindu.

REMEMBER

Detachment in this context acknowledges the spirit of Karma Yoga, which wants you to lovingly focus on what you need to do. Hindus are urged to do their duty and not be attached to what may or may not be the outcome.

The path of knowledge

Another path toward moksha is defined as the path of knowledge, known as *Jnana Yoga*. Through this path, the individual strives to obtain knowledge of the Brahman through appropriate austerities such as through studying under a teacher with dedication to serve the Lord, and through service to other aspirants. The path requires a high level of intellect and determination. It involves rigorous self-discipline and dedication as the mind engages in unraveling complex issues pertaining to the self.

Individuals on this path cultivate such austerities as the practice, on a daily basis, of doing no harm, meditating deeply, controlling passion, avoiding harsh foods that aren't conducive to a healthy body, and so on. This path requires the mental capacity to go deep into the philosophies of life; for that reason it is most suitable for those with a scholarly or intellectual bent.

The path of devotion

The third path we present here is that of devotion, known as *Bhakti Yoga*. This path demands total, unconditional surrender to God with the individual completely absorbed in devotion to a chosen deity.

Normally, people who choose this path associate themselves with a temple, take part in worships, assist in maintenance of the shrine, and take an active part in the service, treating the deity as though it is a person with whom they are in love and to whom they have surrendered in a visible way.

Translating Beliefs into Core Values

Based on the set of core Hindu beliefs discussed earlier in the chapter, several values flow out. Such values are how the beliefs get translated into action and are visible in Hindu society on a daily basis. In this section, we introduce three such values, which are representative of a much larger group of values.

Exercising tolerance

One fundamental aspect of Hinduism is its tradition of tolerance. Ancient universities and religious centers in India attracted students and visitors from many parts of the known world. These institutions invited debate and inquiry into religious ideas. With this same spirit, modern Hindus accept all religions to be true and self-contained. Hindu thought is ingrained with the idea that other ways of life leading essentially to the same goal may be equally good.

TECHNICAL STUFF

One particular Hindu hymn translates this way:

> As the different streams, having their sources in different places, all mingle their water in the sea, O Lord, the different paths which men take through different tendencies, various though they appear, crooked or straight, all lead to Thee.

Similarly, a verse *(shloka)* in the Rig Veda declares that "Flowers and bees may be different, but the honey is the same." And the Lord has declared in the Gita that "Wherever thou seest extraordinary holiness and extraordinary power rising and purifying humanity, know thou that I am there."

Showing respect for elders

Although every culture, every faith, and every society teaches its young to have respect for their elders, Hindus have made an art of this value. The outward signs are clear: In orthodox families, youngsters prostrate before elders, touching their feet. People of any age prostrate this same way in front of holy individuals (and sometimes wash their feet). Even strangers who are elders are greeted by everyone, young and old, with the familiar sign of bringing palms together and bowing heads down. Standing aside and making way for older people is common. Blessings of elders in an assembly are invariably sought during special ceremonies such as weddings.

Many Hindu families (though not all of them) still adhere to what's called the *joint family system*, which means that the family cares for and attends to its elderly members at home. (See the nearby sidebar "The joint family system: The more, the merrier!")

THE JOINT FAMILY SYSTEM: THE MORE, THE MERRIER!

In a joint family system, brothers, their wives and children, and unmarried sisters live with their parents, their paternal uncles, and the uncles' families, all under one roof. Sometimes there may be 15 to 20 people in one household sharing resources, problems, successes, and failures. Having so many family members under one roof can be a lot of fun (of course, not always!) — and there are never any babysitting issues! Free counseling is available 24/7 with no need for psychiatrists. This system is gradually vanishing in favor of the nuclear family, but the model is still the choice for business families and many others in villages and small towns in India.

Treating all life as sacred

Hindus grow up learning that any and every living being is part of creation, and all creatures share a certain mutual dependency. This value is clearly visible when you see Hindus offer worship (and/or showing respect) to trees, crops during harvest, monkeys, cattle, and even snakes.

The implied belief is that an ecological balance is mandated and gratitude needs to be shown to preserve such balance through respect and/or worship. By specifying vehicles to gods and goddesses such as the eagle (Garuda) for Vishnu, a bull (Nandi) for Shiva, and a mouse for Ganesha, Hindus demonstrate the concept of acknowledging that all life is indeed sacred.

REVERING BHARAT MATA (MOTHER INDIA)

When the Pope arrives in another country, the first thing he does is kiss the ground. With this gesture, he shows respect for the host country. From a Hindu's viewpoint, this act is a familiar and fitting show of respect for Mother Earth. The feeling of connection between humans and the Earth seems natural.

Hindus have a deity known as *Bhudevi* (Goddess Earth). They offer a prayer ("forgive me for stepping on you") begging her forgiveness. Before beginning any sort of construction, Hindus do a *bhumi puja* (worship of the Earth) on the land. Before plowing a field, they offer prayers to Mother Earth. This reverence for the Earth extends to identifying the entire country as a goddess: *Bharat Mata*, or Mother India.

(continued)

(continued)

Such connection and identification with the entire nation took firm hold during India's independence movement in the late 19th century into the 20th century. During this movement, a poem known as *Vande Mataram* ("I Salute the Mother") by Bankim Chandra Chatterjee (1838–1894) became very popular and inspired thousands of young people to embrace the cause. In this poem, the country is visualized as goddess Durga (a symbol of female power). The song almost became the national anthem except for the compromise made by Hindu leaders to accommodate the sentiments of Indian Muslims with regard to idol worship implied in the poem. Nevertheless, the first two stanzas of the poem continue to be sung and used on some occasions because of the meaning and the beauty of the music to which it is set:

> I bow to you Mother enriched with bountiful waters, bountiful fruits, cool winds, and great harvests. Rejoicing in the glory of moonlight, the whole country adorned with the beauty of trees and flowers, great sounds of laughter and pleasant speech — the Mother bestowing bliss (on the land and its people).

IN THIS CHAPTER

» Reviewing the four major Hindu denominations

» Examining their core beliefs and practices

Chapter 3
Major Hindu Denominations

Hindu denominations resemble, to a large extent, denominations in Christianity, Judaism, and other religions. That is, they are distinct communities of believers within the larger religious tradition. But differences are significant, complicated, and even confusing to an outsider. Whereas the denominations in, for example, Christianity differ (even vehemently) on how to interpret the Bible, what rituals to follow, or how to attain salvation (good works versus belief), they still all agree that God is God and Jesus is His son.

While all Hindu denominations agree that there is only one Supreme Being (Brahman) and acknowledge the Hindu Trinity (Brahma, Vishnu, and Shiva), they each prefer to believe that their own chosen deity, be it Vishnu (or one of his many forms) or Shiva or Shakti, embodies all the cosmic functions of creation, sustenance, and dissolution. Other differences, such as the individual's approach to worship and the relationship between the individual soul and the supreme soul, also play a major role.

In this chapter, we explain what led to the development of different Hindu denominations and also discuss their subsects.

Understanding the Origin of Hindu Denominations

As explained in Book 1, Chapter 1, Hinduism is based in the Vedas: eternal, sacred scriptures that were revealed to the sages and that outline the spiritual laws that Hindus follow — specifically, the rules regarding how rituals and sacrifices are to be conducted. Early Hindus worshipped forces of nature, such as Surya (or Soorya), the sun; Indra, god of rain and thunder; Vayu, the wind god; and Agni, god of fire. The Rig Veda, the earliest known religious document, is full of hymns of praise for these gods.

Yet Hinduism proclaimed early its openness in allowing and welcoming different approaches to salvation. Therefore, it wasn't surprising that religious thinkers developed different schools of thought and choices of worship. These post-Vedic ideas sought alternate, more personal objects of worship in addition to (or instead of) the Vedic approach of rituals and sacrifices aimed at natural forces.

All these ideas and preferences served as the foundation of Hindu denominational thinking. Over time, in the post-Vedic era (500 BCE to 500 CE), and based on these choices, Hindus developed four major denominations, some with their own subdivisions:

- Vaishnavism (followers of Vishnu)
- Shaivism (followers of Shiva)
- Smartism (worship of Vishnu, Shiva, Ganesha, Surya, and Devi)
- Shaktism (worship of Devi, female power)

Note: The terms *Shaivite* and *Shaiva* are interchangeable; both words refer to someone who is affiliated with Shaivism. Similarly, the terms *Vaishnavite* and *Vaishnava* are interchangeable; they refer to followers of Vaishnavism.

REMEMBER

All these denominations subscribe to the broad basic beliefs and principles of Hinduism, as we outline in Book 1, Chapter 2; each denomination essentially accepts the authority of the Vedas. In addition, all four of these denominations emphasize devotion to their chosen deity as an essential requirement. Vaishnavism, Shaivism, and Shaktism each adhere to the strong belief that their god/goddess alone is the Supreme Being totally in charge of all the three primary functions: creation, protection, and destruction. Smartism, on the other hand, is more liberal and is based on *smrti* ("remembered") scriptures: the Puranas, epics, and myths. Smartas worship, in addition to Vishnu and Shiva, other deities: Ganesha, Surya, and Devi.

Vaishnavism, Shaivism, Smartism, and Shaktism have all developed their own literature and detailed procedures to guide devotees on a variety of worship services along with the mantras associated with each. Sophisticated devotional poetry describes in touching terms the typical loving relationship between the devotee and godhead, akin to that between lovers, with the pain of separation clearly spelled out.

REMEMBER

The primary difference between Vaishnavites and Shaivites is in their approach to attaining salvation. Shaivites emphasize knowledge as the path to salvation, while Vaishnavites emphasize love of God and surrender to God as the path to salvation.

Following Vishnu: The Vaishnavas

Vaishnavas are Hindus who worship Vishnu and his incarnations, principally the avatars Krishna and Rama. (An *avatar* is a physical manifestation of the godhead.) They may also worship other gods, including, for example, a deity known as Satyanarayana, who is believed to be a combination of the Hindu Trinity (Brahma, Vishnu, and Shiva). In addition, Vaishnavas worship the female consorts of Vishnu, including Lakshmi, goddess of wealth and wellbeing; Bhu Devi, the earth goddess; Sita, wife of Rama; and Radha, beloved of Krishna.

For Vaishnavas, salvation means that upon death of the body, the individual soul arrives at Vishnu's heaven called *Vaikunta.* In Vaikunta the soul is united with the Supreme Soul — Vishnu himself — even as it retains its own individuality. This assumes that the individual has lived a meritorious life deserving of such a union. According to Vaishnavas, the individual soul does not *merge* into the soul of the almighty; it *unites* — a subtle difference.

In this section, we outline the worship traditions of the Vaishnavas, as well as the various subsects of this denomination.

Worship traditions

The distinctive mark of Vaishnavas is what orthodox men may wear daily on their foreheads after morning *ablutions* (ritual cleansing): Three vertical lines, two white and one red, that are drawn on the forehead. These lines are known as *Nama.* The red center line is known as *Sricharanam,* a symbol of the goddess Lakshmi. The outer lines represent the feet of Vishnu. The marks worn by a Tengalai SriVaishnava, a subsect of Vaishnavas, are applied on 11 other places on the upper body and both arms; it's quite a sight to see. (Women and non-orthodox

Vaishnavas don't wear these marks, although they may wear only the central red mark during religious events.)

Vaishnavas are known to install intricately carved sculptures (typically stone) of the deities, decorate them lavishly with colorful clothing and flowers, and perform elaborate 16-part ceremonies of worship (called *Shodasha Upacharas*) offering a variety of cooked foods, fruits, and so on.

Vaishnava subsects

Vaishnavas are further divided into subsects, which differ in philosophy pertaining to the relationship between the individual soul and the Supreme Soul, worship different forms of Vishnu, and look to different sacred scriptures for guidance. In this section, we introduce you to all the major Vaishnava subsects.

The Madhvas

The Madhvas are named after their spiritual leader, Madhvacharya, who lived around 1200 CE. Madhvacharya was a proponent of Dwaita philosophy (Dualism), which maintains that an individual soul is distinct from the Supreme Soul. (The philosophy of Nondualism makes no distinction between the individual soul and Supreme Soul.)

Subsects based on Krishna worship

A form of Vishnu that plays an important role in Vaishnavism is Krishna, an avatar of Vishnu — especially his portrayal as a playful cowherd adored by local milkmaids. Krishna's flute-playing attracts young women, and he enchants them with songs and pranks that would make lovers today blush. Such intense interaction between the lovers is interpreted as divine love, not erotic love, and was portrayed in an extraordinarily beautiful and sophisticated poem called the *Gita Govinda* composed by Jayadeva in the 12th century CE. The poem evokes the joy of lovers being together, as well as the pain of their separation. You can read more by looking for a copy of *Song of Love: The Gita Govinda*, translated by George Keyt.

THE HARE KRISHNAS

A Hindu saint named Chaitanya (1486–1533) established the subsect known as the Gaudiya Vaishnavism of Bengal. Chaitanya was regarded by his followers as an incarnation of both Krishna and his beloved, Radha. Followers of Chaitanya viewed the love they shared with the Lord as mirroring the love between Krishna and Radha. The result was an expression of love for the Lord that bordered on infatuation, which was evident in worshipful prayers and dances performed at temples and on street corners.

Today, Chaitanya's followers head the Hare Krishna, or the International Society for Krishna Consciousness. The West became aware of this subsect during the 1970s, when saffron-clad young men with shaven heads began collecting money for Krishna at U.S. airports. Dedicated to a *semimonastic* (somewhat cloistered) lifestyle, this group has built beautiful temples worldwide and practices the intricacies of Vaishnavite rituals with devotion and grand style.

THE VALLABHAS

Another noteworthy movement that also focused on Krishna worship was founded by the intellectual Vallabhacharya (1479–1531). His approach to the worship of Krishna does not call for any self-denial or practices such as, for example, fasting. The approach is obviously a bit easier for the average person to follow, and it maintains that this world is not illusory but real. Scholars have described this approach as the way of enjoyment that occasionally has led to irreligious and corrupt tendencies.

THE SWAMINARAYANS

Under the leadership of Swaminarayan (1781–1830), another movement emerged that was somewhat corrective in nature to the Vallabha movement; it encouraged a more puritanical approach to worship. With an emphasis on *asceticism* (rigorously abstaining from self-indulgence and being fully absorbed in meditation and worship), Swaminarayan claimed that he, not Vallabhacharya, was the true incarnation of Krishna, and he attracted a large following.

Centered mainly in the state of Gujarat in western India, the movement now is a popular organization whose tight-knit followers build huge temples around the world with guidance from their current head.

The SriVaishnavas

Vaishnavas who owe allegiance to the 11th-century Hindu saint named Ramanujacharya are known as SriVaishnavas. They worship Vishnu and his different incarnations. Ramanujacharya advocated the Vedantic philosophy of *Qualified Monism*: the belief that Brahman has attributes, a major departure from Shankaracharya's thesis of Nondualism and Brahman with absolutely no attributes.

Ramanujacharya made no distinction among different castes. (We outline the Hindu caste system in Book 1, Chapter 1.) In fact, he sought the help of his disciple Pillan, a shudra (fourth in the hierarchy of castes), to have an authoritative commentary written on a sacred scripture in praise of Vishnu known as *Tiruvaymoli*, which combines Tamil and Sanskrit. (Tamil is the language of the southern India state of Tamilnadu.) Including a nonbrahmin in an intellectual task was an extraordinary step a thousand years ago!

The Ranganathaswamy temple at Srirangam in the state of Tamilnadu in South India is the origin and center of this sect. The Sri Ranganatha Temple in Pamona, New York (`www.ranganatha.org`) replicates the original temple at Srirangam and displays the principal emblems and symbols of the SriVaishnava tradition.

DIVISIONS BASED ON PATHS TO SALVATION

TECHNICAL STUFF

After the death of Ramanujacharya in the 12th century CE, SriVaishnavas considered and debated the concept of surrender to the almighty stated in the Gita:

> Abandon all duties and surrender to me.
>
> I shall absolve you of all sins. Fear not.
>
> Bhagavad Gita, Chapter XVIII, Verse 66

This verse, which seems to provide a direct approach to salvation, has been a subject of interpretation by scholars over centuries. Does surrender imply no effort on the part of the devotee? Is that even possible? The debate led to two schools of thought:

- **The Cat School:** This school concluded that surrender to the Lord is total and requires no effort on the devotee's part. Everything depends on God's grace, and all a devotee needs to do is simply put faith in it. This school is also called the Southern School and is known as *Tengalai* (meaning southern).

TECHNICAL STUFF

Southern refers to the town of Srirangam in Tamil Nadu, which is south of the town of Kanchipuram where the school known as *Vadagalai* developed. The Tengalai and Vadagalai classification is unique to SriVaishnava brahmins known as *Iyengars,* most of whom live in the Indian states of Tamil Nadu and Karnataka. (See the next section.) The corresponding sect in Shaivite brahmins is known as *Iyers.*

- **The Monkey School:** Also dubbed the Northern School, this school believes that effort on the part of the devotee is a prerequisite for obtaining the Lord's grace.

IYENGARS

Iyengar (or Ayyangar) is an important subsect of SriVaishnavas that came into vogue about ten centuries ago. In the Tamil language, the word *iyengar* refers to five duties. An orthodox Iyengar is required to undertake these five duties:

- Getting the marks of a conch and discus (symbols that appear on a Vishnu deity) branded on their shoulders by an *acharya* (religious head).
- Wearing the namam mark on the forehead and 12 other locations on the upper body.
- Adding and using the adjective *dasan* as an ending to the last name. (*Dasan* means "servant" in Tamil, as in servant of the Lord.)
- Learning and chanting mantras used in a variety of Vaishnava worships.
- Performing a detailed worship every morning.

Being devotees of saint Ramanujacharya, Iyengars are followers of the Qualified Monism philosophy.

The branding ceremony takes place under the direction of an ordained acharya. Metallic emblems of a conch and disc are heated until red hot and are pressed on the top left side of the left arm (conch) and top right side of the right arm (discus) to make permanent impressions. This action qualifies as an initiation into the fold and is performed by authorized religious heads only. It serves to openly proclaim the individual's religious affiliation, and it denotes certain privileges and authority to perform formal rituals both at home and at temples.

CATS AND MONKEYS

Why name these schools of thought after cats and monkeys? Consider the way kittens and baby monkeys are transported by their mothers. A kitten is picked up by its mother. As the kitten lies limp in her mouth and trusts her totally, all is well — no effort on the kitten's part! The baby monkey, on the other hand, clings tightly to its mother as they both move along branches and trees. The baby monkey feels fear and must make considerable effort to reach other destinations safely.

Following Shiva: The Shaivas

The Shaivas or Shaivites are followers of the god Shiva. Their denomination is known as Shaivism. In this section, we touch on the broad spectrum of worship traditions within Shaivism, and we introduce you to the two primary subsects: Ati Marga and Mantra Marga.

Worship traditions

Shaivas vary in their worship practices according to the form of Shiva they revere: Shiva as Rudra (storm god), Shiva as Pashupati (lord of animals), Shiva in a ferocious form known as Bhairava, Shiva as an ascetic, or Shiva as one of the Hindu Trinity.

TIP

As you read about the variety of sects and subsects within Shaivism, keep in mind that the practices described are confined to strict adherents of these subsect approaches. What do the large majority of Shaivite householders do? They go about their religious life by offering daily worship to Shiva, visiting a Shiva temple, fasting on days prescribed by their denomination, and taking part in a Shiva-oriented festival. Life for them is normal without any of the extremes you read about next.

Shiva worship has been continuous since prehistoric times. Its popularity increased starting around the first century CE as an alternative to more prescriptive approaches to Hinduism. Shaiva religious practices run the gamut from one extreme to another, from celibacy and total withdrawal to profane graveyard and Tantric cults. (*Tantric cults*, commonly understood to involve a combination of religion, astrology, spells, charms, and occult rites, emerged around the fifth century CE, centering around *Bhairava* [a ferocious version of Shiva] and *Bhairavi* [a ferocious form of Shakti]. These cults allowed for physical and sexual freedoms as ways of opening a path to self-awareness.)

For a Shaivite, salvation means that the soul, upon death of the body, arrives at the abode of Shiva called *Shivaloka*. Shivaloka is believed to be located on Mount Kailash in Tibet.

You can recognize orthodox Shaivites much the same way you do Vaishnavites: by the markings on the face (and arms and upper body as well). The difference is that Shaivite markings use three white horizontal lines drawn from left to right on the face using ash. The markings are known as *Vibhooti* and are believed to represent the three qualities inherent in humans: Sattva (noble), Rajas (vibrant), and Tamas (inert).

Shiva is often portrayed as a *lingam* — a stone pillar — or as Nataraja, the lord of dance, in a dancing stance.

Other deities included in Shaivite worship are his sons, Ganapati (also called Ganesha) and Murugan (who goes by many names).

Subsects of Shaivism

We now introduce you to two primary subsects of Shaivism within its broad umbrella. One of them is known as *Ati Marga* (extreme path) and originated at a time way, way back before the Vedic period. The second one, known as *Mantra Marga* (ritualistic path), developed later, past the Vedic period. Adherents to these practices are almost always men.

What do these two subsects have in common? Both paths revere the example of Shiva in his ascetic aspect: celibate, living away from civilization, eating very little, covered with ash, wearing animal skins as clothing, and in deep meditation.

What do the followers of these two approaches do that is different from each other and why? We begin with the first group.

The pre-Vedic approach: Ati Marga

We begin with the pre-Vedic Ati Marga subsect. Within this subsect, there are branches known as *Pashupatas* and *Kapalikas*. Although both groups want to disassociate themselves from society, they differ in practice in how they go about it. In addition, there is a branch called Veera Shaivas or Lingayats. We introduce all three here.

PASHUPATAS

Pashupatas follow some deliberate (some may think almost outrageous) steps aimed primarily at disconnecting themselves from society. Their thinking is that, because the bonds between an individual and his family, caste, community, and society at large are strong, extraordinary efforts need to be made to cut them. These extraordinary efforts involve inappropriate laughter, singing or dancing uncontrollably, making uncalled-for advances toward women, taunting others, speaking incoherently, and so on.

Pashupatas appear to perform these acts with a passion, and the objective is accomplished when persons exposed to their pranks gladly withdraw. Mission accomplished! Links are destroyed. Freed thus, the Pashupata can now resort to austerities through Yogic practices with the hope of acquiring magical powers (such as immunity from heat and cold and from extreme pain inflicted on the body) on the path to union with Shiva.

These practitioners have been seen in and around the famous pilgrimage center Kashi (in the holy city of Benares in North India), where Shiva is worshipped 24/7. Here they practice what appear to be strange austerities such as gazing on the sun, standing on one leg for months and years, and lying on beds of nails. These recluses have helped fill pages in *Ripley's Believe It or Not* and in travelers' tales.

KAPALIKAS

Shaivites who embrace this approach live on the edge of society, naked and covered with ash, observing asceticism on cremation grounds. They carry a staff with a skull attached to the top and a begging bowl made of a human skull. To please their deities (Shiva in the form of Bhairava and his equally ferocious consort Bhairavi), they worship them with blood and offerings of meat, alcohol, and bodily fluids obtained through ritual lovemaking. This subsect has all but vanished in India except in the city of Benares.

VEERA SHAIVAS OR LINGAYATS

The Lingayats are Shaivaites who worship Shiva in the form of a *lingam*, a stone pillar. They wear a metal replica of the pillar as an amulet around the neck. They generally reject caste distinctions and accept women as equals.

The post-Vedic approach: Mantra Marga

The post-Vedic approach, called Mantra Marga, is a branch of Shaiva philosophy and lifestyle generally practiced by South Indian and Sri Lankan Shaivite Hindus. It started as ritual-based worship, and the emphasis shifted to devotional *(bhakti)* approach, similar to that of the Vaishnavas.

Shaiva Siddhanta philosophy, which is part of Mantra Marga, is *Dualistic:* It makes a distinction between the individual soul and the Supreme Soul. The adherents follow an intense three-fold daily practice through methods that include the following:

- Purifying the body with total commitment to a spiritual path.
- Seeking divine energy in the body through such rigorous yogic practices as Kundalini Yoga. This is a rigorous and very powerful form of yoga which, through intense practice under guidance from a competent teacher, allows the life force within the body to move up the spine. In the process, the aspirant may obtain some magical powers.

» Awakening the soul with one's own intellect, breath control, and visualization of Shiva's trident.

Like the Vaishnava *alwars* (poet-saints), Shaiva saints known as *nayanars* created stirring Tamil poetry attracting a large following. A good example of a Shaiva Siddhanta center in the United States today is the Kauai monastery in Hawaii.

Integrating Vaishnava and Shaiva Ideas: The Smartas

Smartas are brahmins who follow *smrti* texts: post-Vedic scriptures that are considered to be "remembered" (as opposed to *shrutis*, which are considered "revealed" or "seen"). Smartas have special interest in adhering strictly to the concepts of dharma (see Book 1, Chapter 1). This denomination successfully integrates the ideas contained in the Vedas with those of the post-Vedic literature (texts that came later than the Vedas), bridging Vaishnavism and Shaivism.

Smartas worship five gods and goddesses: Ganesha (Ganapati), Durga, Surya, Shiva, and an avatar of Vishnu (of the devotee's preference). The worship traditions largely resemble those of the Vaishnava sect. The followers believe that the individual soul aspires to merge into Shiva as a river merges into the ocean.

The followers of Smarta tradition generally adhere to beliefs propounded by the renowned Adi Shankara (788–820 CE), an *acharya* (religious guide) known for his *Advaita* (Nondualism) philosophy, which makes no distinction between the individual soul and the Supreme Soul.

Worshipping Devi, the Female Power: Shaktas

REMEMBER

A unique feature of Hinduism is that the adherents worship both gods and goddesses. Hindus whose main worship is directed to a goddess are called *Shaktas*. The word *Devi* is a generic term for the goddess, although the same word is used as an ending to the name of any goddess: For example, *Lakshmi Devi* means the goddess Lakshmi. Two forms of Devi predominate in these worships, and we introduce them here.

In one approach, Hindus revere the concept of Mother and the associated love and compassion. They recognize the female partner of any male godhead as the creative aspect of (and support of) her consort, be it Brahma, Vishnu, or Shiva. Examples of this form of Devi are the goddesses Mahalakshmi, Saraswati, Sita, Radha, and a host of others who are worshipped by millions of Hindus around the world. Earth is worshipped as Bhumi Mata, Mother Earth.

In the other (even more common) approach, Devi is associated with awesome strength and power in her own right. She is recognized most often in this aspect as the goddesses Durga or Kali.

Both these aspects of Devi — motherly and powerful — represent to the Shaktas all that is beautiful, fearful, and awe-inspiring in nature and the universe.

Ritual worship of goddesses such as Lakshmi and Saraswati includes a ceremonial offering of clothing, ornaments, sanctified water, fruit, flowers, incense, and food. This is also true of the public worship of Durga in her benign aspect. However, worship of other forms of Shakta goddesses (either Devi or many regional and village patroness goddesses) may include offerings of sacrificial animals.

IN THIS CHAPTER

- » Discovering Hindu ideas about worship
- » Conducting mealtime worship
- » Offering prayers morning and night
- » Focusing on deities
- » Looking at temple ceremonies
- » Understanding different festivals

Chapter 4
Worshipping at Home, at a Temple, and on Holydays and Festivals

Hindus worship a variety of gods and goddesses in a variety of ways in a variety of settings and at different times during a day. While orthodox Hindus adhere to a strict schedule and pay attention to details prescribed by tradition, the majority of Hindus simply acknowledge a higher power and use a variety of gestures and salutations as they go through their daily routines. As they pass in front of temples or other worship centers, for example, they may pause momentarily and close their eyes in a few seconds' meditation before they move on. But home is where most Hindus keep up the formal family tradition of worship.

In this chapter, we discuss the daily religious practices that devout Hindus perform at home, in temples, on holydays, and at festivals.

REMEMBER

Our goal in this chapter is to give you an idea of the rituals and steps involved in Hindu worship. Whether each set of steps in this chapter is followed strictly or modified depends on individual preferences based on family tradition and the time available each day for such practices.

Discovering the Components of Hindu Worship

For most Hindus, worship is a priority in life. That being the case, worship is not reserved for a particular day or week; it's a daily routine, built into the mindset of Hindus and prescribed by family tradition and belief system. Hindu festivals, temples, rituals, observances, music, clothes, food, and social gatherings are principally the external expressions of this basic belief.

The prayers

Prayers may have different objectives. Some Hindus pray for enhancement of their faith and commitment. Some may pray for specific reasons such as for a loved one's recovery from illness, the smooth delivery of a baby, or a family member's safe journey. The Hindu calendar (called *Panchangam* in Sanskrit, one of the oldest languages in the world) provides auspicious times and dates for certain prayers based on the year, month, position of the sun, phase of the moon, and season and correlates the same with respect to festivals and rituals.

Two important steps or procedures are basic to all prayer rituals and are often repeated. One uses water and the other air. We explain them next.

Procedures using water: Achamana

Hindu prayer rituals include using water to purify the immediate space and performing what is called *achamana*, which involves these steps:

1. Using a ceremonial spoon known as *uddharana* and your left hand, scoop water from a ceremonial cup and dispense it into your right hand, which is cupped by drawing the index finger in and holding it by the thumb.
2. Chant *achyutaaya namaha* (I salute god Achyuta) and take one sip of water.
3. Scoop more water from the ceremonial cup into your cupped hand, chant *anantaaya namaha* (I salute god Anantha), and take a second sip of water.

4. Scoop more water from the ceremonial cup into your cupped hand, chant *govindaaya namaha* (I salute god Govinda), and take a third sip of water.

Note that the names of gods used here are different names of Vishnu.

Procedures using air: Pranayama

A sacred mantra (chant) known as *Gayatri* is meditated upon during different times in prayer rituals using a controlled breathing technique known as *pranayama*. The mantra is translated as follows:

> Om. That which pervades earth, sky, and heaven, which is worthy of worship, that has no beginning; that which is the light of wisdom and truth; Let us meditate on the radiance of that divinity. May that brilliance help inspire and illuminate our minds. That One which represents water, light, and is the quintessence in all things; May that almighty spirit pervading the earth, atmosphere, and heaven bless us with enlightenment.

While meditating on this mantra (saying the words in your mind), you follow these steps:

1. Close your right nostril with your right thumb (with the fingers naturally bent slightly inward except for the middle finger, which is drawn completely in toward the palm).
2. Draw air through the left nostril as long as you can.
3. Then block the left nostril with the ring finger as you release the air through the right nostril.
4. With the left nostril still blocked, draw air through the right nostril.
5. Now block the right nostril with the right thumb, unblock the left nostril, and release the air through it. After you release the air thus through the left nostril, you've just completed one pranayama.

TIP

We offer these steps so you can visualize what prayanama involves, but if you want to practice this technique, you can refer to a Yoga book or a teacher.

The arrangement of an altar

Most Hindu households set up an altar (or shrine) at a special place in the home dedicated to offer prayers. This area can be elaborate or simple. For example, some households may reserve a shelf in the bedroom or the kitchen for daily worship. Large households may set aside a separate room with a tier of shelves or a *mantap:* a four-pillared wooden gazebo-like structure, within which a statue of a deity stands. If an altar is not permanently set up inside the home, Hindus put one up for special occasions when they perform a *puja* (worship) and invite friends and extended family members to participate.

Regardless of the size of the altar, this shrine is always in the inner part of the house that is less exposed to noise and traffic than other living quarters. Such a location provides a sense of privacy and sacredness. The altar also generally faces the eastern direction.

You find the following objects on a Hindu altar in most homes of devout Hindus:

- A clean cloth to drape over the altar
- A picture of the main god or goddess to be worshipped, as well as pictures or statues of the family godhead and guru
- Two stainless steel or silver vessels for water and a metal spoon called an *uddharana*
- A cloth piece to symbolize clothing
- *Kumkum* (the red powder that Hindu women use on their foreheads) and *haldi* (turmeric) in small cups
- Jewelry, to serve as the symbolic offering
- *Akshata* (a dry mixture of turmeric-tinted uncooked rice) in a cup
- Sandal paste, incense sticks, and camphor
- Fresh flowers, fruits, coconut, and leaves on plates, as well as fruit juice in a cup
- Lamps with wicks soaked in oil or *ghee* (clarified butter)
- An *arati* plate (a metallic plate containing in it a small cup or spoon-like receptacle into which a small lamp with wick and oil or a few crystals of camphor are placed and lit at the conclusion of a puja)

The rituals

Worship ceremonies may be simple or elaborate and take from just a few minutes to an hour or two. A simple ceremony may involve no more than the devotee (and their family) standing in front of an altar, lighting and placing an incense stick at the altar, and uttering a couple of prayer mantras before leaving home in the morning. An elaborate ceremony, on the other hand, can last longer, use many objects of symbolic importance, and follow a lengthy series of prescribed steps. Several of the following sections describe such ceremonies.

Conducting Mealtime Worship

In the Hindu epic called the *Mahabharata*, prince Yudhishthira is quizzed by the Yaksha (a forest spirit) with this riddle: "Who is happy?" Yudhishthira answers this way: "That person who is free of debt, not in constant travel, and who eats a frugal, satisfying hot meal in his own home every evening." In this section, we explain Hindu mealtime rituals and the rituals associated with the monthly fast day.

Following mealtime procedures

Orthodox Hindus, especially males in the brahmin (priestly) caste, are brought up to regard eating as a ritual. For the two major meals of the day — lunch and supper — they begin with the ritual known as *parishechanam*. This ritual follows these steps:

1. Pour a couple spoons of sanctified water into your cupped right hand.
2. Sprinkle this water over the entire set of food items served (on a banana leaf or perhaps a plate), circling the items three times clockwise and chanting and addressing the food itself: *You are the Truth. I circle you with dharma.*

   The intent of this mantra is to create a boundary around the food with sanctified water to ward off any bad vibrations.
3. Sip the remaining drops after chanting *Let this be the nectar spreading through the food inside.*

   Amrita (nectar) is considered to be the preferred drink of the gods. The intent of this chant is to pray for infusing nectar throughout this food.
4. Take no more than a grain of rice (or other staple) from the banana leaf (or plate) and swallow it without chewing. Do this five times, one after another, as offerings to each of the wind elements inside the body that control various bodily functions: *prana* (main breath), *samana* (digestive system), *vyana* (circulatory system), *udana* (respiratory system), and *apana* (eliminatory system).
5. Now it's time to eat!
6. Indicate the end of the meal by sipping a few drops of water and chanting *Let this protective nectar infuse the food eaten.*

A night to fast: Ekadashi

Some days, Hindus just don't eat, at least not a full meal. The eleventh day on the Hindu lunar calendar is known as *Ekadashi*. Each month, that day is set aside for contemplation and fasting. (*Note:* Fasting doesn't mean what you probably think. Hindus, at the end of that day, can look forward to a light meal of delicious snack items, warm milk, and sweet drinks.)

Typically, when only a light meal is served on the evening of Ekadashi, a feast is cooked the next day (Dwadashi). An orthodox Hindu family, after fasting on Ekadashi, will enjoy that sumptuous meal on Dwadashi after completing morning *ablutions* (washing, bathing), getting dressed, and worshipping at home.

REMEMBER

All meals that are eaten as part of worship contain only vegetarian items. In a typical South Indian home, the dishes include items such as seasonal and seasoned curried vegetables; *sambar* (a thick soup prepared with spices, lentils, and a vegetable); and a milk-, fruit-, or cereal-based sweet dish. The dishes do vary from region to region in India, but when they're part of worship, they remain vegetarian.

Praying Morning, Noon, and Night

Devout Hindus begin and end the day with prayers. Here, we explain the mantras they use upon waking and through the rest of the day until bedtime.

A simple morning prayer

Upon waking, most Hindus ask forgiveness for stepping on Mother Earth by chanting a mantra that translates this way: *I offer my salutations to the Consort of Vishnu, Mother Earth, asking her to forgive me for stepping on her, whose body is clothed with oceans and mountain ranges.*

Next, Hindus open and look at the palms of their hands, chanting the following: *At the tip of my fingers resides Lakshmi, Saraswati in the center of my palms, and Govinda at the wrist. Thus I view my hands with reverence in the morning.*

Now the day can begin. After a bath and before breakfast, many Hindus offer a simple puja by standing in front of the altar, lighting an incense stick, and chanting a mantra or two. An example of such a mantra is this: *May Brahma, Vishnu, and Shiva along with the planets Sun, Moon, Mars, Mercury, Jupiter, Venus, Saturn, Rahu, and Ketu grant this to be a good day for me.*

TECHNICAL STUFF

Rahu, the eclipse, is represented as a mouth that threatens to swallow the sun and moon. His image in temples, a head with no tail, never faces that of the sun or the moon. *Ketu*, the comet, is the unlucky trailing tail with no head attached. These are malign influences that need to be appeased by invocation and prayer, along with the benign "planets."

At this point, many Hindus are ready to be on their way. But the orthodox need to do more, as the next section explains.

Sandhya vandanam: Worship for orthodox Hindus

Sandhya refers to that particular period of time when the day breaks and the sun rises. The same word is used to identify the time when the sun sets. *Vandanam* means "salutations." Thus, *sandhya vandanam* is a celebration saluting the sun god. Orthodox Hindus perform this celebration three times every day: at sunrise, noon, and sunset.

The ceremony is based in the Vedas and involves no physical form of a deity. No altar is required, and it can be performed in the open as long the environment is conducive to worship (it's quiet and clean). All that is needed is a cup of water and a spoon. The ceremony requires the worshipper to stand, sit, and turn toward the four directions during different parts of the puja.

Before the ceremony

Before beginning the worship, orthodox Hindus follow specific instructions that include minute details, such as the following:

- Washing hands and nails 12 times
- Rinsing the mouth 12 times and brushing their teeth
- Immediately after doing an achamana (refer to the earlier section "Procedures using water: Achamana"), taking a bath while chanting a declaration that the bath is being taken under the orders of the Almighty and to please the good Lord Narayana (another name for Vishnu) in order to absolve all sins
- Invoking and saluting the river Ganges while pouring water on their bodies and completing the bath

The worshipper then dons clean clothes and applies denominational marks on the forehead and other parts of the upper body, as we explain in Book 1, Chapter 3.

Meanwhile, to get ready for the morning puja, they may clean the areas around and inside the prayer room by lighting an incense stick or two along with a lamp and setting up the altar with puja materials and flowers for offerings. They may also typically decorate either the front steps of the house or the entrance to the puja room with what is called a *rangoli* pattern drawn with chalk or rice flour.

The principal steps

The worshipper starts with achamana (explained in the section "Procedures using water: Achamana"). Then they follow these steps (note that each chant involves the names of gods who are all forms of Vishnu):

1. Using the right thumb, touch the right and left cheeks while chanting *Keshavaaya namaha* and *Narayanaaya namaha* respectively. The translation of this chant is "I salute Keshava and Narayana." (The other chants in this list have the same meaning addressed to the other names of Vishnu.) This is a typical salutation to a godhead.
2. Using the ring finger and chanting *Maadhavaaya namaha, Govindaaya namaha,* touch the right and left eyes, one at a time, with eyes closed.
3. Touch the right and left nostrils with the index finger while chanting *Vishnave namaha* and *Madhusudanaaya namaha.*
4. Touch the right and left ears with the little finger while chanting *Trivikramaaya namaha* and *Vaamanaaya namaha,* respectively.
5. Touch the right and left shoulders with the middle finger while chanting *Sreedharaaya namaha* and *Hrisheekeshaaya namaha.*
6. Finally, using all fingertips, touch the navel and head while chanting *Padmanaabhaaya namaha* and *Daamodaraaya namaha.*

REMEMBER

The belief is that these contacts with the right-hand fingers energize the seats of energy in the upper body.

7. Say this prayer to remove all obstacles in the way of this ceremony: *I meditate on Vishnu clothed in white, the color of the moon, four-armed, of pleasant aspect, so that all obstacles may be lessened.*

The worshipper then declares their intention through a chant to perform the ceremony by specifying the time (morning, noon, or evening). After doing so, the worshipper follows these steps:

1. Perform the pranayama three times (see the earlier section "Procedures using air: Pranayama.")

2. Sprinkle a few drops of water on the head while uttering a chant in praise of water itself.
3. Do an achamana and sip water (see the earlier section "Procedures using water: Achamana") while making prayers to banish any anger from yourself and asking for forgiveness for any sins committed the previous night.
4. Say a prayer to the Supreme Being.
5. Stand up and offer a palmful of water (facing east in the morning, north at noon, and west at sunset) while chanting the pranayama (Gayatri) mantra.
6. Sit down and declare that you, the worshipper, are indeed Brahman, followed by an achamana.
7. Salute, by chanting each name, each of the nine planets and the forms of Vishnu named in steps 1 through 6 of the preceding list. Dispense water, as you chant, by pouring it into the cupped right palm and offer it through the fingertips by emptying the slightly bent hand.
8. Chant the Gayatri mantra in a meditative pose (facing east in the morning, north at noon, and west at sunset).
9. Worship the very word Om by
   - Touching the head and meditating on Brahman
   - Touching the upper lip and meditating on Gayatri
   - Touching the chest while meditating on the Supreme Soul
   - Touching the head again to salute the Seven Sages
   - Touching the chest to show reverence to the fire god Agni, wind god Vayu, god of waters Varuna, and the chief of gods Indra
10. Perform three pranayamas.
11. Meditate on Gayatri.
12. Meditate on and chant salutation to the sun god.
13. Salute gods that protect each direction, spaces above and below, and the Hindu Trinity.
14. Salute Yama, the judge of the dead.
15. Conclude with a dedication offering everything that was done by your deeds, mind, and speech to the Almighty.

This completes the worship ceremony for an orthodox Hindu.

Ready to call it a day? Bedtime prayers

At bedtime, Hindus say another prayer to ward off bad dreams. Some Hindus chant a praise to several forms of Vishnu as follows and then go to sleep: *I meditate on Achuta, Keshava, Vishnu, Hari, Soma, Hamsa, Janardhana, Narayana, and Krishna in order to rid myself of bad dreams and sleep at peace.*

Formally Worshipping a Deity

Many families learn how to conduct a formal worship to their family god/goddess by watching their elders. These ceremonies use simple Sanskrit chants even though the family members may not be able to read or write Sanskrit. (It's not uncommon to see worshippers use notes written in the worshippers' own language.)

Pujas, such as the one that follows, may take place on birthdays, anniversaries, or other special occasions. Sometimes a priest may be invited to come and perform the puja. Some householders prefer to do a puja to their family godhead daily at the end of the day.

In the following section, we show the steps used to conduct a simple and typical worship ceremony by the family without the assistance of a priest.

The worship begins by invoking the godhead, followed by a series of invitations, prayers, and offerings described by the Sanskrit word *shodasha upacharas*, meaning "16 offerings." The following sections take you through the worship of goddess Lakshmi to show how Hindus perform a typical 16-step puja.

Prayers to Ganapati, guru, and the family godhead

Before starting the puja, you have to contemplate Ganapati (Ganesha), the lord of obstacles, to ensure that no obstacles interfere with a smooth performance of the puja rituals. Thus, with folded hands, you say the following: *So that the ceremonies we are about to undertake proceed to completion without any obstacles, we contemplate on Mahaganapati.* (*Note:* Hindus always chant the equivalent of these words in Sanskrit.)

You also invoke the *grhadevata*, the family godhead, who bestows protection to the family at all times, by saying *I respectfully contemplate our family godhead.*

Finally, you pay respect to the family guru and offer prayer before beginning the ceremony by saying *Salutations to the preceptor who is verily Brahma, Vishnu, and Maheshwara (Shiva) and who personifies the Supreme Being.*

Shuddhi (cleansing)

To be sure that any and all evil tendencies are removed from the worship room, start with a prayer to Shiva whose very invocation is believed to clear out any troubling vibrations. Say *I salute the Lord of the Southern direction who is the very embodiment of the sacred symbol Om and of pure knowledge and eternal peace.*

Next, invoke and invite the seven sacred rivers to fill the metallic vessel. (A typical vessel is a rounded, narrow-necked urn or bowl.) You use this water, now sanctified, to cleanse and offer throughout the worship. Start pouring water from one vessel into the smaller one as you say *O Ganga, Yamuna, Godavari, Saraswati, Narmada, Sindhu, and Kaveri waters, please be present in this place.*

After you receive the sacred waters, symbolically cleanse your hands by offering a spoonful of water into the hands of the other worshipers and by wiping the hands with reverence as you say *May anything unholy become holy, may all lower tendencies depart, cleansing both inside and out as we remember the Lord.*

Prayer of invocation to Goddess Lakshmi

Say this prayer to invoke the Goddess Lakshmi:

> I worship Mahalakshmi, daughter of the king of the Milky Ocean, queen of the abode of Mahavishnu, who is served by the consorts of all the Gods, who is the one light and point of origin of the universe, through whose benign grace Brahma, Indra, and Shiva attained their exalted positions, who is Mother of the Three Worlds, who is called Kamala, and who is the beloved consort of Mukunda.

The 16 upacharas

Now you're ready to invoke Mahalakshmi and offer upacharas — in other words, you're ready to receive the goddess and make offerings with reverence.

1. **Avahana — Greeting and welcoming:** With folded hands, focus on the picture of the deity as you say *I offer my salutations to Goddess Mahalakshmi* (you repeat this before each step). Then offer a few grains of akshata with your right hand such that the grains fall on the picture gently as you say *I offer an invocation to you.*

REMEMBER

Be sure to make the offerings using your right hand only and with your palm facing upward.

2. **Aasana — Offering a seat:** Offer akshata as before such that the grains fall on the altar as you say *I offer a seat for you.*

3. **Padyam — Washing the feet:** Offer an uddharana-full of water at the feet of the deity or picture as you say *I offer water at your feet.*

4. **Arghyam — Washing the hands:** Offer an uddharana-full of water to the hands of the deity or picture as you say *I offer water for your hands.*

5. **Aachamanam — Offering water to drink:** Offer again an uddharana-full of water to the hands of the deity or picture as you say *I offer water to quench thirst.*

6. **Madhuparkam — Offering a sweet drink:** Offer fruit juice or honey-sweetened beverage as you say *I offer some sweet drink.*

7. **Snaanam — Bathing:** Symbolically offer water to bathe or pour water over the deity to bathe as you say *I offer clean water to bathe.*

8. **Vastram — Offering clothing:** Symbolically offer a clean piece of cloth to represent gifts of clothing, and say *I offer clothing.*

9. **Aabharanam — Offering ornaments:** Symbolically offer a jewel or two (a necklace or a bangle) to be placed around the neck of the statue or in front of the picture of the goddess while saying *I offer jewels to you.*

TIP

You use the Aabharanam only for goddesses. For male gods, you use the Yagnopaveetam (offering the sacred thread) and say *I offer the sacred thread.*

10. **Gandham — Offering perfume (sandalwood paste):** Apply to the forehead some sandalwood paste as you say, *I offer sandal paste.* Then apply some kumkum to the forehead as you say, *I offer kumkum to you.*

11. **Pushpam — Offering flowers:** Offer flowers or petals to the picture or the image of the deity, saying *I offer flowers in worship.* Then with folded hands say the several names of Lakshmi as follows: *I salute Mahalakshmi who is known as Kamala (lotus lady), Ramaa (beautiful lady), who is Mother of the Universe, daughter of the Lord of the Milky Ocean, who sees everything, and who is sister of Chandra (Moon).*

12. **Dhoopam — Offering perfumed incense:** Offer incense by motioning incense smoke with your right hand toward the altar, saying *I offer fragrance in worship.*

13. **Deepam — Offering a lighted lamp:** Lift the lamp and show it to the picture or deity such that it illuminates the face and say *I offer sacred light.*

14. **Naivedyam — Offering food:** Lift the plate of fruits, leaves, and flowers in reverence and offer them saying *I offer a variety of flowers, leaves, and fruits.* Then lift the cover off the *prasadam* (food offered to the god), such as a cooked dish of sweet rice, and offer it as you say *I offer delicious food to you.*

Then sprinkle a few drops of water with the uddharana on the food as you hail the various wind elements in our bodies that promote digestion. The final hail is to the creator Brahma. Continue to offer water as you say *I offer more water as you partake the foods.*

15. **Suvarna - Offering gold:** Offer a coin as you say *I offer gold to you.*

16. **Pradakshina — Circumambulation and salutation (prostration):** Stand up and do a *pradakshina* (circumambulation, or walking around something) three times turning to your right, saying *Whatever sins I have committed in all my lives may all of them be absolved as I circumambulate in worship.*

Conclusion

You complete the puja with an *arati:* a metallic plate containing a small cup or spoon-like receptacle into which a few crystals of camphor are placed and burned. Use your right hand to lift the arati with the burning flame and wave it up and down in an elliptical form clockwise to light up the deity's face, while you ring a ceremonial bell with your left hand. When that is done, take the arati plate around so that the devotees can receive the blessing by reverentially cupping their hands downward and receiving the warmth of the flame and touching their eyes with the cupped hands inward.

As the arati is being performed, the devotees may sing devotional songs depending on the family practice. You conclude the puja ceremony by saying:

You alone are our mother and father

You alone are our sibling and friend

You alone are our knowledge and prosperity

You alone are everything to us my Lord my Lord

Whatever I have performed through my action,

speech, thought, knowledge, or my natural habit,

may all that be surrendered to Srimannarayana (another name

for Vishnu).

The *prasad* (offered food) may now be distributed and enjoyed after chanting the Shanti Mantra:

May Brahman protect us

May we dine together

May we work together with great energy

Let us be illumined together

Let us live in harmony

Peace, Peace, Peace!

Reviewing Temple Ceremonies

Hindus have been worshipping in a community setting since the fire altars of the Neolithic age (6000–4000 BCE). The earliest temples were probably constructed of wood to house a particular deity, and there are still many famous caves with natural rock formations revered as images of gods.

A Hindu temple is known as *devasthanam* in Sanskrit, meaning "abode of God." (In northern India, the word *mandir* is more commonly used.) In other words, Hindu temples aren't merely places where devout Hindus go to worship; they are the earthly homes of the gods.

Specific rules must be observed in choosing a principal deity and associated deities; selecting the materials for sculpting the statues to be installed for worship; choosing the right month, day, and time to break ground; preparing the deities for installation; performing a host of other related tasks; and sanctifying the shrine.

This section presents temple worship practices prescribed in ancient manuals.

Temple protocol

WARNING

Almost all religious spaces have rules about the conduct and demeanor of people visiting them. Hindu temples are no different. So if you are visiting a Hindu temple, please keep these points in mind:

- You must remove your shoes upon arrival at the temple.
- No smoking is allowed. Nor can drugs, alcohol, or meat products (meat, fish, eggs, poultry) be brought in or consumed on the temple premises.
- Remain quiet and contemplative inside. Worshippers may recite the appropriate prayer(s) silently, especially if other people are present. No loud noises, text messages, or conversation! (Please turn off your cell phone before entering a temple.)
- If a puja is in progress, you may stay, participate, and receive the blessings and offering *(prasadam)*. Otherwise, you may pray and/or observe and proceed to the next sanctum.

» Worshippers may circle the shrine three times clockwise, keeping the main sanctum to their right, and prostrate before leaving the temple. Flowers and fruits may be offered or left just outside the sanctum, before circling the shrine. Please do not touch the *vigrahas* (images).

Daily worship

The daily rituals vary, but in general, prayers are offered consistent with the time of day: at sunrise, at noon, and at sunset.

Morning worship includes chanting of *suprabhatam:* hymns in praise of the deity and glorifying the morning that is holy. This worship praises the Lord and sets the stage for other rituals. A chant of 108 names of the Lord, as described in the next section, concludes with an *arati:* a plate with a flame waved up and down clockwise in front of the deity at the conclusion of a worship.

The different worship rituals use additional chants from different scriptures, such as the Vedas. In the morning, the additional chants come from the Rig Veda; at noon, they come from the Yajur Veda; and at night, the Sama Veda. Occasionally a devotee may show up with a new car and request a puja to be performed for it! The priests oblige and do a worship ceremony asking gods to bless the vehicle to ensure safety and performance.

SALUTATIONS USING 108 OR 1,000 NAMES

Orthodox Hindus, particularly in southern India, used two sets of chants commonly practiced and chanted at home but mostly used at temples in front of the deity being worshipped. These chants are salutations to the godhead using either 108 names or 1,000 names.

So what is special about the number 108? There is no clear answer and all sorts of convoluted explanations. Here, for example, are a few facts that may or may not have had an impact:

- The distance between Earth and the sun is 108 times the diameter of the sun.
- The distance between Earth and the moon is 108 times the diameter of the moon.
- There are 108 stitches in a baseball. (Okay, this one could not have been a factor!)

(continued)

(continued)

All major and some minor gods (and goddesses) are described with 108 names, as well as 1,000 *(Sahasra Nama)* names. Using Lakshmi as an example, her 108 names/attributes include: Well-wisher of all life, Supreme Soul, Speech, Lotus, Purity, Auspicious, Inauspicious, Nectar, Fulfilled, Golden, Wealth, Strong, Radiant, Bright wife of the sun, Light, Earth, Earth-borne, Wife of Vishnu, Beautiful-eyed, Granter of wishes, Intelligent, Sinless, Nine-Durgas, Wife of Hari, Sorrowless, Nectarlike, Remover of miseries, Abode of morality, Kind, Mother of the universe, Beloved of god Padmanabha, Virtuous, Fragrant, Giver of boons, Sister of the moon, Doer of auspicious things, Mother of the universe, Remover of poverty, Earth's daughter, Protector, Lover of palaces, Daughter of the milky ocean, Vishnu's chest jewel, Consort of Vishnu, Kali, Friend of the Trimurti.

Hindus don't necessarily stop at 108 names. They have a thousand ways of praising a godhead.

Chanting the names of God

Worshipping Hindu gods, especially in temples, includes almost always a chanting that is known as *Ashtoththara Shata Namavali,* meaning "chanting the 108 names." All major gods/goddesses are greeted with a set of 108 names frequently chanted by priests at temples and by devotees (see the nearby sidebar, "Salutations using 108 or 1,000 Names"). The event is called *archana,* meaning "offering of praises." When these worship services are conducted, the devotees and their families stand in reverence in front of the sanctum while the priest chants the names one at a time, offering a few petals of flowers or a few grains of akshata.

In South Indian temples, the archana is commonly sponsored by a devotee family to celebrate an event (the birth of a child, passing an examination, a new job, or marriage, for example).

If there is a front office at the temple, you can buy a ticket to have the archana performed for a fee and take it to the deity of your choice and present it to the priest in charge. You will then be asked for your name, lineage, birth star, and the name of the person for whom this worship is being offered.

With these details established, the worship begins. Each chant starts with the sacred symbol Om followed by the particular name of the god or goddess, followed by the Sanskrit word *namaha,* which means "I salute." Using the goddess Lakshmi as an example, the chant would be *Om prakrtyai namaha.* Translation: "Om I salute Nature." Nature is one of Lakshmi's names, and this chant means "O Lakshmi, You are Nature and I salute you as such."

Special days for individual deities

Certain days are considered special for certain deities. For example, Friday night is a time to welcome and worship Lakshmi, the goddess of good fortune and well-being. Mondays are for Shiva. Full moon nights are celebrated with an elaborate worship of Satyanarayana. Worships also are conducted after eclipses.

Temples are set to perform elaborate pujas to these deities on special days and nights as well as on days that mark a festival.

Recognizing a Few Festivals Celebrated Throughout India

The most important driver determining the size, scope, and ritual in a festival is family tradition, which explains why these observances vary so much from region to region (and sometimes within a region, too). Non-Hindus can feel confused by this variety, struggling to see a unifying principle beneath it all. But Hindus simply accept the diversity — even relish it — and don't mind if the family next door practices the same festival in a different manner. The word *uniformity* hardly exists in the Hindu world! But don't worry; in this section, we help you figure out the fundamentals about Hindu festivals and holydays.

As you read this section, keep two points in mind:

- The underlying theme of all festivals is the same: the triumph of good over evil and establishing and restoring *dharma* (moral order).
- Three main categories of festival exist: those commemorating the birth or triumph of a god or goddess, those celebrating a lunar or solar event, and those celebrating a harvest.

All the festivals listed throughout this section are observed by Hindus, irrespective of where they live or what language they speak. However, certain regions emphasize some festivals and are known for special celebrations that attract people outside the region.

Makara Sankranti

Makara Sankranti is both a harvest festival and a celebration of the winter solstice. *Makara* is the name of the zodiac phase the sun enters into in mid-January. Sometimes this festival is simply referred to as *Sankranti*.

Hindus view the winter solstice as the time when Surya, the sun god, returns from his journey south, and his journey in a northern direction begins. The journey south is called *Dakshinayana*, and the journey north is referred to as *Uttarayana*. The six months it takes for this journey to end so that the direction may change to north from south is the equivalent of a single night for the gods. In essence, therefore, the six-month night of the divine ends, and Makara Sankranti marks the dawn of a new day — a new sixth-month day of the gods (because one year for us humans equates to one day for the gods).

This celestial event provides a green flag for individuals and families to undertake important or auspicious events. For example, in many parts of India, no marriages are negotiated or performed until after Makara Sankranti.

REMEMBER

As with most festivals, Sankranti celebrations vary from one region to another.

Shivaratri: The grand night of Shiva

Shivaratri is a solemn celebration of Shiva, one of the Hindu Trinity. During this holyday, devotees (mainly Shaivas; see Book 1, Chapter 3 for more information on the various Hindu sects) stay up all night fasting, praying, meditating, and worshipping in the belief that doing so absolves them of all sins.

Shivaratri falls on a moonless night in February or March in the dark waning moon fortnight. Some Hindus believe that on this day, god Shiva married Parvati. Others believe that this was the day of Shiva's cosmic dance of creation *(Tandava nritya)*.

REMEMBER

Simplicity is the guiding principle during this festival, from the rituals to the foods, and contemplation and meditation are the order of the day. The most familiar representation of Shiva is the iconic *lingam* — a phallic symbol. Temple priests, on behalf of devotees, offer elaborate ritual baths, followed by an arati, to the lingam every three hours. Flowers, kumkum powder, and bilva (bael) leaves are offered. (Bilva trees are commonly found on the grounds of Shiva temples, and the leaves are highly valued by the Hindu medical system of Ayurveda.)

The highlights of this festival include holding a night-long vigil, singing *bhajans* (rhythmic phrases in Sanskrit or local vernacular in praise of gods) that praise Shiva, repeating *om namah shivaya* (Om, I salute Lord Shiva), participating in temple worships until morning, and breaking the fast with a final worship and frugal meal.

Ramanavami: Rama's birthday

Ramanavami is nine days of festivities in April (the Hindu month of Chaitra) that celebrate the birthday of Rama, an avatar of Vishnu and hero of the *Ramayana*. During Ramanavami, it's customary to read the poet Valmiki's version of the epic in Sanskrit. On the ninth day, the entire festivity reaches a climax with a great feast. Skillful storytellers relate the nearly infinite substories that bring the theme back and forth to the main story, the *Ramayana*.

Rama is usually portrayed as a handsome young warrior armed with a bow. The *Ram Parivar* is a popular pictorial grouping of Rama with his wife Sita, his brother Lakshmana, and Hanuman the monkey god. Rama stands with Lakshmana on his right (also armed with a bow), Sita on his left, and Hanuman kneeling at his feet.

During this festival, temples perform ceremonial divine weddings of Rama to Sita. These weddings use brass or bronze images of the two (known as *utsava murthis*, or processional images) and are performed in great detail. After the wedding, the images are carried out in a public procession.

Festivals marking the spring equinox and lunar new year

New Year celebrations have always had a religious undertone among Hindus. This event, which is called different names, is not celebrated on the same day by all Hindus. Family traditions, as well as whether a family follows a lunar calendar or solar calendar, determine the timing of the celebration:

- Tamilians observe *Varshapirapu* (birth of a new year) in mid-April.
- Kannadigas (people from Karnataka, who speak Kannada) and Andhras (Telugu-speaking folks from Andhra Pradesh) celebrate *Yugadi* in mid-March.
- Maharashtrians call this celebration *Gudi Padwa* and observe it in mid-March.
- People in northern India consider Diwali, which occurs in late October or early November, as their New Year celebration. For more on this festival, see the later section "Diwali."

Regardless of what this celebration is called or when it is celebrated, all practices include worshipping at home or a temple followed by a special feast. A special feature in some parts of India is to make sure everyone gets a taste of a mixture of *jaggery* (brown sugar) and leaves of bitter *neem* (a tree from the mahogany family) to drive home the point that life in the New Year will include both sweet and not-so-sweet experiences.

Dressing down for the occasion: Holi

Holi, a festival celebrated all over northern India, is essentially thanksgiving for the end of the winter crop harvest of wheat. This is a free-for-all fun time, caste no bar, for men and women.

TIP

During this festival, you'd be wise to dress casually when you step out of your house. You are liable to be met with shouts of *"Holi hai!"* ("Holi's here!") and a shower of red, orange, or yellow color by pranksters (your friends and neighbors, dressed in their worst) ready to throw or spray colored powders or water on one and all.

Krishna Janmashtami: Krishna's birthday

If one Hindu god's name is known and recognized throughout the world, it's Krishna, an avatar of Vishnu (see Book 1, Chapter 5). The most observed celebration during the summer is Krishna's birthday.

Krishna's birthday, known as *Janmashtami* (as well as *Krishna Jayanti* and *Gokulashtami*), is celebrated on the eighth day *(ashtami)* in the darker fortnight of the month Bhadrapada (August/September), in the middle of the monsoon season. The festival celebrating Krishna's birth occurs in the late evening to late night because Krishna is believed to have been born at midnight.

REMEMBER

Indian summers begin with torrid heat: In the northern plains, it's a dry, scorching 100- to 120-degree F; the coastline gets a soggy, humid 90-degree heat. Beginning around the end of March, this heat continues unabated until relieved by torrential monsoon rains in late June. During the hot season, few major festivals are conducted, and even weddings cease from mid-March to mid-April.

Janmashtami is a popular festival celebrated throughout India and other parts of the world. In temples where the presiding deity is Krishna, the rituals begin in the evening with a variety of worship ceremonies that include a royal bath *(abhishekam)* for the deity followed by dressing the deity with new colorful clothing, flowers, and jewelry. *Harikathas* (tales of Krishna rendered by professional storytellers) and music concerts all culminate with the grand finale comprising lighting camphor in an arati plate and waving it up and down ceremonially three times clockwise as priests chant prayer mantras at midnight. A small baby statue of Krishna in silver is set up in a decorated cradle and rocked during the final arati and treated to lullaby songs.

TIP

In South India, you can tell that a family is celebrating Janmashtami just by looking at the front door step in the family home. You'll see a drawing of the two small feet of a child decorating the front in a rice flour rangoli pattern. The joy and anticipation resemble that felt at the birth of a baby in the family!

And the food? Where to begin? Janmashtami is often a favorite holiday because no festival exceeds this holiday in the number of delicious items prepared! Families, especially those with children, prepare 15 or more delicious sweet and savory special dishes. These are mostly finger foods. In a popular arrangement in Iyengar households (those from a subsect of the Vaishnava denomination; see Book 1, Chapter 3), one of each item is tied to a piece of string and hung from a low ceiling frame in front of the altar specially set up for worship that night with a cradle, pictures, and small statues of baby Krishna. Celebrations include an evening puja and chanting from sacred scriptures.

Ganesha Chaturthi: Ganesha's birthday

Ganesha Chaturthi falls on the fourth day *(Chaturthi)* in the second (brighter) fortnight of the Hindu month of Bhadrapada (August/September), near the end of the monsoon season and close to the autumnal equinox. This all-India festival is especially popular in Mumbai and the western Indian state of Maharashtra. It celebrates the birthday of Ganesha (also known as Ganesh, Ganapati, Mahaganapati, Vinayaka, and Vighneshwara), one of the few major godheads who is a combination of man and animal form. Even Westerners who have little exposure to Hinduism recognize the elephant-headed god.

REMEMBER

Irrespective of the region of India, irrespective of special affiliation to any aspect of Hindu religion, Hindus offer their first prayer to Ganesha, Lord of Obstacles, before any auspicious tasks are undertaken. Hindus believe that Ganesha's blessings at the start of an endeavor will help the rest of the mission to proceed smoothly and without incident. For example, most concerts of Indian classical music begin with a composition in praise of Ganesha. This genial, kindly god occupies a very special place in the hearts of Hindus, and almost all Hindu households and places of business display his picture or statue in a prominent setting.

Although Ganesha is a favorite of Hindus worldwide, the festival celebrating his birth is especially popular in Maharashtra in the tradition begun by Lokamanya Balgangadhar Tilak (1856–1920), considered to be the father of the *swaraj* (Indian freedom) movement. To this day, the ten-day festival takes place in grand style, attracting millions to Maharashtra's capital Mumbai, and this religious fervor unites Hindus everywhere as no other festival does.

Beginning the celebration: The homecoming

The festival begins with buying and bringing home a clay sculpture of Ganesha, colored in gold, yellow, pink, and red, from the market and installing it at home in an inner room, along with all the paraphernalia needed to perform daily worship ceremonies. Then each day during the celebration begins with worship to Ganesha. When the festival is held in a temple, the daily worship continues with *darshans* (visiting the divine) by devotees, a storytelling session, a music concert, and a concluding brief worship ceremony at the end of the day.

Send-off ceremony

The ten-day celebration ends with a send-off ceremony called *visarjan* in which the image of Ganesha is immersed in a body of water, preferably a sacred river or lake. In Mumbai, this ceremony becomes an amazing public spectacle in several parts of the city in which a gigantic Ganesha is mounted on a moving chariot. The decorated throne is drawn through the streets by thousands of followers who finally carry it down to the beach and launch it into the ocean.

Navaratri

The Navaratri festival combines fun and frolic, grace and dignity, community involvement and participation, religious fervor and worship, display of power, plenty and pageantry, and connection with epics and legend.

Navaratri ("nine nights") is part of the ten-day event that begins on the first day *(Prathama)* of the bright half of the lunar month of Bhadrapada-Ashvayuja (September or October, depending on the lunar calendar). A concluding festival is tagged on to the tenth *(Dashami)* day known as *Vijayadashami* (Victorious Tenth Day) and pertains to victory of good over evil in the context of local lore. In between are sandwiched worships and celebrations directed toward the *devis* (principal Hindu goddesses): Durga, Lakshmi, and Saraswati.

Based on the Hindu calendar, the current practice is to worship Durga on the first three nights, Lakshmi on the second three nights, Saraswati on the seventh night, and Durga on the eighth night *(Ashtami)* celebrating her killing the demon Mahisha Asura. The ninth night is *Ayudha Puja* dedicated to the worship of martial arms and implements — namely guns, vehicles, elephants, and horses.

On the last day of the festival is the Vijayadashami, a celebration of the victory of good over evil. The victory is realized in hundreds of stories from the two epics, the *Mahabharata* and the *Ramayana*. For example, Hindus celebrate (from the *Ramayana*) the victory of Rama at Lanka, his grand entrance to his realm after 14 years in exile, and the rescue of Sita, as well as (from the *Mahabharata*) the recovery of precious arms that the Pandavas had hidden in the shami tree. All are cause for celebration and a triumphant display of power and plenty.

The most famous Navaratri: Dasara in Mysore

Although Navaratri and Vijayadashami are celebrated throughout the Hindu world, the Dasara at Mysore is without question *the* celebration that has made a mark on Navaratri celebrants around the world. (Think Times Square on New Year's Eve spread over ten nights!) No city celebrates this festival better than Mysore. Each night during Navaratri, the entire boundary of the famed Mysore Palace is illuminated with thousands of electric bulbs. (It's often called a sight for gods to see.)

The presiding deity in Mysore is Chamundeshwari, a form of Durga also known locally as *Mahishasuramardini*, slayer of demon Mahisha of local lore from whom the name Mysore is derived.

To pull off this grand celebration, the Karnataka state government goes all out, involving upward of 150 to 160 high-level officers of the government (you can only imagine the number of assistants in each such office). The result? The usually laid back, somewhat sleepy town comes alive and greets thousands of visitors with activities and events, including hundreds of games (soccer, volleyball, badminton, regional sports called khokho and kabaddi, wrestling, and so on), juried competitions, concerts, and dances, all culminating in the grand finale on the tenth day.

In Mysore on the tenth day, the Vijayadashami procession — beautifully decorated elephants, horses, chariots, men in uniform, government officials, and prominent citizens — assembles on the palace grounds and then winds its way through the town to the indigenous shami tree to the tune of many bands.

TECHNICAL STUFF

When the *maharaja* (king) ruled, he would sit in the *howdah* (a specially designed throne-like seat that fits on the back of an elephant) on the royal elephant and the entire procession would wind its way a couple of miles from the palace to the *Banni Mantap* (a gazebo type of structure) where the shami tree is worshipped. Then the maharaja would "slay the demon" by chopping down a banana tree with the ceremonial sword, and the festival would be over.

Celebrating Vijayadashami in North India

North India in general and Delhi in particular celebrate Vijayadashami as Rama's victory at the battle of Lanka by erecting huge effigies of the demons Ravana, Kumbhakarna, and Meghanada (see Figure 4-1). At the climactic moment, an individual playing the role of the hero Rama shoots flaming arrows, and the effigies catch fire and burn, symbolizing to all that dharma has been restored once again by their beloved king!

FIGURE 4-1: The effigies to be burned at the Vijayadashami festival in New Delhi. Photo by Government of India Department of Tourism.

Navratri at Wesleyan University, Connecticut

Lest you think that this festival is celebrated only in India, consider an example closer to home. Navaratri at Wesleyan is a tradition established there in the 1960s by Professor Robert Brown and two music teachers (professors Tanjore Visvanathan and Tanjore Ranganathan visiting from India). A series of concerts are arranged several evenings during a week in the fall, kicking off the entire season with a student performance.

For a glimpse, go to any search engine and type "Wesleyan Navratri YouTube 2009" and listen to students performing. The festival concludes with a puja performed on the last day to goddesses Durga and Saraswati. It's traditional for teachers to give a brief lesson to their students after the puja.

The doll festival

As part of the Navaratri festival, many families, especially in rural areas in India, celebrate a doll festival. The doll festival is called Gombe Habba or Bombe Habba in Kannada (*bombe* and *gombe* mean "dolls," and *habba* means "festival"), Kolu Pandigai in Tamil Nadu, and Bommala Koluvu in Andhra Pradesh. The festival serves as a vehicle to introduce children to the world of animals, myth, legends of ancestors, and the modern world.

TECHNICAL STUFF

The doll festival is celebrated in the United States partly as a way to help children remember and enjoy the great events from their heritage. Through the doll festival, Hindu children get to see traditional folk-art renderings of musical instruments, soldiers, elephants, horses, chariots, and scenes with a host of details depicting traditional stories and teaching them about life in India and the past with all its wonders and grandeur.

A BIT OF NOSTALGIA: SETTING UP THE DOLLS

Since the days before Sesame Street and radio and television — in fact even before electricity — Gombe Habba (the festival of dolls) has been celebrated. Gombe Habba was mostly for young girls, but young men helped because it required setting up. Beginning in the morning, the men in the family would set up a tier of steps much like the bleachers in a stadium, using wooden planks about 15 to 20 inches wide, 8 to 10 feet long, and about an inch or so thick. After the steps were covered with white sheets, they were ready for dolls to be arranged on them according to size.

By noon, all the arrangements were complete and the dolls would be in their assigned places, ready to be viewed. In the evenings, neighborhood children — young girls who looked like dolls themselves, dressed in fine silks of green, blue, red, and pink — came and sat on mats spread in front of the staircase of dolls. The children were urged to sing and were given small toys, as well as a mixture of sugar crystal, fried *chana dal* (lentils that look like yellow split peas), and chunks of dry coconut mixed with sesame. It was a sight to see: these beautiful girls, dressed in their finery, moving about in the neighborhood visiting their friends and relatives. No television program comes close to providing the joy and peace that the doll festival brought, and life in the village became richer because of Navaratri.

Diwali

Diwali is India's festival of lights. The literal meaning of the word *diwali* is a "row of lamps." Earthen lamps (small enough to fit in a child's palm) are still used in rural India. Filled with a couple tablespoonfuls of oil and a cotton wick, they're lit and arranged in a pattern or rows on a home's or public building's threshold, roof edges, window sills, and front porch. In urban areas, electric bulbs are used. The row after row of these lights, in every building, proclaim a happy occasion for one and all. The event is celebrated in the Hindu month of Kartika in the dark fortnight that falls in late October or early November.

So, what does Diwali celebrate?

- **The return of the epic hero Rama to his kingdom after 14 years of exile:** North Indians associate the Diwali festival with Rama. They consider Diwali to be the day when he made his triumphal entrance to his capital Ayodhya after 14 years of exile. Legend has it that the overjoyed citizens decorated their homes and lit hundreds of lamps to greet their king.

» **Dhanalakshmi, the goddess of wealth:** Merchants and businessmen worship Lakshmi in the form of Dhanalakshmi (Lakshmi, the goddess of wealth) during the Diwali festival. In fact, businesses use this special day of celebration to close the books for the year and make preparations to begin the new fiscal year. The day is believed to coincide with the emergence of the goddess from the milky ocean during the great churning event when gods and demons churned the ocean to recover the many precious items that had been lost during the great flood.

In addition to the rows and rows of lamps or light bulbs, fire crackers are lit and displayed by children. Wearing new clothes and jewelry is a must, as is distributing a variety of sweets. The excitement among clothing and jewelry merchants is palpable as they expect to make a lot of money during the week before Diwali!

The Diwali season is also a bonanza for those who sell sweets. Many varieties of aromatic, colorful, and delicious sweets are made fresh just for this season, and thousands of pounds of these delicacies are bought and distributed among family and friends. In large cities, the whole city erupts with gaiety, color, smiles, and sweets.

IN THIS CHAPTER

» Understanding that everything evolves from Brahman

» Identifying the major Hindu gods and goddesses

» Reviewing the Hindu firmament and Vedic gods

» Recognizing beliefs about where Hindu gods reside

Chapter 5
Hindu Gods and Goddesses

Hindus on their way to worship a deity call the event a *darshan*, meaning an auspicious visit to "see" God. And they do visualize and "see" many gods. The word *Hindu* and the idea of multiple gods and goddesses are synonymous. When people of other faiths think about Hinduism, the images that come to mind must be the variety of idols and pictures depicting deities.

This chapter introduces you to Hinduism's key gods and goddesses, from Brahman, the One Supreme Soul, to the gods that comprise the Hindu Trinity (Brahma, Vishnu, and Shiva), and many others besides. We also explain how you can identify the gods and goddesses you see in pictures and statues, and we describe where Hindus believe their gods reside.

Starting with the One Supreme Soul

Early Hindus had a clear focus on the One Supreme Soul, identified as *Brahman*, referred to in the Chandogya Upanishad as the "One without a second." Brahman is the sole, self-existing, Supreme Universal Soul. It manifests itself without limit, creating, destroying, and re-creating forever and ever. In other words, Brahman is the universe and all the forces in it.

REMEMBER

Unlike the conceptualization of God in monotheistic religions such as Christianity, Brahman does not interact in human lives. The Brahman is simply there, forever, the pure spirit of the universe, and the goal of Hinduism is to reach back to that Brahman.

The root word for Brahman in Sanskrit is *brih*, meaning "to grow" or "to burst forth." This fact is the basis for the saying that Brahman is expansive. ("All indeed is this Brahman," says the Mandukya Upanishad, a sacred Hindu scripture.) The word *brih* is gender-neutral, which is why we refer to Brahman as "It."

Out of this entity issues every visible and conceivable object, from the lowest level of a cell, to all that we see in nature, to demigods and spirits and a variety of gods. At the apex of all these aspects of Brahman are three principal gods and their consorts. These gods are defined as *Trimurti* and sometimes referred to as the Hindu Trinity:

- Brahma, the creator. (Note that Brahma is not the same as Brahman.)
- Vishnu, the preserver or pervader.
- Shiva, who is in charge of the process of destroying all creation before another time cycle begins.

While these gods and their functions appear distinct, Hindus believe that they constantly exchange these roles as situations demand. In addition, any interaction between humans (or other creatures) and the divine starts at the Trimurti level and below, meaning visualization of physical representations of these gods and other demigods in worship. We discuss these three gods in more detail later in this chapter.

REMEMBER

The Trimurtis share in the tasks of creating, caring for, and completing the lifecycle of a timespan of four yugas. A *yuga* is an era. As we explain in Book 1, Chapter 1, there are four yugas:

- Krita Yuga, which lasts 432,000 × 4 years
- Treta Yuga, which lasts 432,000 × 3 years
- Dwapara Yuga, which lasts 432,000 × 2 years
- Kali Yuga, which lasts 432,000 years

A complete cycle from one creation to another therefore lasts about 4.32 million years. Hindus believe that our present age is Kali Yuga.

Identifying Gods by Their Portrayals

The first time you look at a picture of a Hindu deity in a book or on an Indian calendar, or the first time you see the sculpture of a deity, your reaction may be "Wow!" That's because such representations often feature a multitude of colors, more than a single pair of arms, a variety of weapons or animals, and specific gestures (called *mudras*).

All these elements may seem confusing to a non-Hindu, but for a Hindu, they make the god instantly recognizable.

REMEMBER

As you try to comprehend this busy and complex portrayal, keep in mind the Hindu's desire to see divinity in superhuman form. The goal is to feel the presence of a higher power that invokes a certain level of reverence. To the Hindu, these complex portrayals most certainly accomplish that function.

TIP

The very first thing to note when you look at a picture or sculpture of a male deity is the type of mark that has been applied to the forehead. It's your first clue in classifying its sectarian identity. (As we explain in Book 1, Chapter 3, Hinduism has four major denominations and myriad sects and subsects.)

- **The mark of Vishnu:** Male gods that are forms or incarnations of Vishnu (such as Rama, Krishna, and Venkateshwara) typically carry three nearly parallel vertical lines known as Nama drawn on the forehead; the two outer ones in white, about two to three inches apart, and the center one in red. With minor variations, this symbol is typical of the Vaishnava denomination; the attending priest normally has the same pattern applied to his forehead.
- **The mark of Shiva:** The mark worn by a male deity who is a form or incarnation or son of Shiva (such as Murugan or Ganapati) consists of three horizontal white/gray lines (made with ash) that span the entire width of the forehead. The mark is known as *Vibhooti*. The priest at a *sanctum* (holy space) of the Shaivite denomination will draw the same three horizontal lines on his forehead, and sometimes on his arms and upper body. The three lines are believed to represent the three qualities inherent in humans: Sattva (noble), Rajas (vibrant), and Tamas (inert).

Brahma, the Creator

Brahma is the first member of the Hindu Trinity. He is often shown emerging from a lotus flower growing out of god Vishnu in his form as Narayana, floating on the vast causal cosmic ocean.

Hindus consider Brahma to be the Golden Embryo from which all the forms in the universe developed. He was, according to Hindu mythology, the first ever person, and all beings are considered his progeny; he is therefore referred to as Lord of Progeny *(Prajapati)*.

Attributes of Brahma

Brahma has the following attributes in visual representations:

- He has four heads. The heads face each of the four directions, and they are believed to represent the four Vedas (Hindus' most sacred texts), the four yugas (which we explain earlier in this chapter), and the four divisions in the Hindu societal structure.
- He has four arms. He may be shown holding a rosary (representing the counting of time) or a sheaf of grass, ladle, or water pot, all of which are used in Vedic sacrifices. He also holds a book, which represents knowledge.
- The palm of one hand faces forward in a gesture called *abhaya mudra*, which means "fear not."
- He is sometimes portrayed as seated on a swan.
- His consort is Saraswati, the goddess of learning. The next section has more information about goddess Saraswati.

There are very few temples for Brahma. Those that do exist include a temple in Pushkar in the state of Rajasthan, India, and one in Angkor Wat in Cambodia. Based on the *vastu shastra* (a Hindu architectural manual), a space for Brahma is reserved at the center of the base of the main sanctum in every Hindu temple. In addition, an outline of Brahma is included at the center of the shrine in every sanctified Hindu temple. This image helps locate all sanctums in the temple with reference to Brahma's location. However, while other sanctums are built and the specified deities are installed, Brahma is there only in spirit.

Brahma's consort: Saraswati, the goddess of learning

The goddess Saraswati is the consort of Brahma the creator and is worshipped as the goddess of learning, wisdom, speech, and music. Hindus offer prayers to Saraswati before beginning any intellectual pursuit, and Hindu students are encouraged to offer prayers to her during the school/college term and especially before and during examinations!

Saraswati is portrayed as a beautiful, white-clad goddess, exemplifying serenity and wisdom. She has four arms and holds a *veena* (lute), a pearl rosary, and a manuscript. She is sometimes seated or riding on a swan or peacock.

Annual festivals to celebrate Saraswati emphasize Hindus' recognition of the need to acquire *jnana* (wisdom) as an indispensable tool of life. The very first stanza in the great Hindu epic called the *Mahabharata* is an invocation to Saraswati:

> Upon saluting Narayana and Goddess Saraswati, as well as the noblest of men, Arjuna, shall one undertake the study.

Vishnu, the Preserver

Vishnu is the second member of the Hindu Trinity; he maintains the order and harmony of the universe periodically created by Brahma and periodically destroyed by Shiva (to prepare for the next cycle of creation). Vishnu is worshipped in many forms and in his several *avatars*, or incarnations.

In the Vedas (one of Hindus' most sacred texts), Vishnu is an important, somewhat mysterious god. Less visible than many of the nature gods that preside over elements, such as fire, rain, and storms, Vishnu is the *pervader* — the divine essence that pervades the universe.

Vishnu and his forms are worshipped primarily (but not exclusively) by Vaishnavites and Smartas. (See Book 1, Chapter 3 for details about these Hindu denominations.)

Attributes of Vishnu

Through the ages, whole treatises, stories, and poems have been written on Vishnu's attributes. Here are just the highlights:

- He has an erect, forward-looking stance and wears a benevolent expression on his face.
- He is dark blue in color. On his chest is a jewel, and a five-row garland of flowers or jewels hangs around his neck.
- He has four arms. He holds his lower right hand in an *abhaya mudra* (gesture), meaning "fear not." In his upper right hand, he holds the *discus*, a circular, saw-toothed weapon useful in battles fought to preserve dharma. The upper left hand holds the conch, which symbolizes victory and the five elements (air,

ether, water, fire, and earth). His lower left hand holds a mace, which represents the power of knowledge and protection. Sometimes the lower right hand simply points to his feet, suggesting surrender by the devotee.

» His vehicle is the eagle Garuda.

Divinities related to Vishnu

Vishnu is more often recognized and worshipped by other names (Venkateshwara, Balaji, Srinivasa, Satyanarayana or Narayana, and Jagannath) and through his ten avatars. Here, we explain the divine forms Vishnu takes and two of the avatars, Rama and Krishna, which have developed large followings over the centuries.

Vishnu as Venkateshwara, lord of the seven hills

Venkateshwara is worshipped by all devout Hindus, irrespective of their special and regional affiliations. The very name (which is a combination of *Venkata* and *Ishwara*) may also imply a unification of Vaishnavite and Shaivite beliefs. (See Book 1, Chapter 3 for details about these beliefs.)

The most famous shrine to Venkateshwara is at Tirupati on the crest of the Seshadri Hills in the southern Indian state of Andhra Pradesh. Here, he gives *darshan* (blessed sight) to millions of devotees from all parts of India and the world. Venkateshwara's blessings and his worshippers' generosity have been so abundant that a university, a hospital, and a host of other institutions are all funded by the temple and managed under its direction.

Vishnu as Narayana

Narayana is another name for Vishnu, identified as one whose abode is the primeval waters. As Narayana, floating in the primeval ocean, Vishnu has two forms:

» An infant lying on a lotus leaf, foot held in mouth, signifying time with no end and no beginning.

» Vishnu reclining, dreaming, on the serpent *Ananta* (whose name literally means "endless") while Lakshmi, his wife, holds his feet.

Vishnu as Jagannath, lord of the universe

A chariot festival in the Indian state of Orissa is centered around this form of Vishnu (and his avatar Krishna). Jagannath's brother Balabhadra and sister Subhadra also feature in this event.

HANUMAN, THE DEVOTED SERVANT

Like Rama, Hanuman, the monkey god, is featured in the epic called the *Ramayana*. Hanuman has earned his own path to deification and has many temples built for his own worship. His qualities are dedication, loyalty, courage, intelligence, and determination. Anecdotes featuring Hanuman are often used in Hindu households to encourage the younger generation when they are not living up to their potential. Elders cite the time when the monkey leader Jambavan cajoled Hanuman for not recognizing his inherent extraordinary strength. Hanuman was then inspired to help Rama in countless exciting incidents leading up to the battle of Lanka. Hanuman went searching for Rama's beloved wife, Sita, who had been kidnapped and hidden in Ravana's palace. He located her and assured her of rescue. Before leaving, he set fire to the city. During the final battle between Rama and Ravana, Hanuman was sent to bring an herb to help revive the wounded Rama, Lakshmana, and many of Rama's soldiers. Not sure which herb was the right one, Hanuman lifted the entire mountain and brought it to the battlefield. These feats of strength, devotion, and lively courage have endeared Hanuman to many and brought him followers and temples in his own honor.

Vishnu as the avatar Rama

Rama is the prince of Ayodhya whose story is told in the Sanskrit epic called the *Ramayana* ("The Story of Rama"). Hindus have moved this hero up to the status of a major deity because they revere the qualities he represents: the ideal qualities of a king, spousal love, fraternal devotion, and the proper relationship between subjects and their king.

TECHNICAL STUFF

The historical dating of the reign of an actual prince of Ayodhya by the name of Rama is uncertain, although recent excavations claim to have found the structure raised over his birthplace.

In pictures and statues, Rama is represented as a young warrior holding a bow who is flanked on the right by his brother Lakshmana (who also holds a bow) and on the left by his wife, Sita, a beautiful woman with a mild expression. Also in the grouping is his faithful servant, the monkey god Hanuman, who kneels at Rama's feet.

Vishnu as the avatar Krishna

If the name of one Hindu god is known and recognized throughout the world, it is Krishna, the eighth avatar of Vishnu. The form of Krishna most familiar to Hindus is that of Gopala or Govinda, a handsome young cowherd with a cow close behind and a flute held at his lips. His head gear is crested with a peacock feather, he is a cloud blue color, and his clothing is saffron. Another popular depiction shows him embracing his lover, Radha, in a circle of adoring dancing milkmaids *(gopis)*.

REMEMBER

Students of the Bhagavad Gita know Krishna as the charioteer friend, cousin, and mentor of Arjuna. Students of the epic *Mahabharata* know him as the pivot around which hundreds of ugly events occurred — events that were resolved through his intervention and guidance. But most of all, Lord Krishna's promise to humanity that he will return to save the world whenever dharma declines has sustained Hindu belief in the Supreme Being over thousands of years.

Krishna is also the divine child as described in the story of his birth. For his devotees, Krishna is a delight because of his playful, childish pranks. Hindus enjoy recalling how, when baby Krishna ate mud and his mother asked him to open his mouth, she saw the three worlds (earth, ether, and heavens) revealed.

Vishnu's consorts

Vishnu has two consorts: the goddesses Lakshmi and Bhu Devi. Bhu Devi is the earth goddess, who was rescued from the primeval ocean by Varaha, Vishnu's third incarnation — an avatar in the shape of a boar.

Lakshmi (also known as *Mahalakshmi*, meaning "great goddess Lakshmi") is the goddess of good fortune, wealth, and wellbeing. She is depicted as a beautiful female form with four arms, standing or seated on a lotus and holding lotuses or showering gold pieces. She is sometimes flanked by two elephants. She is also referred to as Sri (pronounced *shree*) and Kamala, among many other names.

REMEMBER

The goddess Lakshmi bestows both wealth and wellbeing on her devotees. She is the consort of Vishnu, a role she plays in every incarnation. For example, she is Sita, wife of Rama; Rukmini, wife of Krishna; and Dharani, wife of Parashu Rama, another avatar of Vishnu. She was one of the 14 precious items recovered during the *Amritamanthana*, the famous churning of the milky ocean, and she emerged with a lotus in her hand.

A wide variety of prayers describing her various attributes are found in the *Sri Sukta*, a series of hymns in praise of Lakshmi. The practice of worshipping Lakshmi is a testimony to the importance ancient Hindus placed on the practical aspects of life. For example:

» Hindu practice includes meditating first on Lakshmi upon waking up in the morning. Hindus open and hold their palms up together and recite the following:

  At the top of the hands resides Lakshmi

  And at the center Saraswati

  And at the base resides Govinda.

  Thus we should look at our palms in the morning.

- » Among the days of the week, Fridays are most auspicious for the worship of Lakshmi. Hindus light lamps or turn on lights at dusk on Fridays to welcome Lakshmi.
- » At temples where an image of Lakshmi has been installed, an elaborate ceremony of worship to Lakshmi takes place on Friday evenings.
- » In traditional South Indian weddings, musicians perform a special song in praise of Lakshmi as the bride enters the wedding hall with her entourage because, on her wedding day, the bride is considered to be the embodiment of the goddess herself.

In addition, as goddess of wealth, Lakshmi holds a special role for merchants and businesses, especially at Diwali. This annual festival of lights coincides with the New Year in many parts of India. Merchants and businesses use this special day of celebration to offer worship to Lakshmi, to close the books for the year, and to make preparations for the new fiscal year.

Shiva, the Destroyer

Shiva, whose name means "auspicious," is the third member of the Hindu Trinity. He is tasked with the unmaking of the universe in order to prepare for its renewal at the end of each cycle of time (at the end of the fourth yuga). A key point to remember about Shiva is that his destructive power is *regenerative*: It's the necessary step that makes renewal possible.

The power of Lord Shiva's eternal penance (he is depicted as always in deep meditation, the disturbing of which causes major havoc) is such that Hindus customarily invoke Shiva before the beginning of any religious or spiritual endeavor. Hindus believe that any and all bad vibrations in the immediate vicinity of the worship venue or practice are eliminated by the mere utterance of Shiva's praise or name. Shiva and his forms are worshipped primarily (and mostly) by Shaivites and Smartas (see Book 1, Chapter 3).

Shiva is represented as Rudra, the howler among the Vedic gods (whom I introduce in the later section "Gods and Goddesses of the Hindu Firmament). He is red with a blue throat and four arms. In his hands, he holds a trident. Above his brow is a crescent moon; in his hair is the River Ganges, and around his neck is a snake and a necklace of *rudraksha beads* (prayer beads) or pearls. He owns a spear called *Pasupata* (the herdsman's staff). Shiva's vehicle is a bull named Nandi. The most identifiable of his features, however, is his third eye, which he almost always keeps closed. When it does open, it is a disaster to anyone within its gaze; they simply burn away instantly.

HOW SHIVA GOT HIS BLUE THROAT

The Amritamanthana, or the churning of the milky ocean, is a story from the *Mahabharata*. The story goes that the serpent Vasuki, used as a churning rope, was so tired and sick from the repeated action of churning that he vomited the most potent poison into the ocean of milk. Fearing the destruction of the world through this pollution, Shiva immediately drank the poison. He himself would have succumbed were it not for the timely intervention of Parvati, his wife. Parvati held Shiva's throat tightly to prevent the poison from entering into his body. It is said that the arrested poison turned Shiva's throat blue. Another name for Shiva is *Nilakanta*, meaning "blue-throated."

Forms of Shiva

Millions of devotees around the world worship Shiva. Each year, a certain night in February is devoted to celebrating *Shivaratri*, the "great night of Shiva." Shiva has many forms, from a simple stone representation (called a *lingam*) to an ash-covered *mendicant* (beggar) deeply absorbed in meditation. Here are four forms of Shiva to remember:

- **As Kaala or time, the destroyer of worlds:** At the end of Kali Yuga, the fourth age of the world (which Hindus believe we are in right now), evil threatens to overtake all of creation. Shiva, as Nataraja (Lord of Dance), performs the dance that undoes all forms and ends the yuga. This iconic image of Shiva shows him within a circle of fire with one leg raised and one resting on a recumbent body; Shiva holds a drum in one hand and a flame in the other.
- **As ascetic:** In this form, Shiva spends eons in deep meditation in his abode called Mount Kailas (or Kailasa) in the Himalayas. He is clothed in animal skins, his body is covered in ash, his hair is bound up on top of his head, and he sits with legs folded in the well-known yoga stance. His eyes are closed, shielding the unwary from his terrible third eye.

  Several stories and dramas portray attempts to distract Shiva from his meditative trance. Most such stories end in disaster. An example is the tale of how the gods attempted to help Parvati, daughter of the mountains (Himalayas), tempt Shiva. Cupid (Kama), the lord of desire, was sent on this errand with his bow made of five flowers, but he was burnt to a cinder when Shiva opened his third eye. In time, Parvati was able to overcome Shiva by her power of true devotion.
- **As Pashupati, the herdsman (or lord of beasts):** Shiva has an ancient task in which he roams the wild jungles using his healing powers for animals.

SHIVA WORSHIPPED IN THE LINGA FORM

Temples to Shiva, including wayside shrines and other sanctums, invariably present the deity in the sculptural form of a *lingam* (or *linga*): a stone that represents a phallus or a pillar. The Sanskrit word means "gender." This ancient representation of the generative organ crosses all cultures from the Stone Age onward and demonstrates the very ancient lineage of the worship of Shiva. Devotees accept this simple elemental form as symbolic of fertility, growth, and strength.

- **Shiva the Terrible (Bhairava):** Shiva's task as destroyer of a universe that has reeled beyond help at the end of the fourth era (the Kali Yuga) is helped by his role as midnight haunter of graveyards, a fearful being, controlling the forms of death and decadence.

The consorts of Shiva: Parvati and Sati

Both Parvati and Sati are Shiva's consorts. Parvati (whose name literally means "the daughter of the mountain," referring to the Himalayas) is a peaceful, domestic form of the goddess known as Devi. (Devi's other forms are described in the upcoming section "The Feminine Divine.") Parvati created Shiva's son Ganapati (or Ganesha) — the elephant-headed god — from her bath lotions, turmeric paste, and skin rubbings because she needed a guard for her chamber door.

TECHNICAL STUFF

Sati, worshipped as a paragon of virtues idealized by Hindu women, was a daughter of King Daksha. According to legend, when Daksha organized a great ceremony of sacrificial rituals, he did not invite his illustrious but questionable son-in-law because he had heard about Shiva's occasional association with strange, dark spirits that tended to disrupt such rituals. In anger and shame over such disrespect for her husband, Sati threw herself into the ritual fire. Enraged and grief-stricken, Shiva disrupted Daksha's sacrifice, took up Sati's body over his shoulder, and moved north. As he traveled, Sati's body fell to pieces in places that are now associated with Sati or with pilgrimage. Shiva sank into deep meditation in the mountains until he was finally revived by Parvati's devotion. This story is considered the origin for the practice of *suttee*, or the voluntary burning of widows on their husband's funeral pyre. The practice was never sanctioned by the Vedas or basic Hindu scriptures and is now outlawed.

Shiva's sons

Shiva has two sons: Ganapati and Murugan. Ganapati is worshipped as the lord of obstacles. He is invoked by most Hindus before starting any auspicious undertaking; they pray for a smooth and flawless performance of the task at hand. Murugan is worshipped mostly by *Tamilians* (people who speak the language Tamil). We relate stories of these two sons of Shiva in this section.

Ganapati: The remover of obstacles

Ganapati is referred to reverentially as *Maha Ganapati* ("great Ganapati)" but is equally well-known as Ganesha and also known as *Vighnaraja* ("lord of obstacles"). Lord Ganapati occupies a very special place in the hearts of Hindus. Most Hindu households have a picture or statue of this godhead, and it's not uncommon to see small replicas of Ganapati hanging from rearview mirrors of cars and trucks! The elephant head is the obvious clue to identifying this godhead.

The form of Ganapati with his elephant head and portly belly invokes enormous reverence *(bhakti)* among Hindus. Consider these examples:

- Most Hindus, except for the Vaishnava denomination (generally speaking), believe that worshipping Ganapati first before any worthwhile undertaking is a must so that their task is blessed to proceed toward a successful conclusion.
- Every September, a special festival is held throughout the Hindu world to make images of Ganapati in clay; color them in gold, yellow, pink, and red; worship the same image for ten days; and at the end perform what's called a *visarjan* by immersing the image in a body of water. The festival is especially popular in the Indian state of Maharashtra. To this day, the festival takes place in grand style attracting millions to Maharashtra's capital Mumbai. This religious fervor unites Hindus everywhere as no other festival has.

Murugan

Shiva's second son, Murugan (or Muruga) is a popular deity worshipped by Hindus, especially Tamilians, around the world. He is known by several names: Skanda, Kumara, Kartikeya, and Subrahmanya.

He was created when Shiva, disturbed by Kama Deva (Cupid) at the bequest of Parvati, opened his third eye and reduced Kama instantly to ashes. The ball of fire emanating from Shiva's fury fell into a pool in Saravana, a forest of arrow-like grass in the Himalayas. Six sparks of fire turned into six babies, who were nursed by six mothers. When Parvati gathered the six babies and made them into one, the child was known as *Shanmukha* ("six faces").

HOW GANAPATI LOST AND GAINED HIS HEAD

Ganapati's mother, Parvati, asked Ganapati to guard the entrance to her apartments and admit no one while she took a bath. When Shiva, Ganapati's father, tried to enter, Ganapati stopped him. No amount of persuasion or threats helped, and a furious Shiva cut off Ganapati's head. A grief-stricken Parvati demanded that Shiva find a way to restore the boy's life. Shiva instructed his staff to find anyone, human or animal, sleeping with its head pointed in the southern direction and to bring that creature to him. As it happened, the first creature to be found sleeping with its head toward the south was an elephant, whose head was duly severed and brought to Shiva. Shiva positioned the new head onto the body of Ganapati, and, lo and behold, the boy came alive as the handsome elephant-headed god.

TECHNICAL STUFF

As interesting as Shanmukha/Murugan's birth is, his story really begins with the havoc caused by an asura known as Taraka. Hindus believe that *asuras*, which are like demons, are power-seeking deities that acquire enormous strength through their devotees' austerities and prayers. They generally long for supremacy over the *devas* (gods), tormenting humans and creating havoc during sacred ceremonies. They also are not easy to defeat. Taraka set out to conquer the entire universe and nothing, it appeared, could stop him. But Murugan became a general of Shiva's army, and his mother Parvati gifted him with a powerful lance called *Vel*. He and his army destroyed Taraka in a six-day battle, and the devas were liberated.

The Feminine Divine

A unique feature of Hinduism is the worship of goddesses as well as gods. Lakshmi, Saraswati, Sita, Radha, and a host of other goddesses are worshipped by millions of Hindus around the world. Earth is worshipped as *Bhumi Mata*, Mother Earth. The aspect of mother and the associated reverence, love, compassion, and respect are clearly implied in these rituals.

The female form, especially in the case of the deities we list in the previous paragraph, is generally accepted as representing a role supportive of a male deity, be it Brahma, Vishnu, or Shiva. In temples throughout India and abroad, sanctums of female consorts usually flank those of the major male deities, even if the goddesses have a substantial personal following themselves.

At the same time, the female form is associated with *shakti*, awesome creative strength and power — a resource that the gods recognize and depend on. This is particularly true of regional forms of Parvati, the wife and consort of Shiva. These forms include Durga Devi and Kali, which we discuss in detail next.

Durga Devi

Durga Devi is *the* goddess who signifies the shakti aspect in all its implied creative and destructive power. The mission of Durga is primary, not supportive, and therefore her actions are not typical of a female consort. Because of this independence, she is powerful, even frightening at times, with an unusual spirit to fight fiercely in order to restore *dharma* (moral order). Yet, while Durga is at once a terrifying *Shakti Mata* ("powerful mother") to her adversaries, she is full of compassion and love for her devotees.

Durga is visualized as a beautiful, powerful female divinity riding a lion and fully armed in all her hands. Festivals to celebrate Durga each year emphasize Hindus' recognition of the need for strength to protect dharma. In worshipping Durga, Hindus celebrate the feminine principle for its strength and fortitude as well as compassion, and they seek her grace and blessings.

THE STORY OF DURGA'S BIRTH

The manner in which the manifestation of Durga came about is unlike that of other goddesses. When the demon Mahisha Asura conquered the heavens and drove Indra (lord of gods) out of his kingdom, the gods began to descend to earth. Brahma and Shiva knew they could not bear this assault on dharma anymore. All the gods and demigods visited Vishnu to discuss the news of Mahisha's onslaught and the resulting lack of balance between forces of good and evil. The recounting of events angered the assembled gods so much that bolts of light began to issue from their bodies. The fusion of these lights gave birth to a feminine form known as Durga, who was gifted with immense power. Each part of the goddess was formed from bolts of light emanating from individual gods. For example, her face came into being by Shiva's light, her hair from Yama's light, her arms from Vishnu's light, her feet from Brahma's light, and so on! In addition, the gods offered her a variety of weaponry: a trident from Shiva, a discus from Vishnu, a conch from Varuna, a spear from Agni, a bow and quiver full of arrows from Vayu, a thunderbolt from Indra, a noose from Yama, and more.

Fully armed, Durga roared with anger, and the three worlds (the earth, ether, and heavens) shook. There ensued a fierce battle between her and the asura forces of Mahisha. Thousands of asuras were slain in the gruesome battle, and the enormous loss of his army brought forth Mahisha himself to the battlefield. He had supreme confidence that he could never die in battle because he had, through his own penance, received a *boon* (gift) from the gods that no man could kill him ever. He was immensely satisfied with that boon because he had never thought to include freedom from death at the hands of a woman! Mahisha assumed several animal forms in an attempt to overcome her, but finally Durga slew Mahisha by stomping on him and driving a trident through his heart. Thus ended the saga of Mahisha, which restored dharma, returned the three worlds to order, and restored the balance of good against evil.

Kali, the destructive power of time

Kali is the terrifying aspect of Durga. While Durga is strong and even violent in action, a militant power against evil, she is beautiful in form. Kali, while basically attractive, has some ugly attributes in her battle against evil and against illusion.

Kali's appearance is fearsome: She is dark in color to represent that, at the end of the fourth yuga, all forms dissolve into a dark night and all colors disappear until the next creation. Her tongue hangs from her mouth to indicate a loud laugh. She stands on a corpse that represents what is left of the nonexistent or destroyed universe. Although she is clad in space (that is, naked), she wears a necklace of skulls and a belt of arms. She has four arms, two of which hold a head and a sword; the other two are positioned in the "fear not" and the "giving of boons" gestures *(mudras)*.

The boon that Kali offers is that knowledge and perspective pertaining to the passage of time, with no illusions, remove fear. This understanding allows bliss to be granted by Kali's giving hand. She is frightful because of the illusion that must be abandoned and the fear that such a loss entails, but Kali destroys despair.

VILLAGE GODDESSES

It is not uncommon to see simple temples on the outskirts of villages to house a village goddess. These temples are, more often than not, planned, constructed, and maintained by castes other than brahmin. These goddesses, unlike major Hindu gods and goddesses, are believed to demand and receive animal sacrifices, such as chickens, lambs, and buffalos. The devotees believe that bad things happen to a community when a goddess is angered by some failing in sacrifices, and so the goddess must be appeased. These goddesses are looked upon as guardians of a town or village, and their temples generally face away from the towns they protect as though keeping an eye on evil forces that may bring a disease or similar harm to the town. People who believe that evil forces brought about cholera, plague, or smallpox look to these goddesses to ward off the evils and protect their community.

Introducing the Gods and Goddesses of the Hindu Firmament

The gods named and described in this section, and many others connected with households and communities, are found in the Rig Veda, the earliest book of Hindu sacred scripture. Known and revered as the *Vedic gods*, they are invoked and worshipped daily in all household and many temple rituals. As such, they are basic to the living, ritual culture of Hinduism. Except for Surya the sun, these gods have no temples built to them or personal following, although Hindus revere them deeply.

The Vedic gods fall into these general categories:

- Nature gods, especially gods connected with weather and climate
- Planetary gods who feature in destiny and the composition of horoscopes
- Gods who rule over household health and wealth and community values

Although separated and categorized here for convenience, all these areas of human concern are considered to influence each other in the Hindu universe.

Indra and the Vedic storm gods

Indra, the king of heaven and lord of the gods, wields a thunderbolt and brings rain. He is a hero and a warrior mounted on a white horse or immense white elephant. His bow is the rainbow, and he resides in Amaravati ("immortal city") near the mythical Mount Meru. His wife is Indrani (also called Sachi). More hymns are addressed to Indra than to any other god in the Rig Veda because he is the chief of gods and provider of rain.

TECHNICAL STUFF

Legend has it that with all this adoration and his position as the head of all gods, Indra became arrogant. Thus, when the folks in Lord Krishna's kingdom offered worship to a local hill known as Mount Govardhan instead (on Krishna's advice, no doubt) because they recognized the true source of rain, Indra became furious and sent continuous rain, thunder, and lightning to scare the populace. Krishna came to their rescue and held up the entire mountain to shelter them from Indra's onslaught. It was then that Indra understood the source of the problem — his own arrogance and Krishna's plan to teach him a lesson. He begged Krishna to forgive him. Lord Krishna forgave Indra and allowed the worship of Indra on that particular day in winter at a festival known as *Bhogi*.

Indra is not the only Hindu god associated with weather. The weather above the earth is controlled by Vayu (wind lord), the Maruts (storm gods), and the fearful deity called Rudra, the howler, who was later associated with Shiva. Varuna, who is lord of the waters that circle the earth and rivers, is also seen as affecting the waters of heaven.

The sun and planets as rulers of destiny

The planetary gods are the *navagrahas* (literally, the "nine planets"):

- **Surya,** the sun, is a golden warrior arriving on a chariot pulled by seven white horses; his color is gold or copper; his favored grain for offering is wheat.
- **Chandra,** the moon, is a gentle sage dressed in white, riding a deer or a three-wheeled chariot; his color is pearl white; his favored grain is rice. The moon, also called Soma, is the timekeeper who counts out the years; he is also the cup of immortal ambrosia from which the gods drink periodically and which then fills up again.
- **Angaraka,** or Mangala, the planet Mars, is a young warrior armed with a spear; his color is red; his favored grain is red or toor lentil.
- **Budha,** the planet Mercury, is a gentle sage; his color is green; his favored grain is moong lentil.
- **Brihaspati,** the planet Jupiter, is the guru of the gods; his color is saffron yellow; his favored grain is peanuts or chickpeas.
- **Shukra,** the planet Venus, is the guru of the asuras; his color is diamond white; his favored grain is a small bean.
- **Shani,** the planet Saturn, is the son of Surya and brother of Yama, judge of the dead; his color is dark blue; his favored grain is sesame.
- **Rahu,** the eclipse, is represented as a mouth that threatens to swallow the sun and moon. His image in temples, a head with no tail, never faces that of the sun or the moon. His color is smoke grey; his favored grain is urad lentil.
- **Ketu,** the comet, is the unlucky trailing tail with no head attached; his color is khaki green; his favored grain is horse gram.

These deities are invoked in rituals and are also studied avidly by astrologers who provide horoscopes at the birth of a child. (Ancient Hindus believed that the position of planets at the precise moment of birth launched a life into a dynamic system and that the subsequent fortune of that person depended upon the initial conditions of the total system.) Many Hindus today continue this custom, seeking astrological advice before undertaking a task or a journey or any important step in life or before exchanging and studying horoscopes in the proposal stage of an arranged marriage.

Agni and the Vedic gods of home and community

Agni, the fire god, holds a special place in Hindu ritual as

- **The sacrificer:** The priest who performs the ceremony as specified in the Rig Veda (Book I, Hymn 1, Verse 1)
- **The sacrifice:** The ritual fire and the offerings made into it.
- **The witness:** The one who sees all rites. For example, Hindus consider Agni to be the witness to a wedding.

The Sanskrit word for the fire ritual is *homa* (related to the word for "home") or *havan* (related to the word for "oven").

Not long ago, the fire initiated for Hindu wedding rites was kindled from the bride's parents' home fire and carried carefully with her to her husband's home. A beautiful hymn from the Rig Veda tells how the daughter of the sun went to marry Soma, the moon god. The description of her escort is a catalogue of the household virtues and guardian deities of the early Vedic world:

- **The Ashwins,** twin heavenly horsemen who heal horses and cattle
- **Mitra,** god of friendship and god of contracts
- **Varuna,** here referring to divine law
- **Aryaman,** the personification of family honor
- **Bhaga,** the personification of ancestral share of property
- **Pusan,** the guardian of the roads and nourisher
- **Purandhi,** abundance
- **Matarisvan,** spark of conception
- **Dhatar,** sustainer
- **Destri,** a form of Saraswati (goddess of learning) associated with easy birth

Many of these household deities, some better known than others, are still invoked during Vedic wedding fire rituals today.

Discovering Where the Gods Reside

Where can all these Hindu gods be found? The heavens? Special worlds? Mountaintops? Yes! Hindus sum it all up by saying that God is everywhere. Still, Hindus recognize special abodes for gods. The belief is to allow for a gradation of higher worlds to accommodate both the divinities and humans (including insects, animals, and so on) and lower worlds for subhuman and demonic types.

Thus, Hindus speak of a total of 14 worlds called *lokas* with the earth situated in the middle. In a simpler version, there are three worlds. We explain both mythologies here, starting with the simpler version.

Introducing the three worlds

Hindus define three worlds inhabited by people and gods:

- The physical world of the universe (known as *bhur* in Sanskrit).
- The world of atmosphere *(bhuvas).*
- The realm of the gods *(svar).* The Sanskrit word *swarga,* for heaven, comes from this root word.

Humans live in the physical world, performing actions and enjoying the world within the framework of acceptable codes of conduct. Gods descend to this world in some form whenever there is an unacceptable imbalance between good and evil.

The world of atmosphere exists above the physical world. Here live the demigods and spirits, such as Indra (god of thunder, lightning, and rain), Rudra (destroying and dissolving power), and Vayu (the wind god).

The realm of the gods is above the world of atmosphere. In this topmost world resides Vishnu, along with other major gods such as Rita (the god of righteousness), Dyaus (the god of the sky), Varuna (the god of the waters), and Mitra (the god of day). This location up above is popularly referred to as *Vaikunta,* to which a departed soul can enter if conditions are right.

Magnificent mountains are also identified as abodes of gods. For example, Mount Meru is considered to be the abode of Brahma and Indra. Shiva is believed to reside in Mount Kailash in Tibet.

Looking at all 14 worlds

In another version, Hindu mythology recognizes worlds above and below the earth. Specifically, the six worlds above the earth are the preferred ones for the soul and the seven below are to be feared.

The lowest of the higher worlds is the earth *(bhu)*. The six worlds above the earth are called *bhuva, suva, maha, jana, tapa,* and *satya*. The highest, not surprisingly, is the abode of Brahma and is known as the world of Truth *(satya loka)* reached after successfully passing through the worlds of a hierarchy of gods as the result of living a purer and purer life on earth.

Below the earth are the seven hells called talas: *atala, bitala, sutala, talatala, rasatala, mahatala,* and *patala*. These hells are inhabited by those who need to undergo suffering based on the level of their condemnable actions while on earth. The lowest is considered an abode of demons and serpents and is reached successively through a hierarchy of hells due to worsening lives on earth birth after birth.

2

Taoism

Contents at a Glance

IN THIS CHAPTER

» Tracing Taoist history

» Considering Taoist ideas

» Examining Taoist practices

» Experiencing your first encounter with Taoism

» Becoming familiar with Taoist terminology

» Establishing a School of *Yin-Yang*

» Seeing the world as fluctuations of *ch'i*

» Replicating the movement of the cosmos

Chapter 1
An Introduction to Taoism

Today nearly 5.2 million Chinese people (or people of at least partial Chinese descent) live in the United States, and Chinese people may make up close to 5 percent of the Canadian population. And you may have heard somewhere that China is now an important global economic and political power, too!

So, what can possibly be a better time for picking up a few pointers on Taoism, one of China's oldest (and most interesting) indigenous religious traditions?

But what is Taoism? Taoism is a religious tradition that is native to China. It's about 2,000 years old (though many of the sources that inspired and influenced it go back at least several hundred years before that, so it's also okay to think of Taoism as about 2,500 years old). Taoism has spread to other parts of Asia, including Japan, Korea, Malaysia, the Philippines, Singapore, and Vietnam. In recent years, it has found its way into European and North American countries as well.

In this chapter, we offer some pointers to help you navigate the tradition a lot more smoothly. Here, you discover exactly why Taoist resources can initially come off as misleading or confusing, and you pick up some important vocabulary and categories for keeping track of things.

Delving into the Evolution of Taoism

If you have an idea that history is a lot of dull stuff — names, dates, facts, and figures — you're not alone. And trying to memorize a collage of uncoordinated details can be about as snooze-worthy as it gets. Fortunately, you'll find it hard to nap through the story of Taoism. Colorful characters, dramatic innovations, and unexpected augmentations to the tradition show up at just about every turn! And the more you can fill in the historical background, the more things start to make sense.

Taoist origins and development

The assorted texts, practices, and cultural traditions that we call Taoism had their earliest rumblings close to 2,500 years ago, even though it took several hundred years before any people thought of themselves as Taoists or developed any sense of shared Taoist identity. The tradition more or less began during a period of tremendous intellectual ferment in China, an extended time when numerous philosophical schools contended with one another for intellectual supremacy and political power. The Taoist texts from this period, including Lao Tzu's Tao Te Ching and the *Chuang Tzu* still rank among the most stimulating and entertaining works in all of Chinese literature. These authors failed to "win" the debates from the Hundred Schools Period (as it is now known) in the sense that they never convinced the political leaders of the time to adopt their teachings, but they briefly influenced the ruling ideology of the early Han Dynasty (206 BCE–220 CE) in a short-lived movement called Huang-Lao Taoism, and left a permanent mark on later Chinese religion and culture.

The first documented record of anything we can call a Taoist community or institution took shape a few hundred years after that, and it represents the first sharp right-angle turn in Taoism's history. This all began with the emergence of a charismatic teacher and healer named Chang Tao-ling, who founded a tightly knit society called, alternatively, the Way of the Celestial Masters, the Five Pecks or Rice Sect, or somewhat later, the Way of Orthodox Unity. This group

» Worshiped Lao Tzu as a divine figure (along with many other deities)
» Publicly recited the Tao Te Ching
» Believed in the coming of a "new age"
» Developed both a hierarchical priesthood and series of secretive rituals that continue to shape Taoism today

The community didn't last, but its forms and surviving members mixed and mingled with other people in different regions, and over the next several hundred years, the tradition eventually accumulated many new sacred texts (like the Highest Purity and Numinous Treasure revelations), practices (like alchemy), and deities (like the Heavenly Worthy of the Primordial Beginning). By the 12th and 13th centuries, many new Taoist sects — such as the Correct Method of the Celestial Heart, and the Perfect Great Way — were in competition with one another.

Tao now (brown cow)

Taoism in China suffered terribly during large swaths of the 20th century, to the point that Mao Tse-tung and his Cultural Revolution nearly wiped it out altogether by the mid-1970s. But since then, Taoism has mounted a vigorous comeback, including the restoration of many temples, the resumption of priestly ordination, and the performance of public ceremonies.

REMEMBER

Although a wide range of people claim various Taoist affiliations — some more legitimately than others — most Chinese Taoism today falls into two distinct denominations or lineages:

» **The Way of Orthodox Unity:** The liturgical and ritualistic branch that is more common in southern China and Taiwan
» **The Way of Complete Perfection:** The monastic branch that is more common in northern China

Although these divisions pretty much define Taoism in modern China, the vast majority of Westerners — even those who've read the Tao Te Ching for years and fancy themselves enthusiasts of Taoist philosophy — have never heard of either sect.

Speaking of the West, the history of Taoism isn't limited to China — it has begun to sprout legs and start walking around North American countries as well. The face of American Taoism is very different from that of China, which leads (some) people to debate whether it even "counts" as Taoism. For many years, Taoism's main presence in the West was through texts, including the many (if not always accurate) translations of the Tao Te Ching and *Chuang Tzu* and creative popular writings like Benjamin Hoff's *The Tao of Pooh*, though Taoist temples, study centers, and online marketplaces have begun popping up over the last few decades. For the most part, these American venues focus on historically marginal Taoist practices like *t'ai-chi* (more on that later in this chapter) and *ch'i-kung*, and have found some unanticipated alliances with many of those involved in the New Age Movement. American Taoism often includes other Chinese resources, such as meditation, acupuncture, traditional herbal medicine, and sexual techniques.

Considering Taoist Ideas

Taoists do think about a lot of interesting things, and many Taoist texts contain some of the most philosophically rich thinking you'll find in any tradition. For the most part, Taoist ideas don't involve litanies of doctrinal formulations that people have to say they believe in order to be good Taoists as much as observations and interpretations of the world that translate into specific ways that people should act, whether out of their own enlightened self-interest or out of interpersonal obligation. Just as Taoism changes over time and produces contending lineages, ideas also change over time and vary according to the different lineages. You'll always be better off if you make peace with Taoism's internal diversity instead of trying to get everything to fit together into one "essence."

It all begins with the Tao

You probably already have an idea that Taoism has to do with the *Tao*, just as Christianity has to do with Christ and Buddhism has to do with the Buddha. But Taoism isn't really about a belief in the *Tao* or anything like that. That's because the term *Tao* simply means "the Way," and it was already part of the Chinese worldview well before Taoism came into existence. What's more, other non-Taoist Chinese traditions lay equal claim to ownership of the term, because almost all expressions of Chinese religion and philosophy in one manner or another have something to do with figuring out the "ways" of the universe (possibly including deities) and what "ways" human beings can follow. And Chinese frequently think of various other "ways" that don't have much to do with religion or philosophy either. In other words, the term *Tao* extends well beyond Taoism, well beyond Chinese religion.

WARNING

But *Tao* is an especially loaded term in the Taoist context, and discussions of it in the Tao Te Ching and *Chuang Tzu* waste no time letting you know something funny's going on. First, they tell us that conventional language isn't sufficient for describing it, that those who claim to understand it couldn't possibly have it right, and that dim-witted people who hear about it won't be able to do much more than laugh. And then, they illustrate it through colorful, often paradoxical, figures of speech and continually remind us how difficult it is to comprehend its mystery. It's as though the authors are in on some secret joke, and they keep redirecting you someplace else every time they think you're getting too close to the punchline. If you're not in a hurry, you may end up hitting your head against the *Tao* for a *very* long time.

Even with all the paradoxes and apparent narrative dead ends, some fairly clear characteristics of the Taoist concept of the *Tao* do come through in the texts:

- It represents a creative principle, and the authors frequently allude to it through the metaphor of a procreative mother and other feminine imagery.
- It somehow owes its creative power to being empty, which explains why so much Taoist philosophy deals with discussions of "non-being" or the relationship between "being" and "non-being."
- Whatever the *Tao* may be, human beings habitually lose sight of it and need to recover it through a process of *returning* (a process that many people are convinced involves some type of mysticism).

You can get your *Tao* on in Book 2, Chapter 2.

The Taoist process of following the Way can't really be reduced to one or two things; it's no exaggeration to suggest that every aspect of the Taoist tradition in some measure addresses following the Way, whether it involves praying to deities or engaging in the smelting of metals in a laboratory. But in the Tao Te Ching and *Chuang Tzu* especially, the concept of *Tao* attaches very closely to a truly mind-boggling principle for moral action: that of *wu-wei,* which people alternately translate as "non-doing," "doing nothing," "actionless action," and dozens of similar phrases. The basic idea here is that although the creative power of the *Tao* lies in its emptiness, humans can only "plug in" to the *Tao* by taking on that very quality of emptiness. This translates into acting in a way that comes not from personal desire or affect, but by emulating the empty, impartial qualities of the *Tao* itself, so you don't even feel like you're the agent of your own action. To boot, this non-doing is utterly effective — so both the *Tao* and the person who correctly follows the *Tao* "do nothing, yet nothing remains undone."

The discussions of non-doing introduce a roster of memorable metaphors for accomplishing such a state. The "uncarved block" refers to an object that exists in a natural state of simplicity and perfection, not yet structured (and limited) by human intervention. Bending along the "hinge of the Way" refers to the ability to adapt flexibly and fluidly to the constantly shifting circumstances of existence. And the "mind as a mirror" (which also gets a lot of mileage in Zen Buddhism) alludes to reflecting and responding to reality as it is, without superimposing any of your own interpretations or motivations onto it. We discuss all this in Book 2, Chapter 3.

The expansion of the Tao

Although the concept of the *Tao* and the principle of non-doing are profound, provocative innovations, it would be hard to imagine enduring religious communities based entirely on those ideals. First-time readers of the Tao Te Ching may be disappointed to learn not only that *wu-wei* in isolation isn't really viable as universal public morality, but also that the text never really functioned as a Taoist "Bible," providing a social blueprint for how people should live their day-to-day lives. To understand Taoism in Chinese culture over the last 2,000 years, you need to look at different ideas and resources.

One development that fits somewhat congenially with the original ideas of *Tao* and non-doing is the integration of *yin-yang* and "five phases" (or "five elements") theory into almost all forms of Taoism. By explaining the function of the *Tao* in terms of interactions of *yin* and *yang*, or more complexly as the cycles of five active "agents" — wood, fire, earth, metal, and water — Taoists eventually came to understand everything from imperial history to medical science through elaborate systems of correspondence and resonance. Later in this chapter, we talk about the nuances of *yin-yang* theory and how that creates the basis for many Taoist practices.

TECHNICAL STUFF

The first actual Taoist community believed in a coming "new age," and although the new millennium may never have actually come, Taoists over the next several centuries wrote (or received revelations through) hundreds of new texts. This may come as a surprise if you think the only significant Taoist texts are the Tao Te Ching, the *Chuang Tzu*, and *The Tao of Pooh*. In fact, there are nearly 1,500 volumes in the Taoist Canon, the comprehensive collection of books used by various Taoists from different time periods, most of which have never seen the light of day in English translation. The vast majority of these texts don't discuss philosophical matters like the *Tao* — in fact, most of them don't actually *discuss* anything. Instead, they include guides to performing rituals, formulas meant to be recited or chanted, aids to meditation, alchemical manuals, and documents covering a variety of disciplines (like numerology, geography, and medicine).

Looking at the Practice of Taoism

You're probably getting the idea that if there are well over a thousand texts dealing with Taoist practice that most Westerners don't know, it stands to reason that most Westerners don't know much about Taoist practice! In fact, many people are mistakenly convinced that Taoists have no practices (and no doctrines, no deities, and no clergy, for that matter) of any kind, apart from the vague goal of non-doing. In fact, there's probably no greater "undiscovered country" in Taoism, no territory where scholars are still learning more every day, than the world of Taoist practice. And not coincidentally, there's probably no aspect of Taoism that can be any more difficult to understand.

Methods of personal cultivation

It's hard to tell exactly when something we can categorically recognize as Taoist practice first began, but regardless, it's still pretty clear that many of the earliest Taoist practices took the form of applying techniques of physical and spiritual self-cultivation. Some of these techniques resembled meditation in that they involved a prescribed posture, emphasis on the development of mental discipline, and sometimes even the familiar Buddhist focus on your own breath. Two practices in particular, both described briefly in the *Chuang Tzu,* involve the systematic de-conditioning of all your cognitive and intellectual machinery, the undoing of destructive mental habits in order to return to the original *Tao.* One of these, "sitting and forgetting," is just what it sounds like: gradually peeling away what you already know through an introspective quiet sitting. A related practice, the "fasting of the mind and heart," involves "starving" your ordinary forms of perception until you can develop an entirely different type of immediately, intuitive perception.

Many of the techniques of Taoist self-cultivation involve training of the physical body, and some of these have goals ranging from basic physical health and longevity to attaining an "immortal" status after death. Taoists haven't always spoken with one voice on matters of life and death, and they almost certainly imported their first immortality practices (and generous amounts of related folklore) from a number of non-Taoist sources.

Over time, the most important immortality practices had to do with variations on *alchemy* (the concocting and combining of various substances in the laboratory), which adepts believed they could use to cure illnesses, gain the protection of spirits, and, of course, transform their own postmortem status. There have been many kinds of alchemical practices in Taoism, but they fall roughly into two categories:

- **Exterior alchemy:** The literal alchemy involving preparing and ingesting substances
- **Interior alchemy:** A practice in which alchemical formulas and instructions serve as metaphors for techniques of cultivating and transforming your body's internal energies

Among the many physical practices in Taoism, a handful that have functioned somewhat on the periphery of the tradition have caught on big time in the West.

Practices like *t'ai-chi*, *ch'i-kung*, and a range of other techniques that combine martial arts and spiritual teachings all had loose connections to Taoism in China, but they have, in many ways, become the primary faces of Western Taoism.

The ritual process

Ever since the beginnings of the Way of the Celestial Masters, various forms of ritual — atonement of sins, purification rites, ceremonies on behalf of the dead — have been hugely important in Taoism. When Taoist initiates achieve ordination or advance in priestly rank, they effectively receive authorization to participate in or conduct specific rituals, which almost always involve gaining access to esoteric ritual secrets. Many of the texts in the Taoist Canon actually function as guides or companions to these ritual performances, which is why they're virtually impossible to understand if you just "cold-call" them, but also why they're such a valuable (and understudied) resource for understanding the realities of Taoist practice.

TECHNICAL STUFF

Although most of the rituals have an esoteric component, many are dramatic and colorful, even if you don't understand what's going on. This is particularly true of rites of "cosmic renewal," some of which occur only once every several years, take days to perform, and include the participation of dozens (or hundreds) of priests. In Book 2, Chapter 5, we try to make some of these impenetrable ritual processes a little easier to understand.

Encountering Taoism for the First Time

A lot of what people say and write about Taoism contains overgeneralizations, personal impressions, and preformed assumptions about the tradition, Chinese religion, and religion in general. But believe it or not, you can blame a huge chunk of the apparent chaos on the term *Taoism*, which is itself ambiguous and which people tend not to use very carefully, even in China.

Seeing how Taoists are like Yankees

TIP

You'll probably be happy to know that we don't really want to convince you that Taoists are anything like Yankees, but we do want to show you how the terms *Taoist* and *Taoism* are an awful lot like the term *Yankee.*

If someone were to ask you what a Yankee is or what the word *Yankee* means, your answer would probably depend on a few things, including where you live and whether you like sports:

- **If you live in the southeastern part of the United States,** a *Yankee* is a "northerner," but you almost certainly wouldn't mean people from Oregon or Montana. More likely, you'd mean people who live in or come from the northeastern part of the country, especially people in or originally from states north of the Mason–Dixon Line, or states that aligned with the Union during the Civil War.
- **If you're Mexican or European, or you live in any country that has an unwelcome U.S. military presence,** a *Yankee* is someone from anywhere in the United States.
- **If you live in New England,** the term *Yankee* may be reserved for people who come from old, established, northeastern families, especially those descended from colonial English settlers. This is the origin of the term *Connecticut Yankees.*
- **If you live anywhere in the United States (except probably the southeast),** you can use *Yankee* as an adjective to describe a way to prepare food ("Yankee pot roast"), to solve problems ("Yankee ingenuity"), or even to manage money ("Yankee frugality").
- **If you're a sports fan,** the term *Yankee* can really only mean those guys who play baseball and make a lot of money doing so! Babe Ruth was one real Yankee who probably ate a lot of Yankee pot roast but didn't practice Yankee frugality.

In other words, the term *Yankee* can mean very different things, sometimes because of specific political or social concerns — things that may end up being only slightly related to each other. And if you hear someone use the term one way when you don't know that usage or think they mean something else, you're sure to stumble into a comedy of errors. Imagine what would happen if you heard someone say that the Yankees walked a dozen Tigers, when you thought that person was talking about the Civil War! Or if you were in a baseball frame of mind and heard someone say that the Yankees attacked and burned the city of Atlanta!

As you may expect from this exercise, *Taoist* and *Taoism* can also mean a lot of different things, depending on who's using the words. And just as with Yankees, you'll want to be careful not to mix up the various things that get called "Taoist" for one reason or another, which may not even be very good reasons. One person may be practicing Taoism by moving to the country, spending more time with nature, and making art out of stones and unfinished wood. Another person may be practicing Taoism by joining a monastery, wearing their hair tied up in a bun, and abstaining from sex. They're both Taoism all right, but they're not the same Taoism.

At this point, you've probably figured out that you'll be getting much less of a headache if you start resisting any temptation to try to find any "essence" of Taoism, or to look for things that all Taoists have in common. In fact, there's probably not a whole lot that everything called *Taoist* has in common (just like New York baseball players don't have a lot in common with pot roast), and things they do have in common may just be coincidental rather than meaningful.

The words *Taoism* and *Taoist* may sometimes refer to very different things. There are, in fact, many different "Taoisms." Be careful not to assume that something true of one type of Taoism is true of every other type of Taoism. In fact, try not to even think of all these different Taoisms as variations of one Taoism. There really is no one Taoism.

Playing fast and loose with Taoism

Just because the word *Taoism* is ambiguous doesn't guarantee that people will use the term more carefully. When you're tuned in to how books and websites make generalizations about Taoism without specifying which way they're using the term or what kind (or kinds) of Taoism they're addressing, you'll start to notice that many of these claims just come off like little slogans or sound bites. Some of the following descriptions may sound familiar to you, and they may actually sound very appealing when you first hear them, but when you listen closely, you'll notice that they don't really say a whole lot:

- » Taoism is a religion that teaches the natural way.
- » Taoism is all about being spontaneous and going with the flow.
- » Taoism imparts an experience that is beyond words.
- » Taoism conveys a universal wisdom.
- » Taoism emphasizes the balance of *yin* and *yang*.
- » Taoists avoid religious dogma and organizations.
- » Taoists are peaceful, calm, and in harmony with the universe.
- » Taoists try to live simple, uncomplicated lives.

Every one of these jingles contains at least a grain of truth and reflects genuine familiarity with some Taoist texts, historical figures, or practices. But they also don't take into account all the ways they distort Taoism, the ways they may not apply at all to certain types of Taoism. Yes, one Taoist text cautions that we can avoid government and military affairs, but how does that explain Taoist-led rebellions or Taoist-run states? Yes, Chuang Tzu seems to turn up his nose at institutions of any kind, but then how do we square that with organized Taoist temples that have hierarchies of priests and structured daily rituals? Now that you know there are many different Taoisms, you can bring a much more critical eye to these types of clichés.

Making Sense of the Chaos: Some Important Distinctions

It's time to start looking at some of the different Taoisms and at some of the most important ways that people use the term *Taoism*, but this is actually a little more complicated than just listing different Taoist denominations. One big reason for that is that more than one Chinese term routinely translates into the English word *Taoism*, and those original Chinese terms came about for different reasons and had completely different frames of reference. To muddy things even further, the Chinese have sometimes mixed up these terms, used them interchangeably, or applied them to people or situations where they really didn't belong. Add to that all the Western translators who made careless use of language or misinterpreted the Chinese background, and you've got a real mess.

From library classification to school of philosophy

When people talk about different kinds of Taoism, a term you'll hear often is *philosophical Taoism* or *Taoist philosophy*. What does it mean to say that there is a Taoist philosophy? You may imagine that this term refers to the underlying philosophy behind Taoist practices, or to a systematic and coherent school of Taoist wisdom, or even just to a general way of thinking about life "Taoistically." And why shouldn't we think of Taoist philosophy this way? It certainly makes sense to picture that the great Taoist thinkers developed a consistent intellectual system, which gave rise to a set of religious practices and which any one of us can adopt in our own lives.

Unfortunately, the term *Taoist philosophy* is something of a misnomer, which lends itself to a bunch of misinterpretations. You can even say that it's a translator's invention. In this section, we explain the origin and meaning of the term, introduce you to some of the key figures from this type of Taoism, and give you a brief look at some of the important themes you'll run into when you look at Taoist philosophical texts.

The place of philosophical Taoism

The terms *Taoist philosophy* and *philosophical Taoism* are somewhat awkward approximations of the Chinese term *Tao-chia,* which actually has a narrow, fairly technical meaning. *Tao-chia* translates literally as "family of *Tao,*" but it means something more along the lines of "school of *Tao*" or "lineage of *Tao.*" When an astrologer and librarian hired by the emperor first used that expression a little more than 2,100 years ago, he was marking out one category for classifying earlier authors and texts in terms of how they approached the question of governing the country. These authors may never have considered that they were participating in a single "school of thought," and their texts often contradicted one another. But they sounded enough alike that people who made lists of such things began to think of them as all on the same philosophical page. And so, the Chinese had themselves a retroactive "school of *Tao.*"

What's more, for all the talk of a "school of *Tao,*" there doesn't seem to have ever been any self-conscious "school" that continued after this first round of writings. Yes, Taoists studied and took inspiration from the main texts for centuries, but they never continued any sustained philosophical tradition in the same vein. When you look at the history of Chinese philosophy and religion across 2,000 years, you really won't find any "philosophical Taoists" or people creating "Taoist philosophy."

TECHNICAL STUFF

The invented Western terms *Taoist philosophy* and *philosophical Taoism* pretty much refer to a cluster of thinkers and texts from what we know as China's "Classical Period," the stretch from the late sixth century BCE until the end of the third century BCE. It's probably more accurate to think of the writings from this period simply as "Classical Taoism."

Important names in Classical Taoism

Classical Taoist thought exerts a tremendous influence on Chinese culture and education, and it has so fascinated Western audiences that you may get the idea that it's the be all and end all of Taoism. However, only a handful of thinkers actually seem to fall into this category. Here are the names that you'll hear most often, in roughly descending order of importance:

- **Lao Tzu:** The legendary founder of Taoism who was the supposed author of the Tao Te Ching, the best known and most widely translated Taoist text. Most classical Chinese texts are simply named after their author, so the Tao Te Ching is also known as the *Lao Tzu.*
- **Chuang Tzu:** The author of the most important chapters of the *Chuang Tzu,* a funny and often brilliant text that contains allegorical stories, poems, imagined dialogues, and essays about logic and language. Chinese often refer to

Classical Taoism as "the Lao-Chuang Tradition," because of the importance of Lao Tzu and Chuang Tzu.

- **Lieh Tzu:** An author who may have written in a style similar to that of Chuang Tzu, but whose writings did not survive. There is an existing book called the *Lieh Tzu,* but it's most likely a much later forgery (though still a fun read).
- **Yang Chu:** A mysterious figure who is sometimes described as a "hedonist." He's the focus of one chapter of the *Lieh Tzu,* and a few chapters by his followers are tucked into the *Chuang Tzu.* The Confucians gave him a pretty bad reputation for his emphasis on physical pleasure.
- **Shen Tao, T'ien P'ien, and P'eng Meng:** Thinkers who get mentioned in other texts but whose writings are either lost or survive only in fragments that are quoted elsewhere. It's hard to tell how many others there were like them whose names were simply lost to history.

REMEMBER

Classical Taoism, philosophical Taoism, Taoist philosophy, and the *Lao-Chuang tradition,* as well as a few other terms you may bump into every once in a while (for example, *Hundred Schools Period Taoism, Warring States Taoism,* and *Pre-Han Taoism*), all refer to more or less the same thing.

Important themes in Classical Taoism

Lao Tzu, Chuang Tzu, and the other Classical Taoists may not always put forth the same philosophy, but they do all address a number of recurring themes. Here are some of the topics you'll find most often:

- ***Tao:*** *Tao* translates literally as "the Way," the empty, timeless principle underlying all of existence. Classical Taoists talk about experiencing the Way, harmonizing with the Way, becoming one with the Way, and so forth.
- **Skepticism:** The Classical Taoists do a lot of questioning, and they can sometimes get pretty snarky about it. They question the value and purpose of language, learning and knowledge, and moral categories. They even question their own questioning. This can start to make your head hurt.
- **Returning:** Lao Tzu and Chuang Tzu are convinced that our conventional intellectual and moral habits have dragged us down to a state in which we're distant from and out of touch with the original Way. They chide us to return to that original state of perfection.
- **Unlearning:** If everything we've learned has distanced us from the original Way, the only method for getting back to it is to unlearn everything we already know. Classical Taoists talk about abandoning knowledge and intentionally striving to forget.

» **Spontaneity:** Once we've gotten back in touch with the Way, we can act in a way that harmonizes naturally and effortlessly with the flux and flow of the cosmos. Lao Tzu especially introduces the ideas of "doing nothing" or "actionless action," which he paradoxically understands as an effective way to rule a country.

» **Simplicity:** The spontaneous life brings us back to our original, simple natures, free of scheming, calculating, and conniving. Lao Tzu and Chuang Tzu usually portray this as living an unambitious and uncluttered life, not bothered by fame, rules, or social obligations. Sometimes, they suggest this may look like a kind of primitive utopia.

The fuzzy line between philosophy and religion

Another important term you hear a lot is *religious Taoism* or the *Taoist religion*. If the word *religion* brings to mind deities, priests, rituals, sacred scriptures, organized institutions, and places of worship, you wouldn't be too far off. Religious Taoism refers to actual religious stuff, not just ideas in old texts — the historical and living practices and communities that you can see, visit, and maybe even join. It only gets tricky when you assume certain things about it just because we call it "religion," or try to put together the relationship between Classical Taoism and religious Taoism. In this section, we talk about the term *religious Taoism*, how it relates to Classical Taoism, and some of its most significant types and characteristics.

The development of the Taoist religion

Just as *philosophical Taoism* is an imperfect translation of a Chinese phrase, *religious Taoism* and the *Taoist religion* are also approximations of specific Chinese terminology. The original expression *Tao-chiao* literally means "the teachings of the *Tao*," which over time came to refer to a range of organizations and practice groups that traced their origins back to one specific social and religious movement that began almost 2,000 years ago. And to some extent, almost everything Taoist that occurs after the Classical Period now falls under the heading of "religious Taoism."

TIP

Don't be fooled into thinking the Chinese came up with this term to distinguish religious Taoism from philosophical Taoism. They were actually differentiating the teachings of the *Tao* from the teachings of the Buddha, the missionary Buddhism that had been coming into China during much the same period. Eventually, the Chinese would think of "three teachings" — the "teachings of the *Tao*," "the teachings of the Buddha," and "the teachings of the Confucian scholars." You may recognize these as what people today sometimes call the "three religions" of China: Taoism, Buddhism, and Confucianism.

So, what's the relationship between Classical Taoism and religious Taoism? There isn't really a clear answer, though there are plenty of people fighting about it, and some Chinese even use the terms *Tao-chia* (see "The place of philosophical Taoism," earlier in this chapter) and *Tao-chiao* more or less interchangeably! Sometimes, it seems that there are really obvious connections, like when you see images of Lao Tzu in Taoist temples, or Taoist monks studying the Tao Te Ching. But other times, it's much harder to put them together, such as when Taoist practice focuses so much attention on healing, longevity exercises, and the search for immortality, which doesn't square with Chuang Tzu's argument that we should be indifferent to matters of life and death.

TIP

Try not to think of religious Taoism as the outward expression of Taoist philosophy, or of philosophical Taoism as the intellectual basis of the Taoist religion. They really aren't just two versions of the same thing. *Taoist philosophy* refers to classical texts from a specific period; *Taoist religion* refers to a complicated and diverse set of practices and organizations spanning a much longer period.

Important subdivisions of religious Taoism

So, *Taoist philosophy* is a misnomer, but is it okay to use the terms *Taoist religion* or *religious Taoism?* Mostly, yes, but because this category covers such a huge range of Taoist religious practices, communities, and lineages, it's usually more helpful to think of these terms as just umbrella terms for the many different flavors of Taoism, which people sometimes sort out by historical period (for example, "Six Dynasties Taoism"), region ("Mao-shan Taoism"), and social structures ("monastic Taoism"). But even with all this diversity, you really only need to keep track of a manageable number of specific sects and denominations. Here's a sampling of the most important ones, listed in roughly chronological order of their formation:

- **The Way of the Celestial Masters:** The first organized movement that can really be called Taoist. It formed in about 142 CE, and almost all subsequent Taoist organizations are in some way descended from it.
- **Highest Purity and Numinous Treasure:** Self-cultivation groups that began in the fourth and fifth centuries and produced a large number of revealed texts and practiced meditation or alchemy. They imported many ideas and practices from the Celestial Masters tradition.
- **Celestial heart, Spiritual Firmament, and Perfect Great Way Taoism:** Some of the short-lived sects that arose from the 11th through 13th centuries. They didn't last long, but they provided important links between the earlier sects and the two lineages that still exist today.

- **Orthodox Unity Taoism:** One of the two Taoist denominations that survive in China today. This branch is primarily *liturgical,* which means that its members conduct rituals and preside over various public and private ceremonies. It understands itself as the direct descendant of the original Way of the Celestial Masters.
- **Complete Perfection Taoism:** The other Taoist denomination that you can find in China today. This branch is primarily *monastic,* which means that its members receive their training or live in monasteries. Founded in the 12th century, this is the newest existing branch of Taoism.

Important characteristics of religious Taoism

In some ways, there's nothing at all mysterious about the different branches of Taoism; they look a lot like other religions you may already know, particularly some of the others from East Asia, like Buddhism or Shinto. Here are some of the characteristics that show up in most religious Taoist lineages:

- **Deities:** There are numerous Taoist gods and goddesses, but not every denomination venerates the exact same figures. Some of the most important include the "Three Pure Ones," one of which is a deified Lao Tzu, and various historical and legendary persons.
- **Scriptures:** There are well over a thousand sacred Taoist texts, though almost certainly no single person has ever read them all from cover to cover. They deal with subjects as diverse as ritual formulas, alchemy, morality, and physiology.
- **Priests:** Taoist organizations developed an intricate and elaborate hierarchy of different priestly ranks. Ordained priests wear special clothing, have access to secret interpretations of texts, and preside over ritual functions.
- **Sacred places:** Through most of its history, a big part of Taoism has been its "sacred geography," places that are considered to possess a special religious charge. Several important Taoist temples are built into the landscape of sacred mountains.

Knowing that for Every Yin, There is a Yang

If you've read classical Taoist texts, taken classes in *t'ai-chi* or *ch'i-kung,* or heard bits and pieces about Taoist physical cultivation practices, you've probably gotten the impression that the concepts of *yin* and *yang* figure pretty prominently in

Taoist thought and practice. You may also have an unspecific sense of what those terms mean: *Yin* is the "feminine principle," associated with things like night, coolness, and receptivity, while *yang* is the "masculine principle," associated with things like day, heat, and activity (see Figure 1-1). And you may even have a fuzzy understanding that the goal of Taoism is somehow to keep (or put) these two principles in some kind of balance. If this is what you're thinking, you're actually not too far off, but there is, of course, a whole lot more to it.

FIGURE 1-1: A typical *yin* and *yang* symbol.

© John Wiley & Sons, Inc.

For starters, try to think of *yin* and *yang* — which originally meant nothing more complicated than, respectively, the shady and sunny sides of a hill — not so much as aspects of uniquely Taoist doctrine, but as ingredients within a general Taoist worldview that helped to shape not only Taoism, but also the Buddhist and Confucian traditions, as well as other disciplines like medicine, psychology, and even political history.

REMEMBER

The theory of *yin* and *yang* is not exclusively Taoist, though there's really no doubt that Taoism takes the *yin-yang* ball and runs with it much farther and to more interesting (and often obscure) places than just about anyone else.

Exploring the School of *Yin-Yang*

Although the ideas of *yin* and *yang* did get swallowed up by Taoism, and other Chinese traditions as well, they really did much more than just float around as a pair of vague ways of classifying specific entities or configurations of *ch'i* (more on that in the upcoming section "Understanding the Concept of Ch'i: The Psychophysical Stuff of Existence"). They also figured prominently as the foundational terminology of an elaborate philosophy. In fact, the same historians of the Hundred Schools Period, referring to a time of cultural development in China around 500-221 BCE, who first classified Lao Tzu, Chuang Tzu and others into a "School of *Tao*" also created a category called the "School of *Yin-Yang*," which is sometimes translated as the "Naturalists." When you hear that Taoism incorporates *yin-yang* thought, or something like that, it really means that it incorporates the original teachings (and later interpretations) from this School of *Yin-Yang*.

The five elements theory

Although there's considerable doubt about the extent of Chinese scholar Tsou Yen's contributions to the School of *Yin-Yang*, traditional histories credit him with one especially important innovation in the naturalistic system: the pairing of *yin-yang* theory with another theory that may have had its own historical roots, that of the "five elements." Where the basic dualistic *yin-yang* theory understood existence as the alternation of two rising and falling complementary configurations of *ch'i*, the five elements approach allowed for a much more complex and potentially expansive network of interactive cycles.

TECHNICAL STUFF

In actuality, the term *wu-hsing* is more accurately translated as "five phases" or "five agents" rather than "five elements," a suggestion that may make a little more sense once you understand that the idea of *ch'i* concerns processes and patterns of relationships, not atoms or molecules. Try thinking of them as *phases* of transformation, or *agents* of mutual influence, rather than static *elements*.

So, what are these five phases? They're usually listed in this order:

- **Wood:** This phase refers to much more than two-by-fours, including a whole range of vegetation, minerals, and even substances such as wax or carbon.
- **Fire:** This includes various things associated with heat and light, such as the sun, lava, and smoke.
- **Earth (or soil):** This can include things blended to form soil, such as clay, rocks, dust, sand, and even bone.
- **Metal:** This phase incorporates the various metals the early Chinese knew about — such as gold, silver, copper, and bronze — but it also includes their properties like magnetism and conductivity.
- **Water:** Liquid comes in many different forms, including vapor, the oceans, precipitation, and condensation.

Again, the significance of these phases is not that they represent separate components of reality, but that they interact with one another through a set of predictable cycles and relationships.

Production and generation

The first type of interaction among the five phases is what the Taoists identify as a *generative* or *productive cycle*, the specific ways that the phases continually give rise to (and are dependent on) one another. Here's the most common synopsis of that type of cycle:

- **Water generates wood.** Water doesn't really turn into wood, but you can certainly see how trees (wood) depend on water to grow.
- **Wood generates fire.** Well, you can watch a tree for days and it probably won't spontaneously burst into flames, but fire requires fuel (wood) in order to burn.
- **Fire generates Earth.** When fire consumes a substance, it produces ashes, which settle back into the soil.
- **Earth generates metal.** Okay, this one's not really obvious, until you consider how, in much of the ancient world, people believed that metal grew in the ground. Got it?
- **Metal generates water.** This one may not be obvious either, until you pick up a cold tin cup on a humid day. It must have certainly looked to a lot of people like the metal actually produced the liquid.

Conquest and overwhelming

One of the things that makes the five-phase cycle so interesting, and gives it so much potential for variation and application to different circumstances, is the way the Taoists also imagine a conquering or overwhelming cycle. When they jog the sequence of phases, you get the following relationships:

- **Water conquers fire.** And it's a good thing it does. If we didn't have easy access to an abundant substance to control fire, things would get pretty hot, pretty fast.
- **Fire conquers metal.** At first glance, metals seem fairly solid and permanent. That is, until you apply some heat to them. Use enough fire, and the metal melts.
- **Metal conquers wood.** Implements made of metal are your best bet for felling trees or fashioning things out of wood.
- **Wood conquers Earth.** This refers to how wooden implements can dig up soil. Just don't tell Tsou Yen about the problems for homeowners of Earth-to-wood contact!

» **Earth conquers water.** Water can be a furious force that's difficult to maintain, but the natural banks of a river or an earthen dam can rein it in and even redirect it.

The Taoists sometimes illustrate the two directions of influence through a circle containing a five-pointed star, with each of the stars' vertices representing one of the five agents. Arrows on the circle pointing in a clockwise direction illustrate the generative cycle, while arrows on the star indicate the directions of the conquest cycle. Like the *yin-yang* symbol shown in Figure 1-1, this diagram indicates a dynamic, constantly moving, and internally complete system.

Yin-yang and five phases

So, how does this all connect with *yin-yang?* By identifying the phase of lesser *yang* with wood, greater *yang* with fire, *yin-yang* balance with Earth, lesser *yin* with metal, and greater *yin* with water. Some of this may seem intuitively obvious. The Tao Te Ching says that nothing is more yielding than water, so it makes sense to identify that with a preponderance of *yin.* Fire can be blindingly bright and is so frenetic that you can't even make out its borders, a natural match with *yang.* And the Earth is where you can be, quite literally, *grounded,* a place of balance between *yin* and *yang* (and perhaps) other dualities as well.

When Tsou Yen (or whoever) first started making connections between cycles of *yin-yang* with the five-phase cycles, he may have started speculating about how these progressions related to other things he studied, like history, ethics, and science. In particular, he may have associated the phases of generation and destruction with the rise and fall of successive dynasties.

Understanding the Concept of *Ch'i:* The Psychophysical Stuff of Existence

Whenever you read a Taoist reference to *yin* and *yang,* unless it's using the older and more conventional meanings of dark and light (or night and day), chances are that it's referring at least implicitly not just to general ideas of femininity and masculinity, but specifically to *yin ch'i* and *yang ch'i.* This concept of *ch'i,* which goes back at least as far as the earliest Taoist texts, has one trait in common with other Asian religious terms like *Tao, karma,* and *nirvana:* It has pretty much made its way into the English language and even shows up from time to time in crossword puzzles and Scrabble tournaments. But it's a tough term to define exactly.

What is *ch'i*?

In one way, this is an incredibly easy question to answer. In modern Chinese, the word simply means "air" or "breath." The Chinese term for *balloon* is a "*ch'i*-ball," and your trachea is your "*ch'i*-pipe." When Chinese Americans first encounter lectures or essays on this mystical theory of *ch'i*, they're often amused (and baffled) that anyone's making such a fuss over it.

In religious and philosophical texts, and as a technical term in a number of fields, *ch'i* is, indeed, virtually untranslatable, not because there's anything magical about it, but because there just isn't one single English word that captures all its nuances. For the last hundred years, translators have driven themselves crazy trying to find the best equivalent of this term, and they've generally settled on language that wasn't exactly wrong but just didn't quite tell the whole story. Here are some of the most common choices, any one of which is plausible in its own way:

Breath	Energy	Ether
Life force	Matter	Passion-nature
Pneuma	Substance	Vital energies

If we adopt sort of an all-of-the-above approach, maybe you can see that *ch'i* refers to some kind of "stuff" but also seems to cut across the conventional Western boundaries separating matter from energy, or physical substance from spirit. So, yes, all types of what you think of as *matter* — solids, liquids, gases — are *ch'i* (or, more accurately, composed of *ch'i*), but so are more tenuous "substances" like energy, thought, or will. In short, *ch'i* really is the "stuff" of existence, the raw materials (though not necessarily "material" materials, if that makes any sense) from which everything in the universe is put together.

One really helpful translation of *ch'i* is "psychophysical stuff" because it captures the idea of "substance" that is simultaneously psychological and physical. If the Western term *psychosomatic* indicates an interest in how the mind and body relate to each other, the term *ch'i* indicates how Taoists never really separated mind and body in the first place.

What isn't *ch'i*?

If *ch'i* runs the gamut of everything from matter and physical substance to energy and thought, it doesn't leave a whole lot of room for anything that isn't *ch'i*, does it? Well, no, it doesn't. Taoists have never conceived of anything (or any "thing") that doesn't consist of *ch'i*, and they haven't wasted a whole lot of time trying to speculate abstractly about what kind of *ch'i*-less materials may exist somewhere in the universe. Not all *ch'i* is as hard as concrete, but Taoists generally think pretty concretely about it.

But on the other hand, for about the last thousand years anyway, Taoist thinkers did find it helpful to conceptualize the principle (or principles) that govern *ch'i* and make it function coherently as somehow "above form," while *ch'i* itself was "below form." And so, you may occasionally hear someone say that *Tao* is not composed of *ch'i*, but that it somehow is inherent in the *ch'i* or is somehow manifest in it.

Or, you can try thinking of it this way: You'll never find any existing thing, any configuration of *ch'i* that doesn't embody some underlying or organizing principle (or replicate the *Tao*, as some Taoists may be more inclined to say). On the other hand, such an underlying principle doesn't ever really exist abstractly or independently of reality; there must be some real *existence* that this principle actually underlies.

Contrasting *ch'i* and atomic theory

Once you hear that "everything is made up of *ch'i*," you may be inclined to suspect that what they're really talking about are molecules, atoms, quarks, subatomic particles, and so on, but that they're doing so in a kind of romantic and impressionistic way. In other words, it may sound like the theory of *ch'i* isn't much more than a pseudo-scientific version of atomic theory. That's actually a pretty natural conclusion to draw, but it misrepresents the Taoist worldview in some subtle ways.

The main differences really concern what people mean when they say "everything is made up of" something else and how they understand the significance of that information. At some risk of overgeneralization, Western atomic theory is concerned with the *composition* of matter, of definitively identifying exactly what the smallest building blocks are that combine to form more complex substances or organisms. It also investigates the *properties* of these building blocks, explaining how and why they function, combine (or not), and so forth. It's really like taking something apart to find out what it's made of and why it works.

On the other hand, the theory of *ch'i* is concerned much less with figuring out the *structure* of existence than with recognizing patterns of how different aspects of existence relate to one another, much less with isolating what the stuff *is* than with gaining insight into the *processes* of change and interaction. Taoists generally think of existence as a fluctuating field of various configurations of *ch'i*, not as an accumulation of completely separate entities; so, *ch'i* refers more to shifting states than to static elements. At any moment, *ch'i* can have a preponderance of *yin*, a preponderance of *yang*, or an equal balance between the two, but this can ebb and flow over time. It can be refined or crude, clear or dense, active or sluggish, but those describe *conditions*, not essential realities.

Oh, and what's more, your *ch'i* and our *ch'i* are in some ways the very same stuff. For that matter, your *ch'i* and our *ch'i* and a rock's *ch'i* and the Earth's atmosphere are all the same stuff. They're all parts of the same living organism and participate in the same cosmic processes.

REMEMBER

In Taoism, *yin* and *yang* are not abstract principles of femininity and masculinity; they're ways of characterizing specific configurations of *ch'i*.

Discovering *T'ai-chi Ch'üan:* The Boxing of the Great Ultimate

Despite the vast majority of Chinese martial arts and physical health exercises not being Taoist, we couldn't have an introductory chapter on Taoism without including the one Taoist practice most people think of: *t'ai-chi*.

REMEMBER

Ironically, American Taoism is more closely connected to *t'ai-chi* and *ch'i-kung* than Chinese Taoism is. And the reverse is true, too — American *t'ai-chi* and *ch'i-kung* are probably more consciously Taoist than Chinese *t'ai-chi* and *ch'i-kung* are.

But what are these practices with Chinese roots that have made such a splash in the United States and Canada? And how did they transform after they were transplanted into a new context? As you've no doubt gathered, China has produced a great number of personal practices that employ complicated maps of the body, combine the pursuits of physical and spiritual health, and cut across different religious traditions. Of all these, the one that is probably the best known worldwide is officially called *t'ai-chi ch'üan*, though it's often abbreviated in the West simply as *t'ai-chi*.

TECHNICAL STUFF

The often-ignored *ch'üan* part translates literally as "fist," which is important because, by extension, "*t'ai-chi* fist" refers to a particular type of boxing (there are others, like "eight extremities boxing" or "chop-hanging boxing"). No matter how much people employ it for health, spiritual wholeness, or fun, the name certainly suggests that it's a *martial* art.

So, what type of boxing is *t'ai-chi ch'üan?* It's an "inner boxing" — that is, one that is driven more by the internal circulation of *ch'i* than brute strength, where the practitioner tries to tap into, align oneself with, or replicate the movement of *t'ai-chi*, the "Great Ultimate." And what's the Great Ultimate? The concept appears in many Chinese traditions (though it possibly originated in Taoism), and it refers to a kind of metaphorical cosmic ridgepole that binds and orients the universe. So, to practice *t'ai-chi* is to perform the boxing of the Great Ultimate, to engage in the stylized physical movements that are characterized by fidelity to the cosmos itself.

The roots of *t'ai-chi*

Many people in China who teach *t'ai-chi* understand themselves to be heirs to and transmitters of a distinct training lineage that goes back to a 14th- or 15th-century figure named Chang San-feng. Like many Taoist "founding fathers," Chang may or may not have really existed, though he was actually already a legend in his own time, and more than one Chinese emperor unsuccessfully sent emissaries out to find him. Different popular accounts portray him as blind, funny-looking, and adept at internal alchemy, Taoist sexual practices, and ordinary feats of magic. After these stories had circulated for some time, he achieved widespread recognition as a Taoist immortal, and you can find images of him at mainstream Taoist temples today.

The only problem with this version of the story is that there's no historical evidence that *t'ai-chi ch'üan* actually goes back that far, and the welding of the practice to a Taoist lineage seems to be a somewhat later invention. The earliest credible evidence of an actual *t'ai-chi* practitioner was a 17th-century former military officer named Ch'en Wang-t'ing, who may have learned from a teacher but also may have synthesized the various gymnastic methods popular at the time with his own military sensibilities. Ch'en passed the teaching down in his own family for several generations, and to this day "Ch'en style" endures as a popular form of *t'ai-chi*.

Several other styles of *t'ai-chi* also flourish today, and they, too, can be traced either directly or indirectly to Ch'en Wang-t'ing, including Yang Style, Wu Style, Li Style, Hao Style, and Sun Style.

The steps of *t'ai-chi*

Practitioners of *t'ai-chi ch'üan* learn several postures and movements called *forms*, each of which unfolds like a carefully choreographed cross between dance and gymnastics, which then combine into more complicated routines. Because there are so many different styles and sub-styles (which are still undergoing considerable change), there's really no one fixed "master list" of all the *t'ai-chi* forms and routines, and most students learn only a handful, at least for starters. Some styles have supposedly boasted routines with well more than 200 forms, but as the practice has grown more popular and more mass marketed, it's become pretty common for teachers to pare it down to a much smaller number. You can almost certainly find videos online that will teach you a half-dozen or so forms, spelled out in easy steps.

Many of the forms vaguely resemble pantomime of particular actions, and their names describe them nicely: pounding the ground, needle at sea bottom, step up to seven stars, tornado kick, and playing the lute (sometimes called playing the guitar). Probably the best-known forms allude to animals in motion, or to the human interaction with animals, and their names conjure up some truly delightful images:

- White crane spreads its wings
- Step back and repulse the monkey
- Parting the wild horse's mane
- Golden rooster stands on one leg
- Tiger and leopard spring to the mountain
- Snake creeps down
- Green dragon shoots out pearl

REMEMBER

Depending on who's doing the talking, the goal of learning these *t'ai-chi* forms can range from achieving a sense of "oneness" with the universe to cultivating the body's *ch'i* to obtaining a harmony of *yin* and *yang* to improved balance, flexibility, and circulation.

IN THIS CHAPTER

» Putting the *Tao* into words

» Thinking of the *Tao* as the source of existence

» Getting inside the empty *Tao*

» Experiencing the *Tao*

Chapter 2
What Is the *Tao*, and What Does It Mean to Follow It?

In some ways, the concept of the *Tao* is incredibly easy. It simply means "the way," and there's nothing particularly mysterious about it. Much like the word *way* in English, the modern Chinese *Tao* can connote a path (a way to get someplace), a direction (which way to go), a method (which way to do something), or a principle (a way to act). Modern Chinese people probably use the term dozens of times a day, without thinking that it carries any particular mystique.

But in religious or philosophical circles, the term turns a bit more nuanced. It still means "the Way," but it can refer to matters of ultimate truth (the way of the universe) and matters of human moral responsibility (the way you ought to act). And very often, the natural and the ethical aspects of the Way tie in closely to each other: The way the cosmos is structured and functions (the "way of Heaven") determines the way that human beings are supposed to behave. But it may come as no surprise that not everyone has agreed on exactly what the "Way" is or how you can follow it. In the Classical Period, the Confucian Way differed considerably from the Mohist Way, which in turn differed from the Legalist Way. And in later centuries, when the Chinese begin to speak of the "three teachings," Confucians,

Taoists, and Buddhists argue among themselves about the "Way," just as Jews, Christians, and Muslims argue with one another over doctrine. They all use the term *Tao*, and they all agree that it somehow provides the blueprint for human obligations, but in terms of what it actually means, well, for that the devil really is in the details.

In this chapter, we unpack the single term that seems to lie at the heart of this complicated and diverse tradition. You get a feel for the Taoist attitudes toward language, the creative (and procreative) aspect of the *Tao*, the importance of the *Tao* as "empty," and what Taoists mean when they talk about following or harmonizing with the Way.

Understanding the Paradoxical Language of the *Tao*

You can probably understand why people have come up with all sorts of bizarre definitions of *Tao*. Just look at the first chapter of the Tao Te Ching:

> As for the Tao, the Tao that can be expressed is not the constant Tao.
>
> As for names, the name that can be named is not the constant name.
>
> As for the nameless, it is the beginning of the 10,000 things.
>
> As for the named, it is the mother of the 10,000 things.
>
> Therefore, be constantly without desire, and by this perceive its subtlety.
>
> Be constantly with desire, and by this perceive its manifestations.
>
> The two emerge together.
>
> They have different names, but are called the same.
>
> A mystery of mysteries.
>
> The gateway of all subtleties.

Probably the first thing that jumps out at you in the opening lines is the idea that you can't really talk about whatever it is they're talking about. Both Lao Tzu, the legendary founder of Taoism and supposed author of the Tao Te Ching, and Chuang Tzu, the author of the most important chapters of the *Chuang Tzu*, mention a "wordless teaching," which is, of course, paradoxical. After all, why would they spend so much time — Lao Tzu's 5,000 characters and Chuang Tzu's 33 chapters — talking about what can't be spoken?

On the one hand, this may come as a surprise. Almost a century ago, a German scholar noticed that whenever someone says something can't be described, that person pretty much always has a "copious eloquence" in spite of their supposed linguistic shortcomings. On the other hand, this also carries an implicit warning that the reader should take the texts cautiously, perhaps reading them as containing allegories and figures of speech, as evocative and suggestive of moods and feelings rather than only descriptions of ideas.

Those who know do not speak, those who speak do not know

You don't have to turn too many pages of Taoist texts to find that the authors regard language as inadequate. But inadequate for what? Somehow they keep telling us not just that words miss the point or garble the real meaning, but also that people who use words must not really get it. It's certainly possible that they're putting forth a sophisticated theory of language or a general skepticism about the relationship between words and actualities, but whether or not that's the case, they mainly just come off as pretty suspicious of language. Just look at some of the words Lao Tzu uses to describe words:

- Beautiful words can be bought and sold.
- Sincere words are not beautiful, beautiful words are not sincere.
- Correct words say the opposite.
- To speak seldom is naturally so.

So, what exactly is wrong with words and language? Why does speaking about the *Tao* fall short of describing the "constant *Tao*"? Why does applying a name fall short of the "constant name"? Probably for the same reason that classical Taoists say Confucian or Mohist morality falls short of capturing the true way. Both specific language and defined morality narrow and restrict something that, in the case of the *Tao*, doesn't lend itself easily to such restrictions. By its very nature, language creates discriminations between ideas and conceptual borders between phenomena — and that's a good thing, because these discriminations and borders allow us to function concretely, sort out the world in useful ways, and know the difference between a bicycle and a persimmon. But if the *Tao* is something that is somehow "beyond" discriminations or borders, then applying any language to the *Tao* — at least the way we normally apply language — will necessarily distort its meaning. Or, to put it more simply, if language is finite and the *Tao* is infinite, then the one can't possibly do justice to the other. That isn't actually too far from a basic principle of Kabbalistic mysticism. The early Jewish scholars (more on Judaism in Book 4) described God as *ein sof* (literally, "without limit"), but they always added that even saying that God is without limit is already saying too much about God!

This guarded attitude toward language also relates to Chuang Tzu's observation that any localized, specific perspective on reality — any concrete "situatedness" — inherently creates limited perceptions, attitudes, and ways of understanding. Any use of language — the specific vocabulary, the grammatical structures, the symbolic associations, even the linguistic habits that reinforce the unquestioned distinction between "self" and "other" — localizes you in your own linguistic universe and, therefore, determines (at least partially) the intellectual structures you use to construct and even experience reality.

Lao Tzu and Chuang Tzu tell us that if we use our customary linguistic and cognitive mechanisms to try to know the *Tao*, doing so may accomplish something, but it won't work for knowing the "constant *Tao*."

REMEMBER

Classical Taoists express suspicion of language not only because the *Tao* is somehow beyond words, but because language itself is one human resource that habitually binds us to particular perspectives and narrows our range of possible experience.

Effing the ineffable

Scholars sometimes use the word *ineffable* to describe something that language can't describe satisfactorily. To some extent, lots of things and experiences are actually hard to describe. If you think about it, how would you describe the taste of coffee, the feeling of love, or even the sensation of a sneeze? You don't really have to sit at the feet of a sage to understand some of the limitations of language.

But the implication throughout the classical Taoist texts is that there's much more at stake if you don't understand the *Tao* than if you can't find just the right language to describe a sneeze. When people don't know the Way, they have to deal with confusion, disorder, disharmony, or coming to an early demise.

REMEMBER

Both Lao Tzu and Chuang Tzu seem to be writing, in part, to rescue a world that's being misled by the fraudulent (or incomplete) "ways" of the Confucians and Mohists. This sets up quite the catch-22. It's absolutely crucial that we know the *Tao* but utterly impossible to describe it. Quite the no-win situation, to say the least.

Fortunately, for every time Lao Tzu or Chuang Tzu say something like "those who speak do not know," they also remind us that "those who know do not speak." This may not inspire any great confidence in the power of language. However, at least it acknowledges that there really are, somewhere, "those who know," and there really is something to know. And as frustrating as it is to keep running into red flags about language, it's equally intriguing to chase down clues about the "constant *Tao*," the "nameless," or the "mystery of mysteries," and to get some sense of what it means to enter the "gateway of all subtleties." Regardless of whether the *Tao* falls into the philosophical category of "ground of being" or "principle of reality," Lao Tzu and Chuang Tzu seem intent on reminding their readers at every turn that it holds the key to some mysterious and extraordinary type of knowledge or experience. And you can even say the classical Taoist texts represent the authors' best attempts to "eff" that mysterious and extraordinary ineffable.

The gateway of all subtleties

At times, Lao Tzu almost sounds like he's having a ball dangling the *Tao* right in front of us, dropping little hints without actually giving away the answer, the way a mystery writer builds suspense while narrating a whodunit. But Lao Tzu's whodunit is really more of a "whatisit" (or a "howdoyougetit") where he gradually reveals tantalizing details about the *Tao*. In one passage, he describes it as something "undefined and yet complete" that was "born before Heaven and Earth," something "silent and shapeless" that "stands alone and doesn't change." But even Lao Tzu acknowledges that it's somehow beyond even him, that he doesn't know its name and simply makes use of linguistic convention to identify it as "*Tao*." And when push comes to shove, if he has to call it something, the best he can dredge up is to regard it simply as "great."

Lao Tzu reinforces the sense of mystery by suggesting that it's more than just our language that's in the way — it seems that none of our other regular cognitive or sensory processes is sufficient for grasping this "silent and shapeless" *Tao* either. If you look for it, he says, you can't find it. If you listen for it, you can't hear it; if you reach out to touch it, you can't hold onto it.

Chuang Tzu also gets in on the fun, in one place characterizing the *Tao* through a series of baffling paradoxes:

- *Tao* has actuality and reliability but no action or form.
- *Tao* can be transmitted but can't be received.
- *Tao* can be gotten but can't be seen.
- *Tao* is above the Great Ultimate, but you can't call it high.
- *Tao* is beneath the six extremes, but you can't call it deep.
- *Tao* was born before Heaven and Earth, but you can't call it longstanding.
- *Tao* is elder to antiquity, but you can't call it old.

What's more, Lao Tzu says that the *Tao* is the good person's "treasure." And the person who knows this treasure is "subtle," "profound," "mysterious," and "wise." And what's the payoff for this knowledge? Well, if kings and their ministers can somehow maintain it, Heaven and Earth can "unite to disburse sweet dew." How's that for a beautiful image of a cosmos working generously and beneficently?

Understanding the *Tao* as the Source of Existence

It's a good idea to stay away from jargonistic descriptions such as "ground of being" or "ontological reality," but it probably doesn't push too many esoteric buttons to say that Taoist texts frequently describe the *Tao* as a creative principle. This doesn't necessarily mean that the *Tao* created the universe the way God does in the Bible or the Qur'an or that the *Tao* has any specific will or interest in creating things, but it does point out how the classical Taoist authors often associate the *Tao* with creation and with the idea of creativity itself. The *Tao* is not only the way of existence; it's somehow also the source of that existence. Without the *Tao*, there would be no cosmos.

HERE'S SOMEONE WHO CALLS IT MORE THAN "GREAT"

In a 1974 episode of the classic *Kung Fu* television series titled "The Cenotaph" (a cenotaph is an empty tomb), David Carradine's character, the half-Chinese Shaolin monk Kwai Chang Caine, quotes almost an entire verse of the Tao Te Ching, a passage that describes the mysterious *Tao* as "silent and shapeless." Mistaken for a "Sasquatch priest" by a guilt-ridden Scotsman with an enigmatic past (and an unusually phony-sounding accent), Caine presides over the mock funeral of the man's imaginary wife, Anna White Eagle. Except that after he recites the line "for lack of a better word, I call it great," he tacks on the coda, "for lack of a better name, we call her Anna," which brings a tear to the Scotsman's eye.

It was a pretty amazing piece of dramatic entertainment (and really ahead of its time) for a TV character to be quoting the Tao Te Ching in 1974. This was back when China was still a pretty bewildering entity for most Americans. The press (and politicians) still called it "Red China," and Richard Nixon made his presidential visit there only two years earlier. In fact, the taciturn hero quotes from the Tao Te Ching in several episodes, usually in that pinched, fortune-cookie dialogue that became his trademark. In one scene, he sums up his entire character with a Tao Te Ching sound bite: "I was taught a good soldier is not violent. A fighter is not angry. A victor is not vengeful."

But in retrospect, it's even more amazing that while the action on *Kung Fu* was supposed to be taking place sometime in the 1870s, Caine quotes a translation that is obviously adapted from the 1972 version by Gia-fu Feng (a Chinese-born crony of many of the Beat writers) and his wife Jane English. Now, that's ahead of its time!

The mother of the 10,000 things

Lao Tzu frequently describes the *Tao* as "mother" or uses more generic feminine imagery, but he also states right off the bat that these are metaphorical, not literal, images. We can regard the "nameless" *Tao*, the ineffable *Tao*, as simply the beginning of the 10,000 things — with some saying the 10,000 things refers to the first 10,000 things in existence and others saying it refers more loosely to everything in existence or an approximation of that, like some say a "bajillion" when referring to an overly large, unfathomable number. It's only when we start talking about the named (which is not the "constant name"), that we can think of the *Tao* as the "mother of the 10,000 things." So, the *Tao* may be a *creative* principle, but it's certainly not anthropomorphic — and it's technically not really a *procreative* principle, at least not in the way we conceptualize ordinary human procreation.

REMEMBER

The classical Taoist reference to the *Tao* as "mother" is almost certainly a metaphorical way of conveying the idea of the *Tao* as a source of existence, as a principle that somehow enables the process of creation.

Despite his suggestion not to go too far overboard with the mother metaphor, Lao Tzu puts it to ample use throughout his text. Here are some of the ways he spins that particular image:

- **Symbolizing originality and antiquity:** Perhaps one-upping Chuang Tzu's paradoxical references to the *Tao* as "born before Heaven and Earth" (though "not long-lasting") and "elder to antiquity" (though "not old"), Lao Tzu alternately refers to the *Tao* as the "mother of Heaven and Earth," "mother of the world" (literally the mother of "that which is under Heaven"), and "mother of the kingdom." The *Tao* is in some way *prior* to everything, including Heaven and Earth, and in some way lying at the basis of their creation.
- **Functioning as a nurturing source:** Although the mother imagery naturally suggests a progenitor, don't overlook the role of the *Tao* as *nurturer* (something

that you can tap into for nourishment or sustenance). Lao Tzu periodically talks about the positive things that occur if you "attain," "hold onto," or "possess" the mother, often in terms of avoiding harm or living an extended period.

- **Feminizing the *Tao*:** Whether or not Lao Tzu is talking specifically about the maternal images of creativity and nurture, he also employs more generically feminine metaphors when he describes the *Tao*, ascribing to it the qualities of receptivity and tranquility. In one instance, he relates the "valley spirit" to the "mysterious female," equating them both with the "roots of Heaven and Earth." In another, he casts the "female of the world" as the "meeting point of the world," which can overcome the male with stillness.

WARNING

The Tao Te Ching (more on that in Book 2, Chapter 1) may seem to put forth what was then a fairly radical view of the "feminine," but that doesn't quite justify seeing it as explicitly supporting any kind of feminist revolution. In fact, there's no evidence that the authors of the text didn't share most of the basic Hundred Schools Period assumptions about a stratified social order, a male king, and the role of sons in carrying on the family name and legacy. Some modern feminists do embrace the Tao Te Ching for its feminine images, but it would require a pretty free-wheeling imagination to view it as challenging traditional Confucian gender roles.

Spontaneous self-generation and self-perpetuation

The role of the *Tao* as creative principle is very different from the role of a creator God in the monotheistic traditions. By identifying the *Tao* as the source of existence, this doesn't really serve the purpose of explaining why things are as they are, establishing humankind's place in a divine plan, or even instilling any sense of gratitude in the created beings — all of which are common associations in Jewish, Christian, and Muslim thought. The metaphor of the *Tao* as the "mother of the 10,000 things" doesn't mean that we should accept as an article of faith that the universe was created that way, that we were forged in the *Tao*'s image, or that we should give thanks to the *Tao* for creating us. As Lao Tzu says, "The 10,000 things rely upon it, yet it does not act as their ruler."

So, what, then, does it mean to characterize the *Tao* as a creative principle? What are the implications of imagining the *Tao* as the mother of the 10,000 things? The main point seems to be that the entire cosmos, the ongoing transformations of the universe, somehow participate in a single order, by virtue of their flowing from a single source. What's more, the *Tao* — which has no action or form, can't be seen or received, and can't be called old, high, deep, or longstanding — doesn't seem to *do* anything to or impose itself on these transformations. Yes, the *Tao* lies somehow at the root of all existence, but because of that, the universe takes care of itself perfectly well, on its own accord. In that sense, it is the way of the universe for it to be in spontaneous self-generation and self-perpetuation. That is to say, the cosmos is, the cosmos transforms, and the cosmos endures. The *Tao* is the source of that existence, transformation, and endurance — to know the *Tao* is to be able to understand that self-generating and self-perpetuating process and to take your place in it.

That's why Lao Tzu says that the *Tao* "accomplishes tasks and completes affairs," that it's by virtue of the *Tao* that Heaven is clear and Earth is stable. Chuang Tzu has his own language for characterizing the hundredfold transformations: "As for things alive or dead, square or round, none knows its source, yet from antiquity the 10,000 things have remained firmly in existence."

Chuang Tzu adds, "There's nothing under Heaven that doesn't float or sink, remaining unchanged throughout its lifetime," and though the *Tao* doesn't seem readily apparent, it is indeed the source of this ebb and flow.

TECHNICAL STUFF

The idea of the *Tao* as a single source of a perpetually transforming universe sets up a really interesting tension between the unity of the *Tao* and the obvious diversity of phenomena in that universe. On the one hand, everything springs from and participates in the single source. On the other, nothing remains the same from moment to moment. The Chinese see this not as any kind of contradiction, as much as a creative ambiguity. One *Tao*, but 10,000 things.

The temptation to think of the *Tao* as a deity

If your primary exposure to religion is one or more of the monotheistic religions of the West, you may have initially read the Tao Te Ching and the *Chuang Tzu* and come to the conclusion that they must mean that the *Tao* is some kind of a god or spirit. On the surface, this doesn't seem like a particularly bad interpretation of the texts. After all, the *Tao* is older than Heaven and Earth and the mother of the 10,000 things. It's the mystery of all mysteries that goes beyond language or conventional boundaries, and it's the formless "something" that stands alone and doesn't change. That describes a deity, doesn't it? Well, if you thought so, you'd have plenty of company. Some Christian theologians have asserted that *Tao* (as well as plenty of other charged terms from various traditions) is just another name for the monotheistic God, and some early translators even rendered *Tao* simply as "God."

But of course, there's almost no way that either Lao Tzu or Chuang Tzu intended the term theistically. For one, most of the Hundred Schools Period thinkers — Mohists,

Confucians, Legalists, and Dialecticians — regularly employed the term (as did plenty of others engaged in non-philosophical and non-religious conversations), and none of them seemed to have a deity in mind. What's more, the various commentaries on the text never talk about the *Tao* as a deity, and there's no evidence of anyone from that period ever worshipping the *Tao* itself.

We bring up this point not to rub anyone's nose in this (or any other) misinterpretation of the texts, but to point out how the early Taoists didn't seem to share the common (though not unanimous) Western impulse to ascribe certain processes, like creation and cosmic order, to a deity. Today's advocates of "intelligent design" often justify their position by noting that certain aspects of existence are so microscopically complex, so delicate in their construction and subtle in their functioning, that they must have some kind of intentional, willful, and personal engineer behind them. But one of the most fascinating aspects of classical Taoist philosophy is the idea that the source of existence is utterly without intent, will, or personality, which is why the process of transformation is equally "soulless."

Still, if you initially gave the *Tao* a theistic spin, you can take some solace that the concept of the *Tao*, though not exactly becoming a deity in and of itself, eventually takes on a close association with the later Taoist pantheon. Barely a century after the unofficial conclusion of the Hundred Schools Period, many saw Lord Lao — the deified Lao Tzu — as somehow synonymous with (or at least an incarnation of) the *Tao*. And when the Way of the Celestial Masters established its own roster of gods, it understood those as manifestations of the *Tao*, in contrast to the ordinary popular spirits worshipped by local cults. So, while you can't really say that the Taoist philosophical discussions of the *Tao* are describing it as a deity, you do have to acknowledge that the modern worship and channeling of Taoist deities is really the worship and channeling of the manifest *Tao*.

THE *TAO* WORKS IN MYSTERIOUS WAYS

Mistaking the *Tao* for the Biblical God is not just a peculiar misreading that some spiritual dabblers produce the first time they read the Tao Te Ching — it's a habit that actually enjoyed a long history in European theological circles. Perhaps the earliest scholar to try to identify the *Tao* with God was the early 18th-century Parisian Jean-Pierre Abel-Rémusat, who noticed that the initials of three Chinese characters used to describe the Tao in one chapter of the Tao Te Ching — *yi (level)*, *hsi (rare)*, and *wei (subtle)* — bore a superficial resemblance to the *Tetragrammaton* (the four Hebrew letters in the Old Testament, YHWH, that represented a liturgical name for God). Somewhat later, a German translator of the Tao Te Ching, Victor von Strauss, backed off a bit on the relation between the Chinese terms and YHWH, but he still basically viewed the *Tao* as a metaphor for God.

In one of the first English language translations of the *Huai Nan Tzu*, the Welsh scholar Evan Morgan translated *Tao* as "cosmic spirit." And in addressing Lao Tzu's identification of the *Tao* as "great," Morgan wrote, "This word great may be compared with *Lord*. In a way, it may be synonymous with Jehovah." His comparisons are quite telling. Traditional Bibles still substitute the word *Lord* for *YHWH*, which is actually the source of the name Jehovah.

Seeing Emptiness as the Wellspring of Power

REMEMBER

One important implication of identifying the *Tao* with creativity is the idea that it's effective, that the *Tao* is the creative impetus that informs the universe and its flow. In that sense, you can also understand the *Tao* as a source of power, not necessarily political or social or even hydroelectric power, but the source of real, concrete, and effective transformations of the 10,000 things. That's why it's such a big deal to know or experience the *Tao* — to have access to the *Tao* is to be able to tap into cosmic power par excellence.

But one of the overarching paradoxes of classical Taoism — and this is not just an odd theoretical point, but something that genuinely matters for Taoist practice — is that the texts repeatedly describe the *Tao* as "empty," as a "void," or as a field of "non-being." This doesn't seem to be just another strategic way of expressing ineffability and mistrust of language. Instead, Lao Tzu and Chuang Tzu are emphatic that the quality of emptiness is itself the *Tao*'s source of creative power. Of all the Taoist paradoxes, all of the "elder to antiquity but not old" formulations, this one may seem the most boggling and counterintuitive. How can a creative principle actually be empty, and how can emptiness actually be effective? And why does any of that matter?

Thirty spokes unite in one hub

If you don't quite get how something empty can be a creative source, you may want to think again about the metaphor of the *Tao* as mother of the 10,000 things. In human procreation, the womb, an empty space, is quite literally the cradle of life. And if a womb weren't empty, it wouldn't be able to accomplish what it does. Just as a womb engenders, nurtures, and transforms a single life, the *Tao* engenders, nurtures, and transforms all of existence.

Lao Tzu drives this point further home by using the image of a wheel. The most visible parts of a wheel — at least of wheels from 2,500 years ago — are the spokes, the physical material that makes up the wheel itself. But what makes those materials function, what makes them actually a wheel rather than just a pile of metal or stone, is the empty center around which the spokes converge. The spokes all stem from, revolve around, and return to that center. Even in simple geometry, you can see the curved line that makes up the outside of a circle, but it's the fact that every point on that line is the same distance from the empty center that makes it a circle. And just as it's the empty hub that gives a wheel its potential to turn, and the empty center that gives a circle its definition, it's the empty *Tao* that gives the universe its potential to transform.

Lao Tzu employs several similar images throughout the Tao Te Ching, each one illustrating how an empty space actually provides the value or usefulness of something. Here are a few examples:

- **Clay pots and other vessels:** As with the wheel, we notice the physical materials used to make a pot or other vessel, but it's the emptiness of the pot that allows it to hold things. Think about it — people may compliment the materials in your coffee mug or the design on it, but when's the last time you heard someone compliment the empty space that holds the coffee?
- **A room inside a building:** For all the decorations and furniture you move around a room (through *feng-shui*, perhaps?), it's only the empty space itself that actually makes it useful as a room. And of course, it's an absolute necessity to carve out spaces for windows and doors, all of which are, when you think about, empty spaces themselves.
- **A pair of bellows:** There's nothing inside of a bellows — well technically, there's air, but we don't have to go there — but the bellows always has the capability to blow wind, to stoke a fire, or perhaps to move an object. What's more, it's because the bellows is empty that it can never be depleted; using it never actually drains it in any way. That's why Lao Tzu says that although the *Tao* is empty, you can use it without ever having to fill it and that someone who preserves the *Tao* doesn't need to be renewed.

Because emptiness represents the effective aspect of the *Tao*, Lao Tzu admonishes the reader to "attain emptiness to its utmost limit" and "maintain stillness to the utmost." Chuang Tzu has his own spin on this, pointing out that few people have the capacity to understand the "use of the useless." As always, part of Chuang Tzu's point is that we should question how we make determinations of "value" and "utility," but he's also mirroring Lao Tzu's idea that the source of effectiveness is actually something empty and "useless."

The idea of the *Tao* as the source of creativity and effectiveness is closely tied to the idea of the *Tao* as empty.

Heaven and Earth are not humane

Okay, you've probably got it down by now that the *Tao* is nameless, formless, and shapeless; that it has no discriminations or borders; and that its very emptiness is essential to its creative functions. Even when Lao Tzu and Chuang Tzu make suggestions that the *Tao* ultimately enables the health of the universe or is somehow on the side of the sagely person, they're still quick to remind you that it's dull, bland, and even insipid. What can they have possibly been thinking by arguing that the most important principle in their entire philosophy is insipid? You've got to wonder if the classical Taoist public relations experts were taking an extended lunch break.

They seem to push this to an almost comical extreme when Lao Tzu volunteers things like "Heaven and Earth are not humane." It's one thing to say that human beings "miss" the *Tao* when they pursue conventional virtues like humaneness or ritual propriety — that's just part of the whole critique of Confucian and Mohist ethics — but it's quite another to say that the ongoing transformations of Heaven and Earth (which is basically the movement of the *Tao*) are themselves not humane. What can this possibly mean? Does this say that the universe treats us callously, without feeling, indifferent to our happiness or prosperity? Actually, some translators of the Tao Te Ching seem to go out of their way to give us that idea, rendering the key phrase as "Heaven and Earth are inhumane," "Heaven and Earth are ruthless," or "Heaven and Earth are heartless." So, not only is the *Tao* empty, but it doesn't give a hoot either?

Of course, Lao Tzu really does have a method to his apparent madness, and his point is not that the *Tao* is evil, cruel, or any such thing, but that any expectation we may have that the *Tao* is a moral principle or that the flux and flow of the cosmos is in any way invested in the lot of humankind comes only from our own human-centeredness. It's actually an act of vanity, of human narcissism, of trying to construct a *Tao* in our own moral image — to imagine that the human virtues we recognize somehow apply to the *Tao*. But the *Tao* really is empty; it really is bland and insipid. And it engenders the 10,000 things and their continuous transformations, without will, without intention, without any sense that the created universe fulfills any moral plan or carries any moral obligations, at least not "moral" in the sense that humans ordinarily use the term. The *Tao*, Lao Tzu tells us, is impartial; it truly plays no favorites, and simply treats the 10,000 things as *straw dogs*, as ceremonial objects that wear lavish adornments during the ritual but afterward get discarded with other trash out in the back alley. The straw dogs are not "sacred" during the ceremony, not "profane" in the aftermath; they're just neutral (and temporary) participants in the process at hand. Likewise, the 10,000 things enjoy no special status under Heaven; they're just impersonal participants in the transformations of existence.

Theologians and scholars sometimes talk about what they call *teleology* or a *teleological* view of the world. This is the perspective that there is a *telos* (an end purpose) of existence. If theology examines questions like who the gods are, how they created the universe, and what they expect of created beings, then teleology asks why the universe exists and what divine plan the deities had in mind when they created it. For the most part, the classical Taoist texts seem to be non-teleological — they portray the *Tao* as a natural principle, a principle that lies at the source of existence and that forms the basis of the spontaneous creation and perpetuation of the universe, but has, so to speak, no horse in the cosmic race. The *Tao* is impartial, soulless, and uninvolved.

When you hear quick summaries identifying the *Tao* as a "natural" principle or the principle of "nature," it's tempting then to ask if this nature is good or bad, if the universe that has the *Tao* as its source is ultimately a good or bad one. The classic Taoist answer is neither — the question is itself badly framed and misleading. "Good" and "bad" are moral categories, and those rubrics simply don't apply to the *Tao* or to nature. If you need to characterize nature, just think of it simply as, well, natural. Nothing more, nothing less. This is one more explanation for why harmonizing with the *Tao* requires something other than moral conduct; if the *Tao* is natural and amoral, it stands to reason that humans should be as well.

The sun and moon can only go their courses

When you watch television news coverage— whether about truly important matters like presidential elections or global warming, or trivial tabloid fare like the man who ate an entire lawnmower or the woman who raised hyenas as family members and taught them all Pig Latin — sooner or later one of the reporters is bound to ask the question on every viewer's mind: "How did you feel about this?" Along those lines, how do you feel — or rather, how *should* you feel — about the Taoist ideas of the *Tao* and a non-teleological universe? Or, to put it more broadly, where does it leave us, knowing that the Way of Heaven and Earth doesn't particularly care too much about us? Should we be jumping for joy at this revelation or crying in our beer?

If you come from a religious tradition that has a decidedly teleological bent — traditional Judaism, Christianity, Islam, Hinduism, and many others fall into this category — this may seem like a pretty harsh, cold, or lonely understanding of humankind's place in the cosmos. Instead of a just, wise, compassionate, loving, salvific, and good creator god, you've got an empty source of existence and a cosmos that treats you like a straw dog. Who wouldn't feel a little unnerved by that? If our world had once seemed to us like a bountiful, nurturing greenhouse where we were secure and protected, now it seems like a borderless vacuum, void of any underlying meaning or purpose. Indeed, we wouldn't be surprised if some readers find this a pretty terrifying thought.

And yet, the classical Taoist texts convey an overall mood that there's no reason in the world why anyone should have the slightest problem with any supposed teleological shortcoming. The universe may not, technically, be good or meaningful or purposive, but it does still reflect, for lack of a better way to put it, a fundamental "okey-dokey-ness"! Yes, we know *okey-dokey* isn't exactly a technical term, but it does capture the Taoist idea that there's something basically healthy, intact, and otherwise just fine about a universe that operates this way — insipid *Tao*, impartial universe, amoral cosmos, and all. This is, of course, another typical Taoist paradox; absolutely everyone, every single one of the 10,000 things is an equally straw dog, an equally comfortable and appropriate co-participant in this fine mess we know as existence. In other words, the universe really is okey-dokey, but we have the challenge of following its rhythms and adapting to its movements.

Chuang Tzu especially finds this whole deal not a cause for despair, but an endless succession of opportunities to celebrate the transformations with a kind of intoxicated glee. Why else would he be having so much obvious fun reveling in every offbeat butterfly dream and chattering songbird, while impishly upsetting as many philosophical apple carts as he can? He even has the *cojones* to insist that the *Tao* is to be found in urine and excrement. "Heaven cannot but be high, Earth cannot but be broad, the sun and moon cannot but go their courses, the 10,000 things cannot but prosper. Is this not *Tao*?" When you put it this way, the universe sounds like a pretty cool place after all.

Following, Experiencing, and Harmonizing with the Way

REMEMBER

Keeping with the traditional Chinese emphasis on concrete realities, the classical Taoist texts discuss the *Tao* not in order to indulge the authors' abstract philosophical yearnings, but to offer instructive lessons to their audience. There's speculation about the nature of the Way and how it works — but this only matters to the extent that living human beings can apply what they learn to their own lives in the here and now.

For Confucian and Mohist authors, learning and following the Way was pretty much synonymous with inculcating discrete virtues and cultivating your character, but the kind of application to your own life that the classical Taoist authors have in mind — what exactly you're supposed to do with the *Tao* — isn't always totally clear. Yes, the texts talk about "following" the Way or "knowing" the Way, but they also conjugate a boatload of other interesting verbs. You can "practice" the Way, "devote yourself" to it, "hear it," "possess" it, "preserve" it, "submit" to it, "care about" it, "draw close" to it, or "use it to govern." And as you've probably come to expect by now, Lao Tzu and Chuang Tzu employ some characteristic metaphors to illustrate the uniquely Taoist understanding of what it means to *experience* the Way.

The theme of returning

Once you're comfortable with the idea of the *Tao* as the source or principle of creation, it's probably not such a huge leap to consider the value of getting back to that original source. But this isn't just the intellectual process of doing an end run around all the "false *Taos*," all the mistaken ways you've been taught. This really involves somehow tapping directly into that primary source, experiencing the *Tao* in its fullest, most foundational power. And why shouldn't you want to do that? The *Tao* is the creative principle at the root of all existence, the cosmic impetus informing the transformations of things, the wellspring of power par excellence. To return to that source is in some way to harness that creative power.

REMEMBER

It's really important to keep in mind that the image of returning to the *Tao* isn't just an accidental or strategic one, or just another enigmatic turn of phrase; Lao Tzu really does reiterate that the movement toward the *Tao* is a type of backward movement toward the source. In fact, Lao Tzu even says that "the movement of the *Tao*" is itself "reversal," and he illustrates vividly the multifold transformations as a process of returning.

The classical Taoist version of "knowing the Way" does not involve the acquisition of moral knowledge or the development of character, as much as it involves the direct, experiential return to the *Tao*, to a more pristine state than humans ordinarily occupy.

The emulation of the *Tao*

To a great extent, the real significance of every quality of the *Tao* — its mystery, its ineffability, its role in creation, its emptiness, its amoral impartiality, and its power — points to the implication that it could (or should) be the goal of your life to emulate the *Tao*, that you should seek in some way to embody the *Tao* by returning to it, and in that way, have access to its creative potential. That's why when Lao Tzu and Chuang Tzu ascribe qualities to the Way, they often follow up those descriptions by ascribing similar qualities to the sagely person. So, just as Heaven and Earth treat the 10,000 things as straw dogs, the sage also treats the "common people" as straw dogs. Just as Heaven and Earth live and endure without concern for themselves (which would actually sound kind of strange), the sage thrives by eliminating their own private interest. Just as the *Tao* is empty and without purpose, the sage chooses not to strive or contend with other people or things.

One particular passage from the Tao Te Ching sets this idea of emulating the *Tao* in a deceptively simple series of relationships, starting with humankind and metaphorically working "up the ladder":

> Humanity takes on the pattern of (or models itself on) Earth.
>
> Earth takes on the pattern of Heaven.
>
> Heaven takes on the pattern of *Tao*.
>
> And *Tao* takes on the pattern of that which is so of its own accord.

TECHNICAL STUFF

Try to think of this as kind of a progressive telescoping of the pattern from microcosm to macrocosm, which is actually a reversal of the creative process of the *Tao*. Whoa! Getting a little too jargonistic here? Let's try again without quite so much metaphysical gobbledygook. If you start with the *Tao* as the source, as a sort of cosmic blueprint of or template for existence, it somehow imparts its own pattern — which is, of course, utterly empty and insipid, the simple quality of being "so of its own accord" — onto all aspects of the cosmos, beginning with Heaven. And then Heaven, as a kind of conduit of the Way, transmits that same pattern to Earth. And finally, Earth, which functions as the (metaphorically) tangible "theater" where the transformations of existence occur (and where the 10,000 things cannot but prosper), likewise transmits that pattern to humankind. So, to put it simply, in this ongoing metaphysical drama, the pattern of the original blueprint flows from the macrocosm (the *Tao*) through Heaven and Earth, all the way to the microcosm (each individual person).

When you turn this process around, it more or less summarizes the human potential for returning to the *Tao* and at least one way such a return can occur. Maybe you wouldn't have the slightest idea how to emulate the ineffable *Tao*, but humans can discern, adapt to, and ultimately take on the patterns of Earth because we're all participants in its multifold transformations. And the patterns of Earth are nothing other than the imprinted patterns of Heaven, which are nothing other than the imprinted patterns of the *Tao*, which are ultimately nothing other than the patterns of empty, spontaneous creativity. The ability to return to the Way is inherent in all of us — it's like a metaphysical birthright — because the Way lies at the root of our very existence and the existence of all other beings as well.

The question of mysticism

All this talk of emulating the *Tao*, progressive telescoping, and metaphysical birthrights must make it obvious why many people, both scholars and dabblers in the *Tao*, are quick to portray Taoism as a "mystical tradition" or espousing a "mystical philosophy" or "mystical practice." And to tell you the truth, it's probably more accurate than not to portray at least some aspects of Taoism as mystical. But it's also unfortunate because most sources that use the terms *mystic*, *mystical*, or *mysticism* don't really have a clear, critical sense of how to define the terms, a working knowledge of how mystical traditions have operated historically, or an understanding of the relationships between particular mystics and their broader traditions. They also tend not to recognize ways that the category of mysticism can actually be problematic and misleading, especially when it's applied indiscriminately to any tradition or historical figure whose ideas seem paradoxical, not entirely rational, or boasting "transcendent" insights. Unfortunately, you'll far too often hear people talking about "mysticism" as a substitute for analyzing something critically and carefully.

Because mysticism is so important for understanding Taoism, but is also such a widely misunderstood concept itself, we take some time in this section to walk the conversation back to a more realistic and helpful starting place. You'll come away with a working definition of mysticism and a bit of a road map for exploring whether it's helpful to think of Taoism as a mystical tradition.

A number of people who represent Taoism as a mystical tradition usually tell you that the goal of Taoism is "union with the *Tao*," "becoming One with the *Tao*," or "merging with the *Tao*." And although these descriptions may not be entirely inaccurate, they can potentially create more confusion than clarity. For one, different mystical traditions may have radically different understandings of *oneness* and what they mean by things such as *union* or *merging*.

Authors who aren't familiar with these types of subtleties may use an expression like "union with *Tao*" without making explicit what it means for a human being to "unite" with an ineffable principle or explaining how it differs (if at all) from a Christian understanding of "union with God" or a New England Transcendentalist's understanding of "communion with nature." In any event, this is especially problematic for discussions about Taoism, mainly because the Taoist texts most often regarded as mystical don't particularly use that kind of language. Yes, Lao Tzu and Chuang Tzu do use expressions like "become one with spirit," "come into accord with the great thoroughfare," and "deem the 10,000 things as one," but these aren't necessarily even saying the same thing as one another, let alone just describing "union with the *Tao*" in different ways. It's important to resist the temptation to spiritualize such passages into a single homogenized "oneness."

So, what types of mysticism can we find in Taoism? Unfortunately, there isn't just one answer. With more than a thousand texts in the Taoist Canon (many of which have very little to do with mysticism) and at least a half-dozen different authors of the *Chuang Tzu* alone, there's really no reason to expect that all of them are describing the same kinds of experiences. And even when there's widespread consensus that something mystical is going on (like with the *Chuang Tzu*), no one can really seem to agree on anything. One important scholar describes Chuang Tzu as an *intraworldly mystic* — that is, someone who doesn't seek any kind of unity, but rather, in line with the idea of the *Tao* as transformative process, develops a new way of being present in the changing world. Such a mystic is fully involved with, fully attached to, each moment as it comes, and then fully detached from that moment as it passes, turning life into an endless slide show of new beginnings. However, another scholar argues that Chuang Tzu is a *bimodal mystic*, who eases back and forth between, on the one hand, an introverted loss of self and individuality and, on the other hand, a concrete apprehension of the oneness of the *Tao* in all things. And regardless of what type of mysticism Chuang Tzu actually practiced (if he did at all), at least one linage of Orthodox Unity Taoists today regard the first seven chapters of his book as a coded meditation manual, leading to a kind of "union" based on exorcising both *heterodox deities* (deities not part of the official Taoist pantheon) and one's own selfish desires.

REMEMBER

The *Tao* is not necessarily a "mystical" concept in Taoism, but there certainly are Taoist authors, texts, and practices that point toward experiences of the *Tao* that are, indeed, mystical, in the sense that those who have those experiences understand them as revelatory of a higher reality or the true character of reality.

IN THIS CHAPTER

» Introducing actionless action

» Ruling by doing nothing

» Seeing non-doing in everyday life

Chapter 3
Doing Everything by Doing Nothing

All that talk in Book 2, Chapter 2 of the "creative and empty source of existence," or the "spontaneous self-perpetuation and self-generation of the cosmos," or the "emulation of the *Tao*" may be all well and good, but where does this leave human beings in terms of their day-to-day lives? After Lao Tzu and Chuang Tzu reject all the conventional human virtues, what does the Taoism of the classical texts have to say about ethical conduct, interpersonal relations, or social organization? Doesn't religion usually include at least a couple paragraphs about what people are supposed to *do*? Or is mulling over how to return to the *Tao* doing enough?

The classical Taoist answer sounds astonishingly similar to one you may expect to hear from certain politicians, enthusiasts for mind-numbing video games, and couch potatoes of all persuasions: There's no problem anywhere — ethical, social, governmental, or whatever — that's so big that it can't be solved by doing absolutely nothing! That's right, you heard correctly. Although other Hundred Schools (more on that in Book 2, Chapter 1) thinkers debate which actions will best transform society and solve the world's ills (and later texts from the Taoist Canon offer no shortage of ethical precepts), Lao Tzu and Chuang Tzu seem to be advocating not just taking no action, but actively pursuing the task of taking no action. And no, they're not just messing with your head either.

In this chapter, we do everything we can to make some sense of this peculiar Taoist idea of "doing nothing." You see exactly what the classical texts mean by *wu-wei*, as well as how this idea relates to government and military affairs. You also see examples of how this is supposed to work when you're dealing with ordinary matters, and how some strands of Taoist thought translate this into a kind of primitivist revolt against technology and progress.

Considering the Counterintuitive Concept of *Wu-wei*

The Chinese term that appears nearly a dozen times in the Tao Te Ching (and frequently in both the *Chuang Tzu* and *Huai-nan Tzu* as well) is the ordinary two-character couplet *wu-wei*, where the first character translates easily as "not" or "without," and the second means either "do" or "make." (The latter can also mean something like "on behalf of," but the grammatical structure indicates that's not what they have in mind here.) So, in its most basic sense, *wu-wei* really does mean "not doing," "not making," "not acting," or something very similar. It seems like a pretty straightforward concept, even if a slightly dull one.

But naturally, the Taoist texts wrap up this concept in their usual predilection for paradox and counterintuitive formulations. For one, Lao Tzu talks a couple times about *wei wu-wei*, about "doing the non-doing," or "acting without acting," which suggests that the non-doing actually entails some kind of doing, and possibly even that there's something intentional or willful about this puzzling type of "deed." Hmmm. So, what kind of doing can non-doing possibly be? Looking at the Chinese characters again, maybe you can think of it as *wei*-ing in a *wu* way — that is, acting, but in a "without" kind of way! A "without" *what* kind of way, you may ask? Without intention, without affect, without calculation, in short, without any specific cognitive motivation that brings you out of synchronicity with the *Tao*. This may be why some translators have chosen to render *wu-wei* as "actionless action" or "non-ado," to differentiate it from a kind of mindless passivity.

Nothing left undone

Probably the most important and compelling characteristic of Taoist *wu-wei* is the idea that somehow the proper performance (using the term "performance" very loosely) of this non-doing is effective, that it actually accomplishes particular ends more efficiently and more thoroughly than ordinary action does. The texts explain this point best in a few different places, where they say that the *Tao* (or Heaven and Earth) *wu-wei er wu pu-wei* ("does nothing and yet nothing remains undone"). And by extension, the sagely person, who aspires to emulate the *Tao*, likewise strives to do the non-doing and likewise accomplishes the same end of leaving nothing undone.

So, how does non-doing work? What's the mechanism by which nothing remains undone? It sounds like the classical Taoists are promising the philosophical equivalent of lowering taxes and increasing human services, claiming that you can accomplish more by actually doing less. Of course, they never quite explain this in so many words, but the entire calculus is implicit in the basic understanding of the *Tao*. Because the *Tao* is empty, impartial, insipid, and soulless, because it gives rise to and sustains the 10,000 things (more on the 10,000 things in Book 2 Chapter 2), the ongoing transformations of existence without conscious will, moral investment, or anything remotely resembling effort, the process of purging yourself of willful intent, of the accumulated human cognitive "stuff," is tantamount to "plugging yourself into" the *Tao* and, therefore, plugging yourself into its all-encompassing efficaciousness.

REMEMBER

Just as the *Tao* accomplishes infinitely by virtue of non-doing, so, too, can the sagely person successfully leave nothing undone in the same manner. This may not exactly explain the messy details of how tasks get fulfilled when no one's making a conscious effort to do them, but it does explain the philosophical basis that informs the overall idea.

The spontaneous and the natural

You may be getting the message from this discussion of non-doing that our ordinary doing is somehow unnatural, that action following from our own cognitive habits and values are artificial, manufactured, contrived actions, as opposed to actions in step with the *Tao*. The implication throughout is that "*Tao*-ful" action, the action accomplished through non-doing, is genuine, authentic, and, of course, utterly natural, in that it harmonizes with the wholly natural flow and rhythm of the cosmos. In this way, you can think of returning to the *Tao* as a return to your authentic self. And there's probably no Taoist expression that captures this idea better than *tzu-jan*, yet another confusing term that's boggled generations of well-intentioned translators.

TECHNICAL STUFF

You can best understand the term *tzu-jan* not through its usual translations — such as "spontaneity," "naturalness," or "the course of nature" — but through a more direct look at the Chinese characters themselves. The first one, *tzu*, means "self," but not in the sense of, say, "understanding your true self." It's really more like "I accidentally poked myself in the eye," what your grammatically correct friends would call a reflexive pronoun. The second character, *jan*, means "such" or "so," like the way Captain Jean-Luc Picard of the USS *Enterprise* gives an order to "make it so," or Kurt Vonnegut muses that "so it goes," where "so" simply refers to the quality of being as it is. Together, *tzu-jan* translates into something like "of itself, so" or "so, of its own accord" or more descriptively (if more ponderously) "that which follows by virtue of its own nature." On balance, "naturalness" isn't such a bad translation after all, as long as you keep in mind that this describes harmonizing with the creative and shifting flow of existence, not simply eating granola, doing wilderness exploration, or hanging out at "naturist" (a.k.a., nudist) camps.

The hard part, of course, lies is differentiating what is genuinely natural from what "feels natural," in not confusing true spontaneity from knee-jerk reaction or mere impulsiveness. You may then want to think of Taoist non-doing, the following of what is "so, of its own accord," as something of an *enlightened* spontaneity, a heightened (yet direct and intuitive) apprehension of how to "act" that (quite ironically) doesn't come easily, thanks to all the dysfunctional habits we've acquired all our lives. In short, the path of simplicity isn't always easy.

The metaphor of the uncarved block

One of the recurring metaphors for the *Tao* in the Tao Te Ching is *p'u* (the probable inspiration for *The Tao of Pooh*), which translates as something like "unhewn log," "uncut wood," or, most often, "uncarved block." You can probably imagine why this metaphor has historically been so compelling, how a raw, unfinished piece of wood poetically captures much of what is so difficult to express about the concept of *Tao*: its basic simplicity and naturalness, its utter lack of specific features or characteristics, and its potential for creative manifestation. But most important, this image serves as an important reminder that when you start differentiating the *Tao*, when you start carving it up into particular virtues, goals, or purposes, you've somehow lost that pure, original, whole. It is, in fact, the uncarved quality of the block that makes it so special.

If the uncarved block acts as a metaphor for the *Tao*, then emulating the uncarved block acts as a metaphor for returning to the *Tao*, for settling into a state of pure non-doing. Lao Tzu mentions this image half a dozen times, in each case subtly reinforcing this principle:

- **Describing the ancient sages who were adept at the Way:** Lao Tzu says these shadowy figures were subtle, profound, and wise, but also so profound that you could barely recognize them. Still, if you look closely, you notice that they're tentative, cautious, solemn, broad, and genuine. And also elementally plain, like an uncarved block.
- **Abandoning virtues and calculations:** Lao Tzu repeatedly tells the reader to cast off virtues like humaneness and rightness, to eliminate selfish desires for profit or material gain. So, what's left? Embracing the simplicity of the uncarved block.

- **Maintaining the original integrity:** Lao Tzu notes that you can certainly start carving the block, but doing so will produce "vessels," which may indeed be conditionally useful but which will no longer be the original block. Great carving, Lao Tzu tells us, doesn't involve any actual cutting apart.
- **Enabling spontaneous transformation:** Lao Tzu describes the uncarved block as small and insignificant, but if rulers could somehow harness it, the 10,000 things would all fall in line of their own accord.
- **Setting right the universe:** Building on the previous reference, Lao Tzu notes that once the 10,000 things transform (more on the 10,000 things in Book 2, Chapter 2), their desires may yet become active. The solution? Subdue them with the uncarved block, and then Heaven and Earth will spontaneously be rectified.
- **Transforming the people:** When the sage engages in non-doing, holds fast to tranquility, detaches from ordinary affairs, and desires not to desire, the people transform, repair, and enrich themselves, ultimately taking on the quality themselves of the simple uncarved block.

The role of feminine imagery

Taoism has never been shy about pressing feminine imagery into service, whether in the form of the procreative "mother of the 10,000 things," as half of the *yin-yang* dyad, or as sexual energy in esoteric alchemical practices. But when the Tao Te Ching encourages you to "know the male, yet hold onto the female," this is one piece of a sustained strategy to illustrate how something as counterintuitive as *wu-wei* actually works.

The Chinese of this time identified the female as quiet, receptive, and submissive, and yet just as non-doing accomplishes more than emotionally invested doing, the female overcomes the male *through* (not in spite of) its stillness. Along these same lines, Lao Tzu presents several narrative sequences where something less powerful or possessing less overt physical potency unexpectedly proves to be more effective than its more powerful, more potent counterpart. Taken together, these vignettes reinforce the image of effective non-action.

Here are some of the parings that Lao Tzu has in mind, where the "victorious" side is analogous to the female:

- **Low vs. high:** Whether a low-lying river or a state lying low before doing battle, it's always the lower one that ultimately commands and controls the other. This recurring emphasis on staying low is one theme some interpreters pick up on to justify claims that the text is encoding secret messages about military strategy.

» **Soft vs. hard:** Softness, suppleness, weakness, and flexibility are all characteristics of life, while hardness, firmness, and rigidity are characteristics of death. That's why, Lao Tzu tells us, the softest things under Heaven can often run roughshod over the hardest and stiffest things. It's hard (so to speak) not to relate this particular pair directly to female and male.

» **Weak vs. strong:** Just as reversal is the movement of the *Tao,* so, too, weakness is its application. That's why Lao Tzu claims one whose muscles are weak and pliant nevertheless has a firm and tight grip on the *Tao.* The weak-strong couplet shows up frequently in the text.

» **Water vs. solidity:** Toward the beginning of the text, Lao Tzu compares the highest good to water, as it passively and effortlessly brings benefit to the 10,000 things. What's more, while nothing is softer and weaker than water, its relentlessness will allow it to eventually overcome any other substance, no matter how dense. The British-born, San Francisco philosopher Alan Watts labeled Taoism the "watercourse way," the same title used for an album by the New Age music band Shadowfax in the 1970s.

Ruling by Not Doing

When you first hear about the doctrine of non-doing, you could easily come to the conclusion that classical Taoism supports a kind of radical anarchism or individualism and that the intended audience must be a whole slew of hermits, anti-government libertarians, and social dropouts. But the Taoist idea of *wu-wei* seems less to be advocating your right to be left alone, your right to be free from political intervention or social coercion, than demonstrating how much you can accomplish by leaving others alone, by engaging the world in a non-coercive, non-interventionist manner. After all, Lao Tzu and Chuang Tzu were writing during Axial Age China (a time of cultural change in China around the eighth to third centuries BCE), not 21st-century America or Europe, and they never really questioned the basic political and social givens, like a dynastic ruling family or hierarchical family-centered relationships.

When you look at it this way, it starts to make sense that the Tao Te Ching introduces non-doing not primarily as an individual ideal, but as a model for ruling society (or the world), as the guiding principle that can produce a stable (but not static) social harmony. Why else would Lao Tzu say that it's through quietude and stillness that you can become the one who rectifies the world? And just in case you don't get the point, consider the following sequence from the Tao Te Ching:

1. The Way is great.
2. Heaven is great

3. Earth is great.
4. And the king, also, is great.
5. This realm possesses four greats, and the king occupies one place among them.

REMEMBER

When the Tao Te Ching mentions the king and how to rule, these aren't incidental, passing references just to placate some bureaucratic eavesdropper or metaphorical allusions to being the master of your own fate or anything like that. The text really does assume that ruling is a primary concern, and the adoption of *wu-wei* is the primary means of doing it well.

The trouble with laws and government

Why do governments institute laws? Why does every school, church, and social organization have policies, guidelines, or by-laws? Why do games and competitive sports have rules? Why do you have to produce an electronic signature certifying that you've read and understand the "terms of use" every time you do something on a commercial website? I'm sure a lot of readers will think these questions are too obvious to take seriously. If you don't have these kinds of rules, they're probably thinking you have no way to make sure that (other) people do what they're "supposed to do" or prevent them from doing what they're "not supposed to do." In other words, laws, rules, and regulations all represent attempts to control how people act or don't act, which seems like a pretty important thing if people have to live together, share resources, and so forth.

But the classic Taoist logic dictates that anything you attempt with self-willed, goal-oriented motivations will ultimately backfire. Consciously adopting a particular virtue will miss the mark, seeking valuable goods produces no satisfaction, and even something as basic as looking to gratify your senses only dulls and confuses them. That's why Lao Tzu points out that laws and other methods of control invariably bring about the opposite effect:

- The more taboos and prohibitions in the world, the more the people will be poor.
- The more sharp weapons the people possess, the more the states will be confused.
- The more skill and artistry the people have, the more peculiar things emerge.
- The more legal decrees become pronounced, the more robbers and thieves come to be.

In other words, the wrongdoers only exist because, well, we've just concocted so many wrongdoings! But this isn't just a dash of armchair psychological speculation that people don't like to be told what to do and will violate rules as an act of rebellion or self-assertion. Instead, it's keeping in tune with the idea that deliberate action doesn't work because it deviates from the Way; attempts to control people through laws represent the imposition of an artificial order onto society, a situation that's always doomed to fail. If Confucian virtues like humaneness and ritual propriety fail to live up to the Way, then laws fail even to live up to Confucian virtues.

The sage-king as the empty center

So, if Classical Taoism has a profound distaste for rules and regulations, what exactly is a sagely king supposed to do? You may have guessed that the answer is to engage in non-doing. And yes, Lao Tzu says that ruling a state is like cooking a small fish, that indifference to affairs will both reinforce the ruler's power and benefit the people and that not pursuing greatness is the paradoxical means by which to accomplish greatness. But more importantly, by positioning himself as the human embodiment of the *Tao*, as the empty center that lies at the source of all creative transformation, the sage-king extends the "nothing left undone" dynamic beyond his immediate sphere, expediting (through non-doing) the spontaneous accomplishment of everything in the kingdom or perhaps the world. In short, non-doing is generally efficacious, but non-doing in the hands of the ruler effectuates the wide-ranging common good.

So, the kingly person should be impartial, like the *Tao*, exercising remote and seemingly insubstantial leadership, which causes the people to be genuine and honest. There's also a recurring whiff in the Tao Te Ching that this figure should adopt a paternalistic posture in relation to the masses, "emptying their minds" and "filling their bellies," so they respond like children who attentively "fix their eyes and ears on him," but without recognizing that he's the actual source of their strength. Lao Tzu's ideal world seems to flow as smoothly as the mutually attuned members of an improvisational jazz band, where the solos melt into one another effortlessly, coordinated only by a subliminal nod from the bandleader who lurks quietly in the shadows. Maybe that's why Lao Tzu "ranks" various types of rulers in the following way:

1. With the best kind of ruler, those below know only that he exists.
2. With the next kind, they feel intimately connected and offer praise.
3. With the next kind, they fear him.
4. With the last kind, they insult him.

REMEMBER

The ideal ruler portrayed in the Tao Te Ching is one who's out of sight and out of mind. His emptiness and *wu-wei* facilitate the well-being of the people, who barely notice him and experience all accomplishments simply as their own.

Mixed messages on military affairs

When you think of a non-interventionist doctrine like *wu-wei*, it would seem to be a no-brainer that classical Taoism should have a pacifistic bent. After all, what can be more intrusive and coercive than a military campaign? But the Tao Te Ching especially comes off as unresolved on warfare and military matters. On the one hand, it contains numerous passages that put forth the Gandhi-esque non-aggression and non-violence you may expect:

- Those who assist their rulers in the Way do not employ the force of weapons in the world.
- All the fine weapons are ill-omened instruments.
- Those who are strong and violent do not come to a natural death.
- Those who act upon the world under Heaven are defeated by it.

And yet, Lao Tzu often seems utterly resigned to the necessity of military battle, counseling that we should respond to the killings of masses of people with sobs of grief and sorrow, and treat victories in battle with the gravity of a funeral ritual. What's more, he even seems to be offering subtle suggestions that *wu-wei* is the best strategy for accomplishing those lamentable ends, advocating the use of surprise tactics when employing troops, indifference to affairs in order to gain control of the world, and the concealment of weapons from the people once you're actually in power. In short, Lao Tzu presents non-doing as something that can accomplish a lot, and that holds true for political and military undertakings as well.

When you look at *wu-wei* in this light, it starts to make sense why many legalist philosophers and rulers took such a keen interest in the Tao Te Ching, how Huang-Lao philosophy integrated Taoist thought so easily into a political ideology, and what various interpreters were thinking when they started seeing the text as a blueprint for guerilla warfare. The main themes of guerilla tactics — flexibly employing fewer combatants, harassing and withdrawing quickly, concealing obvious targets, advancing only after the enemy has exhausted itself — show up throughout the text, though not necessarily in so many words. Using typical paradoxical language, Lao Tzu suggests that armies go into battle without armor or shields, that you should retreat a foot rather than advance an inch, that a good warrior doesn't appear militaristic, and that you can defeat an enemy without actually engaging him. In some ways, it reads like one long reflection on a rope-a-dope strategy, where a reader who sees mysticism rather than militarism may actually be the one getting roped!

SO, WHAT'S THE POINT OF FOLLOWING THE *TAO*?

You may have noticed that the doctrine of *wu-wei* seems to come equipped with more potential for self-contradiction than any of the other Taoist paradoxes, especially with regard to political or military affairs. For example, the country should only be run by someone who doesn't want to run the country, right? If you want to run it, the logic goes, you can only accomplish this end if you don't want to run it. But doesn't choosing not to want to run the country for the sole purpose of getting to run the country kind of defeat the whole idea of *wu-wei?* If you do non-doing for a particular purpose, then is it even really non-doing?

One scholar, whose name you don't hear much these days but who was quite influential a half-century ago, tried to find some rhyme or reason in this apparent contradiction. His name was Herrlee Creel, and he spent nearly 40 years as one of the big China cheeses at the University of Chicago. Creel noticed that you can find side by side in the classical texts — not just the Tao Te Ching — one voice that seems to be pushing *wu-wei* simply because it harmonizes you (and/or society) with the Way and another that seems to be encouraging *wu-wei* as an effective strategic means to an end. Creel thought that the former expressions came out of something he called *contemplative Taoism*, and he imagined that followers of this approach sought to ponder and experience the *Tao* for the sheer contemplative delight of it. On the other hand, he thought the latter represented a "purposive Taoism," populated by calculating strategists and entrepreneurs who sought to ply the Taoist philosophy toward specific ends. He speculated that contemplative Taoism was chronologically and intellectually primary, that purposive Taoism represented a later, degenerate attempt to cash in on the philosophy, and that both were still superior to the missing-the-point "immortality Taoism" that would later become the dominant historical and cultural face of the tradition.

Creel was almost certainly incorrect to imagine distinct contemplative and purposive lineages and wrong-headed to assume uncritically that "immortality Taoism" lacked the depth of the "original" philosophy, but he did correctly identify that the formative texts of Taoism didn't speak with one voice, contained internal contradictions, and anticipated the diversity that would characterize the tradition in subsequent generations. But it's probably best not to try to figure out which strain of Taoism represents its "essence," and instead to let go of the idea that Taoism (or any other tradition, for that matter) has to possess such an essence.

Adapting to the Existential Circumstances

Although Chuang Tzu doesn't employ the term *wu-wei* as often of Lao Tzu does, he does capture the spirit of non-doing in a number of places throughout his text. But rather than offering provocative ruminations on the efficacy of *wu-wei* or its application to political and military affairs, Chuang Tzu is more concerned with modeling how you should adapt to the puzzling circumstances that real life seems to present at every turn, including the contending ethical positions of the Confucians and Moists, the mysteries of life and death, and even the challenges of ordinary, mundane tasks. For Chuang Tzu, the question in each instance is how to follow not your own (or someone else's) private motivations, but the natural and non-affected movement of the Way.

The hinge of the Way

If Lao Tzu was troubled that our acquired intellectual habits produce actions that don't easily fall into line with the Way, Chuang Tzu was equally troubled that every single human perspective on reality seemed to be somehow "stuck" in a localized, situated viewpoint. These lenses for interpreting and orienting to the world may superficially make life easier to negotiate — they offer a kind of conditional validity and comfort — but none of them puts you in a position to follow the natural intricacies of the Way. As Chuang Tzu saw it, our biggest impediment to engaging in genuine, spontaneous action was what brainiac philosophers would identify as *epistemological* — the root of the problem lies in how we perceive, learn, process, and integrate information. The only way to engage in *Tao*-ful, non-purposive action is somehow to arrive at a place that isn't locked into a fixed, inflexible perspective, but that liberates you to participate in that "free and easy wandering" that harmonizes naturally with the Way.

So, where is this perspective-less place, and how do we get there? In one passage, Chuang Tzu describes it as the "hinge of the Way" (or "axis of the Way"), a state that doesn't demand the selection of a cognitive affirmation of either something or its opposite, but instead lets you hold the world up to the light — actually, the light of Heaven — and proceed with lucid clarity. The image of a hinge or axis is such an effective metaphor because it illustrates an ability to pivot effortlessly with the changing circumstances, that quality of malleability and adaptability that both Lao Tzu and Chuang Tzu value. When you position yourself on the hinge of the Way, you can always discern the answer to that timeless bumper-sticker question — what would the *Tao* do? — and spontaneously act in a manner guided by that, rather than your own (or someone else's) personal motivations.

Chuang Tzu employs similar language later in the same chapter when he encourages you to deal with contending voices by "harmonizing them on Heaven's whetstone." With just a slight variation, he also says that the sage harmonizes the different alternatives and "comes to rest on Heaven's potter's wheel." Collectively, these three images — hinges, whetstones, potter's wheels — suggest that constructive action should be based on intuitive and aesthetic out-of-the-box insights, rather than conventional and deliberate decision making. Of course, none of these vignettes actually tells you how to get to such a place, and it's hard to imagine that Chuang Tzu just thinks he can grab you and shake you into a new perspective — but certainly, intellectual honesty about your own limitations is a good starting point.

THE POTTER'S WHEEL OF HEAVEN REVISITED

The Chinese terms that translate as the hinge of the Way, Heaven's whetstone, and Heaven's potter's wheel are actually quite obscure and have given translators fits for at least a century. If you compare translations side by side, you'll find that one version translates Heaven's whetstone as "Heavenly equality," while another renders it as "framework of nature," both of which improve on an older version that tried "invisible operation of Heaven." For the reader who doesn't know Chinese, it can be kind of a crapshoot.

But the particular term t'ien-chün, the potter's wheel of Heaven, which appears on two occasions in the *Chuang Tzu*, has gained some modicum of Taoist immortality in modern American popular literature thanks to a wonderfully memorable mistranslation. The 19th-century missionary-scholar James Legge, who translated both the Tao Te Ching and the *Chuang Tzu*, committed what today would be an elementary faux pas of translation when he translated the same phrase two completely different ways. In the first instance, he rendered t'ien-chün as the "equal fashioning of Heaven," which was relatively consistent with the way he was translating similar terminology. But in the second case, perhaps because it appeared in one of the later mishmash chapters and was threatening what would happen if you couldn't get things harmonized, Legge came up with a pretty menacing-sounding sentence: "Those who cannot do this will be destroyed on the lathe of Heaven."

Does this sound familiar? That's the translation that inspired the title of Ursula K. Le Guin's short novel, *The Lathe of Heaven*, and Legge's phrase actually gets quoted early on in the story. The irony here, which Le Guin has since acknowledged and rolled with in characteristically Taoistic fashion, is that Chuang Tzu really couldn't have possibly intended the term chün to mean "lathe," because the lathe hadn't been invented yet during that period in ancient China! But to tell you the truth, we're not sure "Heaven the Equalizer" or "Potter's Wheel of Heaven" would have made as compelling a title.

A BUDDHIST REFLECTION ON THE MIRROR-MIND

If you've dabbled in more than one Eastern religion, you may already know that the image of the mind as a mirror gets considerable mileage in Buddhist, as well as Taoist, traditions. This holds especially true for Zen, the lineage of Buddhism that originated in China (under the name Ch'an), and came to be pretty much synonymous with rigorous meditation practices. Scholars used to think that Ch'an-Zen developed in China as a result of the crosspollination of Buddhism with Taoist philosophy, though that's probably an oversimplification. Still, there's no question that a lot of terminology and some key practices bounced back and forth between the two traditions.

The mirror-mind plays a crucial role in one of the most important early Ch'an-Zen Buddhist texts, *The Platform Sutra of the Sixth Patriarch*, which chronicles a (probably fabricated) leadership struggle in the Buddhist monastic community. As the story goes, the patriarch of the lineage announced an "open call" for poetic submissions, soliciting poems from monks on the "Buddha-nature" that he would judge in order to designate a successor. The heir-apparent wrote a lovely tetrad where he compared the mind to a clear mirror, which each person must constantly polish so no dust (that is, mental defilements) accumulates to obscure the original pure nature, a perfectly reasonable take on the process and goal of Buddhist meditation. But in response, an illiterate, ethnically mixed novice composed his own poem, stating that the original mirror was so clear and pure that there wasn't even any room for dust to gather, effectively "out-Buddha-ing" the earlier entry. Taoism is Taoism, and Buddhism is Buddhism, but it's hard not to notice how they both relate the mirror metaphor to the realization of one's pure, original nature.

The mind as a mirror

Another useful metaphor that Chuang Tzu employs briefly, but significantly, is the image of a mirror. Later Taoism would come up with various ritual and symbolic functions for mirrors, but Chuang Tzu brings it up for much the same reason that he introduces the hinge of the Way — that is, to describe a condition where you respond to the world not by constructing your own ideas and preferences, but by *reflecting* whatever presents itself to you. In the key passage, Chuang Tzu reminds you to let go of desire for fame, of purpose-driven calculations, of investment in ordinary affairs, and of the accumulation of knowledge, directing you instead to use your mind like a mirror, neither being effected by impressions as they come or holding onto them as they go. And echoing the language of *wu-wei*, doing this accomplishes every end without taking any toll on yourself. The passage on the mirror-mind is certainly one of the places where it makes great sense to think of Chuang Tzu as putting forth some type of mysticism, though not in the sense of either merging with things or dissolving one's self. If anything, it describes a quality of presence and the accompanying ability to adapt reflexively and spontaneously to the passing present moments.

TIP

You may be able to get a better grip on the mirror-mind metaphor if you contrast it with some other ways that people have understood the functioning of the human mind. One image is of the mind as a lamp — something that sheds light on objects of its awareness, that helps to differentiate one object from another, and selects which objects are more deserving of attention. Another image, which is popular in some philosophical circles, is of the mind as a transformer — something that processes outside stimuli and converts them into symbols, perceptions, sensations, and so on. Both of these images, to a lesser or greater extent, depict the mind as an active agent, which brings a constructive element to its engagement with (and subsequent action in) the world. By contrast, the mirror-mind is receptive and attuned, not passively being blown over by the world, but fluidly reflecting and responding to it.

The connection between *wu-wei* and nurturing life

Many of Chuang Tzu's best-loved vignettes fall under the heading of "skill" or "knack" stories, where characters like the ox-carving Cook Ting and the cicada-catching hunchback accomplish their mundane tasks to perfection. Whether it's the elderly fisherman who reluctantly takes the reins of government or the picture-painter who's so oblivious to the demands of the moment that he nonchalantly doffs his clothes, all these figures have a few important things in common:

- **Zero expenditure:** Neither the heroes of the stories nor the tools they employ ever seem to expend any energy or exhibit any signs of being worn down. This may not really be possible — at least not according to modern laws of thermodynamics — but it makes for a striking image that Cook Ting can go nearly 20 years without ever sharpening his blade.
- **Ambiguous personal agency:** In most of the stories, the main characters deny that they possess any special skills, instead suggesting that they're merely following the Way or yielding to the "spirit-like" qualities that possess them. Whatever personal will or agency they have, it doesn't stand over and against the function of the Way.
- **Superhuman success:** None of these fables would be worth telling if they didn't end magically, with perfect executions of what the *Chuang Tzu* calls "nurturing life." The individual feats mirror the accomplishments of Heaven — which consequently casts the individual artisans as companions of Heaven in the cosmic processes.

In short, these three qualities together embody the *wu-wei* principle, the effortless, egoless, and effective performance of basic human functions. Those who perform the tasks experience them as though they're doing nothing, like the way Artisan Ch'ui can replicate both the straight lines of a T-square and the curves of a compass with his fingers simply following the natural transformations and his mind tucked safely out of the way. And at the same time, the actors never show any surprise that their performances leave no task undone, no chore unaccomplished.

REMEMBER

Although the characters in Chuang Tzu's "knack" stories partake in various discrete actions, they illustrate perfectly the principle of non-doing. Perhaps they provide a glimpse of what society may look like if everyone were to follow classical Taoist notions.

IN THIS CHAPTER

» Unlearning what you already know

» Learning to forget

» Following the stages of forgetting

» Forgetting in the modern West

Chapter 4

Remembering to Keep Forgetting

When you look at the sheer diversity of specific practices in the many religious traditions of the world, you've probably noticed that they range from the explosively dramatic to the quietly contemplative. In short, religious practices can include everything from fire rituals, acrobatic parades, and snake handling, to silent prayer and meditative visualizations. If you're looking from the outside at practices from traditions other than your own, you can often get a pretty good sense of what's going on, although sometimes superficial similarities may make it harder to notice important differences. For instance, Hindu temple *puja*, hospitality rites for images of a deity (see Book 1, Chapter 4), varies considerably from Christian church prayer (see Book 5, Chapter 3). On the other hand, there are some practices, especially those that are open only to initiates or priests, where even followers of the particular tradition may not fully understand exactly what the ritual participants are hoping to accomplish through the ceremony.

And every once in a while, you come across some practices that simply boggle the mind, not because they're offensive or dangerous or anything like that, but because they just seem completely antithetical to everything you've ever heard about religion. In this case, we're talking about the Taoist practice of "sitting and forgetting," an idea that first appears in the *Chuang Tzu* and still shows up in some Taoist circles today.

REMEMBER

On the surface, it may sound a lot like daydreaming, developing dementia, or simply spacing out, but "sitting and forgetting" refers to a meditation that involves the systematic deconditioning and removal of what you already know. And if you stop to think about it, that's certainly not easy. How can you actually let go of something that's already found a comfortable resting place in your memory and working knowledge?

In this chapter, we talk about the Taoist practice of sitting and forgetting. You get to see its philosophical background, its development in the classical texts, its formalization in an important later scripture, and some of its unexpected applications in modern Western interpretations of Taoism.

Experiencing Return, Reversal, and the Idea of Unlearning

One recurring theme in the classical Taoist literature is that attaining or experiencing the *Tao* involves a backward movement, a return or reversal to the original source of existence. In several texts, especially the Tao Te Ching, the authors connect this explicitly to a process of unlearning — mainly, the unlearning of the dominant Confucian (and sometimes Mohist) virtues of the day. This creates an odd kind of literary device, which basically denigrates knowledge, cultural literacy, and educated people — in short, the widely accepted image of the wise, virtuous sage-king — and presents an alternative picture of the sage as one who appears simple, confused, or (in many of Chuang Tzu's stories) grotesque and outcast.

The farther you go, the less you know

Lao Tzu, the legendary founder of Taoism and supposed author of the Tao Te Ching, begins one chapter with a counterintuitive admonition:

> Don't exit your doorways, and by this know the entire world. Don't peer through your windows, and by this know Heaven's Way. The farther you go, the less you know.

And similarly, "those who work at learning increase daily, while those who hear the Tao decrease daily." Obviously, this flies in the face of conventional wisdom, whether it's speaking to ancient China, which valued hard work and cultural refinement, or the contemporary West, which holds "progress" as a high ideal. On the other hand, it may provide some solace to unmotivated couch potatoes, who like the idea that their own lack of intellectual curiosity and drive ultimately works for the good of humanity!

REMEMBER

Lao Tzu isn't just bashing intellectuals and eggheads for the fun of it — he's genuinely concerned that conscious, directed, affected learning drives one farther from the *Tao*, and he comes up with lots of ways to drive home this point:

- When knowledge and wisdom arise, there is then great artificiality.
- To use knowledge to order the state, is to be its thief; to use a lack of knowledge to order the state, is to be its benefactor.
- Those who know are not educated; those who are educated do not know.
- Too much learning produces frequent exhaustion and is no match for holding to the center.

REMEMBER

In a typical Taoist paradox, Lao Tzu reiterates that you can't "learn" the Way through "learning." Routine learning not only misses the point, but also can drain you, produce artifice, and harm the community.

Learning not to learn

Because Lao Tzu has such low regard for learning, it makes sense that he tasks the reader with figuring out some way to "love the people," to "revive the state," and to "illuminate the four directions," all without the benefit of knowledge. But if this gives you the idea that he's proposing an easier, less-rigorous way of getting to where you want to go, you may want to take a closer look. It's not enough for Lao Tzu that you simply stop learning; you also need somehow to undo all the learning you've already done. That's why the Tao Te Ching says that only by "eliminating sagehood" and "discarding knowledge" can someone truly bring benefit to the people.

So, how do you unlearn everything you've learned? The almost comically puzzling answer is that you have to "learn not to learn." In other words, you can't just sit around waiting for all your intellectual apparatus simply to dissolve on its own accord — you actually need to take part in some specific practice that enables your mind to operate completely differently. In effect, you need to retrain the cognitive faculties of your own mind so that you are, in a sense, perceiving and processing the world completely differently from the way you did before.

The funny thing here is that while Lao Tzu and Chuang Tzu warn us that our regular learning is somehow not "natural," the more natural experience of the Tao doesn't actually come naturally. Or at least, we've gotten ourselves to such a place — so far from the *Tao* — that it no longer seems to come naturally. And so, we have to take active, conscious steps to return to the *Tao* — we need to learn how to reclaim the quality of naturalness that we've lost!

TIP

Try not to get too hung up on asking whether learning not to learn is still a type of learning and, therefore, contradictory. The point is not really that there's something wrong with "learning" — that is, in the broadest sense of understanding the world and discerning how to act in it — but that what we ordinarily think of as "learning" is not the right way (and may actually inhibit our ability) to accomplish those ends. It may be more helpful to think of the classical Taoist approach as a different kind of learning.

Discovering the Goal of Unlearning and the Task of Forgetting

It's often difficult to tell if the classical Taoist authors themselves really engaged in directed practices, or even had any secondhand knowledge of others engaged in such practices, but Chuang Tzu especially seems to offer the best testimony that at least a handful of practices meant to facilitate the task of unlearning were probably circulating during his time. And at least some of them continue, or resurface, considerably later on, providing one thematic thread that connects the classical texts to the later religious practices.

In this section, we talk about two particular (though related) practices that initially show up in the *Chuang Tzu* and that form the basis for later methods of meditation. You get an up-close look at the memorable vignettes that describe "sitting and forgetting" *(tso-wang)* and the "fasting of the mind and heart" *(hsin-chai).*

Forgetting virtue and forgetting everything

In one of Chuang Tzu's short but utterly delightful dialogues, he concocts an intriguing sequence of conversations between Confucius and Yen Hui, who is remembered historically as Confucius's favorite disciple. The dialogue takes place over several days, with Yen Hui initiating each day's encounter with the claim that he's "progressing." In each case, Confucius asks about the nature of the progress, Yen Hui responds, and Confucius offers some modest encouragement but judges that his student hasn't quite hit the nail on the head and needs to try again. As this Confucian version of the Socratic method (repeatedly peppering someone with questions in order to stimulate critical thinking) unfolds, Yen Hui reports the following three distinct stages as indicators of his progress:

Meeting #1: I've forgotten humaneness (*jen*) and rightness (*yi*).

Meeting #2: I've forgotten ritual propriety (*li*) and ceremonial music.

Meeting #3: I just sit and forget (*tso-wang*).

When Confucius pushes Yen Hui further about what he means by sitting and forgetting, the latter replies that he lets go of his body, physical form, sense perceptions, and knowledge and by this "comes into accord with the great thoroughfare," which is likely a metaphor for following the *Tao* (or working harmoniously with the transformations of Heaven and Earth). At this point Confucius recognizes that Yen Hui has moved beyond ordinary cognitive habits and humbly asks if he can switch roles and become Yen Hui's disciple.

Even with such a brief back and forth, it's possible to glean a few features of what this sitting and forgetting entails:

- **Gradual process:** The fact that it takes Yen Hui several tries suggests that the process of unlearning is not simply one massive "memory dump" — like the way a *Star Trek* starship ejects the entire reactor to avoid a "warp core breech" or some such thing — but involves undoing successive layers of cognitive misdirection, like peeling away the concentric layers of an onion.
- **Confronting conventional norms:** It's certainly no coincidence that Yen Hui's first successful "data dumps" are the most often cited Confucian virtues. The process of forgetting seems to begin not with some arbitrary or inconsequential detail to try to forget, but with the dominant public standards toward which most people aspire. For people of Chuang Tzu's era, to forget humaneness and ritual propriety was tantamount to letting go of a shared reality.
- **Contemplative practice:** Perhaps it's obvious to point out that one part of sitting and forgetting is the "sitting" part, but this places the practice as one variety of those introspective techniques we often identify as meditation or contemplation. That means that the process is, more likely than not, specifically structured and directed, even if the first people to employ it may have discovered it through trial and error.
- **Peak experience:** It would be premature (and probably projecting other religious sensibilities where they may not belong) to conclude that the process culminates with anything like an ecstatic union or dissolution of one's self, but the final lines do suggest that the successful practitioner is conscious of moving beyond conventional perception and knowledge and achieving some kind of heightened experience of the Way.

REMEMBER

Based on one brief passage, Chuang Tzu's "sitting and forgetting" appears to be a contemplative practice that gradually unravels conventional norms and cognitive points of reference, ultimately returning the practitioner to the *Tao*, which allows for a dramatically different experience of and orientation toward reality.

The fasting of the mind and heart

Chuang Tzu also describes another technique that seems to have much in common with sitting and forgetting. In another one of his concocted conservations between Confucius and Yen Hui — this one much longer — Confucius continually berates his student for planning to meet with an immature, irresponsible local ruler, without having settled on an appropriate strategy for swaying him ethically. He eventually admonishes him to engage in "fasting," not the fasting from certain food or drink in preparation for a religious ceremony, but what he calls the "fasting of the mind and heart," for which he must first "unify" his will. As with sitting and forgetting, the fasting of the mind and heart also entails a sequence of steps, though this time they come in the form of specific (if not particularly easy) instruction from Chuang Tzu to Yen Hui:

- Don't listen with the ears, listen with the mind and heart.
- Don't listen with the mind and heart, listen with the *ch'i*.

The problem with the ears, Chuang Tzu explains, is that they can do little more than (literally) listen; likewise, the mind and heart (conceived of as one single organ) can do little more than calculate. But your *ch'i* (see Book 2, Chapter 1) can *attenuate* (that is, become empty), and the basis of the *Tao* is emptiness, so it is by "listening" with your *ch'i* (however that works) that you can become attentive to the *Tao*.

In other words, your mind and heart — that is, your cognitive and emotional faculties — follow particular habits, in the way they translate the world to you and orient you to that world. But "fasting" your mind and heart shuts down those ordinary habits and allows you to develop new ones. If this strikes you as kind of a cryptic explanation, think about the various reasons that people ordinarily engage in religious fasting:

- **Purification:** People sometimes fast before religious rituals, or fast *as* a religious ritual, in order to attain a more *pure* state. The idea is usually that abstaining from ordinary stuff like food and drink can create the sense of being clean, fresh, or renewed, but also being in a proper or worthy state for a particular function.
- **Purgation:** Some religious fasts serve to *purge* you of something, perhaps as concrete as evil spirits or as abstract as sin or negative feelings. Whether you

think of it as a form of penance or as a spiritual cleansing, the goal is to expel something unwanted from your physical body or holistic self.

- **Focus:** In some cases, people fast simply to redirect their attention away from stuff that's distracting or less significant and toward matters of greater spiritual interest. Christian monks would sometimes practice austerities not for reasons of atonement or ritual purity, but simply because they wanted to get out of the habit of thinking about food and into the habit of thinking about God.

It may help you make sense of mind-heart fasting if you take all three of these into account. First, fasting helps return your mind-heart to its original, pure state, before it lapsed into the unhealthy mental habits that make it so hard for you to follow the Way. Second, it ejects all the clutter and bogus knowledge that have accumulated since you first began to think and feel. And finally, it redirects the mind-heart to pay attention in a totally different way — what Chuang Tzu calls "listening with the *ch'i*."

TECHNICAL STUFF

The Chinese character *chai*, translated here as "fasting," also refers to the specific purification rituals and community retreats practiced by the later Taoist communities such as the Way of the Celestial Masters, the first actual Taoist community that was founded by Zhang Daoling early in the second century. At some points in history, it also acted more or less as the generic term for Taoist ritual. Because of this, mind-heart fasting eventually evolves into one type of ritual practice, albeit an advanced one that followed more "concrete" fasting practices used to atone for sins and confer physical health benefits.

MIND-HEART FASTING: REDUX

The place of Taoism in Chinese religious *syncretism* — the blending of practices from multiple sources — can sometimes be difficult to untangle, especially when an idea or practice develops in one Taoist context, enters the "public domain" of raw materials and methods in the general Chinese religious "toolbox," and then reemerges some time later in a different form and with different ingredients added to the mix.

A fascinating case in point involves a late 19th-, early 20th-century figure named Ch'en Ying-ning, who put forward a modern spin on mind-heart fasting. Ch'en had a diverse scholarly background, studied extensively in the Complete Perfection Taoist linage, and was involved in founding the Chinese Taoist Association. But mostly, he identified with many of Chuang Tzu's teachings and devoted himself to learning various alchemical techniques, with the intention of making the search for immortality a national priority, presumably because of his lifelong battle with poor physical health.

(continued)

(continued)

Ch'en saw mind-heart fasting as an addendum to *ch'i-kung* practice, with a few dashes of Buddhist philosophy thrown in for good measure. Quoting the key passage in the *Chuang Tzu*, Ch'en recast the practice as a five-step process:

1. **Unify the will.** The first step involves focusing the mind-heart and letting go of distracting thoughts.
2. **Don't listen with the ears, listen with the mind-heart.** Perhaps taking a cue from Buddhism, this stage refers to "listening" to your own breath, which is silent and, therefore, can't be "heard" through the ears alone.
3. **Don't listen with the mind-heart, listen with the *ch'i*.** At this point, the function of the mind-heart is identical to the movement of your *ch'i*.
4. **Your ears are limited to listening, your mind-heart is limited to calculating.** In the fourth stage, the practitioner does not feel as though they have any distinct cognitive identity.
5. **The attenuation is the fasting of the mind-heart.** The process concludes with a Buddhist-style elimination of individual self and an all-consuming experience of emptiness.

Understanding the Treatise on Sitting and Forgetting

Of the 1,400-odd texts in the Taoist Canon, many of them present commentaries on the *Chuang Tzu*, and many of those specifically address the practice of sitting and forgetting. Because many of the commentators were writing at a time when Buddhism first started making significant headway in China and Taoism was still developing its own institutional identity, they often grafted Buddhist ideas onto the theory and interpreted the practice in terms resembling Buddhist meditation. Because of this, it's sometimes difficult to separate Chuang Tzu's sitting and forgetting from the "Buddha-fied" version of it.

The most important later Taoist to write about this practice was Ssu-ma Ch'eng-chen, a seventh- and eighth-century Taoist priest in the Highest Purity tradition, a Taoist movement based on received revelations of sacred scripture. Like other Highest Purity adepts, Ssu-ma engaged in alchemy and other esoteric practices with the hopes of achieving postmortem immortality, so he pretty much viewed sitting and forgetting (and just about everything else in the entire body of Taoist literature) as connected to that end. He eventually recorded his interpretation — or perhaps, his students recorded his lectures — in the *Treatise on Sitting and Forgetting*, which provides an important glimpse into at least one aspect of medieval Taoist practice.

The seven stages of forgetting

Now that you've gotten used to relating sitting and forgetting to the classical Taoist understandings of the *Tao*, returning, and unlearning, you may have some trouble buying Ssu-ma's interpretations of it, particularly his goals of leaving your corporeal body behind and roaming in the Heavens with various spirits. Some of the language does echo that of other Highest Purity scriptures, but it's also so Buddhist in places that it would be pretty hard to justify any claims that this represents the original meaning of the practice that first appeared in Chuang's Tzu dialogue. But, of course, that's part of the fun of studying Taoist history, which teems with these types of twists and turns in the development and reinterpretation of tradition. In any event, Ssu-ma's version of forgetting is a little more complicated than Chuang Tzu's.

Here's a summary of Ssu-ma's seven stages of forgetting, which chronicles a gradual process of realizing the *Tao*. Keep an eye out for ways the terminology means something different from what you would've expected.

1. **Respect and faithfulness:** Though the language sounds like a title for one of the popular "morality books," this stage actually refers to building self-confidence in your ability to know the Way (and presumably become a Taoist immortal) and trust in the teachers and texts that are there to guide you.
2. **Cutting off karma:** If you don't remember Chuang Tzu talking about the Buddhist concept of karma, that's because Buddhism wouldn't enter China for several hundred more years, though Ssu-ma doesn't seem to have been bothered by that fact. In this stage, you try to block off your own willfulness and intentionality — Buddhists generally define karma as willful (or volitional) action — which the author also explains using the traditional Taoist idea of non-doing *(wu-wei)*.
3. **Collecting the mind-heart:** Though it isn't obvious, this, too, borrows a Buddhist idea: the aspect of meditation that involves concentration. This stage can occur most easily in a secluded setting, where you develop *one-pointedness*, the ability to gather your mind to a single object of attention and sever any distractions.
4. **Simplifying affairs:** At this point, having developed an ability to concentrate your mind, you can divest yourself of the ordinary affairs of the world (including things like career and social relationships) and begin to identify your own destiny as in harmony with the movements of the *Tao*.

5. **Perfect observation:** This is the stage that probably most resembles Buddhist "insight meditation," where the goal is to develop an ability to observe carefully the affairs from which you've already divested (and are continuing to divest) with complete detachment. When you're in this stage — and this is actually straight from Ssu-ma's text — you can walk into a fish market and not have any sense that it stinks!
6. **Utmost steadfastness:** When you look at the last couple stages, the descriptions start to get increasingly more jargon filled and difficult to sort out. At this point, it seems like you're so in tune with the *Tao* that you effectively experience the processes of your own mind as indistinguishable from those of the *Tao.*
7. **Grasping the Way:** The last stage is the final realization of the *Tao,* which Ssu-ma describes with just about everything exciting in the Highest Purity Taoist cookbook: longevity, the attainment of magical powers, direct communication with spirits, and so forth.

As you can see, the *Treatise on Sitting and Forgetting* departs from the fairly vague bare bones of Chuang Tzu's fasting of the mind and heart — like the language of unlearning and returning, or the critique of Confucian virtue — and adapts the process to a more elaborate (and considerably more esoteric) set of practices more in tune with Ssu-ma Ch'eng-chen's Highest Purity Taoist sensibilities. But he also rewrites the story in terms that often look surprisingly Buddhist, including aspects of Buddhist meditation (like single-pointed concentration and detached observation) and stages that almost resemble the selfless bliss of a Buddha. Here, sitting and forgetting is not a universal technique of just gradually forgetting things you've learned, but a practice deeply embedded within a particular medieval Taoist religious context.

WARNING

You may enjoy reading the *Treatise on Sitting and Forgetting*, and you may even feel that doing so enhances your sense of spiritual well-being or inspires you to try out some different meditation techniques. But more importantly, it's really a perfect example of how the vast majority of texts in the Taoist Canon were written with a very particular audience in mind and were mainly employed by people with extensive (and often secretive) training in specific ritualistic contexts. Texts like this are usually pretty hard to penetrate, and you're often at the mercy of translators who may inadvertently embed their own interpretations into the translation.

From forgetting to spirit liberation

Sitting and forgetting began as the subject of one passing reference in the *Chuang Tzu* (a nearly identical passage also appeared in the *Huai Nan Tzu*), but it eventually took on a life of its own, as evidenced by Ssu-ma Ch'eng-chen's *Treatise on Sitting and Forgetting*. It also drew considerable interest from other authors of the Highest

Purity era, including one anonymous writer who composed a short but intriguing text called the *T'ien Yin Tzu*, the *Master of Heavenly Seclusion*. In this text, instead of identifying specific stages of sitting and forgetting, the author identified sitting and forgetting as one specific stage of an even more comprehensive process. Once again, the procedure has gotten still more complicated.

Ssu-ma Ch'eng-chen must have found this text congenial with his own thinking about the subject because he wrote an enthusiastic introduction (which is now officially part of the text) where he explains that the teachings go back to Lao Tzu and Chuang Tzu (and even the *I Ching*), deal with such things as the harmony of *yin* and *yang* and the nourishment of *ch'i*, and point toward the Highest Purity concerns for longevity and the path to immortality. Here are the five stages, according to the *T'ien Yin Tzu:*

1. **Fasting and abstaining:** This basically uses the five elements theory to explain proper dietary habits, which includes avoiding foods that are uncooked, overly spiced, fermented, or spoiled. It also talks about properly cleaning and massaging your body.
2. **Dwelling peacefully:** Perhaps because of associations people had about monastic life, the author explains that he's less interested in where you dwell than in how you dwell, including which directions you face when you sit or sleep, how to arrange furniture and allow the right balance of light and dark, and where to place windows and curtains.
3. **Visualizing and contemplating:** This is the most obvious meditation stage of the process. It includes closing your eyes and calming the mind in order to visualize your own "spiritual" essence. The author relates this stage to the classical Taoist ideas of returning to the original source and discovering the "gateway of all subtleties."
4. **Sitting and forgetting:** The author describes this stage as one where you perfect your visualizing and contemplating by — what else? — forgetting visualizing and contemplating. Like Ssu-ma's *Treatise*, it also spins in the Buddhist ideas of letting go of self and of the distinction between self and other.
5. **Liberating the spirit:** After the adept completes the previous four steps, they are ready to free their spirit to enjoy an immortal existence, independent of the affairs of the world and the bondage of life and death.

REMEMBER

Chuang Tzu appears to have related sitting and forgetting to the more basic task of unlearning and returning, but Highest Purity practitioners like Ssu-ma Ch'eng-chen and the author of the *T'ien Yin Tzu* understood it as part of a broader process of Taoist self-cultivation.

Contemplating Contemporary Forgetfulness

As you can see, the Taoist theme of sitting and forgetting has undergone some pretty interesting transformations over time, and it's still showing up in new guises and new venues, particularly in the West. This may strike you as a little strange, because when most Westerners think of Taoism, they probably tick off a lengthy list of more common talking points — the *Tao, wu-wei, yin* and *yang,* the uncarved block (more on these in Book 2 Chapter 1)— before they ever get anywhere near sitting and forgetting. But, in fact, interest in this fairly obscure Taoist practice has recently created something of a cottage industry, and you don't have to do too much looking around online to locate several small but enthusiastic networks of private teachers, multimedia resources, quasi-official Taoist organizations, and online discussion groups devoted to 21st-century forgetfulness.

Certainly, many people first come to sitting and forgetting through recent English translations of Ssu-ma Ch'eng-chen's *Treatise,* but it's safe to say that most modern *tso-wang* enthusiasts don't know much about the history of the practice in China (including its role in Highest Purity Taoism and the assimilation of Buddhist ideas) and instead take cues from the *Chuang Tzu* passage, *ch'i-kung* and *t'ai-chi* classes, and perhaps even New Age literature and generic discussions of meditation.

An issue of *Dragon's Mouth Magazine,* the journal of the British Taoist Association (BTA), featured an article on sitting and forgetting, written by one of the founders of the BTA. Although the author was an ordained Taoist priest, he presented the material in highly universalistic, spiritualized terms, almost completely downplaying Taoist technical language — certainly a far cry from the *Treatise on Sitting and Forgetting.* He also did everything he could to make it seem incredibly easy for anyone to do — you don't need to do any of the usual hard work like counting breaths or taking inventory of your own wandering mind. But that seems to be the trajectory of contemporary forgetting — finding aspects of the practice that can be easily related to other forms of meditation, that can apply concretely to today's problems, and that aren't bound up in Taoist jargon or ritual.

Here are some Western outlets for sitting and forgetting, each of which spins it in a slightly different way:

» **EnerQi Healing Arts Center** (www.enerqihealing.com)**:** This California school of "healing energy" teaches classes in *ch'i-kung, reiki,* and yoga — but it also includes on its website a primer on sitting and forgetting, explaining it with a mix of language drawn from classical Taoism, Taoist physiology, and modern astronomy, and identifying the goal as elimination of the ego and participation in the "fabric of Tao."

- **Old Oak Taiji School (www.oldoakdao.org):** This California practice center also offers an online primer, but it spends a little less time on the Taoist philosophy behind the practice and more on the specific posture you need to do it right. This includes instructions for how you should orient your tailbone, *perineum* (the general area between your butt and genitals), belly, chest, spine, arms, shoulders, eyes, tongue, and *occiput* (the back of your skull).
- **Instituto Qigong Chikung de Barcelona (Barcelona Institute of Ch'ikung; www.institutoqigong.com):** Not all modern Western purveyors of sitting and forgetting are American; some of them are Western European. This Spanish center teaches *tso-wang* as one of seven "static" (that is, motionless) types of *ch'i-kung*. They understand it as an utterly down-to-earth teaching, explicitly rejecting that it leads to any "transcendent" experience, and instead emphasizing how it leads to intuition and creativity.

TIP

Most of the Western sources on sitting and forgetting use the *pinyin* system of Anglicizing Chinese characters. So, if you're looking for *tso-wang*, you'll probably have to look for *zuowang*.

IN THIS CHAPTER

» Untangling Taoism and ritual

» Purifying the self and renewing the cosmos

» Looking out for the deceased

Chapter 5

Cosmic Renewal and Other Rituals

Many Taoist concepts — the *Tao*, *wu-wei*, unlearning, the tension between being and non-being — present philosophical paradoxes, the kind that really make your head hurt when you try to make some kind of intellectual sense out of them. But Taoist ritual presents a different kind of paradox, what you may call a paradox of perception and interpretation. On the one hand, ritual constitutes a crucial aspect of Taoist practice. On the other hand, Taoist ritual remains obscure or unknown to Western audiences, and it will almost certainly remain that way, no matter how many books are written about it or how exciting we can make it sound in this chapter. In fact, you'll probably find no shortage of people who will still insist that "Taoist ritual" is an oxymoron, that there's not really any such thing as Taoist ritual and that the stuff you find Taoist priests doing today isn't "real" Taoism.

In this chapter, we talk about the basic relationship between Taoism and ritual, as well as some of the most common (and dramatic) forms of Taoist ritual you may be lucky enough to see if you happen to be in China at the right place and time.

Untangling the Truth about Taoism and Ritual

So, what is the truth about Taoism and ritual? As always, there's not always one answer to a question like this. A big part of the answer depends on which types of Taoism you mean and what definition you have in mind for *ritual.* This is an easy place to get confused if you think someone's talking about one kind of Taoism, or has one understanding of ritual, when that person actually has something very different in mind.

What is ritual?

It seems like ritual is one of those "you know it when you see it" ideas. Just about everyone has some intuitive idea of what a ritual is, but they may get a little wobbly when they try to come up with an exact definition or list its specific qualities. Most people probably say it refers to some kind of repeated, orchestrated religious act, like taking communion in church or kneeling in prayer in a mosque. But do you also call it a ritual when you stand up for the national anthem or receive your diploma at a graduation ceremony? For that matter, how about some uncomfortable but equally formalized processes, like performing the public execution of a prisoner? When does something qualify as a ritual, and when is it simply a "custom" or a "tradition?"

Sometimes, people refer to their daily habits — like doing morning exercises or drinking coffee while listening to their favorite podcast — as rituals, and psychiatrists are quick to identify certain obsessive-compulsive behaviors as ritualistic. Is a ritual, then, the same thing as a "routine?" If not, what would be the difference? Does there have to be something "sacred" about a ritual, and how do we judge what qualifies as sacred? Suddenly, knowing it when you see it gets a little fuzzier.

As it turns out, sociologists, anthropologists, psychologists, theologians, and religion scholars have been debating the nature and functions of ritual for a long time, sometimes coming to dramatically different conclusions. Some zero in on how ritual ties into the participants' established mythology, while others focus on the emotional and experiential aspects of participating in a ritual. That said, it may not be so easy to settle on one definition that will make everyone happy, but it's still very possible to tease out some general, recurring qualities that can serve as kind of a framework for thinking about ritual actions and their consequences.

REMEMBER

Here are a few of the more important ones to keep in mind:

- **Participant roles:** In order for people to perceive that a ritual is being done right, that it will accomplish whatever it's supposed to do or even just have the appropriate effect on the mood and personal imagination, it's necessary for ritual *functionaries* to play their prescribed roles. These functionaries can be people with special recognized religious status — such as priests, monks, or rabbis — but people undergoing rites of passage or just laypeople participating in a ceremony also need to "follow the rules." If you have any doubts about this, see what happens when rituals don't go according to plan and how shaken up some of the participants may get.

» **Materials and objects:** There's a reason why you place a ring — and not a rubber band, a cigar band, or a finger-puppet — on your spouse's finger during a wedding ceremony. Or why the Hanukkah menorah (more on the menorah in Book 4, Chapter 3) must have a certain number of candles lit on the right day. Or even something as simple as how the officiant of a ceremony dresses. The sense that you're using "the right stuff" (the "rite" stuff?) adds to the feeling and importance of the experience.

» **The right place at the right time:** Religious rituals often depend quite a bit on time and space — it matters both when and where you perform them. The most obvious cases concern ceremonies associated with a particular holiday, performed in a neighborhood temple or church. But some rituals depend on the exact moment — like an evening vigil anticipating the midnight arrival of the baby Jesus — or may be held in more exotic places, like on mountaintops or sites where religious heroes or martyrs left their historic marks.

» **Language, gestures, and movements:** Very often, the communities that utilize rituals expect that those carrying them out use specific language — either through a language not native to the participant (such as Latin in a Catholic Mass, more on that in Book 5, Chapter 4, or Hebrew in a Jewish prayer) or customary choice of words in the participant's own language (like beginning a wedding ceremony with "dearly beloved"). The same is true for hand gestures and physical body movements, like when the pope offers a blessing or when observant Muslims (more on Islam in Book 6) prostrate themselves during prayer.

» **Shared understanding of the meanings or results:** This can include a collective understanding that:

- Someone has changed official status through a rite of passage (like a boy becoming recognized as a man or a bachelor transforming into a married man)
- Sharing a Passover Seder (see Book 4, Chapter 3) at the family dinner table establishes a connection to the Israelites liberated from Egyptian slavery more than 3,000 years earlier

* Burying a beloved relative through prescribed methods both expresses feeling toward that relative and offers hope for the future

Not every participant necessarily interprets every ritual or ceremony the exact same way, but the key is that they're generally on the same page and can "speak the same ritual language" with one another.

TIP

In general, it may be helpful to think about a ritual as a routinized action or set of actions that:

* Assigns specific roles to those who participate in it
* Makes use of a broad "vocabulary" of tools — objects, language, gestures, physical movements, and so on
* Is attentive to proper time and location
* Points toward some concrete or symbolic meaning that can be understood by the participants and members of the community in which it occurs

Attitudes toward ritual in the classical texts

One funny thing about classical Taoism and ritual is that for all the general impressions people may have about Lao Tzu and Chuang Tzu (more on them in Book 2, Chapter 1) being anti-ritualistic, their texts don't really take that explicit position all that often. Yes, Lao Tzu calls the Confucian ideal of ritual propriety the "thinnest husk of loyalty and sincerity," and Chuang Tzu praises the character who forgets ritual propriety (along with all the other standard Confucian virtues). Those are both in the context of a larger, more general indictment of Confucian morality, without really targeting the concrete stuff of ritual performances. Still, the texts do give the general impression that they've got bigger fish to fry than conducting or taking part in rituals.

It's probably fair to say that the classical Taoist rejection of ritual comes not from any inherent distaste for specific ritual acts, but from a sense that Confucian ritual propriety can serve as a convenient stand-in for many of the world's ills. By (sort of) trashing ritual, Lao Tzu and Chuang Tzu can go after the real "villains":

* **Conformity:** If you want a symbol of something that's the opposite of healthy, critical skepticism, you probably can't find anything that fits the job description better than ritual. People often accept and perform rituals blindly and uncritically — to those who don't share in the ritual's language or reject its significance, ritual participants must look like the original zombies.

- **Artificiality:** If you're trying to encourage genuine, spontaneous actions and responses to given situations, you certainly don't want anything that smacks at all of being "pre-programmed." By its very nature, ritual is the reenactment of an already established form.
- **Superficiality:** You must have encountered situations where you felt like you were (or sensed that someone else was) "only going through the motions" or where a prescribed act became "only a symbol" rather than something truly substantial. And rituals, especially those that incorporate micromanagement of minutia, seem to be inviting that.
- **Publicity:** Because the classical Taoist authors generally identified ritual as the ceremonial activities of government and other public figures, they no doubt equated it with the desires for reputation and power, and especially with the personal presumption of thinking oneself deserving to rule the country. If ritual carries a sense of urgency, of gravity, and of self-importance, Lao Tzu and Chuang Tzu want none of it.

The bare facts of Taoist ritual

Before plunging into the somewhat daunting task of describing the various types of Taoist ritual, it is helpful to consider the subject a bit more generally, in terms of who the basic players are, when and why they perform ritual functions, and what elementary characteristics appear most often. This way, even if you're not quite sure exactly what's going on in a particular ritual, the overall rhythm and texture won't feel quite so unfamiliar.

TECHNICAL STUFF

If it seems like there's a huge jump from Lao Tzu and Chuang Tzu rejecting ritual propriety to members of the Way of the Celestial Masters participating in public confessions of sins and consumption of talisman water to the various colorful rituals that Taoist priests preside over today, it may be helpful to make a quick note that the ritual propriety that gets trashed in the classical texts isn't quite the same operative ritual that shows up in later Taoism. When the classical Taoists talk about letting go of ritual propriety, they're invoking the Chinese term *li*, which refers specifically to ritual acts associated with dynastic functions, aristocratic social relationships, and Confucian values more generally.

But the later Taoists don't normally label their performances as *li*; instead, they use a variety of different terms that describe the specific operations, like *chiao*, which translates (sort of) as "offering," or *chai*, which translates as "purification" (or "retreat"). You'll also hear the more generic term *fa*, translated as "ritual," but that may be a little bit of a misnomer because it really means something more like "way" or "method," which underscores the *operative* and *instrumental* purpose of Taoist ritual. This term for method, *fa*, shows up in a lot of ritual places.

Ritual specialists, whether Taoist, Buddhist, or "redhead Taoist," are sometimes called *fa-shih*, ceremonial objects are *fa-ch'i* (ritual-method tools), and certain exorcisms are called *lei-fa* (thunder ritual-methods).

No matter which ritual functions we're talking about, you'll probably see some combination of the following:

- **Altars:** Some ceremonies are performed at elaborate, sometimes multilevel altars, with intricate symbolism that's usually intelligible only to those with specific training. Symbols can include *yin-yang* cosmology trigrams, images of animals (often the dragon and tiger), various high or regional deities, and implicit divisions that mirror things like Heavenly compartments, cinnabar fields in the body, and so on.
- **Officiants:** Depending on the ceremony and the lineage, there may be anything from a small group to a huge entourage taking part, where each person occupies a different priestly rank. They all wear ritual vestments, enact specific movements, and possibly play musical instruments (with distinct *yin* and *yang* tones) or speak or chant in dialects specific to the ritual. The different functionaries may have the authority to play particular roles by virtue of the registers that have been conferred on them.
- **Channeling:** All rituals involve some type of communication with Taoist deities, and many of these involve summoning specific deities to the ceremony, with a priest or assistant acting as the spirit medium. Priests only have the authority to summon specific deities, so they sometimes have to summon other deities to do the summoning. It's not all that common, but priests occasionally have to kick out a wrong spirit who shows up by mistake!

You may be noticing by now that just about every aspect of the ritual requires some kind of special authorization even to participate and some kind of "insider knowledge" to understand what's going on, whether it's the symbolism on the altars, registers possessed by the priests, or the interior conversations between a medium and a channeled spirit. And that's not an accident. Taoists have always protected their lore and rituals, demanding years of esoteric training before extending the privilege of ritual access. For this reason, the *laypeople* — that is, the "ordinary" people who attend such events — usually have a sketchy (at best) idea of what's going on during the ceremonies. They may attend out of a vested interest in the anticipated effects of the rituals, respect for the officiants doing the work, a sense that something "big" is happening, or even just to witness a colorful spectacle.

THE RITUALS OF THE ANTI-RITUALISTIC

Religious traditions, or sects within traditions, sometimes distinguish themselves by maintaining a public position that they reject certain trappings of "ordinary" traditions, like language, scripture, priesthood, or — you guessed it — ritual. More often than not, these "anti-dogma dogmas" don't really reject completely all the stuff they say they do, as much as they force a different way of imagining those things. For instance, the Tao Te Ching may make a big fuss about the limits of language (as do many other supposed mystical texts) and excoriate those who presume to talk about what can't be spoken, but that didn't stop the anonymous authors of the text (and subsequent generations of Taoists) from using an awful lot of words and spilling an awful lot of ink. Ironically (and obviously, once you think about it) using language to make a point about the limitations of language is a wonderfully strategic use of language.

There's probably no single tradition more identified with this kind of iconoclasm than Zen Buddhism (more on Buddhism in Book 3), which talks about the direct personal transmission of an intuitive, experiential insight outside of scriptures, outside of rituals. What's so striking is just how convincing this "official" line has been. It's extraordinary how often you'll see people reading Zen texts and then claiming that Zen Buddhists don't use scripture, or observing monks enter a meditation hall in ritual fashion, or ritualistically approach a teacher for a personal interview but then claim that Zen Buddhists don't practice any rituals. In fact, you'd probably be pretty hard-pressed to come up with any religious tradition that doesn't have some kind of ritual component, however clear the participants are that what they're doing doesn't "count" as ritual, whether it's the silent waiting of Quakers for the spirit to come upon them or the gathering of a regional Baha'i community in order to elect a new Local Spiritual Assembly.

TIP

Because of all this — as well as the fact that a great many of these practices are closely tied to regional geography and history, local gods and spirits, and specific family and community interests — you probably don't want to hold your breath waiting for these to show up in your hometown. However fascinating these Taoist rituals may be, their esoteric quality and regional particularity make them an unlikely fit for Western audiences. If Chinese laypeople don't really understand them, the many Westerners who appreciate Taoism as a *spiritual* resource understandably have a hard time making heads or tails of them.

Swords and plaques and implements of petition

Even if you don't really follow the *yin* and *yang* (so to speak) of Taoist ritual, the performances are seldom less than intriguing to watch, if only for the music, decorations, and ceremonial objects, which can be quite the feast for the senses. Here's a quick inventory of some of the auditory and visual effects you're likely to encounter:

- **Music:** This often includes sophisticated ensembles of bells, stone chimes, hollow wood blocks (usually shaped like fish), gongs, cymbals, drums, bamboo flutes, and various exotic reed instruments. Sometimes a single priest will play a buffalo or ox horn (though called a dragon horn) to call for good spirits or drive away evil ones.
- **Mood:** Some rituals are adorned by objects that have a kind of background symbolic function, in that they're necessary for the ceremony even if priests don't actually do anything with them during the performance. This can include paintings, banners, plaques, mirrors, lamps, and copies of scriptures and texts.
- **Tools:** These are a variety of basic objects — which often have symbols or inscriptions on them — that the priests move and employ in various ways. These may include a measuring stick for exorcizing spirits, a seal for stamping documents, a wooden-handled whip (styled to look like a snake), a bowl of purified water, an incense burner, and gizmos used for divination.

Understanding Rituals of Purification and Offering

In line with basic Chinese religious sensibilities, Taoist rituals are never merely decorative, never just to make you feel good or give you a sense that you're carrying on a tradition for its own sake. Taoist specialists perform rituals for the same overall reasons they venerate spirits or engage in personal cultivation: to accomplish concrete, tangible ends (or at least what they perceive as concrete, tangible ends), though this may be quite high-minded, like the health of the community or even the entire cosmos. In very broad strokes, most rituals involve some kind of transactional quality, where participants are petitioning or in some other way asking something of the deities, in exchange for veneration or offerings they give to the deities. The rituals may be esoteric and require years of training to perform optimally, but they still pretty much replicate some version of a cosmic "you scratch my back and I'll scratch yours" religious drama.

REMEMBER

Specifically Taoist (as opposed to generically Chinese) ritual probably traces back to the practices of the earliest Way of the Celestial Master community, which involved:

- Ordinations and advancement in the priestly hierarchy
- The employment of registers and talismans for healing and the safe passage of the dead
- The meditation on and confession of sins
- Participation in public feasts

All these things influenced the forms that later rituals would take. As the tradition expanded over the next several centuries, it took on ritual forms developed within the Highest Purity and Numinous Treasure cultivation groups, as well as those related to both external and internal alchemy.

Nearly two millennia of historical growth have produced a dazzling variety of Taoist rituals, but Chinese Taoists have generally sorted them into two distinct categories: rituals of purification *(chai)*, and rituals of offering *(chiao)*.

Rituals of fasting, purification, purgation, and retreat

The rituals referred to as *chai* normally translate as purification, purgation, or fasting — it's the same *chai* from Chuang Tzu's "fasting of the mind and heart" — but they can also refer to retreats, where groups of people withdraw to specific ritually pure places to practice abstinence and purification of the body, always in the hope of a tangible benefit. It was probably within the Numinous Treasure cultivation group that they adapted the older Celestial Masters rituals of repentance and created newer formalized practices.

Here are a handful of typical retreat rituals:

- **The Mud and Soot Retreat:** Just like it sounds, this extended ritual involved smearing mud on your face and rolling around on the ground (and possibly some more disgusting punishments), presumably to atone for the sins you've committed and to dispel the unhappy fate that may await you. A priest performing the ritual can do so on behalf of those who are already dead, a motif that will persist in Taoist ritual.
- **The Three "Register" Retreats:** This trio of retreats — the Yellow Register Retreat, the Jade Register Retreat, and the Golden Register Retreat — lasted several days and were performed at specified times during the year. Priests performed the Yellow Register Retreat for the well-being of the dead, the Jade Register Retreat for the well-being of dynastic officials and the wife of the emperor, and the Golden Register Retreat for the well-being of the emperor

(which would presumably protect the people and guarantee the stability of the community).

» **The Great One Retreat:** The performance of this purgation was limited to the emperor, who, as the son of Heaven, was supposed to perform this ritual on behalf of *T'ai-i,* a name given to the "oneness" of the cosmos or to the deity by that name who personifies this unity and serves as a kind of celestial overseer.

THE DEITIES, SPIRITS, AND THE CONCERN FOR CONCRETE EFFECTS

Chinese religion has always included many deities, spirits, ghosts, and other beings whose presence isn't obvious to the naked eye. If you want to know every deity the Chinese have ever honored, you'd probably need a scorecard or the kind of computer program that keeps track of complicated family trees. But for the most part, you can keep track of them by sorting them into the following categories:

- **A high god:** The Chinese name *T'ien* translates literally as "Heaven" or "the Heavens." This deity is more impersonal than anthropomorphic, which is to say that it doesn't really possess human features. Heaven is associated with things like fate, cosmic order, and the protection of a righteous ruling regime.
- **Sectarian gods and goddesses:** These are deities that originated from particular religious traditions, like the Buddha named Mi-lo (that's the round, smiling guy you may see on the counter in Chinese restaurants), a compassionate female Buddhist goddess named Kuan-yin, or Hsi Wang Mu, the Taoist Queen Mother of the West.
- **Functional and local deities:** These deities fulfill particular purposes (such as healing, agriculture, or protecting travelers) or occupy and protect particular regions. Rural villages would often have their own earth gods, and individual families to this day may still have images of kitchen gods in their homes.
- **Deified historical or legendary figures:** Most deities are thought to have once been people who, for one reason or another, earned "promotions" to god status over time. The best known of these is Ma Tzu, an ordinary fisherman's daughter from the tenth century, who is now honored as the goddess of the sea.
- **Spirits of ancestors:** Your parents and grandparents continue to deserve your respect, even after they die. The Chinese holiday called Ch'ing Ming is a time when people visit their family cemeteries, light firecrackers, burn incense, and make other offerings to their ancestors. Spirits of the dead who have no descendants or have been forgotten by their descendants turn into unhappy, restless ghosts.

So, which of these deities are the most important in Chinese practice? You may be imagining that the most powerful ones or the ones commanding the most territory get the most attention, but actually the exact opposite is true. Think of it this way: The most powerful person in the country is (depending on which country) the president, the prime minister, or maybe the chief justice of the highest court. So, naturally, whenever you need something from the government — like getting your dog released from the pound or acquiring a building permit — you get on the phone and call the president, right? Well, no. Instead, you call the local official — the animal control officer or the director of planning and zoning, whoever has the direct authority to take care of your particular problem. The Chinese think of their deities much the same way, as though they were organized like a government bureaucracy. People pay less attention to the higher and more remote figures and more attention to the ones that influence their immediate concerns. The Chinese worship deities based not on their overall importance, but on their *ling*, their "spiritual efficacy," the quality the deities possess to bring concrete effects into people's lives.

But remember, for the Chinese, the deities that matter most are the ones that *matter* — that is, the ancestors, local spirits, and other figures who have the spiritual efficacy to influence their day-to-day lives. If they don't think a spirit is efficacious, they won't worship it.

Because the Chinese measure deities by their efficacy, they may have some religious habits that strike non-Chinese as strange, until you remember that they tend to employ religious resources that have a practical, concrete value. For example, if they think that a deity isn't "doing its job," whoever is in the position of authority to make such decisions can simply replace that deity with a different spirit who's more up to the task. The relationship between humans and deities is mutual; each side has its obligations to fulfill, and even deities are held accountable if they don't fulfill theirs.

The rite of cosmic renewal

Technically, Taoist rituals of offering serve to cement the connection between a community and the deity or deities with whom the people have a special symbiotic relationship, though the best known and most important version of these are also called rites of cosmic renewal, because the elaborate, multi-day (or multi-week) events are designed to do just what the name suggests: to make the cosmos a newly fresh, harmonious organism that nurtures the well-being of the community. You may read somewhere that *chiao* rituals are only offered on a 60-year cycle and are, thus, quite rare, but it appears that the term now pretty much applies to many different types of offering-based rituals and even the special type supposedly offered every six decades shows up a little more often and at odd intervals.

The major *chiao* rituals can have it all, like a boatload of priests taking part, the ceremonial marking off of sacred space, construction of temporary altars, performance of ceremonial music, presentation of petitions to Heaven, lighting ritual lamps and incense burners, reciting moral precepts, summoning deities to present them with offerings, and so forth. Often, these rituals are preceded by lengthy periods of repentance and purification — that's the *chai* piece — and conclude with an addendum straight out of Buddhism, a prayer for universal salvation.

The great offering for a peaceful world

The great-granddaddy of all the rituals of offering is the *Lo-t'ien Ta-chiao*, the Great Offering to All-Encompassing Heaven, which historically attracted the involvement of dozens of priests and supposedly addressed offerings to well over a thousand deities. The first of these extravaganzas may go back as far as the eighth century, but the modern history of it really begins when Chang En-p'u, the 63rd Celestial Master, presided over one in Shanghai in 1933, a decade or so before he escaped to Taiwan and revitalized Taoist practices there.

In the aftermath of the Cultural Revolution, as Taoism began to regroup in China with the refurbishing of temples and ordination of new priests, the China Taoist Association (CTA) made efforts to revive the *Lo-t'ien Ta-chiao* as an ecumenical Taoist mega-event that would unite both major branches of modern Taoism — Orthodox Unity and Complete Perfection — and bring together representatives from the pan-Chinese Taoist world and the various local Taoist associations. In 1993, the White Cloud Monastery in Beijing — with the co-sponsorship of abbots from temples all over China, Taiwan, and Hong Kong — hosted the ten-day Great Offering, constructing ten new shrines where they installed some 1,200 deities.

The CTA co-sponsored a second Great Offering in 2001, this time attracting more than 300 clerics from as far afield as Macao, Singapore, and Korea and constructing 15 new altars. The ceremony was specifically dedicated to "praying for world peace, state prosperity, national reunion, and the people's happiness." But the Taoists pulled out all the stops for the biggest Great Offering yet, which occurred in Hong Kong in 2007. Commemorating the tenth anniversary of Chinese rule over Hong Kong, and with the overall goal of praying for world peace (as well as the elimination of natural disasters), this event topped out at more than 400 priests and acolytes (including many women) and coincided with various other cultural and educational activities.

TIP

The reemergence of the *Lo-t'ien Ta-chiao* may be the biggest and best indicator that Taoism really is in for a comeback in China. It will be interesting to see if the CTA's ecumenical undertakings continue to bear this kind of fruit, and if events like these inspire any widespread renewed interest in Taoism.

Observing Taoist Funeral Rituals

Apart from the seasonal cycles of rituals of purification and offering, Orthodox Unity priests also preside over highly complex funeral rites, which are necessary for guaranteeing a peaceful afterlife for the recently deceased. Because the death of one's parents constitutes a major generational breach, the rituals reflect the seriousness and gravity of the situation. The services can be extravagant and expensive — employing talismans, exorcism, and the construction of large altars — but families usually consider it an important-enough investment that they may even go into debt to pay for it if necessary.

Negotiating a treacherous journey

You can never be sure how much of this is understood metaphorically, but Taoist funeral rituals portray the soul of the deceased person as in a kind of postmortem limbo, stuck in a netherworld purgatory (some sources translate it as "Hell," but that's a little bit misleading). The purpose of the ritual is to make merit on behalf of the deceased, essentially earning them a spiritual "pardon" from the interim subterranean prison and safe passage to some kind of Heavenly paradise (or to a good rebirth, if the priest has had some Buddhist influences).

The narrative crux of the ritual is the symbolic dispatching through the netherworld of a horse rider bearing a "writ of pardon," which the priest has procured through access to spirits. Often, the rider is symbolized by a paper effigy carrying straw (for the horse), an alchemical elixir for the welfare of the deceased, or ceremonial paper money for bribing inhospitable spirits along the way. The ritual enactment of this journey involves the usual assortment of esoteric gestures, theatrical movements, and perhaps even acrobatics.

Crossing the bridge to Heaven

The process of releasing the soul of the deceased person from limbo and enabling the final exodus to Heaven involves several more dramatic steps, the most striking of which is called "attacking purgatory." During this part of the ceremony, the presiding priest engages in feverish, sometimes almost violent actions that symbolically break open the walls of purgatory and release the trapped soul.

In many performances of this ritual, family members actually take a small role — just about the only time laypeople actually participate in, rather than just watch, a Taoist ceremony — gathering in a circle around a paper model of the underworld fortress and literally extending their hands to assist in the destruction of the walls. One ethnographer researching this ritual observed that of all the times during the extensive funeral and mourning ceremonies, this moment most inspires a sense of grief in the family members, whose physical actions literally facilitate the departure of the loved one and, in effect, force the family to say goodbye.

The final stage of the ceremony, at least the final stage before the actual burial, involves leading the newly liberated spirit of the deceased across a bridge to Heaven, which is also usually symbolized by a paper model. The ritual may also include paper models of a palatial estate, representing just how spectacular this Heavenly paradise will surely be. If the ritual is conducted properly, the dollars paid and the emotional efforts expended by the family prove to be well worth it!

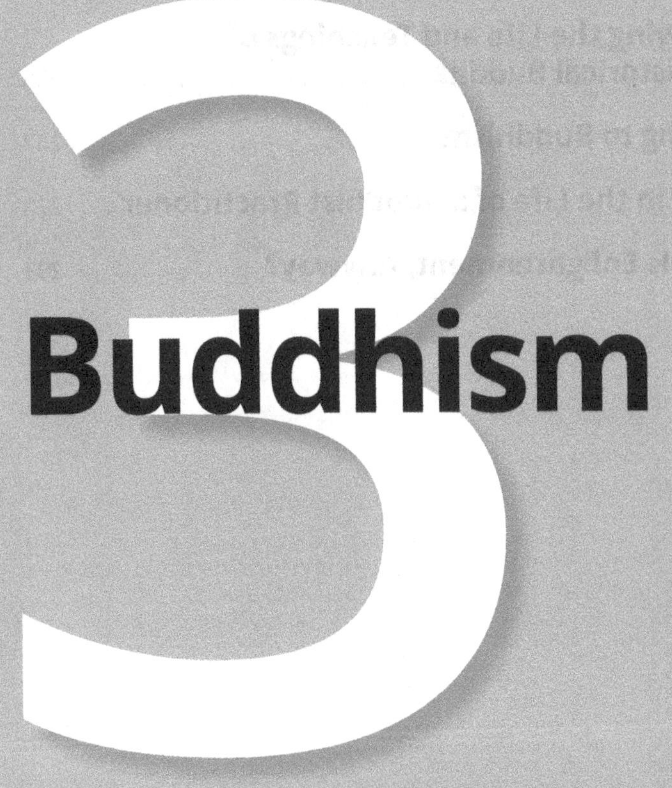

Buddhism

Contents at a Glance

IN THIS CHAPTER

» Considering whether Buddhism is a religion

» Examining the role of the Buddha

» Understanding the significance of Buddhist philosophy

» Exploring Buddhist practices

» Discovering the Buddhist mindset

» Laying down the law — what goes around comes around

» Acting ethically

Chapter 1 Entering the World of Buddhism

Not too long ago, the West was virtually unfamiliar with the teachings of Buddhism. Back in the 1950s and 1960s, for example, you may have gone about your life scarcely hearing the word *Buddhism* mentioned. Sure, you may have come across Buddhist concepts in school in the writings of American Transcendentalists such as Thoreau and Emerson (who read English translations of Buddhist texts in the mid-19th century). But the fact is, if you were like most middle-class people then, you may have grown up, grown old, and died without ever meeting a practicing Buddhist — except perhaps in an Asian restaurant.

If you wanted to find out about Buddhism in those days, your resource options were few and far between. Aside from a rare course in Eastern philosophy at a large university, you would have to dig deep into the shelves and stacks at your local library to discover anything more than the most basic facts about Buddhism. The few books that you could get your hands on tended to treat Buddhism as if it were an exotic relic from some long-ago and faraway land, like some dusty

Buddha statue in a dark corner of the Asian section of a museum. And good luck if you wanted to find a Buddhist center where you study and practice.

Today the situation is much different. Buddhist terms seem to pop up everywhere. You can find them in ordinary conversation ("It's just your *karma*"), in popular songs (like Taylor Swift's "Karma"), and even in the names of rock groups (Nirvana). Famous Hollywood stars, superheroes, space pioneers, and pop singers practice some form of Buddhism. (We're thinking of Orlando Bloom, Benedict Cumberbatch, George Takei, and Tina Turner, but you may be able to come up with a different list of celebrities on your own.)

Bookstores and libraries everywhere boast a wide range of Buddhist titles, some of which — like the Dalai Lama's *Art of Happiness* (Riverhead Books, 1998) — regularly top *The New York Times* best-seller lists. And centers where people can study and practice Buddhism are now located in most metropolitan areas (and many smaller cities as well).

What caused such a dramatic change in just a few decades? Certainly, Buddhism has become more available as Asian Buddhist teachers and their disciples have carried the tradition to North America and Europe. But there's more to the story than increased availability. In this chapter, we try to account for the appeal this ancient tradition has in today's largely secular world by looking at some of the features responsible for its growing popularity.

Figuring Out Whether Buddhism Is a Religion

Wondering whether Buddhism is actually a religion may seem odd, especially in a book devoted to world religions. However, if you consult any list of the world's major religious traditions, you inevitably find Buddhism mentioned prominently alongside Christianity, Islam, Hinduism, Judaism, and the rest. No one ever questions whether these other traditions are religions. But this question comes up repeatedly in relation to Buddhism.

WARNING

The answer depends on how you define *religion*. Ask most people what comes to mind when they think of religion, and they probably mention something about the belief in God, especially when discussing the creator of the world or universe. Our dictionary agrees. *Webster's New World College Dictionary* defines *religion* as a "belief in a divine or superhuman power or powers to be obeyed and worshiped as the creator(s) and ruler(s) of the universe." If this definition were the only definition of religion, you'd definitely have to count Buddhism out! Why? Well, we have two reasons:

- **Worship of a supernatural power isn't the central concern of Buddhism.** God (as this word is ordinarily used in the West) is absent from Buddhist teachings, although some Buddhists do worship gods and celestial Buddhas.
- **Buddhism isn't primarily a system of belief.** Although it teaches certain doctrines, many Buddhist teachers actively encourage their students to adopt an attitude that's the opposite of blind faith.

Many Buddhist teachers advise you to be skeptical about teachings you receive. Don't passively accept what you hear or read — and don't automatically reject it, either. Instead, use your intelligence. See for yourself whether the teachings make sense in terms of your own experience and the experience of others. Then, as the Dalai Lama of Tibet often advises, "If you find that the teachings suit you, apply them to your life as much as you can. If they don't suit you, just leave them be."

TECHNICAL STUFF

This more practical approach agrees with both the spirit and the letter of the Buddha's own teachings. The Buddha is believed to have declared, "Do not accept anything I say as true simply because I have said it. Instead, test it as you would gold to see if it is genuine or not. If, after examining my teachings, you find that they are true, put them into practice. But do not do so simply out of respect for me."

Buddhist teachings therefore encourage you to use the entire range of your mental, emotional, and spiritual abilities and intelligence — instead of merely placing your blind faith in what past authorities have said. This attitude makes the teachings of Buddhism especially attractive to many Westerners; although it's over 2,500 years old, it appeals to the postmodern spirit of skepticism and scientific investigation.

REMEMBER

If Buddhism is not primarily a belief system and isn't centered upon the worship of a supreme deity, then why is it classified as a religion at all? Like all religions, Buddhism gives people who practice it a way of finding answers to the deeper questions of life, such as "Who am I?" and "Why am I here?" and "What is the meaning of life?" and "Why do we suffer?" and "How can I achieve lasting happiness?"

In addition to fundamental teachings on the nature of reality, Buddhism offers a method, a systematic approach involving techniques and practices, enabling its followers to experience a deeper level of reality directly for themselves. In Buddhist terms, this experience involves waking up to the truth of your authentic being, your innermost nature. The experience of awakening is the ultimate goal of all Buddhist teachings. Some schools emphasize awakening more than others (and a few even relegate it to the background in their scheme of priorities), but in every tradition, it's the final goal of human existence — whether achieved in this life or in lives to come.

THE HISTORICAL BUDDHA

Most scholars believe that the Buddha's life largely falls within the fifth century BCE, although the exact dates of his life are unknown. According to tradition, he died at age 80, and recent research puts the year of the Buddha's death not much later than 400 BCE.

The accounts of the Buddha's life aren't historical. The earliest ones date from several centuries after his death and consist mainly of legends, some of which have striking parallels in others told about Mahavira, a religious figure of Jainism (another religion spawned on the Indian subcontinent). The legendary material on the Buddha's life is summarized briefly in this chapter and presented in more detail in Book 3, Chapter 2.

Writing wasn't in use at the Buddha's time. Because the earliest Buddhist texts were orally transmitted and written down only many centuries after the Buddha's death, scholars aren't certain about what the Buddha himself taught and what was later ascribed to him.

Recognizing the Role of the Buddha

Buddhist systems are based upon the teachings given 2,500 years ago by one of the great spiritual figures of human history, Shakyamuni Buddha, who lived in the fifth century BCE. According to legendary accounts of his life (see Book 3, Chapter 2), he was born into the ruling family of the Shakya clan in today's Nepal and was expected to someday succeed his father as king. Instead, Prince Siddhartha (as he was known at the time) quit the royal life at the age of 29 after he saw the reality of the extensive suffering and dissatisfaction in the world. He then set out to find a way to overcome this suffering.

After many hardships, at age 35, Prince Siddhartha achieved his goal. Seated under what became known as the *Bodhi tree* — the tree of enlightenment — he achieved the awakening of Buddhahood. Today a stone platform known as the diamond seat *(vajrasana)* near the Bodhi tree in Bodh Gaya marks the spot. From then on, he was known as *Shakyamuni Buddha*, the awakened (Buddha) sage *(muni)* of the Shakya clan.

Prince Siddhartha spent the remaining 45 years of his life wandering the northern part of the Indian subcontinent, teaching anyone who was interested in the path that leads to freedom from suffering. The famous Buddha statue in Sarnath (India), the place where he gave his first sermon, shows the Buddha making the gesture of turning the wheel of his teaching. After a lifetime of compassionate service to others, Shakyamuni died at the age of 80.

The question is often asked, "What kind of being was Shakyamuni Buddha — a man, a god, or something else?" Some biographical accounts state that the Buddha was once a human being with the same hang-ups and problems as everyone else. He didn't start out as a Buddha; he wasn't enlightened from the beginning.

Only through great effort exerted over a long period of time — over many lifetimes, as the Buddhist texts tell us — did he succeed in attaining enlightenment. However, the later tradition clearly considered the Buddha an exceptional human being and elevated him to a special status. Legendary accounts of his life emphasize, for example, his miraculous birth in the Lumbini grove from his mother's side, the 32 marks of a "great man" that were found on his body, and his ability to work miracles.

The Buddhist spiritual community *(Sangha)* took great pains to preserve and transmit his teachings as purely as possible so that they pass from one generation to the next. These extensive teachings were eventually written down, producing a vast collection (or *canon*) of the Buddha's discourses (Pali: *suttas*; Sanskrit: *sutras*).

Over the centuries, the Sangha also erected burial monuments *(stupas)* in honor of the major events in their teacher's life, which allowed later practitioners to make pilgrimage to these honored sites and receive inspiration. (Book 3, Chapter 4 has more information on Buddhist devotional practices and rituals.)

Thanks to the efforts of teachers and their disciples, the Buddha's teachings (known as *Dharma*) have been handed down from generation to generation up to the present day. That's why, after 2,500 years, Buddhism is still a living tradition, capable of bestowing peace, happiness, and fulfillment upon anyone who practices it sincerely.

REMEMBER

The legends about the life of the Buddha have been a source of inspiration for Buddhists. When the Buddha is considered a mortal, he's a vital example of what each of us can achieve if we devote ourselves wholeheartedly to the study and practice of his teachings.

Understanding the Function of Philosophy in Buddhism

Socrates, one of the fathers of Western philosophy, claimed that the unexamined life isn't worth living, and most Buddhists would certainly agree with him. Because of the importance they place on logical reasoning and rational examination, many

Buddhist traditions and schools have a strong philosophical flavor. Others place more emphasis on devotion; still others focus on the direct, nonconceptual investigation and examination that take place during the practice of meditation.

Like other religions, Buddhism does put forth certain philosophical tenets that sketch out a basic understanding of human existence and serve as guidelines and inspiration for practice and study. Over the centuries, a variety of schools and traditions came into existence, each with its own fairly elaborate and distinct understanding of what the Buddha taught. In addition to the discourses memorized during the founder's lifetime and recorded after his death, numerous other scriptures emerged many centuries later that were attributed to him.

Despite all its philosophical sophistication, however, Buddhism remains at heart an extremely practical religion. In the *Dhammapada (Words on Dhamma)*, an ancient collection of verses on Buddhist themes, his followers have summarized the teachings as follows:

> Abstaining from all evil, undertaking what is skillful, cleansing one's mind — this is the teaching of the Buddhas. (Verse 183)
>
> Not blaming, not harming, living restrained according to the discipline, moderation in food, seclusion in dwelling, focusing on the highest thoughts — this is the teaching of the Buddhas. (Verse 185)

The Buddha has often been called the Great Physician, for good reason: He avoided abstract speculation and made his chief concern identifying the cause of human suffering and providing ways to eliminate it. (See the sidebar "The parable of the poisoned arrow" for details.) Likewise, his teachings are known as powerful medicine to cure the deeper dissatisfaction that afflicts us all. The Buddha's first and best-known teaching, the four noble truths, outlines the cause of suffering and the means for eliminating it. All subsequent teachings, such as the 12 links of dependent arising, merely expand and elaborate upon these fundamental truths.

REMEMBER

At the core of all genuine Buddhist teachings is the understanding that suffering and dissatisfaction originate in the way your mind responds and reacts to life's circumstances — not just in the raw facts of life. In particular, Buddhism teaches that your mind causes you suffering by superimposing permanence and constructing a separate self where, in fact, neither exists.

Reality is constantly changing; as the Greek philosopher Heraclitus said (and Disney's Pocohantas sang about in "Just Around the Riverbend"), you can't step into the same river twice. Success and failure, gain and loss, comfort and discomfort — they all come and go. And you have only limited control over the changes. But you can exert some control over (and ultimately clarify) your chattering, misguided mind, which distorts your perceptions, mightily resists the way things are, and causes you extraordinary stress and suffering in the process.

TIP

Happiness is actually quite simple: The secret is to want what you have and not want what you don't have. Simple though it may be, it's definitely not easy. Have you ever tried to reign in your restless and unruly mind, even for a moment? Have you ever tried to tame your anger or your jealousy, control your fear, or remain calm and undisturbed in the middle of life's inevitable ups and downs? If you have, you've no doubt discovered how difficult even the simplest self-control or self-awareness can be. To benefit from the medicine the Buddha prescribed, you have to take it — which means that you have to put it into practice for yourself.

Appreciating Buddhist Practices

Anyone interested in benefiting from the teachings of Buddhism — beyond simply discovering a few interesting facts about it — has to ask, "How do I take this spiritual medicine? How can I apply the teachings of Shakyamuni to my life in such a way to reduce, neutralize, and eventually extinguish my restlessness and dissatisfaction?" The answer is spiritual practice, which takes three forms in Buddhism:

- Ethical behavior
- Meditation (and the wisdom that follows)
- Devotion

Living an ethical life

Ethical behavior has been an essential component of the Buddhist spiritual path since THE HISTORICAL BUDDHA first cautioned his monks and nuns to refrain from certain behaviors because they distracted them from their pursuit of truth. During the Buddha's lifetime, his followers collected and codified these guidelines, which eventually became the code of discipline *(vinaya)* that has continued to shape the monastic life for more than 2,500 years. (The term *monastic* describes both monks and nuns.) From this code emerged briefer guidelines or precepts for lay practitioners, which have remained remarkably similar from tradition to tradition.

THE PARABLE OF THE POISONED ARROW

Since intellectual activity has had such a significant place in the history of Buddhism, it may be tempting to classify Buddhism as a philosophy rather than a religion. But Shakyamuni Buddha himself warned against getting caught up in philosophical speculation. This attitude is clearly illustrated in the oft-told story of a monk named Malunkyaputta (we'll just call him the Venerable Mal, for short). Venerable Mal approached the Buddha one day complaining that he'd never addressed certain philosophical questions, such as "Is the world eternal or not?" and "Does the Buddha exist after death?" Venerable Mal declared that if the Buddha wouldn't answer these questions once and for all, he would abandon his training as a Buddhist monk.

In response, Shakyamuni described the following hypothetical situation. Suppose, he said, a man had been wounded by a poisoned arrow. His concerned relatives found a skillful surgeon to remove the arrow, but the wounded man refused to let the doctor operate until he had received satisfactory answers to a long list of questions. "I will not have the arrow taken out," the wounded man declared, "until I know the caste to which the man who wounded me belongs, his name, his height, the village he comes from, the wood from which the arrow was made, and so forth." Clearly, such a foolish person would die long before his questions were ever be answered.

"In the same way," Shakyamuni advised Venerable Mal, "anyone who says, 'I will not follow the spiritual life until the Buddha has explained to me whether the world is eternal or not or whether the Buddha exists after death' would die long before he ever received satisfying answers to his questions." The truly spiritual or religious life doesn't depend at all on how these questions are answered. For, as Shakyamuni then pointed out, "Whether or not the world is eternal, you're still faced with birth, old age, death, sorrow, grief, and despair, for which I'm now prescribing the antidote."

Far from establishing an absolute standard of right and wrong, ethical guidelines in Buddhism have an entirely practical purpose: to keep practitioners focused on the goal of their practice, which is a liberating insight into the nature of reality. During his 45 years of teaching, the Buddha found that certain activities contributed to increased craving, attachment, restlessness, and dissatisfaction, and led to interpersonal conflict in the community at large. By contrast, other behaviors helped keep the mind peaceful and focused, and contributed to a more supportive atmosphere for spiritual reflection and realization. From these observations, not from any abstract moral point of view, the ethical guidelines emerged.

Examining your life through meditation

In the popular imagination, Buddhism is definitely the religion of meditation. After all, who hasn't seen statues of the Buddha sitting cross-legged, eyes half closed, deeply immersed in spiritual reflection; or picked up one of the many titles available these days devoted to teaching the basics of Buddhist meditation?

But many people misunderstand the role meditation plays in Buddhism. They falsely assume that you're meant to withdraw from the affairs of ordinary life into a peaceful, detached, and unaffected inner realm until you no longer feel any emotion or concern about the things that once mattered to you. Nothing could be further from the truth.

REMEMBER

According to several Buddhist schools, the main purpose of meditation isn't to calm the mind (though this result may happen and is certainly conducive to the meditative process), nor is it to become uncaring. Instead, the purpose is to experience the profound and ultimately liberating insight into the nature of reality and yourself that we talk about in the section "Understanding the Function of Philosophy in Buddhism," earlier in this chapter — an insight that shows you who you are and what life is about and frees you from suffering once and for all.

Meditation facilitates this insight by bringing focused, ongoing attention to the workings of your mind and heart. In the early stages of meditation, you spend most of your time being aware of your experience as much as you can — an almost universal Buddhist practice known as *mindfulness*. You may also cultivate positive, beneficial heart qualities like loving-kindness and compassion or practice visualizations of beneficial figures and energies. But in the end, the goal of all Buddhist meditation is to find out who you are and thereby end your restless seeking and dissatisfaction.

Practicing devotion

Devotion has long been a central Buddhist practice. No doubt it began with the spontaneous devotion the Buddha's own followers felt for their gentle, wise, and compassionate teacher. After his death, followers with a devotional bent directed their reverence toward the enlightened elders of the monastic community and toward the Buddha's remains, which were preserved in burial monuments known as stupas.

As Buddhism spread throughout the Indian subcontinent and ultimately to other lands, the primary object of devotion became the *Three Jewels* of the Buddha, Dharma, and Sangha — the great teacher, his teachings, and the spiritual community, which preserves and upholds the teachings. To this day, all Buddhists, both lay and monastic, *take refuge* in the Three Jewels (also known as the Three Treasures or Triple Gem).

Eventually, in certain traditions of Buddhism, a host of transcendent figures came to be revered. These figures include other enlightened beings (Buddhas), bodhisattvas (beings striving for enlightenment; see the next section), and celestial figures such as the goddess Tara. By expressing heartfelt devotion to these figures and, in some traditions, by imagining yourself merging with them and assuming their awakened qualities, you can ultimately gain complete enlightenment for the benefit of yourself and others — or so these traditions teach.

Study and reflection help clarify the Buddhist teachings, but devotion forges a heartfelt connection with the tradition, allowing you to express your love and appreciation for the teachers (and teachings) and to experience their love and compassion in return. Even traditions like Zen, which seem to de-emphasize devotion in favor of insight, have a strong devotional undercurrent that gets expressed in rituals and ceremonies but isn't always visible to newcomers. For lay Buddhist practitioners who may not have the time or inclination to meditate, devotion to the Three Jewels may even become their main practice. In fact some traditions, like Pure Land Buddhism, are primarily devotional.

Dedicating Your Life to the Benefit of All Beings

Mahayana ("The Great Vehicle" or "Great Path"), a major branch of Buddhism, encourages you to dedicate your spiritual efforts not only to yourself and your loved ones, but also to the benefit and enlightenment of all beings.

Many Buddhist traditions teach their followers to actively cultivate love and compassion for others — not only those they care about, but also those who disturb them or toward whom they may feel hostility (in other words, enemies). In fact, some traditions believe that this dedication to the welfare of all forms the foundation of the spiritual path upon which all other practices are based. Other traditions allow the love and compassion to arise naturally as insight deepens and wisdom ripens, while instructing practitioners to dedicate the merits of their meditations and rituals to all beings.

REMEMBER

Whatever the method, the teachings often emphasize that all beings are inseparable. Some traditions even counsel that, in the end, you won't be able to achieve lasting happiness and peace of mind until all beings are happy and peaceful, too. From this realization arises the vow of the *bodhisattva* (Sanskrit for "enlightenment-bound being") who dedicates their life to the enlightenment of all (more on enlightenment in Book 3, Chapter 5). Until all beings are liberated, the *bodhisattva* believes, their work isn't yet done. Though not every Buddhist tradition views the *bodhisattva* in quite the same way, all would agree that this spirit lies at the heart of Mahayana Buddhist teachings.

Recognizing How Your Mind Shapes Your Experience

Your mind shapes and colors all your experiences, without a single exception. The ancient collection of verses on Buddhist teachings, the *Dhammapada* (Pali: *Words of Dhamma*), verses 1–2, begins with this statement:

> Phenomena are preceded by mind, led by mind, formed by mind. If one speaks or acts with a polluted mind, suffering follows him, as a wheel follows the foot of a draught-ox.
>
> Phenomena are preceded by mind, led by mind, formed by mind. If one speaks or acts with a pure mind, happiness follows him, as an ever-present shadow.

From the Buddhist point of view, then, what goes on inside you (in your mind) is much more important in determining whether you're happy or miserable than any of the outer circumstances of your life.

Hold it right there. Does what you just read sound reasonable? Do the inner workings of your mind really have a greater effect on you than, say, your possessions or your surroundings? After all, big companies and advertising agencies spend billions of dollars every year trying to convince you that the opposite is true! In their eyes, your best shot at achieving happiness is to buy whatever they're selling. They appeal to what some call the "if only" mentality: If only you drove a fancier car, lived in a bigger house, gargled with a stronger mouthwash, and used a softer toilet paper — then you'd be truly happy. Even if you don't believe everything advertisers tell you, don't you believe that the external conditions of your life determine how well off you are?

TIP

To get into a Buddhist mindset, get into the habit of asking yourself these types of questions when you come across new information. Investigating points brought up in a book that you're reading or teachings that you hear isn't an intellectual game or idle pastime. If done properly, such questioning becomes a vital part of your spiritual development. Merely accepting certain statements as true, while rejecting others as false without examining them closely, doesn't accomplish very much.

In this case, examination is particularly important because the questions concern the best way to live your life. Should your pursuit of happiness focus mainly on accumulating possessions and other "externals"? Or should you focus on putting your inner house in order?

To get a feel for how to start examining this issue, consider the following situation. Two friends of yours, Jennifer and Laura, take a vacation together to Tahiti.

They stay in the same luxurious guesthouse, eat the same food prepared by the same master chef, lounge on the same pristine beaches, and engage in the same recreational activities. But when they get home and tell you about their trip, their stories sound like they vacationed in two completely different worlds! For Jennifer, Tahiti was heaven on earth, but for Laura, it was pure hell. For every wonderful experience Jennifer brings up, Laura tells you about two awful ones. This situation is hypothetical, of course, but doesn't it sound familiar? Hasn't something like this happened to you or your friends?

Consider one more scenario. During wartime, two friends get thrown into a prison camp. As in the previous example, both soldiers end up in identical situations, but this time, the outward conditions are miserable. One soldier experiences extreme mental torment due to the horrible physical conditions and ends up bitter and broken in spirit. The other manages to rise above their surroundings, even becoming a source of strength for the other prisoners. True stories like this scenario aren't rare, so how can you account for them?

These examples (and relevant ones from your own experience) demonstrate that the outer circumstances of your life aren't the only factors — or even the most important ones — in determining whether you're content. If external conditions were more important than the condition of your mind, both Jennifer and Laura would've loved Tahiti, both prisoners would have been equally miserable, and no rich and famous person would ever struggle with their mental health.

REMEMBER

The more closely you look, the more clearly you'll see that your mental attitude is an important factor in determining the quality of your life. We're not saying that your outer circumstances count for nothing, nor are we implying that people have to give away all their possessions to be sincere spiritual seekers. But without developing your inner resources of peace and mental stability, no amount of worldly success — whether measured in terms of wealth, fame, power, or relationships — can ever bring real satisfaction. Or, as someone once said, "Money can't buy happiness; it can only allow you to select your particular form of misery."

Contrasting the body and the mind

Even if you have a general idea of what the mind is, you may have difficulty identifying it exactly. After all, you can't point to something and say, "This is my mind." Why not? Because unlike your brain, heart, or any other bodily organ, your mind has no color, shape, weight, or other physical attribute.

But as long as you're alive, your body and mind remain intimately interconnected and have a powerful influence on one another. For example, everyone knows that drinking too much alcohol can have a potent, harmful effect on the mind. The physical properties of alcohol dull your mental capacities, lower your inhibitions, and even cause you to hallucinate.

The mind–body influence works the other way as well. For example, worrying too much can contribute to many physical ailments, including stomach ulcers, colitis (inflammation of the large intestine), and high blood pressure. This connection hasn't been lost on medical professionals. Every day, more medical professionals recognize that a patient's mental state can have an enormous effect on recovery from disease. Many hospitals now provide a variety of mind–body treatment options, including hypnotherapy, support groups, and individual counseling, to help patients heal more rapidly and completely. And a quick trip to your local bookstore presents you with even more evidence of the mind's role in the health of the body — dozens of books about the healing influence of visualizations, affirmations, and a positive state of mind line the shelves. A well-known writer even claims to have cured himself of cancer by watching one Marx Brothers movie after another! In his case, laughter really was the best medicine.

They're interconnected, but the body and mind aren't the same thing. If they were, your mental states would be nothing more than the nerve cells, electrical activity, and chemical reactions of your brain. But is this definition an adequate and satisfying explanation for what actually goes on in your mind? Can such varied and richly colored experiences as falling in love, feeling embarrassed, and getting a flash of artistic inspiration be reduced to molecular interactions?

Buddhism teaches that your mind (which is conscious of all your experiences) is formless. Hence, you can't see your mind or touch it. But being formless doesn't prevent your mind from doing what only it can do — being aware! In fact, the job of the mind is just that: to be aware (or conscious).

Approaching the mind from three different Buddhist perspectives

The various Buddhist traditions have their own particular way of talking about the mind and its role in spiritual development. To give you some idea of the richness and variety of these views, we briefly mention the approach of the three main Buddhist traditions in the West today:

- In texts of the *abhidharma,* or "higher teachings," section of the canon of the Theravada Buddhist tradition, we find a detailed analysis of the mind. These extensive teachings divide the mind's functions into different categories, such as primary and secondary, skillful and unskillful, and so on. This psychological analysis can help you precisely understand which of the many different mental functions (one abhidharma system identifies nearly 50 of them!) are arising in your mind at any given moment. The more skillful you become at identifying the complex and ever-changing nature of these mental functions as they arise, the more thoroughly you can cut through the harmful illusion of a solid, unchanging ego-identity and achieve spiritual liberation.

- Many serious followers of the Vajrayana Buddhist tradition also study the abhidharma teachings dealing with the mind, the many different mental functions, and so forth. In addition, the Vajrayana offers techniques for contacting what it calls the *mind of clear light,* a blissful state of consciousness residing at the core of your being that's far more powerful than any ordinary state of mind. By gaining control of this hidden treasure, skillful meditators (or *yogis* of clear light) can burn through mental obstructions rapidly and completely. This act brings them face to face with ultimate reality and, eventually, to the supreme enlightenment of Buddhahood itself.
- According to some masters in the Japanese Zen Buddhist tradition, *big Mind*, or Buddha nature, pervades the whole experienced universe. Everything you experience, both inside and outside yourself, is nothing other than this Mind (with a capital *m*). By contrast, the *small mind,* the analytical, conceptual mind, tends to identify itself as a limited, separate ego or self. Spiritual awakening involves a shift in identity from small mind to big Mind and to what has been called "no Mind" in Zen traditions.

You have a choice in the way you experience your life. Your mind can be obscured or unobscured, limited or vast. The first option involves frustration and dissatisfaction. The second brings freedom and fulfillment. The so-called spiritual path enables you to shift your vision of life from the obscured to the unobscured, from the limited to the vast. And that's what Buddhist teachings are about.

Recognizing the six major types of consciousness

Because the human body comes equipped with five senses, you have five types of sensory awareness, sometimes referred to as the *five sensory consciousnesses.* In some Buddhist texts, they're given the following rather technical names, but their meaning is quite simple, so don't sweat the Latin-sounding names:

- **Auditory consciousness:** Aware of sounds
- **Gustatory consciousness:** Aware of tastes (such as bitter, sweet, and sour)
- **Olfactory consciousness:** Aware of odors
- **Tactile consciousness:** Aware of bodily sensations (such as hot and cold, rough and smooth, and so on)
- **Visual consciousness:** Aware of colors and shapes

DISTORTED APPEARANCES

Needless to say, the five types of sensory awareness depend on the conditions of their related sense organs. When you have a cold, for example, you may lose your sense of smell entirely; the olfactory consciousness continues to function well, but the nasal congestion interferes with your nose's ability to smell. Similarly, as every cook who has ever added too much salt to a soup knows, the tongue can become accustomed to certain tastes. Consider one more example: Press your finger against the side of your eye socket in a certain place and then look up into the night sky; you may see two moons rather than one. These examples demonstrate that you can't always trust the way things appear to your mind. If you add to the mix the various distortions created by your preconceptions and expectations, you can see that clear, undistorted perceptions aren't as common as you may think.

These five types of sensory awareness, or sensory consciousness, obviously depend upon the health of your body and your sense organs. But a sixth type of awareness does not rely so directly on your physical senses to function. This sixth consciousness is called mental consciousness. *Mental consciousness* can be aware of *all* the previously listed items — sights, sounds, odors, tastes, and sensations — and a lot more.

Seeing how certain factors affect mental consciousness

When people speak about the mind, they're generally referring to the sixth consciousness — mental consciousness. For example, if you think about your mother, even if she lives hundreds of miles away or is no longer living, you may say, "My mother has been on my mind lately." And if you think about her so strongly that her image appears to you, you're then *seeing* her — not with your *visual* consciousness, but with your *mental* consciousness. Or, as the old expression goes, you see her in your *mind's eye*.

This sixth consciousness functions in many different ways and affects everything about you, including the five sensory consciousnesses. For example, *attention* — the ability to turn your mind in a particular direction — is just one of the many different qualities associated with mental consciousness. While you're awake, all five types of sensory awareness continually receive information from your environment in the form of raw sensory data, but the amount of attention your mind pays to each piece of information in this constant stream of data can vary quite a bit.

As you read this book, for instance, you pay attention to the shape of the letters and words on the page with your visual consciousness. But how aware are you of the tactile (touch) sensations being produced as the chair (couch, bench, or patio swing) that you're sitting on makes contact with your buttocks? Pause for a moment and think about this. Until we directed your attention to these sensations just now, you were probably oblivious to them. (Of course, the situation would be different if you suddenly sat on a splinter. You wouldn't need anyone's help raising *that* kind of sensation to full awareness.)

This brief demonstration just goes to show that the quality of your sensory awareness varies greatly, depending on many factors. In some cases — such as when you look at optical illusions — you can completely mistake what you're aware of. Sense impressions are notoriously unreliable. But under certain very specific circumstances, you may experience a truly astonishing level of heightened sensory awareness. For example, professional athletes often speak about being "in the zone." When this happens, all the action (and time itself) seems to slow down, no matter how furious it may be. Athletes claim that they can see everything clearly, as if events were in super-slow motion. The entire playing field and all the other players come into sharp focus. Miraculous things can happen then.

Such dramatic changes result from an increase in your concentration, another aspect or function of your mental consciousness. *Concentration*, according to some Buddhist authorities, is the mind's ability to be steadfastly rooted in the present moment and remain fully aware of many objects. Similar to other mental abilities, concentration can be developed. Most of the time, your concentration is rather scattered — soft and fuzzy, like the light of an ordinary light bulb. By contrast, some master meditators achieve a particularly concentrated state of mind, *samadhi*, in which their mind is capable of gaining profound insights into reality. (People report that when Einstein was occupied with a particular theoretical problem, he would slip into a *samadhi*-like state of mind for long stretches of time. While in this state, he would remain motionless, oblivious to what was happening around him.)

Feeling around for your emotions

So far, in this introduction to the mind, we've emphasized certain mental activities — such as investigating and concentrating — but these activities are certainly not the only functions of the mind. Mental consciousness also includes your attitudes and emotional states, both positive and negative.

When Buddhists speak of mental development, they're not talking about becoming smarter. Mental development includes such practices as relaxing the hold that the "negative" states have on your mind and increasing the strength of your mind's "positive" qualities. (We put those words in quotation marks because "negative" and "positive" are just relative terms; don't think that one part of your mind is inherently "good" and another part inherently "bad.")

Tapping your emotional intelligence — to borrow a phrase that's become popular recently — is a large part of your mental and spiritual development.

MIND, HEAD, AND HEART

In the West, the tendency is to think of the various aspects of mental consciousness as residing in one of two locations: the head or the heart. Functions such as knowing, thinking, reasoning, remembering, and analyzing — in other words, functions that most people generally think of as mental in nature — are assigned to the head. If someone has sharp academic intelligence, for example, they're often called "a real brain." When people try to figure out a difficult problem or remember something they've forgotten, they often scratch their heads, as if this activity can somehow help them jump-start their thought processes.

The emotional center of your being, on the other hand, is often assigned to the heart. When caught in the grip of strong emotions, many people grab or beat their chest. Love, bravery, and a host of other feelings are commonly said to have their home there. In fact, the heart has become the symbol of romantic feelings (think of all those Valentine's Day cards), and the English word *courage* — a brave attitude of mind — is related to the French word *coeur,* meaning "heart."

(It's interesting to note that organs other than the heart have historically been considered the seat of different emotions. In Shakespeare's day, for example, people thought of the liver as the seat of passion. This usage survives today in the insult *lily-livered,* meaning "cowardly" or "timid." Additional expressions, such as "don't vent your spleen" and "you have a lot of gall," indicate that, at one time, specific emotions were associated with other internal organs.)

Note that this sharp distinction between the emotional nature of the heart and the more intellectual qualities associated with the brain and the head doesn't exist in Buddhism. The Sanskrit word *chitta* is translated as "mind," "heart," "attitude," or "consciousness," depending on its context. Similarly, the Japanese word *shin* can be translated as both "mind" and "heart."

Appreciating the Law of Karmic Cause and Effect

One of the most fundamental principles of Buddhist practice is being careful about your actions, words, and thoughts. Or, to put it another way, minding your karma. Most practitioners of South Asian religions (Buddhism, Hinduism, and Jainism) assume that your present life situation is the result of actions you committed in past lives. Your conduct in this life will have an influence on your future lives. In that sense you're ultimately responsible for your own life.

REMEMBER

Buddhists believe that when you behave in a certain way and with a certain intention, certain results will eventually follow. If you act compassionately, in a beneficial way driven by positive motivations, the long-term results you experience will be pleasurable. But if your behavior is harmful or downright destructive, harm will come back to you in the future. This pattern is called the *karmic law of cause and effect.*

Karma is similar to other types of cause-and-effect relationships, such as the relationship between a seed and a sprout. As a song from the long-running musical *The Fantasticks* says, if you plant a carrot, you'll get a carrot, not a Brussels sprout. Buddhist teachers even talk about planting the seeds of karma and experiencing the future results (or effects) in terms of these karmic seeds ripening.

But according to Buddhist teachings, the intentions that drive the actions are more important than the actions themselves. If you accidentally squash a bug, it is believed, you bring minimal or no karmic consequences to yourself because you didn't see it and, therefore, didn't mean to hurt it. But if you crush an insect deliberately, especially out of anger or malice, you'll experience the karmic consequences of your action.

REMEMBER

We're not talking about rewards and punishments here when we talk about karma. You're not a bad person if you cheat on your taxes or a good person if you help an old timer across the street. The law of karma doesn't carry that kind of judgmental baggage; it's much more practical and down to earth. The point is simple: If you act with aversion, you'll experience negative results in the future. If you act with love, you'll experience a positive outcome. Or, to continue the metaphor of the seeds: As you sow, so shall you reap.

WARNING

According to popular notions, karma can develop (or ripen) in a number of ways. For example, consider an extremely negative action, like brutally and angrily murdering someone. According to some Buddhist traditions, if you don't cleanse yourself of this powerful negativity — in other words, if you don't purify this karma — you can experience its results in any or all of the following ways:

- It is believed that in this lifetime, you may experience painful, turbulent emotions such as guilt, terror, and more rage. And because of the negativity you project, you're more likely to be the victim of a violent act yourself.
- After this life, you may be reborn in a realm filled with extreme suffering.
- When you're born as a human again, you may have a short life filled with sickness and other difficulties.
- In your future life as a human, your surroundings won't be conducive to good health. For example, food will lack nutrition and medicines will lack the power to cure disease.
- Even as a young child in a future life, you may display a sadistic nature — taking delight in killing small animals, for example. With this kind of negative predisposition to harm others, you continue to plant the seeds for more suffering in the future. Of all the results of negative karma, this outcome is the worst because it just perpetuates misery for yourself and others.

Another reason karma can be difficult to understand is the time lag between the cause and its effect. This delay is the reason that cruel, corrupt people may thrive (at least temporarily) while compassionate, ethical people may suffer. A tremendous amount of time may pass between your action (cheating someone) and the reaction you experience (someone cheating you).

The same idea is also true for positive actions; the results may take a long time to show up. Even though some karmic effects ripen rather quickly, you don't experience most of the outcomes for one or more lifetimes! Talk about waiting (and waiting) for the other shoe to drop. As one Buddhist teacher is fond of saying, if your own back began to break just as you started to crush a bug, no one would have to warn you to stop. The connection between cause and effect would be obvious to you, and you'd naturally change your behavior. Unfortunately, the law of karma doesn't necessarily provide such immediate feedback.

Following the Buddha's Ethical Guidance

According to tradition, as Shakyamuni Buddha sat under the Bodhi tree on the night of his enlightenment, his mind achieved an extraordinary level of clarity. Among other things, he saw the pattern of cause and effect in his previous lives. He saw how his actions in earlier lifetimes led to results he experienced in later ones. Buddhists believe that he was able to perceive this pattern as clearly and directly with his mind as you can perceive colors and shapes with your eyes.

When the time came for him to provide spiritual guidance, the Buddha was able to see how the law of karmic cause and effect also shaped the lives of others. He could see the exact historical causes of their current problems and understand the reasons behind their good fortune. Because he understood their past so well, he intuitively knew the most effective way for each of them to progress spiritually. You may say that because the Buddha saw how each person tied their own karmic knots, he gave precise advice on the best way to untie them.

Buddhist texts give extensive guidelines that regulate the conduct of monks and nuns. Fully ordained monks and nuns must follow a large set of rules. Lay practitioners generally follow a number of ethical guidelines, or *precepts*, as outlined in the next section.

Exploring the Buddhist precepts

The five basic precepts recited by laypeople throughout the Buddhist world are probably the simplest and most universal place to start:

- I undertake to abstain from taking life.
- I undertake to abstain from taking what is not given.
- I undertake to abstain from sexual misconduct.
- I undertake to abstain from false speech.
- I undertake to abstain from taking intoxicants.

Different traditions have embellished these five precepts in their own unique ways. For example, in the Theravada tradition, novices in a monastery first take eight precepts (with the lay vow to abstain from sexual misconduct changing to abstaining from any sexual conduct); later, they take ten precepts, adding the following to the initial five:

- I undertake to abstain from eating at the wrong time (that means, after midday).
- I undertake to abstain from dancing, singing, instrumental music, and watching shows.
- I undertake to abstain from using garlands, perfumes, cosmetics and adornments.
- I undertake to abstain from using high or luxurious beds.
- I undertake to abstain from accepting gold and silver (now commonly interpreted as referring to money).

In Zen and certain other East Asian Buddhist traditions, the ten *grave precepts*, which are followed by both monks and nuns and laypeople, consist of the universal first five plus the following:

- Refrain from speaking of others' errors and faults.
- Refrain from elevating yourself and blaming others.
- Do not be stingy.
- Do not give vent to anger.
- Do not defile the Three Jewels of Refuge (the Buddha, Dharma, and Sangha).

The full precepts ceremony as part of a layperson's ordination or formal entry into the practice of the *bodhisattva* precepts (see Book 3, Chapter 4) includes the three refuges of the Buddha, Dharma, and Sangha, the three pure precepts (do not create evil; practice good; and actualize good for others), as well as the ten grave precepts.

Arranging the precepts behind three doors

In the Vajrayana tradition, the ten primary precepts, which are quite similar to Zen's precepts, are described as the ten *nonvirtuous actions* to avoid if you want to stop suffering. (The ten virtuous actions are simply the opposite of these nonvirtuous actions.) The Vajrayana tradition arranges these actions according to the three doors through which you make contact with your world:

- **Door number one.** The three actions of your body:
  - Killing
  - Stealing
  - Sexual misconduct
- **Door number two.** The four actions of your speech:
  - Lying
  - Divisive speech
  - Harsh speech
  - Idle gossip

» **Door number three.** The three actions of your mind:

- Craving
- Aversion
- Delusion

REMEMBER

Buddhist teachings don't reveal the workings of cause and effect or identify actions to be avoided to scare practitioners. Their goal is to protect people from unwanted suffering.

IN THIS CHAPTER

» Glimpsing the early life of Prince Siddhartha

» Leaving the royal life behind

» Becoming the Buddha

» Practicing what he preached

» Waiting for the future Buddha

Chapter 2

Surveying the Life and Teachings of the Historical Buddha

Gautama the Buddha, whose teachings the different schools of Buddhism developed, is thought to have lived in the fifth century BCE. We don't know when he was born, but tradition holds that he died at age 80. Scholars are still debating the year of his death. Born Prince Siddhartha, the heir of a ruling family, he gave up the royal way of life in his search for an end to all suffering. This search eventually brought him to the foot of the famous Bodhi tree — *bodhi* means "awakening" or "enlightenment" — where he reportedly reached the awakening of Buddhahood at the age of 35. This awakening earned him the title Buddha ("Awakened One"). He is also known as Shakyamuni, Sage of the Shakyas (Shakya was the name of the clan to which he belonged). He then spent the remaining 45 years of his life teaching those who were drawn to the path that leads from suffering and dissatisfaction toward genuine spiritual fulfillment.

On one level, Buddhism is the record of these vast and profound spiritual teachings. (On another level, of course, it's the living embodiment of these teachings in the lives of spiritual practitioners through the ages, including right now.) The accounts of the Buddha's life date many centuries after his death and include many legends. This legendary material includes inspiring teachings attributed to Shakyamuni. As in the case of Jesus (more on him in Book 5, Chapter 1), Shakyamuni's life story has been told repeatedly during the past 2,500 years, and each culture Buddhism has entered has responded to his life in its own distinctive way.

In this chapter, we give you a glimpse of the Buddha's basic teachings and some of the most significant and inspiring episodes in his life story as it has been passed down through the ages.

The historical Buddha is known by different names, though we have mostly referred to him as Shakyamuni (Sage of the Shakyas) thus far. Texts also refer to him as the ascetic *Gotama* (Pali) or *Gautama* (Sanskrit), Gotama/Gautama being his family name. His personal name was Siddhartha (Sanskrit; Pali: *Siddhattha*, meaning "he whose aim is accomplished"), or according to some traditions, *Sarvarthasiddha* (Sanskrit: "all aims accomplished"). After his enlightenment, he became known by the title *Buddha* (Sanskrit: "Awakened One").

Revealing the Buddha's Early Life

Even within the traditional forms of Buddhism, you can find different ways of interpreting the events in the Buddha's life and the meaning of his enlightenment.

- An early tradition teaches that Shakyamuni was an ordinary person like you and me who happened to have uniquely favorable life circumstances (that is, plenty of spare time and energy) and an unflagging dedication to achieve full spiritual realization. This characterization suggests that, like him, you also can attain enlightenment.
- Many traditions believe that Shakyamuni began his spiritual journey a long time before his lifetime (in the fifth century BCE) and achieved significant levels of realization, but he didn't actually complete his journey until he sat under the Bodhi tree in the 35th year of his historical lifetime.
- Some traditions claim that the person who was honored as Shakyamuni actually achieved Buddhahood (that is, complete and supreme enlightenment) during a previous lifetime. He then hung out with a host of other Buddhas until the time came for him to descend to earth and demonstrate to others the spiritual path that he'd already completed.

Some traditions elevate the Buddha to mythic proportions and others view him as an exceptional human being, but they all agree that he exemplifies the ultimate fulfillment of the human condition: complete liberation from confusion and suffering.

DEALING WITH CONTRADICTIONS

The fact that you can interpret the Buddha's life story in different ways raises an interesting point. When you have two different and contradictory ways of explaining something, most people assume that if one explanation is right, the other must be wrong. For example, when you solve the equation $2 + x = 5$, you have only one correct answer; anything other than 3 is wrong. If you're in the habit of applying this strict "mathematical" approach to everything, the different ways of viewing the Buddha's life story may make you uneasy. "Only one of those interpretations can be correct," you may insist. "If he's a Buddha, he reached enlightenment either during his life as an Indian prince or before it. If one answer is right, the other must be wrong. So which is which?"

Buddhist teachers don't seem to feel uneasy at all about giving different explanations for the same event. We don't mean to imply that they're careless with the truth. A large part of their training involves keenly intelligent investigation of the nature of reality, so their thinking certainly isn't fuzzy. But they accept that the value of a particular explanation depends to a great extent on the intended beneficiary of that explanation. Because people have such different attitudes and inclinations from one another, the explanation that's best for one person may not be particularly helpful for another.

On one occasion many years ago during an interview, the Dalai Lama brought up the name of Tsongkhapa, a great Tibetan master born more than 600 years ago who had been the teacher of the very first Dalai Lama. Successive Dalai Lamas have always had the utmost respect and devotion for this particular master, and the current Dalai Lama — the 14th in this lineage — is no exception.

In general, Tibetans have great reverence for Tsongkhapa and think of him as a human manifestation of Manjushri, the *bodhisattva* of wisdom. But on this occasion, the Dalai Lama was reported to have said, "I prefer to think of Tsongkhapa as a regular human being who, through great effort, was able to complete the spiritual path in his lifetime. I find this way of thinking about him more inspiring than thinking that he was born already enlightened."

The various Buddhist traditions broadly agree on the events of Shakyamuni's life. To begin, they say, he was born the son and heir of King Shuddhodana of the Shakya clan in the northern part of the Indian subcontinent.

A miraculous birth

The Shakya clan lived in the part of the Indian subcontinent that lies in the southern part of present-day Nepal. The clan's leader, King Shuddhodana (shoe-*doe*-da-na), didn't have an heir to his throne. Then one night, his wife, Queen Maya (or Mahamaya), had a dream in which a beautiful white six-tusked elephant appeared to her and touched or entered her body. The wise men at court all recognized this dream as a sign that the queen was pregnant with a special child who would someday grow up to be a great leader.

Toward the end of her pregnancy, the queen left her husband's palace in the capital city of Kapilavastu and, with her entourage, headed for her parents' home to give birth — a custom that expectant mothers in many parts of India still follow today. As they passed Lumbini, the queen realized that she may give birth at any minute. So she entered the Lumbini grove and, while standing and holding on to the branch of a tree, gave birth to her son in a miraculous way: He emerged from the right side of her body without causing any pain. The child took seven steps and proclaimed that this was going to be his last life.

By all accounts, the child was extremely beautiful, although you'd expect nothing less from the protagonist of this story. Numerous promising signs accompanied his birth, and in recognition of this, his proud father named him *Siddhartha* (sid-*hart*-ta), which means "he whose aim is accomplished." In some Buddhist traditions, the name appears as *Sarvarthasiddha* ("all aims accomplished").

Shortly after Siddhartha's birth, Asita (a-*see*-ta), a widely respected senior religious hermit, unexpectedly arrived in Kapilavastu. He, too, had seen the signs of an auspicious birth and had come to the royal household to check out the child for himself. King Shuddhodana greeted Asita with great courtesy and had the baby brought to him. Imagine, then, the proud parents' shock and fear when the old hermit burst into tears after taking a long look at their cherished boy.

But Asita quickly assured the royal couple that he hadn't seen anything wrong with the child, nor any signs that a disaster awaited him in the future. Quite the contrary! Asita said that the boy displayed remarkable qualities — qualities that would make him an even greater ruler than his father. And if Siddhartha were to leave the royal life and become a seeker of the truth, he would become even greater than a mere emperor: He'd become the source of spiritual guidance for the entire world!

As for his tears, Asita said, he was weeping for himself. All his life, he had wanted only to follow the spiritual path. But now that he'd met the one person who could reveal this path to him, it was too late. Asita knew that by the time Siddhartha was old enough to begin teaching, he himself would already have died.

An overprotective father

Asita's prophesy both encouraged and bothered the king. He wanted nothing more than to have his son inherit his throne and bring added glory to the royal family.

Afterward, when he was an old man like Asita, Siddhartha could retire to the religious life if he wanted. But the king's priorities were clear: His son was to become a powerful and universally admired monarch.

Although he showed signs of great intelligence early on, something in the young prince's character worried his father. The child, who was brought up by his aunt, Mahaprajapati Gautami (*maha-praja-patee gau-ta-mee*), after his mother died, was extraordinarily kind and sensitive, too gentle to be a ruler of nations. He wasn't interested in the rough games of his playmates and preferred to spend his time caring for the animals that lived on the palace grounds. In one famous episode, the prince saved the life of a swan that his mean-spirited cousin, Devadatta (day-va-*dah*-ta), had shot. (Throughout Siddhartha's life, Devadatta keeps reappearing as his jealous rival.)

REMEMBER

The king was afraid that Siddhartha's sensitive nature would lead him to abandon the royal life prematurely, so he did everything possible to hide the harsh realities of life from his son. For example, if a servant fell ill, the king removed the individual from the palace until the illness had passed. According to the stories, one of the king's gardeners was responsible for clipping and removing any flower the moment it began to wilt. In this way, the prince would be spared the pain of encountering even natural signs of decay.

The prince marries: Imprisoned in palaces of pleasure

Eventually, Siddhartha became old enough to get married and raise his own family. The king was sure that these responsibilities would keep him from abandoning the royal life, so he arranged an event where his son could meet the eligible young women in the area. (Think of the ball held in Prince Charming's honor in *Cinderella*, and you get the idea.)

At this event, Siddhartha met Yashodhara (yah-*sho*-da-ra), the daughter of a neighboring king. It was love at first sight for both of them. (Later, when fully enlightened, Shakyamuni explained this instant attraction by saying that he and Yashodhara had been married to each other in a number of previous lifetimes. They'd even mated for life as tigers at one point along the way!) But before they could marry and live happily ever after, Siddhartha had to prove that he was worthy of Yashodhara by defeating rival suitors in contests of strength and martial skill. As you may have guessed, Siddhartha was victorious, and he and Yashodhara celebrated a joyous wedding. Siddhartha was 16 years old at that time.

Soon Siddhartha and his bride were living in the three pleasure palaces (one each for the hot, cool, and rainy seasons) that his father had built for them. The palaces were all located in a vast park surrounded by a wall. In fact, the king had imprisoned Siddhartha in the palaces without the prince realizing it. Because everything and everyone inside these prisons was attractive and captivating, Siddhartha would surely never want to leave — at least, that was the king's plan. And when Yashodhara gave birth to a son, Rahula (rah-*hu*-la), the plan seemed complete.

Forbidden knowledge revealed: The four visions

But even the best-laid plans of courtiers and kings sometimes go astray. One day, a palace musician serenaded Siddhartha and his wife with a song about the beauties and wonders of the world. Intrigued by the descriptions, the prince asked his father for permission to journey beyond the palace gates to see for himself what was out there.

By this time, Siddhartha was 29 years old, and his father realized that the time had come for him to see the kingdom he would someday rule. So the king gave permission for the excursion, but not before he arranged for the removal of all unpleasant sites in the area of town that his son would visit. Finally, when everything was prepared, the prince and his charioteer, Chandaka (Sanskrit; in the Pali tradition: Channa), rode into town.

At first, the visit went very well. The people greeted Siddhartha with great joy and affection, and Siddhartha liked everything that he saw. But then Siddhartha and Chandaka ran into something that only the two of them seemed to notice — an unfortunate person who was bent over in pain and racked by cough and fever.

Siddhartha asked his charioteer to explain the meaning of this unexpected vision. "This is sickness, my lord," Chandaka replied. He then went on to explain that, sooner or later, nearly everyone experiences such disease and discomfort. The prince was startled upon realizing that, at any time, his family, friends, or companions, or he himself, could experience pain and misery. Suddenly, all his happiness and joy faded away, and he could think only about the suffering he'd just seen, a suffering that threatened everyone.

The next two times Siddhartha rode out into the city, he encountered even more disturbing sights: old age and death. The prince was devastated. He wondered how people could act so carefree and happy with the threat of sickness, old age, and inevitable death hanging over their heads.

Finally, on his fourth excursion, he discovered what he had to do. On this occasion, he saw a homeless wanderer. Despite his shabby appearance, the man possessed remarkable calm and determination. When the prince asked him who he was, the man replied, "I am one who has given up the household life to search for a way out of the suffering of the world." Siddhartha's destiny was suddenly revealed to him. He knew that he, too, would have to give up his way of life and devote himself completely to the spiritual quest.

Beginning the Quest

The four visions of sickness, old age, death, and a homeless seeker of truth (which we cover in the previous section "Forbidden knowledge revealed: The four visions") mark the beginning of the prince's spiritual quest. Their importance to the history of Buddhism is undeniable, and depictions of Siddhartha's crucial encounters with them often adorn the walls of Buddhist temples.

Renouncing the royal life

When Siddhartha knew that he could no longer stay cooped up within the confines of royal life, he went to his father and asked for his permission to leave. The king reacted as many fathers would in similar situations: He blew his stack! He forbade the prince from leaving and posted a guard at all the palace exits to prevent his departure.

But the prince was determined to go. Siddhartha wanted to hold his infant son in his arms before he left, but he decided against it, fearing that he'd awaken the sleeping Yashodhara. He silently made his way past the sleeping musicians, dancing girls, and attendants and went outside, where he roused Chandaka (his charioteer) and asked him to prepare his horse, telling him that he wanted to ride out that night. Chandaka was surprised, but he obeyed the prince.

All the people in the palace, including the guards, had fallen asleep (think of the scene in *Sleeping Beauty* in which everyone is suddenly overcome by drowsiness), so Siddhartha was able to escape. He and Chandaka rode through the night, and when they stopped, the prince told Chandaka to take his horse and his royal jewelry and return to the palace without him. Chandaka began to cry and asked what he should tell the prince's family, who were sure to be devastated. "Tell them," Siddhartha replied, "that I have not left because I do not love them. It is because I do love them all that I must find a way to overcome the sufferings of sickness, old age, and death. If I am successful, I shall return. If I am not, then death would have eventually parted us anyway." Chandaka could do nothing but return alone.

Siddhartha was now on his own, and the first thing he did was cast off the signs of royalty. He cut his long hair, exchanged his silk clothing for the rough garb of a forest dweller, and, renouncing his former way of life completely, went in search of someone who could help him in his quest.

After his great renunciation (see the sidebar "The meaning of renunciation," later in this chapter, for more details), Siddhartha met and studied with two renowned spiritual teachers, Arada Kalama and Udraka Ramaputra. He quickly mastered the meditation techniques they taught him, but he realized that, though helpful, the techniques were insufficient to bring him the complete liberation from suffering that he desired. He'd have to go deeper.

Going to extremes and discovering the middle way

Siddhartha heard of a forest in the kingdom of Magadha where *ascetics* (people who practice austerities to attain religious insight) often gathered to practice and immediately decided to join them. On the way, he caught the attention of the ruler of Magadha, King Bimbisara (bim-bi-*sa*-ra). The king was so impressed by the young man's demeanor and dedication that he asked Siddhartha to stay and help him rule. But Siddhartha politely explained that he'd already given up one royal position and had no desire to assume another. Bimbisara then told Siddhartha that if he ever found what he was looking for, he should return and teach it to him.

When Siddhartha arrived at the forest, he found five other ascetics already engaged in strict practices. The ascetics hoped to overcome suffering by winning complete control over their senses and enduring extreme pain and hardship. Siddhartha adopted these practices, and soon, his extraordinary concentration and determination convinced his new companions that if any one of them was going to reach the final goal, it would be the newcomer.

Thus began what later became known as the six-year fast. Siddhartha sat exposed to the elements day and night. He ate less and less, eventually consuming nothing but the few seeds that happened to blow into his lap. His body, once so glorious and attractive, became withered and shrunken. Eventually, the practice reduced Siddhartha to little more than a living skeleton, but still he persevered.

Finally, one day Siddhartha took stock of himself. He discovered that, in his weakened condition, he couldn't think as clearly as before; therefore, he was further from his goal than when he'd started six years ago. Tired and dirty, he decided to refresh himself in the nearby river but nearly drowned before he could pull himself out. As Siddhartha lay on the bank recovering, he realized that if he were ever going to succeed, he'd have to follow the middle way between self-indulgence and extreme self-denial. (Later this phrase, the *middle way*, took on more meaning and became the expression that the Buddha himself often used when referring to his teachings. Even today, Buddhism is widely known as the middle way that avoids all extremes.)

Siddhartha sat up again, and the wife of a local herdsman soon entered the forest with an offering for the local spirits. Her name was Sujata (*sue*-ja-ta), and she had often prayed to the spirits of the forest for a baby boy. Now that she'd given birth to the child she desperately wanted, she came to the forest with a bowl of specially prepared milk rice to thank the spirits for granting her wish. When she saw Siddhartha sitting there, she mistook him for the king of the spirits who had helped her and presented the nourishing offering to him with great devotion. When his five ascetic companions saw him accept this fine meal, they were deeply disappointed. Thinking that Siddhartha had abandoned his quest, they left the forest in disgust, determined to continue their practices somewhere else.

After he'd eaten and his body regained its radiance and strength, Siddhartha thanked the woman. He told her that he wasn't the spirit she thought he was; he was just a human being searching for the path that would end all suffering. And because of her offering, he felt that he was now strong enough to succeed.

THE MEANING OF RENUNCIATION

Long hair was one of the prominent signs of Indian royalty, and Siddhartha's decision to cut his hair symbolized his strong determination to change the entire pattern of his life and devote himself to the spiritual quest. Even today, the ceremony marking someone's formal decision to enter the Buddhist way of life often includes having a lock of hair snipped off, in imitation of the Buddha's great renunciation. Followers who choose to become ordained as a celibate monk or a nun have their entire head shaved, as a sign that they have completely renounced the life of a layperson.

But renunciation isn't really a matter of having your hair cut or changing your outward appearance in some other way. Nor does it mean that you necessarily have to give away your possessions.

The true meaning of renunciation is the decision to give up attachment. The cause of suffering and dissatisfaction is attachment, so you need to give up attachment. If you can possess something without becoming attached to it — without letting it become an obstacle to your spiritual progress or a waste of your time and energy — you don't need to give it up.

Sitting in the Shade of the Bodhi Tree: The Defeat of Mara

Siddhartha crossed the river and made his way to a large fig tree that later became known as the Bodhi tree — the Tree of Enlightenment. With some bundles of grass he'd received from a local grass cutter, he prepared a cushion and sat down with the confident determination that he wouldn't get up from that seat until he reached enlightenment.

The classical Buddhist texts describe what happened next with barely contained excitement. The accounts say that the world held its breath as the moment that would transform history approached. Siddhartha sat under the Tree of Enlightenment, and the gods rejoiced.

But not everyone was overjoyed. Mara the Tempter, the embodiment of all evil, was terrified. He knew that if Siddhartha gained enlightenment, his success would threaten the power that delusion holds over the world. Traditional texts use dramatic imagery to depict the events. As Siddhartha sat in meditation, the sons and daughters of Mara — the whole host of demonic interferences — began their attack, trying to disturb his concentration.

Violent storms of hatred arose, but beneath the Bodhi tree, all remained calm. The demonic forces unleashed a barrage of weapons, but they turned into flower petals that fell harmlessly at the feet of the determined meditator. Visions of the most enticing sensual delights then appeared to Siddhartha, along with images of his wife and son, but nothing could break his concentration.

Mara had just one weapon left: the seeds of doubt. Dismissing his legions, Mara appeared before Siddhartha and addressed him directly. "Show me one witness who can testify that you deserve to succeed where all others have failed," he demanded mockingly. Siddhartha responded wordlessly. He simply stretched forth his right hand and touched the earth, because the earth itself was the witness that Siddhartha had practiced the virtues (over countless lifetimes) that would now empower his attainment of Buddhahood. Mara was defeated and faded away like a bad dream.

It was the night of the full moon in the fourth Indian month (which falls in May or June of our calendar). As the moon rose higher in the sky, Siddhartha's meditative concentration deepened. He passed through different stages of deep meditative absorption. The fire of his growing wisdom burned away whatever layers of unknowing still obscured his mind. He directly and unmistakably perceived the stream of his past lives and understood exactly how past actions lead to present and future results. He saw how craving, the source of suffering, is rooted in ignorance. Gradually, he penetrated subtler levels of ignorance. Finally, as the moon was setting and the sun of the next day was rising, Siddhartha attained the ultimate goal: full and complete enlightenment. He was now an Awakened One, a Buddha.

Benefiting Others: The Buddha's Career in Full Gear

For seven weeks, Shakyamuni, Sage of the Shakyas, now known as the Buddha, remained in the vicinity of the Bodhi tree, absorbed in the limitless awareness only a fully awakened being experiences. According to traditional accounts, the Buddha thought that because no one else was likely to exert the extraordinary effort required to achieve the goal he'd attained, enjoying the fruits of enlightenment himself would be the best way to go.

As if in response to this unspoken thought, the god Brahma Sahampati appeared to Shakyamuni and, on behalf of the world, begged him to reconsider: "While it is true that beings' minds are obscured, the coverings of some are less thick than others. Certainly, there are those who can benefit from your realizations. For their sake, please teach us what you have learned." The Buddha agreed only after some hesitation. He was concerned that people would be unable to grasp the depth of his teaching.

Providing spiritual guidance: Turning the wheel of Dharma

When the Buddha thought about which individuals would be ready to receive his initial teachings, he first considered the two teachers he had studied with but realized that they had already died. So he chose his five former companions, who were continuing their strict ascetic practices without him in Sarnath, near the ancient Indian holy city of Varanasi.

The five ascetics were staying in the Deer Park at Sarnath when they saw the Buddha approach. Still believing that he'd given up the spiritual quest, they resolved not to welcome back this "quitter." But they couldn't help noticing, even from a distance, that a profound change had come over him. He radiated such peaceful assurance and benevolence that they had to greet him with great respect and offer him a seat of honor among them. Then in response to their request to reveal his experiences, he delivered his first formal teaching as an Awakened One, a Buddha.

Of all the activities of a Buddha, *turning the wheel of the Dharma* (giving spiritual instruction) is number one because an enlightened being is most helpful to others when providing instruction. As Shakyamuni himself later pointed out, a Buddha can't remove another's suffering the way you can remove a thorn from another's flesh. (If he could, everyone's problems would already be gone; the compassionate Buddha certainly would've removed them all by now.) But what a Buddha can do — and do with matchless skill — is reveal the path to others in ways that are best suited to each person's individual makeup.

Not every teaching that a Buddha gives is verbal. A Buddha provides spiritual inspiration and instruction by his presence and can convey great meaning even through silence. But during his lifetime, Shakyamuni Buddha did deliver many formal discourses, the first of which he gave at the Deer Park in Sarnath. The theme of this discourse was the *four noble truths*, a theme that he elaborated on and refined in the countless other teachings he gave during the remaining 45 years of his life. (The section "Understanding the Four Noble Truths," later in this chapter, delves into this subject in greater detail.)

Founding the community

As the Buddha had predicted, his five former companions were particularly ripe for spiritual instruction. Just a few words by the Buddha were enough to trigger deep insights into his teachings. They gave up all activities that the Buddha taught were harmful to the welfare of others and to their own spiritual evolution. They took ordination as monks and became the first members of the *Sangha*, the Buddhist spiritual community.

As more people became inspired by the Buddha's wisdom and compassion and benefited from his teachings, the community grew larger. This growth attracted the attention (and often aroused the jealousy) of other established teachers who, together with their own disciples, came to test and challenge the Buddha. Recognizing that the Buddha was indeed the real thing — a fully awakened master — many of the rival teachers and their followers became the Buddha's disciples. The spiritual community grew by leaps and bounds, eventually numbering in the tens of thousands.

In many respects, this community was quite revolutionary. The Buddha accepted disciples from all levels of society and treated them with equal concern and respect. His acceptance of women as disciples and his belief that they were as capable of spiritual development as men was equally unusual, given the male-dominated society of the time.

Knowing that the more conservative elements of Indian society would have great difficulty accepting a monastic community that included women, tradition has it that the Buddha hesitated for quite a while before ordaining any of his women followers. But eventually he established an order of nuns, and the aunt who raised him became its first member.

In addition to a growing community of monks and nuns, many laypeople became followers of Shakyamuni Buddha. One of these individuals was King Bimbisara of Magadha, the monarch who'd offered to share his kingdom with Prince Siddhartha before the six-year fast began. When the king became a disciple and patron of the Buddha, a large number of his subjects followed suit, and the Buddhist community suddenly grew even larger.

Eventually, the Buddha visited Kapilavastu, where he grew up and where many members of his family and clan still lived. Many of them became his followers, including his son, Rahula, who received ordination as a monk. His father, who'd wanted Prince Siddhartha to rule his kingdom, also became one of his son's disciples, though his pride in being known as the father of the Buddha hampered his spiritual progress somewhat. Devadatta (the Buddha's cousin and lifelong rival) also joined the community, but jealous of the Buddha's popularity, he eventually set himself up as a rival teacher, causing a split within the monastic community.

Listening to the Buddha's final message: All things must pass

Finally, at the age of 80, after a lifetime of selfless, compassionate service to others, Shakyamuni fell ill. He died at the village of Kushinagara. Yet even on the last day of his life, the Buddha continued to help others, clearing away the doubts a renowned ascetic named Subhadra had about the teachings and leading him onto the path to liberation.

Finally, with many of his disciples and the people of the nearby villages gathered around him, the Buddha spoke his final words, reminding them all of the essential truths he'd been teaching throughout his life:

> Decay is inherent in conditioned things,
>
> strive with vigilance.

Entering increasingly deeper meditative states, the Buddha died. Many of his followers were overcome by grief. But some — those who understood his teachings well — remained at peace. His disciples cremated his remains and placed his ashes within burial monuments *(stupas)* throughout the lands that he'd blessed with his presence.

Understanding the Four Noble Truths

In his first discourse at the Deer Park in Sarnath (see the section "Providing spiritual guidance: Turning the wheel of Dharma," earlier in this chapter), Shakyamuni introduced the *four noble truths*, the basis of all the rest of his teachings. The more you understand these four truths, the better you can understand what Buddhism is all about. They are the truths of

- Suffering
- The cause of suffering
- The cessation of suffering
- The path that leads to the cessation of suffering

The truth of suffering

The first of the four noble truths acknowledges the widespread experience of what is called *duhkha* in Sanskrit. (In Pali, the other ancient Indian language in which the Buddhist teachings are recorded, the term is *dukkha*.) This term is most commonly translated as "suffering," but it has a much broader range of meaning. In particular, *duhkha* conveys a sense of dissatisfaction about things not being the way you want them to be.

Certain experiences in life are so obviously painful and miserable that no one has any difficulty identifying them as suffering. For example, a headache isn't fun. When you have that familiar throbbing in your skull, sometimes all you can think about is how much you want the pain to go away. You demand relief immediately. And a headache is relatively minor compared to many physical illnesses.

Even when physical discomfort is absent, countless mental and emotional difficulties arise. In his teaching at Sarnath, the Buddha specifically mentioned that the following are unpleasant:

- Birth
- Aging
- Sickness
- Death
- Meeting with what you dislike
- Being parted from what you like
- Not getting what you want

From this list, it's clear that the term *duhkha* covers practically everything pertaining to the human existence.

But if Shakyamuni Buddha was as compassionate as he's made out to be, why did he draw attention to something as distasteful as suffering and make it the first of the noble truths? Partly because humans have such a large capacity for self-deception. Like the person who refuses to admit to himself that he has a life-threatening disease until it's too late to do anything about it, many people will do almost anything to avoid taking a close look at themselves and the way they truly live their lives. They just stumble along from one unsatisfactory situation to the next. Whenever they get a whiff of the flawed nature of their existence, they shrug it off and reach for another drink — or another cigarette, or TV show, or some similar distraction.

The Buddha's intention was to help people wake up from their denial and follow the path that leads to the cessation of suffering.

TAKING MYTH AND DOCTRINE WITH A GRAIN OF SALT

We mix the practical teachings of the Buddha, designed to help you deal with your suffering and confusion, with the mythology and Buddhist doctrines that have accrued over several thousand years. Though the elaborate stories and myths may inspire you to put the teachings into practice, you don't have to believe them to practice Buddhism. In addition, the Buddha himself didn't teach doctrine or dogma that he required his disciples to believe. Instead, he constantly encouraged them to question any concept, to make sure that it agreed with their own experience and understanding. Then he recommended that they put the ideas into practice, to make sure that they actually worked.

In one famous story about a poisoned arrow (see Book 3, Chapter 1 for details), the Buddha was asked a series of theoretical questions, such as whether the world is eternal. Instead of answering in his usual way, he remained silent. When pressed, he told the following story. Suppose someone shoots you with an arrow that you know to be laced with a fast-acting poison. Do you spend time trying to find out the name and caste of the archer, where he comes from, and of what materials his bow and arrow were constructed? Of course not. Instead, you act as quickly as possible to remove the arrow and find an antidote to the poison.

In the same way, argued the Buddha, pursuing the answers to certain theoretical questions that are irrelevant to your own salvation can be a waste of precious time when you've been shot with the poison arrow of greed, hatred, and ignorance — you have only so much time to put an end to your suffering!

THE TRUTH ABOUT THE FOUR TRUTHS

Many writers and teachers have their own favorite English translations for the key terms that crop up repeatedly in the traditional Buddhist texts. For example, when talking about what's known as *dana* in both Pali and Sanskrit — the two major Indian Buddhist languages — one person may call it "generosity," another "charity," a third "giving," and a fourth "open-handedness." Plenty of other examples of the translation question abound. For instance, although *patience, tolerance,* and *forbearance* mean quite different things in English, they've all been used to translate the Sanskrit term *kshanti,* one of the main antidotes to anger. Even the Sanskrit word *duhkha* (*dukkha* in Pali), which is central to Buddha's teachings and has generally been translated as "suffering," has been rendered as "misery," "dissatisfaction," "stress," and even "oppression."

But very little variation is found from one writer to the next when it comes to the four noble truths. Almost everyone refers to them simply as the *four noble truths.* Yet something is misleading about this phrase. These words seem to imply that suffering, its cause, and so on are themselves noble, but this isn't the intended meaning at all.

The terms can be translated and interpreted in several ways, including the following:

- The truths of the noble one (the Buddha)
- The truths for the nobles
- The truths that ennoble (a person)
- The noble truths

In the Buddhist scheme of things, an *arya* (a noble one) is someone who has peeled away the layers of misconception blanketing the mind and who can, therefore, for the first time look upon ultimate reality directly. With this clear understanding, certain truths that previously had been hidden from view finally appear directly and unmistakably. So the four noble truths are actually the four things that the noble one (the Buddha) sees as true. But we stick with the more compact term *four noble truths,* the conventional translation of these terms.

The truth of suffering's cause

Having pointed out how pervasive suffering is, the Buddha addresses the unspoken question, "Where does all this misery come from? What is its origin, its cause?" To answer this question, he states the second noble truth: All suffering, without exception, comes from desirous attachment or craving (Sanskrit: *trishna;*

Pali: *tanha*). In other words, as long as you allow insatiable desires for this and that to lead you around by the nose, you'll be dragged from one unsatisfactory life situation to the next, never knowing true peace and satisfaction.

In essence, the Buddha is saying that if you want to find the true source of your problems, you have to look inside yourself. Suffering isn't a punishment inflicted upon you by other people, life circumstances, or some supernatural force outside yourself. Nor does suffering come to you for no reason; suffering isn't a random occurrence in a meaningless universe governed by the laws of chance (even if it has become fashionable to think so). Instead, the suffering or dissatisfaction that you experience is directly related to attitudes that arise within your own heart and mind. (See Book 3, Chapter 1, where we discuss the karmic laws of cause and effect in more detail.)

You can get an idea of the relationship between attachment and dissatisfaction by thinking of some common, everyday occurrences. For example, many people head for the nearest mall when they feel restless or dissatisfied. They look for something, anything, that can fill the hollow feeling inside of them. Perhaps they spot a shirt and think how great it'll look on them. They begin to fantasize, imagining how this piece of cloth will bolster their self-esteem, make them attractive to others, and perhaps even help them catch the person of their dreams and change the course of their lives!

This example may seem exaggerated, but that's exactly what desirous attachment does. It exaggerates everything. You cling to your possessions, your appearance, and other people's opinions of you in the hopes of satisfying a deep inner longing. But the more you cling, the more disappointed you become. Why? Because everything is constantly changing, and nothing can possibly live up to the unrealistic expectations you place on it. You may walk out of that mall holding the new dress or sweater you just bought, but you're really grasping an illusion. And sooner or later — usually sooner — the illusion will let you down.

REMEMBER

So the problem isn't the piece of clothing or even the fact that you find it attractive and derive pleasure from it. The problem is your attachment to it and the unrealistic expectations this attachment can cultivate. All the grief that you experience afterward — when the dress or shirt reveals its impermanent nature by fading, fraying, or going out of style — is the direct result of your clinging.

When the Buddha spoke about desire, or clinging, as the cause of suffering, he was thinking of a lot more than the effects of mall fever. Ultimately, he was talking about the way all unenlightened beings (that is, all people who've not yet fully awakened to reality — see Book 3, Chapter 5 for more on the meaning of enlightenment) cling to an unrealistic image of who and what they are. Behind the thought, "I hope I look attractive in that shirt," is a much deeper level of grasping for one's overly concrete sense of "I" itself. By clinging to this false sense of self, you not only set yourself up for disappointment and suffering as you go through this life, but you also condemn yourself to wander endlessly from one unsatisfactory life to the next.

The truth of suffering's cessation

The third of the noble truths is the Buddha's bold declaration that there's indeed an end to suffering. (What a welcome relief after the first two rather sobering truths of suffering and its cause!) We're not talking about just a brief vacation from the cycle of dissatisfaction; we're talking about a complete cessation. The Buddha was confident in this declaration because he'd experienced this liberation and saw clearly that nothing prevents everyone else from doing the same.

REMEMBER

Because suffering comes from desirous attachment or craving, eliminating craving leads to an end of all suffering. Craving, according to the Buddha, is eradicated by removing its cause, which is defined as ignorance (Sanskrit: *avidya*). The complete cessation of suffering is nirvana (Sanskrit). Book 3, Chapter 5 explains this complex term, meaning "extinguishing," in detail. Here it means the complete eradication of greed, hatred, and delusion.

The truth of the path

The fourth and final noble truth contains the do-it-yourself instruction manual that leads to the cessation of suffering and the experiences of spiritual liberation and enlightenment that go along with it. (See Book 3, Chapter 5 for more about the various levels of spiritual attainment.) These instructions are presented in terms of the eightfold path, symbolized by the eight spokes of the wheel of Dharma, which we outline later in this section.

REMEMBER

The spiritual life, whether Buddhist or otherwise, is often referred to as a path because it leads you where, in your heart of hearts, you want to go. But don't make the mistake of thinking that this path is outside you. As with the cause of suffering, the path that leads to the highest spiritual goals is within you — in what you think, say, and do.

With this in mind, consider the eight divisions of the path leading to the cessation of suffering:

- **Right view:** The path begins when you see for yourself that suffering and dissatisfaction infect the entirety of ordinary, unenlightened existence and when you understand the four noble truths.

- **Right intention:** Right intention — or right thought — involves giving up selfish attitudes that lead to further suffering and replacing them with their opposites. In place of thoughts that cause harm to yourself and others, you cultivate the intention to bring happiness to all.
- **Right speech:** Because what you say can have a powerful effect on others and can affect your own spiritual evolution as well, cultivating right speech is important. This cultivation involves speaking words that are true and not hurtful, as well as refraining from idle chatter.
- **Right action:** Just as right speech means to avoid causing harm with what you say, right action means to avoid causing harm with what you do. So in place of physically hurting others through your actions, you seek to help and protect them. In particular, you refrain from killing, stealing, and engaging in sexual misconduct.
- **Right livelihood:** You can earn your living in many different ways, but if you're intent on gaining more than just material wealth, avoid occupations that involve harm and deception. Naturally, a profession in which you can be of service to others is an excellent way of supporting yourself. But even if you don't have that kind of job, you can make sure that your dealings with others are honest and kind.
- **Right effort:** This type of effort concerns your spiritual practices. Instead of being lazy, exert continuous yet relaxed (some would say effortless) effort to be aware of what's arising in your mind. If it's negative, don't let it overwhelm you; if it's positive, rejoice!
- **Right mindfulness:** Mindfulness — paying close attention to what's happening right now — is essential at all levels of spiritual practice. *Mindfulness* here means constant awareness with reference to the body, the feelings, the mind, and psychic factors that lead to bondage or release.
- **Right concentration:** To develop deep insight into the nature of reality, the focus of your mind must become sharp and free of distraction and dullness. Through practicing one-pointed concentration, you will eventually be able to attain the four meditative absorptions (Pali: *jhana*).

Those elements, in brief, are the major elements of the Buddhist path, but later masters elaborated upon them and shaped them into the various Buddhist traditions that have appeared over the past 2,500 years.

THE BUDDHA IMAGE

We don't have any idea what the Buddha looked like. In early Buddhist art, the Buddha wasn't shown in human form. Symbols, such as a wheel, a set of footprints, or the Bodhi tree, indicated his presence. The earliest Buddha images originated only several centuries after the Buddha's death, around the first century CE. They were manufactured in two places: in the region of Gandhara (in the northwestern part of the Indian subcontinent) and in Mathura (in the northern part of the subcontinent). The images from Gandhara are stylistically influenced by Greek art. Later artists depicted the Buddha with specific physical signs. These include the 32 marks of a "great man," such as elongated ear lobes, a small circle of hair between the eyebrows (Sanskrit: *urna*), and a protuberance (Sanskrit: *ushnisha*) on the top of his head. The Buddha's hands frequently display meaningful gestures, such as the gesture of turning the wheel of the teaching; the meditation gesture, with both hands cupped and placed palms upward in the lap; the gesture of invoking the earth as a witness, with one hand touching the ground; or the gesture of protection, with the palm of one hand turned toward the devotee. Buddha images vary in style among Asian countries. Buddhists worship them widely, often with elaborate rituals.

Tradition has it that the Buddha recollected his past lives when he became enlightened. These lives, in which the Buddha strove as a *bodhisattva* (a being who has vowed to attain enlightenment), mostly in animal or human form, to acquire the moral perfections *(paramita)*, are the subject matter of the Jataka tales, a specific genre of Buddhist literature. These stories are extremely popular and are frequently represented in sculpture and painting.

Envisioning the Future

Shakyamuni Buddha never said he was unique.

When one of his disciples praised him extravagantly, claiming that no one anywhere was like him, the Buddha admonished him, pointing out that the disciple had no way of knowing whether the statement was true. "Instead of praising me," the Buddha suggested, "it would be far more beneficial for you simply to put my teachings into practice."

Some Buddhist traditions believe that Buddhas repeatedly appear in different times and in different places throughout the universe to help awaken those who are ready to benefit from spiritual instruction. In Theravada Buddhism, Shakyamuni is considered the 25th in the succession of Buddhas. Dipankara was the first Buddha. It is said that Shakyamuni, as the brahmin youth Sumedha in his former life, worshipped Dipankara and resolved to become a Buddha. (The past lives of Shakyamuni are described in the Jataka tales, a genre of Buddhist literature.)

Maitreya (also known as Maitri) is believed to be Shakyamuni's successor, the future Buddha in this world. We deal with this 26th Buddha in the next section.

The advent of Maitreya

TECHNICAL STUFF

The name Maitreya comes from the Sanskrit word *maitri*, which means "loving-kindness." Maitreya received his name because loving-kindness — goodwill — was his main spiritual practice. (In Pali, the term for this virtue is *metta*.)

The future Buddha Maitreya is a source of inspiration and hope for many of Shakyamuni's followers. Realizing that they may not be able to complete the spiritual path in their present lifetime, they pray to be reborn in the first circle of Maitreya's disciples when he reappears as a Buddha, to complete their training under his guidance.

Different beliefs abound concerning when Maitreya is due to reappear on earth. Some people think that he won't be here for several thousand years, but others say the wait is just a matter of a few hundred years.

All this speculation aside, some traditional Buddhist sources say that Maitreya currently resides in Tushita Heaven. He'll remain in this cosmic way station (as Shakyamuni did before him) until the proper moment arrives for him to descend to the human realm to be born.

Degeneration followed by hope

According to considerably later accounts, the era of Shakyamuni's teachings is half over; in another 2,500 years, the Dharma he introduced will disappear from this planet completely. As the times grow more degenerate — in other words, as hatred, greed, and ignorance increase in strength — the world will be transformed into a battlefield. Epidemic diseases and natural calamities will become more severe and frequent, and people will begin dying of old age while they're still relatively young.

When things become as bad as they're bound to get and people have grown stunted and deformed by their overwhelming negativities, Maitreya will show himself.

Although fully enlightened, he won't appear as a Buddha at first. He'll simply show up as someone taller and more attractive than everyone else. Impressed by his beauty, people will ask him how he got to be so good-looking. He will reply, "Through the practice of morality, avoiding giving harm to any living being."

As more people are inspired to take up the practice of morality and loving-kindness, the age of degeneration will come to an end. Peacefulness will replace belligerence, and as a result, people's life span, health, and general good fortune will increase. Finally, when all the proper conditions are in place and potential disciples are sufficiently ripe for guidance, Maitreya will reappear as a glorious wheel-turning Buddha and usher in the next golden age of Dharma.

IN THIS CHAPTER

» Making your way through the initial levels of involvement

» Checking out the Buddhist teachings to see if they interest you

» Committing yourself to Buddhism as a lifelong path

» Considering the wholehearted path of the monk or nun

Chapter 3
Turning to Buddhism

When you know a little something about Buddhism (conceptually, at least), you may want to explore the teachings in greater detail — and perhaps even sample a Buddhist practice or two for yourself. But where do you go and what do you do to get started? "Do I need to shave my head and run off to some monastery in the forest?" you may wonder. "Or can I get a taste of Buddhism right here at home?"

Buddhism comes in many shapes, sizes, and flavors, and a Buddhist center is more than likely located somewhere near you. (So the answer is, no, you don't have to head for a monastery just yet.) But before you get on the Internet to locate your closest center, you may want to read the rest of this chapter. Why? Because we think you'll enjoy it. And because this chapter offers guidelines for approaching Buddhism gradually and thoughtfully — from your initial contact, through progressive stages of involvement, and on to the (altogether optional) moment of formally becoming a Buddhist.

Proceeding at Your Own Pace

When you first start exploring Buddhism, remember that the Buddha wasn't technically a Buddhist. In fact, he didn't consider himself a member of any religion — he was a spiritual teacher who traveled around sharing some important truths about life. So you don't have to be a Buddhist, either. Buddhists and non-Buddhists alike can enjoy and put into practice the many valuable teachings that the Buddha and his disciples have provided over the centuries.

TIP

Even one of the best-known Buddhists in the West today, the Dalai Lama, advises that you don't have to change your religion to benefit from the teachings of Buddhism. In fact, the Dalai Lama generally discourages seekers from other faiths from becoming Buddhists — at least until they've thoroughly explored the tradition into which they were born. When asked to identify his own religion, the Dalai Lama frequently responds quite simply, "My religion is kindness."

REMEMBER

The message of Buddhism is clear:

- Proceed at your own pace.
- Take what works for you and leave the rest.
- Most important, question what you hear, experience its truth for yourself, and make it your own.

"Ehi passiko," the Buddha was fond of declaring. "Come and see." In other words, if you feel an affinity for the teachings of Buddhism, stay for a while and explore them. If not, feel free to leave whenever you want.

Taking responsibility for your own life

REMEMBER

Ultimately, you're responsible for deciding how you spend your life. In Buddhism, no guru or god watches over you, prepared to hand out punishment if you stray from the path.

The Buddha never insisted that his followers, even those who chose to join the monastic order by becoming monks and nuns, remain physically close to him or the rest of the spiritual community. Many of his followers wandered from place to place, meditating and sharing their understanding with others. They gathered just once each year during the rainy season to meet, receive teachings, and practice them together.

At the heart of this approach is the understanding that life itself provides the motivation you need to turn to Buddhist practice. If and when you pay close attention to your circumstances, you may gradually discover that the Buddha had it right: Conventional life is marked by dissatisfaction. You suffer when you don't get what you want (or you get what you don't want). Often your happiness doesn't depend on external situations; it depends on your state of mind. When you realize these simple but powerful truths, you naturally look for a way out of your suffering.

Some traditions of Buddhism encourage followers to fuel their motivation — and, therefore, their devotion — to practice by remembering certain fundamental truths. The Vajrayana (the "Diamond Vehicle") refers to these truths as the *four reminders*, which we outline in the following list.

- **Your human rebirth is precious.** Because you now have the perfect opportunity to do something special with your life, don't waste it on trivial pursuits.
- **Death is inevitable.** Because you won't live forever, don't keep putting off your spiritual practice.
- **The laws of karma can't be altered or avoided.** Because you experience the consequences of what you think, say, and do, act in a way that brings you happiness rather than dissatisfaction.
- **Suffering (or more broadly interpreted: the feeling of dissatisfaction) permeates all limited existence.** Because you can't find lasting peace as long as ignorance veils your mind, make efforts to win true release from suffering.

These reminders can keep you from being distracted by materialistic culture and its many seductive appeals to your craving, lust, and fear. They can help you stay focused on taking responsibility for your own happiness and peace of mind.

Determining your level of involvement

Given their emphasis on self-motivation, Buddhist groups naturally open their doors to all seekers at every level of involvement. Traditionally, teachings on Buddhism and meditation instruction are offered freely — and, generally, free of charge — to anyone who wants to receive them. (In return, offering some form of material support, such as money, is customary.)

You can attend Sunday services at many Christian churches without becoming a member or declaring yourself a Christian, and the same goes for Buddhism. You can receive meditation instruction, listen to teachings, and even participate in meditation retreats without officially becoming a Buddhist. Some well-known teachers, like the Indian *vipassana* (insight meditation) master S. N. Goenka, even hesitate to use the term *Buddhism* because they believe that the teachings extend well beyond the confines of any one religion and apply universally to everyone, whatever their religious involvement.

The Buddha is traditionally described as a great healer whose teachings have the power to eliminate suffering at its root. Like any compassionate healer, he shared his abilities with anyone who approached him, regardless of religious affiliation. But the Buddha also made it clear that you can't benefit unless you take the medicine — in other words, unless you put the teachings into practice.

Getting Acquainted with the Teachings of Buddhism

As so often happens with any involvement, people are drawn to Buddhism for a variety of reasons. For example, consider your favorite sport. Perhaps you learned to play it as a child, and you've been involved with it ever since. Or maybe a good friend turned you on to the sport later in life. Possibly you were inspired to learn by a spectacular match you saw on TV — perhaps by the enjoyment of a family member. Or maybe you simply saw a flyer about a class at a local rec center and decided you needed the exercise.

Believe it or not, people turn to Buddhism for similar reasons. The following examples illustrate that idea.

- Some people read a book or attend a talk by a particular teacher and get so captivated by the teachings that they decide to pursue them further. Other folks tag along with a friend, without knowing anything about Buddhism, and find themselves suddenly enthralled. Still others first seek out meditation practice because they've heard that it's an effective way to reduce stress or improve their health; as meditation begins to have its desired effect, these people read more and discover that the teachings also appeal to them.
- A few folks, like the Buddha himself, have an early insight into the universal suffering of human life and feel compelled to find a solution. Even more common are the many people who experience their own deep suffering in this lifetime, try other remedies (such as psychotherapy or medication, for example), and find only temporary relief. For these seekers, Buddhist teachings offer a comprehensive approach to identifying and eliminating the fundamental cause of their suffering.
- Some people, for whatever reason, believe that their purpose in this lifetime is to practice the teachings and that Buddhism is the tradition they were born to study.

Whatever your particular reasons for getting acquainted with Buddhism — all are equally valid and worthwhile — this initial stage of involvement can actually last a lifetime. Some devoted, long-time meditators choose to never formally declare themselves Buddhists, even though they've studied the teachings and engaged in the practices for most of their adult lives.

The following sections examine a few of the many possible ways to get acquainted with Buddhist teachings. We present them in the order in which they often occur, but you can begin getting to know Buddhism in any way you see fit. And you may keep returning to some, if not all, of these points of contact throughout your life.

Reading books on Buddhist teachings

TIP

Many excellent books on practicing Buddhist teachings are currently available, which makes this entry point a readily accessible and enjoyable place to start. You may want to stick to more popular fare at first instead of getting bogged down in the difficult language of the sutras or the riddles of the Zen masters.

At this stage of your involvement with Buddhism, you definitely want to keep your intellect engaged as you investigate and interpret the teachings. Does what you read make sense to you? Does it mesh with your experiences and understanding? Does it shed new light on the relationship between your thoughts, feelings, and experiences? As you read, make note of any questions you may have and make sure that they eventually get answered.

TIP

In the long run, books won't provide you with satisfying answers to all the deeper questions of life: Who am I? Why am I here? How can I realize lasting happiness? You may need to experience the answers directly for yourself, which is why Buddhism emphasizes putting the teachings into practice rather than merely speculating upon them intellectually.

Choosing a tradition

As you check out different books on Buddhism, you may find teachings and traditions that particularly appeal to you. Are you drawn to the practical, progressive approach of insight meditation (*vipassana*), which offers a variety of accessible practices and teachings for working with your mind? Or are you taken with the more enigmatic, formal path of Zen, with its emphasis on awakening here and now to your innate Buddha nature? Or maybe you're attracted to the elaborate visualizations and *mantras* of tantric Buddhism (*Vajrayana*), which use the power of the spiritual teacher and other awakened beings to energize your journey to enlightenment.

A few Buddhist traditions, such as the Pure Land schools, even de-emphasize meditation in favor of faith in the saving grace of Buddhist figures known as *bodhisattvas*. If you have a strong devotional nature, you may find one of those traditions particularly appealing.

If you came to the path through the influence of a teacher or friend, you may clearly feel that this person's tradition is the one you want to pursue. But if you're still shopping around, you may find it helpful to zero in on a particular approach before you take the next step of receiving meditation instruction. We're not saying that you can't shift directions at any point along the way or that basic Buddhist practices and meditation techniques aren't remarkably similar across traditions. But the styles of practice, which may differ only slightly at the outset, begin to diverge rapidly as you become more actively involved in a particular tradition.

Receiving meditation instruction

If you live in a large city, you may be able to locate a class on basic Buddhist meditation at your local community college or adult education center. Nowadays, Buddhist meditation also comes in a package known as Mindfulness-Based Stress Reduction (MBSR), a program developed by researcher and longtime Buddhist meditator Jon Kabat-Zinn (born in 1944), a retired professor of the University of Massachusetts Medical School.

As a method for reducing stress, MBSR introduces basic Buddhist teachings and applies the fundamental practice of mindfulness to reduce stress. Research has demonstrated that MBSR is effective in alleviating a host of stress-related health problems.

If you can't locate a basic class in Buddhist meditation (or if you're already drawn to a particular tradition), search the Internet for Buddhist centers and churches. Then be sure to ask whether they provide meditation instruction to the general public.

TIP

If you can't find what you're looking for under the heading "Buddhism," check for "Meditation" instead. Many vipassana and Zen groups that meet to sit together believe that this category more accurately describes what they do. After you make a connection, don't be afraid to ask a few questions to make sure that the organization teaches the kind of meditation you want to master. Then go ahead and take the leap!

Developing a meditation practice

REMEMBER

Expect to work on and develop your meditation practice for as long as you continue to meditate. Even the most accomplished meditators are constantly refining their technique. One of the joys and satisfactions of meditation is that it offers the opportunity for endless exploration and discovery.

In the beginning months of your encounter with meditation, your focus will be on finding the time and a suitable location to practice and on familiarizing yourself with the basics, such as following your breath or generating loving-kindness. You'll almost certainly have questions like the following:

- What do I do with my eyes or my hands?
- My breathing seems labored and tight. Is there any way to loosen it up?
- How can I keep from losing track of my breath entirely?

Having these kinds of questions is perfectly normal, which is why follow-up guidance is crucial. More people give up meditating because they lack proper guidance than for any other reason.

In addition to technique, the teachings of Buddhism inspire and inform the practice of Buddhist meditation. Attending talks, reading books on Buddhist teachings, and meditating regularly work in combination with one another. As your meditation skills improve, the teachings make more sense to you — and as your understanding of Buddhism progresses, your meditation naturally deepens.

Finding a teacher

You may be able to meditate quite happily for months or years without feeling the need for a teacher. After all, with all the books on Buddhism available these days, the most profound teachings are just a click away at an online bookstore (or a few miles away at an offline bookstore). Sure, you may already consult a meditation instructor every now and then or attend an occasional talk by a Buddhist teacher, but choosing someone to guide you on your spiritual journey — now, that's another level of involvement entirely!

REMEMBER

In the various Buddhist traditions, the role of teacher takes different forms.

- **Theravada:** The Theravada tradition of Southeast Asia, for example, regards the teacher as a *kalyana-mitra* (Sanskrit: good friend, spiritual friend). Essentially, they're a fellow traveler on the path who advises you to "go a little to the left" or "head right a bit" when you veer off course. Other than providing this type of input, a teacher has no special spiritual authority, aside from the fact that they may be more experienced than you. The words *preceptor* and *mentor* may be the best everyday English equivalents to describe this teaching role.
- **Vajrayana:** In tantric traditions (Vajrayana), the spiritual teacher has considerable authority over their disciples. Instead of merely standing witness to vows, they initiate their disciples, of whom strict obedience is expected. The life stories of many Buddhist saints illustrate this special teacher-student relationship. Naropa (ca. 1016–1100), one of the 84 Mahasiddhas ("great accomplished ones"), had to suffer many hardships during the 12 years he served his teacher Tilopa (tenth century). Likewise, the Tibetan yogi Milarepa (1040–1123), founder of the Kagyu lineage, was made to undergo a series of ordeals by his teacher Marpa (1012–1096). Best known is the story of the four stone towers that Marpa ordered Milarepa to build and which Milarepa was then asked to tear down before they were completed.

In the Tibetan traditions, teachers come in several shapes and sizes, including the following:

- **Meditation instructors:** These teachers provide expert guidance in developing and deepening your practice. They may be monks or nuns or merely experienced lay practitioners.
- **Lamas:** These teachers are often, but not always, monks. Lamas have extensive meditation training and accomplishment and are revered by their disciples as the embodiment of wisdom and compassion.
- **Geshes:** These teachers, who are usually monks, have extensive academic training and are experts in interpreting and expounding on the scriptures.

When you accept someone as your religious teacher, you're generally making a lifelong commitment. Although you can alter or terminate your involvement, developing hostility toward your teacher while you are in an active working relationship with them is believed to have serious negative karmic consequences (see Book 3, Chapter 1).

» **Zen:** In Zen, practitioners regard the teacher or master (Japanese: *roshi;* Korean: *sunim*) as having considerable spiritual power and authority. Disciples deem the master to be enlightened, with the capacity to awaken similar realizations in students through words, gestures, and bearing. Close personal study with a Zen master is an essential component of Zen practice and training. Zen also has its meditation instructors and junior teachers — but behind them all stands the spiritual presence of the master.

Ordinarily, the teacher you choose depends on the tradition that appeals to you. But sometimes the process works the other way around — you're drawn to a teacher first, through their books or talks, and then you adopt the tradition the teacher represents. An ancient Indian saying makes the point, "When the student is ready, the teacher appears."

Formally Becoming a Buddhist

You don't need to declare yourself a Buddhist to enjoy and benefit from Buddhist practices and teachings. Some traditions even reserve formal initiation for individuals who choose the monastic life and simply ask laypeople to observe a few basic precepts. But the step of becoming a Buddhist can have profound personal significance, solidifying your commitment to a teacher or tradition and energizing your practice. For this reason, many people consider taking this significant step at some point or another in their involvement with Buddhism.

Focusing on the importance of renunciation

Many people associate renunciation with giving up material possessions and involvements and pursuing a life of detachment and withdrawal. But true renunciation is an internal (rather than external) movement or gesture — although it can certainly express itself in action. In many traditions, becoming a Buddhist involves the fundamental recognition that *samsaric* existence — the world of getting and spending, striving and achieving, loving and hating, and so forth — doesn't provide ultimate satisfaction or security.

In other words, when you commit yourself to Buddhism as a path, you don't renounce your family or your career; you renounce the conventional view that you can find true happiness in worldly concerns. You renounce the relentless message of the consumer society that the next car or house or vacation or accomplishment will finally relieve your dissatisfaction and bring you the contentment you so desperately seek.

Instead, you adopt the radical view that you can achieve lasting peace and happiness only by clearing your mind and heart of negative beliefs and emotions, penetrating to the truth of reality, opening yourself to your inherent wakefulness and joy, and experiencing what some Buddhists have called the "sure heart's release."

Taking refuge in the Three Jewels

The same 180-degree turnaround in consciousness that's necessary to formally become a Buddhist lies at the heart of many of the world's great religious traditions. For example, Jesus (more on him in Book 5, Chapter 1) asked his disciples to renounce worldly concerns and follow him, and many Christian churches still require their members to acknowledge Jesus as their only salvation. In Buddhism, this turning (*metanoia,* literally "change in consciousness") often takes the form of taking refuge in the Three Jewels (or Three Treasures): the Buddha, Dharma, and Sangha. This is done by uttering the formula

> I take refuge in the Buddha.
>
> I take refuge in the Dharma.
>
> I take refuge in the Sangha.

This formula is repeated three times ("For the second time I take refuge. . .; for the third time I take refuge. . .").

REMEMBER

In many traditional Asian countries, taking refuge defines you as a Buddhist, and laypeople recite the refuge vows whenever they visit a monastery or receive Buddhist teachings. For Western lay practitioners, the refuge ceremony has become a kind of initiation in many traditions, with far-reaching significance. Although it may simply involve the repetition of a prayer or chant, taking refuge implies that you turn to the Buddha, Dharma, and Sangha as your source of spiritual guidance and support. When you encounter dissatisfaction and suffering, you don't immediately assume that you can resolve it by making more money, taking the right antidepressant, or getting a better job — although these can be helpful to a limited degree.

You instead reflect on the example of the enlightened teacher (the Buddha, who discovered the path to a life free from suffering), find wise counsel in his teachings (known as the *Dharma* in Sanskrit and *Dhamma* in Pali), and seek support in others who share a similar orientation (the Sangha, or spiritual community). Many Buddhists repeat their refuge vows daily to remind themselves of their commitment to the Three Jewels.

The ancient collection of Buddhist sayings, the *Dhammapada*, emphasizes the special nature of the threefold refuge in verses 188 to 192:

> Often do men, driven by fear, go for refuge to mountains and forest, to groves and sacred trees.
>
> But that is not a secure refuge, that is not the best refuge. Having gone to that refuge a man is not freed from all suffering;
>
> He who goes for refuge to the Buddha, the Dhamma, and the Sangha, sees the four noble truths with clear understanding;
>
> The four noble truths: suffering, the origin of suffering, the cessation of suffering, and the noble eightfold path that leads to the quieting of suffering;
>
> That is indeed the secure refuge, that is the best refuge. Having gone to that refuge, a man is freed from all suffering.

When you take refuge, you may appear to be relying on forces outside yourself for your peace of mind. But many great masters and teachers suggest that the Three Jewels are ultimately found inside you — in the inherent wakefulness and compassion of your own mind and heart, which are identical to the Buddha's.

Receiving the precepts

In addition to taking refuge, making a commitment to abide by certain ethical *precepts*, or guidelines, signifies an important step in the life of a Buddhist. Different traditions may emphasize either refuge or the precepts, but at their core, the traditions agree that both taking refuge and committing yourself to certain precepts mark a participant's entry into the Buddhist fold. You can read more about the precepts in detail in Book 3, Chapter 1.

But if you're a Vajrayana practitioner, for example, you generally formalize your involvement by taking refuge — and later by taking what are called the *bodhisattva vows,* in which you vow to put the welfare of others before your own. When you take refuge, you generally receive a Buddhist name to mark your new life as a Buddhist.

In the Zen tradition, you deepen your involvement by undergoing a ceremony in which you agree to abide by 16 precepts and receive a new name. (See Book 3, Chapter 4 for more on this ceremony.)

Interestingly enough, the Vajrayana refuge ceremony includes a commitment to act ethically, and the Zen precepts ceremony includes refuge vows. In the Theravada ceremony for becoming an *upasaka* (male lay practitioner) or an *upasika* (female lay practitioner), as conducted in certain communities in the West, participants ask to receive both the refuge vows and the precepts. Throughout Buddhism, refuge and precepts work hand in hand and reinforce each other.

Monks and nuns, for their part, adhere to a lengthy code of conduct (the *vinaya*) that includes hundreds of regulations.

Exploring further stages of practice

Traditionally, laypeople engage in devotional practices rather than in meditation. They chant and listen to religious sermons. They worship Buddha images with flowers, incense, and lights, and acquire religious merit (Sanskrit: *punya*) by making offerings to the community of monks and nuns. These can be offerings of food made to individual monks on an alms round or donations to the community. Rejoicing (Sanskrit: *anumodana*) in the merit earned by others is another way to acquire merit.

Generosity (Sanskrit and Pali: *dana*) is one of the *perfections* of the practitioner in Theravada and Mahayana Buddhism. It is said that Shakyamuni practiced generosity and the other perfections for many lifetimes before attaining enlightenment. The Jataka tales of his past lives illustrate this virtue through stories in which he gives away everything, including his own body, to help others. The famous Vessantara Jataka tells the story of the last life of Shakyamuni before he became the Buddha. He was born as Prince Vessantara who attained perfection in generosity by giving away all his possessions and even his wife and two children.

REMEMBER

Although some traditions of Buddhism believe that becoming a monk or nun tends to accelerate your spiritual progress, they all agree that you can achieve the pinnacle of Buddhist practice — enlightenment — whether or not you become a monastic. In particular, the Mahayana tradition offers compelling portraits of laypeople who were also great bodhisattvas, suggesting that you, too, can follow in their footsteps.

When you've become a Buddhist by taking refuge in the Three Jewels and receiving precepts, you devote the rest of your life to living according to these principles and teachings — not a small undertaking by any standards! In most Zen centers, everyone in the meditation hall, both monks and laypeople, chants some version of this bodhisattva vow in the Mahayana tradition at the end of meditation:

> Beings are numberless; I vow to save them.
>
> Mental defilements are inexhaustible; I vow to put an end to them.
>
> The teachings are boundless; I vow to master them.
>
> The Buddha's way is unsurpassable; I vow to attain it.

With these kinds of promises to inspire your meditation, you definitely have your life's work cut out for you. By setting your sights on lofty goals like compassion, selflessness, equanimity, and ultimately, enlightenment, you commit yourself to a lifetime of spiritual practice and development.

Of course, you're welcome to terminate your involvement in Buddhism at any time without karmic repercussions — other than those that may reverberate through your own mind and heart. (In the Vajrayana, after you become deeply involved with a teacher, forsaking your vows gets a bit more complicated.) In fact, in Southeast Asia, especially in Thailand, it's customary and considered spiritually beneficial for laypeople (and sometimes children) to shave their heads and become monks or nuns for a few days, weeks, or months. After practicing in the monastic community briefly, they give back their robes and return to ordinary, everyday life — indelibly changed by their experience!

Entering the Monastic Way

In a number of the world's great religious traditions, the monk or nun stands as the embodiment of the spiritual ideal — the one who has given up all worldly attachments and devoted their life to the highest pursuits. Although Buddhism acknowledges the merit of lay practice, it, too, has traditionally placed the highest value on the acts of shaving the head, taking the full monastic vows, and entering a monastic community.

People are drawn to monastic practice for the same reasons they're attracted to Buddhism in the first place: the desire to eliminate suffering, benefit other beings, and achieve ultimate clarity and peace. Add to this mix a certain distaste for (or downright abhorrence of) conventional worldly life, and you have a good feel for the monastic impulse. Of course, in some Asian countries, people become monks and nuns for other reasons as well, such as to escape worldly obligations, fulfill parental wishes, and so on.

Renouncing the world

When you take monastic ordination, you leave behind the comfort and familiarity of family and friends and enter an entirely new world where the old rules no longer apply. You give external expression to your inner renunciation by cutting off your hair (a mark of personal beauty and pride), giving up your favorite clothes, and letting go of your prized possessions. (Compare these acts with Shakyamuni Buddha's own renunciation, which we describe in Book 3, Chapter 2.) In essence, you strip yourself of the signs of your individuality and merge with the monastic collective, where everyone wears the same robe, sports the same haircut, sleeps on the same thin mat, and eats what is offered to sustain the body.

In the time of the Buddha (and in the traditions that continued to adhere to the full monastic code — the *vinaya*), monks and nuns were prohibited from handling or soliciting money and were allowed to own just a few simple belongings, which included items like several robes, a bowl, a razor, and an umbrella for protection from the sun. They took vows of celibacy, ate only before noon, and received their food from laypeople, either during alms rounds or through offerings brought to the monastery. The point of these regulations wasn't to cause hardship or suffering; in fact, the Buddha's approach was known as the "middle way" between asceticism (severe restrictions in the comforts of life) and materialism. Instead, the point was to free the monastics to dedicate their life to practice and teaching.

The vinaya regulations, which the Theravada tradition of Southeast Asia still follows, have been adapted somewhat in other traditions, such as Zen and Vajrayana. For example, in Japan (home to the Zen tradition), the priest, who has largely replaced the monk, trains for a period of months or years and then returns to his home temple to marry, raise a family, and serve the lay community. In Tibetan Buddhism, some lineages emphasize full monasticism (although they're not nearly as rigorous in their interpretation of the monastic code as their Theravada counterparts), but others encourage sincere seekers to combine married life and dedicated spiritual practice.

Ordaining as a monk or nun

The ceremony of ordaining as a monk or nun is a solemn and auspicious occasion marking the participant's entry into an order that dates back 2,500 years. In the West, ordination generally occurs as the culmination of years of practice as a layperson, although some people bolt from the starting gate like thoroughbred horses and head full speed for the monastery.

If you want to receive ordination, you must first ask a senior monk — often, though not always, your current spiritual teacher — for permission. Then you obtain the required robes, shave your head (in some traditions, you keep a lock to be shaved off during the ceremony itself), and set your life in order. During the ceremony, you recite the refuge vows and receive the appropriate number of precepts, depending on the level of your ordination and the tradition you follow.

For example, there are 16 precepts (including the three refuges) in the Zen tradition, 36 vows for the novice nun in the Vajrayana tradition, and 227 vows for the fully ordained monk in the Theravada tradition, just to name a few. After taking refuge and receiving precepts, you assume a new name (which, when translated into English, often expresses some aspect of the Buddhist path, such as "stainless love," "pure mind of patience," "holder of the teachings," and so on). At that point, you've crossed from one world into another, and your life as a monastic begins.

Dedicating your life to Buddhist practice

If you enter a Buddhist monastery, you do so because you're eager to devote all your time and energy to the practice and realization of the teachings. To accomplish your goals, you rise early, day after day, and follow a routine consisting exclusively of meditation, chanting, ritual, study, teaching, and work. You may have limited contact with the outside world (generally, monasteries are more open to lay practitioners at certain times of the year than at others), but for the most part, you turn your attention inward, toward spiritual matters.

In both their structure and purpose, Buddhist monasteries resemble their Christian counterparts. Western Buddhist monks have even become interested in the Rule of Saint Benedict, the official code that has governed Catholic (more on Catholicism in Book 5, Chapter 4) monasteries for centuries. Yet, whether the goal is to get closer to God or experience enlightenment, monasteries throughout the world have a remarkably similar role to play — they're places where people get to dedicate themselves wholeheartedly to truth.

WOMEN IN BUDDHISM

Like many religions, both Eastern and Western, Buddhism has traditionally failed to give women equal status with men. Buddhists over the centuries more or less mimicked the attitudes of their respective cultures, where women have traditionally been regarded as inferior and subservient. (The historical record does show that, despite the rampant sexism of the times, certain women emerged as accomplished *yoginis* — female practitioners of yoga — and masters.)

According to tradition, the Buddha created the female monastic order at the request of Mahaprajapati Gautami, his foster mother (see Book 3, Chapter 2), and his disciple Ananda. But the full monastic ordination for women (Sanskrit: *bhikshuni;* Pali: *bhikkhuni*) died out on the Indian subcontinent. It has survived only in certain Mahayana countries (including China, Korea, and Vietnam). Instead, women in the Theravada tradition like that of Myanmar who seek to practice as nuns receive ten precepts, as well as numerous other more informal regulations.

In recent decades, however, Western women Buddhists of every persuasion have strongly criticized the institutional sexism and required their teachers and communities to recognize their full equality. The result has been the rapid emergence of women as powerful practitioners, scholars, and teachers. Clearly, Western Buddhists, like their Eastern ancestors, are adapting to the culture of their times.

IN THIS CHAPTER

» Examining the function of monasteries

» Exploring practice in a Theravada monastery

» Extending Zen to everyday life

» Walking in the shoes of a Vajrayana practitioner

» Spending a day with followers of the Jodo Shinshu tradition

» Getting into meditation practices

Chapter 4

A Day in the Life of a Buddhist Practitioner

Buddhism evolved in Asia, grew into various different traditions, and made its way to the West. But how do you actually practice the Buddhist teachings? Sure, many Buddhists meditate, but how exactly do they meditate? What else do they do? How do they spend their time? How do their daily lives differ from yours?

In this chapter, we answer these questions by giving you a firsthand look at Buddhist practice through detailed day-in-the-life accounts of practitioners from four different traditions practiced today in the West. Buddhism comes in many different shapes and sizes, but the one thing that all these traditions have in common — and that makes them quintessentially Buddhist — is the importance they place on basic teachings. Examples of these teachings include the four noble truths and the eightfold path (see Book 3, Chapter 2), the three marks of existence (impermanence, no-self, and dissatisfaction), and the cultivation of core spiritual qualities such as patience, generosity, loving-kindness, compassion, and insight.

Surveying the Role of Monasteries in Buddhism

Buddhist monks and nuns have traditionally relinquished their worldly attachments in favor of a simple life devoted to the three trainings of Buddhism:

- **Moral discipline:** Ethical conduct
- **Concentration:** Meditation practice
- **Wisdom:** Study of the teachings and direct spiritual insight

To support these endeavors, monasteries are generally set apart from the usual commotion of ordinary life. Some monasteries are located in relatively secluded natural settings like forests and mountains; others are situated near or even in villages, towns, and large cities, where they manage to thrive by serving the needs of their inhabitants for quiet contemplation and the needs of lay supporters for spiritual enrichment.

REMEMBER

Wherever they're located, monasteries have traditionally maintained an interdependent relationship with the surrounding lay community. For example, in the Theravada tradition, monks and nuns rely exclusively on lay supporters for their food and financial support. The tradition prohibits monastics (a catch-all term for monks and nuns) from growing or buying food or earning or even carrying money. So monks and nuns often make regular alms rounds to local villages and towns (during which they receive food from their supporters) and open their doors to the laity to receive contributions of money, food, and work.

Likewise, Tibetan Buddhist monasteries are often situated near towns or villages. The monasteries draw both their members and their material support from these nearby communities. The exchange works both ways. The laity in both Tibet and Southeast Asia traditionally benefits from the teachings and wise counsel that the monks and nuns offer.

In China, the monastic rules changed to permit monks and nuns to grow their own food and manage their own financial affairs, which allowed them to become more independent of lay supporters. As a result, many monasteries in China, Japan, and Korea became worlds unto themselves, where hundreds or even thousands of monks gathered to study with prominent teachers. Here the eccentric behavior, paradoxical stories (Japanese *koan*; see the sidebar "Entering the gateless gate: *Koan* practice in Zen," in this chapter for more information), and unique lingo of Zen flourished. (See the section "Growing a Lotus in the Mud: A Day in the Life of a Zen Practitioner," later in the chapter, for more details.)

Despite their doctrinal, architectural, and cultural differences, Buddhist monasteries are remarkably alike in the daily practice they foster. Generally, monks and nuns rise early for a day of meditation, chanting, ritual, study, teaching, and work.

Renouncing Worldly Attachments: A Day in the Life of a Western Buddhist Monk

An excellent model of Buddhist monasticism in the West is Abhayagiri Buddhist Monastery, a Theravada monastery situated in Redwood Valley, in the woods of northern California, about a three-hour drive north of San Francisco. It is one of the main monasteries of the worldwide monastic community associated with Ajahn Chah, a Buddhist monk, teacher, and founder of two prominent monasteries.

Scattered around Abhayagiri's 280 forested acres are little cabins that house the monastery's fully ordained monks and junior monastics in training. As in the forest tradition of tropical Buddhist countries like Thailand, each practitioner has a sparsely furnished cabin for individual meditation and study.

The monastics at Abhayagiri didn't choose their strict lifestyle on a whim. The fully ordained monks began as novices by adhering to first 8 and then 10 precepts before they committed to the full *vinaya* (monastic discipline), consisting of 227 rules for restraint of body, speech, and mind. That's no small task, as you can imagine: Just memorizing and keeping track of all those rules can be a major undertaking! The monks recite the 227 rules on the full moon and new moon days to remind them of their conduct. After confessing any transgressions of minor rules, the monks assemble in close proximity while one monk recites the 13,000-word *Patimokkha* (Pali: *Monks' Code of Discipline*) in the ancient Pali language from memory. Another monk corrects any omissions or mispronunciations. During the 50-minute recitation, the monks may not leave the area nor may anyone else enter or the recitation must begin again. The tradition of reciting the *Patimokkha* has continued for more than 2,500 years.

REMEMBER

According to the rules laid down in the *Patimokkha*, monks must abstain from sexual activity of any kind and refrain from physical contact with the opposite sex. They can't eat solid foods after midday, sell anything, ask for or handle money, or go into debt.

Needless to say, these regulations shape monastic life in significant ways. For example, monks must rely on laypeople to deal with monastery finances, and they can't engage in any project unless the monastery has money on hand to fund it. No movies, no TV, no music, no midnight snacks. Most laypeople can't even begin to imagine a life of such utter simplicity and discipline! Yet Abhayagiri merely follows the time-honored model for Buddhist monastic life that's been passed down for thousands of years.

REMEMBER

Although Abhayagiri is a monastery devoted to the spiritual pursuits of its monks, laypeople come and go regularly to offer food, participate in practice, renew their precepts and refuge vows, and receive teachings from the resident instructors.

TIP

Men visiting for the first time can also arrange to stay at the monastery for up to one week, so long as they agree to follow the schedule and participate in practice. For people who've stayed at the monastery before, longer visits are possible. Because the monastery isn't very old (it was founded in 1996), accommodations are quite limited.

Following a day in the life

As a monastic at Abhayagiri, you follow a schedule that's typical of Buddhist monasteries the world over. You rise at 4 a.m. — well before the sun — shower, dress, and walk the half-mile from your cabin to gather with your colleagues at the main building for chanting and meditation, which begins at 5 a.m. For the first 20 minutes, you chant various scriptures that express your devotion to practice and touch on familiar themes, such as renunciation, loving-kindness, and insight. After taking refuge in the Three Jewels (the Buddha, Dharma, and Sangha), you meditate silently with the other monastics for an hour and then participate in more chanting.

Following chores from 6:30 to 7:00 a.m., you meet to discuss the morning work assignments over a light breakfast of cereal and tea. After you determine your responsibilities, you work diligently and mindfully until 10:45 a.m. and then don your robes for the main meal of the day, a formal affair that laypeople offer you. After you and the other monastics help yourselves, the laity take their share and eat with you in silence. Everyone helps wash up and put things away. You then spend the afternoon meditating, studying, hiking, or resting on your own. Remember, you've seen the last of solid food until 7 a.m. tomorrow morning — and private stashes are definitely not allowed!

Tea and fruit juice are served in the main hall at 5:30 p.m., followed by a reading of a Buddhist text and discussion at 6:30 p.m., and meditation and chanting at 7:30 p.m. Sometime between 9 and 10 p.m. you're off to your cabin to continue your meditation or to rest in preparation for yet another long day that begins at 4 a.m.

REMEMBER

Though fixating on the rigors and relative strictness of such a routine is easy, we want to emphasize the joy and fulfillment that accompanies a life of such purity, awareness, and devotion to truth. Without the many distractions of postmodern lay life, the subtle insights and revelations of the spiritual life come more quickly and easily into focus. That's why the Buddha recommended the monastic life and why so many devoted practitioners have followed his example.

Punctuating the calendar with special events

In addition to the regular daily schedule we outline in the preceding section, the lunar quarters (that is, the days corresponding to the quarter, half, and full phases of the moon) and the three-month rainy-season retreat punctuate the monastic calendar.

On the lunar quarters (roughly every week), you observe a kind of Sabbath: You get up when you want, set aside the usual program of meditation and work, and refrain from touching computers or phones. Instead, you go on alms rounds with the other monastics — you walk the streets of the local town in your robes, begging bowl in hand, receiving food from anyone who wishes to offer it. Then you devote the rest of the day to personal practice.

In the evening, one of the resident teachers offers a talk that's open to the lay community. Laypeople who attend and stay the night take the three refuges (the Buddha, Dharma, and Sangha) and commit to following 8 precepts for the duration of their stay — the usual 5 precepts for laypeople (with monastic celibacy in place of the customary precept governing lay sexual behavior), plus 3 precepts with a "twist" of renunciation: no eating after noon, no entertainment or self-adornment, and no lying on a high and luxurious bed (also understood as no over-indulging in sleep). (You can read more about the precepts in Book 3, Chapter 1.) Both laity and monastics practice meditation together until 3 a.m., followed by morning chanting. The rest of the day is completely unstructured, and monastics often use it to catch up on their sleep.

On Saturday nights, the monastery hosts a regular talk on a Buddhist theme that draws even more of an outside audience than the lunar gatherings.

REMEMBER

The high point of the year at Abhayagiri comes at the beginning of January, when the three-month rains retreat begins. Fashioned after the traditional monsoon assembly in India, when the wandering monks gathered to practice together, the retreat coincides with the rainiest time of the year in northern California. It gives the monks an opportunity to observe noble silence, turn their attention inward, and intensify their practice. Overnight guests and outside teaching engagements are prohibited, and the schedule becomes more rigorous, with many more group practice sessions scheduled throughout the day. In addition, monastics take turns retiring to their individual cabins during this period for solitary retreats.

VIPASSANA CENTERS FOR LAYPEOPLE

In addition to monasteries, the Theravada tradition in the West supports lay practice centers, much like Zen centers (see the section "Growing a Lotus in the Mud: A Day in the Life of a Zen Practitioner," later in the chapter). At these practice centers, laypeople can gather to learn how to meditate, listen to talks, attend workshops on Buddhist themes, and participate in retreats of varying lengths (from one day to three months). Frequently using the term *vipassana* (insight) rather than *Theravada,* Western teachers (some of whom have trained in Asia) staff these centers, which may be closely affiliated with nearby monasteries.

TAKING A BOW

Some teachers say, "Buddhism is a religion of bowing." By this they mean two things:

- Bowing expresses the surrender of self-centered preoccupation, which is one of the core teachings of Buddhism.
- Buddhists bow a great deal.

Both statements are true. In every tradition of Buddhism, bowing plays an important role. Buddhists bow to their altars, their teachers, their robes, their sitting cushions, and one another (see the following figure of a Theravada monk bowing). As a traditional expression of gratitude, respect, veneration, acknowledgment, and surrender, bowing occurs both spontaneously and in prescribed situations and contexts. In other words, sometimes you bow because you feel like it, and sometimes you bow because you're expected to.

Bowing is also a common practice in traditional Asian societies. Buddhism, bowing, and Asian culture are inextricably entwined.

Bowing in Buddhism takes different forms, depending on the culture and circumstance.

- In Southeast Asia, for example, you show respect by holding your hands in prayer position to your slightly lowered forehead. For a full bow, kneel in that position (sitting on your buttocks), lay your palms on the ground about 4 inches apart, and touch your forehead to the ground between your hands.

- In Japanese Zen, execute a half bow by holding your hands together at chest level and then bowing from the waist. For a full bow, start off with the half bow and then continue with the Southeast Asia style of bow, except with palms up rather than down.
- In Tibetan Buddhism, show respect by touching your joined hands to your forehead, throat, and heart (indicating the dedication of body, speech, and mind) and executing a full prostration by (more or less) extending the full bow of Zen until you're lying face down on the ground.

Though bowing may lapse into mere formality, the deeper intention is to express heartfelt respect and devotion. The regular practice of bowing in Buddhist monasteries and communities contributes to an atmosphere of harmony, loving-kindness, and peace. As a Westerner taught to "bow down to no one," you may find yourself resistant to the practice at first. But you may soon discover that it encourages a flexibility and openness of mind and heart that feels good inside — and it's Buddhist to the core!

Photo courtesy of Jay Carroll/JFoto.com.

Growing a Lotus In the Mud: A Day in the Life of a Zen Practitioner

Zen first gained a foothold in North America around the turn of the last century, but it didn't achieve widespread popularity until the 1960s and 1970s, when Zen teachers began arriving in larger numbers and young people (discontented with the religion in which they were raised) began seeking alternatives.

Since that time, the uniquely Western expression of a place for Buddhist practice known as the *Zen center* has appeared in cities and towns across the North American continent. Like monasteries, Zen centers offer a daily schedule of meditation, ritual, and work combined with regular lectures and study groups. But unlike their monastic counterparts, the centers adapt their approach to the needs of busy lay practitioners who must balance the demands of family life, career, and other worldly obligations with their spiritual involvement.

Though Zen temples in Japan and Korea have lay meditation groups, nothing quite like the Zen center has ever emerged in Asia. The reason is quite simple: Lay practitioners who fervently commit themselves to Buddhist practice are far more common in the West than in Asia, where serious practitioners generally take monastic or priestly vows. Maybe this phenomenon is the result of the Western belief that we can have it all: spiritual enlightenment and worldly accomplishment. (The Judeo-Christian ethic so prominent in North America teaches that daily life is inseparable from spiritual practice.) Or perhaps Westerners simply have no choice: In a culture where the monastic style of practice isn't widely acknowledged or supported, practitioners have to make a living while studying the teachings.

REMEMBER

In any case, Buddhism has its own strong precedents for this approach: The Mahayana tradition, of which Zen considers itself a part, views lay and monastic members as equal in their capacity to achieve enlightenment. The Zen tradition, in particular, has always emphasized the importance of practicing in the midst of the most mundane activities, such as washing the dishes, driving a car, and taking care of the kids. The Mahayana tradition expresses the idea in this way:

> Just as the most beautiful flower, the lotus, grows in muddy water, so the lay practitioner can find clarity and compassion in the turmoil of daily life.

Though Zen centers form the spiritual hub of their respective communities, members continue their practice throughout the day by applying meditative awareness to every activity.

Following a day in the life

At the heart of Zen practice is *zazen* (literally, "sitting meditation"), a form of silent meditation understood by some traditions to be both a method for achieving enlightenment and an expression of your already enlightened Buddha nature. In other words, you can be the truth and seek it, too! How's that for a two-for-one deal?

As a Zen practitioner, you're encouraged to practice zazen on your own, but sitting with other members of the *Sangha* (spiritual community) is considered particularly effective and favorable. (Sangha is regarded as one of the Three Jewels of Buddhism, along with the Buddha and Dharma.) So, most Zen centers offer daily group meditations — usually in the early morning before work and in the evening after work. Depending on how much time you have to spare and the schedule at your local center, you can spend from one to three hours practicing Zen with others.

At *zendos* (meditation halls connected with Zen centers) across the country, meditators repeat the familiar ritual of gathering in the predawn dark to practice together.

Though Zen is best known in the West in its Japanese form, and we use Japanese terms throughout this section, remember that Zen began in China and that Korean and Vietnamese teachers introduced it to the West.

After entering the zendo, you bow respectfully to your cushion or chair and then position yourself in preparation for zazen. Even in its Western incarnation, Zen is notorious for its careful attention to traditional formalities. Meditation begins with the sounding of a bell or gong and generally continues in silence for 30 to 40 minutes. Depending on the school of Zen to which you belong and the maturity of your practice, you may spend your time following your breaths, just sitting (a more advanced technique involving mindful attention in the present without a particular object of focus), or attempting to solve a *koan* (a paradoxical story; see the sidebar "Entering the gateless gate: *Koan* practice in Zen," for more details). Whatever your technique, you're encouraged to sit with an erect spine and wholehearted attention.

Between meditation periods, you may form a line with other practitioners and meditate while walking mindfully around the hall together. Following a period or two of sitting, everyone generally chants some version of the four *bodhisattva vows:*

- Beings are numberless; I vow to save them.
- Mental defilements are inexhaustible; I vow to put an end to them.

» The teachings are boundless; I vow to master them.

» The Buddha's way is unsurpassable; I vow to attain it.

During the service that follows meditation, you bow deeply three or nine times to the altar (which usually features a statue of Shakyamuni Buddha or Manjushri Bodhisattva, flowers, candles, and incense) and chant one or more important wisdom texts, which generally include the *Heart Sutra*. These texts offer concise reminders of the core teachings of Zen, and the altar represents the Three Jewels of Buddhism, the ultimate objects of reverence and refuge: the Buddha, Dharma, and Sangha.

When you finish your morning meditation, your Zen practice has just begun. Throughout the day, you have constant opportunities to be mindful — not only of what you're doing or what's happening around you, but also of the thoughts, emotions, and reactive patterns that life events trigger. Whether on the cushion or on the go, this steady, inclusive, mindful awareness lies at the heart of Buddhist practice in every tradition.

REMEMBER

In particular, the Zen tradition emphasizes taking mindful care of every aspect of your life because the deeper truth is that you're not separate from the tools you use, the car you drive, the dishes you wash, and the people you meet. The world is your very own body! For example, when you get behind the wheel of your car, stop to sense the contact of your back against the seat, listen to the sound of the engine as it starts, pay attention to the condition of the road, and notice the state of your mind and heart as you head down the street. When you stop at a traffic light, be aware of the impatience you feel as you wait for the light to change, the sounds of the traffic around you, the warmth of the sun through the window, and so on. As you can see, every moment, from morning to night, provides an opportunity to practice.

TIP

In addition to meditation and service, most Zen centers offer weekly talks by the resident teacher and regular opportunities for private interviews with the teacher to discuss your practice. These face-to-face encounters may touch on any area of practice, including work, relationships, sitting meditation, and formal *koan* study. The Zen master isn't a guru endowed with special powers. Practitioners regard the master as a skilled guide and an exemplar of the enlightened way of life.

If you're a serious Zen student but can't practice at the center, because you're sick, you live too far away, or you can't arrange your calendar to include it, you can generally follow some version of this daily schedule on your own by sitting in the morning and again, if possible, in the evening. Then to energize and deepen your practice, you can make it a point to attend one or more intensive retreats each year.

ENTERING THE GATELESS GATE: *KOAN* PRACTICE IN ZEN

When you think of Zen, what image comes to mind? Perhaps it's the shaven-headed monks in black robes sitting silently facing the wall. Or maybe it's the Zen master making some enigmatic statement or engaging in some unusual behavior designed to rouse students from their spiritual slumber.

This last image figures prominently in the paradoxical stories known as *koans,* which teachers have used for centuries (especially in the Rinzai Zen tradition) to serve as a catalyst for awakening their students. More than an intellectual exercise, *koan* study is a process of spiritual reflection designed to confound the conceptual mind, bypass the intellect, and elicit a direct insight *(kensho)* into the nondual nature of reality — that is, our inherent oneness with all of life.

Some masters, especially those in the early years of Zen in China, didn't need such stories. In direct contact with their disciples during day-to-day monastic life, they had ample opportunity to transmit the teachings through their spoken words, gestures, behaviors, and, above all, their silent presence. But as monasteries grew and teachers became less accessible, the teaching encounter became increasingly confined to public dialogues and the interview room, where masters challenged and encouraged their disciples and tested their understanding.

In this context, Zen masters began using traditional questions and true stories of classic teacher–student encounters, initially to provoke kensho and then to teach different aspects of the multifaceted jewel of *prajna* (enlightened wisdom). Over the centuries, these stories and questions were collected and systematized into a kind of graduate program in living from the enlightened perspective. With Zen's emphasis on "direct transmission outside the scriptures," *koans,* along with the transmission stories and poems of the great masters, became the focal point of study for serious Zen practitioners, and they're still widely used today in Asia and now in the West. Among the best-known *koans* are "What is the sound of one hand [clapping]?" and "What was your original face before your parents were born?"

Attending silent retreats

Most Zen centers in the West offer regular one- to seven-day retreats (Japanese: *sesshin*) featuring as many as a dozen periods of meditation each day, morning and evening services, daily talks on Buddhist themes, and interviews. (Korean Zen also offers retreats devoted primarily to chanting and bowing.) As a rule, these rigorous retreats are held in silence and offer an opportunity to hone your concentration, deepen your insight into the fundamental truths of Buddhism, and possibly catch a glimpse of your essential Buddha nature (an experience of awakening known in Japanese as *kensho* or *satori*). Retreats of more than one or two days are generally residential, though some centers allow you to attend part time while continuing your everyday life.

In keeping with the Mahayana spirit of general equality among monastic and lay practitioners, larger Zen centers often have country retreat centers that provide monastic accommodations and training for both ordained monks and nuns and lay practitioners. For example, the San Francisco Zen Center — which describes itself as one of the largest Buddhist Sanghas outside of Asia, a diverse community of priests, laypeople, teachers, and students — includes three separate facilities:

- **City Center:** This facility serves urban members.
- **Green Gulch Farm:** This location combines a suburban practice center and a working organic farm.
- **Tassajara Zen Mountain Center:** This facility is the oldest Soto Zen monastery in the United States. It offers teacher-led retreats and Zen Practice Weeks, and visitors can expect to spend time in the meditation hall, cabins, wilderness trails, and hot springs.

All three facilities offer residential retreats, but the program at Tassajara is particularly intensive.

JUKAI: THE BODHISATTVA INITIATION OR LAY ORDINATION

Jukai (Japanese: "receiving the precepts") is the ceremony of a layperson's ordination or formal entry into the practice of the bodhisattva precepts in the Zen tradition. This ceremony involves making a commitment to practice and keep the precepts for life while being a householder. In many American Zen centers, including the San Francisco Zen Center, the ceremony is a shortened version of Zaike Tokudo ("staying at home and attaining the way"). To prepare, a candidate sews a *rakusu,* a five-panel small robe patterned after the Buddha's robe, and studies the bodhisattva precepts. The ceremony then starts with an invocation to all Buddhas and bodhisattvas, to provide a framework of support for the candidates' initiation. Each candidate receives a new name and the robe they have sewn. The candidates then formally don the rakusu with a chant. Next, they avow and repent past actions stemming from greed, anger, and ignorance and are purified with water. Thus purified, they receive the 16 precepts by reciting them after the teacher. They receive the bloodline of the Buddhas and ancestors (Japanese: *kechimyaku*). Finally, the teachers give congratulatory statements, and the ceremony is dedicated to the welfare of all beings.

Devoting Yourself to the Three Jewels: A Day in the Life of a Vajrayana Practitioner

In addition to North American converts to Buddhism, the continent has many thousands of ethnic practitioners who carried their Buddhist practice with them from Asia or learned it from their Asian parents or grandparents.

Some of these Asian American Buddhists are monks and nuns (many come from Southeast Asia) who have transplanted traditional forms and practices to Western soil. But most folks are laypeople for whom Buddhism is often more a matter of devotion and ritual than meditation and study.

For these Asian Americans, being a Buddhist may involve the following actions:

- Going to the temple on the weekend to listen to a sermon
- Chanting Buddhist texts in the language of their homeland
- Participating in the special ceremonies that mark the changing of the seasons and the turning of the year
- Sharing food at temple gatherings
- Helping fellow temple members in times of need

As an ethnic lay practitioner of Tibetan Vajrayana Buddhism now living in the West, you may engage in some or all of the following daily practices:

- You rise early, between 5 and 6 a.m., to begin your day with meditation.
- You walk around *(circumambulate)* your house, which holds a sacred shrine containing statues, scrolls, and other ritual objects.
- As you walk, you finger your mala (a string of beads, a rosary) while chanting a sacred mantra such as *Om mani-padme hum* (the famous mantra of Avalokiteshvara/Chenrezig, the bodhisattva of compassion) or the longer mantra of Vajrasattva, the bodhisattva of clarity and purification.
- After cleaning your shrine, you offer 108 prostrations (see Figure 4-1 to get a glimpse of how they're done) as an expression of your devotion to and refuge in the Three Jewels (the Buddha, Dharma, and Sangha).
- You engage in a particular practice your teacher has given you, often a visualization of a particular deity accompanied by chanting, prayer, and prostrations.

» As you go about your day, you chant *Om mani-padme hum,* either aloud or silently to yourself, while cultivating the qualities of compassion and loving-kindness for all beings.

» You spend an hour or two in the evening studying certain special teachings recommended by your teacher.

» Before you go to sleep, you make offerings of incense and candles at your altar, meditate, do additional prostrations, and recite long-life prayers for your teacher(s).

As you can see, the life of a traditional Vajrayana lay practitioner is permeated by spiritual practice. Of course, some people are more devoted than others, and young people are more inclined to diverge from the traditional ways of their parents. But in general, Tibetan culture, even in exile, is filled with strong Buddhist values that often express themselves in dedicated practice.

WHAT ARE MANTRAS?

Mantras are sacred syllables, words, or sentences. Their literal meaning isn't always clearly understood, but the practice of repeating mantras isn't about an intellectual understanding of the meaning of words. Practitioners of Asian religious traditions often repeat mantras to focus the mind. In this chapter, we mention the mantra of Avalokiteshvara (or Chenrezig), which is popular among Tibetan Buddhists: *Om mani-padme hum.* A mantra that practitioners of the Pure Land schools in Japan chant is *Namu amida butsu* ("Homage to Amida Buddha"). More about it comes in the next section ("Trusting the Mind of Amida: A Day in the Life of a Pure Land Buddhist"). There is also another important mantra in the Japanese Nichiren School (and its offshoots): *Nam* (or *namu*) *myoho renge kyo* ("Homage to the *Lotus of the Good Dharma Sutra*").

Take a look at these characteristic features of mantras:

- Mantras are believed to be invested with divine power. It's assumed that repeating a mantra many times can access this power.
- Counting the repetitions of a mantra is done with the help of a rosary *(mala),* which often has 108 beads (108 is a sacred number).
- Ideally, a spiritual teacher *(guru)* selects a mantra and transmits it to a disciple orally. (Mantras are not meant to be picked up from books.) After receiving the transmission, the student is authorized to repeat the mantra.

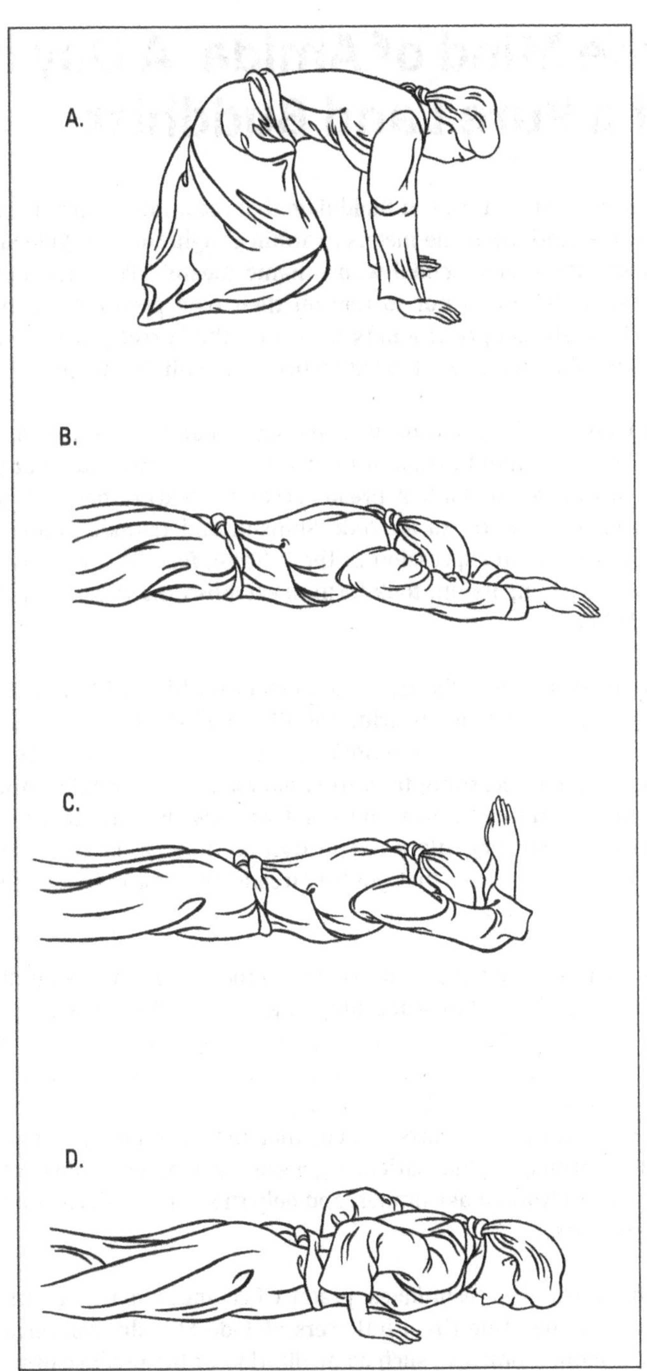

FIGURE 4-1: Performing full prostrations in the Tibetan style.

© John Wiley & Sons, Inc.

Trusting the Mind of Amida: A Day in the Life of a Pure Land Buddhist

Unlike most other forms of Buddhism that recommend spiritual practices (particularly meditation) as the means to attain enlightenment, Jodo Shinshu (a popular Japanese Pure Land school whose name means "The True Pure Land school") teaches its followers not to rely on their own personal practice. Instead, Jodo Shinshu instructs practitioners to rely on the "great practice" of Amida Buddha himself, who took a vow to lead all beings to enlightenment.

As a Jodo Shinshu follower, you're taught that entry to the Pure Land (which is more a state of mind than a future realm) occurs through other power (the power of what Amida Buddha has already accomplished) rather than through whatever you yourself may try to do. Jodo Shinshu understands Amida (or Amitabha, in Sanskrit) to be an expression of the infinite, formless, life-giving Oneness that, out of deep compassion, took form to establish the Pure Land and lead beings to Buddhahood.

REMEMBER

Shinran (1173–1263), the Japanese founder of this tradition, did recommend certain practices, such as "hearing the Dharma" (listening to Buddhist teachings), reading scriptures and contemporary commentaries, internalizing basic Buddhist principles, and "learning to entrust yourself to the mind of Amida" rather than to your own limited effort and point of view. But the point of these practices isn't to eliminate negativity and purify your mind, as in other Buddhist traditions. You practice to realize that you're already swimming in an ocean of purity and compassion.

Shinran himself left the monastic life to marry and raise a family because he felt that making the Buddhist teachings more accessible to laypeople was extremely important. In this spirit, Jodo Shinshu emphasizes that everyday life in the context of family and friends is the perfect setting for spiritual practice. As a result, Jodo Shinshu followers lead ordinary lives that differ little from those of their non-Buddhist counterparts, except that they attempt to put into practice basic Buddhist principles, like patience, generosity, kindness, and equanimity. They get up and go to work, make dinner, and help their kids with their homework just like everyone else.

Without prescribed techniques, practice becomes a matter of attitude rather than activity. At the same time, followers of Jodo Shinshu can engage in any traditional Buddhist practice, such as meditation or the practice of mindfulness of the Buddha *(nembutsu)* by chanting the mantra *Namu amida butsu* ("Homage to Amida

Buddha"), as long as they do it as an expression of their gratitude for the gift of Amida's grace (not as a means to attain enlightenment).

On Sunday mornings, followers generally gather at their local temple to listen to a talk on a Buddhist theme while their children attend the Buddhist version of Sunday school — a short sermon followed by an hour-long class about Buddhist values. If they're strongly motivated, adult members may join a discussion or study group focusing on Jodo Shinshu themes.

Seasonal holidays also bring the community together to celebrate special occasions like the Buddha's birth, enlightenment days, the vernal and autumnal equinoxes, and a summer ceremony honoring the spirits of departed ancestors. For many practitioners, the temple (like the local church or synagogue) is the focal point of social and community life. Temples often offer classes in martial arts, flower arranging, taiko drumming, and Japanese language that instill Buddhist principles and Japanese culture and values.

Taking Part in Meditation Practices

As the rest of this chapter shows, Buddhists around the world engage in a variety of different activities — from reciting prayers and studying religious texts to worshipping an image of the Buddha.

But of all the different activities you can think of, many people identify one in particular as typically Buddhist: meditation. Although not all people who call themselves Buddhists meditate — or make it part of the everyday routine — meditation is an important practice in Buddhism.

But what exactly is meditation and what can you accomplish with it?

Defining meditation

REMEMBER

In Buddhism, the practice of *meditation* basically involves three separate but interrelated aspects or skills: mindful awareness, concentration, and insight. Though the various traditions differ somewhat in the techniques they use to develop these skills, they generally agree that mindful awareness, concentration, and insight work hand in hand and that all three are essential if you want to attain the goal of spiritual realization.

However, meditation is a rather broad term. It denotes diverse techniques and methods developed to calm, fashion, understand, and release the mind. Thus it is usually practiced to attain specific aims, including the following:

- Mental tranquility or purification
- Insight into a religious truth
- The visualization or construction of a special perception

Meditation techniques are found in many religious traditions, but their specifics differ with their associated belief systems. The importance of meditation in Eastern religious traditions has been overrated. (Meditation plays no significant role, for example, in Japanese Amida Buddhism.) Traditionally, Buddhist meditation is viewed as a means of attaining liberation, not as a stress-reduction technique or a form of therapy. Accordingly, it is practiced along these lines:

- Mostly by a few monks and nuns, who usually live a reclusive lifestyle
- As part of a larger system of religious beliefs and (in Vajrayana, highly ritualized) religious practices
- In intensive retreats lasting several weeks or months

Some Buddhist teachers taught that not every type of meditation is appropriate for everyone. In the Theravada Buddhist manual *Visuddhimagga (Path to Purity)*, Buddhaghosa (ca. 370–450) recommended different objects of meditation for different types of individuals, depending on their predisposition. Regardless of the object, meditation is traditionally practiced in Buddhism to purify the mind, attain insight into the Buddhist truths, and ultimately, gain liberation from cyclic existence *(samsara)* for oneself (in Theravada Buddhist tradition) or for all beings (in Mahayana Buddhist tradition).

Practicing meditation

TIP

Meditation can be a method for transforming your view of reality or for getting in touch with parts of yourself that you didn't previously know about. Meditation can also be considered as a method for getting to know your own mind. To include it in your practice, follow these steps:

1. **Begin by finding a quiet place where you won't be disturbed by interruptions or loud noises for 20 minutes or longer.**

2. **Set aside your preoccupations and concerns for the moment and sit down in a position that's comfortable for you.** You may choose to sit cross-legged on a cushion in traditional Asian fashion or on a straight-backed or ergonomic chair. Whatever position you choose, be sure to keep your spine relatively erect (yet relaxed) so you can breathe easily and freely.
3. **Now gently rest your attention on the coming and going of your breath. Some traditions recommend focusing on the sensation of the breath as it enters and leaves your nostrils; others prefer to focus on the rising and falling of your belly as you breathe.** Whatever you choose to concentrate on, stick with it for the full meditation period. Be aware of the subtle changes and shifts in your sensations as you breathe in and out. When your mind wanders off (daydreaming or fixated thinking), gently bring your awareness back to your breath.
4. **Don't try to stop thinking — thoughts and feelings will naturally come and go as you meditate.** But remain uninvolved with them as much as possible. Enjoy the simple experience of breathing in and breathing out.
5. **After 15 or 20 minutes, slowly move your body, stand up, and resume your everyday activities.**

IN THIS CHAPTER

» Figuring out what makes enlightenment so special

» Walking along the Theravada path to nirvana

» Considering the Mahayana tradition

» Exploring enlightenment in the Vajrayana tradition

» Studying the path to enlightenment through the ten ox-herding pictures of Zen

» Identifying similarities within different traditions

Chapter 5

What Is Enlightenment, Anyway?

A few decades ago, few people had heard the word "enlightenment" used in the Buddhist context, and the available books on Buddhism for a general audience may have filled half a bookshelf, at best. Things have really changed in the past 40 years! Today books dealing with aspects of Buddhism regularly make *The New York Times* bestseller lists, and everyone seems to be seeking enlightenment in some form. You can read popular manuals for "awakening the Buddha within" or achieving "enlightenment on the run," and you can take "enlightenment intensives" at your local yoga studio. One perfume company even produces a scent they call Satori, the Japanese word for "enlightenment."

But what does enlightenment (or awakening) really mean in Buddhism? Though the current quick-fix culture has trivialized it, *enlightenment* is often considered the culmination of the spiritual path, which may take a lifetime of practice and inquiry to achieve. In this chapter, we describe (as much as words possibly can) what enlightenment is — and is not — and explain how people's understanding of it has changed as Buddhism evolved and adapted to different cultures.

REMEMBER

As you read this chapter, keep in mind that words can only express so much. To use a traditional Buddhist analogy, words are like a finger pointing at the full moon. If you get caught up in the finger, you may never get to appreciate the magnificent sight of the moon in the sky.

Considering the Many Faces of Spiritual Realization

If you read the stories of the world's great mystics and sages, you find that spiritual experiences come in a dazzling array of shapes and sizes. For example:

- Some Native American *shamans* enter altered states in which they journey to other dimensions to find allies and other healing resources for their tribe members.
- Some Hindus experience visions of deities and feelings of ecstasy through the rising of an energy known as *kundalini,* enter blissful states that last for hours, or merge in union with divinities like Shiva. For more on Hinduism, see Book 1.
- Christian saints and mystics have encountered transformative visions of Jesus, received visitations from angels or the Blessed Virgin Mary, and manifested the *stigmata* (marks resembling the crucifixion wounds of Christ) in their hands and feet. For more on Christianity, see Book 5.
- The Hebrew Bible is filled with tales of prophets and patriarchs who meet Jehovah in some form — as the fire in the burning bush, the voice in the whirlwind, and so on. For more on Judaism, see Book 4.

Though such dramatic experiences can have a transformative spiritual impact on an individual, they may or may not be enlightening, as Buddhists understand this term. In fact, most traditions of Buddhism downplay the importance of visions, voices, powers, energies, and altered states, claiming that they distract practitioners from the true purpose of the spiritual endeavor — a direct, liberating insight into the essential nature of reality.

The basic Buddhist teaching of impermanence (Pali: *anicca*) suggests that even the most powerful spiritual experiences come and go like clouds in the sky. The point of practice is to realize a truth so deep and fundamental that it doesn't change, because it's not an experience at all; it's the nature of reality itself. This undeniable, unalterable realization is known as *enlightenment.*

REMEMBER

Among the Buddha's core teachings are the *four noble truths* (see Book 3, Chapter 2 for more information), which explain the nature and cause of suffering and the "eightfold path" for its elimination. This path culminates in enlightenment.

The Buddha also taught that all beings have the same potential for enlightenment that he had. Among the characteristics distinguishing ordinary beings from a Buddha are the distorted views, attachments, and aversive emotions that block the truth from their eyes.

All traditions of Buddhism would undoubtedly agree on the fundamental teachings about enlightenment that we outline in the two preceding paragraphs — after all, these teachings come from the earliest and most universally accepted of the Buddha's discourses. The traditions differ, however, over the contents of enlightenment and the precise means of achieving it. What is the actual goal of the spiritual life? What do you awaken to — and how do you get there? Believe it or not, the answers to these questions changed over the centuries as Buddhism evolved.

Most traditions believe that their version of enlightenment is exactly the same as the Buddha's. Some claim that theirs is the only true version — the deeper, secret realization that the Buddha never dared reveal during his lifetime. Other commentators insist that the realization of later Buddhist masters carried both practice and enlightenment to dimensions that the Buddha himself had never anticipated. Whatever the truth may be, the traditions clearly differ in significant ways.

REMEMBER

In the rest of this chapter, we offer you a glimpse of enlightenment from three different points of view: Theravada, Vajrayana, and Zen. Though this brief tour certainly can't cover every conception of enlightenment within Buddhism, it does cover the basics — at least, as much as words can. Ultimately, as all traditions agree, enlightenment surpasses even the most refined intellectual understanding and simply can't be contained in our usual conceptual frameworks.

TIP

As you read the following sections, keep this old Zen adage in mind: "A painting of a rice cake cannot satisfy hunger." You can look at pictures of pastries all day long, but you won't feel fulfilled until you taste the real thing for yourself. In the same way, you can read dozens of books about enlightenment, but you won't really understand what they're talking about until you catch a glimpse of the actual experience.

Reviewing the Theravada Tradition's Take on Nirvana

The Theravada tradition bases its teachings and practices on the Pali canon, which includes the Buddha's discourses (Pali: *suttas*) that were preserved through memorization (by monks actually in attendance), passed along orally for many generations, and ultimately written down more than four centuries after the Buddha's death. Because these teachings are ascribed to the historical Buddha, some proponents of the Theravada tradition claim that they represent original Buddhism — that is, Buddhism as the Enlightened One actually taught it and intended it to be practiced and realized.

The Theravada tradition elaborates a detailed, progressive path of practice and realization that leads the student through four stages of enlightenment, culminating in *nirvana* (Pali: *nibbana*) — the complete liberation from suffering. The path itself consists of three aspects, or *trainings:* moral discipline (ethical conduct), concentration (meditation practice), and wisdom (study of the teachings and direct spiritual insight).

Defining nirvana

Because the Buddha considered craving and ignorance to be two of the root causes of all suffering, he often defines *nirvana* as the extinction of craving and eradication of ignorance.

The term *nirvana* literally means "extinguishing," referring to the fires of craving, hatred, and ignorance that keep us unenlightened beings cycling endlessly from one rebirth to the next. Nirvana refers to a condition in which these fires are extinguished, and you're completely free of craving, hatred, and ignorance. Just because the terms used to refer to nirvana emphasize the absence of certain undesirable qualities, don't mistakenly assume that nirvana itself is negative. These seemingly negative terms point to an unconditional truth that lies beyond language and thus can't be accurately described in words. In his wisdom, the Buddha realized that positive terms, which appear to describe a limited state, may be more misleading than helpful because nirvana isn't a state and has no limitations.

Nirvana is indescribable. In the Theravada tradition, it's referred to using negative terms because it's the complete opposite of samsara, the cycle of existence in which we are entangled.

However, if nirvana has a particular feeling or tone, it's generally characterized as unshakable tranquility, contentment, and bliss (see Figure 5-1). Sound appealing?

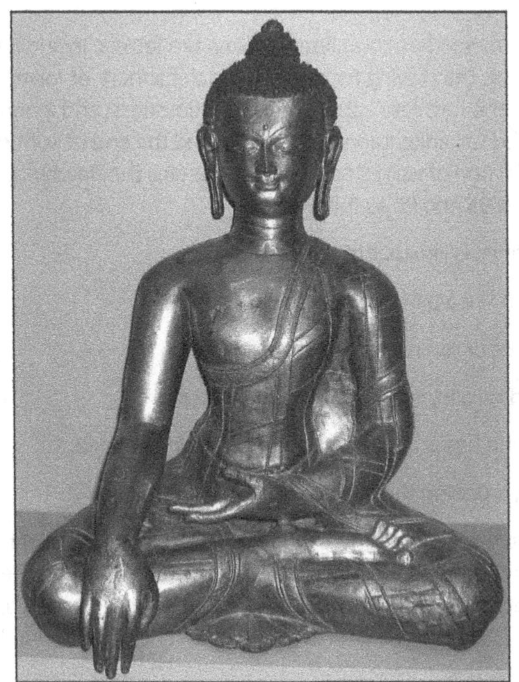

FIGURE 5-1: Shakyamuni Buddha, the classic embodiment of serenity and peace. Photo courtesy of Gudrun Bühnemann.

Revealing the four stages on the path to nirvana

REMEMBER

Early Buddhism recognized four distinct levels or stages of realization, each one marked by the elimination of certain fetters (Pali: *samyojana*), or chains, that bind us.

These types of practitioners have attained the distinct stages on the path to nirvana:

- **Stream-enterer:** The practitioner has broken three of ten fetters: the erroneous view that a personality exists, doubt about the path to liberation, and attachment to rules and rituals. They have thereby entered the stream that leads to nirvana. This person purportedly will attain nirvana within seven lives.
- **Once-returner:** This person has significantly weakened two additional fetters: craving and aversion. They will be reborn as a human being no more than one time before reaching the fourth stage, that of an arhat (see the last bullet point of this list).
- **Nonreturner:** The practitioner has completely eliminated all of the five fetters previously mentioned and will not be reborn as a human being.

» **Arhat:** This person has completely broken ten fetters, including these additional five: the craving for existence in the sphere of form, the craving for existence in the formless sphere, pride, restlessness, and ignorance. They have attained full enlightenment and reached the end of suffering. The ancient collection of verses on Buddhist themes, the *Dhammapada*, describes him in verses 95 and 96 as follows:

His patience is like that of the earth.

He is firm like a pillar and serene like a lake.

No rounds of rebirths are in store for him.

His mind is calm, speech and action are calm

of one who has attained freedom by true knowledge.

For such a person there is peace.

At this point, the circumstances of life no longer have the slightest hold over a person; positive or negative experiences no longer stir even the slightest craving or dissatisfaction. As the Buddha said, all that needed to be done has been done. There's nothing further to realize. The path is complete.

Getting a Handle on Two Traditions of Wisdom

As Buddhism developed over the centuries, various schools emerged that differed in how they framed the path to enlightenment and how they understood the ultimate goal of this path. Some Mahayana ("Great Vehicle" or "Great Path") schools shifted the emphasis from the experience of no-self to the experience of *emptiness*.

The two main commentarial branches of the Mahayana tradition understood emptiness (or ultimate reality) in two quite different ways. The Madhyamika (Sanskrit for "middle doctrine") school refused to assert anything about ultimate reality. Instead, these folks chose to refute and discredit any positive assertions that other schools made. The end result left practitioners without any belief or point of view to hold on to, which effectively pulled the rug out from under their conceptual minds and forced them to, in the words of the great Mahayana text, the *Diamond Sutra*, "cultivate the mind that dwells nowhere" — the spacious, expansive, unattached mind of enlightenment.

By contrast, the Yogachara (Sanskrit for "practice of yoga") school said that the world as we perceive it is only a manifestation of the mind, or *consciousness*. (This view gave rise to the other name for this school, Vijnanavada (Sanskrit for "teaching [in which] consciousness or mind [plays a special role]").

Realizing the Mind's Essential Purity in the Vajrayana Tradition

The Vajrayana (or tantric) traditions of Buddhism, which began in India and flowered in Nepal, Mongolia, and Tibet, retain the basic understanding of no-self and expand on it. (Vajrayana is the name for tantric traditions within Mahayana Buddhism, which we discuss earlier in this chapter.) After you look deeply into your heart and mind (using techniques adapted from different traditions and discover the truth of no-self, you naturally open to a deeper realization of the nature of mind (or consciousness), which is pure, vast, luminous, clear, nonlocatable, ungraspable, aware, and essentially nondual.

Nondual simply means that subject and object, matter and spirit are "not two" — that is, they're different on an everyday level, but they're inseparable at the level of essence. For example, you and the book you see in front of you are different in obvious ways, but you're essentially expressions of an inseparable whole. Now, don't expect us to put this oneness into words the mind can understand, though mystics and poets have been trying their best for thousands of years. If you want to know more, you just may have to check it out for yourself.

Not only is the nature of mind innately pure, radiant, and aware, but it also spontaneously manifests itself in each moment as compassionate activity for the benefit of all beings. Though conceptual thought can't grasp the nature of mind, this mind-nature (like no-self) can be realized through meditation in a series of ever-deepening experiences culminating in complete realization, or Buddhahood.

In Vajrayana, the path to complete enlightenment begins with the extensive cultivation of positive qualities, like loving-kindness and compassion, and then progresses to the development of various levels of insight into the nature of mind. In some traditions, practitioners are taught to visualize themselves as the embodiment of enlightenment itself and then to meditate upon their inherent awakeness, or Buddha nature.

Generally, navigating the path from beginning to end requires a qualified teacher, diligent practice, wholehearted dedication, and numerous intensive retreats. For more on following that path in your daily life, see Book 3, Chapter 4.

Taking the direct approach to realization

Some consider the *Dzogchen-Mahamudra* teachings the highest teaching of the Tibetan traditions. Dzogchen means "great perfection" in Tibetan, and *Mahamudra* is Sanskrit for "great seal." Both terms refer to the insight that everything is perfect just the way it is.

These two approaches are generally considered to be slightly different expressions of the same nondual realization. (For a complete explanation of nondualism, see the second paragraph earlier in this section.) Traditionally, only practitioners who completed years of preliminary practice are qualified to learn about Dzogchen-Mahamudra, but today in the West, anyone sincere and motivated enough to attend a retreat can explore this approach to enlightenment.

In Dzogchen, teachers provide their students with a direct introduction to the nature of mind, known as *pointing-out instructions*. The students then try to stabilize this realization in their meditations and ordinary lives. The goal is to embody this realization without interruption until the separation between meditation and nonmeditation drops away and the mind is continuously awake to its own inherent nature in every situation. In Mahamudra, practitioners first learn to calm the mind and then use this calmness as a foundation for inquiring deeply into its nature. When the mind recognizes its own nature, practitioners rest in this mind-nature as much as possible. (Now, don't ask us to explain what this "resting" involves — like so much else in this chapter, it eludes words.) Though the approach of Dzogchen-Mahamudra may be considered direct, mastering it is extremely difficult and may take a lifetime — at least.

Understanding the complete enlightenment of a Buddha

The Theravada tradition considers the final goal of spiritual practice, exemplified by the arhat (see the section "Reviewing the Theravada Tradition's Take on Nirvana," earlier in the chapter, for a reminder of what arhat means), to be eminently attainable in this lifetime by any sincere practitioner. In the time of the historical Buddha, numerous disciples achieved complete realization and were acknowledged as arhats, which meant that their realization of no-self was essentially the same as the Buddha's.

In the Vajrayana tradition, by contrast, the realization of Buddhahood appears to be a much more protracted path. The completely enlightened ones experience the end of all craving and other negative emotions, but these folks also exhibit numerous beneficial qualities, including boundless love and compassion, infinite, all-seeing wisdom, ceaseless enlightened activity for the welfare of all beings, and the capacity to speed others on their path to enlightenment.

Needless to say, many of the faithful (especially at the beginning levels of practice) may see such an advanced stage of realization as a distant and unattainable dream. Compounding this feeling may be the many inspiring stories of exceptional sages who meditate for years in mountain caves and achieve not only a diamondlike clarity of mind and inexhaustible compassion, but also numerous superhuman powers.

Yet dedicated Vajrayana practitioners do gradually see their efforts lead to greater compassion, clarity, tranquility, and fearlessness, along with a deeper and more abiding recognition of the nature of mind. Indeed, Vajrayana promises that everyone has the potential to achieve Buddhahood in this lifetime by using the powerful methods it provides.

Standing Nirvana on Its Head with Zen

REMEMBER

The teachings about the *tathagatagarbha* (Sanskrit for "Buddha embryo" or "Buddha nature") found in some Mahayana texts have influenced the schools of Zen Buddhism. According to these teachings, all beings have the potential to become Buddhas. Instead of emphasizing a progressive path to an exalted spiritual ideal, some Zen masters teach that complete enlightenment is always available right here and now — in this very moment — and can be experienced directly in a sudden burst of insight known in Japanese as *kensho* or *satori*. Other masters teach a gradual path. Some Zen masters de-emphasize the enlightenment experience altogether, teaching that the wholehearted practice of sitting meditation (Japanese: *zazen*) — or wholehearted practice in any situation — is enlightenment itself.

TECHNICAL STUFF

Zen is filled with stories of great masters who compare their enlightenment with Shakyamuni's enlightenment and speak of him as if he were an old friend and colleague. At the same time, enlightenment (though elusive) is regarded as the most ordinary realization of what has always been so. For this reason, the monks in many Zen stories break into laughter when they finally "get it." Awakened Zen practitioners are known for their down-to-earth involvement in every activity and for not displaying any trace of some special state called "realization."

Tuning in to the direct transmission from master to disciple

A reflection of a certain attitude toward enlightenment may be found in this Chan/Zen slogan:

> A special transmission outside the scriptures,
>
> No dependence on words and letters.
>
> Directly pointing to the mind,
>
> See true nature, become a Buddha.

The verse makes several points, which the following list expands on:

- **Special transmission outside the scriptures:** Zen traces its lineage back to Mahakashyapa, one of the Buddha's foremost disciples who apparently received the direct transmission of his teacher's "mind essence" by accepting a flower with a wordless smile. Since then, masters have directly "transmitted" their enlightened mind to their disciples, not through written texts, but through teachings passed on from mind to mind. But the truth is that enlightenment itself isn't transmitted; it has to burst into flame anew in each generation. The teacher merely acknowledges and certifies the awakening.
- **Directly pointing to the mind:** Masters don't explain abstract truth intellectually. Instead, they point their disciples' attention directly back to their innate true nature, which is ever present but generally unrecognized. With the master's guidance, the disciple wakes up and realizes that they aren't this limited separate self, but is rather pure, vast, mysterious, ungraspable consciousness itself — also known as the Buddha nature or Big Mind.
- **See true nature, become a Buddha:** Having realized true nature, the disciple now sees with the eyes of the Buddha and walks in the Buddha's shoes. No distance in space and time separates Shakyamuni's mind and the disciple's mind. Illustrating this point, some version of the following passage appears repeatedly in the old teaching tales: "There is no Buddha but mind, and no mind but the Buddha."

REMEMBER

The great Zen masters inevitably teach that mind includes all of reality, with nothing left out. This very body is the Buddha's body, this very mind is the Buddha's mind, and this very moment is inherently complete and perfect just the way it is — a truth known as *suchness* or *thusness*. Nothing needs to be changed or added to make this body, mind, and moment more spiritual or holy than it already is — you merely need to awaken to the nondual nature of reality for yourself. (Turn your attention to the sidebar "Pure as the driven snow" for some more info.)

PURE AS THE DRIVEN SNOW

Generations of Zen teachers have told the following story, recorded in the *Platform Sutra* of the Sixth Patriarch, to illustrate the distinction between a partial, progressive view of realization and the view of the Zen masters, who understand the mind to be intrinsically pure — and, therefore, in no need of purification through various methods and practices. The Fifth Patriarch of Zen in China gathered his monks together and asked each of them to write a verse that expressed their grasp of *true nature* (also known as *Buddha nature*). If he found one among them whose wisdom was clear, he promised to pass on his lineage to him and make him the Sixth Patriarch, his successor.

That night, the head monk came forward and wrote the following verse on the monastery wall:

> The body is the Bodhi tree,
>
> The mind is a clear mirror.
>
> We must strive to polish it constantly
>
> And not allow any dust to collect.

When the Fifth Patriarch read the verse, he knew that it showed some relative appreciation of the value of practice, but it also clearly revealed that the person who wrote it had not entered the gate of realization — and he told this to the head monk. In public, however, he praised the verse as worthy of study. Several days later, a young, illiterate novice who worked in the kitchen threshing rice heard someone reciting the verse and asked to be taken to the wall where it was written. There he had someone inscribe the following verse:

> Bodhi [awakening] has no tree,
>
> The mirror has no stand.
>
> Buddha nature is originally clear and pure.
>
> Where is there room for dust to collect?

In other words, your fundamental nature needs no polishing through spiritual practice because it's never been stained — even for an instant. When the Fifth Patriarch saw this verse, he knew that he had found his successor. Even though the young novice couldn't read or write, the Fifth Patriarch acknowledged his enlightenment and made him the Sixth Patriarch of Chinese Zen.

The ten ox-herding pictures

Ever since the ten ox-herding pictures were first created in 12th-century China, Zen masters in China, Korea, and Japan have used them to instruct and inspire their students. The images illustrate the ten stages of training the mind by comparing them to the taming of an ox. They begin with an individual's search for the ox and culminate with the individual's complete liberation.

The images (less frequently known as the cow-herding pictures) depict, in most cases, a water buffalo. After they became popular, numerous artists drew them over the centuries, with only minor differences. There's also a series of six ox-herding pictures in which the color of the ox undergoes gradual lightening from dark to white until the ox disappears. The comparison of an ox that needs to be tamed to a practitioner's unruly mind was already being made in early Indian Buddhist texts. These texts commonly use similes that appeal to a society whose main occupation was agriculture. One example is comparing the concept of karma to a seed that is sown in the ground and eventually bears fruit.

Here we explain the set of ten ox-herding pictures and its meaning:

- **Seeking the ox:** The first picture shows the herder, rope in hand, wandering in search of the lost ox.

  You have the desire to practice the Buddha's teaching and are taking the first steps in Zen practice.

- **Finding the tracks:** In the second picture, the herder finds the tracks of the ox and follows them.

  Having been introduced to the teachings of Zen, you study and practice them diligently and acquire a conceptual understanding of them.

- **Glimpsing the ox:** In the third picture, the herder glimpses the rear of the ox.

  You've clearly seen your true nature for the first time. But this realization quickly slips into the background, and you're still a long way from making it your constant companion.

- **Catching the ox:** In the fourth picture, the herder has caught the resistant ox and holds it by a rope.

  You're aware of your true nature in every moment and situation; you're never apart from it — even for an instant. But your mind continues to be turbulent and unruly, and you need to concentrate to keep from getting distracted.

- **Taming the ox:** In the fifth picture, the herder leads the now-docile ox by a rope.

Finally, as every trace of doubt disappears, the mind settles down. You're so firmly established in your experience of your true nature that even thoughts no longer distract you, for you realize that, like everything else in the universe, they're just an expression of who you fundamentally are.

- **Riding the ox home:** In the sixth picture, the herder has mounted the ox and rides home. The ox moves of its own accord, without being led by a rope.

  Now you and your true nature are in total harmony. You no longer have to struggle to resist temptation or distraction; you're completely at peace, inextricably connected to your essential source.

- **Forgetting the ox:** In the seventh picture, the herder is sitting outside their hut alone at sunrise.

  At last, the ox of your true nature has disappeared because you have completely and inseparably incorporated it. The ox was a convenient metaphor to lead you home. Ultimately, however, you and the ox are one! With nothing left to seek, you're thoroughly at ease, meeting life as it unfolds.

- **Forgetting both self and ox:** The last three pictures describe the state of a Buddha after enlightenment. In the eighth picture, we see an empty circle.

  The last traces of a separate self have dropped away, and with them, the last vestiges of realization have vanished. Even the thought "I am enlightened" or "I am the embodiment of Buddha nature" no longer arises. You're at the same time completely ordinary and completely free of any attachment or identification.

- **Returning to the source:** The ninth picture shows nature in full bloom, without an observer.

  After you've merged with your source, you see everything in all its diversity (painful and pleasurable, beautiful and ugly) as the perfect expression of this source. You don't need to resist or change anything; you're completely one with the *suchness* of life.

- **Entering the world with helping hands:** In the tenth picture, an older big-bellied and bare-chested figure sits happily at rest.

  With no trace of a separate self to be enlightened or deluded, the distinction between the two dissolves in spontaneous, compassionate activity. Now you move freely through the world like water through water, without the slightest resistance, joyfully responding to situations as they arise, helping where appropriate and naturally kindling awakening in others.

Finding the Common Threads in Buddhist Enlightenment

REMEMBER

The experience of enlightenment, though described slightly differently and approached by somewhat different means, bears notable similarities from tradition to tradition:

- Enlightenment signals the end of suffering and the eradication of craving and ignorance.
- Enlightenment also inevitably brings the birth of unshakable, indescribable peace, joy, loving-kindness, and compassion for others.
- Enlightenment involves being in the world but not of it.

4

Judaism

Contents at a Glance

IN THIS CHAPTER

» Understanding the difference between Ashkenazi and Sephardi Jews

» Exploring the wide spectrum from Orthodox to Reform (and beyond)

Chapter 1

Finding Out Who's a Jew and Why

Some people think you can tell if someone is Jewish just by looking at them, that there are characteristics that make someone Jewish. Maybe that's dark wavy or curly hair. Or a certain type of nose. But that's not the case at all.

What many people think of as "Jewish" is just one small segment of a much bigger picture — like finding out that kissing isn't all there is to love. There are blond Jews, Middle-Eastern Jews, Asian Jews, Black Jews, Latino Jews, Jews who look like Arnold Schwarzenegger, and Jews who look like Britney Spears.

What it comes down to is that Judaism isn't a race or even a particular culture or ethnic group. In this chapter, we briefly consider the beginnings of Judaism, some of the different denominations, and what makes someone Jewish.

Meeting the Jewish Tribe

A little over 15 million Jews are spread around the world, including about 6 million in the United States and about 7 million in Israel — so Judaism isn't simply "a nation." And, some Jewish people seem to know more Jews who don't believe in

God or practice Jewish observances than those who do, so being Jewish doesn't even necessarily have to do with religion.

REMEMBER

So what does it mean to be Jewish? Here are the basics:

- **Being *Jewish* (being "a *Jew*") means you're a Member of the Tribe (an M-O-T).** The tribe started with a couple named Abraham and Sarah more than 4,000 years ago, it grew over time, and it's still here today. You can become an authentic part of the Jewish tribe in two ways: by being born to a Jewish mother or joining through a series of rituals (called *converting*). Some folks think there are other ways of becoming a Jew, too; we cover that issue later in this chapter.
- ***Judaism* is a set of beliefs, practices, and ethics based on the Torah (see Book 4, Chapter 5).** You can practice Judaism and not be Jewish, and you can be a Jew and not practice Judaism. Confusing, right? That's why we're starting here for you before diving into the full basics of the religion.

What's in a name?

The word "Jewish" doesn't appear in the Bible at all (see Book 4, Chapter 5 for more on Jewish religious texts such as the Hebrew Bible). For example, the folks who came out of slavery in Egypt in the Book of Exodus were called "Hebrews" or "Children of Israel," and they each belonged to one of the 12 tribes of Israel. Ten of the 12 tribes were dispersed by the Assyrians in the eighth century BCE, but the tribe of Judah and the smaller tribe of Benjamin remained as the Southern Kingdom known as Judea until early in the sixth century BCE.

TIP

When Judea fell to the Babylonians, and the people were taken into exile, they became known as the Judah-ites *(Yehudim)*, since they were the people of Judah *(Yehudah)*. In Hebrew, the name *Yehudim* persists today and simply means "Jews." The religion they practiced was later called "Judah-ism" — which became "Judaism." We prefer to pronounce this word "Judah-ism" rather than "Jude-ism" or "Judy-ism" — which makes it sound like you're talking about Judy Garland.

Jews far and wide

The Jewish people have always tended to fan out across the known world. Evidence indicates that even centuries before Jesus, Jewish communities inhabited the North African and East African coasts, Europe, and Asia. Jews were among the first people to come to the Americas from Europe in the 15th and 16th centuries. Some evidence suggests that there was at least one Jew aboard the ship with Columbus. (Some people suspect that Columbus himself was a Jew, perhaps because Jews were kicked out of Spain in 1492.)

Everywhere the Jews went, their population grew through intermarriage and conversion, and — most importantly — they kept their basic religion while adopting the culture and norms of the local area. That's why up to 20 percent of Jews descended from European ancestors have blue eyes and why some Jews are Black, Hispanic, or Asian. It's also why a Jew from New York looks and acts different than a Jew from Mumbai, but each one can probably fumble along with most of the other's *Shabbat* ("shah-baht") service (the weekly Jewish holiday that lets people take a break from the pressures of the workweek, which you can read more about in Book 4, Chapter 3).

Similarly, Jewish food, music, and humor from Iraq and Yemen is much more Arabic in nature than the Spanish flavor of Jews from Brazil and Argentina, which is different than the borscht soup and klezmer music of Jews from Europe. They even all speak Hebrew with different dialects! Jews just don't fit any consistent set of stereotypes or expectations.

And yet, all Jews are inextricably linked together simply by being Jewish. Perhaps it's a common practice and belief in Judaism; perhaps it's a common sense of history, or a shared sense of being an outsider from the broader culture. Or perhaps it's a deep, innate feeling of connection to the tribe.

Who decides if you're Jewish?

Two years after the new government of Israel came to power in 1948, it passed the Law of Return, which states that anyone born of a Jewish mother or anyone who has converted to Judaism can move to Israel and claim citizenship. This immediately re-ignited a controversy that began much earlier and continues to this day: Who gets to say whether or not someone is really Jewish?

Whether someone practiced Judaism wasn't an issue for citizenship because Israel was founded for the most part by secular Jews. But what about people born Jewish who had been raised as Christians or Muslims or who practiced another religion? Some say you have to not only identify yourself as Jewish, but also not practice any other religion. Others say that religion has nothing to do with it and point out that the Nazis killed thousands of people who were Jewish by birth but practiced some other religion. Each year Israeli courts consider cases arguing over whether someone is or is not Jewish.

And what about people who convert? Technically, someone who converts to Judaism is no different from someone who was born Jewish. However, not everyone sees it that way. In the next section, we discuss the various denominations of

Judaism, including the Orthodox Jews who refuse to acknowledge the conversion of anyone converted by a Reform or Conservative rabbi (A *rabbi* is someone who helps run religious services and serves as an educator and a counselor. For more on the role of a rabbi, see Book 4, Chapter 4.)

Many people say, "I'm half Jewish" (if one parent is Jewish) or "I'm a quarter-Jewish" (if one grandparent is Jewish). Traditional Jews argue that either you're Jewish or you're not. To them, if your mother's mother was Jewish, then your mother is Jewish, and if your mother is Jewish, then you're Jewish. Among Reform and Reconstructionist Jews (more on them later in this chapter), if only your father is Jewish and you were raised Jewish, then you're considered Jewish, too.

It's a small world

Jews have long spread out to the corners of the world, so significant Jewish communities (over 100,000 people) live in France, Australia, Argentina, and South Africa. In America, most people think all the Jews live in big cities such as New York (where there are over 1.5 million Jews). But many also live in the "Wild West" states like Wyoming, the deep south states like Louisiana, and everywhere in-between.

In fact, not only do far more Jewish people live outside of Israel than within today, it has been this way for over 2,500 years. And no matter where they live, most Jews today identify with one of two groups: Ashkenazi and Sephardi.

Ashkenazi

The descendants of Jews who, until around 1900, lived anywhere from northwest Europe (like France and Germany) to eastern Europe (including Russia, Ukraine, and Lithuania) are usually called *Ashkenazi* (pronounced "ahsh-ke-nah-zee;" *Ashkenazim* is plural). The majority of Jews in the world are Ashkenazi.

Sephardi

The descendants of Jews who lived in Spain up until the 15th century are called *Sephardi* (seh-far-dee; *Sephardim* is plural). After the expulsion, these Jews traveled to North Africa, Italy, the Ottoman Empire (Turkey), and back to the Middle East. Of course, many Jews started out in those areas (never having traveled as far as Spain to begin with), but they're generally called Sephardi anyway.

You may also hear Jews from the Middle East called *Mizrachi* ("from the East;" Hebrew has no "ch" sound, so this is the guttural "kh" sound).

Over the past 500 years, the *Sephardim* primarily interacted with Muslims, especially African and Arab Muslims. Today much of their culture (music, language, liturgical melodies, food, festival customs, and so on) is based on those cultures. The Ashkenazim, on the other hand, mostly interacted with European Christian cultures, resulting in a very different ethnic feeling.

Although Israel was founded primarily by Ashkenazi Jews, more than half of Israelis have always been Sephardim. However, the very different cultures have caused a number of difficulties. Many Ashkenazi Jews mistrust Sephardi Jews and think they've "ruined" Israel, and vice versa. Fortunately, as time goes by, things seem to be getting better.

Exploring the Major Branches of the Tree

When we say that Judaism is a set of beliefs and practices, we're glossing over one key point: Judaism encompasses a lot of different sets of beliefs and practices! In some ways, you can see Judaism as a tree with many branches; there's a common trunk and root system, but each sect or denomination is off on its own branch, and in many cases, each synagogue is on its own little twig.

Most Jews see the biggest branches of the tree as Orthodox, Conservative, Reform, and Non-Religious — plus, they may add a few others, like Ultra-Orthodox, Modern Orthodox, Reconstructionist, Renewal, and Humanistic. On the other hand, some traditional Orthodox Jews see it differently: To them, Orthodoxy is the whole tree, and what everyone else is doing is something else — maybe a whole other tree, but certainly not practicing Judaism.

The basic difference between the groups is that while the Orthodox believe that the Torah (both written and oral; see Book 4, Chapter 5) was literally given by God to Moses, word for word, more liberal Jews tend to believe that the Torah and *halakhah* (Jewish law) may have been Divinely inspired but were expressed by humans influenced by their own time and place.

Orthodox Jews

When you hear the term "Orthodox Jew," you probably think of a man in a long black coat, with long locks of hair over his sideburns, a big beard, and a black hat. But in reality, there are dozens of different styles within Jewish Orthodoxy, each of them with a different culture, educational philosophy, leadership model, and set of policies. True, many of them do, in fact, wear black hats and coats, but many others — typically called Modern Orthodox Jews — almost always wear modern dress, and you may not be able to even tell them apart from non-Jews.

However, all Orthodox Jews technically accept the Torah as the word of God. So although you can see a massive cultural difference between the Orthodox Jew who wears a *shtreimel* (the black fur hat worn by some Ultra-Orthodox) and the Orthodox Jew who wears jeans and a T-shirt, most people would find it extremely difficult to discern a difference between their religious beliefs and observance.

TECHNICAL STUFF

Liberal Jews began calling more observant Jews "Orthodox" (which literally means "correct belief" or "proper doctrine") in the late 19th century as a somewhat derogatory term. But to the Orthodox, there's no spectrum of "less Orthodox" and "more Orthodox," so the term didn't really mean anything to them. Nevertheless, the word stuck.

However, most people make a distinction between "Modern Orthodox" Jews (who engage in many aspects of modern, secular culture) and "Ultra-Orthodox" Jews (sometimes called *haredi* or "black hats," who tend to insulate themselves from modern culture). You can always find exceptions, though! Chabad (a Jewish movement centered around turning knowledge into action and intellectual study), for one, falls somewhere between the two.

All the black clothes

We know you're dying to ask: "Why do some Orthodox Jews wear all that black?" The simple answer is that they're in mourning for the destruction of the Second Temple (a place of worship in Jerusalem that was built after the First Temple was destroyed by Babylonians around 586 BCE but that was later destroyed by the Romans in 70 CE), more than 1,900 years ago. However, that doesn't explain what they wear. Although some "black hat" Orthodox communities (such as Chabad Lubavitch and the *Mitnagdim*; see "Hasidim and Mitnagdim," later in this chapter) wear somewhat modern black suits, others — especially *Hasidic* Ultra-Orthodox — consciously try to resist modern influences. Their long black coats, black hats, white stockings, and old-style shoes are a way to hold on to the old eastern European culture of the 18th century. Traditional women don't have the same dress codes, but they do tend to dress more modestly.

Ultra-Orthodox Jews set themselves apart in other ways, too. Many Ultra-Orthodox Jews minimize their contact with the "outside world," so they usually don't have televisions in their homes, they tune their radios to religious programming, they don't go to movies, and at least one group has ruled that its members shouldn't use the Internet.

For many people, these restraints seem extreme. On the other hand, think of it this way: How much pornography do you want your family exposed to? For some folks, much of the secular world is pretty pornographic and offensive, and they wonder "Why even be tempted by it?"

Different groups, different interpretations

Even in a relatively small Jewish community with few Orthodox Jews, you may find several Orthodox synagogues. Two reasons explain this: First, the Orthodox have to be able to walk to the synagogue on Shabbat; second, each Orthodox congregation has its own particular culture, ideas, interpretations, and style.

For example, one Orthodox rabbi may say that the biblical commandment "Don't round off the corner of your beard" means don't cut the *earlocks* (the hair that grows to the side of the forehead). Another rabbi says, "No, the commandment means that men should not shave." A third rabbi may chime in with this interpretation: "You can't shave with an instrument with a single cutting edge, but you can use a rotary-blade shaver."

Similarly, some groups are staunch *Zionists* (supporters of a Jewish state of Israel), and others don't believe that Israel should exist (because the Messiah hasn't come yet). Some believe that their children should get a secular education as well as a religious education, and others say that only a religious education is important. Some socialize with non-traditional Jews or visit a non-Orthodox synagogue, and others refuse.

REMEMBER

There is no ultimate authority for Judaism; so each Jew must decide whom and what to follow.

Hasidim and Mitnagdim

A "who's who" of all the different Orthodox groups and their doctrines would fill a small book by itself. However, they all basically fall into one of two types: *Hasidim* and *Mitnagdim* (also pronounced "misnagdim" by many Ashkenazi Jews). Because the word "*Hasidim*" (plural of "*Hasid*") is pronounced with the "kh" sound at the back of the throat, like the Scottish "Loch Ness," some people spell it *Chasidism.*

Hasidism was a movement founded in the 18th century by the Ba'al Shem Tov (a.k.a. Rabbi Israel ben Eliezer [1700 to 1760]) focusing on sincere, joyful, and intense prayer — including ecstatic dancing, singing, and storytelling as a way to connect with God. Shortly after 1760, when the Ba'al Shem Tov died, *Hasidism* splintered into a number of other groups, like *Chabad Lubavitch*, *Belzer*, *Satmar*, and *Breslov* (which all still exist today). Hasidism appeared at a time when traditional Judaism focused on an ascetic, scholarly approach to Torah and Talmud (see Book 4, Chapter 5). Most rabbis of the time insisted that only learned, critical, and erudite study was important, in contrast to the simple and sincere devotion of Hasidism. Elijah ben Solomon Zalman, known as the Vilna Gaon, was the driving force behind these ascetic Jews, who became known as Mitnagdim (which literally means "opponents"); he even went so far as to prohibit interactions with the *Hasidim*, fearing that their ecstatic worship and lack of intellectual focus was a danger to Judaism.

Fortunately, by the end of the 19th century, most of the antagonism subsided, especially as the two groups formed a common front against religious reformers and anti-Semitism. Since then, the *Hasidic* and Mitnaggid movements have greatly influenced each other. There are still differences, though. While the Mitnagdim tend to focus on the head of a particular *yeshivah* (school), the Hasidim tend to focus on their particular *rebbe* (what they call their rabbis), who acts almost as a guru does in some Eastern traditions. Mitnagdim tend to base their study on Talmud and *halakhah*, and *Hasidim* tend to study the writings of their rebbe (and his rebbe, and so on, as well as other traditional texts).

Breakaway denominations

How does Judaism deal with the fact that times and people change? Traditional Jews tend either to avoid the changes or — more commonly — to apply established interpretations of Torah, Talmud, and previous *halakhah* to modern issues. However, in the early 19th century, many Jews began to rethink this position, arguing that these sources weren't actually Divine after all, but rather very human responses to Divine inspiration. If the Torah, Talmud, and *halakhah* are human creations, these reformers reasoned, then they can be inspected, judged, and understood to be affected by their particular time and place of creation.

REMEMBER

These folks weren't saying that the traditional texts had no meaning; they still studied Torah, Talmud, and *halakhah*, but they insisted that some passages were more meaningful for particular timeframes than others and that individuals are responsible for finding what's relevant in their own time.

These groups are usually lumped together under the umbrella of "Liberal Judaism," although there is a wide spectrum of belief and observance among the groups. The best-known groups are Reform, Conservative, Reconstructionist, Renewal, and Humanistic. Most of these groups are American and — to a lesser degree — European movements. They do exist in Israel, where they're gradually becoming more established.

Reform

Reform Judaism (yes it's Reform, not Reformed!) — probably the largest Jewish group in America — rests on the idea that all Jews have the responsibility to educate themselves and make decisions about their spiritual practice based on conscience rather than simply relying on external law. In Reform Judaism, the Torah, Talmud, and *halakhah* are necessary resources, but Reform Jews tend to focus on social and ethical action based on the writings of the Prophets rather than the ritual observance of the Torah and the *halakhah* of the Talmud.

Unfortunately, many Jews today associate the Reform movement — which outside of North America is usually called Progressive or Liberal Judaism — with empty and meaningless services or congregations that want to retain a sense of being Jewish without actually following any practice other than the Passover seder and Friday night services. We won't deny that some groups are like this, nor that the Reform movement of the 1950s and 1960s often lacked a sense of spirituality, but the Reform movement has changed radically in recent decades. Today, many Reform congregations are deeply committed to a living and evolving sense of Judaism and Jewish spirituality.

Reform Jews tend to strip away what they consider to be unessential elements of Judaism in order to more closely observe the kernel of the tradition. For example, when the movement began in the early 19th century, Reform synagogues started seating men and women together, pretty much dropped the dietary laws, and encouraged instrumental music at Shabbat services. Clothing customs — such as *yarmulkes* (small, brimless hats) and prayer shawls — were discouraged (though today growing numbers of Reform Jews wear them).

REMEMBER

In 1972, the Reform movement became the first Jewish movement to ordain women as rabbis. Although the Reform movement, which is currently the fastest-growing group in American Jewry, continues to innovate, it has also started to embrace more traditional practices, as reflected in the 1999 revision of the basic principles of Reform Judaism.

Conservative

The Conservative Judaism movement (which is often called Historical Judaism in Europe and is called *Masorti* in Israel) is reminiscent of the fable of the Three Bears, in which Goldilocks said, "That one was too soft, that one was too hard, but this one is just right!" Since the late 19th century, many Jews have felt that the Reform movement went too far in its rejection of traditional observance, but also that Orthodox communities were unrealistic in their restrictions regarding modern life.

Conservative Jews tend to respect many Jewish laws, like keeping *kosher* (which means adhering to the dietary standards set out by Jewish law), observing Shabbat and other religious holidays, and performing daily prayers. At the same time, they agree with the Reform movement that *halakhah* has its basis in history and therefore needs to be reconsidered in each age. Conservative rabbis ruled that when Jews live too far from a synagogue, they can drive there (but they encouraged walking when possible), and some wines and cheeses that were ruled kosher for Conservatives have not been accepted by Orthodox Jews.

Conservative synagogues have sometimes been perceived as being inconsistent on Jewish legal issues. Some people have accused Conservative Jews of hypocrisy because their rabbis appear to tend toward Orthodox practices while the congregants appear to tend toward Reform practices. But there are some Conservative congregations that are virtually indistinguishable from Modern Orthodox groups, so you just can't tell without walking in, sitting down, and seeing for yourself.

Conservative Judaism flourished during the 20th century and was, for a long time, the largest Jewish movement in the United States. However, some reports indicate that its size has been shrinking in recent years as many Conservative Jews find themselves increasingly drawn to Reform, Renewal, or Orthodox congregations. (People who were offended when the Conservative movement began ordaining women rabbis in 1985 were especially drawn to the Orthodox community.)

Reconstructionist

When the 17th-century Jewish philosopher Baruch Spinoza announced that God was not a separate being but rather nature itself, the Jewish community was so outraged that they excommunicated him, declaring that no other Jew could even talk with him, much less read his writings. Skip ahead 300 years, and you find the 20th-century theologian Mordecai Kaplan taking Spinoza's theories even further. The result? A group of Orthodox rabbis excommunicated him and burned the prayer book that he had published.

Today, no one remembers the names of those book-burning rabbis, but every philosophy student in the world reads Spinoza, and Kaplan is the founder of the fourth major Jewish movement: Reconstructionist Judaism.

Kaplan was a Conservative rabbi, and during his long tenure at the Conservative rabbinical seminary, he began to teach that God wasn't a Being, but rather the natural, underlying moral and creative force of the universe, the force that creates order and makes for human happiness. He also taught that each generation of Jews had the obligation to keep Judaism alive by "reconstructing" it — not by stripping away the practices and words like the Reform movement, but by reinterpreting them, in order to find new meanings that are relevant for the time.

Reconstructionism, as a separate movement, developed in the late 1920s but didn't establish a rabbinical school until 1968. Today, the movement counts about 100 congregations. Reconstructionist congregations tend to see the rabbi as a facilitator and a valuable resource, but not necessarily the leader; they encourage a lot of lay participation and creative reworking of both ritual and worship.

Renewal

Jewish Renewal sprang from the philosophies of Martin Buber and Abraham Heschel, as well as the "Neo-Hasidic" teachings of Reb Shlomo Carlebach and

Reb Zalman Schachter-Shalomi. It teaches that people can draw wisdom from a variety of diverse sources, including *Hasidism*, *Kabbalah*, feminism, the Prophets, environmentalism, and the writings of the ancient rabbis.

Renewal focuses on a welcoming, egalitarian, hands-on approach to Jewish worship and community. It encourages mixing both traditional and feminist ideals. What's more, Renewal congregations have embraced lessons from diverse spiritual traditions, such as Eastern philosophy and both Eastern and Jewish meditative practices. Renewal programs support a spiritual ecology, relating Jewish practices to both political as well as ecological action.

The 40 or 50 Jewish Renewal congregations and *chavurot* (friendship groups) around the world (mostly in America) vary widely in their observance of traditional liturgy and ritual. In fact, the group defines itself as "transdenominational," inviting Jews from all aspects of the greater Jewish community to reconnect, learn, and celebrate together.

Humanistic Judaism

What do you do if you feel Jewish — you like the Jewish holidays, food, music, sense of ethics and social involvement, humor, and so on — but you're not into the idea of God? You're certainly not alone. The Humanistic Jewish movement, also called Secular Humanistic Judaism, was established in 1963 by Rabbi Sherwin Wine and is based on Humanist ideals of rational, critical thinking, as well as developing the depths and dimensions of both individuals and communities.

Humanistic Jews focus on Jewish culture and civilization, celebrating Jewish heritage as a way to find meaning in life and minimizing the role of God or any cosmic forces. In fact, Humanistic Jews define a Jew as pretty much anyone who identifies with the history and culture of the Jewish people. They completely remove any theistic language from their liturgy.

Humanistic congregations around North America celebrate the Jewish holidays, Bar and Bat Mitzvahs, and other Jewish traditions, although they ascribe non-religious interpretations to everything. These Jews tend to be very involved with social action, and it's probably no coincidence that the first ordained Humanistic rabbi was a woman.

MESSIANIC JEWS

Despite the historical fact that almost all early Christians, like Jesus himself, were Jews, today Judaism is completely incompatible with a belief in Jesus as Messiah. However, a tiny minority of Jews and non-Jews who observe Jewish traditions — like wearing yarmulkes and prayer shawls, reciting the *Sh'ma*, and celebrating the Jewish holidays — do believe that Jesus is the Jewish *Mashiach* (Messiah).

People who believe in both Jewish observance and that Jesus brings redemption are called Messianic Jews. (Some folks call them "Jews for Jesus," but that's just the name of their biggest outreach organization, not the denomination itself.) Some of them go to Messianic synagogues, others go to church, most call Jesus "Y'shua," and like other Christians, they're all waiting for Jesus to return.

Jewish groups and rabbis almost universally condemn *Messianic* Judaism (sometimes called *Nazarene Judaism*) as a Christian movement or even a cult, and they insist that the movement is an abomination and a threat to Judaism. Many Christians also find Messianic Judaism confusing and un-Christian, and so the group's beliefs place it between a rock and a hard place.

IN THIS CHAPTER

» Tracing Judaism from Abraham through Moses

» Fleeing Egypt to David's kingdom

» Replacing older beliefs with faith in God

» Enduring and thriving despite persecution

Chapter 2
Judaism's Deep Roots in History

During a trip to New York, you may be walking down a Manhattan side street when you notice an old synagogue under repair. New York is dotted with these old buildings that have been refurbished after hundreds of years of use.

Wondering about the old synagogue, you may ask an elderly man standing nearby, one who clearly belongs to a group of religious Jews called Hasidic (more on them in Book 4 Chapter 1) since he's wearing a black hat, has a beard and unruly sideburns, and fringes poke out from under his coat in accordance with biblical law.

If the man were to tell you what was inside, he may describe men wearing a skullcap (*kepot*) and prayer shawl (*tallit*) and standing in a small chapel inside a nondescript brick building. A very young man, maybe 12, is leading prayers to honor his late father. Although, to be a valid service, the congregation needs ten adult Jewish males (called a *minyan*).

What he describes is one of the oldest forms of worship still functioning anywhere in the world.

In this chapter, you find out more about how Judaism started and has endured for close to 4,000 years.

WHAT'S IN A NAME?

Names used in the Bible for Jewish leaders and for God have various origins.

- The original name for Jews, *Hebrew*, is of unknown origin. It is thought to translate "from across the river," a reference to people who crossed the Euphrates River, which waters the land around Babylon. Abraham would have had to ford the Euphrates and its sister waterway, the Tigris, when he left Ur.
- The name *Israel* was given to Jacob, Abraham's grandson. It's believed to mean "he who strives with God." The reference is to a story in the Bible where Jacob wrestled all night with an angel of God. (You can read the whole story in Genesis 32:22–32.)

  Eventually, Israel replaced Hebrew, and the Jewish people became known as *Israelites*.
- The familiar words *Jew* and *Judaism* are derived from the name of the most powerful of the 12 tribes of Israelites, Judah.
- Another name that rings in Jewish history is *Moses*. His name is not Hebrew for "lifted from the water," as the Bible says, but rather is a perfectly good Egyptian name.

  It exists in Raamses, the supposed Pharaoh of the era, and in Thutmose, a great Pharaoh of another era. *Moses* means "son of." Raamses means "son of Ra," the Egyptian word for spirit. Thutmose means "son of Thoth," the god of wisdom.

From Abraham, Judaism Takes the Long Road

You may be so used to religions centered around the idea that there is one God that you may not be aware that religions based on this idea had to struggle to survive. That was particularly true for Judaism, the oldest of the three great monotheistic faiths (with Christianity and Islam being the other two — and which you can read more about in Books 5 and 6, respectively).

When Abraham, the first Hebrew patriarch who God called to found a new nation, decided to follow a god named Yahweh about three millennia ago, he didn't think anyone else would join him. He didn't preach to anyone. His children adopted their father's belief, but no neighbors did.

REMEMBER

Abraham didn't develop any rules for his new religion either. The laws and customs that comprise Judaism today developed over centuries, finally becoming recognizable to modern eyes around the sixth century BC.

Initially, the people who became Jews were called *Hebrews*. They claimed Abraham as their father and lived as shepherds around the area now known as Israel.

TECHNICAL STUFF

The dates for early Jewish history are tentative, simply because time has erased many of the landmarks that would help locate people and places. Worse, many cities were destroyed or now exist under different names.

Like father, like son: The leaders after Abraham

After Abraham died, Jewish history shifts its focus to his son Isaac's family. Jacob, Isaac's youngest son, took center stage, and he was followed by Joseph, Jacob's second-youngest son, who rose to be second in command in Egypt.

Egyptian historians have insisted that Joseph never reached any position of authority within the government. The Egyptians detested and feared the Semites, which is a term used to describe people who spoke a related language, like the Hebrew of the Jews. They weren't likely to let a Semite like Joseph become one of their primary rulers. Their dislike was understandable. At one point, Semitic raiders, known to the Egyptians as *Hyksos* (foreign conquerors), overthrew the native pharaoh and ruled the country between about 1750 and 1550 BCE.

Given the native Egyptians' animosity toward Semites, some scholars have proposed that Joseph may have reached power during the time of the Hyksos.

Over the river and through the desert, to Pharaoh's land we go

According to the Bible, Joseph was his father's favorite and was given a special colorful coat to reflect that feeling. His brothers were jealous and sold Joseph into slavery. After a series of adventures, he finally came to the attention of the ruler of Egypt, the Pharaoh. Joseph reached his high office among the Egyptians by interpreting a dream that frightened Pharaoh, predicting a terrible seven-year famine throughout the land. The Bible reports that when famine struck the region, Jacob and his sons were forced to seek food in Egypt where Joseph was overseeing food storage and distribution. The Bible says the family then settled in Egypt at the invitation of Pharaoh, who extended the offer because he respected Joseph and wanted to help him reunite with his family. (Tim Rice and Andrew Lloyd Webber wrote a hugely popular Broadway musical back in the 1960s called *Joseph and The Amazing Technicolor Dreamcoat.*)

TECHNICAL STUFF

The purpose of the story may be to explain how the Jews ended up in Egypt. Many Jewish customs and rituals seem to have an Egyptian tinge. Historically, Egypt was the dominant nation in the region. Many of its ideas would have naturally filtered into surrounding cultures, especially when carried along by powerful armies. No one had to live in Egypt to adopt them. That's why some historians argue that the Jews never actually settled in Egypt.

Moses, Receiver of God's Laws

After the Jews had made Egypt their home for many years, a new leader arose among them to lead the Jews to the *Promised Land*, today known as Israel. Someone who could lead the Jews out of Egypt was needed because the Israelites didn't enjoy their stay in their adopted homeland.

After Joseph died, a new pharaoh of Egypt came to power and didn't know how Joseph had helped save the Egyptians from starvation and death. The new pharaoh enslaved the newcomers. The Israelites were forced to build cities, and they became embittered by the experience that lasted, according to accounts written much later, about 400 years. They thought God had forgotten them, and they prayed for rescue.

Eventually God responded. He sent Moses, the son of slave parents. Raised in the palace, according to the biblical account in the book of Exodus, Moses didn't know his parentage until he killed a vicious overseer and fled into the desert after discovering the truth.

In the arid land of Midian, he had a face-to-face meeting with God before a bush that was on fire yet remained unscathed by the flames. God ordered Moses to return to Egypt. There he confronted the pharaoh and demanded the slaves be set free.

Relying on plagues and walls of water to escape slavery

Armed with a staff that reverted to a snake upon command and performed miracles, Moses succeeded in freeing his countrymen from captivity with the help of God, who sent ten consecutive plagues:

- The Nile River turned to blood
- Frogs
- Lice
- Flies
- Sick animals
- Boils
- Hail
- Locust
- Darkness
- Death of the firstborn

The Jews remember the plagues every year during the Passover holiday, which commemorates the Exodus of the Jews from Egypt. (See Book 4, Chapter 3 for more about Passover.)

The plagues convinced the pharaoh to allow the Jews to leave Egypt. However, he changed his mind and chased them to the Sea of Reeds — some people mistranslate the words as the Red Sea. The Suez Canal now sits where the Sea of Reeds once was. Moses parted the waves so the Jews could cross, and the pursuing Egyptians drowned in the returning waters.

A song that Miriam, Moses's sister, reportedly sang as the Israelites rejoiced on the opposite bank of the waterway is still repeated in Jewish houses of worship around the world. Its age adds authenticity to the account, although archaeology has found no evidence for an actual exodus.

In the biblical account, after Moses and the Jews left Egypt, they spent 40 years wandering through the Sinai Desert before they reached the Promised Land (Israel).

Counting on the Ten Commandments

During the Jews' long trek through the desert, God called Moses up to Mount Sinai for a little chat. There, according to the biblical text, Moses accepted the Ten Commandments from God. They have been the guiding moral precepts for Western society ever since.

REMEMBER

The commandments, as written in the biblical book of Exodus, Chapter 20, go like this:

1. You shall have no other gods before Me.
2. You shall not make for yourself a carved image.
3. You shall not take the name of the Lord your God in vain.
4. Remember the Sabbath to keep it holy.
5. Honor your father and your mother.
6. You shall not murder.
7. You shall not commit adultery.
8. You shall not steal.
9. You shall not bear false witness against your neighbor.
10. You shall not covet.

Joshua takes control

Moses died overlooking the land that the residents then called Canaan after turning over his leadership to Joshua. Moses was not allowed into Israel because he had disobeyed God, according to the Bible. The text says he banged a rock to bring forth water instead of letting God's word suffice.

Joshua, who had been Moses's assistant, guided the Israelites in their conquest of Canaan, a land described as flowing with milk and honey. He parted the water of the Jordan River so the people could pass, directed attacks on major cities, and then distributed the captured land among the 12 tribes of Israel.

WARNING

In the biblical account included in the book of Joshua, the escaped slaves overwhelm major Canaanite cities and take control of the land. However, historical findings to date don't support that tale. No evidence of an invasion of the land has ever been found. The conquest should be easy to prove. Every cultural group produced its own ceramic pots with a unique design. Canaanite ceramics then should be different from the ones produced by the former Hebrew slaves. Unfortunately, ceramics found by archaeologists are unchanged for centuries. Moreover, some cities supposedly destroyed by Joshua and his army — like Jericho and Ai — were already in ruins during the era when Joshua must have lived. The debate is not settled, and supporters of the account continue to dig for evidence.

This issue is significant because Jewish claims for Israel date from God's promise to Abraham and continual Jewish occupation of the land after the Exodus. The lack of a conquest would create a shadow over Jewish claims.

The Days of the Judges

After the Exodus from Egypt, the Israelites lived in Canaan and adopted the gods of other residents there, including deities like Moloch who demanded human sacrifice. Their leaders in those confusing days were called *judges*, individuals who arose when trouble threatened and would save their people.

Judges were colorful people who did all sorts of things to help get rid of foreign conquerors. One of them was Samson, who, like a sun god, lost his power when his hair (rays of the sun) was shorn by a devious mistress. He was strong and eventually destroyed a temple filled with enemies.

Another was Gideon, who may have been a real king and whose name has been borrowed in modern times by earnest folks who pass out Bibles worldwide. Gideon led an army to rout enemies of his people.

The last judge was named Samuel. Unhappy with continual invasions by enemies, the people pressed him to find someone to rule over and protect them. He finally agreed after warning them that a king would raise taxes and use their young men in his army.

The Time of Kings

Samuel first chose a tall man named Saul to be king. Saul had lots of problems, both with rebellious followers and with his own mental health. His favorite son, Jonathan, even supported a fella named David, who played musical instruments for Saul and would succeed him as king one day.

Eventually Jonathan and Saul were killed by the Philistines, the chief enemy of the Jews at the time. David seized the throne but is credited with the immortal lament: "How the mighty have fallen."

David starts a dynasty

David had played many roles before becoming king. He even fought on behalf of the Philistines before seizing the throne after Saul died. Just to be safe, David also killed virtually all of Saul's relatives.

REMEMBER

David is considered Israel's greatest king. His descendants were expected to rule the land. That's why Jews, in later times, looked to David's family for a new anointed king (or a *messiah*) to arise to throw off foreign control. Jesus was thought to be of the line of David.

David had a successful reign. He subdued enemies along Israel's border, captured Jerusalem and made it his capital, and brought back the holy carrying case (called an *ark*) of the Lord.

David was also the first king to be guided by *prophets*, holy men who told the people what God wanted of them.

Solomon rules wisely

King David was succeeded by his son, Solomon. He built the holiest building in Jewish history, the Temple, also known as the First Temple or Solomon's Temple. It was a place of worship and considered incredibly holy because God was supposed to live there.

Solomon had many wives, reportedly entertained visiting monarchs like the Queen of Sheba, and lived lavishly. He imported wood and materials from around the known world and became famous for his wisdom.

Splitting into two kingdoms

The Jewish kingdom did not endure, but split into two parts after Solomon died: Israel in the north; Judah in the south.

Israel had a series of kings, while Judah was led by David's descendants. Neither land was strong enough to defend itself long against the huge empires that began to appear on the horizon.

WHO WERE THE PROPHETS?

Jews recognize major and minor prophets. The distinction isn't a reflection on what the individual said, but how much of his writings survived the passage of time.

Major prophets are:

- Isaiah
- Jeremiah
- Ezekiel

Minor prophets include:

- Amos
- Habakkuk
- Haggai
- Hosea
- Joel
- Malachi
- Micah
- Nahum
- Obadiah
- Zechariah
- Zephaniah

Getting Conquered: The Jews Find Themselves in Hot Water

Abraham probably thought he had bought himself a pack of trouble when he loaded up his ox cart and headed east from Ur into the unknown wilderness. Actually, he had it easy compared to his descendants who have been conquered and attacked by many different countries and people ever since they moved into Canaan perhaps 3,000 years ago.

The list of conquerors includes:

» Assyrians, a tribe located in what is now Syria, who swept over Israel. The residents were forced to leave, becoming the Ten Lost Tribes.

» Babylonians, who captured Judah and sent its residents into captivity.

» Persians, who let the Jews return home about 60 years after the Babylonians drove them away.

» Greeks, led by Alexander the Great.

» Syrians, who succeeded the Greeks after Alexander's kingdom shattered.

» Romans, who created an enormous empire throughout Europe, northern Africa, and the eastern portion of Asia.

WHAT HAPPENED TO THE ISRAELITES?

Historians speculated for years about the fate of Israelites after they were overwhelmed by the Assyrians around 723 BCE. Writers as late as the 1800s thought the Native Americans were descendants of the missing tribes. Today, by using chemical markers in blood, scientists have traced the last descendants of those Israelites to a tribe living in South Africa.

Monotheism arrives

From Moses to the time of the Babylonians in the sixth century BCE, the Israelites weren't *monotheists* (people who worship only one god). They believed that their God was supreme, but they recognized the existence of other gods and worshipped them.

Jewish teachers, called prophets, continually called on believers to put their faith totally in God, who, they said, would protect his people from foreign invaders.

In those days, people accepted whichever god seemed the strongest. Conquerors had no trouble imposing their religious beliefs. After all, the winner's god definitely had to be stronger than the god of the losing side.

Besides, no one wanted to be wrong. Why not keep all the gods happy, just in case one of them actually had some power? As a result, a famous prophet, Jeremiah, in the sixth and seventh centuries BCE complained that God was using the Babylonians to punish the Jews for maintaining the snake god of Moses and other idols in the Temple. Soon after, King Josiah ordered all the foreign idols destroyed.

REMEMBER

As a result of prophets, the old idols were banished in the seventh century BCE, and Jews became true monotheists. Never again would they turn to another deity, even after their land was finally conquered by the Babylonians late in the sixth century BCE.

Living under foreign rule

Conquerors, typically on their way to Egypt, besieged tiny Judah and dominated the landscape. As a result, Jewish leaders were forced to write down their history so their traditions wouldn't die out. Eventually, many of those writings would be collected into a book today known as the Bible.

REMEMBER

At the same time, guided by prophets, Jews began to see themselves as a nation of priests instructed by God to carry his message to the world. They created laws to isolate themselves from others, banning intermarriage, for example. They wanted to remain pure and to avoid violating rules that may lead to problems. They saw the various conquests as divine punishment for their own misbehavior, and they studied the holy texts to figure out exactly what they must do to avoid more punishment.

The Babylonian invasion was enough. That meant they must live in the Holy Land, which is another name for Israel. Jews who chose not to were (and are) said to be living in *diaspora*, which comes from the Greek and means "to sow" or "to scatter." The belief is that they have chosen temporary living quarters elsewhere and will eventually join other Jews in Israel.

Jews did manage to shake free of conquerors briefly from about 142 BCE to 63 BCE. Then until 1948, Israel remained under foreign control.

While the Romans ruled Israel, Christianity developed. As this new faith grew stronger, Jews fought three wars against the Romans and lost them all. Still, the Romans didn't hate the Jews.

They teased them about taking a day off every week and didn't understand their dietary restrictions (learn more about these in Book 4, Chapter 3). But the Romans actually catered to such religious convictions. Food normally distributed to the poor on Saturdays went to impoverished Jews on Sunday. Roman emperors were clearly aware of Jewish laws.

Even when Emperor Caligula ordered his statue placed in the Temple of Jerusalem around 40 CE to the outrage of the Jews, the Roman regional officer in Judea delayed long enough to avoid offending the Jewish residents, even at the risk of his own life. The officer's decision was vindicated when the emperor was assassinated. The demand for a statue died with him.

Christianity's Emergence Puts the Jews on the Defensive (Yet Again)

The Romans' live-and-let-live attitude toward the Jews changed with the advent of Christianity. In an effort to hold back views believed to be contrary to the fledgling church, leaders of the new faith developed rules to control and eliminate what they saw as heresies. The new Christians were particularly upset that Jews didn't accept Jesus. Many did, of course, but others refused to abandon their religious views.

In time, Christianity grew much bigger than Judaism. Christians began to attack Jews, accusing them of killing Jesus.

WARNING

Jewish persecution (called *anti-Semitism*) has lasted 2,000 years and has occurred in many forms:

- Christian church leaders eventually passed laws restricting where Jews can live and work. Ironically, many of the laws were based on restrictions that Jews originally used against their non-Jewish neighbors.
- Jews were often sent to isolated living areas called *ghettoes*.
- They were attacked in murderous raids called *pogroms*. Crusaders heading to the Middle East often massacred Jews as they passed through cities and villages on the way.
- If Jews were allowed to live in a country, they were required to take hated jobs, like money lending or tax collecting. Those responsibilities didn't endear them to anyone. Because they were outside the church, Jews may charge interest on loans, whereas Christians weren't allowed to collect interest. However, after the businesses were established, Jews often would be ordered out and their goods and money confiscated.
- For many centuries, Jews were invited into European countries to help develop the commercial part of society. After they succeeded, they were forced to depart and leave everything behind.
- In 1492, all Jews were ordered out of Spain and banned from living in most European countries. However, the English statesman Oliver Cromwell let Jews return to England in the 1600s.
- During the 1930s and 1940s, an estimated 6 million Jews were killed by German Nazis as part of the Holocaust. More on that later in this chapter in the section called "The Holocaust."

Jews endured all these persecutions because, when one area closed to them, another may be available. As a result, at one time, Spain was a haven. Then Poland took over. No place stayed open for long. America was the first region that permitted them religious freedom, and that wasn't until the 1600s.

WHAT IS ANTI-SEMITISM?

The word "anti-Semitism" was coined in the mid-19th century, most likely by a renowned anti-Semite as a less-offensive substitute for the German word *Judenhass* ("Jew-hatred"). The problem is that these people don't hate Semites, they hate Jews. The word "Semite" includes all the descendants of Shem — who was the eldest son of Noah in the Bible — including both Jews and Arabs (and all the other tribes originally from the Middle East). Of course, there now are plenty of Jew-hating Arabs, so the word "anti-Semite" doesn't really make any sense.

Some folks now say "Jew-hater" to be more specific, and others have begun to write "antisemite" as a single un-hyphenated word in order to downplay the idea of a separate "Semite" population.

The Holocaust

WARNING

Jewish history in the past 500 years has been a rollercoaster of events, with thrilling highs and catastrophic lows. And one of those terrible, terrible lows is what is today generally called the "Holocaust" and, by many Jews, the *Shoah* (Devastation). The Shoah is just too big to truly do it justice. But here, we attempt to briefly tell you what happened and explain how this nightmare became reality.

In the mid-1930s, the German Nazi party instituted laws that were meant to make the Jews miserable enough to emigrate. Laws prohibited Jews from work for the government, placed boycotts on their businesses, expelled their children from schools, and so on. The government created concentration camps to hold anyone, Jewish or non-Jewish, considered dangerous: political activists, communists, members of trade unions, Romani, homosexuals, Jehovah's Witnesses, and many Jewish journalists, lawyers, and community leaders. These concentration camps were basically prisons and were different from "death camps," which appeared later and were specifically designed to kill people. Some concentration camps also became death camps, but some were simply sources of slave labor for the Germans.

Too little, too late

In 1935, the Nazis instituted the *Nuremberg Laws*, which stripped Jews of their citizenship and prohibited mixed marriages. The Jews had no choice of converting; the Nazis considered anyone who had Jewish blood (meaning at least one grandparent was Jewish) to be racially impure.

Many Jews left Germany during this time. Other well-off, assimilated Jews were optimistic enough to believe that their enlightened neighbors would never stand for this kind of behavior for very long. However, many thousands of Jews couldn't leave simply because no other country would take them in. As Chaim Weizmann, who later became the first president of Israel, said in 1936, "The world is divided into places where [the Jews] cannot live and places into which they cannot enter."

For example, when one Canadian official was asked how many Jewish refugees his country could take, he answered, "None is too many." When the ship *S.S. St. Louis* was turned away from Cuba (even though its 937 German Jewish passengers held valid Cuban visas), America not only refused their entry but even fired a warning shot to keep them away from Florida's shores. The ship finally had to return to Europe, where over a quarter of the passengers were later killed in death camps.

The final straw for most German Jews came on November 9, 1938, which will forever be known as *Kristallnacht* ("night of broken glass"). That evening, a nationwide pogrom was unleashed against the Jewish community, smashing windows, burning buildings, killing 91 Jews, and arresting 30,000 others who were taken to concentration camps. To add insult to injury, the German government then imposed a billion mark fine on the Jews, arguing that the pogrom was their own fault.

Immediately, most Jews in Germany tried desperately to escape, selling their homes and businesses for a pittance. But for most of them, it was too late.

The war against the Jews

By the end of 1939, emigration out of Germany was nearly impossible for the Jews, and the German government decided it was time to change their policy from terror to murder. Many Jews were routinely tortured and shot both in Germany and Poland (which Germany had annexed), and the Nazis killed more than 250,000 Jews in their communities within a few months. Other Jews were forced to move into ghettos (they were shot if they left the walled neighborhoods), where they were kept in a state of perpetual starvation. The Germans, like the Romans 2,000 years earlier, conscripted thousands of Jews to work as slave labor for the war effort, where they were worked so hard and fed so little that most died within a year.

As World War II broke out, the Nazis instituted the same policies wherever they conquered — Hungary, the Netherlands, Czechoslovakia, Greece, Italy, and so on. The governments and people of some countries (often called "Righteous Gentiles") were clearly opposed to the anti-Jewish persecution and refused to cooperate. For example, the people of Denmark helped transport almost every Danish Jew to Sweden, where they were safe. Years later, when the Jews returned, they found that the Danish people had even saved their property from vandals and promptly returned it to the rightful owners.

On the other hand, the Nazis found that many people in other countries were all too willing to help. Many French citizens enthusiastically rounded up Jews to offer to the Germans. Some French citizens were clearly more compassionate, but try asking any Israeli over age 70 what they think of the French (but get out of the way fast in case they spit).

After Germany invaded the Soviet Union in 1941, the Nazis accomplished even larger-scale murders. Squads of trained killers, typically with the help of the local non-Jewish community (whether Ukrainian, Russian, Latvian, Lithuanian, Romanian, or whatever), rounded up Jews, Romani, and communist officials and killed them, typically by machine gun, drowning, or asphyxiation with truck exhaust. In a single September weekend in 1941, on Rosh Hashanah (see Book 4, Chapter 3), the Germans and Ukrainians murdered over 33,000 Jews in the town of Babi Yar.

The death camps

WARNING

To most people today, the Nazi machine makes no sense at all. How could Germany, the center of rational thought, suddenly unleash such centuries-old irrational anti-Semitism? But the greatest villains never think of themselves as evil. The Germans seemed to feel that they were being sensible; they seem to have truly believed that the Jews were subhuman parasites that would destroy the world if they weren't wiped out.

In 1942, Hitler met with a group of high-ranking officials to prepare what they considered "the final solution of the Jewish problem." They would now systematically kill them, as efficiently as possible. The goal: The "extermination" of every Jewish person in Europe (and ultimately, the world).

The Nazis had already turned some concentration camps into death camps. For example, at Ravensbrük, an all-women's camp, they began using lethal gas to kill Jewish women who were pregnant or chronically ill. They had also added crematoria to several camps in order to more easily dispose of the large number of people who were dying. Now, they devised methods to murder not just thousands, but millions, of Jews. Typically, a group of 700 or 800 Jews were brought to a facility to be "deloused," and, believing that they were going to get showers, they dutifully undressed and entered a large room. The door was closed behind them and the room was filled with Zyklon-B gas, an extremely toxic insecticide that killed every person after four or five excruciating minutes. The bodies were then buried in giant pits or cremated.

Unbelievably, the Germans actually forced other Jewish prisoners to perform most of this work. Those who refused were killed immediately. Those who did the work were typically killed after a month or two, anyway.

Jews who had escaped Germany to other European countries were captured and killed. Entire communities that had prospered for hundreds of years — like the incredible Sephardic community of Salonika, Greece, with over 65,000 Jews — were wiped out.

Those who survived often became the subjects of insane tortures. Nazi doctors injected Jewish men and women with slow-acting poison or placed them in freezers to test how long it would take for them to die. Some surgeons tried to create conjoined twins by sewing people together.

TIP

Jews endured so many other horrors — each one as sad and frightening as the last — that we can't describe them in this short space. If you get a chance to visit Yad Vashem in Jerusalem, the National Holocaust Museum in Washington, D.C., or the Simon Wiesenthal Center in Los Angeles, you'll get a better idea of the scope of this horror. Among the artifacts there are letters from people who knew their fate but were powerless to stop it, and many of them wrote of their greatest fear: that their lives and deaths would simply be forgotten by future generations.

The fall of the Third Reich

The idea of killing the Jews wasn't a secondary objective during World War II; the Germans were so obsessed with the Jews that they threw resources at this goal even when it was tactically stupid to do so. For example, trains that should have been used to help German soldiers retreat in the final months of the war were directed instead to transport more Jews to their deaths. Army officials who suggested that they put military aims over anti-Jewish actions were demoted. While the world was at war with Germany, Germany was at war with the Jews.

Many Jews did fight back against the Nazi machine through guerilla action or by working with the resistance movement. One of the most important battles the Jews fought began on April 19, 1943 in the Warsaw ghetto. There, young Jews who had smuggled in a small stash of arms fought off the German army. The Germans burned the ghetto down, and after several weeks, killed all the Jews. But news of the battle spread and was an inspiration to Jews in other communities, even in the concentration camps.

The German army, weakened by the long war and fighting in Russia, finally fell in 1945. Adolf Hitler, still raging against the Jews in his final days, committed suicide as the Allied forces marched on Berlin. The American, British, and Russian soldiers who liberated the concentration and death camps were shocked and sickened at what they found. While rumors had spread for years about what the Germans were doing to the Jews, the "final solution" had largely been kept a secret from most of the world.

In the year following the war, many Jews, perhaps forever optimistic, returned home to their villages in Poland and the Ukraine. Sadly, killing the head of the beast didn't kill the spirit of the people, and many of these Jews were murdered by their old neighbors.

REMEMBER

In the end, some 6 million Jews — over a million and a half of whom were children — brought three new words into modern common language. The first word is *genocide*, the extermination of an entire people, which had never been attempted on this scale before. The second word is *Holocaust*, which, two millennia earlier, had been used to describe the ancient sacrificial offering that was completely burned when offered at the Temple. Even later, the tragedy became known by the Hebrew word, *Shoah*, which means "devastation." Today, *Yom Ha-Shoah*, Holocaust Remembrance Day, is marked each year in the spring.

Flying the Blue and White Banner of Israel

While Jews were developing their own identity across countries, they also gained a homeland. For centuries, many Jews wanted to go to Palestine, the name given to what had been Israel. However, that was very difficult. In the late 1800s, wealthy Jews began to buy up land in Palestine and welcomed Jews to settle it. However, that only increased anger between the new settlers and the long-term residents, the Arabs.

As a result, moving to Palestine grew harder in the 20th century. Great Britain, which controlled the Holy Land after World War I, was caught between the demands of the Arab herdsmen and the newly arrived Jewish settlers. Small bands representing each interest blew up buildings and each other in desperate efforts to get the British to turn the land over to Jewish or Arab control.

Eventually Great Britain, which had been battered physically and financially during World War II, turned the matter over to the United Nations.

REMEMBER

In April 1948, in perhaps the most dramatic single political event in the history of the United Nations, the General Assembly overwhelming voted to divide Palestine into two units:

- Jordan, to house Arabs
- Israel, to serve as a Jewish homeland

For the first time since 63 BCE, the Jews had regained control of the Holy Land.

From Religion to Race: Anti-Semitism in Modern Times

Before the 19th century, most anti-Jewish feeling was based on religious belief — if a Jew truly converted to Christianity, the persecution would likely end. However, with the rise of nationalism in the 19th century, anti-Semitic attitudes shifted from the focus on religious beliefs and practices to the theory that the Jews comprise an inferior race. This focus on ethnic Judaism led anti-Semites to use slurs such as *kike*, *yid*, *hebe*, and *sheeny*. Or, on a more humorous note, the satirical description of a Jew in the Monty Python film *The Life of Brian*: "a Red Sea pedestrian."

In his book *To Life!*, Rabbi Harold Kushner remembers Mordecai Kaplan saying that "expecting the antisemite to like you better because you were a nonobservant Jew was like expecting the bull not to attack you because you were a vegetarian." And social class didn't matter — because of the distribution of Jews throughout every level of society, rich Germans could hate the poor Jews, and poor Germans could hate the rich Jews. The epitome of this hatred, of course, was the Nazi charge not only to remove Jews from their lands but to actually kill every single Jewish person.

Israel and anti-Semitism

The establishment of the State of Israel in 1948 led to the rise of anti-Semitism in Arab communities, where it had been less prevalent. People often forget that Jews and Muslims — members of sibling religions, each tracing their ancestry back to Abraham — lived peacefully together for centuries. In fact, Jews tended to live much better in Muslim countries than Christians lands. However, based on political realities, anti-Semitic feelings began to rise in Arab countries. Following the establishment of the State of Israel, the number of Jews expelled from Muslim countries was approximately the same as the number of Palestinians disenfranchised by the Jewish population.

REMEMBER

Many contemporary attacks on Jews (whether verbal, written, or physical) have an anti-Zionist basis — that is, the attacker is angry at the country of Israel (its politicians, its actions, or even just its existence). However, the anger is unfairly expressed at Jews as a whole. For example, in 2011, soon after Israel's defense forces stopped a ship from bringing supplies to the blockaded area of Gaza and nine pro-Palestinian activists were killed, anti-Semitic propaganda increased around the world, including swastikas painted on Jewish gravestones and hateful comments written on online forums.

On the other hand, some attacks are clearly anti-Jewish but are targeted at Israel as a country. Ultimately, untangling the two is usually considered impossible.

The color of anti-Semitism

Although people of African descent tend to see Jews as simply part of the white majority, from the standpoint of white racists, Jews are more or less the same category as those with darker skin — a nonwhite inferior "race." Even though they share a minority status, many African-Americans have held anti-Semitic beliefs over the past 50 or 60 years.

For example, some people have claimed that the majority of slave holders were Jewish or that Jews created the slave trade, even though very few Jews were involved in the slave industry. Others claim that Jews have long oppressed the African-Americans in their communities, even though the Jews were often the only "white folks" who would hire their black neighbors for decent jobs at decent wages. Undoubtedly, suspicion and racism existed among many Jews (thus, the Yiddish epithet *shvartze*, which literally means "black," but usually holds negative connotations), and it's easy to point to business practices among some in the Jewish community that were racially unfair. But on the whole, the Jewish community has long been much more accepting than most other people.

REMEMBER

Many people today don't remember that Jews (identified as liberals) were among the forefront of those helping African-Americans gain basic civil rights, marching alongside Martin Luther King, Jr., and risking their lives (and losing them, in some cases) in order to help voter registration in the southern states. In fact, the NAACP — America's leading black rights organization — had prominent Jews among its founders, and from 1966 to 1975, a Jew — Kivie Kaplan — was the group's president.

In the 1960s, as some African-Americans became increasingly interested in Islam, they began to identify more strongly with Arab nations and therefore became more anti-Israel and anti-Jewish. In the past 30 to 40 years, groups such as the Nation of Islam have spread significantly more anti-Semitic propaganda, such as Reverend Louis Farrakhan's comments that Jews "are the most organized, rich, and powerful people, not only in America but in the world. . . . They are plotting against us even as we speak." Other black leaders have announced that Jewish doctors caused AIDS by injecting it into black people and that Jews "undermined the very fabric of the society" in Germany. Somehow, even some Christian African-Americans seem to believe these outrageous claims.

Some black organizations feel they need to build cohesiveness by rallying against a common enemy, and perhaps they feel that the Jew is an easier target than the larger "white power structure." Whatever the case, it's clear that an increasing divide exists between these two groups that were once bound together by similar experiences of oppression.

Toward Healing

TIP

We believe that there is healing to be done on all sides. Clearly, Jews need to become less focused on past victimizations and more willing to forgive. Non-Jews need to become more educated about the realities of Jews and Judaism in order to dispel old stereotypes and myths. Ultimately, we must all remember that creating any enemy called "them" dehumanizes everyone.

IN THIS CHAPTER

» **Understanding Jewish beliefs about God**

» **Discovering daily practices**

» **Appreciating Jewish holidays and their origins**

» **Exploring rituals that date back centuries**

» **Interpreting symbols that reflect Jewish beliefs**

Chapter 3

Finding God in Everything

Would you be disappointed if we said that Judaism couldn't care less what you think about God? Or would you be outraged if we insisted that Judaism absolutely requires you to believe in God? In many ways, both of these statements are true: Judaism essentially believes that there is a God — and only One God — but not only leaves *what* God is completely up in the air, but allows for Jews who don't believe in God at all.

Most people are surprised to find out that some practicing Jews are agnostics, insisting that you simply can't know whether or not there's a God. Some Jews are atheists, not believing in God at all. However, when people say, "I don't believe in God," they're usually saying, "I don't believe that God is an old guy sitting on a throne, looking down on us and making decisions about our lives." These same folks can wander out into nature, take a deep breath, and experience a profound sense of wonder about the mystery of life, the unknowable depths of this incredible universe, and the majesty of everything — from a blade of grass to the vastness of a supernova. If you ask us, these people believe in God, they just interpret the word *God* differently.

Fortunately, as we show you in this chapter, Judaism not only allows for all kinds of interpretations of God, but encourages people to wrestle with this issue personally. Do you disagree with somebody about the nature of God? If so, you're getting the hang of Jewish theology!

A Little of This, A Little of That

Judaism has been something like a sponge, quickly absorbing new ideas from surrounding cultures and then transforming them to meet the needs of Jews. Egyptians, Babylonians, Greeks, and other long-forgotten ancient people provided concepts that Jewish leaders transformed into today's rituals and holidays. As a result, the religion has developed a singular set of beliefs that has allowed it to endure for thousands of years.

REMEMBER

The basic tenet of the faith is that there is one God who is intricately involved in daily life. His presence remains the one truth first revealed by Abraham — and the underlying basis of Judaism today. Jews believe that God rescued their ancestors from Egyptian captivity, "choosing" them to carry his word to the rest of the world. That's why they are called the *chosen people.* Although now divided into multiple sects, they are steadfast in the belief that God created man and entrusted Jews to tell mankind of his presence and his requirements for proper behavior.

They celebrate God with daily prayers of thanks, many of which are taken directly from a collection of ancient texts called the *Bible*. The prayers are placed on the walls of homes and recited during religious services.

Their enduring faith in a single God allowed Jews to reject the pagan beliefs of powerful cultures, such as the Greeks and Romans, and to survive centuries of persecution and hatred in the Christian era. Today, that faith links them in an unbroken line back to Abraham, the man credited with first heeding God's call. (See Book 4, Chapter 2 for more on Abraham's life and descendants.)

Pondering Jewish Beliefs about God

Judaism was the first tradition to teach *monotheism*, the belief that there's only one God. As Judaism evolved, the idea of God evolved, too, focusing on a single unknowable, universal, image-less Being, Who, because the universe is framed in Love, requires justice of human beings.

DENYING THE EXISTENCE OF GOD

Jewish tradition allows that there can even be some purpose for not believing in God. Here are the words of a Rabbi Moshe Leib, a great Hasidic teacher:

> To what end can the denial of God have been created? If someone comes to you and asks your help, you shall not send him off with pious words, saying: "Have faith and take your troubles to God!" You shall act as if there were no God, as if there were only one person in all the world who could help this man — only yourself.

Although some religious traditions consider belief alone to be adequate, Judaism isn't one of them; to Jews, belief is only really significant in light of the actions motivated by that belief, which is why we cover many Jewish traditions, rituals, and symbols in this chapter.

REMEMBER

Although the idea of a complete surrender to faith, a surrender to God, is harmonious with many Christian and Muslim beliefs, it's much less comfortable for most Jews, who are traditionally taught to question in order to learn more deeply. Judaism tends to encourage individuals to explore their own personal relationship with God. For people who are comfortable with the idea of surrender, God-wrestling isn't an easy concept.

Some Jews see God as an external force, a Being outside of the universe Who listens to prayers, controls lives, creates miracles, and judges. But that doesn't mean that when the Bible talks about "the outstretched arm of God," they think that God literally has an arm. In fact, Jewish thought is very clear on this: Any reference to God being like a human should be taken as poetic metaphor — as though it were followed by the phrase, "so to speak."

Some Jews say that God contains the Universe, but is infinitely greater. Other Jews say that God is the universe, and the universe is God. Some folks say that all these ideas are true. The one thing that Jews won't argue about, period, is that God — whatever you imagine God to be — is ultimately unknowable and therefore can't be captured by any name.

Calling One God Many Names

In the ancient world, naming something meant that you had power over it. Even today, naming implies both understanding and control. What, then, do people do about naming a God Who is beyond full understanding, certainly beyond control, and generally perceived to be far more powerful than puny humans?

A longstanding Jewish tradition states that each name of God (like *Ha-Rakhaman*, "the Merciful One") refers to an aspect or quality of the Divine. The name defines the ways humans experience God rather than limiting God's Unity.

In fact, you may say that God has all names, so the simplest name of God in Jewish tradition is *Ha-Shem* (literally "The Name"). Many traditional Jews say *Ha-Shem* instead of any other name of God, except in the context of worship or group study. In the Jewish mystical tradition, God is often referred to as *Ain Sof* ("Without End"), though sometimes this is shortened simply to *Ayin* ("Not" or "No-Thing") to indicate how far beyond words the Reality of God is.

TECHNICAL STUFF

Most traditional Jews won't even write out the English word "God," so many Jewish books and periodicals print it "G-d." Just as the four-letter name of God isn't supposed to be pronounced (we talk about that in a moment), some Jews extend this restriction to writing names of God. Also, the restriction ensures that a name of God won't be defaced or erased if the paper is ripped up, soiled, or thrown away.

The *Shem Ha-M'forash* ("The Ineffable Name") is the *Tetragrammaton*, the four-letter name of God comprised of the Hebrew letters *yod-hay-vav-hay* (YHVH), and it's never pronounced as written. Instead, the Jewish tradition teaches that anytime YHVH appears, it should be read *Adonai* (ah-doh-nai; another word entirely that actually means "Lord, or "my Lord"). However, it's important to remember that the name *Adonai* replaces doesn't mean "Lord."

More importantly, no one knows for sure how this word is actually supposed to be pronounced. Historically, YHVH was misread as "Jehovah," and many scholars now think it may be read "Yahweh," but even if it were, we think there is something sad about not honoring the intention of the tradition. This was to be the Name beyond pronouncing, to remind people that God is beyond the limitations implied in being named. The four-letter Name is a form of the Hebrew verb "to be" that signifies Unlimited Being. That's why we translate it in this book as "the Eternal" or "Eternal One."

Looking behind the Name

Naming an Ultimate Reality is one thing; determining the nature of that Reality is another. In many ways, the names themselves speak the nature of the Being and the kinds of relationships experienced between human and Divine.

Jewish tradition holds that any attempt to know God is bound to fail. Perhaps any view of God says more about the person doing the viewing than about the Ultimate Reality. But that hasn't stopped millennia of philosophers and theologians from trying!

The God of the philosophers, of course, tends to be somewhat different from the God of the worshipers. Maimonides, the greatest Jewish theologian of the Middle Ages, understood God as the Prime Mover, the "Uncaused Cause," different not only in degree but in essence from humankind. Maimonides' God was the God of reason, the God of the intellect, appreciated according to the scientific axioms of his time. Humans can't really say anything about the nature of this God because adjectives simply can't apply to God in the same way they apply to people. Since God is unlimited and all-powerful, God can't "want" or "need" anything from humanity.

The God of the mystics, on the other hand, has a very complementary relationship with humankind. For the mystic, there is a profound interrelationship between God and person — one in which each party affects the other. God's Presence (*Shekhinah*) actually participates in the experience of exile with the Children of Israel. Similarly, each person's actions make a cosmic difference. The mystics see the actions of humans (especially those relating to performing the *mitzvot*, "commandments") impacting the nature of God's Being because God and people are one.

And the God of the believer — the God of those many generations of Jews who contributed to the continuity and to the expansion of Judaism — is the One Who Creates, the One Who Reveals, and the One Who Redeems. We use capital letters for these terms to remind us that God's actions may be vastly different from the human actions described by these same words.

God creates

Some Jews say that God started the Big Bang and then walked away from the universe, letting it unfold like a scientist watching a magnificent experiment from a distance. Other Jews insist that God is a more involved Creator. The *Midrash* (more on this in Book 4, Chapter 5) describes a remarkable image: When God decided to create the world, He opened the Torah scroll and read the beginning of *Bereisheet* (Genesis) as though the Torah were an instruction manual or set of blueprints. You'll get your brain tied in knots if you try to work this out literally or logically; remember that this stuff is meant to be poetic.

Of course, just as scientists try to figure out how the universe began in order to understand better where humankind is today, Judaism focuses on Creation not just as a historical event, but as an ever-blossoming act. To many thinkers, God is the Creator and the constant source and resource of creation. God is more like a Natural Force behind all life, expressing Itself as that life and sustaining the rhythms and the order of the universe.

THE PROBLEM OF EVIL

Everyone asks the question sooner or later: If God is good, why is there so much evil in the world? Couldn't God have created a universe in which there simply is no pain, no grief, no violence? After the Holocaust (see Book 4, Chapter 2), with over six million Jews murdered, some people noted that humans simply can't understand God or God's "decisions," and there were some who gave up on God entirely, proclaiming, "God is dead!"

For many others, however, it wasn't a matter of God's dying as much as a time to adjust the human, childlike understanding about the nature of God. Maybe God doesn't have "all" the power after all, since human beings are quite literally given the power to create for good or for ill. The Talmudic rabbis noted that the *yetzer tov* ("inclination toward good") and the *yetzer ha-ra* ("inclination toward evil") live within each human being. While "ra" means "evil," this refers to acts that are solely self-serving, like greed. It is crucial that we learn to balance our instincts toward self-satisfaction with our yearnings to be of service to others and to our world.

While some faiths imagine an evil being, a "Satan," with whom God contends, this idea never really developed within Judaism. A character named "Ha-Satan" (pronounced "ha-sah-tahn") appears in the Book of Job, but this Satan is literally "the adversary" or "the accuser" and functions as God's prosecuting attorney and not the demonic archangel in which some people believe. In some respects, you can say that Ha-Satan is actually part of God, too — the aspect of God that tests humans to see what they do with their free will.

God reveals

An old joke, based on a Talmudic story, says there once were two rabbis arguing over a detail in the Torah. The debate almost came to physical blows when, suddenly, there was thunder and lightning. As the rabbis looked on, amazed, a giant hand came down from the Heavens and pointed to one of them. "He's right," said the massive Voice of God. After a moment, the other rabbi shrugged his shoulders and said, "Okay, fine, so it's two against one. Let's ask somebody else."

Some say this story demonstrates how each Jew is ultimately responsible for their own interpretations, even if it means arguing with God. Other people see it as a lesson that it's more important to interpret — and reinterpret — the words of the Torah (the oral, as well as the written Torah; see Book 4, Chapter 5), rather than appeal to new heavenly voices. Either way, there's an underlying message that God Reveals.

Revelation is the channel through which a human being "hears" the Divine word. The Bible is full of revelations, of course, from the first communication to Adam, to Moses and the giving of the Torah at Sinai, to the profound messages of the great Prophets. The big question, however, is did God once speak "openly" to human beings, and then decide not to any longer? Or perhaps people could "hear" differently back then. The scholar Julian Jaynes postulated that in biblical times, the human brain itself was in the process of evolving, so that what people now know as intuitive insights may have been experienced as an outer "Voice of God."

The kabbalistic tradition has long taught that God speaks the same today as God always did, but that humans both hear and interpret what they hear differently. They imagine that revelation is always happening, like a "revelation channel" that's always broadcasting, waiting for humans to become sensitive enough to receive and understand its message. Once received, the messages are filtered through the language, culture, and belief of that time in order to make them understandable.

Of course, for some Jews, God doesn't communicate through words, but through relationship. In the experience of love, compassion, and creativity, realizations of God unfold. And for still others, revelation is contained in the beauty of the natural world, so that by relating to that greater world, people can realize the communication.

God redeems

The phrase "God Redeems" doesn't imply that the Universal Being clips coupons or brings glass bottles into a recycling center. Unfortunately, while the idea of redemption is a core concept of Judaism, what, exactly, that means is subject to interpretation. Most Jews agree that redemption is different from the Christian idea of salvation from sin, especially because Christians tend to see it as a result of right belief rather than acts.

The key redemptive event in Jewish history, the event that in many ways created the Jewish people, was the exodus from Egypt (see Book 4, Chapter 2). Traditional Judaism teaches that God redeemed the Children of Israel from the great hardships of enslavement and celebrates this event each year during Passover (see the section "Observing Jewish Holidays" later in this chapter). In that redemptive moment lies the beginning of the essential journey of a People in quest of their God. And yet, Jewish tradition also holds that God didn't simply free the slaves; God created a set of options, and each person had to make a choice from free will: Moses, the Pharaoh, and even the Hebrews. For example, biblical commentators note that the majority of Hebrew slaves chose not to leave Egypt!

Throughout biblical history, this theme continues and is deepened through the developing relationship between the Jews and God. It becomes clear that the people have responsibility for following divinely inspired paths and living in accord with principles of justice and compassion, in service to the One God. When they fail in this responsibility, there is punishment, including exile. But even from the midst of such exile, redemption awaits if they reform.

Visions of redemption

Some Jews see this as a metaphor for personal redemption from exile, such as making choices to live in ways that release them from slavery (whether that's addictive behavior, bad habits, anger, fear, or whatever). Redemption is a process of becoming more human and more able to freely experience the world and act more consciously. In this way, perhaps redemption is another word for self-actualization, enlightenment, or God-consciousness.

Others insist that redemption cannot be achieved by the individual alone, but will come all at once to the entire People of Israel, or the entire world. In this traditional interpretation, God guides history through an ever-unfolding path, and the final act will be the redemption of humankind, brought about by a Jewish king called the *Mashiach* (Messiah). At that time, all Jews will return to the ways of Torah (even the "wicked" ones) and be led out of exile to return to the land of Israel. For traditional Judaism, this promise of redemption translates to a future Messianic Age, including the resurrection of the dead.

The paths of redemption

The future promise of redemption provides the idea that history is purposeful, that there is direction and intention involved, rather than simply being chaotic and purposeless. The primary paths toward redemption — whether personal or communal — involve following the *mitzvot* (see Book 4, Chapter 4), and performing acts of *tikkun olam*, the healing of the world through a life-long series of socially responsible actions and intentional blessings.

Embarking on a Quest for Ultimate Reality

The spiritual experience, in which a person or a group opens to a Greater Presence, seems a natural part of human consciousness. Throughout the ages, men and women have been touched by this ineffable Presence, and often had the directions of their lives altered forever. This is certainly the experience recounted time and time again through the literature of the Bible and many texts of the Jewish tradition.

Although Judaism doesn't lack for those inquiring into the specific nature of that Divine Being, it tends to focus more on discovering ways to connect that Holiness to ordinary life. God is experienced through fulfillment of the *mitzvot* as well as through awakening to the wonders of relationship to others and to the natural world. Life is made holy by realizing the ever-present connection to a Greater One. And that can be furthered through rituals, practices, and other displays of faith.

Maintaining Daily Practice

Jewish sages have developed a variety of rituals over the years designed to remind believers of God's presence in their lives. You may leave a note on the refrigerator or tie a string around a finger to remember something. Jews do similar things. Leather straps wrapped around the arms of devout Jews, for example, are shaped into Hebrew letters to reflect religious messages. Even a children's game is played with a top that bears Hebrew letters. They are the initials for "A great miracle happened there" and are meant to remind participants (who are often more focused on winning chocolate) of the Jewish victory over the Syrians almost 2,200 years ago. With such a long history, Jews can link every religious activity to some historical event or ritual.

Let us pray

Jews consider prayer the most important daily ritual. They believe they are on earth to praise God. As a result, their prayers, some of which are thousands of years old, are typically designed for that purpose. Even the *Kaddish*, a mournful sounding prayer said at funerals and during the portion of services to remember the departed, only praises God and has no mention of death.

Jews do pray for the rain in the proper season, for good health, and for the safety of loved ones. Like Christians and Muslims, they have prayers when they wake up, prayers when it's time for a little shut-eye, prayers during weddings, and prayers for new seasons, new moons, and other special events. Jews have a prayer over bread, over wine, and for just about every other kind of food.

Unlike other religions, however, Jews don't have prayers for personal property. In World War II, U.S. General George Patton asked a Christian padre to write a prayer for good weather so the Allied pilots may see to provide protection for the soldiers on the ground. He couldn't have asked a rabbi for a prayer like that.

The Shema

The most important Jewish prayer is known by its first word in Hebrew, *Shema.* That means "hear." The full prayer in English is: "Hear, oh, Israel, the Lord, our God, the Lord is one." This prayer is considered the watchword of the Jewish faith and reflects the belief begun by Abraham that there is only one God.

The prayer adds, "These words which I command this day shall be in thy heart . . . and upon the doorposts of thy house." So observant Jews place the prayer in a box called a *mezuzah* and nail it by their front door. Over the years, Jews began to decorate *mezuzahs*, and they have become works of art in themselves.

The *Shema* shows up somewhere else, too. Orthodox Jews wear *tefillin*, which is a long leather strap with a tiny box connected to each end. A Jew slips a copy of the *Shema* in each of the boxes and wears the tefillin during prayer, with one box dangling between his eyes and the other in the left hand. The leather strap winds around the worshipper's left arm. Why? Because the Shema requests that its words be kept in the "forefront of thy eyes" and near the heart. The left arm is closest to the heart. (Find out more about special prayer garb in the upcoming section, "Exploring the worship wardrobe.")

No kneeling please, but you can rock away

TIP

You won't find Jews kneeling down to say the *Shema*, no matter how important the prayer is. In fact, you won't find kneeling benches in a synagogue, unlike churches. Traditionally, Jews don't believe in bowing to man or God. They don't bow in a synagogue in case someone may think they're bowing toward the rabbi.

A story in the Bible tells of a man named Mordecai who gets into serious trouble because he declines to bow to the Persian Prime Minister Haman. Haman threatens to kill all the Jews because of Mordecai's faux pas. Of course, Haman loses in the end. (You can read the details of Mordecai's predicament in the book of Esther in the Bible.)

Many Jews tend to rock back and forth during prayer in a kind of meditation. Jews call it *davening* and say it allows them to gain a mystical connection with their inner feelings. To an outsider, davening creates an image in a synagogue of a misguided chorus line. Christian services tend to be highly organized with everyone on the same page. In orthodox Jewish services, members of the congregation rock back and forth while murmuring their own prayers from the prayer book. No one seems to be doing the same thing, except for an occasional "amen" when a prayer is completed.

Exploring the worship wardrobe

Jews have developed special clothes for prayers. One difference between sects of Judaism is how much ritualistic clothing is required. The most liberal Jews, called *Reform*, dress in standard clothes for religious services. They don't wear the religious get-up. Other Jews, whether praying at home or in a synagogue, typically put on a prayer shawl and a skullcap.

The prayer shawl, called a *tallis* or *tallit*, is a thin cloth that goes around a man's shoulders and can stretch to the waist. Orthodox Jews use the tallis to cover their heads when praying. Because Judaism is a male religion founded and run by men, women (with the exception of female rabbis) don't have to worry about wearing a tallis.

The corners of the tallis always feature tassels (called *zizit*), like the ones on a mortar board at graduation. That's because the Bible contains an order that clothing must have tassels or fringe. Because clothing these days doesn't come with that ol' time frizzy styling, the shawl itself contains fringe and fulfills the law. No one knows anymore why the Bible contains such a demand, but, as with many laws, precedent is sacred.

Devout Jews wear a tallis under their regular clothes. The fringes poking out under the coat fulfill the biblical injunction without messing up a nice suit.

The skullcap, called a *kepot* or *yarmulke*, also has a very old history. In ancient times, people carefully covered their heads when entering a sacred building or shrine. Veils worn by religious women in Catholic Masses carry on that tradition. However, in time, people started removing their hats to indicate their devotion. Jews retained the old tradition, though, and now they place skullcaps by the entrance to the synagogue's sanctuary so male Jews can cover their heads during services. More orthodox Jews never remove their skullcaps, which have become works of art.

The skullcaps may also be linked to the power invested in hair. Orthodox women shave their heads to eliminate hair, which may lure men away from their religious studies. They wear wigs instead. (Sometimes these wigs are quite beautiful, which may cause problems anyway.)

Keeping kosher

Jews got a lot more than prayers from the Bible that also served up menu options. These requirements were organized in the Talmud and are collected under the heading *kosher*, meaning ritually prepared. Some foods that are commonplace in restaurants, such as ribs, shrimp, and oysters, can't be eaten by Jews; other foods are perfectly acceptable. (Chapter 11 in the biblical book Leviticus and Chapter 14 in Deuteronomy outline Jewish dietary habits.)

TIP

Acceptable foods:

- Jews can eat any animal that has cloven hooves and chews its cud. So sheep, cattle, goats, deer, and bison are kosher.
- Jews can dine on chicken, geese, ducks, and turkeys. Some people avoid turkey, however, because it's not mentioned specifically in the Torah.
- Anything in the water with fins and scales is okay.

WARNING

Forbidden foods:

- The rules bar dining on camel, rock badger, rabbit, and pig.
- All the prohibited fowl are birds of prey or scavengers.
- Sharks are out. So are shellfish such as lobsters, oysters, shrimp, clams, and crabs.
- Don't even think of grabbing a handful of chocolate-covered termites. Of the "winged swarming things," only a couple are specifically permitted. However, the great sages had to put on their thinking caps for this rule. Even 2,000 years ago, they had no idea what insects the biblical text referred to. To avoid breaking the law, they forbade eating any insect.
- Rodents, reptiles, and amphibians are all no-nos.

WARNING

Jews can't eat milk, eggs, fat, or organs from banned animals. That can create some problems. For example, rennet, an enzyme used to harden cheese, usually is derived from non-kosher animals. That makes kosher hard cheese difficult to find. Certain parts of animals also aren't kosher, such as the sciatic nerve in the hindquarters. Unfortunately, not only are these parts difficult to remove, they also include some of the choicest cuts, which is why it's rare to find kosher filet mignon, rump and sirloin steaks, leg of lamb, or London broil. Additionally, animals that are diseased or have physically flawed organs aren't kosher (called *trayf*, from the Hebrew word *terayfa*, meaning "torn"). When the lungs of animals are examined for irregularities, and none are found, the animal is considered *glatt* ("smooth"). If there is any question about the quality of the meat, even if it proves to be just fine (kosher), it isn't considered glatt kosher.

No one is really sure why some animals were considered worth eating and others were not. Modern scholars believe there were religious reasons behind the rules. Say a nearby pagan tribe worshipped crabs. To prevent Jews from falling into the error, their leaders banned the animal from the dinner plate. The rules may also have been designed to keep Jews ritually pure. Kosher laws definitely serve as a reminder. Any Jew who follows the rules can't forget their religion.

Kosher laws affect more than the dinner plate:

- Animals destined for the dinner table must be killed in accordance with Jewish law. That means all blood must be drained from the meat or broiled out of it before it is eaten.
- Fruits and vegetables are permitted, but must be inspected for bugs.
- Meat can't be eaten with dairy products. At home, a Jewish family that keeps kosher has two sets of dishes: one for food with milk elements; one for food with meat. There are two sets of silverware and utensils, too. That way, there's no danger the wrong foods can meet.

  This rule outlaws cheeseburgers, chili with cheese, meat tacos with cheese and a whole bunch of other delectables.
- Grape products (jelly, juice, wine) made by non-Jews may not be eaten.

Finding God in Everything

To be sure no kosher laws were violated, even by accident, Jewish sages eventually clarified some of the rules to indicate precisely how long after eating meat a person can also dine on cheese; how dishes can be cleaned to eliminate possible contamination; and so on.

TIP

Today, it's easy to find kosher food in a grocery store. Just look for a certain "seal of approval" called a *hekhsher*, which typically appears as a symbol on the food's packaging. The most famous hekhsher symbols are OU or OK (an "O" with either a little "U" or "K" inside), but dozens of different symbols exist. To ensure these foods are kosher and aren't just given the *hekhsher* by the manufacturer, a trained rabbi, called a *mashgiakh*, supervises and certifies that the food is indeed kosher.

Remembering the Sabbath

The one holiday followed by Jews and Christians alike is called *Sabbath* (*Shabbat* in Hebrew). That's a day of the week dedicated to God. It's the day of rest; no work and no play — just rest. No holiday is more identified with the Jews than this day of rest. To the Greeks and Romans, the Sabbath was proof that the Jews were crazy. Who took a day off? And *every* week, too? They probably shuddered to think slaves may pick up that routine.

KOSHER RULES CHANGED JUDAISM

The kosher laws help explain why Jews split into sects. In the 1700s, all Jews were orthodox and followed biblical rules, like the kosher laws. However, Jews who came to this country sometimes settled in tiny, rural communities. They found it impossible there to find a kosher butcher or to hunt up enough appropriate food. As a result, far-sighted rabbis suggested that some laws didn't need to be followed in the modern world. That led to the Reform and Conservative movements. Jews in those sects rarely keep kosher.

Kosher laws also are linked to animal rights. The Bible orders Jews to kill animals with the least amount of suffering. They also were banned from eating blood. Jews combined the two requirements by killing animals by slitting their throats. The animals bled to death with minimal suffering. In time, sages added other laws to reduce animals' suffering. In ancient times, when hungry people would simply slice meat off a living animal, kosher rules represented a major step against cruelty to animals.

Yet, the day is honored with its own commandment: "Remember the Sabbath and keep it holy." The Bible gives two reasons for Sabbath:

- In Genesis, God rests on the seventh day after creation.
- In Deuteronomy 5, the Sabbath is tied to the *Exodus* when the Jews hurried out of Egypt ahead of the Egyptian army. Jews are supposed to use the Sabbath to remember this important event and to thank God for his help.

TECHNICAL STUFF

The two explanations imply an earlier meaning. In the ancient Babylonian account of creation, historians found several similar concepts. All of them, including Sabbath, are derived from the Babylonian word meaning "to cease." In the Babylonian story, called the *Enuma Elish*, the gods destroy humankind and then cease working on the seventh day. Also, in Babylonia, the last day of the week was dedicated to Sin, the moon goddess whose name lives on in the word "Sinai." The Babylonians considered it an unlucky day, like we may think of Friday the 13th. Jews probably reversed the idea to give it a nicer meaning. After all, living in Babylon, they would see the day commemorated no matter what they did.

Jews still chose the last day of the week, Saturday, for their day of rest. Early Christians held their Sabbath prayers on Saturday and Sunday, before shifting to Sunday only.

Because the Jewish day begins at sundown, religious Jews start their prayers Friday night and end their worship at sundown the next day. Many go to religious services or pray at home.

DON'T FLIP THAT SWITCH!

How does someone avoid working on the Sabbath? Better yet, what's work? Early Jewish sages spent a long time on both questions. Some of their rules were translated in American culture as *blue laws*, which prohibited stores from opening on a Sunday. Those laws finally were erased after World War II.

Although Reform and even Conservative Jews today don't follow the "no work on Saturdays" rule, Orthodox Jews won't work on Sabbath to this day. Many won't even drive cars on the Sabbath. As a result, devout Jews often live near their synagogues so they can walk to services.

Really pious Jews won't cook or turn on lights on the Sabbath because the smallest action of flipping a light switch is considered "work." Instead, they may hire a non-Jew to flip on a switch. Clever! That's not the only ingenious way Orthodox Jews avoid work. Elevator call and floor buttons are also off limits for Orthodox Jews on the Sabbath. Imagine living on the 50th floor of a high-rise building. Walking up several dozen flights of stairs hardly seems like less work than pushing an elevator button. In high-rise buildings inhabited by stricter Jews, an elevator often is kept running all day, and it simply stops on every other floor. Residents need only walk up or down one level to catch a ride, and they never have to push a button. These very observant Jews have therefore exercised no intention and done no work by pushing the button to go up, and they are absolved from breaking a rule. An interesting — and sneaky — solution!

Observing Jewish Holidays

Jewish holidays developed in rhythm with the seasons. Born in a farming culture, Judaism built on that environment for spring and fall holidays, but it also drew on significant events to fill the calendar with festivities and remembrances.

High Holy Days: Rosh Hashana and Yom Kippur

The two most important religious holidays on the Jewish calendar are *Rosh Hashana* and *Yom Kippur*, which are ten days apart in late September or early October. Rosh Hashana, which is the Jewish New Year and means "head of the year," kicks off the annual cycle of prayer and religious thought called *Days of Awe* or *High Holy Days*. Yom Kippur, also called the *Day of Atonement*, ends the holidays. Even nonreligious Jews crowd synagogues during these times.

Although Rosh Hashana marks the beginning of another year, the holiday doesn't resemble anything like the huge celebrations held around the world on December 31. Jews don't set off fireworks or gather for big parties with noisemakers and balloons. Instead, they go to synagogues to thank God for whatever happened the previous year and to look forward to a better new year.

Yom Kippur is even more solemn. Religious Jews don't even eat all day, cleansing their bodies while asking God to forgive their sins. For Catholics (more on them in Book 5, Chapter 4), this would be like a one-day confession that takes care of the whole year. Jews pray that God will enter them in the Book of Life for another year. They are also required to ask other people they may have wronged for forgiveness.

REMEMBER

On both Rosh Hashana and Yom Kippur, children are expected to take off from school, and devout Jews don't work. This can cause problems in the secular world. In the 1960s, Los Angeles Dodgers pitcher Sandy Koufax, who is Jewish, kicked off a furor by refusing to pitch on Yom Kippur, despite a tight pennant race.

Passover: Recalling the great escape

This eight-day spring holiday is directly linked to the most significant event in Jewish history: the Exodus from Egypt led by Moses. In fact, Passover is probably the oldest, continually celebrated holiday on earth. However, it originally had nothing to do with Jews or Egypt.

WHY EIGHT-DAY HOLIDAYS?

Jewish holidays are of varied length. Originally, many were seven days long — especially those related to planting and harvesting. That's because of the astrological link to the sun, moon, and five visible planets.

The actual date for the holiday to start was announced by sages in the holy Temple, based on their computations. However, when the Temple was destroyed in 70 CE, Jewish leaders feared that Jews now scattered would not begin the holiday on the correct day. So they added one day to every holiday except the Sabbath.

So the spring planting holiday became eight days long. A later holiday, like Hanukkah, also became eight days long.

The old candelabra, which was the symbol of Judaism, also went from seven candles to eight.

Centuries before Abraham, Middle Eastern shepherds used to sacrifice a lamb to their deities every spring. Then as Judaism began to develop, the annual shepherds' lamb roast was combined with an otherwise unknown holiday for dry bread and adapted to the Jews' miraculous escape from Egypt. That took place around the eighth century BCE. Passover has been an important Jewish holiday ever since.

REMEMBER

Passover simply wouldn't be a Jewish holiday if it didn't involve food restrictions and special rituals:

- Religious Jews carefully clean their houses before the start of the holiday to be sure no unacceptable foods are still around when Passover starts.
- During the holiday, Jews often use a different set of dishes to prevent contact with the wrong food.
- The menu is limited. Jewish sages noted that the fleeing slaves wouldn't have had time to cook properly or gather up vegetables difficult to harvest. So they banned potatoes and carrots, among other foods, that have to be dug up.
- No bread is allowed because there wouldn't have been time to bake. According to the story in Exodus, Jews had to flee Egypt in a rush, what with the Egyptians chasing them and Moses parting the Red Sea. Therefore, they had no time to wait around for their morning dough to rise, or *leaven*. Instead, they simply packed it up and carried it out, pronto. As a result, the hot sun baked this unleavened dough into crackers called *matzoh*. Jews eat matzoh during Passover to remind themselves of their ancestors' escape from the Egyptians. Matzoh can be crumbled into cereal, mixed with eggs, toasted, or used like breading.

The holiday includes prayer and a family gathering, called a *Seder*, where the story of the Exodus is retold. Seders are held the first, second, and last days of the holiday. Symbols of the Exodus are placed on a large Seder plate. Items include a bone to signify the sacrifice of a lamb; an egg, which symbolizes spring; a sprig of parsley, also a symbol of spring; horseradish, which reflects the tears that the slaves shed before they were rescued; a concoction of apples, walnuts, wine, and cinnamon, which resembles the mortar used by slaves to build Egyptian buildings; and several pieces of matzoh.

Each participant at the Seder also drinks four cups of wine. An additional cup is left out for Elijah, the biblical prophet whose return is expected to introduce a golden age of peace.

One piece of matzoh is hidden for children to find later for a reward. The meal can't end until the *afikomen* (dessert) is found, ransomed, and eaten. Many families have stories of sitting around the Seder table for long hours while children haggle with whoever is running the Seder.

PARTY LIKE IT'S 5769!

When to celebrate a holiday can be tricky business. The Jewish calendar was developed centuries ago and, like all ancient calendars, was based on the moon. People can see the moon change, while the darn sun seemed to stay the same. So they marked the passing of time by the arrival of the new moon. However, a lunar calendar is shorter than one based on the sun. The moon runs through its cycle in about 28 days. The solar calendar averages 30 days a month. Regardless, the Earth needs 365.25 days to complete one circuit around the sun in a year. The lunar calendar, however, falls short of that requirement. To make up the missing days, Jews add a month (Adar 11) to the calendar seven times every 19 years.

That's why Jewish holidays can occur in different months in the English calendar. Also, because of the lunar calendar, Jewish holidays run from sundown to sundown.

Using the Bible, Jewish sages decided that the world began about 5,769 years ago. That corresponds to 2008 BCE in our English calendar.

Planting and harvesting holidays

Spring planting and fall harvest holidays are normal for many religions. People once lived by the rhythm of the changing seasons. As a result, holidays built around sowing and reaping took on special significance in ancient times. Jews have two such holidays, now both eight days long:

- The spring holiday is called **Shavuot** and marks spring planting. The tail end of Shavuot is called *Shemini Atzeret,* when the Jews remember when Moses received the Torah from God. The final day of Shemini Atzeret is called *Simchas Torah.*
- The fall holiday, **Sukkot,** once required Jews to live in small huts for seven days along with samples of grains being harvested. Devout Jews still build little huts, called *sukkoths,* behind their homes during Sukkot and decorate them with fruits.

Purim: A great reason to party

The early spring holiday of Purim isn't that important religiously, but it has remained extremely popular. Jews dress up in costumes, put on saucy plays, and shake loud noisemakers. It's even permissible to get drunk on Purim.

The holiday supposedly began as a way of recalling a supposed Jewish victory over the mammoth Persian army. In a biblical book that bears her name, Esther rescues the Jewish people after Haman, the evil Persian prime minister, gets the king to approve an order allowing the Persian troops to kill all the Jews. Esther persuades the king to arm the Jews, who then defeat the Persian army. Haman and his sons eventually are hung on gallows meant for the Jews.

The entire episode is a moral tale, not a historical one. *Purim* means "lots," as in "odds," rather than a place to park cars. However, the holiday started out as a pagan event that Jewish leaders branded with a new meaning. Jewish children liked the festival so much that Jewish leaders figured they were better off adopting the holiday and creating some kind of Jewish tie rather than trying to fight it. Jews in the Middle Ages shifted the emphasis of Purim from Persia to celebrating a hoped-for defeat of Christians who harassed them. Even though that meaning has been lost, the festivities roll on today.

Hanukkah: In praise of victory and light

You've probably heard of this holiday because it's celebrated around Christmas in December with candles and gift giving. The holiday, however, has nothing to do with Jesus. It commemorates when Jewish troops retook the Temple of Jerusalem from the Syrians in 165 BCE.

Hanukkah means "redemption," because the Jews were able to clean the Temple and return it to its holy ritualistic standard. The Syrians had allowed the place to be used as a pig sty and deliberately desecrated the building.

Most non-Jews have heard the story that Hanukkah lasts eight days because a small amount of holy oil found in the Temple burned far longer than expected. That tale comes from the Talmud, however, and probably was written years after Jews retook the Temple.

In reality, the soldiers were so busy fighting that they didn't have time to celebrate Sukkot, now an eight-day harvest holiday. So they celebrated it when the Temple was recaptured. The next year, Hanukkah was devoted totally to the big win.

Today, Hanukkah is typically celebrated with songs and fried potato cakes called *latkes*. Jews light candles on a menorah each night and say several holiday-related prayers. In many homes, Hanukkah includes gifts given to children as a substitute for Christmas gifts.

Jews also have a Hanukkah game, which involves a spinning four-sided top called a *dreidel*. Participants create a pot with antes — typically with chocolate coins. Each side of the top contains a different Hebrew letter. Depending on which letter turns up when the top stops, the spinner may win the pot, half the pot, nothing, or have to match the pot.

Other holidays

The Jewish calendar is dotted with at least 36 Jewish holidays every year. They highlight biblical stories and special events in the long Jewish history. Most are commemorated with brief ceremonies or prayers. They include:

- ***Tu B'Shevat,*** which is a festival to honor trees. The first known environmental holiday, it takes place in January or February.
- ***Tisha B'av*** remembers the Temple. The first one was destroyed by the Babylonians. The second one fell to the Romans about 600 years later. Ironically, both temples seem to have been destroyed on the same day of the year, near the end of summer.
- ***Yom HaShoah,*** which honors those killed during World War II in the Holocaust. Held a week after Passover, this holiday recalls the nearly six million Jews massacred by the Germans. It is marked with prayers and candlelight ceremonies.

Understanding Jewish Rituals

Jews have developed a variety of rituals over the centuries for special occasions such as birth, marriage, and achieving adult status. These rites of passage exist in every religion and culture, but those that characterize Judaism are designed to fulfill biblical commands or to acknowledge the presence of God in daily life.

Circumcision: No getting around it

REMEMBER

Circumcision remains the one aspect of Judaism that has endured since the beginning of the faith. To Jews, a circumcision is a joyous event, a *bris,* and usually conducted by someone trained for the procedure, called a *moyel.* In the ritual, the foreskin on the tip of the penis is removed in accordance to biblical commands. Prayers accompany the brief operation.

In the Bible, God orders Abraham to initiate the procedure. Moses is almost ambushed by God for not circumcising his son. His wife, Zipporah, rescues Moses by performing an abrupt operation on her son (Exodus 4:25). Moses apparently did not require circumcision while the Jews wandered the desert for 40 years, but Joshua reinstituted the practice (Joshua 5:2–10).

The idea itself predates Judaism. The operation began in Egypt or even earlier, possibly to reduce pleasure in sexual relations. It may also have developed to replace human sacrifice. This way, only an unnecessary portion of the body was dedicated to a deity, not the whole person. That's why females were circumcised as well, losing their clitoris in what today is considered mutilation.

Cultures throughout time have looked at the ancient ritual in different ways:

- » Greeks and Romans disagreed completely with the procedure. The Romans actually passed several laws banning circumcision, although they did not require Jews to stop. Greeks would not allow it. Jewish athletes actually underwent a procedure to sew on the missing foreskin so they could compete in Greek athletic competitions, which were conducted in the nude!
- » Early Christians objected, too. At the Council of Jerusalem (Acts 15), they joined the Romans in prohibiting the ritual. Paul, the leading missionary, actually separated groups into circumcised and uncircumcised. He told parents not to circumcise their kids (Acts 21:25) and warned his assistant, Timothy, about the "circumcision group" (Titus:1:10–16).
- » Americans didn't mind as much. The practice became very widespread in this country about 1870. It was seen as a way to prevent self-stimulation, then considered a horrible activity with dire consequences for practitioners. Americans carried the surgical procedure with them around the world. For example, Koreans began to circumcise their children after being introduced to American culture during the Korean War.
- » The practice peaked internationally in 1971 after a series of medical reports found no medical evidence to support the operation. However, the American Academy of Pediatrics issued a report that year rejecting circumcision. The number of procedures has declined slowly ever since.

REMEMBER

Circumcision remains the one sure link between Jews of every generation back to the hallowed patriarchs like Abraham, Isaac, and Jacob. It's not an insignificant "slice of life."

Bar mitzvah: All grown up in God's eyes

The one Jewish rite of passage most familiar to non-Jews may be the *bar mitzvah*, which marks the moment when a Jewish boy becomes accepted as an adult in the religious community. In the ceremony, a teenage boy (or girl in a *bat mitzvah*) reads from the Torah and, often, leads the service. When the ceremony is completed, the youngster is considered a full-fledged member of the congregation.

Most people think it's an ancient custom, but a bar mitzvah is a surprisingly new ritual. Christians developed confirmation as a way to mark entry into adulthood, but Jews had no similar event for centuries. A boy was viewed as a man when he was capable of reading directly from the sacred texts. That could be any time. Religion was man's work; women need not concern themselves.

To counter Christianity, in the 12th century, Jewish leaders developed the bar mitzvah ("son of a good deed"). In the early 1900s, a rabbi with only daughters came up with a bat mitzvah ("daughter of a good deed") and guided his girls through the event.

By the 1960s, bat mitzvahs and bar mitzvahs had become standard in the Jewish community. They remain a significant part of Jewish life and are commemorated with parties after the ceremony. Those affairs can be lavish with huge dances and endless presents. The "good deed" these days may refer to property given as a gift.

Mazel tov! Celebrating a Jewish wedding

Jewish weddings follow precise ritualistic rules. The ritual begins when the bride and groom sign a legal document, called a *get*, (ketubah) in front of their rabbi. This document has been very important for millennia. It is a legal contract focusing on divorce. Should the groom die before the nuptials, his fiancé actually was banned under Jewish law from getting married again.

The bride and groom then gather under a canopy, called a *chuppah*, to recite their vows. The chuppah is a remnant from the ancient days when the bridal couple — in what usually was an arranged marriage — met in groom's room or tent. In fact, in those days, two ceremonies took place, one for betrothal, followed as long as a year later by the wedding. Talk about long engagements! At the conclusion of the betrothal period, the community escorted the bride to a room (the chuppah), where the bride and groom consummated the marriage.

These days, the chuppah is just a canopy, and the honeymoon is a private occasion without onlookers to verify the bride's virginity or the groom's virility.

In the final part of the wedding ceremony, the groom breaks a glass by stepping on it. The broken glass has been linked to the memory of the destroyed Temple, or is seen as a reminder that a little sadness accompanies even the greatest happiness. The glass originally was thrown against a wall, as though at a drunken party. In Germany, at one time, the glass was broken on a stone set against the north wall of the synagogue. Supposedly, evil spirits would be scared away by the noise. The breaking of the glass could even represent the end of a wife's virginity The truth is that no one knows how the idea originated, but it's likely to have something to do with evil spirits. They were always spoilsports, and people continually came up with dramatic plans to counter them.

Understanding Jewish Symbols

From candelabras to six-pointed stars, Jews have developed various symbols throughout their long history. The images decorate flags and homes, and are worn on jewelry as constant reminders of a proud heritage.

The menorah

REMEMBER

The *menorah*, a seven-pronged candelabra, has served as a symbol of Judaism for centuries. One is shown in Figure 3-1 and is what most people are familiar with even if different menorahs are used today. It appears in many ancient documents and inscriptions. Today, most Jewish homes have a menorah, which is put out on holidays or placed in the window during Hanukkah.

The usual menorah used today for Hanukkah actually has nine prongs: eight for the candles, and one for the candle used to light the others.

Jewish scholars who have looked at the menorah and its seven candleholders have suggested its design was inspired by a plant. More likely, it's an astrological device representing the five visible planets and the sun and the moon. That would also explain the persistent use of the number seven throughout the Bible, something vegetation would not reflect.

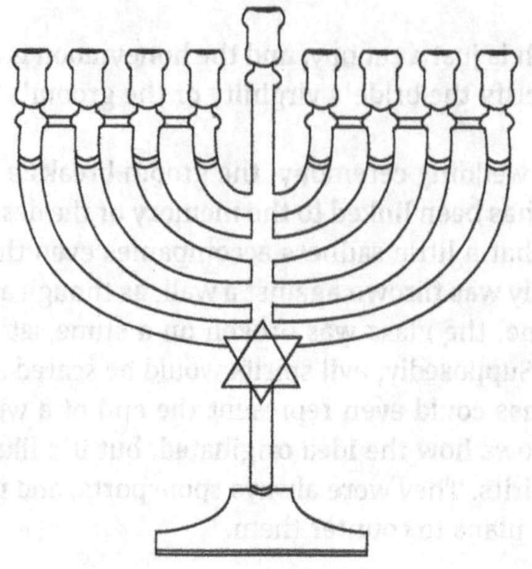

FIGURE 3-1: Menorahs are typically seen during Hanukkah.

© John Wiley & Sons, Inc.

The ark

Every synagogue features a large container placed against the eastern wall to hold the sacred scrolls. It's called an ark, mirroring the wooden box that once carried God around. The word comes up in three stories in the Bible. The great ship of Noah in the flood; the basket that carried baby Moses in the Nile; and the container holding the stone representing God were all called arks.

Arks can look very different depending on the synagogue, but all are made of wood. They typically are located on the back of the altar and can feature huge doors or look like small boxes.

The ark is of Egyptian origin. They, too, carried around gods in similar containers.

The Jewish star

Today, many Jews like to wear jewelry with the six-pointed Jewish star on it (see Figure 3-2). The star became prominent in the Middle Ages as various rulers searched for ways to identify Jews among their people. England's King Edward I forced Jews in the 13th century "to wear a piece of yellow taffeta shaped like the Ten Commandments. French Jews of the 14th century were required to wear circular yellow badges, and Pope Paul IV in the 16th century had Jewish men wear yellow hats and women yellow kerchiefs," according to a historical report. Finally, one of the kings hit upon a six-side star and required his Jewish residents to don it. No one knows who actually began the concept, but the idea spread quickly. In time, the six-pointed star became exclusively connected to Jews.

In the 1890s, Theodore Herzl, the founder of Zionism (the movement to bring Jews back to Palestine), used the star on the masthead of his journal *Die Welt*. The Nazis naturally thought the star was a Jewish image and required all German Jews to wear one. Today, the star, known in Hebrew as *Magen David*, is in the center of the Israeli flag. Despite its name, King David probably never saw one. Still, the star does appear in ornamentation on walls dating as far back as the sixth century BCE.

The six-pointed star was simply another image to be worn by Jews until it became idealized as a symbol of Judaism. There are even Jewish boxers that have had the star sewn on their trunks.

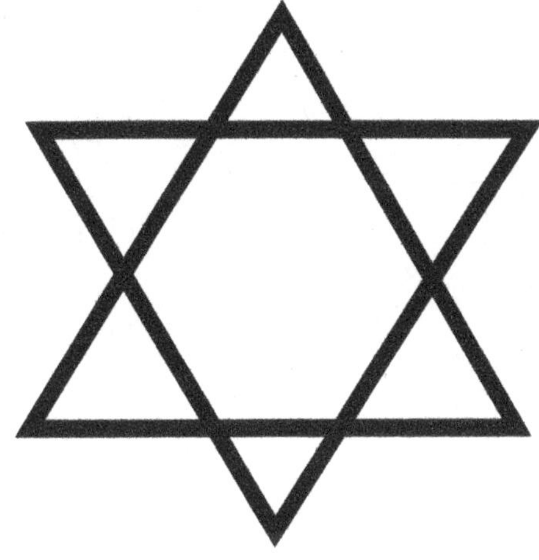

FIGURE 3-2: The six-pointed star is a prominent symbol of Judaism.

IN THIS CHAPTER

» Walking the Jewish path: It's a *mitzvah*

» Connecting through prayer at the synagogue and at home

» Adorning person and place with Jewish symbols

Chapter 4

A Path of Blessing: Judaism as a Daily Practice

Some people are really good at yoga. But for others, it can feel like flopping around like a beached porpoise as more experienced classmates (not to mention the instructor) bend, twist, stretch, and generally look amazing in comparison.

How did those people get so good? The answer is obvious, but frustrating: practice. They showed up day after day, week after week, and slowly got better, looked better, and felt better. But, to those who grew up focusing on getting the job done and reaching the finish line, there's an even more annoying aspect of these activities: There is no finish line. That's why they call yoga — or martial arts, or meditation, or whatever — a practice: You're always practicing, getting better, and going deeper.

Judaism, a religion that focuses far more on deeds than on beliefs, involves practices. When you're new to the practice, it may feel strange. That's okay. Keep practicing anyway. You may be surprised to find yourself opening to deeper meaning in your life — but it probably won't help with your yoga postures.

Connecting With God and Community through Practice: The *Mitzvot*

You may have heard people say that Judaism is a way of life. Referring to Judaism in this way is apt because the religion is a set of practices. These practices, particularly when they're vehicles through which an individual connects more consciously to God, are called *mitzvot* (mitz-vote; it's the plural of *mitzvah*), meaning commandments or religious acts.

How does one discover the *mitzvot*? Through the *halakhah* — walking the talk of Jewish tradition. *Mitzvot* make up the steps on the path of halakhah, along which a Jew discovers their connection to God as well as connections to the past, present, and future of the Jewish community.

Mitzvot consist of ritual as well as ethical acts, and they follow from the principles expressed in the Torah (see Book 4, Chapter 5). Some practices, such as wearing a head covering (*kippah* or *yarmulke*), were developed more recently and fall under the category of *minhag* (custom); however, after so many years of practice these customs have become virtual *mitzvot*.

Undoubtedly the most famous *mitzvot* are the Ten Commandments. In Hebrew, these ten items are called either *Aseret Ha-Dibrot* (The Ten Statements) or *Aseret Ha-D'varim* (The Ten Principles). The Bible never refers to the practices specifically as commandments, perhaps because they were so basic and fundamental to the community. Here are the Ten Principles, numbered according to Jewish tradition (the Christian divisions tend to differ slightly):

1. I am the Eternal your God, who brought you out of the land of Egypt.
2. You shall have no other gods before Me. You shall not make a graven image.
3. You shall not use the name of the Eternal in vain (literally, for nothing).
4. Remember (and Observe) the Sabbath day to keep it holy.
5. Honor your father and your mother.
6. You shall not murder.
7. You shall not commit adultery.
8. You shall not steal.
9. You shall not bear false witness.
10. You shall not covet.

These are the central principles (*mitzvot*) that serve as the foundation for all the other *mitzvot* of Jewish living. According to Jewish tradition, there are 603 more.

613 habits of highly effective people

In the third century, Rabbi Simlai taught that God gave 613 commandments (also called the *taryag mitzvot*) in the Torah. He further divided them into 248 positive commandments (thou shalt's) and 365 negative commandments (thou shalt not's). The number 248 was believed to correspond to the number of organs and sinews in the human body; the number 365 corresponds to the number of days in a solar year.

Examples of positive *mitzvot* include

- Believe in God
- Love God
- Study and teach Torah
- Build a sanctuary for God
- Participate at synagogue services
- Say the blessing after meals
- Spiritually cleanse in a ritual bath (*mikvah*)
- Leave gleanings for the poor
- Tithe to the poor
- Rest on Shabbat
- Eat matzah on Passover
- Fast on Yom Kippur
- Give charity

Here are some negative *mitzvot*:

- Don't believe in any other god
- Don't worship idols
- Don't get tattoos (or decorative scars)
- Don't enter the sanctuary intoxicated
- Don't delay payment of vows

Don't eat an unclean animal

Don't eat blood

Don't eat leavened products on Passover

Don't fail to give charity

Don't convict someone on the testimony of a single witness

TECHNICAL STUFF

Of the 613 commandments, over 200 of them can no longer be observed because they require the ancient Temple that was destroyed in 70 CE. Additionally, some say 26 of the commandments require living in Israel (like the *mitzvah* to leave a portion of a field unharvested so there's some left for the poor).

Mitzvot are scattered all over the Bible, so different rabbis include slightly different *mitzvot* in their lists and order them differently. For example, Maimonides' 12th-century *Sefer Ha-Mitzvot* (Book of the Commandments) and the Chafetz Chayim's 20th-century *Sefer Ha-Mitzvot Ha-Kitzur* (The Concise Book of the Commandments) number the commandments differently. The *mitzvot* are also codified in the 16th-century *Shulchan Aruch* (The Arranged Table) by Joseph Caro, which still serves as the basic authority in matters of traditional practice.

Women and *mitzvot*

All the negative commandments pertain to both men and women, but women are exempted from the positive, time-specific *mitzvot* because of the demands of child-rearing and taking care of the home. For instance, women aren't required to wear the *tallit* (prayer shawl) or attend daily synagogue worship. Although no specific injunction forbids women from doing these *mitzvot*, more traditional communities tend to discourage women from doing them; these same communities are troubled by some women's interest in exploring these practices. In less traditional communities, where women are treated with far greater equality, don't be surprised to see a woman wearing a tallit at worship.

The reasons for *mitzvot*

For traditionalists, the answer to the question "Why perform *mitzvot*?" is easy. They say that the commandments of the Torah represent the will of God and the covenant between the Jewish people and God. However, even traditionalists make exceptions; in a crisis, you're actually required to violate the *mitzvot* if it means you can save a life. The exceptions to that exception are the *mitzvot* prohibiting idolatry, murder, and adultery or incest, which aren't allowed under any conditions.

Many (perhaps most) non-traditional Jews actually have little or no inclination to perform *mitzvot* or to follow *halakhah* and consider themselves Jewish because of birth or cultural identity (see Book 4, Chapter 1). Others observe only those *mitzvot* that are most meaningful to them and choose not to follow the rest.

Rabbi Arnold Jacob Wolf compares the *mitzvot* to precious jewels that appear on the Jewish path: Some of them — like lighting Chanukkah candles, eating matzah on Passover, and lighting a memorial candle for a deceased parent — are easy to pick up and carry. Others — such as observing Shabbat more fully and eating according to the Jewish dietary laws of *kashrut* — require special persistence, but they may well be wonderful jewels to carry.

REMEMBER

The Jewish Way is defined by studying and embracing the jewels — the *mitzvot* — along the path. Those jewels can deeply illuminate your life and connect you more meaningfully to God and to the Jewish people.

SWEET CHARITY'S JUSTICE

One of the most basic themes of the *mitzvot* has to do with providing for those unable to provide for themselves, whether financially, physically, emotionally, or mentally. The Hebrew term for this kind of giving is *tzedakah,* and although it's usually translated "charity," the word literally means "justice." In Jewish tradition, such charitable actions aren't simply a matter of a kind heart. Instead, Jews see them as right actions in the world that are just as important as any other *mitzvah*. For example, Jewish tradition institutes a tithe for those in need (called *ma'aser kesafim*) as a primary social obligation.

Here are Maimonides' (a Jewish theologian of the Middle Ages) famous eight degrees of *tzedakah*, beginning with the lowest level:

- Give only grudgingly.
- Give willingly, but less than is appropriate.
- Give only after being asked.
- Give before being asked.
- Give so that the donor doesn't know who the recipient is.
- Give so that the recipient doesn't know who the donor is.
- Give so that neither donor nor recipient knows the identity of the other.
- Help the poor to rehabilitate themselves by lending them money, taking them into partnership, employing them, or giving them work, for in this way the end is achieved without any loss of self-respect at all.

Connecting With God and Community through Blessings and Prayers

If you live along the coast in New York, and your friend lives near the bay in San Francisco, and you both step into the ocean, you may appreciate that you're actually connecting to one another. Anytime you enter the ocean, you're in touch with others all over the planet. That's how it is with prayer: When you enter into the depths of prayer, you're connected with all others in that space, including those who inhabited that space in the past. Prayer helps you connect with a shared Being, a Universal Presence through Whom all people are connected.

In Jewish tradition, the holy space of prayer is always available. You can access the holy space through daily communal prayer services and through private prayers and blessings that hallow even the most ordinary moments of daily life. Such regular prayers (*t'fillot*) and blessings (*b'rakhot*) keep you conscious of the bigger context in which you live. Unfortunately, one problem with praying so regularly is the very human tendency to go on automatic — observing the outer form while forgetting the inner content. This is why *kavvanah* is so crucial.

Kavvanah is the intentionality with which the prayers and blessings, and even your acts and your words, are to flow. Tradition often teaches how important *kavvanah* is with respect to the observance of all *mitzvot*, including the *mitzvot* of blessings and prayers.

Sometimes you see Jews rhythmically rock and sway in deep concentration (it's called *shuckling*) while they pray (called *davening*). This is a way of entering prayer with the whole body (see Figure 4-1). Similarly, during worship service you may see Jews participate in a subtle choreography, in which they bend their knees and bow, or take several steps forward and several steps back. These actions help Jews pray with *kavvanah*.

TIP

These movements are all customs, not commandments, but if you feel comfortable doing them, you can easily learn them by watching other folks.

Private worship

Although Jews are encouraged to pray in a community, nothing stops them from praying on their own. Judaism recognizes a number of different kinds of prayer — including praising God, petitioning for help, giving thanks, and even just wrestling with the often-difficult issues in our lives.

FIGURE 4-1: A traditional Jew performs his morning prayers at the Western Wall in Jerusalem. Stuffed in the wall are small pieces of paper on which prayers are written.

© Photo courtesy David Blatner.

REMEMBER

Prayers are almost always directed to God, but Jews disagree on what that God is. The important thing is that you find an interpretation that feels right to you (see Book 4, Chapter 3).

In addition to the many blessings traditionally recited during group worship, many blessings are meant to be recited alone. For example, many Jews say blessings at the beginning and the end of the day. Also, although silence isn't part of the traditional communal worship, Jews treat silent meditation as an important part of private worship.

The community worship service

By the time of the *Mishnah* (a codification and expansion of traditions completed around 200 CE), the synagogue worship services that Jews practice were, for the most part, set. On most days, traditional Jews can attend any of the following three services:

- ***Arvit*** or ***Ma'ariv***: Evening service (remember that the Jewish day begins at sundown)
- ***Shakharit***: Morning service
- ***Minkhah***: Afternoon service

On Shabbat and festival days, Jews celebrate an additional service:

» ***Musaf***: An additional service, which takes place after the morning service

The first-century rabbis noted that the Sh'ma was to be recited twice daily (as it had been even in the days of the Second Temple, a place of Jewish worship until it was destroyed by the Romans in 70 CE), with specific blessings before and after. And the daily Amidah (see the following section) was also already pretty much set by 100 CE. The opening formula for a *berakhah*, a blessing (*Baruch Atah Adonai . . .*, "Blessed are You, Eternal One . . ."), became popular following the destruction of the Second Temple and enabled a series of blessings to be developed for the service. In addition to public prayer, individuals added their own private prayers, often reciting Psalms.

Traditional services are conducted entirely in Hebrew, although most prayerbooks in North America include English translations, too.

REMEMBER

Jewish law insists that people understand what they're praying, so the law allows for people to pray in whatever language they know (except for the Sh'ma). Nevertheless, most congregations (even Reform) tend to use Hebrew these days.

Traditionally, you need a *minyan* (min-*yahn*, meaning "quorum") of ten men to pray as a community, but non-Orthodox communities now count women as well. Once you've got a minyan, a service usually begins with a few psalms, poems, and readings that are appropriate for the particular service. Several other elements are always included (which we discuss in the following sections), including the recitation of the *Sh'ma*, the *Amidah*, the *Aleinu*, the *Kaddish*, and sometimes a reading from the Torah and other books of the Bible.

Sh'ma and its blessings

Jews recite the *Kriyat Sh'ma* (Declaration of the Sh'ma) during the morning and the evening services. The Kriyat Sh'ma contains three sections from the Torah:

» **Deuteronomy 6:4–9:** The first passage declares the Oneness of God and promotes love as the way of remembering, teaching, and acting in the world.

» **Deuteronomy 11:13–21:** The second section again stresses the love of God and reminds us that human actions make a difference in the world.

» **Numbers 15:37–41:** The final passage encourages worshippers to remember God's redemption by wearing fringes, called *tzitzit,* on the corners of their garments.

Additionally, Jews always include in the *Sh'ma* blessings that are appropriate to the morning or the evening, as well as blessings for Torah, for redemption, and for protection.

The Amidah

The *Amidah* (literally, the "standing," because worshippers always stand while reciting it) is the central prayer of the worship service. It's often also called the *Tefillah* ("the Prayer") or *Shemonah Esray* ("the 18," referring to the 18 original benedictions it originally contained, even though a nineteenth was added long ago). First you read it silently (move your lips while reciting just loudly enough for you to hear), and then the service leader repeats it aloud.

The 19 blessings of the *Amidah* consist of three sections that reflect the three basic modes of Jewish worship:

- » ***Shevakh***: The first three blessings express praise for the Jewish patriarchs, the wonders of God, and God's holiness.
- » ***Bakashah***: The middle 13 blessings speak petitions, broken up as follows:
  - A set of petitions for knowledge, repentance, forgiveness, redemption, healing, and prosperity.
  - Seven petitions relating to the restoration of Jerusalem, justice, heretics (this is more of a curse, actually), converts, the righteous, God's Presence in Israel, and restoration of the Davidic line of kings.
  - A final petition that God hear all prayers.
- » ***Hoda'ah***: Three blessings of thanksgiving concerning acceptance of the worship, expressions of gratitude, and blessings of peace.

REMEMBER

On Shabbat or other holidays Jews replace the middle section, *Bakashah*, with a single blessing focusing on the holiness of that particular day. They do this because these petitionary prayers are contrary to the spirit of Shabbat — a spirit that imagines the day already to be Eden-like.

Following the Amidah, congregants usually have time for silent worship or personal prayers.

Reading the Torah

During the morning service on Mondays and Thursdays, and on Shabbat afternoons, a rabbi, cantor, or a learned congregant reads sections of the weekly Torah portion. The entire weekly portion is read on Shabbat morning, followed by the

Haftarah, which are complementary readings from the Prophets. The Torah is also read on festival mornings, along with a number of prayers of praise (*hallel*).

Aleinu

Toward the end of each traditional service comes the *Aleinu*, in which worshippers affirm God's Oneness and pray that God's Oneness may one day truly connect all people.

Kaddish

The *Kaddish* is basically a prayer, written mostly in Aramaic, expressing praise of God and the yearning for the establishment of God's Kingdom on earth. Jews recite the *Chatzi Kaddish* (a shorter version of the prayer) to separate the major sections of the worship, so you hear it more than once during a service.

Finally, at the end of the service, worshippers recite the last Kaddish, called the *Mourner's Kaddish*. Traditionally, only those who are mourning the loss of a close relative rise and recite this Kaddish, but today in many communities, everyone rises. The prayer became associated with memorializing the dead because it came at the very end of the service — when by custom the names of those recently deceased were read. Interestingly, the Mourner's Kaddish makes no mention of death; instead, it focuses on praise of God.

Going to Synagogue

Most Jews don't call the house of worship a temple, preferring instead to reserve that word for *The Temple* in Jerusalem (the one that was destroyed by the Babylonians in 586 BCE, was rebuilt, and was then destroyed by the Romans in 70 CE). Some Reform congregations still use "temple," but it's becoming increasingly rare.

Today, English-speaking Jews tend to call the Jewish place of worship a "synagogue" (which actually comes from Greek meaning "gathering" or "assembly"). The Hebrew language has a number of different words for *synagogue*, including *Beit Midrash* (House of Learning), *Beit Tefillah* (House of Prayer), and *Beit Knesset* (House of Assembly). These names reflect the various activities that take place at synagogue: education, prayer, and community gatherings. Many people also use the Yiddish word *shul* (from the German word for "school") to refer to synagogue.

TIP

If you want to attend or join a congregation, look around at different locations (provided that there is more than one where you live). Synagogues can vary significantly not only in their physical appearance, but also in the type of congregation that attends them. Physically, some synagogues rival cathedrals, while others are housed in apartment buildings; some congregations even share space with a church. The type of congregation can range from traditional groups that follow *halakhah* to far less traditional communities that espouse vegetarian, New Age, and feminist values. Take the time to look into your options to find a congregation that best meshes with your own values.

No matter how many differences exist among synagogues, they do share a few commonalities, which we outline in the following section.

Four things you'll find in every synagogue

In every synagogue you usually find the following items:

- **The *Aron Kodesh*:** The ark that holds the Torah scrolls. By convention, in Western countries, it's always on the east wall (so when facing it, the congregation is facing Jerusalem). The ark may have doors and is often covered with a curtain (called a *parochet*), which may be ornately decorated.
- **The *Ner Tamid*:** The eternal light, which often burns above the ark. The light — these days, usually an electric light or oil lamp — symbolizes the menorah (a type of candelabra (which you can read more about in Book 4, Chapter 3) from the ancient Temple and reflects the Eternal Presence experienced through prayer and study in the synagogue.
- **The *bimah*:** The location where the Torah is read and the service is led. It's usually a raised platform, either in the center of the synagogue (this is the Sephardic style) or along the east wall, in front of the Aron Kodesh.
- **Seating area:** All synagogues have a seating area for the congregations. Non-orthodox synagogues (see Book 4, Chapter 1) seat men and women in a shared space. Orthodox synagogues have separate seating areas for men and women, separated by a divider called a *mechitzah* (meh-*kheet*-sa). Often the mechitzah is a low curtain or a partial wall, high enough so that men and women can't see each other during the service. We're not going to get into the volatile political issues surrounding the mechitzah; suffice it to say that while in some synagogues the separation clearly de-emphasizes the role of women, in many other Orthodox synagogues, it's designed so that everyone feels separate-but-equal.

Synagogues, for the most part, reflect the sanctuary style of the dominant culture. Many synagogues in the Middle East resemble mosques, while those in Great Britian tend to look more like churches. However, synagogues rarely feature statues of animals or people, in adherence with the commandment prohibiting graven images. (One notable exception is the often-seen "Lion of Judah," the insignia of the ancient Kingdom of Judea.)

Who's who at shul

A lot of people are involved in running worship services, but the focus is almost always on two people: the rabbi and the cantor.

The rabbi

Although a congregation can conduct religious services without a rabbi, most congregations employ one. The rabbi also serves as an educator and a counselor and officiates at life-cycle events like Bar or Bat Mitzvah ceremonies and weddings (see Book 4, Chapter 3 for more on these).

Rabbinical students typically do five years of post-graduate work before they're ordained as rabbis. Orthodox *yeshivot* (seminaries) tend to have a less formal course of study, but the study is far more extensive in matters of Jewish law. The ordination (as well as the accompanying diploma) is called a *s'mikhah*, literally referring to the laying on of hands through which ordination is traditionally conferred.

REMEMBER

In the past a rabbi was always a "he," but since 1972, non-Orthodox rabbis may be either "he" or "she." Although most rabbis are simply called *rabbi* (a Hebrew term conveying honor, similar to "reverend"), some Jews within the Hasidic and Renewal communities refer to their rabbis as *reb* or *rebbe*. Some people also use the Hebrew word for rabbi, which is simply *rav*.

The cantor

In a traditional synagogue, the cantor (*chazan* in Hebrew) actually leads worship services. In most other synagogues, the cantor performs solo musical prayer selections and leads community singing. The cantor leads the traditional chants for reading the Torah, as well as different musical motifs for daily, Shabbat, festival, and High Holiday worship. Cantors bring great musical and liturgical depth to the community. Many rabbinical schools offer training programs for cantors.

Although traditionally cantors — like rabbis — were all men, today women occupy cantorial positions at many synagogues.

A FIRST-TIMERS' GUIDE TO SYNAGOGUE

Going to any synagogue for the first time can be overwhelming and confusing. If you're familiar with one synagogue, you're sure to wonder why others do the service so differently (adding prayers, leaving prayers out, and so on). If you're unfamiliar with the worship service in general, then keep your eyes and ears open and plan on going a few times before you catch on. Don't be afraid to ask questions, but ask only when people aren't in the midst of prayer. Here are a few other things to think about:

- Wear modest clothing as a sign of respect. If you're male, wear a *kippah* (a head covering; the plural is *kippot*) in the sanctuary; some women in more liberal congregations wear kippot, too. Most synagogues keep extra kippot in the lobby for visitors to borrow. If you're a woman, you may wear a scarf. Men often wear a white or light blue shirt, women often wear a dress or skirt. You don't need a prayer shawl; you probably shouldn't wear one unless you're Jewish, anyway. For more details on the Jewish worship wardrobe, see Book 4, Chapter 3.
- If you don't have a *siddur* (prayer book), ask for one that has an English translation if you don't speak Hebrew. Even better, ask if there's one that has both a translation and a transliteration, so that you can see how the Hebrew is pronounced.
- In Orthodox synagogues, men and women always sit separately. This is uncomfortable for some couples, but that's the way it is. In other synagogues, men and women are almost always mixed.
- The whole thing may look really disorganized, especially in some Orthodox shuls. Some people may be standing while others are sitting, then suddenly everyone comes together for a song or prayer and then people are off on their own again. Remember that Jews are often praying at their own pace, but in the company of other people.
- Try to arrive on time (or early), but if you arrive late, don't walk in while the congregation is standing or during the rabbi's sermon. You may notice other people arriving late (sometimes very late). Instead of just joining in, they often start from the beginning of the prayer service. Sometimes people just leave when they're done, too.
- A collection plate won't be passed around (especially not on Shabbat). However, you may find a box for charitable donations in the lobby.
- Stand up (with everyone else) as a sign of respect when the ark is open. Other times, though, you may see people standing or bowing; you don't have to do this if you don't want to.
- Typically, before the Torah reading, the Torah is marched around the synagogue (an act called a *hakafah*), and people reach out, touch it with their fingers (or prayer shawl), and then kiss their fingers (or shawl). You don't have to do this; it's just a way to make contact with the central symbol of Jewish tradition. After the Torah reading, the Torah is usually lifted up and shown to the congregation (called *hagbah*).

Purifying the Spirit: Rites and Rituals

Nothing brings on transformation like a good, hard rainstorm. After the clouds pass and the sun appears, both air and land seem cleansed, and the earth is nourished once again. Water is the transformer and the giver of life, and for millennia, people have used water to purify their bodies and possessions — literally, figuratively, and spiritually.

Judaism has a long tradition of caring about ritual and spiritual purity, called *taharah*, stemming from the Biblical instructions regarding priests and sacrifices (a priest had to be ritually pure to participate in the Temple service). Because everyday observance of *mitzvot* and worship now replace the ancient sacrifices, you need to be ritually pure to participate properly. For example, Jewish law states that being in a room with (or touching) a dead person or animal makes you ritually impure. When people become impure (*tamay*) for one reason or another, they can use a water ritual to become pure (*tahor*) once again. So, Jews often pour water from a pitcher over their hands before coming into the house of mourning after attending a burial.

Similarly, traditional Judaism states that while women are menstruating, and for seven days after they finish bleeding, they are *tamay* (so men and women don't touch each other during this time). When this period is finished, the women immerse themselves in a mikvah, a ritual bath composed at least in part of fresh water (tap water doesn't count as fresh). Most Jewish communities have a "public" mikvah that people can go to, but any natural spring, river, lake, or ocean will do, too.

The *mikvah* (or the hand-washing ceremony prior to eating) isn't meant to cleanse physically; participants must be physically clean beforehand. The mikvah is meant to provide a *spiritual* cleansing. Many observant Jews, both men and women, visit a *mikvah* each week, before Shabbat. Jews traditionally visit the *mikvah* just before getting married, too.

Many less-traditional women and men view the *mikvah* with suspicion because this ritual cleansing can be interpreted as "women are dirty and untouchable" after menstruation. We believe that *taharah* has more to do with the affirmation of life, and the *mikvah* is a process of being born again and re-focusing on creation. Not surprisingly, the *mikvah* is called for just before the woman is ovulating, and couples are reunited when the chance of pregnancy is highest. Use of the *mikvah* by Reform and Reconstructionist Jews is on the rise, particularly before conversions, wedding ceremonies, and even some holidays. Some liberal Jewish communities have also explored use of the *mikvah* for psychological healing — to help one recover from a trauma, such as rape, for example.

The Jewish Home

Jewish homes are typically similar to other homes in the same neighborhood, inside and out. However, if you keep your eyes open, you may notice a few items that commonly appear in Jewish households. For example, sometimes a piece of art with the Hebrew word *mizrakh* (east) hangs on the home's east wall (facing Jerusalem), and some Jews display their seder plate in a cabinet. The Hebrew word *chai* (life) is a popular symbol in artwork, as is the *hamsa*, an inverted hand, often with an eye in the middle of the palm. The hamsa is shared with other Middle Eastern cultures and isn't exclusively Jewish.

The two most common Jewish items that you may find in a Jewish home are the *mezuzah* and the *menorah*, which you can learn more about in Book 4, Chapter 3.

So Go Now and Live

While antisemites have long used the verb *to Jew* as an insult, the word *Jew* can be verbed in a different way, reflecting a Jewish way of living. Traditional practice is certainly a major part of such "Jew-ing," but it doesn't end there. All Jewish practice is aimed at affirming the One Being Who connects all life with Blessing, Compassion, Justice, and Love. The ultimate goal of Judaism is to awaken to a greater awareness of that One Being.

IN THIS CHAPTER

» Discovering the essence of a faith: The Five Books of Moses

» Looking at the Hebrew Bible

» Uncovering Judaism's oral tradition

» Exploring the Jewish Way

Chapter 5

A Never-Ending Torah: The Unfolding of a Tradition

Judaism has survived for almost 4,000 years, including 2,000 years without a homeland, without the Temple in Jerusalem, without any common geographical location, and without support from the outside. Judaism and Jews survived because of Torah. No matter where they lived, no matter what historical horrors or joys they experienced, the heart of their faith was carried and communicated through the way, the path, and the teachings of Torah.

Torah: The Light That Never Dims

The word *Torah* ("teaching") refers to the first five books of the Hebrew Bible, which are written on a scroll and wound around two wooden poles (see Figure 5-1). Hand-lettered on parchment, the text has been carefully copied by scribes for more than 2,500 years. On one level, the five books narrate a story from the creation of the world to the death of Moses, around 1200 BCE. On a deeper level, the Torah is the central text that guides the Way called Judaism.

FIGURE 5-1: Torah scrolls covered by a richly decorated cloth.

© Tom Le Goff/Getty Images.

The five books of Moses

TIP

The five books are commonly named Genesis, Exodus, Leviticus, Numbers, and Deuteronomy, following the naming in the early Greek translation of the Bible. (These books also appear in the Christian Bible, which you can read more about in Book 5, Chapter 2.) One way to remember the names is with the mnemonic: "General Electric Lightbulbs Never Dim." Note that the Hebrew names for the books are very different (they're taken from the first unique word that appears in each book):

- **Genesis (*Bereisheet*, "In the beginning"):** Deals with the creation of the world, the patriarchs and matriarchs (including Abraham, Sarah, and Jacob), and concludes with the story of Jacob, Joseph, and the eventual settlement of the Hebrew people in Egypt.
- **Exodus (*Sh'mot*, "Names"):** Tells of the struggle to leave Egypt, the revelation of Torah on Mount Sinai (including the Ten Commandments), and the beginning of the journey in the wilderness.
- **Leviticus (*Vayikra*, "And He called"):** Largely deals with levitical, or priestly, matters concerning the running of the Sanctuary, although this book includes some incredible ethical teachings, as well.

- **Numbers (*BaMidbar*, "In the wilderness"):** Begins with taking a census of the tribes and continues with the people's journey through the wilderness.
- **Deuteronomy (*D'varim*, "Words"):** Consists of speeches by Moses recapitulating the entire journey. Deuteronomy concludes with the death of Moses and the people's entrance into the Promised Land.

When these five books are printed in book form (rather than on the scroll), they're usually called the *Chumash* (from *chamesh*, "five"; remember that this "ch" is that guttural "kh" sound), or the *Pentateuch* (this is Greek for "five pieces" and not Hebrew, so here the "ch" is a "k" sound, like "touk"). Because tradition teaches that Moses wrote the books based on Divine revelation, basically taking dictation from God, the books are also called the Five Books of Moses.

If you had your latté this morning, you may have noticed that the Torah is said to have been dictated to Moses, even though it includes the story of his own death and burial. Traditional Jews (see Book 4, Chapter 1) don't have any problem with this contradiction because to a traditional Jew, the words are those of God, not Moses.

The weekly readings

The *Sefer Torah* (Torah book, or scroll) is the most important item in a synagogue, and it "lives" in the *Aron Kodesh* (the "Holy Ark" or cabinet, which is sometimes covered with fancy curtains and decorations). A portion of the Torah is read in every traditional synagogue each week, on Mondays, Thursdays, Shabbat (see Book 4, Chapter 3), and on holidays (see Figure 5-2).

The five books are divided into 54 portions called *parshiot* (each one is a *parashah*), also called *sidrot* (each one is a *sidra*). At least one parashah is read each week of the year; some weeks have two *parshiot* to make it fit the Jewish year correctly. Some synagogues divide the Torah portions differently so that it takes three years, instead of one, to read all five books.

During a synagogue service on Shabbat morning, the Torah reading is followed by the *Haftarah* (see the section later in this chapter). Traditionally, the person who reads the *Haftarah* also repeats the concluding verses of the parashah called the *maftir*.

REMEMBER

Chapters and verses in the Hebrew Bible were a much later invention, when the Latin "Vulgate" translation was created (405 CE). Instead, each parashah of the Torah has its own name, like "*Parashat Noakh*," which corresponds to Genesis 6:9–11:32.

THE MAKING OF A SEFER TORAH

Anyone who's been in the book business knows that a few typos always get by the proofreaders, no matter how carefully they, er, chck. The Torah business is different. The text of each and every Torah is identical because it's copied letter by letter from an original by a *sofer* ("scribe") on to sections of parchment. Even the tiny decorative flourishes on some letters are copied exactly. If the *sofer* makes a mistake, he (traditional *sofrim* are invariably men, though now at least one Torah has been scribed by a woman) has to scratch the ink off the parchment, and if he can't correct the mistake completely, the whole page must be destroyed. In this way, the written Torah has been lovingly preserved for over 2,500 years. It takes about a year to complete a scroll, and the final product can cost $20,000 to over $50,000. (You can usually pick up a used Torah for between $7,500 and $20,000. What a deal!) If a scroll gets damaged or, after perhaps 100 or 200 years, if it wears out beyond repair, it's not thrown away — it's buried in a Jewish cemetery, along with other holy books.

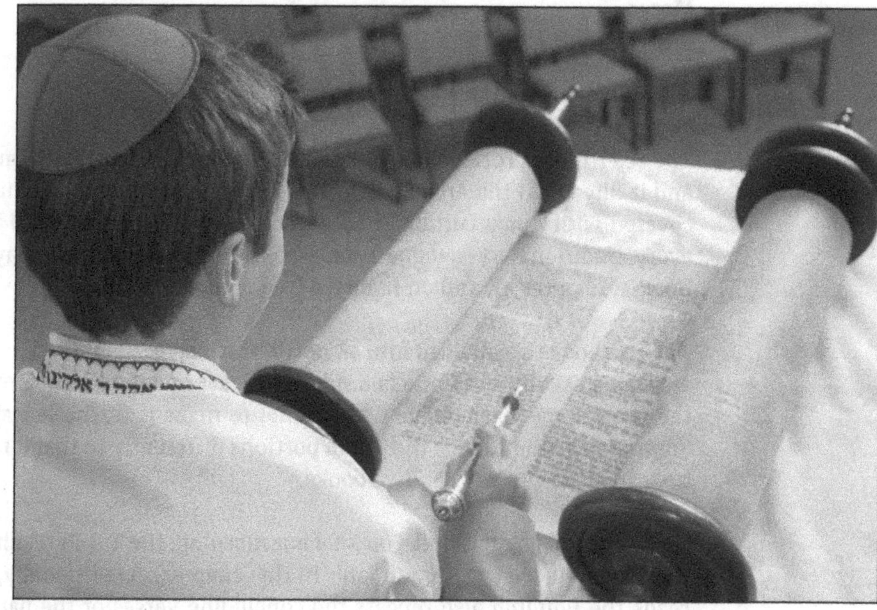

FIGURE 5-2: The Torah scroll is always read with a pointer so that fingers won't touch the type.

© Eric Delmar/Getty Images.

The TaNaKH: The Hebrew Bible

The five books of the Torah appear as the first of three sections of the Hebrew Bible, which contains 39 books reflecting texts that were gathered over almost 2,000 years. Another name for the Hebrew Bible is the *Tanakh*, which is actually an acronym made up of the first letters of the names of each of the three sections: "T" is for *Torah*, "N" is for *Nevi'im* ("Prophets"), and "KH" is for *Ketuvim* ("Writings").

TIP

If you want to sound like a *mayven* (expert), don't call the Hebrew Bible the "Old Testament." The Old Testament is a Christian term based on the idea that there is a *New* Testament that supersedes the Hebrew Bible. Jews prefer to call their Bible either the Hebrew Bible, or simply the Holy Scriptures. What Christians call the New Testament is usually referred to in Jewish settings as the Christian Bible. For more on the Christian Bible, see Book 5, Chapter 2.

Nevi'im ("Prophets")

Nevi'im (neh-vee-eem) contains a record of most of the important history for the roughly 700 years after Moses. The history is told in the Books of Joshua, Judges, Samuel, and Kings. *Nevi'im* also includes the words of the great sixth-century BCE prophets like Isaiah, Jeremiah, and Ezekiel. The last 12 books in *Nevi'im* — from Hosea to Malachi — are much shorter, and they're often grouped together as "The 12 Prophets."

Ketuvim ("Writings")

Ketuvim (keh-too-veem) is a collection of books, but the books don't necessarily relate to one another. Some (Ezra, Nehemiah, and Chronicles) relate history; some (like Proverbs) relate, well, proverbs. The Books of Ecclesiastes and Lamentations express some of the bleaker reflections on life.

The Book of Psalms, the longest book of the Bible, contains 150 poems of praise, yearning, and celebration that form the basis of many prayers and hymns both in Jewish and Christian traditions. The Books of Job, Ruth, Esther, and Daniel record epic moral and religious quests. The Song of Songs is a beautiful love poem that many people read as a metaphor for the relationship between God and the Jewish people.

TECHNICAL STUFF

After being passed down orally for centuries, most of the individual books of the *Tanakh* were written down by the third century BCE. However, Jewish scholars didn't determine the official canon — the list of books that "made it" into the Bible — until 90 CE, in the city of Yavneh (also called Jamnia). The scholars of Yavneh left out several books that came to be included in the *Septuagint* (the Greek translation of the Bible), including the *Apocrypha* ("hidden books"), like the four books of Maccabees. However, Roman Catholic and Greek Orthodox Bibles include these books because they're based on the Septuagint.

The Haftarah

Each of the 54 *parshiot* is associated with a section from *Nevi'im* (historical and prophetic books of the Hebrew Bible). Those 54 sections of the *Nevi-im* are called *Haftarah* (the name "Haftarah" means "taking leave," representing an additional reading following the Torah portion). Most historians think that during a particularly repressive period, perhaps as early as the second century BCE when public reading of the Torah became a capital offense, scholars instead read non-Torah texts that would remind them either by theme or characters of the weekly Torah portion. In this way, people can remember what Torah portion should have been read. Later, when the ban was lifted, this extra reading was retained, so even today, Jews typically read both the Torah and the *Haftarah* texts on Shabbat and festivals.

Interpreting the Bible

Jewish "fundamentalism" doesn't focus on the "literal truth" of the Bible like some other forms of religious fundamentalism do. Although many traditional Jews believe that the *Tanakh* expresses the Word of God, very few Jews would argue that the literal meaning of the words is the right one. An important rabbinic teaching says that there are 70 interpretations for every word in Torah — and they're all correct! Jewish tradition talks of four dimensions of meaning: the literal, the allegorical, the metaphorical, and the mystical.

TECHNICAL STUFF

For example: When Abraham hears *Lekh l'kha may-artz'kha* . . . ("Get you out of your land . . ."), God seems simply to be telling him to move on. But a deeper interpretation encourages the reader to consider the nature of such journeys in a personal context: What is it like to really "leave" a place? Then an even deeper interpretation is addressed to people on a spiritual quest in which they are asked to leave the place of comfort in old ideas and identities and strike out into the unknown. Finally, the first two words (which are usually translated, "Get you out") can also literally be translated, "Go to yourself." On a more mystical level, the call directs us toward an inner journey.

Studying different interpretations is called *hermeneutics*, and it's an important part of the Jewish understanding of Torah. Hermeneutics is why five different rabbis can make five different sermons on the same text. More fundamentalist Jewish groups don't focus on an exclusive interpretation of the Torah text as much as on a very strict application of ritual practice.

A Hidden Revolution: The Oral Torah

The written Torah may be the central text of the Jewish people, but if that's all Jews had, they may be in trouble. For example, the Torah doesn't explain how to perform a religious marriage, what "an eye for an eye" really means, or even how to honor Shabbat and the other holidays (especially ever since the Temple was destroyed and Jews could no longer make animal sacrifices). Think of the Torah as the musical score to an amazing symphony; the written music contains the notes but doesn't say how to play them. Jews need more than the Torah scrolls to know how to "play" Judaism.

The "musical direction" is provided by the "Oral Torah," a set of teachings, interpretations, and insights that complement the written Torah. One seminary professor, Dr. Ellis Rivkin, spoke of the development of Oral Torah as one of the most profound religious revolutions of all time. Without it, he taught, Judaism can hardly have survived for as long as it has.

Traditional, Orthodox Jews believe that Moses not only received what became the Written Torah (*Torah sheh-bikh-tav*) at Sinai, but also the Oral Torah (*Torah sheh-b'al peh*). The oral tradition itself states: "Moses received the [Written and Oral] Torah from Sinai and handed it down to Joshua, and Joshua to the elders, the elders to the prophets, and the prophets handed it down to the men of the Great Assembly . . ." So Jews not only see the Written Torah as the word of God, but the Oral Torah, as well.

This oral tradition would, centuries later, itself be written down in the form of the *Mishnah*, the Talmud, and the *midrash* — only to be further interpreted by countless more rabbis and students, developing into the Judaism of today. Each time the oral tradition is written, it gives rise to the next step of the process.

TECHNICAL STUFF

Liberal Jews tend to discount the transmission of the Oral Torah at Sinai; instead, they believe that the Oral Torah slowly evolved over time. These folks appreciate that pieces of Mishnah, Talmud, and midrash still hold eternal truths, but they also believe that some passages tied to ancient cultural environments are no longer relevant.

The law of the land: The *Mishnah*

The early scholars and teachers (roughly between 100 BCE and 100 CE) developed guidelines for a continuing Way of Life, called *halakhah*. Whether or not halakhah (which is usually translated "legal material" or "law," but literally means "the walk" — as in "walking the talk") was originally divinely given, it provided the structure for the community's practice of Judaism. For more than two hundred years, this body of material developed orally, and because it was considered an oral tradition, Jews were prohibited from writing it down.

GETTING HIT OVER THE HEAD WITH WISDOM

Two of the most influential rabbis in the developing Oral Tradition were Hillel (70 BCE to 10 CE) and Shammai (50 BCE to 30 CE). Perhaps the most famous story about these two rabbis concerns a non-Jew seeking to discover the essence of Judaism.

First, the man went to Shammai, who was in the midst of working (all the rabbis back then had day jobs, too, and Shammai was a house builder). The man asked Shammai, "Tell me the meaning of Judaism while standing on one foot." Shammai stared at the guy and then whacked him on the head with his measuring rod.

Not particularly satisfied, the man then visited the sage Hillel with the same request: "Tell me the meaning of Judaism while standing on one foot." Hillel looked at him for a moment and then said, "What is hateful to you do not do to others. That is the whole of Torah, all the rest is commentary — go now and learn."

Although this is a wonderful story about Hillel, we think that Shammai's teaching has long been unappreciated. You may be aware of the Zen Buddhist tradition in which a teacher may strike a student in order to startle him into a radically new way of seeing things (for more on Buddhism, check out Book 3). Perhaps Shammai knew that understanding the essence of Judaism isn't so much a matter of a gentle principle but rather a matter of deep inner transformation.

But, as you may guess, Hillel's gentle, compassionate, and practical answers, as well as his legal decisions, were virtually always followed. But there are many who suspect that Shammai's teachings were actually more spiritually-based, and tradition has it that while Hillel's decisions are fit for this world, Shammai's will be followed in the World to Come.

However, after hundreds of thousands of Jews were killed by the Romans in the early years of the first millennia, and halakhah continued to become more complex, Jews realized the importance of codifying the expanding traditions in writing. Although some of the earlier rabbis had collected material before him, Judah Ha-Nasi ("Judah the Prince," who is also simply called "Rabbi") finally codified the laws, creating the *Mishnah* between 200 and 220 CE.

The *Mishnah* (the name derives from "a teaching that is repeated," indicating its origin as an oral tradition) includes lessons and quotations by sages from Hillel and Shammai (first-century rabbis) through Judah Ha-Nasi (who lived in the third century). The *Mishnah* contains a collection of legal rulings and practices upon which Jewish tradition still depends. The *Mishnah* is organized like a law book (as opposed to the narrative of the Torah), splitting up the Jewish Way into six basic *sedarim* ("orders"):

- ***Zera-im* ("Seeds"):** Blessings and prayers, agricultural laws
- ***Mo-ed* ("Set Feasts"):** Laws of Sabbath and the holidays
- ***Nashim* ("Women"):** Marriage, divorce, and other vows
- ***Nezikin* ("Damages"):** Civil laws, idolatry, and *Pirke Avot* ("Ethics of the Fathers," which is a collection of ethical quotes and proverbs by the rabbis)
- ***Kodashim* ("Hallowed Things"):** Temple sacrifices, ritual slaughter, and dietary laws
- ***Tohorot* ("Purities"):** Ritual cleanliness and uncleanliness

The teachings explained: The Talmud

The ancient sages feared that once the *Mishnah* was written down it wouldn't meet the demands of changing times, and they were right. Academies of Jewish learning grew in Palestine and Babylonia (modern Iraq) to discuss new issues raised by their consideration of the *Mishnah*. Most of the rabbis had other jobs, but their true love was meeting in the academies to discuss, argue, and debate concerns arising from the text of the *Mishnah*, new legal issues, the Torah, stories of supernatural events, and a host of other matters.

Their dialogues were the beginning of another part of the Oral Torah, the *Gemara* ("completion"). The *Gemara* is basically a commentary on the various teachings of the *Mishnah*. Where the *Mishnah* dealt mainly with matters of halakhah, the *Gemara* contained both halakhah and *aggadah* ("discourse," stories, legends, and pieces of sermons; the tales and the teachings that "read between the lines" of *Tanakh* and Talmud). The *Mishnah* with the *Gemara* became known as the *Talmud* ("teaching").

In size, the *Tanakh* is dwarfed by the massive Talmud, which often appears in as many as 30 volumes (with translations and commentary). Note that most traditional Jews don't focus on "Bible study"; they focus on the study of the Talmud. However, the Bible does tend to be the focus for more liberal Jews.

Reading the Bible is hard, especially without helpful commentary, but reading the Talmud is orders of magnitude more difficult (take a look at Figure 5-3 to see how much information is crammed on to just one page). Discussions frequently contain several radically different opinions, offered by rabbis who appear to be in the same room but actually lived in different centuries. The arguments often appear nonlinear, like a free-association or like surfing on a cosmic Internet. Some people say that you don't read the Talmud, you swim in it. But behind the complexities of the text, the Talmudic scholars find profound insights and deep meaning.

REMEMBER

With the completion of the Talmud, was the oral tradition finished? Of course not. Commentaries, codifications, questions, and answers continue to unfold through books, articles, and rabbinic discussions. This ongoing, unending discussion is also considered part of the Oral Torah.

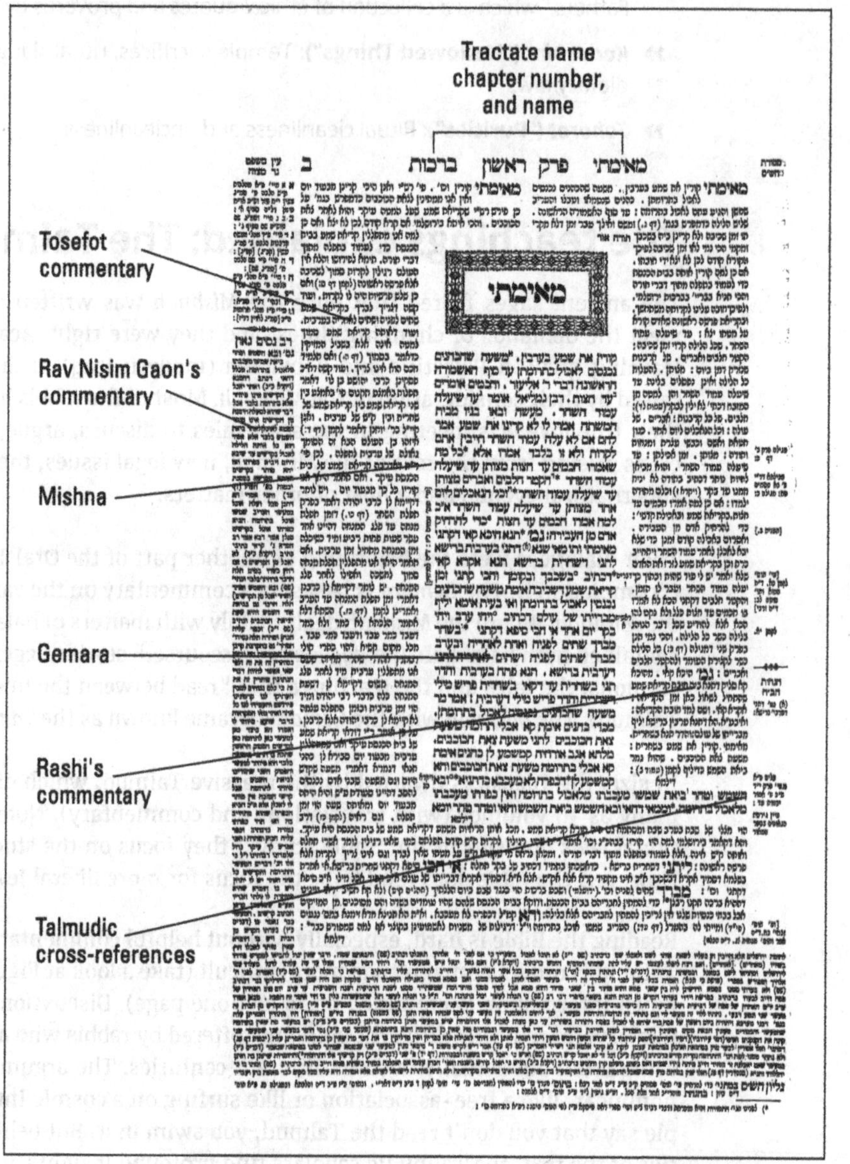

Tractate name chapter number, and name

Tosefot commentary

Rav Nisim Gaon's commentary

Mishna

Gemara

Rashi's commentary

Talmudic cross-references

FIGURE 5-3: A sample page from the Talmud.

A SAMPLE OF TALMUDIC DIALOGUE

Even though few people other than scholars and religious Jews ever read the Talmud, the discussions offer a fascinating window into the essence of the Oral tradition. Here's one small example, focusing on a central Jewish prayer, the *Amidah* ("Standing"), also known as the *Shemoneh Esrey* ("The 18").

***Mishnah*:** Raban Gamiliel says that everyone should pray the "Eighteen [Blessings]" daily. Rabbi Yehoshua says that one should only pray an extract of the 18 Blessings. Rabbi Akiba says that if one knows them clearly one should say all 18, otherwise one should pray the extract. Rabbi Eliezer says that whoever prays "on automatic" isn't really praying at all.

Here, three rabbis from the first and second centuries discuss how to recite the central prayer in a Jewish service. Remember that at that time there were no printed prayer books, so people had to know prayers by heart. Then, generations later in the *Gemara*, rabbis reading this Mishnah wondered why there should be 18 blessings in the first place.

***Gemara*:** On what are these "Eighteen Blessings" based? Rabbi Hillel, the son of Rabbi Shmuel Bar Nachmani, says that they're indicated by the 18 times the name of God is mentioned in Psalm 29. Rav Yosef bases it on the 18 times God's name is mentioned in the *Sh'ma*. Rabbi Tanchum said in the name of Rabbi Yehoshua Ben Levy that the 18 blessings correspond to the 18 major vertebrae in the human spine.

This is interesting because the spine connects the body's lower and higher functions and so symbolizes the link between the physical and the spiritual realms. So now the prayer under discussion, because it has 18 sections, acts as a daily reminder of the Jew's role as a bridge between worlds.

Telling stories: The *midrash*

Perhaps the most fascinating parts of Oral Torah (at least to lay readers) is the large body of *midrash* (from *d'rash*, an "exposition," or "sermon") that contains both halakhic and aggadic materials. Most people focus on the aggadah — those tales and the teachings that "read between the lines" of *Tanakh* and Talmud. The most well-known collections of *midrash* span the years between the fourth and sixth centuries, although the *midrashic* form continued in collections through the 13th century, and *midrash* even exists today in the form of contemporary sermons, stories, and homilies.

ABRAHAM AND THE IDOLS

One of the most famous *midrashic* tales concerns the Patriarch Abraham when he was still a boy. As the story goes, Abraham's father was an idol salesman, with a shop full of stone statues of various gods. One day, his father entrusted the care of the shop to Abraham while he went out. Abraham, looking around the room of idols, took a stick and proceeded to smash all the idols except the largest one, into whose hands he then put the stick.

When his father returned, he looked aghast at the destruction in his shop and exclaimed "What happened?" Abraham calmly replied, "That idol smashed all the others." His father said, "Idols can't do that." And Abraham replied, "That's right, father, idols are powerless."

This story, which beautifully brings aspects of the biblical story to life, is so well known that many people grew up thinking that it was actually written in Genesis.

It is in *midrash* that the great creative and imaginative genius of the Jews blossomed, and you often find psychological, emotional, and spiritual insights in it. A kind of play is possible in aggadah that was usually inhibited in Talmudic legal discussions, and tradition has it that God smiles when people write and discuss aggadah.

For example, one famous *midrash* explains an apparent inconsistency in the Book of Genesis, in which both man and woman are created in the first chapter, but then the man is suddenly alone in the second chapter. A *midrash* says the first woman was named Lilith, but Adam couldn't get along with her. He complained bitterly to God: "We can't agree on anything. She never listens to me!" So, according to that *midrash*, God banished Lilith and replaced her with Eve, with whom Adam could better relate. A very long time later, the Jewish feminist movement embraced Lilith because she was created equal to Adam. Remember, this is *midrash* — just a story.

The Expanding Torah

REMEMBER

The word *Torah* has a third and even larger meaning beyond the written and oral law, too. Torah is the Jewish Way. Torah is the whole thing. Torah is 3,800 years and counting. Torah is the expanding, evolving quest of a people exploring the nature of Ultimate Reality and the responsibilities of Human Being.

5

Christianity

Contents at a Glance

IN THIS CHAPTER

» Becoming familiar with the Trinity's basic meaning

» Looking at each member of the Trinity

» Getting to know Jesus

» Understanding how Christianity developed

» Discovering how the Christian world split apart

» Exploring the role Christianity has played in the world

Chapter 1

God, Jesus, and the Origins of Christianity

For Christians, there is a singular God who is the creator of the universe — because he (yes, Christians refer to God as "he," and some may capitalize those pronouns based on personal preference) is infinite in power and greatness. When you try to wrap your mind around that concept, your mind may go numb. And that's okay. Because to Christians, God is someone whom you'll never fully fathom in your head — but who you can know intimately in your heart. He's more than just some unexplainable Being in the sky; he's profoundly personal.

In this chapter, we explore who Christians believe God is and what he's like. Christianity says that God is a Trinity — one God expressed in three beings. So we'll help you wrap your head around that idea. Then, after getting your feet wet, we'll dive headfirst into getting to know Jesus and the Christian world on a basic level before exploring the divisions within the faith.

Introducing the Trinity

REMEMBER

The basic gist of the Trinity is that one God exists, with three distinct identities (or "persons"): God the Father, God the Son, and God the Holy Spirit. Each member of the Trinity has a unique personality and role, but they are all coequal and unified.

The term *trinity* literally means "three-oneness" — combining the terms *tri* (meaning "three") and *unit* (meaning "one"). Although the idea of the Trinity is plainly rooted in the Bible, the word isn't mentioned in scripture. Instead, it's an attempt by the Church to explain, as much as possible in human terms, the mystery of who God is.

TIP

Think of the Trinity as an equilateral triangle, such as the one shown in Figure 1-1. The triangle consists of three equal, distinct sides that are never separate from each other — the Father, Son, and Holy Spirit. Together these sides form a triangle, the area of which is "one" — God.

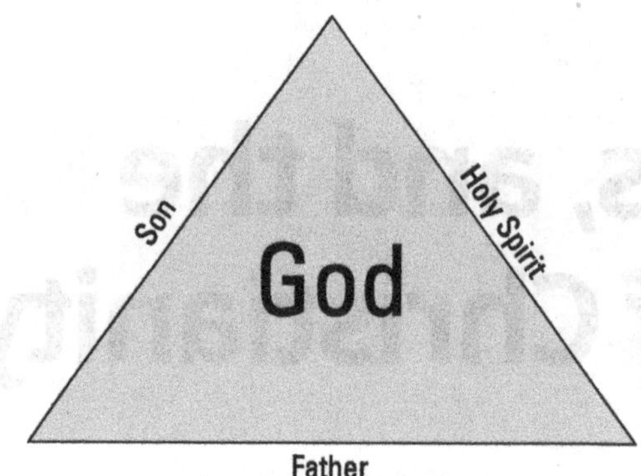

FIGURE 1-1: An equilateral triangle is a helpful illustration of the Trinity.

© John Wiley & Sons, Inc.

Another way to think of the Trinity involves the three states of water — or, for the science buffs, H_2O. Depending on the temperature, H_2O takes on one of three forms: solid ice, liquid water, or a steamy vapor. In the same way, God is "one," but expresses himself in three distinct manners. In the next section, we dive into those distinct parts in more depth.

Examining the Three Parts of God

Although each of the members of the Trinity are equal, the role that each of them plays is distinct. Ephesians 2:18 (a small passage from the Christian holy book called the Bible) provides a good summary when it says, "For through the Son we both have access to the Father by one Spirit." In other words, the Christian has access *to* the Father *through* the Son *by* the Holy Spirit. If all those prepositions have your eyes glazing over, perhaps an illustration will help distinguish among the roles.

Suppose you want to travel to Europe from the United States. Because thousands of miles separate the North American and European continents, you can't just put one foot in front of the other and make it there. An ocean fills the chasm between the continents and connects them together, providing a way to sail a ship to the destination. In this example, you travel *to* Europe *through* the ocean *by* a ship. Similarly, when you approach God the Father, Jesus mediates while the Holy Spirit enables.

Because Christians believe that God the Father plays the leading role, they traditionally call him the "first person" of the Trinity, referring to Jesus as the "second person" and the Holy Spirit as the "third person." (Note that *person* refers to his personality and doesn't imply any idea of humanness.) At the same time, although Father, Son, and Holy Spirit is the most common order, it's not like a law firm where the names are always sequenced in the same way. The Bible has several examples of alternative orders (see 2 Thessalonians 2:13–14, Ephesians 5:18–20, and Jude 20–21).

We explain each of the roles of the Trinity members in the sections that follow.

BIBLICAL CITATIONS

While we cover the Bible more in Book 5, Chapter 2, throughout this book, you may see books of the Bible named followed by some numbers. These are citations that refer you to specific books and passages of the Bible.

To find the mentioned passage in any Christian Bible, locate the named book (keeping in mind that if there is a number before the book name it actually is part of the book name, as some books share the same name and need numbers to differentiate themselves and mark which comes first).

Next, locate the chapter number, which will be listed first. Some citations will end there if they want to direct you to that entire chapter. However, if there is a colon after the chapter number, then the numbers following the colon refer to the verse numbers within that chapter.

So John 3:16 would refer to the sixteenth verse of the third chapter in the book of John. And if the numbers after the colon are hyphenated, it means you're looking for several verses, like verse 11, 12, and 13 if it read 11–13.

God the Father

REMEMBER

The Father is considered the first person of the Trinity. He's the one who people are usually referring to when they say "God." In fact, in the *New Testament* (a newer portion of the Bible focused on the life of Jesus, his teachings, and the early Church, with the other portion of the Bible being called the Old Testament, which focuses on history, prophets, and individuals before the time of Jesus), Paul and other apostles often use the term "God the Father."

The Father is fully in control and is the chief planner (Ephesians 1:3–5). He planned salvation through the Son and is the one who actually does the forgiving, not Christ. God the Father is also the one whom Christians normally direct their prayers to. So, he listens to prayers and answers them according to his will.

Many people assume that God the Father is the Creator of the universe, but that's only partially correct. Although all things originated *from* the Father, all things were created *through* the Son (see 1 Corinthians 8:6, John 1:3, Hebrews 1:2). Therefore, even in regard to the actual creation of the world, you see that two members of the Trinity had distinct roles in the process.

God the Son

REMEMBER

The second person of the Trinity is the Son, Jesus Christ. He's the one who came to the earth as a man to die for the sins of the world. The Son always does the will of the Father and sits at his right hand in heaven. He's the go-between, smack in the middle of a perfect Father and a most unholy people. This mediation played out for all people when he died a sacrificial death on the cross, but he also continues to intercede for Christians on a day-in, day-out basis, as they pray to the Father (Hebrew 7:25).

The Bible indicates that Christians should normally direct their prayers to God the Father, but that's not a hard and fast rule. Occasionally, in the New Testament (such as in Acts 7:39), believers prayed directly to Jesus.

Most Christians tend to feel closest to the Son, identifying with him because he came to the earth as a human and was the one who actually died in their place. What's more, as Hebrews 2:17–18 says, Jesus experienced all the temptations that humans have to deal with. So, he's able to help everyone out because he knows what it feels like to deal with the yucky stuff.

God the Holy Spirit

REMEMBER

The third person of the Trinity is the Holy Spirit (sometimes referred to as the Holy Ghost). The Holy Spirit is said to do the will of the Father and of the Son (see John 14:26). Of the Trinity members, the Holy Spirit is the one that's hardest to relate to for many people because "spirit" is such a vague concept. But, in spite of the mystery, the Holy Spirit performs many critical roles in the lives of Christians.

He has been involved throughout history, such as in revelation to the authors of the Bible and in supernaturally impregnating Mary for the virgin conception of Jesus Christ (see Luke 1:35). He also is actively involved in the life of every Christian. First, he participates in the salvation of a person, which is often referred to as the "baptism of the Holy Spirit" (see Book 5, Chapter 2 for more on baptism). Second, he dwells inside all Christians, filling them with spiritual gifts, giving assurance, convicting them of sins in their lives, helping in worship, and empowering them for service.

The Holy Spirit also plays an important role in a Christian's prayer life. First, the Holy Spirit prompts believers to pray. Second, Christians believe that even when they don't know exactly how to pray for something, the Holy Spirit serves as their translator, so to speak, so that even when they don't know how to express themselves, God the Father understands their needs (Romans 8:26–27).

The Holy Spirit is often depicted in art as a white dove. Ultimately, Christians believe that in order to get to know and understand the personal aspects of God, you should get to know Jesus Christ, who we cover more in the next section.

Studying Jesus's Life and Death

Jesus, the founder of Christianity, has been the subject of many stories and books. He may have been the most important person to live in the last 2,000 years.

A remarkable birth

Jesus arrives on the earthly scene as a beautiful baby, asleep in a manger. His entire life is played out in the pages of the Bible's New Testament. As with the Old Testament, multiple versions of many stories appear in the sacred text, giving us a distinct view of how Jesus was seen by different people in the first century.

JESUS LEFT NO PORTRAIT

Just like no one knows what Abraham looked like, we don't know what Jesus looked like either. However, we can guess. Jesus would have been short — diets in those days had little protein, limiting growth. He would have been dressed in a fringed robe and, as any Jew of his day, worn a skullcap. He would have had a dark beard and long hair because religious figures dedicated to God didn't shave or cut their hair.

Many attempts have been made to construct an image of Jesus by using the descriptions of other Jews living in that era. Because we have yet to uncover a portrait — and probably never will, given the Jewish ban on graven images — every generation has created its own vision of Jesus. Some have been borrowed from other cultures.

The Romans envisioned a "good shepherd," whose gentle gaze and long hair has given rise to similar images of Jesus. A statute of the Egyptian goddess Isis with her son Horus was once mistaken for Mary and Jesus, and widely imitated.

However, some Catholics (more on them in Book 5, Chapter 4) venerate the Shroud of Turin, a piece of Jesus's supposed burial cloth some believe to hold an image of Jesus's face.

For example, two of the four Gospels (the word *Gospel* means "good news" and are books in the Bible written about Jesus's life) include stories about Jesus's birth. In Luke, Jesus's parents, Mary and Joseph, trek to Bethlehem to comply with the demands of a Roman census. There, Jesus is born in a stable with shepherds to welcome him. He then is taken to the Temple (see Book 4, Chapter 2 for more) for the traditional baby-naming ceremony and circumcision. In Matthew's account about the birth, Jesus is born in Bethlehem, and three kings guided by a star bring him gifts. Then he is rushed off to Egypt because King Herod is imitating the Egyptian pharaoh of old and trying to kill all the newborn males. The two stories form the basis of Christmas, the Christian celebration of Jesus's birth.

The Gospels of Mark and John don't include birth stories, and Jesus is presumed to have been born in the obscure village of Nazareth in Galilee.

In another example, the first three Gospels insist Jesus comes from the line of David, while in the fourth, the Gospel of John, a townsperson asks how Jesus can be the Messiah if he isn't related to David. John suggests Jesus is about 50 when he begins to preach; the other three think he is about 30. The age is significant: In Jewish teaching, a man doesn't become wise enough to really understand Scripture until he turns 30.

Still, two millennia later, we can develop a basic understanding of this extraordinary individual, who is believed by more than 2 billion people to be God who came to Earth.

Preaching and teaching God's word

As an adult in Galilee (a region that lies to the north of Jerusalem), Jesus began to preach, speaking out for social justice and expressing love for all mankind.

REMEMBER

Jesus called on his followers to prepare for the coming end of the world and the arrival of a kingdom of God filled with peace. Scholars have identified what they believe is the essence of Jesus's teachings:

- God loves you and is with you.
- Love one another.
- Every person has immense value.
- The kingdom of God has come to earth.
- Believers will face final judgment in heaven or hell.
- God forgives those who ask.

As a result of Jesus's messages, some of his followers thought Jesus was the promised leader sent by God, a person known as the *Messiah*. The Gospel accounts of Jesus are unclear whether Jesus himself claimed that role. In some places, he seems to. In others, he seems to avoid a direct answer. Later, his followers were sure Jesus was that special person.

His status was affirmed to believers by miracles he was credited with, including raising a man from the dead and turning water into wine. These miracles parallel accounts in the Jewish Bible where they are performed by prophets like Elijah. Historians today argue that the miracle accounts are later additions to the Jesus saga.

Jesus's claims stir the pot and create controversy

WARNING

Despite his calls for peace and love, Jesus wasn't especially appreciated by the people of his day.

- **Romans didn't like Jesus or anyone who preached about a new kingdom.** After all, they were quite happy with the current kingdom, which was led by their emperor. They thought their emperor was a god and worshipped him. As a result, they attempted to kill anyone who suggested that someone else was God.

» **Jewish authorities can't have been pleased with Jesus either.** They were trying to accommodate the Romans and avoid bloodshed. They thought Yahweh (one of their names for God) would step in on their behalf eventually and oust the Romans anyway. Jesus's message of a coming end of the world could only heighten unrest, which is the last thing they wanted.

» **Jews who wanted to live in peace with the Romans rejected Jesus, too.** They didn't want the Romans attacking them because of Jesus's insistence on a kingdom of God.

» **Militant Jews rejected Jesus's call for peace.** Some Jews had decided not to wait for Yahweh to return to set the Romans straight, so they formed guerilla units that harassed Roman troops. They thought God would help them defeat their enemies and spurned any idea of peace.

A date with the cross

With so many opponents, Jesus had little chance to be heard or to survive. According to Christian reports, Jesus was eventually arrested and tried for treason by the Romans for claiming to be or being proclaimed as the king of the Jews.

The Romans then crucified Jesus; *crucifixion* was an excruciating manner of death in which a victim was nailed to a cross and left to die. Jesus was buried, but, according to his followers, arose in three days to reappear to his disciples. (You can read the accounts of Jesus's death and resurrection in Matthew 27–28; Mark 15–16; Luke 23–24; and John 19–20.)

REMEMBER

Jesus's disciples (and Christians to this day) believed that Jesus conquered death and, if they followed his teachings and believed in him, they, too, could be saved from death.

No one knows exactly when Jesus died. The conflict in biblical dates has created problems in developing a chronology for Jesus. Many historians use 33 CE as the date of Jesus's death, even if it conflicts with aspects of his life story. For example, Passover that year did not fall on a weekend, but Jesus was supposedly crucified on Friday at the start of the Passover holiday.

REMEMBER

In the first years after Jesus's death, few people knew about him. No writers or historians of the era wrote about him, except for one disputed paragraph in the book by Josephus, the Jewish historian of the first century CE.

As Christians note today, it's remarkable that a man who attracted so little attention in his era has become the center of the world's largest religion. They see God's hand in that situation.

While Christians typically use BC and AD to denote dates, in this book to be consistent and considerate of all religions we use BCE and CE.

Meeting the First Believers

Jesus selected 12 common men from various walks of life to be his *apostles* or *disciples* (students and followers). Jesus and his "band of brothers" traveled throughout Palestine preaching and teaching. Jesus spent a lot of time talking to religious leaders who were suspicious of his claims, but he seemed to prefer hanging out with commoners and people who were looked down upon by the religious authorities.

His principal message was that he was the *Messiah*, the "anointed one" who the Old Testament predicted was going to come and free Israel and serve as king. He performed many miracles (which Christians believe demonstrated that his authority was from God), showing compassion for the hurting.

The apostles include:

- Simon (also known as Peter)
- Andrew
- James the son of Zebedee
- John
- Philip
- Bartholomew
- Thomas
- Matthew
- James the son of Alphaeus
- Judas Thaddaeus
- Simon the Zealot
- Judas Iscariot (who later betrayed Jesus)

Along with the apostles, who were the followers of Jesus before he died, the other earliest followers of Jesus may have been called *Nazarenes*. The term comes from the Old Testament and was used in connection with two important figures there: Samson and Samuel. Samson was a judge who helped the Jews fight off the Philistines. Samuel was a judge and a prophet, linking the eras of judges and prophets together.

The tie between Samson and Samuel was the hair. Both were Nazarenes, a Jewish sect that developed around the concept of holy men completely absorbed in God. They vowed never to shave or cut their hair or nails, leaving their bodies as God created them.

Early Christians may have followed those guidelines because they copied the name. Some argue that the Nazarenes got their name because Jesus supposedly lived in the city of Nazareth.

TECHNICAL STUFF

No trace of historic Nazareth has ever been found. A city in Israel today that bears that name may or may not be the same one. Nazareth may have been a tiny suburb of a larger city, but evidence of its presence is scant until several hundred years after Jesus died.

What the early followers believed

The first Nazarenes lived in Jerusalem and continued to be faithful Jews. Later, they would be called *Ebionites* (meaning "poor ones"), a derisive reference to their communal living and the sharing of their minimal possessions. They viewed themselves as a reform movement within Judaism. They saw Jesus as a prophet and sage.

They gathered together for worship and brought animals for ritual sacrifice at the Temple. They observed the Jewish holy days (more on those in Book 4, Chapter 3), circumcised their male children, followed kosher dietary laws, and practiced the teachings of Jesus as they interpreted them. These Jews truly believed Jesus had warned them about an onrushing end of the world.

The idea that the world was about to end has enjoyed a lot of support throughout history, predating Jesus, but the belief was very current in his day, as it is in modern times. The ongoing religious turmoil, wars, and philosophical differences during the years that the Romans ruled the Jews led to a widespread conviction that God would punish the world with some kind of mass destruction.

REMEMBER

A leader chosen by God was to herald the end of the world, an event known as *Armageddon*. After all, the concept of a final end was so overwhelming that it needed a divine being, a *messiah*, to bring it about. The early followers of Jesus believed he was the person destined to rule the new world that would arise when the old one was destroyed.

But, given the believers' small numbers and isolated position in a tiny country on the eastern rim of the Roman Empire, how would anyone else find out about Jesus and his message?

The first missionary of Jesus

Jesus found his missionary in a man named Paul (previously named Saul before he converted). He took on that task of spreading Jesus's message. In letters (or *epistles*) preserved in the sacred texts, Paul said he was native of the city of Tarsus, in what is now Turkey. He claimed to have first persecuted the fledgling Nazarene sect, and then joined it and traveled throughout the Roman Empire to form small colonies of believers.

Paul believed that Jesus was sent by God in preparation for the coming end of the world. Paul began writing no earlier than 39 CE, at least 30 years before the Gospel of Mark, the oldest book in the New Testament, was written. Some historians put the date of Paul's first letters as late as 50 CE.

REMEMBER

Paul's goal was to reach as many people as possible so that, when the end came, they could be saved. History was not his touchstone; philosophy was.

Paul may not have intended to start a new religion, but his approach opened the door to many people who felt stymied by Jewish laws but wanted to be part of the "Chosen People."

Just as Jesus had in his day, Paul faced many obstacles:

- **He was not well liked within the Nazarene community.** They were the first followers of Jesus, after all, and he was a late arrival. They were downright vicious in their criticism of him. In the surviving *Heresies by Epiphanius*, the Ebionites testified that

  > Paul had no Pharisaic background or training; he was the son of Gentiles, converted to Judaism in Tarsus, came to Jerusalem when an adult, and attached himself to the High Priest as a henchman. Disappointed in his hopes of advancement, he broke with the High Priest and sought fame by founding a new religion.

» **He had never met or even seen Jesus.** That put him at a disadvantage with the original followers of Jesus who did know him and his teachings. Some of the ideas Paul expressed conflicted with what the early Christians were teaching. For example, Church leaders wanted followers to follow Jewish laws, but Paul did not.

» **Paul's ideas about what Jesus taught and meant differed from the Nazarenes' beliefs.** The Nazarenes followed Jewish laws, for example, while Paul thought belief in Jesus without following the laws was enough to guarantee a place in heaven.

» **Paul said he suffered from some kind of infirmity.** Some historians today think he meant epilepsy.

Eventually, Paul was taken into Roman custody after a disagreement with the Nazarene leaders, taken to Rome, and at least according to legends, executed there. Nevertheless, his strenuous efforts to share Jesus's message with the world led to the rise of Christianity.

Tracking the Growth of a New Religion

In spite of Paul's best attempts to reform Judaism through belief in Jesus — or, maybe, because of them — Jesus became the central figure amid a wide array of religious ideas. His followers were still mainly Jewish, but that wouldn't last long.

Many Jews were drawn to Jesus's call for peace and love. They had grown up with a militaristic deity. Jesus reflected a God who preferred peaceful coexistence. Others, called *God-fearers*, appreciated the fact that they didn't have to be circumcised to become a member of the "Chosen People."

Many pagans were attracted to the morality and ethics exhibited by Jesus's followers. Pagan philosophers noted how members of the early Christian community took care of each other; they wished their own religious communities were as loving.

Still, for at least the first decades after Jesus, followers continued to worship in synagogues and in the Temple. They read the same holy texts and followed the same religious practices as other Jews.

The only exception was observing the Sabbath. The early Christians started their Sabbath on Friday night with the rest of the Jewish population, but extended the holiday through Sunday. That may have been because Jesus rose from the dead on a Sunday.

The destruction of the Temple fuels growth

The Christian movement remained part of Judaism until 70 CE, when the Temple in Jerusalem was destroyed by the Romans. To the Jews, the Temple was God's home. Its loss signified his unhappiness with them. To Christians, the end of the Temple implied that God had fled the Jews and that they were the new "Chosen People."

People whom Paul had converted and those living in colonies around the Mediterranean now constituted the bulk of the faith. They no longer had to contend with the Nazarenes.

The Nazarenes, who made their homes in Jerusalem, probably didn't survive the civil war against the Romans or the destruction of the city in 70 CE. Jewish historian Josephus described a desperate group of Jews who made a suicidal charge against the Roman soldiers as the Temple burned. Some historians believe that group to be the Nazarenes.

Christians separate from Judaism

Over time, friction arose between mainstream Jews and the followers of Jesus. For starters, Jews firmly believed that any mistake on their part can cause the wrath of God to descend on them, as had happened in the past.

Moreover, Roman control of their land implied that God was already unhappy. How would he react to believers among them who now worshipped a dead messiah? No prophetic statements had prepared Jews for a messiah who died before achieving the expected goal of ruling over an independent Jewish theocracy.

As beliefs about Jesus solidified, some believers began to argue that Jesus was God incarnate, an idea that Jews rejected. To them, God was a spirit who would never become a man.

Finally, around 90 CE, Jewish religious leaders began to insert into the regular services a prayer that condemned those who taught something contrary to traditional Jewish views. Followers of Jesus knew the prayer was meant for them. They responded by creating their own meeting places for religious services.

REMEMBER

In time, they had a separate religion and a new name. *Christ* is the Greek word for "messiah." Greek was the language of the new religion; so, its followers became known as Christians.

The number of Christians began to grow rapidly and quickly eclipsed Judaism. Jews banned *proselytizing* (an attempt to convert someone to a religion), which had helped build their population to such heights, in fear that Christians were spying on them. Jews still do not recruit converts today.

Christian practices: It's no mystery

Christianity seemed to be part of a large group of beliefs once called *mystery religions.* They were all very different, but shared some common ideas:

- **They all had secret rituals to allow a follower closer contact with a deity.** *Communion,* the central Christian ritual of eating bread and wine in remembrance of Jesus, is one such ritual (see Book 5, Chapter 2).
- **They contained an annual cycle in which life is renewed each spring and dies each fall.** Followers of the mystery cults found deep symbolic significance in the natural processes of growth, death, decay, and rebirth.
- **They included a myth in which the deity either returned to life after death or else triumphed over his enemies.** Implicit in the myth was the theme of redemption from everything earthly and temporal.
- **They were primarily concerned with the emotional life of their followers.** The cults used many different means to affect the emotions and imaginations of their followers and to invoke a "union with the god:" processions, fasting, communion, a play, acts of purification, blazing lights, and esoteric liturgies.

One of the biggest differences between Christianity and the other mystery religions was that the mystery religions didn't emphasize following specific beliefs. The Christian faith recognizes only one legitimate path to God and salvation, Jesus Christ. The other mystery religions were not so straightlaced, so members commonly traipsed from one cult to another.

In addition, other ideas began to circulate around the followers of Jesus, which apparently set off a wave of explanations for his life and death.

Perhaps the largest group that took an interest in the fledgling faith was the *Gnostics*, a philosophical and religious movement with roots in pre-Christian times.

Gnostics claimed that Jesus carried a message from heaven that allowed them to acquire *gnosis*, or inner knowledge. This gnosis was identified as the spark of divine thought that had been obscured by ignorance.

Christian leaders belittled Gnostics and their followers as heretics. By the sixth century, Christianity succeeded in overcoming the Gnostic movement. The only group to have survived into modern times is the Mandaean sect of Iraq and Iran.

The big time arrives: Legitimacy in the Roman Empire

Christians fought for centuries against many faiths that developed around Jesus. After Gnosticism was defeated, the new religion took on other pagan faiths that abounded in the Roman Empire.

A brief attempt under the Roman Emperor Julian late in the fourth century to revive pagan faiths failed after he was slain in battle. With Julian's death, Abraham's sole survivors consisted of a handful of Jews. The swelling multitudes of Christians were now in control of the Empire. To any onlooker, that would have been a strange scenario, considering how hard the Romans originally fought to suppress the faith.

REMEMBER

Early Christians faced persecution because they refused to worship the Roman emperor. Many were killed in terrible ordeals and tortured, including being attacked by wild animals in Roman spectacles. The persecutions continued off and on for several hundred years. Some of the early records that mention Christians are from regional governors writing their emperors for advice on how to deal with Christians.

The outright persecutions ended in the beginning of the fourth century when Emperor Constantine, whose mother was Christian, legalized the faith. About 70 years later, Christianity was declared the only legal religion in the Roman Empire.

Nicene council sets the belief

As Christianity grew in members and power, the religion developed a solid philosophical base. Emperor Constantine invited some 250 to 318 church leaders from countries around the Mediterranean to meet in Nicea in 325 CE to resolve their differences.

More than religion was involved. Early Christians adopted the Roman view that the gods were responsible for the country's stability. If a debate raged, and no one knew who or what was the correct belief, then the country was in grave peril.

The issue of what constituted the true belief was debated widely: "If you ask a man for change for a piece of silver, he tells you which way the son differs from the father; and if you ask for a loaf of bread, you get a reply that the son is inferior to the father," wrote Gregory, Bishop of Nyssa, after visiting Constantinople, the capital of the Roman Empire in the fourth century. "If you ask if your bath is ready, you are solemnly told the son is made out of nothing."

REMEMBER

At the Nicean meeting, after much debate, the Church fathers approved the concept that God the Father, Jesus, and the Holy Spirit formed a single divinity. This is commonly known as the *Holy Trinity.*

The momentous work of shaping the Christian church would continue in future councils (also known as *synods*). Leading bishops met on a pretty regular basis through the fourth century. In time, they became known as Catholics, from the Latin word for "universal." When the religion split, the western side took the Name Roman Catholic; the eastern half, Greek Orthodox.

Over that time, the bishops decided

- » The correct days to celebrate the birth of Jesus, Christmas; and his death, Easter
- » The calendar we use today, including the familiar AD and BC (also known as CE and BCE)
- » Church structure, which was based on the Roman government
- » Procedures to become a priest and the rules that govern the priesthood

The delegates to Nicea in 325 approved a statement that binds all believers together. The *Nicene Creed* is still dutifully recited by the Roman Catholic faithful throughout the world during Mass. Here's the traditional version of the prayer:

> We (I) believe in one God, the Father Almighty, maker of heaven and earth, and of all things visible and invisible.
>
> And in one Lord Jesus Christ, the only begotten Son of God, and born of the Father before all ages. (God of God) light of light, true God of true God. Begotten not made, consubstantial to the Father, by whom all things were made. Who for us men and for our salvation came down from heaven. And was incarnate of the Holy Ghost and of the Virgin Mary and was made man; was crucified also for us under Pontius Pilate, suffered and was buried; and the third day rose again according to the Scriptures. And ascended into heaven, sits at the right hand of the Father, and shall come again with glory to judge the living and the dead, of whose Kingdom there shall be no end.

> And (I believe) in the Holy Ghost, the Lord and Giver of life, who proceeds from the Father (and the Son), who together with the Father and the Son is to be adored and glorified, who spoke by the Prophets. And one holy, catholic, and apostolic Church. We (I) confess one baptism for the remission of sins. And we (I) look for the resurrection of the dead and the life of the world to come. Amen.

The Greeks split while the Romans grow in influence

There were still disagreements between the eastern half of the Roman Empire and the western portion. In the fourth century, Emperor Constantine had created the division by moving his capital from Rome to Constantinople in what is now Turkey.

WARNING

The Greek half of the church eventually split away over the question of whether Jesus was "like" or "as" God. The two factions still disagree. Greek Orthodox Christians have their own leader today, called a *patriarch*, and do not obey the *pope*, the leader of the Roman Catholics (more on them in Book 5, Chapter 4).

Occasional attempts at reconciliation have failed, especially after the Turkish armies overwhelmed Constantinople in the 1400s. The Western world watched the great city fall, ending the last remnant of the Roman Empire. Constantinople's name was changed to Istanbul, and the Christian faith once based there was scattered.

The Roman Catholic Church had similar problems. Various marauding tribes conquered Rome, but the Church leaders took over for the departed Roman authorities and built their own political and social organization. As a result, the Church dominated society. Spreading out rapidly, Church missionaries converted pagan groups and retained the faith of millions until the religion splintered in the 1500s.

Realizing It's Hard to Keep Everyone Happy

The Church leaders knew people weren't happy, but they were surprised when the faith fell apart.

Rumblings against the powerful Roman Catholic Church had radiated through Europe for centuries. Small cults, designed to purify the faith, rose and fell, or cowered in distant mountains after soldiers sent by the pope massacred everyone in sight.

The Church couldn't maintain a united front, making it vulnerable to reformers. During one sorry episode, the pope fled Rome for Avignon, France, and then returned. At one time, three popes were in power simultaneously.

The first Pope John XXXIII was charged with a long list of crimes, including murder and rape. He may have been guilty of most of them.

For a brief period, the Church-led Crusades reconquered the Holy Land. That lasted less than 200 years. Eventually, the Arabs, under Saladin, held off English King Richard the Lionhearted, and Jerusalem once again was under Muslim rule.

Martin Luther spells out his displeasure

Despite the discord, the Church survived and thrived. Then in 1517, it met its match when confronted by Martin Luther, a solemn Catholic monk.

Luther was upset after John Tetzel, a salesman sent by the Vatican to market indulgences, showed up in Wittenberg where Luther was teaching. *Indulgences* supposedly allowed people to rapidly pass through *purgatory*, a kind of unpleasant way station en route to heaven. People bought them for dead relatives. Many people objected to them, including Luther.

Convinced that the Church had lapsed into heresy, Luther decided to mimic Abraham and metaphorically smash the idols. On Halloween, Luther wrote down his complaints in Latin, creating 95 theses attacking the pope and Church practices, and nailed them to a church door that was used for public announcements.

His complaints eventually circled Europe, aided by the invention of the printing press just 60 years earlier.

Instead of being burned for his behavior, Luther was protected by German princes who were upset that the Church controlled a vast percentage of the Germanic land and siphoned off too much of the local proceeds. With Luther, they had a new religious leader to follow.

REMEMBER

Luther's goal was to purify the Church, but, like many reformers before and after him, he ended up creating a new faith that opposed the old one.

Luther was very courageous. Called to answer charges of heresy in 1521, Luther marched bravely, like Daniel, into the lion's den of angry cardinals. Expected to apologize and denounce his own writing, Luther said, "Unless I am convinced by proofs from Scriptures or by plain and clear reasons and arguments, I can and will not retract, for it is neither safe nor wise to do anything against conscience. Here I stand. I can do no other. God help me. Amen."

Protestants reform, the Church counterreforms, and fighting ensues

Luther and his German princes soon had plenty of company as countries around Europe picked sides in what became known as the *Protestant Reformation.*

The name *Protestant* comes from the fact the participants were "protesting" against the Roman Catholic Church.

The Church did not accept this new *schism* (or split) quietly, creating a "counter reformation." The movement led to the founding of new religious orders, the cleansing of existing ones, and the elimination of many of the abuses that had led to the creation of new Christian sects.

France and Spain stayed with the old beliefs of the Catholic Church. The Netherlands and, eventually, England did not. They didn't necessarily become Lutheran either. Luther's bold stance encouraged other theologians to offer their individualized views on God, Jesus, and salvation.

Some of the new leaders, like John Calvin, Ulrich Zwingli, and John Knox, were far more radical than Luther. They attracted followers, too. Soon, the religious conflict sawed Western society in half. No magician could unite the Catholic and Protestant portions.

Christians didn't see Muslims as their worst enemies anymore; their Satan lay within their own ranks. As a result, from the 1520s to 1648, the two sides of Christianity fought with undisguised ferocity.

The Catholic Church created an order of priests called Jesuits to teach the faith, convert nonbelievers, and oppose Protestants. Today, the Jesuits are revered for scholarly and missionary pursuits, but in the early days of that order, they aided the Catholic Church's Inquisition. The Inquisition allowed priests to ask accused people whether or not they really believed in Christianity. The Jesuits were seeking people who claimed to be faithful but really were not or who taught ideas opposed to traditional Catholic teachings. Those who didn't were often turned over to the civic authorities to be burned.

English sailors reported horror stories of comrades captured by Catholic (mostly Spanish) forces and burned at the stake or sent to galleys as slaves. No cruelty on either side was considered sufficient when trying to protect the sainted Prince of Peace from desecration.

Meanwhile, both halves of Christianity fought for control, sparking explorations of the world as well as scientific investigations aimed at discovering God's intentions.

The religious conflicts led to the first "modern" war when Charles VIII of France led his troops across the Alps toward Italy with an eye on conquering the country. From that point on, Europe rang with the clash of weapons as Catholics fought Protestants and each other. Popes even led troops into battle.

The toll was incredible: Germany and Austria together lost 8.5 million people; Bohemia's population dropped from 3 million to 800,000. In Bohemia, a German state, 29,000 of the existing 35,000 villages were deserted. Starvation killed many of the noncombatants.

The rise of science in a Christian world

For centuries, people relied on faith to understand the world. Eventually, scholars began to develop ways to investigate the world. Science expanded rapidly, starting in the late Middle Ages. From Holland came the telescope. Through it, Dutch scientist Anton van Leeuwenhoek revealed far more about the heavens than anyone reading Genesis ever could discover.

WARNING

Although such men of genius as Galileo, Harvey, Newton, Bacon, and Pascal also lived at this time, science often was the subject of fierce criticism. Many of the findings — such as Galileo's discovery of moons around Jupiter, meaning earth's moon is not unique as religious folks thought — seemed to contradict faith. Religion, caught in the backwash of scientific advances, fought to avoid being drowned. Scholars abruptly shifted the earth outside the center of the universe. Other long-held ideas collapsed, too. Evolution provided an answer for how mankind emerged. Space explorations discovered new worlds.

When critics' efforts failed to hold back the scientific tide, science was probed to support religious views. In 1650, the Reverend James Ussher, archbishop of Armagh, issued his famous study in which he "calculated" that the world was created in 4004 BCE. Dr. John Lightfoot, vice chancellor of the University of Cambridge, added to those findings that life began at 9 a.m., October 23, of that year. Ussher's views became thought of as inspired as the Bible itself.

The end result of all that turmoil was the development of many Christian sects. Not until the 20th century did science find the tools to date ancient materials and demonstrate that the world was billions of years old.

Today, the Church endorses scientific exploration.

Looking at Christianity Today

Christianity has moved easily into modern times and is the largest single religion on Earth. Christian concepts remain ingrained in world culture, from art and music to literature and film.

Christian missionaries still fan out across the world to bring the message of Jesus to more people. That has led to occasional conflicts in some countries.

Christian holidays are followed worldwide, even in countries with small or no Christian population. Christian themes radiate through political debates. In many ways, Christianity has evolved into the world's religion.

IN THIS CHAPTER

» Summing up Christian basics

» Putting faith into practice through rituals

» Examining the roots of Christmas

» Looking at other Christian holidays

» Taking a look at the Bible and Christian symbols

Chapter 2
Christian Beliefs and Practices

Christianity is a faith that's all about good news. The heart of the Christian message is called the *gospel*, which means — you guessed it — the "good news." The Christian faith, therefore, claims to offer meaning and hope to people, not just for a day, but for all eternity.

So what exactly is this so-called good news that Christianity claims? How is it different from other religions? And if Christianity is supposed to be about good news, why does it seem that so much bad news — scandalous priests, corrupt televangelists, and so on — flows from the Christian Church these days?

In this chapter, you discover the essence of Christianity and how you can put it into practice. You also explore some popular holidays, rituals, and denominations.

Packing Christianity into a Nutshell

Trying to define Christianity in a single sentence is kind of like trying to cram your family's luggage into the back of your minivan when you go on vacation — an impossible task until you start throwing many bags, even seemingly important ones, out the window. So if you had to pack Christianity into a nutshell, it's the belief that God chose to create and love humans, and — at an incredible cost to himself — frees them from a tight spot if only they, in response, choose to reach out for his helping hand.

Going back to the beginning: People choosing, God responding

REMEMBER

Christians believe in what they call the one True God, who is perfect, has existed forever, and created the world and all its itty-bitty little creatures. But when God created humans, he came up with something extra special; he not only gave people pinky toes and eyebrows, but also the one-of-a-kind gift of *free will* (choice).

God gave people the ability to choose whether to follow him and have a relationship with him or to go our own separate ways. The reason he did this seems pretty obvious: suppose you desired a relationship with special someone. Would you prefer a person who decidedly picked you out of a crowd, or would you rather have a robot that was programmed to do nothing else? We think the choice is obvious. So too, God opted for a humanity with free choice. But when he did so, he took a risk, because people can decide to go their own ways and forget about him.

WARNING

God made it clear from the get-go that following him meant letting the good times roll, while going against him would be a major bummer for all parties involved — yucky stuff like eternal death and judgment (more on this later in this chapter).

The first folks to live out this experiment in freedom were Adam and Eve. The couple had some good times with God for a while. But as the Bible talks about in the Book of Genesis, curiosity got the better of them, and they soon wanted to know what it was like doing what they wanted to do instead of what God wanted them to do. They disobeyed God, setting off a chain reaction of disobedience (or *sin*) that has spiraled through every generation since them.

When people recognize sin in their lives, their natural response is to try to do something to make up for it. Humans have continually tried to earn God's favor by doing good deeds as a payback. Christianity says that payback with God is impossible, though. Think of it like this: Suppose a genie grants you a wish to be transformed into a fish if you want to. Because the genie asks you in the middle of a heat wave, the idea of being a fish surrounded 24/7 by chilly water sounds really cool, so you take the plunge into the deep blue sea. However, after a long swim and an initial fling with a puffer fish, you decide that the fish's life isn't for you. Your natural response may be to swim upstream to where you initially jumped into the water and hope that somehow that action will reverse the metamorphic process. But no amount of swimming against the current will change you back into a human again. Instead, the genie, by their own initiative, has to change you back.

REMEMBER

In the same way, God had to act on his own initiative to allow some way out of the trap that humans found themselves in. Christianity says that he did this by sending his Son, Jesus Christ (more on him in Book 5, Chapter 1), to take the punishment that is due to humans. In his teaching, Jesus made it clear that the Good News of Christianity is simple: Rather than deal with the bad news of sin, confess your sins and believe in Jesus as Lord and Savior. He wipes your sins clean and gives you eternal life. A single Bible verse sums up his message: "For God so loved the world that he gave his one and only Son, that whoever believes in him shall not perish but have eternal life" (John 3:16).

Understanding how Christians define their faith

If you played a word association game with a sampling of Christians who've been touched by God's gospel and asked them to name a single word or phrase that sums up Christianity, you'd get a handful of answers. A few likely candidates are

- Jesus Christ
- Grace
- Truth
- Life
- The Bible
- A transformed life

Each of these words reveals a key aspect of what Christianity's all about. After you begin to paint the terms one on top of another, you begin to see a clearer portrait of the Christian faith.

TIP

If you want to understand what true Christianity is, look first and foremost to what the Bible's New Testament says about Jesus. Explore all of what Jesus did, said, and taught — not just a couple of selected verses. What's more, never look at the actions or words of Christians and conclude that their behavior or attitudes reflect what Christianity is. The Church is often in alignment with Jesus, but Christians aren't perfect and make mistakes as well.

Definition #1: Jesus Christ

Christianity is a faith based on the life, teachings, and resurrection of Jesus, a man who lived in Palestine some 2,000 years ago. Jesus claimed to be the Son of God, sent by his Father in heaven to die on the cross for the sins of all humans.

Definition #2: Grace

You see the word grace sprinkled all around the Christian Church — in the song, "Amazing Grace," in church names, such as Grace Baptist Church, and when Christians say "grace" before a meal, to name a few. Grace is everywhere. In fact, the New Testament mentions it 123 times.

Christians define *grace* as God's undeserved love shown toward humans. They believe that God's grace is what saves humans through Jesus Christ and enables believers to live a Christian life.

Definition #3: Truth

Christians say that their faith isn't just a fairy tale that gives them comfort in times of trouble or blind hope in the midst of tragedy. Rather, they say that Christianity is factual, explaining the way events actually happened in the past, why today is like it is, and what's going to happen in the future.

Definition #4: Life

A central teaching of Christianity has always been that life is more than school, marriage, kids, work, Florida retirements, and hearing aids. Instead, Christianity claims that every person has an eternal soul that will exist even after their earthly body dies. Therefore, those who believe in God's grace through Jesus Christ will have eternal life in heaven and eventually on a new earth, while those who don't will be separated from God forever in hell. As Jesus said, he came so that humans may have life that has meaning, purpose, and joy.

Definition #5: The Bible

Christianity says that God revealed who he is and what his plans are through the written words of the Bible. Christians have historically believed that the Old and New Testaments are the inspired Word of God, are without error in the original writings, and serve as the final authority for the Christian faith. In fact, Christians have traditionally believed that their religion is intricately interwoven with the Bible, so much so that you can't separate them from each other without destroying the fabric of both. See the section "Reading Christianity: The Bible" later in this chapter for more on this subject.

Definition #6: A transformed life

When you know a lot about a subject, it's easy to get lost in the details. For example, if you ask a theologian what Christianity is, and they may go off on the particulars of the Nicene Creed (see Book 5, Chapter 1), when all you want to know is whether the faith brings peace and joy to life.

REMEMBER

Don't forget that, for the average Christian, the Good News of Christianity on a practical, everyday level means a transformed life, from a life that was empty to a life that has meaning and hope, even when tragedies happen.

Being Born with Sin

In the New Testament, humans are definitely born in sin. The idea came from the first book of the Bible. In Genesis, Adam, the first man, disobeyed God and, with his wife, Eve, ate forbidden fruit from the Tree of Knowledge. That, in later Christian thinking, caused the sin that afflicted everyone. In many ways, Adam's behavior led to a legal flaw, a violation of a contract. Paul, an early missionary for the Church, explains the link to Adam in one of his letters: "By one man's disobedience, many were made sinners" (Romans 5:19). At the time he was writing, around 50 CE, the New Testament didn't exist, so his thinking was based on the books that are now part of the Old Testament.

REMEMBER

Christians believe that the only person born without sin is Jesus. In some denominations, his mother, Mary, also falls into the category.

In Roman Catholic theology, Adam and Eve's big oops is called *original sin*, and Catholics believe that all followers of Christ are burdened with this sin. Original sin is different from *actual* or *personal sin*, which refers to evil words, acts, and thoughts. Actual sins can be *venal* (or minor) or *mortal* (major).

Of course, other Christian denominations don't necessarily agree with the Catholic approach. Some sects see other types of sins:

- *Concupiscence* or sexual sin
- *Eternal* or "unforgivable" sin when someone leaves the faith

Evangelical Christians argue that all behaviors not perceived as good are, by definition, sinful. Accidental sins, then, don't exist.

WARNING

According to Christians, a mortal (or eternal) sin must

- Involve a grave matter
- Be committed with full knowledge of the sinner
- Be committed with deliberate consent of the sinner

Clearly, this kind of sin is not a mistake you stumble into. Traditionally, the seven mortal or "deadly" sins are pride, covetousness, lust, anger, gluttony, envy, and sloth.

The apostle Paul didn't stop at seven deadly sins. In two separate letters in the New Testament, Galatians and 1 Corinthians, he came up with a lengthy list of sins bound to send anyone to eternal punishment. They include

- Adultery
- Fornication (sexual relations outside marriage)
- Uncleanness
- Lasciviousness (pornography)
- Idolatry
- Witchcraft
- Hatred
- Variance (choosing another religion)
- Emulation (following someone down an evil path)
- Wrath
- Strife
- Seditions (leading people astray)
- Heresy
- Murder
- Drunkenness
- Reveling
- Effeminate behavior
- Thievery
- Extortion

Paul insisted that anyone who committed one of these behaviors wouldn't "inherit the Kingdom of God."

Enjoying Heaven for Eternity

Christians believe that people are designed by God, not just for seventy or so years on planet earth, but for eternity. The Bible calls the future home of Christians *heaven*. Heaven was seen initially as God's residence alone. Gradually, people began to believe that heaven is where the souls of the righteous go after their deaths.

Jesus serves as the prime example of that view. In Christian theology, Jesus's death, resurrection, and ascent into heaven serve as the model for all true believers.

What heaven is like is largely shrouded in mystery. Great Christian thinkers through the ages have long speculated on heaven and have provided some vivid and imaginative perspectives. Yet, in the end, most of these ideas are simply educated guesses. The Bible fills in some details, but not nearly enough to satisfy curious minds who want to know more.

Christian views about heaven vary by denomination, but most agree on two points:

- Heaven is a great place with no pain, disease, or other human weaknesses.
- People bask in the presence of Jesus.

Being Purged of Sin in Purgatory

One of the key belief differences between Catholics, Protestants, and Orthodox Christians is the issue of purgatory — Catholics believe it exists, but Protestants and Orthodox believers don't.

In general, *purgatory* serves as an interim place for people who will eventually go to heaven but who aren't yet purified enough to do so. In Catholic teaching, purgatory isn't a place where unsaved people get a second chance to avoid going to hell. Instead, it's a place for eventual heaven-to-be's to wait expectantly for the joys to come.

TECHNICAL STUFF

The belief in a place called purgatory evolved over many centuries. Although it's not the Christian Church's official teaching, some early Church fathers and writers believed in an intermediate state that exists after death but before heaven. The Catholic Church made this part of their official doctrine in the 16th century.

Going to Hell: Considering the Underworld

"You can just go to hell." "To hell in a handbasket." "Hell, no." People casually say the word "hell" all the time in expressions like these, but the Christian concept of hell is anything but casual. Frankly, it's a scary business, though one that people outside of the Church find silly, unfair, or politically incorrect. Hell isn't a very popular topic inside church walls, either. People much prefer more positive messages. Go to a thousand churches on a Sunday morning, and for each of the ministers you hear preach on hell, I'll give you a nickel. I suspect that I won't need much spare change to pay you.

Yet, the belief in hell is closely tied to the Christian faith. After all, if Christ died to save people, it follows logically that he had to save humans *from* something. Without hell, the whole notion of Jesus suffering on the cross for humanity doesn't make sense.

All Christians agree on the broad definition of *hell* as being the state of complete separation from God. And yet the specifics of what that separation means have always been the subject of debate. Ever since the first century, three distinct viewpoints on hell have permeated the Christian Church:

- Eternal punishment of the *unsaved* (people who aren't Christians)
- Annihilation of the unsaved
- No punishment, because all will receive salvation from God

REMEMBER

The last perspective — commonly known as *universalism* — may be much more palatable and politically correct than the others, but this view has no biblical legs to stand on and has never been considered a position that's in synch with biblical Christianity. Universalism can't be proven by the Bible, but proponents of the other two perspectives both argue that the Bible supports their hellish claims.

Awaiting the Second Coming of Jesus Christ

Christians believe that Jesus Christ came to earth some 2,000 years ago and lived as a suffering servant, and, before his ascension (when he returned to be with his father), he promised to return to earth one final time (John 14:3) — this time as a conquering and triumphant king. Christians believe that only God knows when exactly Jesus will come back to earth, though most every generation since the early Church looks at the events of their day in light of prophecies in scripture and concludes that surely he'll come within their lifetime.

The Bible talks about several events that will take place surrounding the time of Jesus' Second Coming. However, the Christian Church often debates on the exact timeline, sequence, and meaning of these events.

TECHNICAL STUFF

Some Protestants, called *premillennialists*, believe these are literal events that will take place sometime in the future before the Second Coming. Other Protestants, Catholics, and Orthodox Christians hold *amillennialist* or *postmillennialist* positions, saying that the biblical references are metaphoric, and therefore, the events actually won't take place prior to Jesus' Second Coming.

Recognizing Rituals: Outward Expressions of Faith

Christian *rituals* (ceremonial acts that follow religious customs) often were drawn directly from biblical accounts. The rituals serve as reminders of Jesus's sacrifices — and for some denominations, they can actually help one achieve life eternal in heaven. So they're pretty vital.

Some Christian sects refer to these rituals as *sacraments*.

One bread, one body: Communion

When worshippers observe the central Christian ritual called *Communion* (or sometimes the *Eucharist*), they eat a small wafer and sip from a cup of wine (or grape juice). The bread and wine symbolize the body and blood of Christ. This ritual is based on the biblical account of the *Last Supper* (also called the *Lord's Supper*) when Jesus asked his followers to eat bread and drink wine in memory of him.

This ritual is an integral part of many Christian worship services and is derived from the Latin word for "common." Partaking of the ritual allows a Christian to remember Christ and to contemplate their own life. Many faithful Christians participate in the ritual on a weekly basis.

TECHNICAL STUFF

At one time, the Christian world was hotly divided over the question of whether the wine and bread is actually *transmuted* (changed form) into the real flesh and blood of Jesus after being ingested. While the debate has faded, some Christian faiths still believe in *transubstantiation*. Now most Christians focus on the metaphorical idea that Jesus is the "blood and body" of life — that is his sacrifice represents the essence of existence. No eating of human flesh is involved, an idea that nauseated the Romans and helped fuel their anger against the early Christians.

REMEMBER

For Roman Catholics, they believe they are actually eating the body and blood of Jesus Christ when they receive the Eucharist. This happens through a process called transubstantiation, by which the substance of the bread and wine turn into Jesus's body and blood even though the outward appearance does not change. Although, there have been multiple miracles documented by the Church of the Eucharist bleeding real blood.

Welcoming new Christians through baptism

Baptism is a sacred rite in Christianity. Babies are brought into churches to be welcomed into the faith with holy water. In some sects, adults are led to rivers or to the ocean for ritualistic baths.

Although the Bible never says that Jesus baptized anyone, the sacred texts describe a man named John the Baptist who baptized Jesus in the Jordan River. According to several accounts, John felt that people awaiting the end of the world needed the last baptism as final proof of their belief. Modern baptism serves that same idea: to cleanse away old sins and to symbolize birth. To some, baptism represents their acceptance in the salvation promised by Jesus.

The concept draws on Jewish teachings, which encouraged cleanliness. In fact, Jews were mocked by Romans for insisting on ritual cleanings on a daily basis. John the Baptist, who was Jewish, drew on the ritual cleansing idea, but insisted that one final baptism was necessary for a person to repent of his sins and to seal the individual in preparation for the coming end of the world. That view was incorporated into Christianity.

REMEMBER

The Roman Catholic Church made baptism a sacrament, in accordance with the biblical accounts of Jesus's baptism, and requires infants to be baptized to receive God's saving grace. The debate over whether baptism is for babies or for anyone, however, led to bloody battles in the Middle Ages. Today, baptism remains a key component of Christian faith. Some sects insist on infant baptism; others allow children to be older. A person who feels "born again" — that is, returning with full faith to Christianity — is often baptized again as well to symbolize that status.

Celebrating additional sacraments

Many Christian sects have more than the two basic sacraments of Communion and baptism. The additional ones range from ceremonies involving marriage, confirmation of faith, death, reconciliation to the faith, and the taking of *holy orders* (becoming a priest or a nun). These sacraments are accepted by orthodox Christians and members of the Roman Catholic Church.

Groups such as the Salvation Army and Society of Friends don't see the need for additional sacraments. They believe they are living a sacramental life.

Marking the First Noel: Christmas and the Roots of Christianity

Besides celebrating rituals, every year, Christians celebrate the birth of their founder. Biblical accounts vary, but most Christians believe Jesus was born in the city of Bethlehem in a barn outside an inn. Angels came to visit him, as did wise men or kings bearing gifts. The resulting holiday features seasonal songs called *carols*, as well as religious services, decorations, parties, and other holiday events.

TECHNICAL STUFF

To a somber church father living some 1,800 years ago, today's hoopla around this holy day would be stunning. Christmas wasn't even celebrated with any known festivities for at least 200 years after Jesus was born. Even the term *Christmas*, so familiar to us, was unknown then. The word comes from two Old English words *Cristes moesse*, meaning "the mass or festival of Christ." The suffix *–mas* is derived from the closing Latin words of a religious service: *Ite missa est*, meaning "it is ended."

Because Christianity didn't develop in a vacuum, much of what we take to be Christian started in another culture and was adopted and modified by believers. Christmas is no exception. Many aspects of the festive occasion have antecedents reaching back deep into history.

Santa Claus himself was born in Dutch stories about Saint Nicholas, who brought little children gifts on December 6. When the English conquered the Dutch city of New Amsterdam and changed its name to New York, English children saw their new Dutch friends get gifts and pestered their parents for the same thing. Because the English Christians didn't believe in saints, the closest holiday for which they may give gifts was Christmas. Saint Nicholas's name was *anglicized* (changed to English) to Santa Claus, and he began to deliver presents to good little English children on December 25. In time, he became the internationally recognized symbol of Christmas.

Aspects of today's festivities extend beyond the mandatory red costumes and fake beards of Santa. Christmas add-ons include everything from mistletoe, poinsettias, boughs of holly, eggnog, and fruitcakes to lights, decorations, trees trimmed with ornaments and other decorations, holiday-themed clothing, greeting cards, and, of course, carols.

To some Christians, the secular activities have detracted from the religious aspects. To remember the holy season, many Christians display a *nativity scene* (also called a *crèche*). Figurines of Mary, Joseph, baby Jesus, the three wise men, shepherds, and animals are often set up on church lawns and in private homes. The nativity scene was developed in the Middle Ages to help explain the story of Christ's birth to illiterate parishioners. The popular holiday carols, like "Silent Night" and "Hark! The Herald Angels Sing," reflect the deep feeling Christians have for this sacred day. For many Christians, Christmas is a day for prayer, meditation, and somber reflection on the life and words of Christ.

TECHNICAL STUFF

Some people use *Xmas* as an abbreviation. Actually, the *X* is the Greek letter *chi*, which is the first letter of the word *Christ*. As a result, *Xmas* is actually appropriate usage, despite occasional objections from religious purists.

Why a holiday for the Nativity?

Christmas doesn't show up on the list of Christian festivals described by early Church fathers. Origen, the most prolific writer among the early Church hierarchy, didn't like the idea of a birthday party at all. He noted that the birthdays of Moses, Abraham, and other prophets didn't warrant a single slice of cake. In the holy texts, he added scornfully, only sinners celebrate their birthdays.

Arnobius, another great leader of that day, satirically commented on the "birthday of the gods." He felt that celebrating Jesus's birthday would equate Jesus with the Roman emperors, whom pagans thought of as gods, rather than with God, the Father. After all, Roman emperors enjoyed annual feasts on their birthdays.

However, opposition faded as Christianity began to grow. The new faith smacked into other religions, like those believing in a god named Mithra, which celebrated the birthday of its founder. Roman holidays, such as the Saturnalia, also seemed a lot more fun with parties and special events.

Finally, in the third century, leaders of the Church decided that a day dedicated to the birth of Jesus would help retain and attract members. By that time, many smaller churches had already begun to hold annual celebrations.

Why December?

When the Church finally decided to have a holiday to mark Jesus's nativity, the question was when to celebrate it. In 200 CE, when the holiday finally earned an official mention in the Church, the big day was May 20. Religious leaders thought the ninth month of their calendar corresponded to the ninth month of the calendar at the time when Jesus lived.

Other dates suggested for Jesus's birthday included April 19 and April 20. March 28 earned a vote because that was the day, supposedly, when the sun was created.

(A later study found that Christ's birthday has been earnestly placed on virtually every day of the year, with each claim supported by ample evidence or wise conjecture.)

The issue was debated well into the fourth century. Finally, most Church fathers agreed to observe the birth of Christ on December 25. As a result, Christmas is celebrated then, but in Hispanic countries, the big day is January 6, when the traveling Magi supposedly arrived in Bethlehem to worship baby Jesus.

So the decision to place Christmas on December 25 was political, not religious. Church leaders opted for December for several reasons:

- **They wanted to counter a variety of holidays.** Every year, the Romans celebrated a huge December event called the *Saturnalia,* a wild affair in which slaves and masters may switch roles. In addition, the Romans marched around with evergreen boughs and gave gifts.

  Christians also wanted to overshadow the holiday that celebrated the December birthday of Mithra, the Zoroastrian god of truth and light. Roman soldiers had adopted Mithra, so he was a formidable foe to the new Christian religion.
- **Pagan holidays marked the beginning of winter and, with it, the death of the sun god.** He died on December 22 and was reborn on December 25. The rebirth concept dovetailed with the Jesus story.

REMEMBER

Note that Christmas is more than a single day. Christians use the weeks before Christmas to prepare themselves spiritually to celebrate Christ's birth. After Christmas, they remember special events that took place shortly after Jesus was born. The Christmas season includes

- **Advent,** which marks the start of the Church calendar and spans the four weeks leading up to Christmas. Advent, which means "coming," refers both to the birth of Jesus and his promised return to judge all mankind. Customs vary throughout Christianity, but believers see this holiday as a time to prepare for Jesus.

  Scripture readings for Advent reflect this emphasis with selections focusing on themes of accountability, faith, judgment on sin, and the hope of eternal life. To Christians, Advent signifies Jesus's presence in this world, requiring a focus on ethics and appropriate behavior.

  Specific colors are linked to each of the four weeks of Advent, including blue and purple. At one time, Christians fasted on Saint Martin's Day during Advent and also handed out gifts. The gift portion was later transferred to Christmas. Wreaths and candles are also part of the celebration.

» The **Feast of the Immaculate Conception,** celebrated during Advent on December 8. The day commemorates Mary, Jesus's mother, who herself is believed to have been born without sin by some Christian denominations.

» **Twelfth Night,** which marks the last day of the holiday on January 5. Many of the holiday traditions, such as the wassail drink and fruitcakes, actually began with this holiday. It once marked the end of an ancient pagan holiday that began with Halloween but became absorbed into Christianity. In some countries, Twelfth Night was the last day Christmas decorations can be left up and marked the beginning of festivals leading up to Easter. At one time, baptisms were conducted on this day, but the holiday has lost much of its religious significance.

» **Epiphany,** which is January 6. Epiphany grew out of Hanukkah, the Jewish festival of lights (see Book 4, Chapter 3). Epiphany marks the revelation of God to mankind in the person of Jesus Christ. This is also the day when the *Magi* (the three wise men) visited baby Jesus in Bethlehem, according to the account in Matthew's gospel (see Matthew 2:1–11 for all the details).

Considering Other Christian Holidays

Christians, unlike Jews, recognize very few holidays. In fact, Christianity has so many sects that not even all Christians accept Christmas as a religious holiday. The Roman Catholic faith observes minor holidays that are named for saints whose lives served as an example for others, but Protestants often don't recognize these holidays.

As a result, Valentine's Day, named for the Catholic Saint Valentine, has become a secular romantic holiday. Saint Patrick's Day, named for an Irish Catholic saint, has become another secular holiday with green beer and parades.

Hallelujah! He is risen: Easter

Spring is a time for rebirth, which is why almost every religion has a holiday then. (Passover is the Jewish spring holiday; see Book 4, Chapter 3.)

Easter is a spring holy day that commemorates the death of Jesus and his resurrection. According to the Bible, Jesus was crucified and died on Friday, but he rose from the dead and was seen by his disciples on Sunday. His victory over death provides a model for the faithful to follow. They believe that because Jesus overcame death, they, too, will obtain immortality.

REMEMBER

The only religious holiday accepted by all Christians is Easter.

Easter history

No one celebrated Easter in the early years of Christianity. Instead, when Christians decided to observe Easter, they borrowed elements from other spring holidays. The principal model was Passover, the Jewish holiday, which celebrates the Exodus from Egypt. That's because, according to the Bible, Jesus died during the holiday.

By the fourth century, Church fathers wanted to separate themselves completely from Judaism and decreed that the holiday would fall on a Sunday.

How Easter is celebrated

The days leading up to Easter Sunday are solemn ones, typically used for religious services and contemplation.

Palm Sunday is celebrated the Sunday before Easter and commemorates Jesus's entry into Jerusalem. In Christian tradition, his arrival represents the first time the public welcomed him as their redeemer. In the Gospel of John, palm fronds are laid along Jesus's path. They represent victory and triumph. People lining the streets also waved fronds, adding to the symbolism and giving the holiday its name.

Practices vary according to the sect of Christianity. In the Roman Catholic faith, for example, baptisms are held on Easter. Many groups hold candlelight vigils, read sections from the Bible that concentrate on creation and rebirth, and renew their faith. Many churches will troop down to a body of water to hold group baptisms. Churches are typically festooned with flowers. Easter lilies are a traditional floral arrangement.

The day is not all solemn. Congregations contemplate the great joy that Mary must have felt when greeting her resurrected son. As a result, music plays a big part in the activities.

Easter symbols

Eggs are a symbol of rebirth, and the early Christians worked this pagan symbol into their observances of Easter. But ironically, these eggs (and today, other goodies) are delivered by the Easter Bunny. Rabbits don't lay eggs, but the connection was made through Oester, a German fertility goddess whose name was converted to Easter. Every deity had a *familiar*, an animal that kept them company. Witches had black cats. Oester had rabbits.

WHY IS EASTER ON A DIFFERENT DATE EVERY YEAR?

Easter bounces around the calendar in tandem with the Jewish holiday of Passover. That's because the day when the Passover festival begins is based on the lunar calendar. Aside from some additional complicating factors, the date of Easter Sunday falls . . . follow us now . . . on the first Sunday after the first full moon after the vernal equinox. The vernal equinox is usually March 21, so the earliest possible date for Easter is March 22; the latest possible date is April 25.

Because Jesus died after celebrating Passover, according to biblical accounts, the two holidays are inevitably tied together.

Easter is the only Christian holiday that isn't fixed to a specific day.

A solemn and somber season: Lent

Lent ("spring"), the only other major Christian holy observance, consists of 40 days preceding Easter. It commemorates two aspects of Jesus's life: the 40 days he lived in the desert, fasting and fighting off the devil's temptations; and, in some sects, the 40 hours he was in the tomb before his resurrection.

To Christians, this is a time of sacrifice and prayer. Many give up something they enjoy to emulate Jesus's fast. The money saved is then donated to charity. But Lent, too, grew from pagan and Jewish sources.

Early Christians didn't observe Lent. However, festivals for risen Greek gods such as Osiris, Adonis, and Tammuz all featured 40-day fasts. Jews commemorated a 40-day period leading up to God giving them the Ten Commandments on Mount Sinai. Eventually, Christians felt a need to develop a holiday that countered those of opposition faiths.

There's no definite date when the holiday was initiated, but it became accepted by the fifth century. The Catholic Encyclopedia suggested there was a 50-day festival, of which 40 were set aside to be less of a party and more devoted to prayer.

Many Christians recognize Lent by attempting to give up unhealthy foods, like chocolate, or stop bad habits, like smoking. Others use Lent as a time to take up charitable causes or attempt personal improvement, such as increasing exercise or praying every day.

Lent is more than a 40-day commemoration. It has several holy days associated with it:

- **Fat Tuesday:** This holiday actually precedes Lent, which begins the following day on Ash Wednesday. Also called Mardi Gras, this day is considered the last day for fun and festivities before the serious work of religious contemplation begins, to prepare for Easter. The city of New Orleans marks the day before Ash Wednesday with a big party that's renowned for excessive and perhaps unsavory behavior.
- **Ash Wednesday:** This is the day Lent begins. Christians go to church to pray and have a cross drawn in ashes on their foreheads. The ashes draw on an ancient tradition and represent repentance before God. The holiday is part of Roman Catholic, Lutheran, Methodist, and Episcopalian liturgies, among others.
- **Holy Thursday:** This is one of the important days in the Easter celebration and is tied to four events in Jesus's life: his washing of his disciples' feet; the institution of the Eucharist (ingesting of bread and wine in Jesus's name) at the Last Supper; the suffering of Jesus at the Garden of Gethsemane; and the betrayal of Jesus by Judas Iscariot, who identified him to the Roman soldiers. It is also known as *Maundy Thursday. Maundy* is derived from the Latin word for "commandment."
- **Good Friday:** Another highly significant day, this holiday commemorates the crucifixion and death of Jesus. In some faiths, it is a fast day. For many Christians, it is a day of solemn services and prayer.

A weekly holy day: The Sabbath

Early Christians followed the Jewish tradition of setting aside one day each week for prayer. However, soon after Jesus, historical accounts indicate that his followers expanded the Sabbath to include Sunday. The Bible indicates that Jesus died on a Friday and appeared to his followers on a Sunday. In 325, Emperor Constantine declared Sunday as the official Christian day of rest.

Until the 20th century, so-called *Blue Laws* prohibited American businesses from being open on Sunday. Eventually, that law was challenged in court and ended.

For many Christians, Sunday remains a day for prayer and contemplation of the mysteries of the faith or a day where they opt to or are required to attend Mass or services.

Reading Christianity: The Bible

It's hard to understand the Christian faith without understanding the *Bible*, or Christian holy book. Pick up a Bible today, and you'll find that it has two parts: the Old Testament (the Hebrew Bible) and the New Testament. The New Testament was written after Jesus died and focuses on his message. While Jews only use the Hebrew Bible, Christians use both the Old and New Testaments.

Christian texts appear to have been written to resolve questions arising after Jesus's death. Early followers of Jesus thought the world would end promptly. When it didn't cease with his death, they thought he would return sooner, rather than later, to complete the task. However, as years passed, they began to have questions. The texts may have been written to answer those concerns.

The structure of the New Testament

Here's how the 27 books of the New Testament break down:

Four Gospels

The Gospels are biographies of Jesus, each written by a different author:

- Matthew
- Mark
- Luke
- John

Acts of the Apostles

This book describes events after Jesus died, and concentrates largely on the activities of Paul, the first great evangelist of Christianity. He toured the Mediterranean region in a tireless effort to set up colonies and to introduce Jesus to distant lands.

Epistles

The Epistles are 21 letters. Many are attributed to Paul, although scholars think he wrote six or seven at most. Each is identified by the church Paul wrote to, such as Rome, Corinth, and Galatia. They were edited extensively. The rest of the letters are by unknown writers, although names of famous early leaders of the church, such as James and Titus, have been attached to them.

REMEMBER

Early writers didn't care about who got credit. They just wanted their message distributed, so they often listed a famous person as the author. That's true in the Old Testament, too. The book of Daniel, for example, is named for a famous Jewish prophet who lived hundreds of years before the book may have been written.

The Revelation of Saint John

This book provides a prediction of the end of the world. In it, the author describes a terrible war between heavenly armies ending in the return of Jesus, the reward of heaven for the faithful, and the condemnation of nonbelievers.

Who wrote the books?

As with the Old Testament, no one knows who wrote most of the material in the New Testament. The Gospels each carry a name from their title pages — Matthew, Mark, Luke, and John — but they first appeared without any authors on them. The names, which were chosen from among the followers of Jesus, were added around 150 CE.

The Gospel of Luke and the Acts of the Apostles are thought to have been written by Clement, a doctor in Rome, and may have been combined into a single book at one time.

As noted earlier, Paul did write some of the letters attributed to him. Based on computer analyses of word choice and style, scholars think at least six (and maybe seven) of the epistles in the New Testament are authentic. The rest were produced by people who used Paul's name to get their thoughts accepted by a wider audience. All the epistles were extensively edited, so no one is sure exactly what Paul wrote and what someone else added.

The book of Revelation is attributed to John, a disciple of Jesus, but most scholars believe it was written too late for that to be the case.

Where were they written?

No one knows where Old Testament books were written, although many seem to have originated in Israel. The New Testament contains more clues.

Intense study has concluded that the Gospel of Matthew was probably written in Egypt; the Gospels of Luke and Mark in Rome; and the Gospel of John probably in what is now Turkey. Not all scholars agree, however.

No one is sure where the epistles were written. Only those by Paul contain biographical material, but even that is skimpy. Some scholars believe Acts was written in Rome.

When were the books written?

The New Testament was compiled within a relatively short time — between 70 and 120 CE. By analyzing words that the authors used, events occurring at the same time, and other factors, historians have narrowed down the chronology.

The Gospel of Mark is clearly the oldest book in the New Testament, an idea first suggested in the 1800s, but now universally accepted. That's because 80 percent of the stories in the Gospel of Matthew also appear in Mark, not the other way around. These similarities suggest that the writer of Matthew took the older texts and updated them with additional material or new ideas that had come into the early faith. In addition, Mark is written in rougher language, while Matthew is smoother and written by someone who was better educated.

Mark is dated to about 70 CE because the writer infers that the Temple was destroyed, which took place in 70. Matthew and Luke probably were written in AD 85, which gave the Gospel of Mark time to circulate and reach the authors of those Gospels.

The Gospel of John is the youngest Gospel and dated from 90 to 105 CE. That Gospel writer didn't read the Gospels of Matthew and Luke. His book has more historical data, but Jesus is presented as a divine figure far removed from the earthly figure who walks through Mark.

Paul started writing his letters as early as 39 CE and probably continued until his death around 64 CE. Some of the epistles believed to be written by other early Christians were probably written after the Gospel of John.

Drawing material from many sources

The Old Testament mentions sources, such as the Book of Jasher, that the writers used as reference material. However, those original texts have disappeared in time. The situation is more complex with the New Testament.

REMEMBER

The writers of the Gospels of Matthew and Luke relied on the Gospel of Mark as their source. They also had another document, known as Q (from German for "unknown"), that provided additional information. However, neither writer read the other's book, which is why they disagree in many areas.

In addition, all four Gospel authors draw on various other sources, including

- Word of mouth. People in the first century would memorize and pass on stories to their children.
- Gnostic documents like the Gospel of Thomas, which was rejected as canonical and survived only by being buried in the desert.
- Jewish stories available in what became the Old Testament.
- Writings in pagan texts about their gods.

By the fourth century, despite the lack of a good publisher, many books were floating around. No one knew what to believe. Church fathers were upset, as was Emperor Constantine. He figured that one empire deserved one holy book and demanded that all the philosophical debates stop.

Revising the Bible: Jerome

In 382 CE, Pope Damasus commissioned a young priest named Jerome to revise the Latin versions of the Gospels. Jerome was the pope's private secretary, but he was also a linguist who could speak, write, and understand Latin, Greek, and Hebrew. Jerome even knew Aramaic and was trained in Latin classics.

Jerome began with the Jewish books first, and then went to work on the Christian texts. (Jews had sacred books, but had not decided that more holy texts couldn't be produced. After the destruction of the Temple in 70 CE, Jewish sages met in the small Israeli town of Jamnia to collect the holy books. However, debates recorded in the Talmud show arguments raging as late as the fifth century over which books were truly holy. That implies that the holy men at Jamnia didn't make a final decision on the Jewish Bible. Jerome changed that with his translations.)

Eventually, Jerome's successors produced what became the official Bible. The text became known as the *Vulgate*, because it was written in "vulgar" Latin, rather than the sophisticated Greek language. Suddenly, in the fifth century, as the western Roman Empire was being overrun by pagan hordes, the world had a Bible. The translation wasn't accepted right away by Church leaders, but eventually, it became the primary Bible for millions of Christians through the centuries.

WARNING

Different denominations may prefer different translations of the Bible. So if you open one and go to a chapter and verse, it may read slightly differently in another translation.

Discovering the Symbols of Christianity

Christians have developed many symbols to reflect their beliefs. The most common symbols are the cross, halos, and fish. These symbols can show up on the walls of homes, as well as in everyday life, in religious services, and on clothing or even cars.

The old rugged cross

The cross, which Romans used as an instrument of torture, became the symbol of eternal life for Christians (see Figure 2-1). According to biblical accounts, Jesus died by being nailed to a cross. Because he symbolized victory of life over death, the instrument of his torture took on special significance in the faith that developed around him.

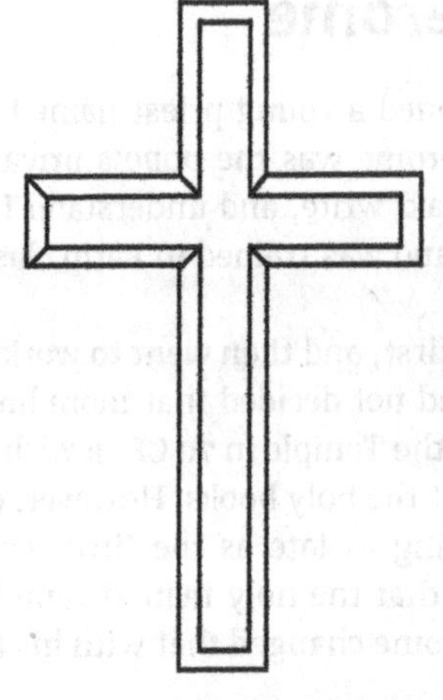

FIGURE 2-1: The cross is a universal Christian symbol.

© John Wiley & Sons, Inc.

In early years, all images of Jesus on a cross didn't depict his suffering. Realism crept into artwork in the Middle Ages, just as it did in other types of paintings. Eventually, some sects refused to show a bloody Jesus and only use a cross as a symbol. Other sects insist that Jesus must be part of the sacred image.

The cross appears in the flags of many countries, including Great Britain and Sweden. Many athletes make the sign of the cross before, during, and after athletic competition. One baseball player used to draw a cross on the ground with his bat before batting. And at one time, the cross was used as a kind of protective mark against illness and was even placed on cattle to shield them.

The biblical description of Jesus's death on the cross fits what we know about crucifixions throughout history, including his *scourging* (whipping) and the use of guards around the cross to prevent a rescue.

The Gospel writers may have added other details based on texts that preceded them:

> He is despised and rejected of men; a man of sorrows and acquainted with grief; and we hid our faces from him; he was despised and we esteemed him not. —Isaiah 53:3
>
> For dogs have compassed me; the assembly of the wicked have enclosed me; they pierce my hands and feet. —Psalm 22:16
>
> Give strong drink to him who is ready to perish. —Proverbs 31:6
>
> They gave me also gall for my meat; and in my thirst they gave me vinegar to drink. —Psalm 69:21
>
> He was numbered with the transgressors. —Isaiah 53:12
>
> The sun and the moon shall be darkened, and the stars shall withdraw their shining. The Lord shall also roar out of Zion, and utter his voice from Jerusalem, and heaven and earth shall shake. —Joel 3:15–16
>
> They shall look upon me whom they have pierced, and they shall mourn for him as one mourns for his only son. —Zechariah 12:10

What's the bright idea behind halos?

Many Christian religious icons and paintings feature *halos*, an aura of light hovering over an angel's (a spiritual being who serves God) or holy person's head. That image was actually banned in ancient times by the early Church because it was used in pagan artwork. After several centuries, Christian artists could use halos, but they had to be square to distinguish them from pagan versions. Finally, around the ninth century, the Church felt that the pagans had been overcome and permitted artists to incorporate the now-familiar round halos.

Fish, lamb, doves, and more

You may have seen a fish on the back of a car or on a necklace. It, too, is a symbol of Christianity. The letters of the Greek word for fish, *ichthus*, spells out the first letters of "Jesus Christ, Son of God, Savior." Early Christians used a fish to symbolize their faith. Today, the image of a fish reflects the Christian faith without the need for words.

Some symbols often associated with Christianity actually have other roots:

- **Lamb:** Jesus is called the "lamb of God," reflecting his role in a sacrifice for man's sins. That idea is borrowed from Judaism and shows up in Passover as the animal sacrificed so the Angel of Death would bypass Jews during the ten plagues.
- **Dove:** A dove appears when Jesus is baptized by John the Baptist. As a result, a dove is often associated with Jesus. Once again, this is a Jewish symbol. Today, the dove represents Israel as well as peace.
- **Rainbow:** This is both a Christian and Jewish symbol, representing God's promise. It comes from the Bible. In Genesis, after a terrible flood destroys all of mankind except Noah and his family, God sends a rainbow as a promise never to destroy all humans again.

IN THIS CHAPTER

» Discovering what worship means and distinguishing Christian worship

» Finding out why Christians worship together

» Exploring the differences between liturgical and free worship

» Finding the right church for you

» Understanding the roles of church leaders

Chapter 3
Making Sense of Worship

Worship is a fundamental part of Christianity — but to some Christians, worship is only pure when you do what the original New Testament Church did. To others, worship may combine the best of the ancient world and our modern world — sound biblical principles mixed with modern creativity and artistry. Still others want to ensure that, regardless of the worship style, they maintain a balance, avoiding the extremes of stuffy and emotionless or emotional and shallow.

This chapter takes a close look at the issue of worship, explaining what worship is, why Christians worship, and how different people express devotion to God — from somber, cathedral-style services to contemporary services with upbeat music played on guitars and drums to charismatic services in which people dance in the aisles. Plus, we delve into who the leaders of these churches may be and what their roles are.

Defining the Christian Tradition: I Worship, You Worship, We All Worship

Compared to people in earlier societies, most modern people have a hard time understanding exactly what worship is. In the past, showing reverence and awe was a normal part of life, whether it was to a king or to a god of one sort or another. Today's highly individualistic society stands in contrast to this lifestyle, tending to view any kind of authority with either skepticism or as irrelevant. As a result, the word *worship* conjures up images of prehistoric folks bowing down before golden statues and revering them like gods. To a society that prides itself on being sophisticated and savvy, the whole worship idea ends up sounding silly.

Although bowing to a golden calf is outdated, the concept of worship is not. Worship is hardwired into the fabric of humanity; all people worship something, whether they realize it or not. Some people worship God, while others worship more earthly gods. The ancients often opted for golden idols, but today people revere money, food, power, fame, sex, celebrities, social media, sports, and so on. In short, people worship whatever captivates their hearts.

Christianity says that a believer's all-consuming focus needs to be the Lord and the Lord alone. In this light, *worship* is the act of showing God that you're in awe of and devoted to him. Christians do this through a variety of practices, including singing, reading the Bible or creeds of the Church, praying, sharing in the Lord's Supper, preaching, and enjoying fellowship with other Christians. Christians believe that worship not only honors God but also empowers the worshiper. Some Christians even believe that the Holy Spirit fills up the spiritual gas tank of the individual who's worshiping, enabling them to be a disciple who's ready to go out into the world and share the gospel.

REMEMBER

The New Testament doesn't provide much specific instruction on what worship may consist of, so the perspectives that developed are based on what the apostles and the early Church did, rather than on the specific teachings of the Bible.

No matter how they do so, Christians agree that they must approach worship with the right attitudes for true worship to occur. These include

» **Being reverent:** Both the Old and New Testaments make it clear that God's faithful must always worship in reverence — they're never to approach worship in a light-hearted or an unwilling manner. After all, the Lord said to Moses, "Don't come close. Take your sandals off of your feet, for the place you are standing on is holy ground" (Exodus 3:5).

» **Being genuine:** Jesus indicated that true worship means doing so in spirit and in truth (John 4:23–24). By *worshiping in spirit*, Jesus meant that the worship originates deep inside of a person rather than through external activity. *Worshiping in truth* indicates being focused on the Word of God and being genuine in what you do, not going through the motions.

» **Being attentive to the Holy Spirit:** Paul tells believers to worship "in the Spirit" (Philippians 3:3). True Christian worship is always inspired by the Holy Spirit, and Christians can acknowledge the Holy Spirit's role as they worship.

» **Being humble and surrendering your heart to God:** The story of the three wise men in Matthew 2:11 reminds believers that true worship means giving:

> The wise men came into the house and saw the young child with Mary, his mother, and they fell down and worshiped him. Opening their treasures, they offered to him gifts: gold, frankincense, and myrrh.

In the same way, when you worship with abandon, you become completely focused on God, not holding back or sitting on the sidelines. Sometimes that involves giving gifts, like the wise men did, and other times, it means giving one's whole self to participate in the service.

» **Being intentional while allowing room for emotion:** Some churches have a tendency to treat worship as a purely outward emotional experience, while others think it's a cerebral activity and much prefer to leave emotion out altogether. But most Christians agree that the Bible points to a balance between these opposing positions.

The Bible indicates that God wants emotion to play a part in worship. Note the word "shout" in Psalm 81: "Sing aloud to God, our strength! Make a joyful shout to the God of Jacob!" In fact, the Old Testament uses "shout" over 20 times and often uses the term interchangeably with "sing" in the original Hebrew.

At the same time, the Bible makes it clear that Christians must not get carried away and let mindless emotion dominate. Paul dealt with this problem in his first letter to the Corinthian church. Their worship services got crazy and out of control, making it impossible for some people in the congregation to worship. As a result, Paul responds in 1 Corinthians 14 about the importance of worshiping in an orderly manner, one that produces a worshipful attitude in everyone, not just a few. As Paul says, God is not a God of confusion, but of peace.

» **Being committed to worship as a lifestyle:** The Apostle Paul reminds Christians in Romans 12:1 that true worship is a 24/7 deal, not something you only do for an hour on Sunday or Saturday:

> I urge you, brothers, by the mercies of God, to present your bodies a living sacrifice, holy, acceptable to God, which is your spiritual act of worship.

Not that Christians feel that worshiping with others isn't important, because they do, but Paul says that the Christian life is, by definition, worship.

Examining the Worship Service as a Whole

TIP

Christians worship God in a variety of manners, performing a variety of practices. But, as author Robert Webber notes in *Planning Blended Worship: The Creative Mixture of Old and New* (Abingdon Press, 1998), you can dissect worship into three distinct parts:

- **Content:** Christian worship proclaims and celebrates God's nature and the gospel of Jesus Christ. It can also serve as a response to what God has done in one's life. This involves all aspects of the service, including singing, Bible reading, participating in sacraments/ordinances, praying, and listening to sermons.
- **Structure:** Church leaders organize worship services in a particular way. Some churches are highly structured and maintain the same order at every service, while others are more loosely structured and often vary the order of a service. For example, Catholics have a very structured worship service, and you can read more about it in Book 5, Chapter 4.
- **Style:** Because Christians don't worship in a vacuum, worship always takes on a cultural style. Some Christians believe that churches today should stick to the style of the early Church's worship services, while others think that style is a far more flexible issue.

WORSHIP THROUGH THE EYES OF THE EARLY CHURCH

Justin Martyr, one of the second century Church fathers, played an important leadership role in the Church when it was working hard to transition from a faith led by the original apostles to an organized Church that would soon spread throughout the world. As Christians in the 21st century deal with the issue of worship, it's helpful to get a perspective from someone who lived just a few decades after the apostles and well before the modern-day divisions of Catholicism, Protestantism, and Orthodoxy. The following comments are taken from Martyr's *First Apology*, a book he wrote concerning worship.

Who should worship together?

On the day called Sunday, all who live in cities or in the country gather together to one place.

On what day should the Church worship?

Sunday is the day on which we all hold our common assembly because it is the first day on which God, having wrought a change in the darkness and matter, made the world; and Jesus Christ our Savior on the same day rose from the dead.

What should a worship service include?

The memoirs of the apostles [the Gospels] or the writings of the prophets are read, as long as time permits; then, when the reader has ceased, the president [preacher/priest] verbally instructs, and exhorts to the imitation of these good things. Then we all rise together and pray, and, as we before said, when our prayer is ended, bread and wine and water are brought, and the president in like manner offers prayers and thanksgivings, according to his ability, and the people assent, saying Amen; and there is a distribution to each, and a participation of that over which thanks have been given, and to those who are absent a portion is sent by the deacons.

How should believers serve others as part of worship?

They who are well to do, and willing, give what each thinks fit; and what is collected is deposited with the president, who helps the orphans and widows and those who, through sickness or any other cause, are in want, and those who are in bonds and the strangers sojourning among us, and in a word takes care of all who are in need.

Worshiping together: Why Christians believe it's essential

Worship can be an individual or corporate act, but the Church — clearly based on New Testament teaching — has always emphasized the importance of worshiping with other believers (often called *corporate worship*). Christians are called to worship corporately as a reminder that the Church is a family of God and because God is glorified when a group of believers gather in unity to worship him. Jesus promised in Matthew 18:20 that when two or more Christians are gathered together in his name, he'll be in their midst. That doesn't mean that Jesus isn't with an individual Christian who's praying and worshiping, but clearly Jesus was emphasizing that there's something special about worshiping together.

During the New Testament times, worship was usually held in homes and occasionally in Jewish synagogues. However, after the Church grew and became more organized, local communities began constructing church buildings for group worship. That same practice continued on through the centuries to the present day.

Some Protestant groups now gather in places outside of church buildings (homes, school gyms, and so on), but the focus remains the same — worshiping together as the Body of Christ.

Deciding when to worship

Protestants commonly call the time when Christians get together to worship a *worship service*, while Catholics refer to it as *Sunday Mass*. Although Jews worship on the last day of the week, Saturday (also called the *Sabbath*, which you can read more about in Book 4, Chapter 3), the early Christians decided to set aside the first day of the week (Sunday) for worship, instead, because Jesus was resurrected on that day. This tradition has carried on through the ages, although rare exceptions exist where believers still observe the Jewish Sabbath as the proper day to worship God.

For Catholics, Sunday Mass can actually occur on either Saturday evening or Sunday morning. The reasoning is that they follow the old Hebrew practice of recognizing a new day at sundown rather than at sunrise.

Many Protestant churches offer Saturday evening services as well. Sometimes, the service helps accommodate people's busy weekend schedules. Other times, the motivation is to appeal to teen or young adult age groups.

Exploring Ways to Worship: Liturgical Versus Free Worship

Although Christians tend to agree on what worship is, exactly *how* to worship is a matter of much discussion and debate. The Church has had different perspectives on this issue for centuries, but these differences seem to have peaked within the past forty years.

REMEMBER

Christians hold two basic viewpoints on how the Church should conduct worship:

- **Liturgical worship:** Embracing tradition, the liturgical (or *high church*) view looks at the early Church model and aims to duplicate it. Not only do proponents of *liturgy* (rituals and ceremony) say that it's the most biblical approach, they also say that only through the liturgy can you worship God in awe and reverence. These Christians believe that repeating liturgy from the early Church strengthens Christians today by providing a link to the past.

» **Free worship:** The free worship (or *low church*) view embraces the adaptability of the gospel in a contemporary setting, saying that modern worship should pull from the practices of the early Church but not clone them. Free worship advocates believe that their worship approach is in line with Jesus' ministry because he spoke against the empty traditions that the religious leaders of his day performed. They see free worship as being flexible to the needs of the congregation and allow for a more informal environment that they believe makes people feel more comfortable opening their hearts.

We discuss these two perspectives more in the sections that follow.

REMEMBER

It's important to note that, although both sides of this debate make important points about what can go wrong using the other worship style, neither side produces an airtight biblical argument in support of its style or against the other. It's important to remember that God didn't use a cookie cutter when he created people. Christians have likes and dislikes that aren't always the same as those of other Christians — a point that they always seem to have a hard time remembering. By and large, Christianity says that so long as worship expression is within the boundaries of biblical teaching, it glorifies God. Ultimately, Christian worship, no matter the style, should emphasize both reverence toward God and a closer personal relationship with the Lord.

Taking the high road with liturgy

A *liturgical church* provides a rigid structure to the order of the worship service and uses liturgy as a key part of the worship experience. Copying the worship patterns of the early Christian Church, they have a set structure for their normal services, often emphasizing written prayers and creeds and a repeated set of music. In general, all churches of the same type (Catholic, Orthodox, and so on) use this structure consistently year after year. Liturgical churches also have an organized structure for special services, such as for baptism, Christmas, Easter, and Palm Sunday. In terms of music, liturgical churches sing traditional hymns, either accompanied by an organ or *a cappella* (without musical accompaniment).

Liturgical churches place a high degree of priority on creating a worship environment that displays grandeur, mystery, and reverence toward God, paying attention to every detail, including the structure of the church buildings themselves. The medieval cathedrals and the traditional American stained-glass-clad churches all reveal this emphasis in the intricacy of their design. Liturgical churches focus their services on expressing reverence and awe to God through these physical surroundings along with the tried-and-true order and ceremonies of worship.

The sacraments play a central role in a liturgical church. Catholic and Orthodox churches, both liturgical, place greater emphasis on the role of the sacraments in salvation than do Protestants (check out Book 5, Chapter 2 for the skinny on the sacraments). Naturally, then, Catholics and Orthodox Christians believe that the purpose of liturgy is to enable Christ to be present through worship in order to produce a saving encounter with God. Many Protestant denominations, however, such as Episcopalian, Lutheran, and United Methodist, have a liturgical style of worship, but see worship as an expression of a Christian's inward saving faith, not as an activity directly related to salvation itself.

TECHNICAL STUFF

Of all the strands of Christianity, the Orthodox Church undoubtedly places the highest value on liturgy. That's because it sees liturgy as a primary way in which one experiences true Christianity. Worship becomes something that involves all the senses — sight (icons, architecture), hearing (music), smell (incense), touch (baptism), and taste (Communion) — to awaken the hearts of believers and wipe away the stains of a sinful soul. The Orthodox Church has performed the same liturgical practices for centuries and is resistant to any change in those practices. Because these practices are the main method of the Church's expression, they see changing the liturgy as equivalent to tweaking the core tenets of the Christian faith. However, it should be noted that Catholics also put a heavy emphasis on the importance of attending Mass. Missing mass knowingly without a valid reason (like illness) is considered a *mortal sin*, or a grave offense against God.

Worshiping freely along the low road

A *free worship church* is more flexible in the order and style of worship and doesn't feel bound to the age-old traditions that liturgical churches do. Services usually follow a general order, but the structure is tweaked as needs arise. Therefore, the focus or structure of a service may change based on what's happening that day — either within the church or in the secular world.

Although in liturgical churches a member of the clergy often reads prayers from a book, free worship emphasizes a scheduled time of off-the-cuff (or unprepared) prayer, which the pastor or even a member of the congregation says aloud.

Free worship services are more informal, relaxed, and even conversational than liturgical services, as these churches believe that Christians can be reverent in an informal setting because true worship is a matter of the heart. This relaxed atmosphere often, but not always, is reflected in the style of dress worn by church attendees. Most free worship churches welcome khakis or even T-shirts, though some hold to a more traditional dress code.

Many free worship churches also believe that the external surroundings are insignificant to worshiping God. That's why they don't have a problem meeting in school gyms if they don't have their own digs or in a multi-purpose sanctuary that they also use for sports. Free worship churches focus on being practical and relevant, all with the aim of reaching out to the world for Jesus Christ and equipping the congregation to be disciples.

This same principle carries over to musical styles and other parts of worship. In light of the fact that the Bible doesn't give specifics on music, many (though not all) free worship churches believe they have the freedom and license to use contemporary music in the services, rather than traditional church music. So too, many free worship churches believe in including skits, plays, and occasionally even interpretive dances as a way to enrich the worship experience.

Free worship churches are predominately Protestant and evangelical and include both *denominations* (groups within the larger Church that express their faith in different ways) that support free worship and many independent *nondenominational* churches (churches that aren't tied to any denomination). Increasingly, some individual churches that are part of a larger liturgical denomination have broken from this tradition and have adopted a more free worship style.

TECHNICAL STUFF

One of the free worship trends over the past twenty years is the idea of a *seeker-sensitive church.* The goal of a seeker-sensitive church is to reach out to non-believers by focusing on their needs and making worship services more relevant to them. These churches often use savvy marketing techniques to attract people to church, worship in auditorium style sanctuaries, and integrate multimedia and entertainment as part of the worship service experience. Most people consider Willow Creek, the *mega church* (a fancy way of saying it has thousands of members) located in suburban Chicago, the granddaddy of the seeker-sensitive movement. Proponents see this as a way to effectively present Christianity to the 21st-century person. Critics, both from liturgical and free worship traditions, say that this emphasis on attracting people waters down the true Christian message by telling people what they want to hear rather than dealing with the full written Word of God.

UNDERSTANDING WHEN CHRISTIANS BABBLE IN A LANGUAGE YOU DON'T RECOGNIZE

Charismatic churches, which are part of the free worship tradition, are those that emphasize worshiping by using spiritual gifts, especially the gift of speaking in tongues. Christians who practice this believe that speaking in tongues is an emotional, spiritual experience that prompts a person to start speaking in non-human speech. The people speaking in tongues understand the words they say to be angelic languages that the Holy Spirit gives to them so that they can pray spontaneously as directed by God.

(continued)

(continued)

Charismatic churches have rapidly increased in popularity over the past several decades. Today, a growing number of Catholics, non-Pentecostal Protestants, and even some in the Orthodox Church widely practice the charismatic gift of tongues-speaking, which was once considered a fringe activity in Pentecostal churches, as a form of worship.

Charismatics see speaking in tongues as being an important component of true worship. Non-charismatics disagree, believing tongues-speaking to either be a minor gift or something that is not biblical in this day and age.

If you'd like to find out more about charismatics and speaking in tongues, check out *Christian Prayer For Dummies* (John Wiley & Sons, Inc., 2011).

Fellowshipping with a Church

For some, faith is a private matter, meaning they don't believe that a Christian needs to be involved with other believers. Within a society that celebrates self and promotes individual expression, it's not surprising that this belief is quite commonplace.

Considering why biblical Christianity says church is necessary

WARNING

This individualistic thinking is the norm today, but it's not authentic biblical Christianity. St. Augustine wrote, "He cannot have God for his father who does not have the Church for his mother." Many Christian thinkers agree, saying that Christianity doesn't even exist apart from the Church. This perspective isn't surprising coming from the Catholic and Orthodox Churches, given the relatively strong role the Church plays in Catholic and Orthodox Christians' lives (see Book 5, Chapter 4 for more on Catholicism). Yet, Protestants, who reject any role that the Church as an institution plays in personal salvation, agree as well. For though salvation is between an individual and God, a key part of living out the Christian faith is being involved in a church home.

TIP

If you're skeptical, take a read through the Bible — church involvement is a given. Jesus certainly worshiped regularly with others (see Luke 4:16), and Hebrews 10:24–25 emphasizes the importance of participating in a church:

> Let us consider how to spur one another to love and good works, not giving up on our meetings together, as the custom of some is, but exhorting and encouraging one another.

REMEMBER

In fact, when you take the New Testament as a whole, you easily see that neither Jesus nor any of the apostles envisioned a stand-alone faith, much less spoke about it.

Consider the following parallel, which sheds some light on the importance of the Church in a Christian's life. Imagine, for example, you're an orphan who's adopted into a new family. Your primary relationship is with your new parents, but because you live in a family environment, you still live day-in, day-out with your new siblings. You won't set up shop in private rooms and live completely apart from each other. No, you develop your relationship with your parents at the same time you develop them with your siblings. In the same way, although Christianity centers on a personal relationship with God, it involves more than that. When someone becomes a new Christian, they're immediately part of a new community, the Family of God. As such, a vital part of a Christian's life is getting hooked up in that community.

Although Christians believe that worshiping together regularly is important, the New Testament model of a church is more than a group of people meeting together for an hour on Saturday night or Sunday morning in which they file in quietly, stand up, sit down, stand up, sit down, stand up, and then head for the exits. Instead, the biblical concept of a church involves *koinonia*, a Greek word that literally means "communion together in God's grace" or simply "fellowship." Biblical Christianity says that God designed Christians with the need for fellowship to be able to grow in their faith. Therefore, when Christians meet together, they are to

- Love one another, being bound in unity (Colossians 3:14)
- Provide opportunities to serve one another (John 13:14)
- Bear one another's burdens (Colossians 3:13)
- Encourage each other (Hebrews 3:13, 1 Thessalonians 4:18)
- Be accountable to each other (Proverbs 27:17)
- Challenge each other (2 Timothy 2:42)

TIP

If you go to a large church, it's not possible to talk with every person in your congregation. That's why meeting together in small groups with other Christians is so critical, whether that interaction is in a Bible study, a home group, Sunday school, or an accountability group.

Finding a church that you can call home

Although you may understand the need to go to church, you may run into barriers to actually finding a church that you want to join. Perhaps the church you attend is so large that it's hard to feel accepted or needed. Maybe the service is so dry that you feel like you get a windburn every time you enter the church doors. Or perhaps your hypocritical neighbor goes there and speaks about how godly their life is, making you want to have one of those bags handy that you find in the backs of plane seats.

On the one hand, it's important to remember that no church is perfect. Although the Church is the Body of Christ, it also is filled with sinners. So you're always going to come up with an excuse as to why you shouldn't go to a particular church. In spite of that, it's important to find a good church that you feel at home in.

TIP

Some tips to keep in mind as you look for a church home are

» **Know where you stand.** Christians have many differences of opinion on certain aspects of the faith. The most obvious ones are those differences between Protestant, Catholic, and Orthodox Christians. Therefore, as you begin to better understand these issues, you need to come to a personal decision on which strand of the Christian faith best expresses what you believe is true.

» **Be wary of labels.** Christian churches have an amazing number of different names. And if you try to understand all the subtle differences among them, your mind will quickly turn to mush. For example, do you think the average churchgoer knows the differences between the Christian Reformed Church, the Orthodox Christian Reformed Church, the United Reformed Church, and the Reformed Church of the United States? No way! In fact, you'd probably have to go to "reformed" school just to figure that out!

  Moreover, even if you got a PhD in Christian Labelology, sometimes the label of an individual church is quite misleading. For example, the beliefs of a United Methodist church in Indiana may be altogether different from the beliefs of a United Methodist church in Massachusetts. Or, take Catholic churches — most are traditional Catholic, but some are more evangelical in nature, and some are even charismatic. Further, Vineyard churches vary wildly in their worship approach. Some are heavy-duty charismatic churches, yet others are mainstream evangelical.

  Therefore, although a label is often a good guideline, never assume. Make sure you check out the particular church in question.

» **Dive into the doctrine of the church.** Although it's easy to assume that all Christian churches are basically the same, just as with worship styles, that's unfortunately not the case. As you decide on a church to attend, be sure to check into the church's doctrine (what the church actually teaches and believes apart from any denominational label they may have outside the door). Ask a church leader for the church's confession of faith (also called a *catechism* or statement of faith), which is usually available in printed form, and inquire as to how much the church pays attention to it. You can also check out the church's website, as more and more churches are providing a listing of core beliefs easily accessible via the Internet.

If you're concerned about finding a church that adheres to "mere Christianity," two of the most important ideas to pay attention to are

- **View of the Bible:** Does the church consider the Bible to be the inspired, authoritative Word of God? Some churches hold to the inspiration and inerrancy of the Bible, but others don't consider the Bible to be God's perfect truth.
- **View of Jesus Christ:** Does the church believe Jesus was simply a good moral teacher or does it say he was literally God in the flesh? Although Jesus' divinity is a basic foundation of biblical Christianity, a few churches that consider themselves Christian don't hold to that perspective.

If you seek a biblical, historical Christian faith, then these two issues are key factors in your overall decision-making process. In other words, make sure the church that you attend considers the Bible the complete, final, and authoritative written Word of God and considers Jesus both fully God and fully man. Biblical Christianity falls apart at the seams when these doctrines are compromised.

» **Be in synch with the worship style.** Churches today have a wide variety of worship and music styles. Some churches are throwbacks to the first-century Church, others are very ceremonial, a growing number of churches are contemporary, and a few have services that resemble a professional performance — complete with a rock band with electric guitars, drums, and a synthesizer. Make sure that you can worship and give honor to the Lord with whatever worship style the church features.

» **Make sure you're challenged.** In some churches, the preaching may be as bland as leftover white bread, or it can have a "feel good" message to pump up the congregation. However, neither of these, on a consistent basis, satisfies the desire in a person's heart to be fed spiritually. Therefore, make sure that you believe you're challenged by the teaching at the church, whether that's during the main weekly service, a Bible study, or Sunday school. When other Christians regularly challenge you and push you to dive deeper, you grow in your faith.

» **Get a sense of the church's spirit.** When you walk through the doors of a church, you often get a good feel for whether the congregation as a whole is earnestly seeking to love God and to serve him. Regardless of whether a church has a liturgical or contemporary worship style, you should sense whether the church is "alive" or whether it's simply going through the motions. You can usually get a strong sense of the church's spirit just by observing how people are worshiping or listening to the minister. Also, when you enter and exit the church, pay attention to whether the church has a spirit of outgoing friendliness or whether people keep to themselves. Finally, look at whether or not the church has a strong missions and outreach program to live out Christ's command of the Great Commission.

- **Visit multiple times.** Unless you discover a major red flag in the church's beliefs or teachings, don't try to make your decision in one or two visits. You should generally attend at least six times to get a good understanding of what the church is like.

Recognizing Christianity's Leaders

In the early years of Christianity, many people taken by Jesus's message began to offer guidance and direction to the fledgling church.

James, the leader of the Nazarenes, was described in the Jewish historian Josephus's account as being so devout that his knees were calloused from so much praying. Paul wrote letters that are now part of the New Testament. His words offered advice and philosophical teachings to converts to Christianity.

Other great teachers included Tertullian, Origen, and Justin Martyr, men who wrote profound arguments in support of Christianity and whose works carried the ideas throughout the Western world. Many such people died in the various Roman persecutions until the religion became legal in the fourth century.

The pope becomes the point man

Initially, the Church was divided into sectors. Leaders in Rome, Alexandria (Egypt), Jerusalem, and the eastern portion of the Roman Empire all jockeyed for power. These fellas were called *bishops*.

In time, the bishop of Rome became the dominant figure. The *pope*, as he was called, gained some of his clout from the legend that both Peter and Paul died in Rome, as well as from living in the empire's capital.

TECHNICAL STUFF

Pope is derived from the Roman word for "father," *poppa*.

The pope took over the title *pontifex maximus*, a title used by priests serving Roman pagan gods and often conferred on Roman political leaders such as Julius Caesar. As a result, today the pope is also known as the *pontiff*.

By the fourth century, the pope had become the leader of the western half of the Roman Empire, negotiating with invading Huns and organizing assistance to residents.

Despite various problems over the years, the pope has remained the central figure for the more than 2 billion Roman Catholics. In modern times, Pope John XXIII reformed the church in the 1960s. One of his successors, Pope John Paul II, revived and energized the religion with his powerful speeches and ceaseless travels.

Historians recognize three great popes:

- **Pope Saint Leo I (reigned 440–461):** In 452, he bravely met Attila the Hun and succeeded in saving Rome from being sacked. He also instituted many reforms, including imposing strict discipline on the bishops.
- **Pope Saint Gregory I (reigned 590–604):** He restored clerical discipline, protected the Jews from persecution, and negotiated peace treaties with the barbarian invaders. A renowned teacher, Pope Gregory wrote a book on the role of bishops that remains necessary spiritual reading. He revitalized the Mass and is credited with instituting a type of singing that is commonly called the *Gregorian chant.*
- **Pope Saint Nicholas I (reigned 858–867):** Like prophets of old, he fearlessly denounced kings. He was a champion of the poor, an art patron, and a reformer.

Christianity's organization

The leadership of Christianity developed a logical hierarchy over time. What follows is a breakdown of the chain of command.

The first heads of Christian congregations were called *presbyters.* That's from the Greek word meaning "leaders." They were responsible for supervising the morals of their members.

As the membership grew, that task became too difficult. So the presbyters began to focus on administrating the sacraments, such as baptism, communion, and the like. Eventually, one person in the congregation was awarded that authority. He became a *priest*, using a word already familiar from pagan and Jewish services.

The financial officer in each community was known as *episcopos* or *bishop.* It means "overseer" in Greek. Initially, the bishop handed out alms to poor Christians in his community. He also had to divvy up money to the various priests in his area. In time, he became their supervisor. When the tasks grew too great, the bishop was able to hire assistants. They were called *deacons* from the Greek word for "servant."

The *archbishop* lived in the capital of a religious region, called a *diocese*. The archbishops began to supervise bishops in smaller communities.

If an archbishop lived in a city tied to an apostle, such as Constantinople, he took on special connotation and was known as a *patriarch*, from the Latin word for "father." Other patriarchs were in Antioch, Jerusalem, and Alexandria.

The patriarch of Rome became the pope, as discussed in the preceding section. He then elevated bishops to serve as his advisors. They became known as *cardinals*.

The patriarch of Constantinople has evolved into the head of the Greek Orthodox Church.

The requirements and roles of Christian church leaders

As mentioned in the last section, while the Church was still getting set up, it borrowed Roman and Jewish nomenclature to create a hierarchy to oversee the faith. Priests lead the people. They are still ordained and, in the Roman Catholic Church, required to be celibate.

To become a priest, an individual must obtain a degree from a seminary. Protestant faiths also require their congregational leaders to have an education. They may be called by a variety of familiar names, including:

- Brother
- Deacon
- Elder
- Father
- Minister
- Reverend

In some faiths, a member of the congregation can be named a minister. That's true for the Unitarian Universalist, but the individual has that position only with the particular Society. Full ordination requires a college degree obtained from the Society's seminary.

Roles vary depending on the denomination. A Roman Catholic priest may not marry and serves as an intermediary between God and man. He has some administrative duties as well. Women aren't allowed to be priests, but some women devote themselves to the Church and are called *nuns*.

In the Methodist Church, in contrast, the minister may marry and is seen as a role model for proper Christian behavior. He also is the administrator of the church and oversees its functions. In the Presbyterian Church, elders are the top officials. Some elders are called ministers; they are responsible for church services and teaching. Others, called deacons, handle administrative duties.

REMEMBER

Women can be ordained in almost all Christian denominations, except Catholicism. However, more conservative churches may discourage women from assuming religious duties.

IN THIS CHAPTER

» Getting a sense of the Catholic perspective

» Introducing Church teachings

» Participating in Catholic worship

» Behaving and praying like a Catholic

Chapter 4
What It Means to Be Catholic

As the saying goes, every square is a rectangle, but not every rectangle is a square. So too, is it true that every Catholic is a Christian, but not every Christian is a Catholic.

Being Catholic means more than attending parochial school or going to religion class once a week, owning some Rosary beads, and going to Mass every Saturday night or Sunday morning. It means more than getting ashes smeared on your forehead once a year, eating fish on Fridays, and giving up chocolate for Lent. Being Catholic means living a totally Christian life and having a Catholic perspective.

What is the Catholic perspective? In this chapter, you get a peek at what Catholicism is all about — the common buzzwords and beliefs — a big picture of the whole shebang.

TECHNICAL STUFF

Many Catholics capitalize pronouns when referring to God, Jesus, and the Holy Spirit. To honor that tradition, uses of those pronouns are capitalized in this chapter. And while we're on the subject of pronouns, just so you're not confused, when Catholics refer to the Church, it's always a "she."

What Exactly Is Catholicism?

The cut-to-the-chase answer is that *Catholicism* is a Christian religion (just as are Protestantism and Eastern Orthodoxy). *Catholics* are members of the Roman Catholic Church (which means they follow the authority of the bishop of Rome, otherwise known as the pope), and they share various beliefs and ways of worship, as well as a distinct outlook on life. Catholics can be either Latin (Western) or Eastern Catholic; both are equally in union with the bishop of Rome (the pope), but they retain their respective customs and traditions.

REMEMBER

Catholics believe that all people are basically good, but sin is a spiritual disease that wounded humankind initially and can kill humankind spiritually if left unchecked. Divine grace is the only remedy for sin, and the best source of divine grace is from the *sacraments*, which are various rites that Catholics believe have been created by Jesus and entrusted by Him to His Church.

From the Catholic perspective, here are some of the bottom-line beliefs:

- More than an intellectual assent to an idea, Catholicism involves a daily commitment to embrace the will of God — whatever it is and wherever it leads.
- Catholicism means cooperation with God on the part of the believer. God offers His divine grace (His gift of unconditional love), and the Catholic must accept it and then cooperate with it.
- Free will is sacred. God never forces you to do anything against your free will. Yet doing evil not only hurts you, but also hurts others because a Catholic is never alone. Catholics are always part of a spiritual family called the *Church*.
- More than a place to go on the weekend to worship, the Church is a mother who feeds spiritually, shares doctrine, heals and comforts, and disciplines when needed. Catholicism considers the Church as important to salvation as the sacraments because both were instituted by Christ.

The Catholic perspective sees everything as being intrinsically created good but with the potential of turning to darkness. It honors the individual intellect and well-formed conscience and encourages members to use their minds to think things through. In other words, instead of just giving a list of do's and don'ts, the Catholic Church educates its members to use their ability to reason and to apply laws of ethics and a natural moral law in many situations.

Catholicism doesn't see science or reason as enemies of faith but as cooperators in seeking the truth. Although Catholicism has an elaborate hierarchy to provide leadership in the Church (see Book 5, Chapter 3), Catholicism also teaches individual responsibility and accountability. Education and the secular and sacred sciences are high priorities. Using logical and coherent arguments to explain and defend the Catholic faith is important.

Catholicism isn't a one-day-a-week enterprise. It doesn't segregate religious and moral dimensions of life from political, economic, personal, and familial dimensions. Catholicism tries to integrate faith into everything.

REMEMBER

The general Catholic perspective is that because God created everything, *nothing* is outside God's jurisdiction, including your every thought, word, and deed — morning, noon, and night, 24/7.

Knowing What the Catholic Church Teaches

The Catholic religion is built (by Christ) on four pillars of faith: the creed (teachings), the sacraments (liturgical worship), the Ten Commandments (moral code), and the Lord's Prayer or Our Father (prayer and spirituality). Church doctrine and dogma can be very sophisticated, which may intimidate some people. But the fundamentals are rooted in the Church's creed: the first pillar of faith. Either the Nicene Creed (see Book 5, Chapter 1) or the Apostles' Creed is said every Sunday and holy day to reaffirm what the Church actually teaches and expects her members to believe and profess. Catholics read the Bible and the *Catechism of the Catholic Church*, the definitive book explaining the official teachings of the Catholic Church on faith and morals.

Grasping the basic beliefs

Catholics are first and foremost *Christians*. Like Jews and Muslims, Catholics are *monotheistic*, which means that they believe in one God. But Catholics believe that Jesus Christ is the Son of God, which is unique to Christianity. Catholics also believe the following:

- **The Bible is the inspired, error-free, and revealed word of God.** See Book 5, Chapter 2 for an introduction to the Bible.
- **Baptism, the rite of becoming a Christian, is necessary for salvation.** This is true whether the Baptism occurs by water, blood, or desire. Though normally it is done with water.

» **God's Ten Commandments provide a moral compass — an ethical standard to live by.** To learn more about the Ten Commandments, see the nearby sidebar, "What are the Ten Commandments?".

» **There is one God in three persons: the Holy Trinity.** In other words, Catholics embrace the belief that God, the one Supreme Being, is made up of three persons: God the Father, God the Son, and God the Holy Spirit (see Book 5, Chapter 1).

REMEMBER

Catholics recognize the unity of body and soul for each human being. So the whole religion centers on the truth that humankind stands between the two worlds of matter and spirit. The physical world is considered part of God's creation and is, therefore, inherently good until an individual misuses it.

WHAT ARE THE TEN COMMANDMENTS?

The Church doesn't see the Ten Commandments as arbitrary rules and regulations from the man upstairs but as commandments for protection. Obey them, and eternal happiness is yours. Disobey them and suffer the consequences.

To help you avoid those negative consequences, here are the Ten Commandments Catholics should follow:

I am the Lord your God, you shall not have strange gods before Me.

You shall not take the name of the Lord your God in vain.

Remember to keep holy the Lord's day.

Honor your father and mother.

You shall not kill.

You shall not commit adultery.

You shall not steal.

You shall not bear false witness against your neighbor.

You shall not covet your neighbor's wife.

You shall not covet your neighbor's goods.

The *seven sacraments* — Baptism, Penance, Holy Eucharist, Confirmation, Matrimony, Holy Orders, and the Anointing of the Sick — are outward signs that Christ instituted to give grace. These Catholic rites marking the seven major stages of spiritual development are based on this same premise of the union of body and soul, matter and spirit, physical and spiritual. You find out more about the sacraments in this chapter's section "Worshipping as a Catholic: The Holy Mass."

REMEMBER

Grace is a totally free, unmerited gift from God necessary for our salvation. Grace is a sharing in the divine; it's God's help — the inspiration that's needed to do His will. Grace inspired martyrs in the early days of Christianity to suffer death rather than deny Christ. Grace bolstered St. Bernadette Soubirous to sustain the derision of the locals who didn't believe she'd seen the Virgin Mary. You can't see, hear, feel, smell, or taste grace because it's invisible. Catholic belief, however, maintains that grace is the life force of the soul. Like a spiritual megavitamin, grace inspires a person to selflessly conform to God's will, and like the battery in the mechanical bunny, grace keeps the soul going, going, going, and going. Because grace is a gift, you can accept or reject it; if you reject it, you won't be saved, and if you accept it, you have to put it into action.

Respecting the role of the Church and its leaders

Catholics firmly believe that Jesus Christ personally founded the Church and He entrusted it to the authority and administration of Saint Peter (the first pope) and his successors. In this section, we explain what Catholics believe the Church really is, as well as how its leadership is structured.

WHY IS THE CATHOLIC CHURCH'S HOME IN ROME?

Saint Peter, the first pope, began his ministry in Jerusalem. Eventually, he ended up in Rome, where he was its first bishop and was then crucified and buried on Vatican Hill. That spot was imperial property, but in the fourth century, the Roman emperor donated the land and buildings to the pope in compensation for property and funds that were seized from Christians during years of Christian persecutions. It's important that the Church continues to have its home in the place where Saint Peter spent his final years and was bishop and pope.

TECHNICAL STUFF

Catholics claim theirs is the true Christian faith due to the fact that they recognize Jesus as their founder and say that other denominations were founded by human individuals (such as Martin Luther for the Protestants, discussed in more detail in Book 5, Chapter 5).

What "the Church" really is

The word *church* has many meanings. Most obviously, it can signify a building where sacred worship takes place. The Catholic Church is not one particular building even though the head of the Church (the pope) lives next to Saint Peter's Basilica in Rome. People who use the church building — the body or assembly of believers — are also known as the *church*. When that body is united under one tradition of worship, it is called a *liturgical church*, such as the Eastern Catholic Church, the Melkite Church, the Ruthenian Church, or the Latin or Roman Rite Church.

REMEMBER

Catholic Churches may differ liturgically, but they're still Catholic. The two main lungs of the Church are the Latin (Western) Church and the Eastern Catholic Church. The *Latin (Western) Church* follows the ancient traditions of the Christian community in Rome since the time of St. Peter and St. Paul; most parishes in the United States, Canada, Central America, and South America celebrate this type of Mass, said in either the location's common tongue or Latin. The *Eastern Catholic Church*, which includes the Byzantine Rite, celebrates its Mass like Greek or Russian Eastern Orthodox Churches. Both Masses are cool by the pope, though.

At an even more profound level, the entire *universal* Church (meaning the Catholic Church around the world) is theologically considered the Mystical Body of Christ. In other words, the Church sees herself as the living, unifying, sanctifying, governing presence of Jesus Christ on earth today. Not just an organization with members or an institution with departments, the Church is an organic entity; it is alive. Its members, as Saint Paul says in his epistle (1 Corinthians 12:12–31), are like parts in a body. Just as your body has feet, hands, arms, legs, and so on, the Church has many members (parts) but is also one complete and whole body.

Unlike a club or association you belong to, the Church is more than an informal gathering of like-minded people with similar goals and interests. The Church was founded by Christ for a specific purpose: to save us. The Church is an extension of Jesus and continues the work begun by Him. He came to teach, sanctify, and govern God's people as the Anointed One (called *Messiah* in Hebrew and *Christ* in Greek).

REMEMBER

The Church is necessary for salvation because she is the Mystical Body of Christ, and Christ (being the Savior and Redeemer of the World) is necessary for salvation because He is the One Mediator between God and humans. People who do not formally belong to the Church are not *de facto* lost, however, because the Church believes in the universal salvific will of God. In other words, God offers salvation to all men and women, yet it is up to them to accept, believe in, and cooperate with that divine grace.

Anyone who has not consciously and deliberately rejected Christ and the Catholic Church can still be saved. In other words, besides the formal members (baptized, registered parishioners), there are many anonymous and unofficial members of the Church who act in good faith and follow their conscience, living virtuous lives. Someone may be innocently ignorant of the necessity of Christ and His Church and still achieve salvation from both.

One body with many members: That is how the Church sees herself. Her mission is to provide everything her members need — spiritually, that is. From the seven sacraments that give us grace to the Magisterium that teaches essential truths to the hierarchy that brings order through laws and governance, the Church is there to give the soul what it needs on its journey to heaven. More than a convenient option, the Church is a necessary and essential society (community) where members help each other, motivated by the same love.

The Catholic chain of command

Every group of human beings needs a chain of command (authority) and a set of rules (laws), which enable the group to maintain security, provide identity, and promote unity. Families depend on parental authority over the children. Nations have constitutions that delineate and define powers. The Church has authority that she believes comes directly from God. For example, the Lord gave Moses not only the Ten Commandments but also many other laws and rules to help govern God's people to keep them safe.

Canon law is the set of rules and regulations the Church enacted to protect the rights of persons and the common good of all the members. The word *hierarchy* means "leveled tier." Like the Roman army of old, the Church adopted a chain of command. The highest authority resides in the person of the pope, who is always simultaneously the Bishop of Rome. He is the Successor of Saint Peter, the man to whom Christ entrusted the keys of the kingdom.

The pope is the Church's supreme lawmaker, judge, and visible leader. He is also called the Vicar of Christ on earth. As the Church's ambassador to the world, he possesses full, supreme, and universal power the moment he takes office. He is elected pope by the *college of cardinals,* which exists to elect a pope after the current one dies (or freely resigns) and also to advise, counsel, and assist the reigning pope.

The terms *Vatican* and *Holy See* refer to the various departments, commissions, congregations, and so on that help the pope govern the Church, evangelize and teach the faith, and maintain and promote justice.

Jesus not only entrusted the Church to Saint Peter and his successors (the popes), but He also had Twelve Apostles whose successors are called *bishops.* A bishop shepherds a local church called a *diocese*, whereas the pope shepherds the universal, global Church around the world. Bishops are helped in each parish church by a pastor who is a priest, and often they are helped by a deacon and/or a parochial vicar (assistant pastor). The bishops of a nation or geographical region form Episcopal conferences, which provide the benefit of pooled resources.

Worshipping as a Catholic: The Holy Mass

The second pillar of faith in the Catholic religion is the seven sacraments — or in more general terms, divine worship of God as celebrated in the sacred liturgy. The ceremonies, rituals, and rites performed for over the past 2,000 years were developed by the Church to render worship of the Almighty, to teach the faith to the believers, and to give moral guidance on how to live that faith.

REMEMBER

The seven sacraments are the most sacred and ancient Catholic rites. They mark the seven major stages of spiritual development:

- **Baptism:** You are born. (You are welcomed into the Church typically by a priest pouring water on your head,)
- **Holy Eucharist:** You are fed. (You receive the Body and Blood of Jesus Christ, typically during Mass.)
- **Confirmation:** You grow. (You confirm the faith given to you in Baptism.)
- **Penance:** You need healing. (You confess your sins to a priest and receive absolution.)
- **Anointing of the Sick:** You recover. (You are given spiritual healing and receive the Holy Spirit's gift of peace and courage to better face any difficulties that accompany illness.)
- **Matrimony:** You need family. (You enter into a covenant with your spouse.)
- **Holy Orders:** You need leaders. (You join the Church as a priest or brother.)

Because humans have five senses and can't physically see what's happening in the spiritual realm, the seven sacraments involve physical, tangible *symbols* (such as the water used in Baptism, the oil for anointing, and unleavened bread and wine). Symbols help connect us to the invisible spiritual reality, the *divine grace* (God's gift of unconditional love) given in each sacrament. Catholics belong to their own churches, called *parishes*, which are local places of worship. The *Holy Mass*, the Catholic daily and weekly church service, is a reenactment of *Holy Thursday* (when Jesus celebrated the Last Supper) and *Good Friday* (when He died to purchase the rewards of eternal life in heaven for humankind). See Book 5, Chapter 2 for more on these.

WARNING

Sunday attendance at a parish isn't just expected; it's a moral obligation. Not going to Sunday Mass without a worthy excuse, such as illness or bad weather, is considered a grave sin. (Note that many Christians attend church services on Sunday, but Catholics can also attend Mass on Saturday evening instead to fulfill the Sunday requirement.)

Bringing body and soul into the mix

Human beings are created as an essential union of body and soul. Material and spiritual worlds are bridged in each and every human person. Because God made us this way, it only makes sense that both body and soul are incorporated in worship.

TIP

Attending Mass requires more than just being physically present in church. That's why Catholics use different postures, such as standing, sitting, kneeling, and bowing, and do plenty of listening, singing, and responding to phrases. For example, if the priest says, "The Lord be with you," Catholics respond, "And with your spirit."

During Mass, the inspired Word of God is read, proclaimed, and heard through people's eyes, lips, and ears. Holy Communion, food for the soul, is given to believers.

Sacred art adorns the worship space (such as stained glass, statues, icons, paintings, mosaics, tapestries, and frescoes), sacred music is played and sung, bells are rung, incense is burned . . . the senses are stimulated as body and soul are united and nourished in the House of God.

Participating inside and out

Catholics are not spectators while at public worship. Yes, there is a distinction between the *clergy* (ordained ministers who perform the sacred rites and rituals in the name of the Church) and the congregants, but the people in the pews are crucial because they represent the entire human race.

Everyone in the church is asked to get involved in sacred liturgy. Divine worship is the adoration of God by man, and *interior* participation is the most important element. Every person at Mass should be open to God's grace to accept and cooperate with it. Interior participation means going to church not for what you get out of it but for what you can give to God.

Of all the sacraments and all the sacred liturgies, the Mass is par excellence, the source and summit of Christian worship. It is more than a mere reenactment of the Last Supper; it is the unbloody representation of Christ's sacrifice on Calvary (Good Friday).

Mass is first and foremost sacred worship, but it also teaches and supports what Catholics believe in terms of the doctrines and dogmas that form the creed of the religion. Mass communicates religious truths and encourages parishioners to respond morally and spiritually by living holy lives.

REMEMBER

One of the reasons Mass is important for Catholics is because they are receiving the Body and Blood of Jesus Christ in the Eucharist. How this occurs is a considered a mystery of the faith — called *transubstantiation* — because the bread and wine do not alter in appearance, only in substance after the priest says the proper words of consecration over them. While many other denominations treat the bread and wine as mere symbols, Catholics hold tight to the belief that it is the true body and blood of their Savior. One passage from the Bible cited for this belief reads, "Then he took the bread, said the blessing, broke it, and gave it to them, saying, 'This is my body, which will be given for you; do this in memory of me.' And likewise, the cup after they had eaten, saying 'This cup is the new covenant in my blood, which will be shed for you'" (Luke 22:19–20). This reenactment of the Last Supper sets up the Catholic faith to be fed spiritually by the Savior, and in this way, Christ is assimilated into each recipient.

Behaving Like a Catholic

The third pillar of the Catholic faith is the Ten Commandments, which represent the moral life of the believer. Behaving as Jesus would want us to is the basic premise. The concept is not puritanical; fun and enjoyment aren't frowned upon. All legitimate pleasures are allowed in moderation — and only if they aren't an end in themselves. The individual's goal is to maintain a happy balance of work and leisure.

As we explain in this section, there are certain activities the Church recommends and encourages, and some she requires and demands. In all places and at all times, being docile to the will of God is paramount.

Following the general ground rules

The minimum requirements for being a Catholic are called the *precepts* of the Church:

- Attending Mass every Sunday (or Saturday evening) and holy day of obligation.
- Going to confession annually or more often (or when needed).
- Receiving Holy Communion during Easter. (Receiving weekly or daily Holy Communion is encouraged, though.)
- Observing laws on fasting and abstinence: one full meal on Ash Wednesday and Good Friday; not eating meat on Fridays during Lent.
- Supporting the Church financially and otherwise.

And, in the United States, the American bishops added two more precepts:

- Obeying the marriage laws of the Church.
- Supporting missionary activity of the Church.

Catholics are also required to pray daily, participate in the sacraments, obey the moral law, and accept the teachings of Christ and His Church. If you haven't grown up knowing and accepting the faith, then you need to make sure you know and agree with all that the Catholic Church teaches before you can truly practice the faith.

Practicing the faith is the most difficult part of being Catholic. Obeying the rules isn't just mindless compliance. It involves appreciating the wisdom and value of the various Catholic rules and laws. Believers are asked to put that belief into action, to practice what they believe. Catholics are taught that all men and women are made in the image and likeness of God and that all men and women have been saved by Christ and are adopted children of God. That belief, if truly believed, requires that the person act as if they really mean it.

TIP

Every organization, society, association, and group has rules. Even individual families and homes have their own rules, which exist for one purpose: the common good of all the members. Just like directions on a bottle of medicine tell you the proper use of something, Church laws are signs that warn you of danger and give you the proper directions to your destination. The laws of God — be they the Ten Commandments, the Natural Moral Law, or the moral teachings of the Church — exist to protect us and to ensure our spiritual safety.

Avoiding sin

Sinning is not only breaking the law of God but also much more. Sin is a disease, a germ, an infection of the soul. Just as tumors can be either benign or malignant, sins can be either venial or mortal, either slightly wounding or actually killing the life of grace in the soul.

The best prevention is to avoid sin just as doctors advise us to avoid disease. Good spiritual health requires more than being free of infection, however. Living a virtuous moral life and maintaining a healthy spirituality, when combined with an aggressive program to avoid sin at all costs, is the best plan to live a holy life worthy of a true follower of Christ.

Heeding the Church's stance on tough issues

Certain topics get much more media attention than the substance of Catholic religion (like doctrine, worship, prayer, and spirituality). These topics include the Church's stance on abortion, euthanasia, contraception, homosexuality, and more.

Many of the tough issues that distinguish Catholicism from other faiths are based on the Church's foundational beliefs. The Church believes that issues such as priestly celibacy are matters of discipline, whereas the ordination of women contradicts a doctrine of the faith. Abortion, euthanasia, contraception, and homosexuality are moral issues that require the application of biblical and doctrinal principals in order to see clearly the spiritual dangers often overlooked by well-meaning people. War and capital punishment are examples where legitimate differences of opinions still exist, yet basic fundamentals must always be respected and upheld.

Praying as a Catholic: Showing Your Devotion

While public worship (such as the Holy Mass) is governed by the official Church, private prayer is more a matter of personal taste and preference. Each person needs to cultivate their own spirituality just as they need to develop a healthy lifestyle for their body.

When it comes to prayer, what works for one person may not work for another, but certain fundamentals almost always apply. Think of it this way: Your choices with regard to diet and exercise may differ from those of your friends and neighbors, but chances are your choices have a lot in common with those made by people of similar physical health. Likewise, your devotional choices (such as how and when to pray) can be tailored to meet your needs, but many similarities exist among people who share a certain faith.

Praying and using devotions

Catholicism promotes both public and private prayer. *Devotions* are prayers or actions devoted to God, which can be private or public as well. Devotions are minor ways that believers cultivate a love and familiarity with theological truths and revealed mysteries of faith and (most importantly) develop a personal relationship with the Lord. Devotions such as *praying the Rosary,* which consists of a series of prayers counted on a string of beads, are some of the more popular and effective ones around.

Realizing the importance of Mary and the saints

The Virgin Mary is the mother of Jesus, and she is also considered one of His most faithful disciples in her own way. While not an Apostle and never holding any authority in the early church, the Mother of Christ nonetheless has always been a model of humility, virtue, and obedience to the will of God.

Mary and the *canonized saints* (individuals who lived exemplary lives) of the Church are not objects of worship (which would be idolatry — something condemned by the First Commandment). Instead, they are living examples and models of holiness and sanctity. They are role models and heroes of faith who, in their own way, tried and succeeded in following Jesus as best they can.

Following traditions

The most visible aspects of Catholicism are not usually the most fundamental theological, doctrinal, or moral teachings. In other words, they aren't necessarily the meat-and-potatoes substance of what it means to be Catholic. But some traditions are so public or well known that people associate them with Catholicism much like people associate Judaism with a man wearing a yarmulke (see Book 4, Chapter 1) or Islam with the use of a prayer rug (see Book 6, Chapter 4).

Some such Catholic traditions include meatless Fridays, ashes on the forehead to begin Lent, palms on Passion Sunday, and blessings (of throats, persons, homes, cars, and so on). Such pious practices are not the core of Catholicism, but they do connect and point in that direction.

IN THIS CHAPTER

» **Considering why Protestants split from the Catholic Church**

» **Exploring what all Protestants believe**

» **Shedding some light on the many Protestant denominations**

» **Discovering what different Protestant labels mean**

Chapter 5
Back to Basics: The Protestant Church

The film *Back to the Future* tells the story of Marty McFly, a typical 1980s teenager who accidentally travels back in time to the 1950s in a rigged-up DeLorean automobile. Once he's there, Marty has to make sure that his presence doesn't prevent his parents-to-be from meeting and falling in love, and then he has to figure out how he can get back to the future and life as he knows it.

Back in the early 16th century, another Marty — Martin Luther — found himself going back in time, figuratively anyway, when he rediscovered the core teachings of the first-century apostles. What he found was far different from the Christianity he'd always known. From Luther's perspective, over the years, the Catholic Church had gotten away from the heart of the gospel that Jesus and the apostles taught. His remedy: Go back to the central teachings of the Bible that he believed the Church had lost, in order to move on to the future. Luther's radical beliefs got him into such a pickle that he may have liked to hop into a DeLorean and escape by time travel. But he made it through the sticky spots and, in the process, kicked off the Protestant Reformation.

This chapter travels through time and explores the key factors of the Reformation, chronicling the rapid growth of Protestantism. It then explores how Protestantism exists today by looking at denominations and notable trends as the 21st century unfolds.

Exploring the Protestant Reformation

Most significant moments in history — whether they're battles, revolutions, or discoveries — have a single individual behind them who spearheaded events and got them rolling. The Protestant Reformation is no different; although the Reformation was expansive and went beyond a single person, Martin Luther nonetheless was the catalyst that set the wheels in motion for a movement to forever change the Christian Church. In the next section, you get to know more about Luther and what caused the Reformation in the first place. Then, you explore how Protestantism expanded into four distinct strands.

Urging the Church to reform

REMEMBER

Martin Luther was a German monk born in the late 15th century who became preoccupied with his own utter sinfulness and God's awesome holiness. The more he studied who God is, the more he became terrified, petrified, mortified, and stupefied about what God's holiness meant for him personally; he wanted to experience salvation and go to heaven, but he believed that he was utterly destined for hell, given his sin. He tried *penance* (confessing his sins to a priest), *self-flagellation* (whipping oneself), and *mysticism* (which distrusted the Christian Church and said that a person achieves salvation by entering their "innermost being"). Performing the Eucharist (see Book 5, Chapter 4) terrified him all the more, because he believed he was doing so unworthily. Martin's superiors urged him to simply love God, yet he found himself resenting and despising the Lord because of the hopeless situation.

Reexamining the Bible

Luther found the hope that he'd been desperately searching for in the pages of the Bible. After he took on a new position heading up biblical studies at Wittenburg University, he began to study the Bible like he'd never done before. He found himself drawn into the Book of Romans and was amazed by what he was reading. He discovered a common theme of the Apostle Paul throughout the book — that God justifies humans by grace through faith, and faith alone. As Luther read, he saw Paul paint a far different picture of the Christian faith than what he'd known. His eternal soul wasn't dependent on his personal worthiness or on the penance he performed. Salvation wasn't something that could be earned. The angst and despair that he felt inside gave way to hope and joy in the idea that people are saved not by anything that they do, but only by accepting in faith the work of Jesus on the cross.

Condemning indulgences and corruption

When Luther glanced at the Book of Romans and then looked up at the Christian Church around him, he did a double take. The two didn't seem to synch up, leaving Luther frustrated over what to do about it. He didn't agree with some of the Church's teachings and had long been dismayed at the spiritual state of the Church, but he certainly didn't see himself as a rebel or revolutionary.

What ultimately set him into action was what he saw as widespread corruption regarding the Church's sale of indulgences. An *indulgence* is time off from purgatory (see Book 5, Chapter 2) that Catholics believe they receive by performing certain acts, such as reading the Bible daily. They believe that these acts help them receive greater sanctification in their earthly lives and thus spend less time in purgatory.

The Catholic Church believed it may dispense indulgences to people because Catholics believed that, as Christ's representative on earth, the Church possessed a storehouse of merit for such purposes. This practice had started centuries earlier to help fund the *Crusades*, which were medieval military campaigns that the Western Church undertook to reclaim the Holy Land from Muslims. Whatever the original intent, by this time, indulgences became as common and as simple as a pill that everyone wanted in order to take care of sins quickly and easily. A person's spiritual state became a non-factor in their forgiveness.

REMEMBER

While Luther was at Wittenburg, a church spokesman came to Germany to raise financial support for the completion of St. Peter's Basilica in Rome. Like a used-car salesman, the spokesman offered not just forgiveness of one's own sins through indulgences, but he went even further — he offered a sort of Get-out-of-Purgatory-for-Free card that people can cash in for their dead loved ones. Luther was horrified by the theology of this teaching. In response, he posted a list of 95 calls for debate on indulgences (known as the *Ninety-five Theses*) on the outside of a church door in Wittenberg, Germany in 1517.

Going to trial

Church leaders denounced Luther for his rebellious act and brought him to trial in 1521 at the Diet of Worms (a name that sounds more like a radical new weight-loss fad than an imperial heresy hearing in the city of Worms). He demanded that the Church provide biblical evidence that his ideas were a *heresy* (false teaching that seriously undermines Christianity) and argued that the Bible is the authority for these kinds of matters, not the pope or anyone else in the Church. In his memorable words, Luther said, "I am bound by the scriptures . . . and my conscience is captive to the Word of God."

The Church declared Luther guilty of heresy at the Diet of Worms and placed him under the emperor's ban, a severe sentence because he was fair game to be killed by anyone at any time. However, Luther was able to escape any sentencing and gain protection from a sympathetic prince in Germany, in whose castle he hid out for many years, spending some of this time translating the Bible from the original Hebrew and Greek to German.

From reformation to separation

REMEMBER

Martin Luther didn't set out to separate from the Catholic Church. Even after the Diet of Worms, he and some of the original reformers of his day hoped that their calls to reform would bring about change within the Church. Yet, as the years passed, they slowly began to give up on that idea and increasingly developed their own churches apart from the Catholic Church.

Martin Luther was the first of what the Catholic Church came to call *Protestants*, a term that comes from the Latin word meaning "one who protests." Over the next fifty years, four initial strands of Protestantism developed: Lutheran, Reformed, Anabaptist, and Anglican. This section discusses each of these strands.

Following Luther: The Lutherans

By the late 16th century, the effects of the Reformation were having a significant impact on much of Europe. Christians who supported Luther's reforms were given the name *Lutheran*, a term that they eventually coined for themselves. Lutheran churches sprang up in Germany, Scandinavia, and other parts of Northern Europe.

Lutheran churches focused on the "saved by grace through faith alone" beliefs that Martin Luther had been fighting for, but they still had many similarities to the Catholic Church. Lutheran churches remained intertwined with the state leaders and politics around them. And although Luther rejected all the Catholic sacraments that he believed didn't have biblical justification, he still was closely aligned with Catholic theology on the nature of the Lord's Supper and baptism (see Book 5, Chapter 4).

Developing five-point Calvinism: The Reformed Church

The second major Protestant movement brought about the Reformed Church, which the Frenchman John Calvin started. Calvin had a reputation as a stern, somber sort of guy who had a liking for tough moral discipline and a strict work ethic. He became famous for his book *Institutes of the Christian Religion* in 1535, roughly 14 years after the Diet of Worms (see the section, "Going to trial," earlier in this chapter). His book became perhaps the most influential piece of writing to describe Protestantism.

Calvin soon moved to Geneva, Switzerland, and was the church leader in that city. During his time there, Geneva became the hip place to be for Protestants. Persecuted Protestants found a welcome mat for them in Geneva. The Swiss city had everything — a missionary training school, a model community for Christian living, and all the cheese fondue you can eat.

REMEMBER

Although Calvin was fully in line with Luther on core Protestant beliefs (see the section, "Examining Core Protestant Beliefs," later in this chapter), he disagreed with him on other issues, such as the nature of the Lord's Supper (Calvin didn't agree with Luther that the body and blood of Christ are spiritually present in the bread and wine). The churches that followed Calvin began to stress that if people are saved by God's grace alone, then God must be the one who takes the initiative for salvation. That is to say, no one can choose God unless God chooses them first. This belief came to be popularly known as *Calvinism* and is often summarized with five points:

- **Total depravity:** Sinful humans are totally unable to save themselves (see Romans 6:20, Mark 7:21–23).
- **Unconditional election:** God's purpose for saving people isn't based on anything that people have done, but solely on his will (see Romans 9:11,15).
- **Limited atonement:** Christ's death was sufficient to save all people, but only actually saves the *elect* (or the people who will be saved; see Matthew 25:32–33). Check out the "Debating on predestination" sidebar in this chapter for more.
- **Irresistible grace:** Those who are elected by God will also choose him with their own human wills (see Romans 9:16).
- **Perseverance of the saints:** Those people who are chosen by God will never opt out, but will persevere in their faith and receive salvation (see John 10:27–28).

TIP

Observant readers will notice that these five points spell out TULIP as an acronym. In fact, five-point Calvinism is often referred to using that acronym.

The influence of Calvin's teaching spread throughout various parts of Europe, notably in regions of France, the Netherlands, and even Scotland. In fact, by the 17th century, the Calvinist movement even surpassed Lutheranism in terms of its influence in the Protestant Church.

Furthering reform: The Anabaptists

As radical as Luther and Calvin appeared to the Catholic Church, they didn't go far enough for other Protestants. Another group, which became known as the *Anabaptists* (a term that means "rebaptizers," given to this group by its opponents), argued that in order to truly seek reform, one must separate the Church from the state altogether. Anabaptists looked at the New Testament Church and saw no intermingling with government authority, no stories of Paul and Peter hobnobbing with Emperor Nero. Instead, the Anabaptists focused on reaching the world with the Good News of Christ. From their perspective, anything else was just a distraction.

Anabaptists had issues that went beyond how the Church relates to state and society. They actually got their nickname because of their stand on baptism. Unlike the infant baptism of the Catholic and Lutheran churches, Anabaptists believed that only adult believers who openly confess Jesus Christ as their savior can be baptized. Because they didn't see infant baptism as legitimate, many of the Anabaptists were baptized again as adults. Their enemies saw this practice as rebaptism, an idea that they considered heretical and punishable by death. Anabaptists countered by saying that it's not rebaptism at all. They believed that baptism at birth isn't really baptism, because baptism implies a conscious faith.

Anabaptists had some extreme fringe groups whose radicalism gave them a bad name throughout parts of Europe during this era. However, some Anabaptists were ahead of their time on several issues that are commonplace today (separation of Church and state, religious diversity, believer's baptism). But like so many mavericks throughout history, they were persecuted, not only by Catholics, but also by other Protestants.

Some Anabaptists were also ahead of their time on the issue of freedom of religious expression. Many believed that a person should be able to worship where they wanted to. To Lutherans and Calvinists in the 16th century who still held to the idea that a single church dominated a geographical area, this smacked of radicalism.

Today, the Mennonites and the Amish are two groups originating from the Anabaptist tradition. The Baptists, a major Protestant denomination, are unrelated to this group, as most Baptists come from a Reformed background.

Taking a middle ground: The Anglican Church

The fourth and final original Protestant movement brought about the Anglican Church. Unlike the previous three, this split from the Catholic Church didn't come about initially due to theological differences, but instead because of that nasty, unseemly business of politics.

Not too long after the Reformation began, England's King Henry VIII wanted to get a divorce, but in order for the divorce to be valid, he needed the pope's approval. Try as he might, he couldn't get it. So, if you're a spoiled king who always gets what he wants, what do you do? Why, of course, you simply tell the Catholic Church to take a hike, form your own national Church (the Church of England), and then get a divorce approved by the head of that Church. And that's exactly what the king did. However, when he took this action, the Church of England didn't immediately become Protestant in orientation, but instead kept a doctrine in line with Catholic teaching.

In time, the Church of England moved closer to the Protestant position, believing that the Bible, not tradition, was the final authority and that the only two legitimate sacraments were baptism and the Lord's Supper. At the same time, the Anglican Church didn't move as far away from the Catholic Church as the other Protestant groups, retaining a "high church" liturgy (see Book 5, Chapter 3), among other ideas.

Examining Core Protestant Beliefs

The original goal of Protestantism was to provide new answers to age-old questions concerning Christianity, for which some people felt the Catholic Church gave unsatisfactory answers. These questions included

- How is a person saved?
- Where does religious authority lie?
- What is the Church?
- What's the essence of Christian living?

Protestants share common answers to each of these questions. They summarize these beliefs as a set of *solas*, a word derived from the plural Latin word meaning "only." These are

- ***Sola Scriptura:*** The Bible is the only authority for Christians to determine God's truth.
- ***Solus Chrisus:*** Jesus Christ is the only mediator between God and man.
- ***Sola Gratia, Sola Fide:*** Salvation is by grace alone through faith alone.
- ***Sola Deo Gloria:*** Only God gets the credit for offering the solution of salvation, not people.

A final core belief, *priesthood of the saints* (all people are considered equals before God) doesn't begin with *sola*, but all Protestants hold it closely.

Together, these core beliefs served as the foundation for Protestantism centuries ago and remain valid to biblical Protestants today. We discuss each of them in this section.

Yielding to the Bible as the one and only authority

Protestants believe that the Bible is the sole and final authority as the written Word of God. They believe that Church tradition (referring to the historical beliefs and practices of the Church) is good and helpful but that it doesn't carry the authority of scripture. The Holy Spirit works through the Bible, never presents truths independent of it, and isn't going to speak new extra-biblical revelations to people today.

In addition, Protestants believe that biblical interpretation shouldn't be reserved for the lofty domains of the clergy and theologians. Instead, they say that each person can interpret the Bible, not simply the Church. But at the same time, the original reformers never believed that this meant a "to each their own" freedom of interpretation. Although one shouldn't ignore the clergy's education and special insight into understanding the Bible, the reformers' initial vision was that the clergy and congregation would work together to reach a consensus on understanding the Word of God. In other words, a Christian shouldn't interpret the Bible outside of the instruction and teaching of the Church. However, as the "Breaking It Down into Denominations" section (later in this chapter) discusses, the belief that all Christians are called to interpret the Bible for themselves had the unintended side effect of creating a multitude of denominations.

Luther's belief regarding the authority of the Bible differed from his more radical contemporaries. Luther believed that although the Bible was the only authority, extra-biblical traditions were legitimate so long as they didn't go against the Bible. On the other hand, the Anabaptists and other radicals claimed that if the Bible didn't specifically command something, it was wrong to practice it. By the 18th century, most Protestants came to emphasize the belief that "only scripture" meant that no authority *except* the Bible may determine God's truth.

Seeing Christ as the one and only mediator

Protestants believe that the sacramental system of the Catholic Church incorrectly puts the clergy as the mediators between God and man. In a Catholic's eyes, the individual Christian is dependent on the Church for matters pertaining to salvation (such as baptism) and the Christian life (such as confession and the Eucharist). But this practice prevents the average Christian from being able to go directly to God without mediation by priests.

In contrast, Protestants hold 1 Timothy 2:5 up as their slogan: "For there is one God, and one mediator between God and men, Christ Jesus." Christians believe that Jesus was the one who lived a sin-free life and sacrificed himself so that people can be justified before God the Father. Therefore, to Protestants, "only Christ" means that Christianity is about Christ and what he's done in order to make salvation possible, not something individuals or the Church can do.

Being saved by grace alone and faith alone

Although all Christians believe that salvation is made possible only by God's grace, they disagree on how he gives that grace. Protestants say that Christians receive grace simply by accepting and believing it, but Catholics believe they receive grace by accepting it in faith and by participating in the sacraments. Orthodox Christians believe that Christians receive grace as they participate with God in the work of salvation through living a life of holiness and worship.

Giving kudos to God alone

The idea behind *Soli Deo Gloria* ("To God Be the Glory") is that humans didn't pick themselves up by their own bootstraps and find God, but instead, God did all the work, leaving nothing for the Christian to do but accept the offer of salvation.

The opposite perspective that Luther noted is what he termed the *theology of glory*, in which humans trust in their own efforts to bring about salvation rather than trust in God alone. This theology of glory also leads people to rely on their own wisdom and understanding rather than be humble before the Lord and trust his wisdom as chronicled in the Bible. Instead, Luther argued for a *theology of the cross*, which states that all humans are miserably sinful and can't ever escape sin, and it's only the saving work of Christ on the cross that can give real hope to people.

Because of what God has done for humans, *Soli Deo Gloria* is the reason and basis for Christian worship. God has done everything, so the natural Christian response is to worship God in gratitude and humility. (Check out Book 5, Chapter 3 for more on Christian worship.)

Considering all Christians as equal in God's eyes

A final classic belief of Protestants is the belief in the priesthood of all believers (Revelation 5:10). That doesn't mean that every Protestant has to go to seminary and wear a collar around their neck. Instead, what Protestants mean by the phrase is that all Christians are the same before God. They don't fit into a holiness hierarchy, and God doesn't make a distinction between those who work in the Church and those who work in the secular world. Relying on the Holy Spirit to guide them, Protestants believe that God uses them as his ambassadors in either of these vocations.

Answering the core questions

REMEMBER

Protestants answer the questions raised at the beginning of this section as follows:

- **How is a person saved?** A person is saved by their faith in Jesus, not by simply doing good deeds or by being a good person.
- **Where does religious authority lie?** Authority lies solely in the inspired Word of God, not in the pope or in the Church.
- **What is the Church?** The Church is an entire community of believers, each of whom is called to go directly to God through Christ as the sole mediator. All Christians, not just the clergy, are called to reach out as Christ's ambassadors in the world. See the section, "Considering all Christians as equal in God's eyes," earlier in this chapter, for more on this idea of the priesthood of all believers.
- **What's the essence of Christian living?** The essence of Christian living is serving God in a calling, whether it's inside or outside of the Church.

WHERE ARE ALL THE PROTESTANTS?

Catholic Christians identify closely with the term "Catholic," and Orthodox Christians embrace the term "Orthodox." In contrast, many Protestants only marginally relate to the term "Protestant." It's not that they don't have Protestant beliefs, but the term itself is so generic that it often holds little meaning to Protestants today. One reason is that no Protestant is just a Protestant, but they instead identify with either a denomination (Methodist, Congregationalist, and so on) or a particular expression of Protestantism (evangelical, fundamentalist, charismatic).

Breaking It Down into Denominations

Protestants and rabbits seem to have something in common, and it's not floppy ears or a love for carrots. Since the beginning of the movement, Protestants have had a knack for multiplying churches. Or, as a cynic may say: Put two Protestants in a room and you'll soon have another denomination being formed.

Denominations rose up within the Protestant Church nearly a hundred years after the deaths of Luther and Calvin. Luther, Calvin, and their predecessors were tied to the medieval concept of *Christendom* (a marriage of Church and state) and a single Church for a geographical area. So, they were strict in combating dissention within these areas. But, over time, an openness to denominations began to develop.

REMEMBER

Denominations are different from sects. Although the term has many meanings and connotations in contemporary society, a *sect* is much more exclusive and tends to distance itself from other Christians, believing that it alone knows God's truth, and everyone else is either outside the Body of Christ or at least on very shaky ground. One may liken a sect to a cult. In contrast, a *denomination* is often more inclusive, believing that different groups can express their faith in different organizational and worshipful ways, but all are part of a larger Body of Christ. In other words, a person in a sect points to the True Church with one finger. Persons in a denomination, although they may believe that their particular brand of Christianity is best, nonetheless use all their fingers and toes (and then some) to point to all the churches of the True Church. Refer to Figure 5-1 to see some of the Protestant denominations that spun off of the original four strands through the years.

TECHNICAL STUFF

The reasons that denominations came about are wide ranging. For example:

- **Some denominations formed based on the government of the church.** Congregationalists believe that independent churches should govern themselves by the congregation apart from a higher authority. Congregationalist pastors, then, are ultimately subject to the congregation. Presbyterians (from *presbyter,* the Greek word for "elder") believe that *elders* (leaders) should govern the church alongside the pastor. Episcopalians, closer to the Catholic model, say that the government should be a hierarchy of regional *bishops* (overseers) over pastors in local churches.
- **Denominations were established due to doctrinal differences**. The Baptist denomination was originally established in the early 17th century by an Anglican pastor named John Smyth. Smyth believed that the Church of England was unbiblical due to its position on *apostolic succession* (the belief that bishops are the anointed successors of the original apostles to lead the Church). In addition, the holiness movement rose up from the Methodist Church in the 1890s, based on the belief that the Church should be primarily dedicated to promoting holiness-based living and teaching.

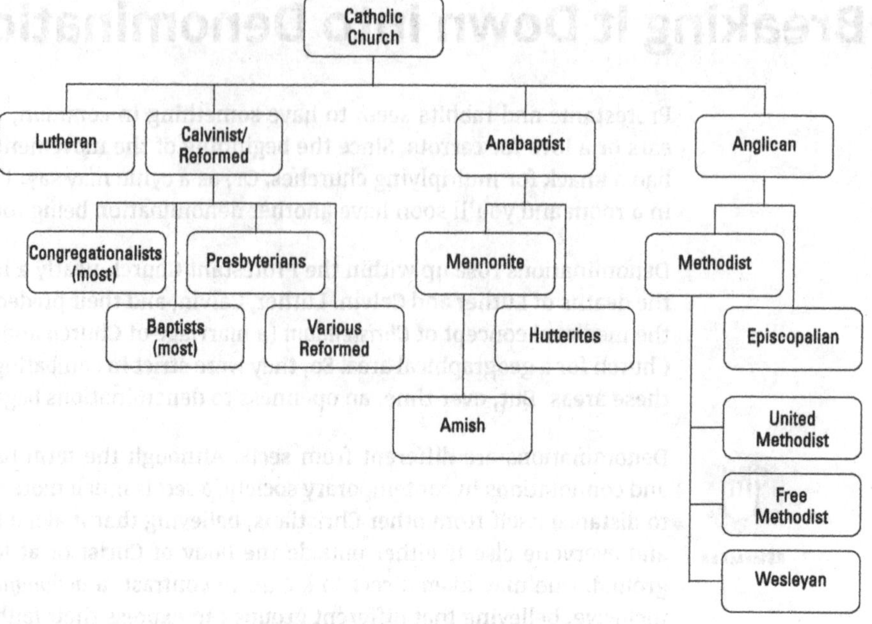

FIGURE 5-1: Protestantism began with one man and evolved into four main strands of belief that further branched over time.

- **Other denominations developed almost organically, springing out of ongoing church activities.** The best example of this is the Methodist denomination, which was started by John Wesley (see the "John Wesley: The Prototype of the 21st-century evangelical" sidebar in this chapter), an Anglican pastor whose missionary activities eventually created a group of Christians that met together outside of the Church of England.
- **Other denominations formed not due to doctrinal differences, but due to geographical considerations.** These include the Dutch Reformed Church in the Netherlands or the north and south churches of the U.S. during the civil war era (Northern Methodists and Southern Methodists). Over the years, some of these geographically-split churches merged together with others (the United Methodist Church).
- **Denominations also sprung up due to ethnic and cultural realities.** The African-American churches that emerged during the 19th century are most notable.

REMEMBER

An adage among Christians is, "Major on the majors and minor on the minors." Biblically-minded Protestants are characterized by agreement on the majors (see the section "Examining Core Protestant Beliefs," earlier in this chapter), but by splitting along the minors. Issues such as how Christians should express their faith outwardly are less important than the major issues pertaining to salvation, but they're not insignificant and trivial and can't be simply brushed aside.

TO NAME OR BE NAMED

Some Christian groups have been stuck with names that people who disagreed with them coined. *Christians* is a label that the Romans first used to condescendingly refer to followers of Christ. *Protestants* is a term that the Catholic Church used when referring to the protestors within the Church. *Anabaptists* got their name too from their enemies, who scathingly were calling them "rebaptizers." But other groups, such as the Catholics, Orthodox, and Presbyterians were more proactive (or had better marketing departments) and got to choose their own names.

Protestants believe that individual Christians should follow what they believe the Bible says and find a church that's in synch with those beliefs. At the same time, they believe that no one church body has a monopoly on God's truth. The result is that the Church inevitably consists of multiple church bodies, not a single one. Still, these separate church bodies can be unified by majoring on the majors while allowing for differences on the minors.

Looking at More Protestant Labels

WARNING

If you talk politics, labels are a given. Conservative or liberal, moderate or extremist, left-wing, right-wing, center-wing, or chicken-wing. Although labels like these are helpful in identifying an individual's political tendencies, they also can be misleading and cause you to stereotype a person rather than understand their true position. Labels are popular in Protestantism, as well, in part because a denominational affiliation doesn't mean much these days. Because some denominations aren't strict on following their confessions of faith (see the sidebar "Confessing a church's beliefs"), the denomination name can mean squat. For example, depending on the particular local church they belong to, two Methodists may have wildly diverging beliefs on the cores of Christianity, due primarily to the issue of modernism.

Therefore, in spite of the risk of stereotyping, understanding these labels is helpful to better understand how Protestants identify themselves (though some people categorize themselves under more than one of these groups). These include the following:

- **Evangelical:** The term *evangelical* comes from the Greek word *evangel,* meaning "gospel." Back in the 16th century, early Protestants used the term to identify their core beliefs about the gospel and to differentiate between the Catholics and the "out in left field" Protestant sects. Traditionally, an evangelical is someone who believes in the five solas discussed in the section "Examining Core Protestant Beliefs" earlier in this chapter. John Wesley is a good example of what evangelicalism entails.

However, the term has also taken on a more specific meaning among American Protestants, so that not every Protestant is an evangelical. The more uniquely American usage is often closely associated with Christians who place emphasis on seeking to share the gospel with the world through evangelistic crusades and missions, being *born again* (meaning to be spiritually reborn by committing your life to Jesus and entering into a personal relationship with him), and prioritizing the issue of *biblical inerrancy* (a belief that the Bible is without fault).

- **Fundamentalist:** Started in the early 1900s, fundamentalism was a reaction against *modernism,* the secularization of society and the Church. *Fundamentalists* believed that modernists (or liberals, see the next bullet) were compromising on key components of the faith, including the nature of sin, the need for salvation through Jesus Christ, and the authority of the Bible. However, although the movement initially focused on "getting back to the fundamentals," fundamentalists took on the stereotype of Bible-belting, narrow-minded anti-intellectuals, a stereotype that still exists to a large extent today, particularly in the media.
- **Liberal:** Within the church context, a liberal is someone who embraces many of the contemporary views of the world (postmodernism, relativism, evolution, and naturalism) and looks at Christian faith through these viewpoints. As a result, liberals question the reliability of the Bible and don't consider it to be the authoritative Word of God in the modern world. They're also more optimistic about the ability of individuals to overcome sin, and they discount the possibility of miracles.
- **Charismatic:** *Charismatics* (which comes from *charisma,* meaning "gift") are Christians who "speak in tongues" — an intense spiritual experience that prompts a person to start talking in non-human speech. Charismatics also emphasize other spiritual gifts, including the ability to *prophesy* (highlighting biblical truths for a specific context), see visions, and heal people physically and emotionally. Although they once made up a small minority of Christians, charismatics have grown significantly since the 1960s.

In the past, speaking in tongues was deemed a fringe activity practiced in a few Pentecostal churches, but it's widely practiced today by a growing number of non-Pentecostal Protestants, Catholics, and even Orthodox Christians.

ORDAINING WOMEN

Although the original apostles were all men, women still played a vital role in the development of the early Church. Women served in various leadership roles in the Church, but they didn't serve as ordained clergy because of biblical teaching against that practice. Specifically, Paul instructed in 1 Timothy 2:12: "I don't permit a woman to teach, nor to exercise authority over a man."

Christians who don't support female pastors say that the issue is straightforward: The Bible teaches against it. They say that Paul's command still applies to the Church today, in spite of whatever's going on in society outside the Church. They're quick to point out that they believe that men and women are equal before God and that women can and should play many key leadership roles in the Church. However, they hold that God has specifically ordained men for public pastoral preaching.

On the other end of the spectrum, Christians in support of female clergy insist that Paul's words were specific to the Ephesian Church and point out other examples of Paul allowing women to teach (see Acts 18:24–26).

The Catholic and Orthodox Churches don't permit female clergy, but Protestant denominations remain divided on this issue. Most mainstream denominations — such as Episcopalian, United Methodist, Congregational, and some Lutheran — allow women in pastoral positions. Other more conservative denominations and nondenominational churches don't.

6 Islam

Contents at a Glance

IN THIS CHAPTER

» Getting an overview of Islamic origins, beliefs, and practices

» Referring to God as "Allah"

» Recognizing the attributes and names of God

» Understanding the role of the Prophet

» Testifying to God

» Discovering different Muslim branches around the world

Chapter 1
Approaching Islam

Islam isn't just a religion of individuals bound together for spiritual pursuits and guidance. Islam attempts to organize all aspects of human society. But some basic beliefs about God are shared by most — and, perhaps, all — Muslims. These beliefs or affirmations are based on what the Qur'an (Islam's holy book) and the traditions (called *hadiths*) say about God.

If you're familiar with Jewish (see Book 4) or Christian (see Book 5) understandings of God, you may find that Islamic views about God are pretty similar. Most of what Muslims say about God would be readily affirmed by traditional Christians and Jews. This contrasts with the situation in Hinduism (see Book 1), in which different people focus their devotion on different Hindu gods, while denying that any of these gods is the ultimate reality.

For Muslims, as for members of Judaism and Christianity, God is the only ultimate reality. God depends on nothing else, but everything else depends on God. To understand all that, in this chapter, you get a quick glance at Islam, what Muslims believe, how those beliefs diverge into various branches of the faith, and where and how many Muslims practice their faith around the world today.

Just like some Christians, many Muslims also capitalize God's pronouns. To honor that, those pronouns are capitalized throughout this Book.

Taking In an Overview of Islamic Origins

In about 610 CE, the angel Gabriel appeared to a man named Muhammad in the city of Mecca (in present day Saudi Arabia). Gabriel told Muhammad that God had commissioned Muhammad as His last prophet. The revelations Muhammad received until his death in 632 constitute the *Qur'an*, Islam's holy book. Muhammad believed that he was restoring and completing the original religion of humanity, that he stood in the line of the Biblical prophets who had also been sent by God to call people to submit to God.

Muhammad's contemporaries in Mecca worshipped many gods and rejected Muhammad's call to worship only one God. In 622, Muhammad and his small band of believers emigrated from Mecca north to the town of Yathrib, which the Muslims renamed Medina. That year would eventually be set as the first year of the Muslim calendar. At Medina, Muhammad established the first Muslim community.

In 630, Muhammad led the army of the growing Muslim community against Mecca, which submitted peacefully. By the time of Muhammad's death, two years later, most of Arabia had accepted Islam and become part of the Islamic community. Muhammad was succeeded by a series of rulers *(caliphs)* under whom Islam burst forth as a new power on the world scene. In less than 100 years, Muslim armies had incorporated most of the lands from the western border regions of northwest India in the East to Spain in the West into a single, great empire usually called a *caliphate*.

Gradually, the original unity of Islam was lost, never to be regained. The caliphate fell before the Mongol onslaught in 1258. Islam continued to spread in the following centuries, but new Muslim kingdoms rose and fell. By the end of the 17th century, the military power of Islam ebbed away and by the end of the 19th and on into the first part of the 20th century, most Muslim countries came under direct or indirect control of European nations. In the second half of the 20th century, Muslim nations gained their independence. Despite political and economic decline, the number of Muslims in the world increased rapidly in the 20th century, and Islam became, for the first time, a truly global religion.

Summarizing Islamic Beliefs

Muslims share many of the same basic beliefs as Christians and Jews, while differing fundamentally from Eastern religions such as Hinduism, Buddhism (see Book 3), and Taoism (see Book 2):

- God created the world and all that is in it.
- God established in His revealed word the principles by which to live, including concern for the poor.
- One shouldn't worship other gods, or money, or power, or oneself.
- At the end of time, God will judge all people.
- If a person had fulfilled the divine command, he or she will go to heaven.

God calls upon all people to submit to His will, as embodied in His revealed law. In fact, the word *islam* means submission; Islam comes from the same root as the word for peace. Islam is often thought of as the religion of submission to God. Basic Islamic beliefs are summarized in the Five Pillars of Islam (see Book 6, Chapter 4).

TECHNICAL STUFF

Islam is the name of the religion. A *Muslim* is the name of a member of the Islamic religion. The word "Muslim" means "one who submits to God." A Muslim isn't a Mohammedan, and Muslims don't belong to a Mohammedan religion because Muhammad is only a man, not a god. Muslims worship God and not Muhammad.

REMEMBER

Basic Islamic practice is summed up in the Five Pillars of Islam (read more about them in Book 6, Chapter 4). Muslims must confess that only God is God and that Muhammad is His messenger. They stop whatever they're doing five times a day to pray to God. Once a year, in the month of Ramadan, they fast from dawn to dusk. Each year, they give a defined portion of their wealth to serve God's purposes. And once in a lifetime, each Muslim who is able must make the pilgrimage to Mecca.

Affirming the Unity of God: Tawhid

Understanding the Islamic view of God is central to understanding the faith. *Tawhid* (unity) is the Islamic term that best sums up the Muslim understanding of God. Sura 112 (the Qur'an is divided into chapters called *suras* and verses), one of the earliest and shortest suras, is titled "unity" (an alternative name is "sincerity"), and because unity is so important, this sura is said to constitute one-third of the faith. Only the *Fatiha*, Sura 1, surpasses Sura 112 in importance. Most Muslims know this sura by heart, just as many Christians know Psalm 23 by heart. Sura 112 begins:

> Say, he is God, One.
>
> God, eternal.
>
> He does not give birth, nor was he born.
>
> And there is none like unto Him.

WARNING

This passage was directed against the people of Mecca, who believed that Allah (which nowadays is simply the name of God for Muslims, which you can read more about in the "Clarifying the Terminology: Allah Equals God" section later in this chapter) was one among many gods and that he had three daughters. To believe that God has a wife or children is to commit the sin of *shirk* (association), the worst sin possible in Islam. *Shirk* also occurs if one believes other gods exist and that they share power with God. Sura 4:116 says,

> God does not forgive associating anything with Him; anything else He forgives according as He wills.

TECHNICAL STUFF

As with the Christian Bible, certain passages in the Qur'an can be located based on chapter numbers and verse numbers usually separated by a colon.

However, Muslims extend their understanding of God's unity and the corresponding sin of *shirk*, which denies His unity beyond simply a denial of literal polytheism. Michael Sells, in his widely praised book on the Qur'an, points out four understandings of God's unity to which we've added a fifth that may help you:

- **The denial of *polytheism*** (a belief in other gods) and the denial of the association of other beings with God. Paganism and popular Hinduism, in accepting a multiplicity of gods, are guilty of association from a Muslim perspective.
- **The denial of absolute loyalty to anything other than to God,** including money, power, or possessions. Of course, most modern Westerners aren't inclined to cling to other gods in the literal sense, but many people put money, possessions, country, family, or reputation ahead of God, making these things into their gods.
- **The internal unity of God:** Not only do no other gods exist external to God himself, no multiplicity exists within God. Sura 112 wasn't originally directed against the Christian concept of the Trinity — one God in three beings (see Book 5, Chapter 1). However, Muslims easily expanded Sura 112 to include a rejection of the Christian concept of the Trinity, which asserts a multiplicity within the nature of God — father, son, and holy spirit.

- **The denial of the permanent reality of the self:** *Sufis* (Islamic mystics) understand Sura 112 to imply that because only God is real and eternal, the goal of spiritual development is a loss of a sense of self. Human egocentricity attests to the existence of something other than God.
- **The assertion of the uniqueness of God:** Nothing else is essentially similar to God. You may say that something is like God in some way — for example, human mercy is like God's mercy — but according to the great Muslim theologian Abu Hamid al-Ghazali (1058–1111), this comparison doesn't mean that human mercy is the same as divine mercy, even though human mercy reflects divine mercy.

TECHNICAL STUFF

Al-Hallaj, the famous Sufi mystic who was martyred in the tenth century, said that Satan was the most consistent *monotheist* (or a believer in a single god or deity). The Qur'an says that when Adam was created, God commanded all the angels to bow down before Adam. Satan refused to do this. Al-Hallaj said Satan was being obedient to God's command not to worship anyone other than God himself. Satan observed this commandment even when it meant his own condemnation.

Clarifying the Terminology: Allah Equals God

The word *Allah* occurs over 2,500 times in the Qur'an. Allah is probably a contraction of two words: the *(al)* and god *(ilah)*. Muslims regard Allah as the original god of the *Ka`ba*, the sacred shrine in Mecca, but in pre-Islamic times, the divinities worshipped by the Meccans were Hubal, the moon god, and al-`Uzza. Still, long before the time of Muhammad, Arabs knew Allah to be an important Arabic deity; in fact, Muhammad's father was named `Abd Allah, which means "servant of Allah."

REMEMBER

Today, in Islam and in the Qur'an, Allah is simply the name of God. In fact, Allah in Arabic is a direct equivalent of the word God (with a capital G) in English. When early Christians translated the Bible into Arabic, they used Allah wherever God stood in the original Greek and Hebrew. Muslims claim that Allah is the same God as the God of the Hebrew and Christian scriptures, thus affirming that Islam stands in continuity with Judaism and Christianity. Muslims believe that all three religions share the same God and the same scripture, but also believe that each, in turn, claims to reform, perfect, and complete what came before.

Christians and Jews naturally think of Islam as a religion, which originates later than Judaism and Christianity. Christians and Jews will also naturally think of Muhammad as the founder of Islam in the same way they think of Abraham,

Moses, and Jesus as the founders of either Judaism or Christianity. Muslims realize that the present form of Islam goes back to the prophetic mission of Muhammad in the seventh century CE. At the same time, Muslims believe that Islam is the original religion of humanity, which Muhammad was sent to restore. In the Qur'an, Adam is the first person to worship Allah/God. Abraham is the essential founder of the Muslim religion. The Qur'an tells the story of Abraham's rejection of other gods in Sura 6:74–79.

Understanding the Core of Islam: One God with Muhammad as His Last Prophet

WARNING

Central to Islamic belief is the absolute power of God. Islam is strictly monotheistic in believing there is only one God, who is omnipotent and merciful. Associating any human being or image with God is an unforgivable sin.

REMEMBER

Muslims believe that Muhammad was the last of a series of prophets that God sent to earth. Although Muslims respect the teachings of the earlier prophets such as Moses, Jesus, and Elijah, they believe that Allah sent his final message to Muhammad to correct the corruption that occurred after previous revelations. Like Christians, Muslims believe that their faith is the whole of God's revelation to mankind, and also its final expression. There is nothing more to be changed or added, in other words.

They revere the Prophet as the embodiment of the perfect believer and accept his actions and words as a model of ideal conduct. Unlike Jesus (more on him in Book 5, Chapter 1), whom Christians believe was truly God's son, Muslims accept that Muhammad was a mortal with extraordinary qualities.

Today, many Muslims insist that pictures of Muhammad are improper and against their faith. However, at one time, they created many images of important Muslim leaders, although none became holy icons, as in some Christian sects.

TIP

A passage in the second sura of the Qur'an sums up what it means to be a Muslim:

> Verily, righteousness is he who believes in God, in the day of Judgment, in the angels, in the Koran, and in the prophets; who bestows his wealth, for God's sake, upon kindred and orphans, and on the poor and homeless, and upon all who ask; also for delivering captives; he who is steadfast in prayer, gives alms, who stands firmly by his covenants once he has entered into them, and is patient in adversity, and in hardship, and in times of trial. These are the righteous, and these are the God-fearing.
>
> — Sura 2:177

At first, Allah was only the god of contracts who watched over travelers. As He became more important in the years leading up to Islam, He assumed other tasks. He became the moon god, a role familiar to Abraham, who grew up surrounded by the rituals for a powerful moon goddess. He also evolved into the god of sky and rain, a key necessity of life in the desert.

REMEMBER

In the view of Muhammad, Allah becomes God of the world, of all believers, the one and only who admits no other associates in the worship of him. This conforms with Jewish and Christian monotheistic views. Muhammad identified Allah as the one God.

The Prophet's mission was not only to proclaim God's existence, but to deny the existence of all lesser deities. The Qur'an regularly refers to Muhammad's adversaries in Mecca, swearing by Allah, invoking him, and recognizing his sovereignty as creator. That's because Allah, to them, was one of many gods, not the sole deity as claimed by Muhammad.

Conflict between Muhammad and the Meccan leaders arose because the people of Mecca didn't understand or allow that Allah alone should be worshipped. They insisted that if Allah had willed it, they would have refrained from believing in other deities (Sura 6:148). The Meccans believed that Allah was okay with their worship of other gods.

Muhammad's success changed that thinking forever. From Muhammad on, Allah was the one true god of Islam.

Testifying to God's Supremacy

How is one to know that there is only one God? How did Muhammad know? How were the people of Mecca to know? The Qur'an calls a proof of God a *sign (aya)*.

- **The Qur'an itself is a sign of God.** The individual verses of the Qur'an are called *signs*, but they're generally referred to as *verses*. More on the Qur'an in Book 6, Chapter 4.
- **The creation of the world is a sign of God.** Sura 13:2 says:

  > God is the one who raised the heavens without pillars that you can see and then seated Himself upon the Throne, ordaining the courses of the sun and moon. He regulates all affairs and sets forth his signs that you may know you're meeting your Lord.

» **The processes of nature provide additional signs testifying to God.** Sura 36:33 says:

> A sign for them is the dead land, which we bring to life and bring from grain, which they eat; and we make in (the land) gardens of palms and vines, from which we cause fountains to flow forth.

Rain falling on the dead land and causing it to turn green did, indeed, appear as a miracle in the desert environment of Muhammad's contemporaries.

» **God's concern for humanity is a further sign of God.** The most important expression of this divine care is God's sending of the prophets to warn people so they may escape eternal damnation, as in Sura 30:47, which says:

> Indeed, we sent before you [that is, before Muhammad came] messengers unto their peoples. And they brought to them the clear signs. Then, we punished those who sinned.

God also provides daily care for people: the night for rest, seas for transport, food to eat, water to drink, and relief to the suffering (see Sura 27:62).

» **Human reason and logic provides proof of God's existence and some basic knowledge of God's attributes according to theologians and philosophers.** The logical proofs of God offered by medieval Muslim theologians are similar to those offered at the same time by Jewish philosophers, such as Maimonides, and Christian theologians, such as St. Thomas Aquinas. Al-Ghazali, the most prominent medieval Muslim theologian, said that when you look at the intricate order of the universe, you can conclude that this universe must have a creator who is different from the universe.

Defining the Attributes of God

The *Throne Verse* (Sura 2:255) is one of the most famous verses of the Qur'an. It's part of a larger group of Qur'anic passages known as *passages of refuge*. The Throne Verse is frequently inscribed on amulets (to protect one from evil) and on tombstones. It reads,

> God. There is no God but Him, the living, the everlasting. Neither slumber nor sleep seizes him. To Him belongs all things in the heavens and the earth. Who may intercede with Him except with His permission? He knows what lies before them [people] and what is after them, and they do not understand anything of His knowledge except what he wills. His throne encompasses the heavens and earth; the preserving of them does not weary Him. He is the all-high, the all-glorious.

Even if one knows from revelation (the Qur'an) or human reason that God exists, people want to know more about God. As the Throne Verse shows, Islam shares with Judaism and Christianity the belief that one can assert certain things about God. Muslim theologians refer to these qualifications of God's nature as the "attributes of God." Through examination of Qur'anic passages that speak about God and especially those which list the various epithets (titles or names) of God, Muslim theologians such as al-Ghazali arrived at lists of the most essential attributes of God. Among these are:

» **Knowledge:** God knows everything.
» **Power:** God can do anything.
» **Will:** Everything happens according to God's will.
» **Life:** God lives eternally.
» **Speech:** The Qur'an is the eternal speech of God.
» **Hearing:** Nothing one says is hidden from God.
» **Sight:** As with "hearing" because God is everywhere nothing is hidden from His sight.

Other attributes are implied by these seven. For example, God's power includes God as creator. God's knowledge and God's will imply the idea of predestination — God both knows and wills who will be saved and who will be damned. God's hearing and seeing implies the attribute of God's justice in rendering judgment. For more on this, see the next section.

Going to Heaven or Hell: From Life to Death to Resurrection

One detailed sequence of events that did emerge early on in Islamic texts is the process regarding death, resurrection, and the final judgment. In this section, we summarize the typical sequence of events, but keep in mind that variations exist both as to sequence and details.

REMEMBER

Islamic portrayals divide the process into two stages: the first is that of death itself and the time in the grave. The second stage includes the sounding of the trumpet, the general resurrection of all peoples in the grave, and the final judgment and dispensation.

Dying and the grave

Muslims believe in an end to history and time at which point occurs the resurrection of all who have lived, the judgment of those now resurrected, and their entry into heaven or hell. However, most people die long before the Day of Judgment. What happens to them in the meantime? Are they simply dead? Do they have some form of intermediate existence in the grave? Do they have any contact with the living? Even where the scriptures have little to say, tradition will supply answers to these questions.

The series of steps is a sequential one, although different traditions may slightly vary both sequence and details.

1. **Forty days before death, a leaf with the name of the person who is to die falls from the tree beneath the throne of God.**

   From this sign, `Izra'il, the angel of death, knows the appointed time has come. God determines both the length of an individual's life (Sura 6:2) and when the universe will cease to exist. When an individual dies, both death and the angel `Izra'il appear to the dead person, who asks, "Who are you?" The person may try to turn away but death (or `Izra'il) confronts them wherever they turn. The two angels who have recorded the person's good and bad deeds show the person the record of their deeds.

2. **`Izra'il extracts the soul of the person from the body.**

   The dying person may resist, but resistance is futile.

3. **Satan tempts the dying person to abandon their faith, perhaps offering a cup of cold water to alleviate their discomfort.**

4. **The person is greeted by the grave, receiving perhaps a glimpse of the future rewards of paradise or of the evils of hell, depending on the future destiny of the person.**

   The grave is a place of darkness and isolation, containing unpleasant insects and reptiles.

5. **The person may then attempt a journey through the seven heavens to see what lies ahead.**

   The condemned person is, of course, denied entrance through the gates of heaven.

6. **The soul is reunited with the body in the grave.**

7. **In the crucial part of this stage, the angels Munkar and Nakir interrogate the dead person.**

   The person, who by now has been buried by his family, is commanded to sit up. "Who is your Lord?" ask the two angels.

   Martyrs and prophets skip the interrogation and go directly to heaven.

8. **The person is punished in the grave — distinct from the final punishment in hell.**

   All those in the grave experience at least a minimal unpleasantness — the pressure of the grave — because all will have committed at least some deeds worthy of punishment.

9. **After usually no more than 40 days, the punishment comes to an end. The person then remains unconscious in the grave until the day of resurrection.**

   This period is called the *barzakh* (Sura 23:100) — the barrier or partition — and is similar to sleep. Theologians raised questions about where the person is during this time, whether spirit and body are together and whether the dead person has contact with or awareness of the living. (No single, consistent answer is given to these questions.)

Approaching Islam

The resurrection and the final judgment

You can think of the events of the previous section as the warm-up act. Now occurs the grand finale. Life, and even the time in the grave, is but a short prologue to an eternity in heaven or hell. On the Day of Judgment, God will conduct a judicial inquiry of each person based on his conduct when alive. Again, the following steps are sequential.

1. **The signs of the end of time appear.**

   Signs announce the approaching end. These signs include the reversal of the order of nature (Sura 81:1–14), such as the rising of the sun in the west rather than the east and the decline of moral order. After a time of troubles involving conflict between the forces of good and evil, God's representatives triumph over evil and the world comes to an end.

TECHNICAL STUFF

As in the case of other religions, the human imagination and the traditions are very creative in filling the gaps of information about what happens in the "last days" or the "end times." In a typical view, a figure usually called the anti-Christ (*al-Dajjal*, mentioned in the Qur'an as "the Beast" — Sura 27:82) appears. He leads people away from Islam during the period of his rule. Jesus returns to defeat the anti-Christ. After a relatively short period of rule according to God's will (as expressed in Islam), time and history end.

2. **The resurrection (*qiyama,* which means standing) begins.**

   The angel Israfil sounds the trumpet to announce the day of resurrection (Sura 69:13–18). The world comes to an end, and with a second sounding of the trumpet, only God remains — "all that is on earth will perish, only the face of God will remain," says Sura 55:26–27. After a period of time, the world is reconstituted, and bodies are reformed in their graves. Israfil is the first of the angels to reappear and Muhammad or one of the Jewish prophets is the first person to be resurrected (spirit rejoined to body). Then comes the resurrection of all the community of Muslims, and finally the resurrection of all others. Only God knows how long a period of fearful anticipation about their fate the resurrected will endure before the actual judgment takes place.

3. **The reckoning (judgment) occurs.**

   At the time of death, the book in which each person's deeds were recorded during their lives was affixed to their necks. Now those destined for heaven receive the book in their right hands; those destined for hell receive it in their left hands. The book, or the deeds themselves, are put on the balance scales of judgment and the result determines the final fate of the person. Good deeds weigh more than bad deeds and one must achieve a minimum total weight known only to God to be worthy of entrance into paradise.

4. **All move across the bridge that goes over the fire of hell and leads to the entrance to heaven.**

   For the faithful, the bridge is flat and broad and the crossing is easy. For sinners, the bridge becomes as sharp as a sword and as narrow as a hair while the passage becomes dark. They fall into hell. Muhammad meets his faithful followers at a pond on the other side of the bridge. The sweetness of the pond's liquid anticipates what the saved will drink in heaven. But the possibility remains that several of those who fell into hell will ultimately be raised from there into heaven by God's mercy (and perhaps with the aid of the intercession of Muhammad).

Facing the unresolved issues

One question leads to another. The outline of the events of the Day of Judgment left many important questions unanswered. For example, what happens to children who die at a young age before clearly formulated belief is possible? These are crucial issues for ordinary, believing Muslims.

» **Intercession:** Intercession refers to the concept that someone of exceptional merit may petition God to reduce the punishment that a believer would otherwise receive for their sins. Strictly speaking, the justice of God demands that each individual receive what he or she deserves, in which case intercession would be pointless. Some early Muslims did deny intercession. However, intercession came to be accepted in the mainstream as a manifestation of God's mercy. Muhammad is the primary intercessor. Tradition says that after the final judgment, Muhammad will encounter his people (Muslims) at the entrance to heaven. Some will ask him to intercede to remove the effects of their sins. Other prophets may also intercede.

- **Children:** If you're a believer but your children die young before they can understand and practice the faith, what happens to them? Popular Islamic belief came to affirm that children of believers would enter heaven. Some said all people are born with a natural faith. In the case of young children, this natural faith that hasn't entirely disappeared will suffice to get them into heaven. Others said that the faith of the parents would enable their children to enter heaven.
- **Spending eternity in hell:** Logic and justice seem to suggest that where one was sent at the judgment is where one would remain for all eternity. But mercy triumphs over judgment in Islam. The common belief is that all sincere Muslims eventually enter heaven despite grave sins (except possibly the sin of denying God). Some say that this mercy will ultimately extend to non-Muslims.

Some Sufis (more on them in the next section) and modernists of the last several centuries have emphasized a metaphorical understanding of the events concerning the final judgment and the final destiny. Other modernists argue that the Muslim view of death and resurrection is supported rather than put in doubt by modern science. Of course, even the strictest traditionalists in affirming the literal meaning of images of heaven and hell in the Qur'an and subsequent tradition would add that these are true "without our knowing how."

Dividing Islam into Branches

Islam has two main branches: the Sunnis and the Shi`ites.

- Sunnis constitute from 87 to 90 percent of the world's Muslims. The term *Sunni* refers to the traditions followed by Muhammad and the early Muslims.
- After Muhammad's death, some Muslims believed that his cousin and son-in-law, `Ali, should have succeeded him (as opposed to the first three caliphs who came after Muhammad). The term *Shi`a* refers to the party of `Ali, those who believed that religious and political leadership of the Muslim community should always remain in the line of `Ali and his wife Fatima. Because of disputes that arose about the line of succession, Shi`ites divided into a number of different groups, such as Ithna`-Ashari (or Twelvers), Isma`ilis, and Zaydis.

Sufis are another large group of Muslims. Sufism is Islamic mysticism, rather than a sect, like Sunnis or Shi`ites. So, a Sufi is normally also a Sunni (or more rarely, a Shi`ite) Muslim. Many Sufi orders exist just like many monastic orders exist in Roman Catholicism.

Believing in the Sufi manner

Sufism, with its emphasis on religious experience, provides a counterbalance in Islam to religious legalism and to theological dogmatism.

The *Sufis* represent a mystical tradition in Islam, seeking an alternative way of approaching the faith through a direct experience of God. Prominent throughout Islamic history, more than half of the male Muslim population was attached to a Sufi order *(tariqa)* in the 19th century. To the Sunnis, Sufism is considered to be an integral part of Islam.

Whirling dervishes, a group known to spin in religious ecstasy until collapsing, are members of this sect. But the early Sufis were *ascetics* (people who practiced physical self-denial) and wore coarse woolen garments. Most likely the word "Sufi" comes from the Arabic word for "wool," although other explanations have been offered. Western scholars of Islam, several centuries ago, first popularized the terms Sufi and Sufism. The Arabic term is *tasawwuf*.

What are some of the features which characterize a Sufi? The following list indicates some of the most important characteristics.

- **Asceticism, self-denial, and purgation:** This relates to renouncing the world's pleasures, denying physical desires, and purging evil traits.
- **Poverty:** "My poverty is my pride," says a Sufi tradition. Physical poverty is linked to asceticism. Spiritual poverty means desiring nothing for oneself, even paradise. Two terms often used for initiated Sufis are *faqir* and *dervish*. The first is Arabic, the second Persian, and both literally mean a "poor person."
- ***Tawakkul,* absolute trust in God, and *rida* (contentment or acceptance):** An acceptance of whatever good or evil happens because it all comes from God.
- **Love for God:** Nizami's version of the folktale of *Laila and Majnun* (1188) became for Sufis an allegory of the Sufi's love of God. Cut off from contact with his beloved, Majnun became a madman (the meaning of *majnun*), wandering the desert like a Sufi dervish, giving up all his possessions, searching for and crying out *(dhikr)* the name of his beloved. She died before they consummated their love, just as the Sufi's search for God finds its final fulfillment beyond death.

- **Abiding in God *(baqa)*:** *Baqa* is what remains after annihilation *(fana)* of self and world. This "goal," which only the most advanced Sufis achieve, is described as a form of experiential union with God, like the moth that is drawn to and consumed in the flame. Others say it is perfect knowledge *(ma`rifa)* of God.
- ***Tawhid* (unity of God):** Sufism understands *tawhid* to mean that only God exists. God is the ultimate reality or truth *(al-haqq)*. If only God exists, then everything in the world mirrors the reality of God.
- **Focus on the interior, spiritual, esoteric aspects of religion and religious texts in contrast to the exterior:** For most Sufis, this was a step beyond, not a replacement for, the religious ritual and law.
- **The master-disciple relationship:** Individual wandering dervishes existed from the early days of Sufism, but for most Sufis, spiritual advancement may take place only under the tutelage of one's spiritual guide *(murshid)* and master. This guide is called the sheikh in the Arabic world and the *pir* in Persian-Turkish-Indian regions.
- **The spiritual genealogical tree (*silsila*, which means chain)** that traces a Sufi's spiritual ancestry from their sheikh back through earlier sheikhs to Muhammad or `Ali.
- ***Dhikr* (recollection), the ritual invocation of a sacred phrase:** Remembering God is important, and *dhikr* is a practice that involves reciting certain prayers and sayings as a way to glorify and remember God in day-to-day life.
- **Stations *(maqams)* and states *(hals)*:** *Stations* are the rungs of the ladder that the Sufi ascends as they mature spiritually. *States* are temporary emotional and psychological experiences associated with each station. As an example, al-Sarraj (10th century) lists the stations (in sequence) as: repentance, watchfulness, renunciation, poverty, patience, trust, and acceptance. Others include gratitude, fear, hope, love, and knowledge.

Worshipping in Twelver Shi`ite fashion

In most areas of belief, law, and ritual, Shi`ites are the same as Sunnis, but most Shi`ites are "Twelvers," meaning they believe in twelve imams who were descendants from the Prophet.

The following sections look at the ways Shi`ites differ from Sunni Muslims.

Remembering Husayn at `ashura'

To an outsider, the *`ashura'* celebrations are the most distinctive aspect of Twelver Shi`ite worship. They commemorate the martyrdom of Imam Husayn, the grandson of the Prophet in a battle at Karbala in 680 CE. During the first two months of the Muslim year, but especially during the first ten days of the first month *(Muharram)*, the events of Karbala are reenacted. The celebration includes:

» Lamentation and wearing of dark clothes.

» Cries of "Ya, Husayn" (to remember and invoke the aid of Husayn).

» Blackening of faces and bodies.

» Erection of tents, pulpits, and special structures (*tekyeh* or *hoseyniyyeh*). Decorative tiles in the *tekyehs* illustrate episodes from Karbala.

» Begging for water (recalling the thirst at Karbala).

» Beating with the fists on one's chest. Men's shirts, which open on the side rather than down the front, make it easy to expose the chest.

» Self-mutilation by males with knives, chains, and razor blades on the last three days. First-aid stations take care of the participants' wounds.

Shi`ite rituals

The differences between Sunnis and Shi`ites in shared rituals are minor but still distinguish Shi`ites from Sunnis. Some differences are:

» In the call to worship, Shi`ites add "I attest that `Ali is close" and when prostrating, may touch their heads to a clod of clay from Karbala.

» Shi`ites combine the second daily prayer with the third and the fourth with the fifth so that they do three ritual prayers a day.

» On the *hajj* to Mecca, Shi`ites make one more circle around the *Ka`ba*. (More on hajj in Book 6, Chapter 4.)

Shi`ite thinking

Shi`ites developed their own brands of Islamic law, theology, philosophy, textual interpretation, and religious leadership.

TECHNICAL STUFF

The Twelver Shi`ite law School is called the Ja`farite School after the sixth *imam*, who is regarded as its founder (more on schools of law in Book 6, Chapter 3). So long as a living *imam* was in their midst, they gave divinely inspired and infallible interpretations of divine law. While the *imam* is in hiding (Twelver Shi`ites believe the Twelfth Imam is currently alive but concealed), the first two sources of law are the same as for Sunnis: the Qur'an and the *hadiths.* Shi`ites have four major collections of traditions *(hadiths);* the oldest was collected by al-Kulayni (tenth century). These collections differ from Sunni collections in containing additional traditions relating to `Ali and in including traditions (sayings and actions) of the *imams.* A group called the *Ashkaris* were strict literalists and believed that an ordinary Shi`ite shouldn't depend on scholarly opinion but only on the Qur'an and the *hadiths.* Their rivals, the *Usulis* (from the word for "root" as in "roots of the law"), prevailed and persecuted the Ashkaris. Usulis use reason *(`aql)* to apply and extend the law so long as the result doesn't contradict the Qur'an and the *hadiths.* For Shi`ites, the "door of *ijtihad* (interpretation)" was never closed. In contrast to Sunni Islam, the decisions of earlier legal scholars weren't binding on the present generation of scholars or believers, although by reason, they may reach the same legal decisions.

REMEMBER

Three areas (excluding rituals and the imams) where Shi`ite law differs from Sunni law are:

- A dead father's brothers have no share in the inheritance.
- The rights of the woman are more strongly protected as regards marriage and divorce.
- *Mu `ta* (temporary marriage) is permitted under Shi `ite law (based on Sura 4:24). It seems the major purpose was to provide a sexual outlet for men when away from home. In the contract, fixed formulas are spoken, a dowry is specified, and a time period is named after which the marriage ends. The woman doesn't inherit and the husband isn't obligated to provide for her. Any children go with the father.

Other Muslim sects

Islam, like Judaism and Christianity, is divided into multiple sects.

The four Sunni schools of law (called *madhahib*) — the *Hanafi*, the *Maliki*, the *Shafi'i*, and the *Hanbali* — are sometimes thought of as different sects, but are not. The schools refer to four great Islamic scholars who may have taught slightly different ideas but were actually students of one another.

The Shi'ites have one major school of thought known as the *Jafaryia* or the "Twelvers" (as discussed in the previous section), and a few minor schools of thought, known as the "Seveners" or the "Fivers." These names all refer to the number of imams Shi'ites recognize after Muhammad's death. The term *Shi'ite* is usually meant to be synonymous with the *Jafaryia*.

Shi'ite and Sunni communities are splintered into thousands of smaller subsects and cults with an incredible diversity of beliefs. The multiple sects have created friction within Islam, just as the various groups in Judaism and Christianity have bred conflict within those faiths.

What follows are descriptions of some of the larger Islamic sects, listed in alphabetical order.

Ahmadiyya

A messianic arm of Islam, the *Ahmadiyya* sect was founded by Mirza Ghulam Ahmad (c. 1839–1908) in India. He claimed to be everything from the biblical Messiah to Muhammad, Jesus, and the Hindu god Krishna. After his death and the death of a successor, the sect divided in two. One recognizes Ahmad as a prophet; the other sees him as only a reformer. Today, about 170 million Ahmadiyya Muslims reside mainly in Pakistan.

Ahmadiyya Islam is also associated with several Sufi orders, most notably the Al-Badawi order of Egypt, named for an Islamic saint who died in 1276.

Ismailis

An offshoot of the Shi'ite sect, *Ismailis* accept the Aga Khan, an honorary title dating back more than 1,000 years, as their spiritual leader and refuse to join other Muslims in prayer. The most recent Aga Khan is a Harvard-educated businessman living in Switzerland. The Ismailis left the fold not long after Muhammad's death by accepting one son of the sixth imam, Ishmail, as their titular head while other Shi'ites accepted a different son.

Ismailis gave birth to their own subsects, including one of the most famous groups in Islam, the *Nizaris.* Formed in the 1200s, they were Shi'ites who would commit murder to protect the interests of Ali's descendants. They fought with the Knights Templar, the power behind the Jerusalem throne, under a leader called the "Old Man of the Mountains."

Kahrijites

In Arabic, the name *Kahrijite* means "to go out." The sect earned that title by leaving the main sects almost as soon as the religion was founded. They simply disagreed with some of the teachings. For example, they originally supported the idea that any Muslim who violated Islamic law should be put to death. Other sects were not as harsh. As a result, Kahrijites believe the members of the main sects have stepped off the true Islamic path.

Kurds

Although not a sect, *Kurds* nevertheless are outside the mainstream because of their insistence of a separate country. Although mostly Sunni with a smaller portion Shi'ite, they inhabit land about the size of Spain that stretches from Turkey through Iraq and Iran.

Many of the residents there follow traditional Islamic and pre-Islamic practices. They also speak a different language related to Persian, not Arabic. Ethnically related to Iranians, the Kurds once had their own country and have endured conquerors of all stripes, including Sumerians, Assyrians, Persians, Mongols, Crusaders, and Turks. Eventually, in the tenth century, the Kurds accepted Islam.

They are prominent now because many supported the Americans in battles with Iraq and even tried to revolt against their Iraqi overlords. Their goal is independence in a new Kurdistan.

Wahhabis (or Muwahiddun)

Wahhabis are strictly traditionalist, an approach popular on the Arabian Peninsula. Founder Muhammad ibn Abd al-Wahhab argued in the 1700s that every concept added to Islam after the first three centuries after the Prophet's death was erroneous. He was objecting to a variety of new ideas that had seeped into Islam, including the worship of saints and sacrificial offerings.

WARNING

The term *Wahhabi* was first used by opponents of the founder, and is considered derogatory and not used by supporters of the sect, who prefer to be called "Unitarians" *(Muwahiddun)*. Also, the terms *Wahhabism* and *Salafism* can be used interchangeably, but Wahhabism is seen by some as ultraconservative.

Locating Islam on the World Map

All Arabs aren't Muslims, and all Muslims aren't Arabs (the original inhabitants of the Middle East who became the dominant population of many Middle Eastern and North African countries, from Iraq to Morocco). In fact, Arabs are only 15 to 20 percent of the world's Muslims. In contrast, South Asia (Pakistan, Bangladesh, and India) has 240 million Muslims. The Middle East has 315 million Muslims, but the two largest Muslim countries in the Middle East — Turkey and Iran — aren't Arab countries. Of course, Arabic is the language of Islam, and Arabic culture has left an indelible impression upon Islam, although most Muslims don't speak Arabic.

Muslims are concentrated in a continuous band of countries that extends across North Africa, the Middle East, South Asia, and then to Malaysia and Indonesia in Southeast Asia. Over time, through emigration and conversion, most of the population of today's Pakistan and Bangladesh became Muslim, while the majority of the population of India remained Hindu (see Book 1). At independence in 1948, the former British colony of India (including all three of the countries named) split into India and Pakistan, resulting in a massive displacement of the population as most Hindus in Muslim-dominated areas moved to India, while a substantial number of Muslims in areas with Hindu majority moved to Pakistan. (Later, a civil war in Pakistan gave rise to the independent nation of Bangladesh in what had been East Pakistan). Since 1948, relations between India and Pakistan have been tense, coming close at times to all-out war. Because a substantial number of Muslims remain in India, clashes at the local level have often broken out between Muslims and Hindus. Both religious factors (for example, some Hindus are offended by Muslims' using cattle for food because the cow is a sacred animal in Hinduism) and political factors (for example, disputes over Kashmir, a Muslim majority area that remains with India) play a role in these conflicts.

THE REALM OF ISLAM *(DAR AL-ISLAM)*

Islam understands its mission as extending God's rule over the entire world. Practically speaking, this means that the entire world should be under Islamic rule. Islam divided the world into Islamic and non-Islamic realms:

- The *dar al-Islam* (realm of Islam) is that portion of the world under Islamic rule. God's intent, according to Islam, is that the *dar al-Islam* should expand until it includes the entire world so that all people live according to God's plan and law.
- The *dar al-harb* (realm of war) is that portion of the world not under Islamic rule. God commands Muslims to bring all peoples into Islam (although not by forced conversion).
- Sometimes a third category is mentioned, the *dar al-sulh* (realm of truce), the portion of the world that exists in a treaty relationship with the *dar al-Islam* but isn't presently under Islamic rule.

Islamic scholars debated which geographical areas were properly considered part of the *dar al-Islam* and under what circumstances an area ceases to be part of the *dar al-Islam.* They also argued about whether an Islamic state should be at war with any adjoining non-Muslim state in order to bring it into the *dar al-Islam.* Another point of discussion concerned whether a person can properly live a Muslim life if they do not live in an Islamic state. Some said that those who, due to changes in political boundaries, found themselves living in a non-Islamic state should immigrate to an Islamic state. These remain relevant issues in Islam today in the light of — for example — large-scale immigration of Muslims to Western countries.

Dar (as in *dar al-Islam*) is difficult to translate into English. The root meaning of the Arabic word is "to surround." Before Muhammad, *dar* designated the circular encampment of a nomadic group. It can also indicate the housing complex of an extended family with its surrounding wall, in contrast to the house proper. Thus, "compound" or "estate" is perhaps the closest you can come in English to this word, which designates a type of dwelling area. *Dar* is frequently translated into English as "land" or "house." Thus, the concept of *dar al-Islam* is a bounded compound in which the entire Muslim community dwells securely under God's law.

IN THIS CHAPTER

» Understanding how the Arab world gave birth to Islam

» Welcoming Muhammad to the ranks of great religious leaders

» Developing two Islamic points of view

» Charting the rise of the Ottomans

Chapter 2
The Birth of Islam: The Prophet Submits to Allah

Years ago, a *Muslim* (a follower of the Prophet Muhammad) in a Western country would have seemed unusual. Today, the Muslim religion, *Islam*, is commonplace. *Mosques*, the Muslim religious buildings, exist in many major cities throughout North America and Europe. In fact, Islam may be the fastest-growing religion in the world.

Yet, Islam started in a small, out-of-the-way community lost in a desert. This chapter explains the origins of the youngest of the major monotheistic faiths and introduces Muhammad, the great prophet of Islam.

Islam: Born in the Desert

Islam is much younger than Judaism and Christianity. This *monotheistic faith* (meaning they believe in a single god) emerged in the Middle East with a distinct face and a solid historical base.

Islam arose in the deserts of the Arabian Peninsula, where ancient civilizations thrived and desert gods ruled the arid land.

But Islam changed everything. Because when Islam was born, it confronted Christianity, which had towered over the religious landscape as the controlling force. Around 391 CE, Emperor Theodosius closed the pagan temples and demanded that all Roman citizens worship one God and his son, Jesus (more on him in Book 5, Chapter 1). For the next 200 years, Christianity tightened its grip on people's lives, even as Goths and Vandals destroyed the Western Roman Empire.

However, in the swirling sands of the Arabian Peninsula, Christianity made only modest inroads. By the sixth century, the last of Abraham's offspring was about to be born (more on Abraham in Book 4, Chapter 2). The entry of Islam continued a pattern of monotheism begun with the Babylonians more than 2,500 years earlier.

All roads lead to Mecca

The Arabian Peninsula, where Islam originated, is mostly desert with sandy dunes, grayish camels, and white stone buildings. Here and there, the green of an oasis sparkles in the sunlight. Most of its residents (then and now) lived along the coast or in a few major cities that served as crossroads for goods heading west to Egypt or east toward Mesopotamia (present-day Iraq). Most of the inland residents were nomads, wandering through the dunes from oasis to oasis in a perpetual search for water and food for their herds.

REMEMBER

The city of *Mecca* served as the heart of the region. Mecca had long been a religious center of Arabic culture and would become the birthplace of Islam. Today, people sometimes call an alluring or popular site a *mecca* (for example, Graceland is a mecca for Elvis fans, and Forks, Washington is a mecca for *Twilight* book fans).

Travelers bringing goods along the desert route that led to Mecca also toted their religions. Books had been invented hundreds of years earlier, so salespeople didn't have to lug around heavy scrolls. Books were still rare and copied by hand, but at least they were available.

As a result, Christianity and Judaism became widely known among the pagan Arabs. Jews dominated some cities, such as Yathrib (later called Medina), while Christians populated many other cities. Both religions had penetrated Arabic culture by the fifth century CE.

The nomadic *Bedouins* (which means "desert" in Arabic) were pagans, believed in many gods, and did far more than shepherding their livestock from one oasis to another. Their most important achievement, however, was the conquest of Mecca by the tribe of Quraysh around 500 CE.

Meccans become traders with the world

The Quraysh turned Mecca into a city-state that was ruled by a council of ten chiefs who enjoyed a clear division of power. A group of ministers aided the chiefs with foreign relations, taking care of the temple, and of course, overseeing the military. The Quraysh developed solid institutions that made Mecca successful.

This organized system helped the Meccans create treaties with distant empires such as Iran, Byzantium, and Abyssinia and to work out pacts with the Bedouin tribes who carefully watched the caravan trade routes. The agreements created a lively import–export business through Mecca and gave residents the ability to travel safely. At the same time, foreigners felt comfortable coming to Mecca.

REMEMBER

The intermixing cultures throughout the Middle East inspired poetry and the growth of folk tales. They also opened the Arabs' eyes, leading to new ideas about the treatment of women, who were usually viewed with contempt by tribal leaders. As a result, women were allowed to own property in Mecca, had to consent to marriage, could divorce their husbands, and could remarry. Many of these ideas would eventually seep into Islam.

The Prophet Arrives

Muhammad, who announced Islam to the world, was born in Mecca, where religions and commerce mixed freely.

Tradition indicates Muhammad's name originally may have been Amin, which means "faithful" or "trustworthy," and was changed later. The moniker *Muhammad* was common then (and still is today) and means "praise" or "popularity." Muhammad was born into a reasonably well-off merchant family in the late 500s, but his circumstances changed quickly.

Historians can detail Muhammad's life because many people in his lifetime wrote biographical sketches. As with the Bible, the stories are often intermingled with mythology and *hyperbole* (exaggeration). Fortunately, Muhammad was also mentioned by non-Arab historians. The resulting merger of evidence creates a clear, consistent account of an extraordinary life.

Muhammad's early life

Muhammad's father, Abdullah, died shortly before his son's birth. So Muhammad's grandfather took him in. By custom, a Bedouin foster mother handled Muhammad's upbringing.

Eventually, Muhammad was returned to his family when he was barely beyond toddler age. His mother, Aminah, took him to his maternal uncles in Yathrib to visit his father's tomb. When Aminah died, Muhammad went back to live with his grandfather, who also died abruptly soon after. Orphaned and alone in a harsh culture, the 8-year-old Muhammad was adopted by his uncle, Abu-Talib.

Starting out as an average guy

As a child, Muhammad didn't attend school. He worked as a shepherd, tending the neighbors' flocks. He also traveled with caravans to Syria. Along the way, he was introduced to a hodgepodge of faiths, including Bedouin polytheism, Judaism, and a little bit of Christianity.

At some point, Muhammad opened a small business in Mecca. He couldn't read or write, but on his travels, he apparently loved to talk with the priests and rabbis he met at caravan trading posts. He must have remembered those conversations. The Qur'an, the Islamic holy text (sometimes spelled Koran) that contains his inspirational thoughts, includes many mentions of Old and New Testament patriarchs and events.

At age 25, Muhammad met and married Khadija, a wealthy widow who eventually presented him with six children. At that point in his life, Muhammad seemed unlikely to achieve greatness. Like Abraham before him, his early years were commonplace and of little apparent significance.

Beginning of a faith

As a young man, Muhammad began to have regular revelations, some apocalyptic in tone:

> And when the book of fate is open wide,
>
> And when the heavens are stripped bare
>
> And when Hell is set ablaze,
>
> And when Paradise comes near,
>
> Each soul shall know what it has done! — Sura 81:10–14

Many of the verses, which Muhammad said were dictated to him by the angel Gabriel, declare that mankind is doomed unless people follow the ways of God.

Muhammad accepted his role as the mouthpiece of God, but like Jewish prophets in earlier times, he wasn't sure how to respond to an inner tugging that called on him to proclaim his message.

Solitude leads to action

Troubled by the revelations but initially reluctant to face down the dominant pagan faith in Mecca, Muhammad spent days quietly thinking about the angelic messages while in a cave, supposedly imitating his grandfather. The tale parallels biblical accounts in which David, Elijah, and Jesus went to mysterious caverns and spent long periods of isolation in prayer (see Book 5, Chapter 1 for more on Jesus).

At age 40, again on a retreat in a cave, Muhammad was visited by an angel who announced that God had chosen Muhammad as his messenger to all mankind. Muhammad said Gabriel told him:

> With the name of God, the Most Merciful, the All-Merciful.
>
> Read: with the name of thy Lord Who created,
>
> Created man from what clings,
>
> Read: and thy Lord is the Most Bounteous,
>
> Who taught by the pen,
>
> Taught man what he knew not. — Sura 96:1-5

After delivering this divine message, Gabriel taught Muhammad how to worship God, pray, and conduct *ablutions* (a religious cleansing of the body). Muhammad shared this revelation with his wife but hesitated to speak out for another three years.

The faith develops: Introducing the Five Pillars of Islam

REMEMBER

Stories about Muhammad and his heavenly visitor began to circulate. In response, Muhammad began to talk first to his family, and then to his friends. Muhammad's message was simple: They were to believe in one God, in the resurrection of believers, and in a final judgment before God. Muhammad also removed all other gods from the Arab world and insisted *Allah* (the Arabic name for God) was alone. Muhammad encouraged charity and proper behavior. In this, he was duplicating Jesus and the Jewish prophets.

The basic rules of behavior were codified into Five Pillars of Islam (see Book 6, Chapter 4 for a more in-depth look at these pillars). The fundamental pillar requires followers to pray five times a day. All Muslims repeat a daily affirmation of faith, called the *Shahadah:*

> There is no God but Allah, and Muhammad is his messenger.

Anyone who cannot repeat this sentence wholeheartedly is not considered a Muslim. Anyone who says it three times in front of witnesses is officially a member of the faith.

Other pillars include

- **Prayer (*Salat*):** These are required daily prayers. The fisherman who Mark saw was fulfilling this requirement.
- **Purifying tax (*Zakat*):** Muslims are required to donate a portion of their income to the needy.
- **Fasting (*Sawm*):** Muslims must fast during the holy month of Ramadan. They eat only after the sun sets.
- **Pilgrimage (*Hajj*):** At least once in a lifetime, a Muslim is obligated to visit Mecca and pray at the holy shrine.

REMEMBER

Muhammad called the resulting faith *Islam* (meaning "submission"), which was based on heavenly dictates.

Like many ancient Jewish prophets, Muhammad was often scorned by those who listened to him and was the subject of bitter jokes.

Writing the Qur'an

Muhammad did something for which later scholars are grateful. He ordered his revelations to be written down and memorized by converts to his new faith.

Muhammad's revelations were dictated and collected in the *Qur'an* (meaning "recitation"), which Muslims believe to be the perfect words of Allah. The Qur'an also accepts Jewish and Christian sacred texts as divinely inspired and even encourages readers to compare the Qur'an's words with those beloved books.

- "If you have any doubt regarding what is revealed to you from your Lord, then ask those who read the previous scripture." — Sura 10:94
- "This is a revelation from the Lord of the universe. The Honest Spirit (Gabriel) came down with it, to reveal it into your heart that you may be one of the warners, in a perfect Arabic tongue." — Sura 26:192–195
- "Say, 'Anyone who opposes Gabriel should know that he has brought down this (the Qur'an) into your heart, in accordance with God's will, confirming previous scriptures, and providing guidance and good news for the believers.'" — Sura 2:97

The Scriptures referred to in the Qur'an are the Torah, the Psalms of David, and the Gospels of Jesus Christ (Sura 4:163; 5:44–48).

The Qur'an, like the Jewish and Christian sacred books, is divided into chapters (called *suras*) and verses. However, the Qur'an is organized by length, not chronologically. The longest suras appear first. No other writers contributed to the text, unlike the Jewish Bible where books are ascribed to David and Solomon, or in the Christian New Testament, where books are ascribed to the disciples of Jesus and to Paul, among others. (For more on Islam's holy text, see Book 6, Chapter 4.)

THE QUR'AN AND BIBLE

Although the Bible and Qur'an recount similar stories, they often contain contradictory details. For example, the Qur'an explicitly denies Jesus's crucifixion (Sura 4:157–158), while all four Gospel accounts clearly portray Christ as crucified. Muslims believe that Jesus is a prophet, and a prophet is always saved by God, not murdered by Romans or others.

One major contradiction in particular separates Muslims and Jews. The founder of Judaism, Abraham, had two sons, Isaac and Ishmael. In Jewish teachings, Isaac is the patriarch of the Jews (see Book 4, Chapter 2).

> And the Lord visited Sarah as He had said, and the Lord did for Sarah as He had spoken. For Sarah conceived and bore Abraham a son in his old age, at the set time of which God had spoken to him. And Abraham called the name of his son who was born to him — whom Sarah bore to him — Isaac. — Genesis 21:1–3

Jews believe that God made an agreement (also called a *covenant*) with Abraham and Isaac: If they worshipped him, he would protect them, bring them to a holy land (see Genesis 12:4 for one example), and make them prosper. (See Book 4, Chapter 2 for more on Jewish history.)

However, the Qur'an insists that Ishmael was the child of promise (Sura 19:54; also compare Sura 37:83–109 with Genesis 22:1–19). Muhammad said Arabs descended from Ishmael, giving Muslims claim to God's promised land. So Muslims believe that God's covenant was meant for Ishmael's descendants, not Isaac's. Since 1948, when Israel was created as a Jewish state by the United Nations, Israel and her Arab neighbors have displayed unceasing hostility toward each other, with major armed conflicts in 1948–49, 1956, 1967, 1973, 1982, 2006, and at the time of writing.

Christianity is caught up in this disagreement. Christians believe that Jesus came into the world through the nation of Israel, and according to Christians, he fulfilled the covenant that God had made with Abraham.

Muhammad Takes Command

As news of Muhammad's revelations spread, people began to join him. With a surge in membership came a violent reaction from authority. Officials tend to get upset whenever someone speaks out against the accepted faith.

The official punishment for a *heretic* (a person who believes or practices things contrary to the generally accepted doctrine) in Mecca was to strip the culprit naked and leave them to die in the desert. City leaders were eager to see how long Muhammad could endure that kind of treatment. He was reportedly subjected to verbal attacks and being doused with dirt. Other Muslims were stretched on burning sands, branded with red-hot irons, and imprisoned with chains on their feet.

Muhammad was spared some agony because he didn't introduce a new god. Instead, he said that Allah, who was worshipped among the pagan gods, was the only deity.

Nevertheless, the threats reached a dangerous level. He had few followers, and authorities were threatening a violent response. Finally, Muhammad ordered his followers to flee. Many did. Ironically, Muhammad's strongest enemies included his uncles. One, Abu-Lahab, took over leadership of the Meccans.

Despite the maltreatment, Muhammad refused to give up. In time, he began to envision himself as an apostle of God like Paul, who had carried the Jewish message of salvation to the Gentiles (more on him in Book 5, Chapter 2). Muhammad would take that same divine information to the Arabs.

After continued harassment and other troubles similar to the ones that the Bible says Jewish prophets and Christian apostles experienced, Muhammad and his few followers finally fled Mecca in 622 and set up a base in the northern community of Yathrib.

REMEMBER

That escape, called the *Hegira*, changed history. Muslims began to follow a cultural path that took them away from Judaism and Christianity. They even have an alternative calendar (see Book 6, Chapter 5). Muslims mark July 16, 622, as the beginning of the new era when, after years of struggle, Muhammad was welcomed to Yathrib as a king.

Muhammad wanted to advance the cause of his new and vibrant religion through conquest. Success followed quickly, including a triumphant return to Mecca, battles against the Persians who ruled the Holy Land, and a showdown with the Byzantine governor of Egypt. Muhammad even sent a letter to the Byzantine emperor, who ruled the last remnant of the great Roman Empire, asking for surrender (the emperor didn't give in).

TECHNICAL STUFF

Although Muhammad encouraged his followers to look at the Jewish holy texts, he did not gain the support of Jews living in Arabia. Disagreement with Jews started soon after Muhammad and his small band arrived in Yathrib. He thought Jewish residents would welcome him in line with other biblical prophets. Instead, one of their leaders, Ka'b ibn al-Ashraf, aligned himself with the Meccans and promised to help kill Muhammad. The basic problem was that the Jews liked their religion, no matter how many times they were conquered or harassed by other religions, and they rejected Muhammad's vision. He also banned alcohol, gambling, and games of chance. Jews could have done without the latter two, but wine was a sacred part of their rituals.

Spreading the new faith

Muhammad was busy sending out missionaries to spread the word of the new faith. As with the early Christian missionaries, the public wasn't ready to endorse his teaching. The Byzantine emperor's daughter accepted Islam but was promptly lynched by the Christian mob. When the leader of Palestine accepted Islam, he was promptly decapitated and crucified by order of the emperor.

A Muslim ambassador was assassinated in Syria-Palestine. The Roman emperor didn't care about this violation of diplomatic courtesy. Instead, he sent an army to battle the angry Muslims.

Considered the last and greatest of all God's prophets, Muhammad himself wasn't sitting back watching everyone else do all the work, however. He led a 10,000-man army into Mecca and conquered the region's key city. People flocked to his side, obeying the age-old view that whoever won the battle must have a stronger god. Muhammad didn't even have to leave any soldiers to guard the city against insurgents when he returned to Yathrib. Mecca was firmly in the Muslim camp.

The Farewell Sermon

Muhammad fought continual wars against non-Muslim forces for more than ten years. By 632, Muhammad met 140,000 Muslim pilgrims from around the Mediterranean region at the Ka'baa. This led to his most famous sermon, the Farewell Sermon, akin to Jesus's Sermon on the Mount (see Book 5, Chapter 1 for more on Jesus).

Muhammad told his followers to obey several important rules:

- Believe in one God.
- Do not use images or symbols.

- Treat all believers as equals.
- Treat life as sacred.
- Treat women better.
- Be sure to help the poor and needy.

REMEMBER

Muhammad insisted that the holy Qur'an and the examples he set of how to live according to Allah's will were to be the basis for laws and behavior in every aspect of human life.

Breaking Down from the Beginning: Sunnis and Shi`ites

On June 8, 632, Prophet Muhammad died. His impact, however, didn't fade. Nor has his presence waned in the last 1,400 years. Modern historian Robert Payne noted that:

Of all the great visionaries who at various times have come to torment an evil world with visions of Paradise, he was perhaps the most human, the most like ourselves.

Muhammad's death unleashed the fury of Arab armies driven by a religious ideal. Many times, Muslims simply approached a country as religious missionaries, only to find the people welcoming them as rescuers. Many of the lands were so badly managed that people were eager for these fiery horsemen from the desert to take control.

As a result, Muslims swept quickly across the Middle East, avoiding only Byzantium, the last remnant of the Roman Empire, and then leaping the Mediterranean Sea into Spain. They were stopped from conquering Europe by a Frankish army at Tours in 732. The Arabs call the battle site "the pavement of martyrs." This battle was a major defining event for the West.

As Arab armies marauded, the religion began to splinter because Muhammad had named no successor. The divisions within Islam echoed what happened to Christianity after the death of Jesus (see Book 5, Chapter 1). Islam was broken in two and never healed. Among Muslims, two factions developed

- **The Shi`ites,** who wanted someone from Muhammad's family to continue in leadership

» **The Sunnis,** who preferred that the most capable individual available at a given time take charge

You can find out more about these and other Muslim sects in Book 6, Chapter 1.

Choosing a leader causes strife

The Shi`ites and Sunnis went their separate ways from the moment Muhammad died. Many members of the faith nominated Ali, Muhammad's son-in-law, cousin, and early convert, to step into Muhammad's leadership role, a position known as the *caliph* (successor). Instead, Ali waited patiently as Abu Bakr (632–634), `Umar (634–644), and Uthman (644–656) served as caliphs. (After Ali finally became caliphs, these four became known as the four rightly guided caliphs.)

When Ali finally became caliph after Uthman was assassinated, he found himself locked in a struggle with Aisha, Muhammad's wife and the daughter of Abu Bakr. Aisha accused Ali of laggardly pursuing Uthman's assassins. After a fierce battle between the two sides, Ali won and forced Aisha into retirement.

However, Ali then had to fight Mu'awiya Umayyad, Uthman's cousin and governor of Damascus. Mu'awiya also declined to back Ali unless the assassins were caught. Once again, soldiers on opposing forces clashed. At the Battle of Suffin, Mu'awiya's soldiers stuck verses of the Qur'an onto the ends of their spears. It was a clever move. Ali's pious troops refused to fight them. Backed into a corner, Ali worked out a compromise with Mu'awiya. His gesture, although politically advantageous, undermined his popular support, and Ali was killed by one of his own men in 661.

Mu'awiya promptly seized the title of caliph. Ali's elder son, Hassan, wanted to do the same thing. His existence threatened Mu'awiya's budding dynasty, but not for long. In a pattern familiar from Roman history, Hassan died within a year, allegedly poisoned. Ali's younger son, Husayn, didn't protest openly, but bided his time. He was sure that the caliphate would return to him when Mu'awiya died. Instead, Mu'awiya son, Yazid, claimed the throne when his father passed away in 680.

Husayn then recruited an army, but it proved no match for his rival. He and his troops were annihilated in the Battle of Karbala. Husayn's infant son, Ali, survived. *Shi`ites* (meaning "party of Ali") rallied around him as a descendant of Muhammad, while *Sunnis* (meaning "custom" or "tradition") went with the strongest man, Yazid. The two political-religious parties have never reconciled.

To complicate matters, Muhammad's line ended in 873 when the last Shi`ite leader, Al-Askari, who had no brothers, disappeared within days of inheriting the leadership mantle at the age of 4. The Shi`ites refused to accept that he was gone, and still insist the toddler is merely in hiding and will return someday.

REMEMBER

Shi'ites currently view virtually all Islamic rule — whether by Sunnis or outsiders — as *illegitimate* (not the real thing), or *provisional* (temporary) at best. The well-known guerilla organization *Hezbollah* follows Shi`ite beliefs.

How Sunnis and Shi`ites practice Islam

First the good news for Islam: Sunnis and Shi`ites do agree on the core fundamentals of Islam and recognize each other as Muslims. Unfortunately, the sects have developed different ways of following Muhammad's directions. Many Sunnis believe that Shi`ites are more interested in the death of their early leaders than in the tenets of the faith.

This is best illustrated at *Ashura*, a ten-day Muslim holiday in which the Shi`ites commemorate the Battle of Karbala. Each evening a wailing *imam* (someone who leads prayers in mosque) whips the congregation into a frenzy of tears and chest beating. (Read more on it in Book 6 Chapter 4).

Sunnis, however, don't consider Ashura a major holiday, nor do they associate it with the battle. Instead, it celebrates several traditional events, like the day Noah left the ark.

The differences between the two sects run deep. Shi`ites, for example, don't believe Muslims will see the face of Allah after death, while Sunnis do.

The two sects have different calls to prayer and follow different rituals. To the horror of Sunnis, Shi`ites combine prayers, sometimes only saying them three times a day, instead of the prescribed five. Sunnis may say different prayers, too, drawing on verses written by Ali and Muhammad's daughter, Fatima, which Shi`ites consider the worst options, unless the writings support their claims that the descendants of Ali should rule Islam. Shi`ite Muslims also permit *muttah* — a fixed-term, temporary marriage — which is banned by the Sunnis, although it was permitted when Muhammad was alive.

For more on the Sunnis and Shi`ites, see Book 6, Chapter 1.

The Ottoman Turks Dominate Islam

Arab power did not last long. In 1273, a group of Turkish tribesmen under Ertughrul came to the aid of the *sultan*, or monarch, in a battle against Mongols, the invaders from the Far East. In 1288, Ertughrul died and was succeeded by his son, Osman — in the West known as Ottoman. The Crusades had brought Christian armies into Jerusalem in the 1100s. For two centuries, the Christians watched as Arabs battled each other. They knew they were no match for a united Arab front.

They were right. Within the next 200 years, the Ottoman Turks seized power in the region. Their approach was simple: They started with cattle raids and then bought land. Neighboring farmers paid *tribute* (a sum of money they were forced to cough up) to avoid being killed and then converted to Islam to avoid further payment. In that way, Islam continued to spread throughout the Middle East. This time, however, the Turks rather than the Arabs carried the Prophet's message.

The Turks built their capital in Adrianople, on the European side of the straits, across from Byzantium. After recovering from fresh attacks by the Mongols under Tamerlane (Timur the Lame) in the early Middle Ages, the Turks resumed their conquests.

In 1453, Byzantium fell, and as a result, all of Asia Minor now belonged to the Ottomans. By 1517, they controlled Egypt, Palestine, Syria, and Iraq. Attacks on Europe followed, leading to an unsuccessful siege of Vienna in 1683. That failure in the Austrian snows — essentially a stalemate — ended Turkish hopes for power outside Asia Minor.

Despite success on the battlefield, the Ottoman Empire was weakened for centuries by ill-suited sultans. Eventually, other countries labeled the empire "the sick man of Europe." The end came after World War I. The Turks were pushed back behind their current border. Modernized in the 1920s by Kemal Ataturk, the residents use a Western alphabet and have moved away from their Islamic roots.

The religion of Islam, however, continues to expand, reaching all areas of the world with the message once heard in a lonely cave in a desert.

IN THIS CHAPTER

» **Grasping the basic Islamic beliefs**

» **Looking at key issues of Islamic theology**

» **Discovering Islamic ethics**

» **Addressing some specific ethical issues from an Islamic perspective**

Chapter 3
What Muslims Believe

The Qur'an intermixes obligations toward God and obligations toward one's fellow humans. Some Islamic introductory ethics manuals for the layperson intermix morals and manners. For example, admonitions to sleep on your right side and not to lie occur in the same book. Therefore, in this chapter, when we speak of *ethics*, we're talking about duties toward other people and toward oneself — social and personal morals.

All religions place emphasis on beliefs and ethics. Indeed, most religions largely agree on the major moral do's and don'ts. What religion, for example, says it's okay to kill, cheat others, lie, oppress the poor, commit adultery, steal, or act harshly toward one's parents? Religions also share similar views about desirable and undesirable character traits — the *virtues* and the *vices* — for example, be generous and don't be stingy; be modest and don't be boastful. The major difference between Islam and some other religions is that ethics in Islam are based on divine revelation — the word of God.

In this chapter, we look at Islamic beliefs, ethics, and theology.

REMEMBER

Although some Western ethicists make a distinction between ethics (theory) and morals (practical guidelines), in this chapter, we use the two terms interchangeably.

Stating the Essential Beliefs of Islam

A well-known *hadith* (tradition) says that the angel Gabriel, dressed as a man in white, once sat beside Muhammad and his companions. He asked Muhammad: "What is Islam?" Muhammad answered with a statement of the five basic ritual requirements of Islam. The man then asked, "What is faith *(iman)?*" Muhammad responded with a list of five basic beliefs. The man commended Muhammad's answer and then asked a third question: "What is virtue *(ihsan)?* Muhammad replied, "That you should worship God as if you saw Him, for if you do not see Him, nevertheless he sees you." The man in white departed.

Gabriel's three questions correspond to the traditional Islamic division of religion into three parts — worship (*`ibada*, literally service), belief about God (*iman*, or faith), and ethics (*ihsan*, literally virtue and including right living). In answering the first question, Muhammad names the *Five Pillars of Islam* (see Book 6, Chapter 4), also sometimes unofficially called the *Five Pillars of Worship* or the *Five Pillars of Faith*. These five pillars are the testimony that only God is god and that Muhammad is His messenger, the five daily prayers, the observance of the daytime fast in the month of Ramadan, the giving of alms, and a pilgrimage to Mecca at least once in one's lifetime. The placing of this question first indicates the priority of these ritual obligations in the life of a Muslim. The ordinary Muslim accepts the basic beliefs of their religion but doesn't spend much time puzzling over them. Their conscious efforts as a Muslim is focused on active submission to God (worship and service) more than on intellectual assent to propositions about God (beliefs).

But if you ask a Muslim about their beliefs, they'll most likely respond with the items mentioned by Muhammad in replying to Gabriel's question about faith. The first three of these beliefs are also stated in Sura 2:285, which says that each Muslim believes "in God, His angels, His books, and His messengers." The Gabriel *hadith* adds two (in some versions only one) additional beliefs to the four in Sura 2:285.

TECHNICAL STUFF

These beliefs are sometimes referred to as the *Six Pillars of Iman (Faith)*. Belief in the books of God and the prophets of God is usually listed as one pillar, but some list it as two. Neither the Qur'an nor the *hadith* of Gabriel specify how to count them and the normal Arabic phrase is *arkan islam* — pillars of faith (without specification of number). But these are not the same as the Five Pillars of Islam that we mention above, which are sometimes unofficially referred to as the Five Pillars of Faith. Actually, different ancient variants of the *hadith* of Gabriel vary in the number of items included in the Six Pillars of Iman (Faith) and in how specifically they refer to each item of belief. But whether five or six, the content is the same.

Believing in God

"There is no god but God" — the first half of the basic testimony of faith *(shahada)* states unequivocally this simple, core belief of Islam. The theological term that expresses this concept is unity *(tawhid)*. *Tawhid* (unity) means a numerical oneness: God is one because no other gods exist beside God. God is one in that He doesn't manifest Himself in different beings. Islam rejects anything similar to the Christian concept of one God in three persons (Father, Son, and Holy Spirit) or to the Hindu concept of the manifestation of the God Vishnu in ten different incarnations. Christians who accept Jesus as a very important prophet of God but reject Him as being the same as God are called *Unitarians*. The Arabic word equivalent to Unitarians *(muwahhidin)* is another Islamic term for Muslims.

God is one because He has no associates — no wife, or parents, or children as gods often have in polytheistic religions.

WARNING

The greatest sin in Islam is "association" *(shirk)*, a term that occurs frequently in the Qur'an in reference to the citizens of Mecca who continued to worship other gods. To be guilty of "association" is to be subject to the penalty of death in this world and spending eternity in hell in the next world (although ultimately God is capable of forgiving even the worst sinners should he choose to do so). To accuse somebody of *shirk* is the worst accusation one can make against a fellow Muslim and a term of derision applied to non-believers. The person who is guilty of *shirk* is a non-believer, a *kafir*.

Some radical Islamic websites today and some decrees *(fatwas)* issued by extreme Islamic organizations refer to all non-Muslims as *kafir* even though the Qur'an allows a special position for Jews and Christians and doesn't accuse them of shirk. Radical Muslims today (and even in the earliest period of Muslim history) at times refer to other Muslims who don't share their particular beliefs or join their cause as *kafir*. It's analogous to what happened during the American Cold War with Russia when some people accused political liberals of being communists. Today, *kafir* is virtually synonymous with atheist. A *kafir* as atheist is one who by his actions actively opposes the will of God more than simply one who rejects the concept of God as a philosophical proposition. Does it seem strange that the same term can designate an *atheist* (one who does not believe in God) and a *polytheist* (one who believes in many gods)? Not to a Muslim. To a Muslim, one who believes in other gods denies the one true God just as the formal atheist who believes in no gods does.

REMEMBER

God is one because He is unique. God is "number one" and no "number two" exists alongside Him. Nothing can be compared to God because nothing is like God. Nothing can be added to or taken away from God that would make Him more perfect, wiser, more powerful, or more knowledgeable. He is perfect and the one entity (living or not) that has existed eternally and will continue to exist eternally.

While believing in God involves intellectual assent to the existence of God, more is involved in saying, "Yes, God exists." If God is what the Qur'an and Islam say He is, then to say you believe and not act on that belief is to demonstrate you don't really believe. If actions do not follow from belief, then one doesn't truly believe. Note that in the division of Islamic religion into worship, faith, and virtue or ethics, belief in God in the sense of submission to the will of God as manifested in worship of God is first in each of these three divisions.

Believing in God's angels

A number of Hollywood movies use the motif of an angel who comes to earth for one purpose or another, reflecting the fascination with angels in popular American culture. Traditional Islamic beliefs about angels are similar to the portrayal of angels in the Bible and in subsequent Christian and Jewish tradition. Eastern religions in general don't have angels, although various gods may exercise some of the same functions as angels in the Western monotheisms. The representation of an angel on a Christian card is of a human-appearing individual with wings. This is the basic portrayal also in the Qur'an where angels are mentioned more than 80 times.

While still basically humanoid, some angels, as described by tradition, are quite fearsome looking. Angels are an order of beings between humans and God. God created angels from light. They don't (normally) sin and have many functions as agents of God. In Islam, angels have three especially important functions:

- They have a heavenly function, praising God, carrying His messages, and supporting His throne.
- They may serve as an instrument of God in human affairs. Angels played an important role at key points in Muhammad's life; each person has two guardian angels.
- Several specific angels play a key role in the events beginning with the death of an individual and ending with the resurrection.

REMEMBER

Satan or Iblis is a fallen angel in Islam who was expelled from the presence of God when he refused God's command to bow down and worship Adam. Until the Day of Judgment (see Book 6, Chapter 1), God allows Satan to tempt humanity and spread mischief on the earth. Although frequently mentioned in the Qur'an, Satan in Islam isn't the powerful, anti-God figure that he becomes in Christian and Jewish traditions. Believing in angels also includes by extension believing in the other major category of non-material beings, the *jinn*. *Jinn* are minor beings who exercise some influence, good and bad, on human affairs.

THE JINN

Although the English word *genie* comes from the Arabic *jinn*, these creatures aren't likely to grant you three wishes. Many cultures have traditions of a group of beings, normally invisible to human eyes, who may cause good or evil for humans — for example, fairies, leprechauns, and trolls. Islam has the jinn, made of fire.

Jinn are intelligent beings, imperceptible to humans. In pre-Islamic tradition, they were spirits of the deserts and springs. In the Muslim tradition, they're more important in folklore and storytelling than in theology.

Jinn are capable of salvation or damnation and, thus, can be good or bad. A group of jinn once overheard Muhammad preaching (Sura 72:1–5). They believed what they heard and accepted Islam at a place called the Mosque of the Jinn in Mecca. Jinn helped King Solomon construct the temple in Jerusalem (Sura 34:12–14).

Jinn have their own tribes and kings. They are male and female, and they marry. Occasionally, they marry humans. And some people even thought Muhammad must be inspired by a jinn when he first began to recite the Qur'an and claimed revelations from God — a perception Muhammad rejected.

Jinn isn't the only term used of such creatures. Several other terms occur for the more troublesome or evil of these creatures. The most prominent are the *shaytans*; this term occurs over 100 times in the Qur'an and refers to rebellious jinn. They try to disrupt the prayers of Muslims. One *shaytan* or jinn sits on the shoulder of each person, tempts the person, and witnesses against him on the Day of Judgment.

Believing in God's books and in God's messengers

REMEMBER

Some list this as one pillar; others list it as two. These two items of belief can be considered separately from one another in that they don't say the same thing; however, they relate logically to one another in a way that's not true of the other pillars. The messengers are the ones who bring the scripture, so to believe in one implies belief in the other. Keeping this connection in mind, we summarize them separately in the following sections.

Believing in the revealed books of God

First and foremost, one believes in the Qur'an, but the "books of God" also include the Mosaic Law, the Psalms of King David, and the Gospel of Jesus. The revealed books are specific manifestations of the heavenly book — the "mother of the

Book." Although the question of the nature of the Qur'an was a hot topic in early Islamic theological debate, the consensus position for the last 1,000 years is that the Qur'an is the literal, eternal, spoken word of God. Just as God has always existed, so has His word, the Qur'an, always existed. When a Muslim recites orally the text of the Qur'an, they are actualizing God's eternal word. In a sense, this is similar to how a sacred mantra may actualize the power of a deity in Hinduism and Buddhism (read more on those religions in Books 1 and 3, respectively). Another way of putting it is to say that as in Christianity God is most fully manifest in Jesus (who is called "the word" in the gospel of John), so in Islam, God is most fully manifest in His word, the Qur'an.

TECHNICAL STUFF

The revelations to Moses, David, and Jesus (all considered prophets) come from the same heavenly book as does the Qur'an. Islam says that these earlier revelations were incomplete in that they didn't contain the entire heavenly book. Muslims also believe that Jews and Christians intentionally or unintentionally corrupted the earlier books they had received. Therefore, Muhammad was sent with an uncorrupted and complete rendition. Muslims believe this Qur'an has remained unchanged since the death of Muhammad. Therefore, no need exists for future revelations from the divine book because in the Qur'an, the whole word of God is already present. Many stories and characters that appear in the Bible also appear in the Qur'an although often with significant changes. Much that is in the Bible isn't paralleled in the Qur'an and much in the Qur'an has no parallel in the Bible.

Believing in the messengers who reveal God's books

The foremost messenger is of course Muhammad himself, as the second half of the *shahada* states: "Muhammad is the messenger of God." A messenger is one who brings a revelation from the heavenly book. God has sent only a limited number of messengers to humanity to reveal His word. Muhammad is also a prophet. God has sent many prophets to warn people of their sinful ways and of the judgment that they'll face if they don't return to worshipping only God. Because Muhammad revealed the perfect and complete form of the word of God (the Qur'an), God will send no further prophets and messengers. The Qur'an itself now stands as a warning and a call to return to the service of God.

REMEMBER

The Qur'an names about 28 prophets, most of whom occur in the Bible. A few references are uncertain so the precise number is uncertain. The Qur'an gives considerable information about some of these prophets and very little beyond their names about others. It mentions some only once and others such as Abraham, Noah, Moses, and Jesus numerous times. The Qur'an is shorter than the Bible, and it relates less about each of the Biblical prophets than what is found in the Bible.

Most of these prophets bring the same message: an exhortation to justice in dealing with others and a call to return to worshipping only God, along with a threat of judgment on the Day of Resurrection if the warning isn't heeded.

Some people called prophets in the Qur'an are prominent in the Bible but not called prophets by the Bible — such as Adam, Noah, Job, Lot, and King Solomon. Along with Abraham and Muhammad, Jesus is one of the most revered Islamic prophets. The Qur'an affirms his virgin birth and his relationship to his mother Mary, who is also highly respected. Most of the story of Jesus' ministry isn't included. In two points, the Qur'anic understanding of Jesus differs radically from the Christian understanding. Like all the prophets including Muhammad, Jesus is only a man. He isn't the son of God or in any sense divine. Islam also denies that Jesus was crucified on the cross and resurrected. While Jesus is very important, he isn't the savior of humankind.

Believing in the last day and the resurrection from the tomb

Muhammad's contemporaries in Mecca apparently didn't have a developed concept of an afterlife. *Fate,* a power greater than the gods, determined everything. If you think this life is all there is, then the temptation is strong to enjoy it while it lasts. If you think this life is only a brief prelude to eternity, then, with hope, you'll live this life in such a way to guarantee a happy eternal life after resurrection. Muhammad warned his contemporaries that sometime after death, the Day of Resurrection would occur. An individual's deeds had been recorded in a book and on the basis of this record, placed in their left hand (a bad sign!) or their right hand, the person would go to hell or to heaven. Islamic views didn't include either a purgatory for those meriting neither heaven nor hell nor a limbo for those who couldn't get into heaven through no fault of their own. Even most Muslims who go to hell will ultimately be admitted into heaven due to the mercy of God.

REMEMBER

The Qur'an presents many "snapshots" of hell but no detailed or comprehensive picture. Both hell and heaven have seven levels. Tradition develops the picture of the torments of hell in graphic detail. Generally, the punishment fits the sin. The picture of the tortures of hell is similar to that found in many religions. Fire is the basic feature of hell. Heaven is viewed as a well-watered garden in which the saved live a serene existence. The purpose of these images of heaven and hell is to motivate those still alive to live in such a way as to avoid hell and merit life in heaven at the final judgment. Although Muslims believe that all rests in the hands of God, most probably believe that as Muslims the mercy of God will eventually result in their entrance into heaven.

Islamic tradition provides a detailed picture of what happens between death and entrance into heaven or hell. Upon death, there is an examination of the person in the grave by two angels that may lead to a limited period of punishment in the grave (see more in Book 6, Chapter 1). Various events signal the coming of the end of time at which point all are resurrected and eventually face the judgment as to their final state.

Every religion faces the problem of the relationship between free will and pre-destination. Most people, at the gut level, feel that their actions in this world affect to some extent their fate in this world. If you don't study, you won't get good grades. If you goof off at work, you won't get promoted. Free will says that each person makes the decision as to whether or not to study or goof off at work. Religions extend this free will concept also to one's eternal destiny. Hinduism and Buddhism share a concept of karma — as you sow, so shall you reap. They also believe in reincarnation or rebirth. What happens to us in this life is simply the working out of the inevitable effects of the actions we have chosen in past lives. If you suffer in this life, that isn't punishment but simply the result of choices made in past lives. Western monotheisms (Judaism, Christianity, and Islam) don't usually believe in reincarnation. A person has only one life and the choices one makes in this life determine one's eternal destiny. To say that a person can freely make those choices is to affirm free will.

But Western monotheistic religions generally affirm that God is ultimately responsible for everything that happens. To say otherwise would be to diminish the power of God. Problem! How can one say that people are responsible for their own actions and still affirm that God is in control of everything? But if divine predestination is overly emphasized, then we can say that our bad (or good) fortune is simply the mysterious will of God. If God determines everything (good and evil), then we may as well do whatever appeals to us because God has predetermined the end result in any case. And if our sinful actions are due to a decision of God, made even before we were born, isn't it unjust of God to condemn us to hell for doing what He had pre-determined that we would do? This is a short statement of what is one of the thorniest theological problems of monotheistic religions but hopefully you'll get a sense of its importance.

This fifth (or sixth) belief affirms that God ultimately is responsible for all that happens. Some Muslims went so far in defending this position as to effectively deny ordinary cause and effect. However, the dominant position tried to defend both free will and divine determinism. The most important ninth-century Muslim theologian, al-Ash`ari, said that although God knows, wills, and determines what people will do, people acquire the responsibility of their actions by freely choosing what they were predestined to choose. We know that to many non-Muslim Westerners today, al-Ash`ari's "solution" will seem more like a semantic trick than a genuine solution. But before you criticize Islam too harshly for failure to reconcile free will with divine determinism, remember that no solution to this perennial problem is able to resolve the problem to the satisfaction of non-believers.

TIP

You've probably heard the expression "if God wills it." Muslims frequently say *inshallah* after any expression of what they'll do in the future. "I'll meet you here at noon tomorrow, *insha'allah* (God willing)." This means that although the speaker makes decisions, the real decision maker even for that meeting with someone at noon tomorrow is God.

The Pillars of Faith represent the starting point as to what a Muslim is to believe. A beginning Muslim accepts these statements on the authority of the Qur'an and of Muhammad. As a Muslim matures in their faith, their beliefs are deepened, and they come to understand at a more profound level the truth of these statements.

TECHNICAL STUFF

Theology *(kalam)* exists among Islamic scholars, but "doing theology" isn't central to Islam. Some Muslims even reject the idea of doing theology, saying that they simply accept the words of the Qur'an and the *hadith* at face value. However, as is the case in other religions, people who claim that they're simply stating the position of the scriptural texts rather than interpreting them are basically not facing up to the reality that other interpreters come up with different views on the basis of the same texts. As soon as one begins to explain a sacred text rather than simply quote it, one is engaged in interpretation and to claim otherwise is intellectually dishonest.

Explaining the Faith to Non-Muslims

The Pillars of Faith present a consensus of basic Islamic beliefs. Two episodes from the traditional biography of Muhammad (more on him in Book 6, Chapter 2) reflect how Islam presented itself to non-Muslims. In both accounts, matters of faith or belief *(ihsan)* are intermixed with items pertaining to worship *(ibada)* and ethics (also *ihsan*). Scholars disagree as to the historic accuracy of the events, but whether historical or not, they reflect an Islamic view of how to present the faith to non-believers or new converts. These narrative accounts supplement the more systematic lists of beliefs and worship in the *hadith* of Gabriel.

The first incident occurs about 616. Muhammad sent 80 of his followers to Ethiopia to escape persecution in Mecca. When the Meccans sent two diplomats asking the king to send the band of Muslims back to Mecca, the king called the leaders of the Muslims before him and his bishops and asked them to tell him about the new religion that had caused them to abandon the gods of their fathers. The response of the spokesman, Ja`far ben Abu Talib, gives us a picture of early Muslim preaching. As a summary of early Muslim preaching, Ja`far's speech recalls sermons of the apostle Paul in the New Testament such as that to the citizens of Athens (Acts 17:22–31). Ja`far begins by referring to Arabian paganism of the fifth century. He continues with God's sending of Muhammad, the demand to abandon the worship of many gods, to be just in dealings with others, and to follow the Five Pillars of Worship. Ja`far says that when he and some others accepted this message, the non-believers in Mecca attacked them and tried to make them abandon their Islamic faith. Because of this, they came to Ethiopia seeking refuge, which they trust the king will grant them. The king asked them to read a passage from their scripture and they read a passage about Mary, the mother of Jesus, from Sura 19. The king and bishops were so moved at these words that they wept. The two emissaries from Mecca then tried to lay a trap by telling the king to ask the Muslims what they thought about Jesus. Ja`far replied that Jesus is the slave, messenger, spirit, and word of God and that God put the unborn Jesus in the womb of the Blessed Virgin Mary. The king was impressed and satisfied with Ja`far's testimony and promised the Muslims protection while they were in his country.

REMEMBER

Ja`far's speech emphasized:

- Oneness of God
- Rejection of worship of other gods
- Concern for the poor and weak (orphans and women)
- Observance of prayer, fasting, and charity
- Honesty in word and in dealings with others
- Hospitality to others (a key virtue of Arabic culture and one which is also important to New Testament Christianity, See Book 5, Chapter 2)
- Avoidance of bloodshed
- Reverence for Jesus and Mary, thus linking Islam to the Biblical tradition

The second example of Islamic missionary preaching comes from the year before Muhammad's death, a year in which most of the remaining tribes of Arabia were accepting Islam and the leadership of Muhammad. The Banu al-Harith, a Christian tribe from the Yemen (in Southwest Arabia) had submitted. As they'd already made their confession of Allah as God and Muhammad as His prophet, Muhammad sent Amr ibn Hazm to instruct them in the faith.

REMEMBER

Muhammad told ibn Hazm to tell the Banu al-Harith that they should:

- Avoid evil actions
- Teach their people the Qur'an
- Know the joys of paradise and the torments of hell

» Fulfill obligations of daily prayer, purification, pilgrimage, and payment of alms and taxes

» Not fight with other Muslims but rather bring disputed matters to God (namely, to Muhammad as God's messenger) for arbitration

» Allow Jews and Christians the freedom to practice their religions

Expounding the Faith: Dealing with Difficult Faith Issues

One of the great contributions of Islam to world civilization was in preserving, transmitting, and developing the philosophical (as well as the scientific and medical) heritage of the Greeks that had largely been forgotten in much of the West. Through their translation of ancient Greek philosophical works, Muslim scholars became familiar with both the nature of philosophical disputation and the conclusions of the Greek philosophers. Some conclusions of Greek philosophers — including whether the world was created or eternal and whether there would be a physical resurrection of the body — were in obvious conflict with the plain word of the Qur'an.

The problem of the relationship between revelation and human reason is a difficult issue in many religions, but especially in the three Western monotheisms. Most Americans are familiar with this problem through issues that arise when the conclusions of modern science contradict statements in the Bible. One example is the account of the seven-day creation of the world (Genesis 1) in contrast to the position of most scientists that formation of the earth took several million years. Another related example that everyone is familiar with is the conflict between the Genesis account of the creation of humanity and the scientific Darwinian view of the evolution of the human species over time. Those who defend the literal truth of these Biblical accounts today often call themselves "scientific creationists." Some Muslims also reject the consensus of modern science in matters of creation.

Muslim philosopher-theologians may deal with such conflicts in three different ways:

» Attempt through the use of human reason to refute the conclusions of the Greek philosophers in places where those conclusions conflicted with the Qur'an.

» Reject philosophy because it conflicted with the revelation of God and then refuse to argue the issues. One should accept whatever the scripture says without even asking how it can be true.

» Accept the positions on these issues of Greek philosophy (as found in the writings of Aristotle, Plato, and the Neo-Platonists) and find a way to reconcile these positions with the Qur'an.

One possible way of reconciling apparent conflicts between reason and revelation — philosophy and the Qur'an — was to say that some statements in the Qur'an are metaphors or poetic language and not to be taken literally. Another way of reconciling seeming contradictions was to say that statements are meant literally, but that when applied to God they don't mean the same thing as in ordinary usage. For example, the Qur'an says God has a face and hands. Early Muslim theologians disagreed as to what this meant. Some said it was a metaphorical way of expressing the nature of God as a personal, active being. Others said the statement was meant literally and must be accepted as true but that Muslims don't know in what sense it's true when applied to God. This position of accepting "without knowing how" became the dominant Islamic position that continues to the present day.

REMEMBER

All sides in this debate accepted the authority of the Qur'an and quoted it freely to support their positions, but they interpreted the specific Qur'anic passages differently to support their positions. All sides also accepted the basic beliefs of Islam, although they may have understood them differently. For 300 years, debates continued until finally, in the middle of the tenth century, a general consensus emerged, and it was known as Sunnism, or *Ahl al-Sunna wa-l-jama'a* (meaning, "people of the tradition and the community"). This consensus position is especially associated with the great Islamic theologian al-Ash`ari (873–935).

Identifying Important Theological Issues

The Pillars of Faith include just the most basic Islamic theological affirmations. These affirmations are probably sufficient for most Muslims. However, other theological issues arose in Islam. We mention some of the important theological issues in this section. Some of these issues are long since settled. Others are still live issues today. Some issues may strike you as obviously important and relevant today. Other issues may make you wonder what all the discussion was about because the issue appears to you as either unimportant or even as a non-issue — but they were important issues in Islamic theology.

REMEMBER

Theology is important in Islam but not nearly as central as it is in Christianity, or as philosophy is in some forms of Hinduism. Islam is closer to Judaism than to Christianity in that it emphasizes other things (such as the law) more than it does doing theology.

Defining a true Muslim

In the past, some Protestants haven't regarded Catholics as true Christians and when Protestantism arose in the 16th century, Catholics didn't regard Protestants as true Christians (more on Catholic beliefs in Book 5, Chapter 4). Many Orthodox Jews don't regard Reform Judaism as a true form of Judaism and do not recognize as valid conversions to Judaism performed by Reformed rabbis (more on them in Book 4, Chapter 3). Even in ordinary conversation, one person may refer to another person (usually not in their presence) as not being a true Christian or Jew, usually meaning they believe the person doesn't actually live their religion. Islam, from the earliest days, debated the issue of who was a true Muslim.

One group that originated in the seventh century, the Kharijites, advocated a puritanical strictness that would exclude from the Muslim community anyone who didn't totally practice their religion — for example, someone who was lax in observing daily prayers. As it turned out, through most of its history and in most places, Islam has accepted as a Muslim anyone who claimed to be a Muslim. Even today, concern for the unity of the Islamic community *(umma)* prevails over imposing uniformity of belief and action in most places. The decision as to who was a true Muslim is left for God to decide on the Day of Judgment. And even a person who is condemned to hell on that day because of their sins may ultimately gain entrance into heaven if they have, while living, sincerely affirmed the *shahada*.

WARNING

Exceptions exist to this general attitude of tolerance and acceptance of all who say they are Muslims. Some Islamist radical groups take a position similar to that of the ancient Kharijites. Members of an extremist Islamist group assassinated President Sadat of Egypt in 1981, having declared him not to be a true believer even though Sadat was known for his personal piety and strict observance of Islamic law and ritual. The Taliban who when they ruled Afghanistan, forced their interpretation of Islam upon all people living in Afghanistan, even issued a decree that Hamid Karzai, the then-president of Afghanistan, wasn't a true Muslim and thus could or should be killed by a true Muslim. To declare someone who claims to be a Muslim not to be a Muslim is to say they are an unbeliever *(kafir)*.

Relating faith to works

The relation of faith to works was another important issue. Islamic texts speak of affirmation by tongue, heart (the seat of understanding), and limbs (that is, deeds). At a practical level, all three types of affirmation are required of a Muslim. But disagreements exist as to whether tongue and heart are minimally sufficient, or whether, without deeds, a person shouldn't be regarded as a Muslim.

Degrees of faith

A related issue is whether faith is an absolute. Some say you either have faith or you don't. The majority position rejects this understanding and says that the faith of a Muslim may increase and deepen or can decrease and become shallower.

Anthropomorphizing God

We've already mentioned this issue, which was very important in early Islamic theological debates, in the section "Expounding the Faith: Dealing with Difficult Faith Issues." When God is described using human terms (this is called *anthropomorphism*) are these descriptions meant literally? The majority position is "yes," but adds that such language doesn't necessarily mean the same thing when used of God as it does when used of people.

Created or eternal Qur'an

Perhaps the most bitterly debated theological issue in ninth-century Islam was whether the heavenly prototype of the Qur'an had always existed or whether God had created it at some point in time. The argument is similar to the crucial argument in early Christianity (as to whether Christ had always existed or whether he was the first of God's works of creation. A group called the *Mu`tazilites* argued in favor of a created Qur'an.

Why was this issue important to Islam? According to the Mu`tazilites, to say that the Qur'an was *eternal* (has always existed) contradicts the basic Islamic concept of the unity of God, which includes the belief that only God is eternal. The Islamic rulers of the time (the caliphs) tried to impose by force the Mu`tazilite belief that the Qur'an was created but weren't successful. Most Muslims since that time accept that the Qur'an has always existed although the specific explanation as to how this is so can get rather complicated. While the idea of a created Qur'an was ultimately rejected, some theologians recognized a distinction between the eternal Qur'an and the Qur'an as manifested in time and space. Read more about the Qur'an in Book 6, Chapter 4.

Knowing what is good and evil

Does God tell people not to kill because killing is intrinsically bad or is killing bad only because God says not to do it? If God said to kill, would killing be good? The answers to this question vary. Some say that even apart from revelation and scripture, an objective standard of good and evil exists that one can at least partially know through reason and intuition. Others take the opposite view and conclude that actions are good or bad only because God says they are. This latter position tended to prevail.

Rejecting Formal Creeds

Islam isn't a creedal religion. It doesn't make acceptance of a *creed* (a statement of a religion's core beliefs) a requirement of being a Muslim. It doesn't incorporate creeds into its worship. It doesn't convene groups of Muslim theologians to write and approve official creeds.

This doesn't mean that Islam produced no creeds, however. The *hadith* of Gabriel summarized amounts to a short creed (*ʿaqida*). The Fiqh Akbar I is another short, early "creed" attributed to Abu Hanifa (700–767). Ultimately much longer creeds were produced — some containing 100 or more belief statements. These creeds summarize the theological position of a particular scholar or school.

To give you a feel for the content and format of these creeds, we reproduce statements from several creeds written during the first 400 years of Islam. This short list isn't an effort to summarize what Muslims believe. To find out more about Muslim creeds and to read the major creeds in their entirety, we recommend reading W. M. Watt's *Islamic Creeds: A Selection* (Edinburgh University Press, 1994).

- "We [Muslims] do not hold anyone to be an infidel on account of sin, and we do not deny their faith."
- "He [God] has always existed together with His attributes since before creation. Bringing creation into existence did not add anything to His attributes that was not already there. As He was, together with His attributes, in pre-eternity, so He will remain throughout endless time."
- "Everything happens according to His [God's] decree and will, and His will is accomplished. The only will that people have is what He wills for them. What he wills for them occurs, and what He does not will, does not occur."
- "People's actions are created by God but earned by people."
- "They [Muslims] confess that faith is both word and deed."
- "People who innovate in religion or do as they please about it go to the fire of hell, in accord with the *hadith*."
- "The Qur'an is the speech of God, not something created which must therefore die out, nor the attribute of something created which must therefore come to an end."

Reviewing the Starting Points for Islamic Ethics

Humans are made in the image of God, and that image includes moral and intellectual capability. According to Sura 33:72, God offered the "trust" to the heavens, the earth, and the mountains. They were afraid and refused it. Only humans were willing to accept it. In other words, morality is a uniquely human attribute and, thus, morality is central to Islam. In contrast, angels can't sin and thus don't make moral choices. (Satan is a unique exception.). Moral action does not always come easily, as Satan and evil spirits *(jinn)* are always tempting people to do evil. According to Islam, people do have the ability to choose good and to avoid evil.

The principles of Islamic ethics

REMEMBER

The Qur'an has a strong ethical thrust. For example, it contains condemnation of the people of Mecca for their oppression of the poor (see Sura 107:3) and the orphans (see Sura 17:34; 93:9) and for cheating in commerce (see Sura 17:35). In the following list, we give what we regard as six basic principles of Islamic ethics:

» Every action has moral significance. Perhaps the phrase most often cited by Muslim ethicists comes from Sura 3:104, where Muslims are told that they're a people who should call all to do what is good and right and forbid what is wrong or dishonorable. This principle of calling to "do good and forbid evil" is a guiding light. Specific "rules" are important, but insight is required to apply the rules (or the general principal of "doing good" in specific cases).

» Moral actions are those which result in justice (*`adl*, see Sura 4:58). In concrete circumstances, an action may involve both good and evil consequences and then one must choose that action which will maximize the good and minimize the evil, resulting in the greatest degree of justice, according to the prominent 14th-century legal scholar, Ibn Taymiyya.

» Faith and works are both required. Sura 2:25 says,

> To those who believe and do acts of righteousness give the good news that they will go to paradise.

The moral choices one makes are serious as they play a role in determining one's ultimate fate — to heaven or to hell.

» Intentions are as important as deeds (as is true also in acts of worship). Sincerity is crucial. The trio of "heart, tongue, and deed" is frequently mentioned. Everyone agrees that it's not enough to advocate moral actions (the action of the tongue) but then act differently. An action done just for external compliance, says Islam, isn't nearly as good as one which comes from the heart. Something that comes from the heart will be accompanied by words and actions. If circumstances prevent accomplishment of the action, then commitment of the heart is still regarded as good.

» When it comes to doing what is morally right, having the proper character (consisting of virtues such as wisdom, concern for justice, modesty, and the avoidance of vices such as lust, greed, and anger) is as important as following a set of rules. In most situations, people act instinctively, in accord with their basic character, rather than by consulting a set of rules. The great 12th-century theologian al-Ghazali wrote extensively on the importance of cultivating virtue and avoiding inclination to vice. Sura 5:105 says,

> Believers, guard your own souls. The person who has gone astray cannot hurt you if you are rightly guided.

» Extremes should be avoided; follow the middle path, the way of balance. One shouldn't be arrogant or exalt oneself in the eyes of others. Sura 31:18–19 says,

> Do not be disdainful of other people, nor walk in arrogance in the earth. God does not love any person who boasts arrogantly. Be moderate in your pace and lower your voice. The most unpleasant of voices is the ass's.

Illustrative texts

According to tradition, Muhammad said, "None among you is a believer until he wishes for his brothers and sisters what he wishes for himself." This is similar to the Golden Rule, versions of which occur in Judaism, Christianity, Confucianism, and most other faiths.

On the other hand, Islam has no Ten Commandments (read more about those in Book 5, Chapter 4), although several Qur'anic texts do summarize basic moral requirements. Sura 23:3–11 says,

> Believers are those . . . who avoid vain talk; who are active in deeds of charity; who abstain from sex except with their wives, or whom their right hands possess. Thus they're free from blame, but those whose desires exceed those limits are transgressors. Believers faithfully observe their trusts and covenants and keep their prayers. They will be the heirs, who will inherit Paradise, where they will dwell.

Sura 70:22–35 has a similar list of good and bad deeds.

REMEMBER

Muhammad gave a summary of some of the moral duties of a Muslim in his farewell sermon on the pilgrimage to Mecca in 632. Along with worship and other obligations, he included the following moral instructions:

- Return any property belonging to others.
- Don't hurt anyone.
- Don't charge interest on money loaned to others.
- Husbands should treat their wives well, as they are partners together.
- Don't make friends with people of bad character.
- Don't commit adultery.

Sources for ethical guidance

TIP

Beyond specific ethical commands in the scriptures, other resources also offer ethical guidelines in Islam:

- The Qur'an is naturally the primary source, with its explicit laws and its moral principles.
- The traditions *(hadiths)* give guidance based on Muhammad's words and actions.
- Islamic legal scholarship, by the use of analogy and other means of argument, derives additional moral directives based on the Qur'an and the *hadiths.*
- Pre-Islamic Arabic virtues, such as honor, courage, loyalty, hospitality, self-control, and endurance, continue to be important in Islam.
- Certain people from Islamic history, such as the four rightly guided caliphs (Abu Bakr, `Umar, Uthman, and Ali). and Fatima (Muhammad's daughter), provide important role models.
- Philosophical reflection on issues of justice and ethics by the Mu`tazilites and others helped refine ethical issues.
- Works of Greek ethicists, translated into Arabic, are another source.
- God's attributes and names (see Book 6, Chapter 1) provide a model for Muslims to imitate in their actions toward one another. Such names include the gentle, the grateful, the just, the giver, the equitable, the loving, and others with ethical implications.
- Sufism cultivates a set of ethical values, including humility and poverty (see Book 6, Chapter 1for more on this).

- *Adab* (etiquette, manners) works were written for various professions and for ordinary Muslims, and they still exist today. Two examples are manuals of advice for kings on how to rule and for physicians on how to care for patients. Works of literature (also called *adab*) provide further moral exemplars.

Dealing with sins, major and minor

Some sins are more serious than others. Like other religions, Islam recognizes gradations of seriousness in sins. Serious sins are those that are most likely to land one in hell on the Day of Judgment. To Muslims, for whom this life is only a prelude to what comes after death, the distinction between more and less serious sins is very important.

REMEMBER

The 12th-century theologian al-Ghazali provides a good example of how Islam organized sins into different categories (although other theologians may express the distinctions somewhat differently):

- The first rank sins are unbelief in God *(kufr)* and idolatry (*shirk*, associating anything else with God, worshipping others in addition to God, see Sura 4:48). These two sins are often regarded as unforgivable and earn a person a stay in hell either permanently or, depending upon the grace of God, for a very long time.
- The second rank sins are against life and family (for example, murder and adultery).
- The third rank sins include wrongful appropriation of property. Perhaps sins of the second and third rank will cause a Muslim to spend some time in the top (and least painful) level of hell, but if they were sincere believers in God while living, they'll eventually make it into heaven.
- The fourth category is a catch-all, including consuming alcohol and lying. While not unimportant, these sins may not keep a Muslim out of heaven on the Day of Judgment.

Applying Ethics to Practical Issues

TIP

What do Muslims think about the hot moral issues of today? As in any culture, expert opinions on moral issues vary widely. Someone may tell you what the Islamic position is on some issue, without a hint that other Muslim scholars may hold a completely different view on the issue. Don't expect all Muslims to agree on any complicated moral issue any more than you and your friends agree on all moral issues. In the remainder of the chapter, we try to give you a sense of where Muslims stand on these issues — but don't expect that all Muslims would agree with our statement of the Muslim position on any particular issue.

Understanding sexual ethics

Ethics concern how people relate to one another, and because sexual relations are the most intimate of human interactions, sexual ethics occupies an important role in most discussions of ethics. To a non-Muslim, Muslim sexual ethics would probably appear fairly puritanical. Sex is good, but is to be expressed only within carefully prescribed limits.

- **Sexual intercourse is a gift of God and is good.** Islam doesn't believe that a *celibate* life (no sexual relations or marriage) is a more holy life. For Muslims, like any other action undertaken in moderation and with the right attitude, sexual relations can be regarded as an act of worship and should be preceded by prayer.
- **Sexual relations cause ritual impurity.** One should perform the major ritual purification after intercourse or the next morning before engaging in ritual prayer. Sexual relations involve bodily emissions and all bodily emissions require purification before acts of worship.
- **Sexual intercourse isn't permitted during menstruation.** In part, this is because contact with blood requires purification.
- **Impotency is a medical problem to be dealt with by the best medical means.** So the use of Viagra is okay if it doesn't lead to unreasonable sexual demands made on a partner.
- **Masturbation (the texts contemplate only male masturbation) is regarded as undesirable (Sura 23:5–7).** However, it's not clear that verse 7 actually refers to masturbation. The Hanbalite legal School allows masturbation in order to avoid committing fornication or adultery when the man is unable to marry.
- **Despite legal penalties for "fornication," Muslim cultures have shown tolerance toward premarital male sexual relations with females.** Premarital sexual relations by females, however, are strongly condemned and bring severe disgrace on the family. (We've never understood how the math works for a society that tolerates premarital sex on the part of young males but not young females.)

WARNING

Premarital sex by a Muslim woman may even lead to an *honor killing*, where in some cases even a woman who has been raped is considered to have shamed the family and a male member of the family may kill her to redeem family honor. Honor killings are contrary to Islamic law but nevertheless sometimes happen in some Muslim countries.

- **Prostitution is morally and legally wrong in Islam.** However, prostitutes exist in Muslim societies. Sura 24:33, along with various traditions *(hadiths)*, condemn forcing female slaves to serve as prostitutes (perhaps for the financial benefit of their owner).
- **Anal sex is wrong.** Islam teaches that some acts are contrary to God's intent as manifested in the created order — a concept similar to what in the West is sometimes called "natural law." To Muslim ethicists, vaginal intercourse between a man and a woman is natural, while anal intercourse isn't.
- **Homosexuality is wrong both because it's contrary to God's intention and because it's explicitly condemned in the Qur'an and the *hadiths*.** In Sura 26:165–175, Lot condemns the male homosexuality of the people of Sodom. Sura 4:16 apparently refers to male homosexuality and says the men involved should be punished but doesn't say what the punishment is. A few *hadiths* recommend stoning people guilty of homosexual practice on the basis that God destroyed Sodom and Gomorrah by raining down stones on the cities. However, while the Hanbalite legal School imposes severe penalties for homosexual acts, the Hanifite School doesn't. You can discover more about these schools in the nearby sidebar "Getting legal: The Schools of law (*madhhab*)".

WARNING

Homosexuality is illegal in some Muslim countries, but it's often tolerated if practiced discreetly. So you won't find many openly gay bars in Muslim countries, but you'll find a few.

REMEMBER

The Qur'an, *hadiths*, and historical records say little about lesbianism. Most Muslims would say that lesbian sexual relationships are sinful. Transvestitism and cross-dressing are also wrong according to Muslim ethicists. Sexual roles should be clearly distinguished and anything which confuses the distinction is wrong.

- **Pornography is condemned because it intentionally excites rather than constrains lust, and also because it degrades women.** In a frequently cited book, *The Lawful and the Prohibited in Islam* (American Trust Publications, no date), Yusuf al-Qaradawi explains that as a general principle, Islam prohibits anything which may lead to sin. Pornography, and less explicit actions which may cause erotic arousal (such as mixed dancing — that is, of a male with a female), are therefore prohibited as a safeguard.

» **Modern birth control methods (other than abortion) are generally accepted in Islam.** Having too large a family to properly care for is a legitimate reason to use birth control, so in the last 50 years the birth rate in a number of Muslim countries has dropped dramatically. Many conservative Muslims joined with Roman Catholics, however, in opposing recommendations for government-imposed birth control at a United Nations population conference held in Cairo in the 1990s.

» **Artificial insemination of the wife with the husband's sperm is usually permitted, although some disagree.** However, use of another male's sperm in the case of the husband's sterility is regarded as adultery. Surrogate motherhood is also illegal under Islamic law. A child born to a surrogate mother is illegitimate according to Islamic law.

» **Islam strongly condemns the use of sex to sell products**. You won't see scantily clad women showing off their wares at car shows or reclining men dressed only in Calvin Klein underwear on billboards in Muslim countries.

GETTING LEGAL: THE SCHOOLS OF LAW (*MADHHAB*)

Every Muslim takes one of the Schools of law as a guide in legal matters. *Madhhab* literally means "direction" and is sometimes translated as sect or rite. Schools aren't religious denominations. Regardless of what branch of Islam one belongs to, each Muslim adheres to one of the Schools. Each School has an accepted body of key texts and cultivates a strong bond between teacher and student.

Most Shi`ites follow the Ja`farite school, associated with the sixth Shi`ite *imam*, but here we discuss the four Sunni Schools that exist today (find out more about Shi`ites and Sunnis in Book 6, Chapter 1).

- **Hanifite School:** The Hanifite School is the most lenient of the four Sunni Schools, partly because of its use of "juristic preference" *(istihsan)* to moderate harsh rulings. It uses the Qur'an and *hadiths*, but it focuses more so on personal belief over strict rules and laws. It was the official School of both the Abbasid and Ottoman Empires. The Hanifite School, by far the largest Sunni law School today, is dominant in most regions that were ruled by these two empires, with the exception of Iran and Saudi Arabia. Iran, as a Shi`ite country, follows the Ja`farite school and Saudi Arabia follows the Hanbalite School. Afghanistan, much of Central Asia, and most of South Asia also follow the Hanifite School.

- **Malikite School:** The fundamental beliefs of this school include the Qur'an, the *sunna (*or the "way of the prophet"), the consensus of the people of Madina, analogy, beliefs or rulings from Muhammad's companions, and public interest, among others. Malikite School is dominant in West Africa and Northwest Africa, and it's prominent in southern Egypt, Sudan, Bahrain, and Kuwait.
- **Shafi`ite School:** This school of thought follows the Qur'an, the *sunna*, the consensus of scholars, and the thoughts of Muhammad's companions, among others. The Shafi`ite School is dominant in lower Egypt, southern Arabia, East Africa, Malaysia, Indonesia, and it's found in central Asia and in parts of the Caucasus mountain region, such as Dagestan.
- **Hanbalite School:** This is the most conservative of the four Sunni Schools, Hanbalite conservatism is evident in its ranking of the Qur'an above *sunna.* This School says that prophetic tradition may not be used to *abrogate* (or do away with) a verse in the Qur'an, and it relies on the precedent set by early Muslims. Although the influence of the Hanbalites remains strong, Hanbalite law today is dominant only in Saudi Arabia, Qatar, and Oman.

Outlining ethics regarding marriage and family

A Frank Sinatra song from 1955, written by Sammy Cahn and Jimmy Van Heusen and entitled "Love and Marriage," says they are linked like a horse and carriage. If you want one, you have to have the other. As the discussion of sex in the preceding section makes abundantly clear, sex and marriage certainly are supposed to go together in the Muslim world.

» **Marriage in Islam is a social contract with divine sanction (Sura 25:54).** A marriage celebration is highly recommended and almost always occurs, but the crucial religious requirement is the contract negotiated by the man and the male representative of the woman and signed in the presence of two witnesses (more on marriage in Book 6, Chapter 5). Elopement is contrary to Islamic practice because marriage is a public event (the celebration feast makes it public). Although prior romantic attachment isn't a basis for marriage, love is important in marriage. Sura 30:21 says that marriage is one of the signs of God's concern for humanity and that God "has put love and kindness between" husband and wife.

» **Marriage is encouraged at an early age — mid- to late teens**. Because the man is expected to support the woman, the realities of modern life, with extended education prior to having a full-time job, may lead to a somewhat later marriage.

» **Islam sanctions polygamy.** Some Islamic modernists say the Qur'an prefers monogamy but allowed polygamy because of the conditions of the early Muslim community. The husband can have up to four wives, but he must treat them equally. "Treating equally" refers to financial support of the wives, not to loving them equally.

Muslims living in non-Muslim countries that prohibit polygamy are expected to obey the law of the host country. Some Muslim countries have limited or even outlawed polygamy.

Women can have only one husband, and most Muslim men today have only one wife. In some cases, a wife may include in the marriage contract a clause that prohibits the husband from taking another wife.

» **Adultery is one of the most severe crimes.** The Qur'an mentions a punishment of 100 lashes (Sura 24:2), but a *hadith* (tradition) supports death by stoning. The *hadith* is normally considered to have superseded (or abrogated) the Qur'anic punishment. In either case, procedural safeguards ensure that the sentence is rarely carried out. A false accusation of adultery is punished by 80 lashes (Sura 24:4).

» **Divorce *(talaq)*, according to a well-known *hadith*, is the most detestable of the permitted actions in Islam.** The Qur'an recommends reconciliation with the help of arbitrators (Sura 4:35). A husband may divorce his wife, basically by saying "I divorce you" during each of three successive months. After the first and second time, the couple may reconcile. During the three months, the wife continues to live in their (husband and wife's) home, and the husband continues to support her financially during this period (see Sura 65:1). After the third time, the divorce is final and the couple may not remarry unless the woman has had another marriage (and divorce) in the interval (these details are specified in Sura 2:228–232, 236–237). Later, custom came to accept saying it three times all at once. This quick divorce was legally permissible but not recommended and lent itself to abuse by the husband. Modern legislation in some Muslim countries provides protection for the wife from arbitrary divorce by the husband.

For a wife to divorce her husband is difficult. Grounds for divorce by a wife include abuse or non-support by the husband, impotency, debauchery, desertion, chronic disease, insanity, or his converting to another religion. In the case of divorce, the woman normally gets to keep her dowry.

» **The husband is responsible for the support of the wife (Sura 4:34).** The wife is responsible for the care of the children and the management of the home. If she fulfills these duties, she may have a job outside of the home. Any income she earns is hers to do with as she pleases; she isn't required to contribute to the basic expenses of the family. Throughout Muslim history and in the majority of Muslim countries, many women have had various occupations.

- **Despite a strong egalitarian emphasis in Islam, the patriarchal family is considered the divine norm.** Everyone submits to God. Citizens submit to the ruler. The wife submits to the husband, and children submit to the parents. Mutuality is encouraged between husband and wife, and the husband normally defers to his wife in matters pertaining to the home and bringing up young children. Still, if a difference of opinion arises and a decision must be made, the husband has the final word (see Sura 4:34, speaking of the righteous women being obedient to their husbands.)
- **Children are a joy.** Children should honor their parents, and parents should treat each of their children equally unless extenuating circumstances exist, such as having a child with a disability. A *hadith* says, "Fear God and treat your children with equal justice." The parents are responsible for meeting the basic needs of the child — food, clothing, shelter, religious training, and education.
- **Islamic law doesn't allow legal adoption (Sura 33:4–5), in which the adopted child has the same rights of inheritance as the other children.** If a child is orphaned, it's the duty of the extended family to care for that child. A childless man may take in and care for an orphan. He can will that child up to one-third of his estate, but the child doesn't inherit in the same way a natural child would.
- **Grown children care for their elderly parents and show them respect.** According to Sura 17:23, "Say not to them a contemptuous word nor repel them, but address them with respectful words." The same respect should be extended to all the elderly.
- **The extended family is morally responsible for the debts of a family member who is poor through no fault of their own and for the debts left behind by a family member who has died.** However, the extended family isn't legally responsible for those debts and can't be made to pay them.

Exploring the role of women

The status of women in Islam is one of the points which most grabs the attention of Westerners and indeed offends many Westerners, who feel that women are second-class people in Islam. We share these concerns, but we also agree with Muslim critics who point out that up until 100 to 150 years ago, women had more legal and economic rights in many Muslim countries than they did in Western countries. Also, both Muslims and many Western scholars agree that at the time of the origin of Islam, Qur'anic stipulations about women marked an advance in the legal, social, and economic rights of women compared to what existed prior to Islam. A view we share is that the position of women subsequently declined in portions of the Islamic world not because of the Qur'an but essentially contrary to the intent of the Qur'an.

REMEMBER

Here are some considerations about women in Islam:

- **Islam claims it has a separate-but-equal policy regarding women.** Interestingly, some Hindu writers have claimed the same about Hinduism (see Book 1) and as in the case of Islam, argue that Western perceptions of unfair treatment of women in Hinduism (or Islam) is due to lack of appreciation of the complementary roles of women and men and the high respect in which women are held. However, we remain suspicious of any claims of separate but equal.
- **Women have the same religious rights and duties as men.** They must, however, remain in separate parts of mosques, and they can't lead a congregation in prayer if a man is present because of the belief that men take the leadership role in the public arena as women do in the domestic area. (Sufis are the exception because mysticism helps dispense with such social boundaries.)
- **Infant girls are to be welcomed.** Because male children were preferred in pre-Islamic Arabia (see Sura 43:17), infant girls were often killed (see Sura 81:8–9). The Qur'an condemns this practice. Prophetic traditions say a Muslim should rejoice as much at the birth of a daughter as of a son. However, cases of female infanticide undoubtedly continued, and as in many societies, traditional Muslim families have continued to rejoice at the birth of a son and regard the birth of a daughter as a burden, regardless of what their religion says they should do.
- **A daughter gets only one-half of the inheritance of a son.** Muslims say this is fair because the son has to support himself and a wife, while the daughter can do whatever she wishes with her inheritance, and she gets a dowry in addition.
- **The Qur'an (Sura 2:221; 60:10) explicitly prohibits a Muslim woman from marrying a non-Muslim man but allows a Muslim man to marry a non-Muslim woman.** The concern is to prevent a Muslim from leaving Islam. The assumption is that a woman is more likely to adopt the religion of her husband than vice versa.
- **Women are to be veiled.** The specific Qur'anic text applies to Muhammad's wives (Sura 33:53). Two other texts (Sura 24:31–32; 33:60) speak of the Muslim women covering their private parts and their bosoms and wearing a cloak when outside. The extreme interpretation is the woman must completely cover herself from the top of the head to the feet including the face. Many Muslim women understand the texts only to command dressing modestly and covering their hands but not necessarily their faces.

The dress requirements for women is an area of dispute within Islam. Over the centuries, head covering and veiling styles for Muslim women have varied considerably. You may have seen pictures of women in Iran, Saudi Arabia, and Afghanistan wearing outer garments which cover them from head to foot, perhaps with only slits for the eyes to see through. This garment may be a single garment or several. *Abaya, chaddor,* and *burqa* are not exact synonyms but all are cloak-like garments which cover the entire body. The *khimar* is a head covering that extends down to the breast and may be combined with the *jilbab,* which covers the rest of the body. *Hijab* is the general term for a veil of whatever type, whether or not it actually conceals the face from view. To affirm their Islamic identity, many women whose mothers or grandmothers rejected the veil, in cities such as Cairo, have now taken to wearing the veil once more.

- **Opinions regarding seclusion of women vary widely.** Extreme conservatives say women should remain secluded in the house, women should go out (including travel) only with their husbands or other male family members, and work environments and schools should be sexually segregated. But in most Muslim countries, you see many more women in public than this view would suggest.

Noting other ethical issues

In addition to the issues discussed in the preceding sections, here are some other ethical issues:

- **Alcohol, drugs, and gambling are all prohibited in Islam.** These activities cater to the vices of greed and cloud the mental faculties.
- **Islam traditionally disapproves of representational art as an effort to duplicate the creative work of God.** Statuary is prohibited because of its use in pagan worship. Children's toys are an exception because Muhammad had no objections to his daughter playing with dolls.

  Mixed opinions exist regarding two-dimensional art. Illustrated epics and stories have flourished in Iran, Turkey, Central Asia, and South Asia. Illustrations are also used in medical and scientific works.

  Photographs, movies, and television shows are acceptable (but not to all Muslims) because they involve mechanical reproduction of a real image rather than creation of an image by an artist.

» **Ecological ethics is a relatively new field in Islamic ethics.** Muslim countries participate in United Nations conferences dealing with ecological issues, such as pollution. Humans can use the earth's resources for the benefit of humankind but have responsibility as God's vice-regents *(caliphs)* not to wreak ecological havoc.

» **Another recent focus in Islamic ethics is animal rights.** Animals are placed on earth for human use according to Islam, yet they shouldn't be abused or made to suffer needlessly. They shouldn't be castrated or neutered. Islam forbids the use of animals for target practice or sports, such as bullfights and cock fights. Animals should be respected and cared for. Although Islam discourages keeping pet dogs, Muhammad was a cat-lover.

IN THIS CHAPTER

» Understanding the core pillars

» Looking at the holidays, rituals, and traditions

» Approaching the Qur'an as scripture and as God's book

» Interpreting and following the Qur'an

Chapter 4
Submission of the Faithful

Muhammad, the founder of the faith and its great Prophet, encouraged education and the accumulation of knowledge. He created many of the rituals, including daily prayers, as well as festivals. Others were added over time.

In many ways, Islam today continues to be a direct reflection of the ideas he presented to the Arab world about 1,400 years ago.

This chapter provides an overview of this robust and expanding faith by looking at traditions, holidays, daily practices, and Islam's holy book.

Discovering the Five Pillars of Islam

Each religion has sacred texts to base its faith on. Judaism stands on the Torah (see Book 4). Christianity has the New Testament of the Bible to support its beliefs (see Book 5). In addition to the Qur'an, Islam has *arkan ud-Din,* or in English, "pillars of faith." These are five religious duties expected of every pious Muslim.

SHI`ITES ERECT A FEW ADDITIONAL PILLARS

All Muslim sects endorse the Five Pillars of Islam. The Shi`ites have increased the total by adding four more:

- The *jihad*: This is a "holy war" declared by a religious leader (*imam*).
- Payment of the *imam's* tax: This is a tax to support the religious leader in addition to tithing.
- Encouragement of good deeds.
- Prevention of evil.

REMEMBER

The five pillars are cited throughout the Qur'an on an individual basis, but Muhammad (see Book 6, Chapter 1) listed them together when he was asked to define Islam. After his death, Islamic leaders designated these pillars as "anchoring points" within the Muslim community. Believers who obey the five pillars are thought to receive rewards both in this life and in the afterlife. The pillars are a ready-made formula for becoming a believer, and they make transitioning to the faith very accessible.

First pillar: Creed (Shahadah)

A Muslim must make a public declaration of the faith (called a *Shahadah*) at least once in a lifetime, although most Muslims recite it daily. Here's the declaration in Arabic:

> Ashhadu al-la ilaha illa-llah wa ashhadu anna Muhammadar rasulu-llah.

In English:

> There is no God but Allah, and Muhammad is his messenger.

TIP

Converts can join the Muslim community simply by reciting the *Shahadah* in complete sincerity. The vow is also echoed in the regular call to prayer, included in the daily ritual prayer, and recited in the moments before death.

Second pillar: Prayer (Salat)

Muslims must pray five times daily — at dawn, noon, midafternoon, sunset, and nightfall. The prayers (*salat* in Arabic) always contain verses from the Qur'an and must be said in Arabic. Muslims believe that prayer provides a direct link between the worshipper and God.

The Muslim holy day is Friday, when congregations gather just past noon in a mosque. An *imam*, or religious leader, gives a sermon and leads the congregation in prayer. As a result, in most Muslim countries, the weekend begins on Friday, not on Saturday as in Western countries.

REMEMBER

The three holiest places of worship in the Islamic world are

- The Mosque of the *Ka'ba* in Mecca
- The Mosque of the Prophet Muhammad in Medina
- The Masjid Aqsa, adjacent to the Dome of the Rock in Jerusalem

Unlike Christian churches and Jewish synagogues, mosques are nondenominational. Traditional Friday prayer services are largely similar in every sect, and Muslims of any background are welcome to attend services at any mosque. Still, some Sunnis only will attend a Sunni mosque. Some Shi`ites feel the same way.

WHY PRAY SO OFTEN?

Muslims are obligated to pray many times each day — the number varies depending on the sect. The inspiration for that requirement may have come from a Catholic saint, Saint Benedict, who set up the rules for monks and died shortly after Muhammad was born.

Benedict ordered prayers seven times a day. He wanted the monks to focus on their religious duties. However, as an unexpected side effect, the bells ringing for prayers served as a clock. No one had wristwatches in those days. Many communities relied on the calls to prayer to know the time of day.

Today, the only vestige of Benedict's required prayers in Christianity is Vespers, the prayers at dusk.

Where do Muslims pray?

Muslims may perform *salat* almost anywhere. At the appropriate time, people stop whatever they're doing and face Mecca, which is the religious center of the Muslim cosmos in what is now Saudi Arabia. The direction toward Mecca is called the *qibla*.

Mosques are planned so that one wall, the *qibla wall*, faces Mecca. In the interior of the mosque, an area on the *qibla* wall — often a semi-circular arched recess — designates the direction toward Mecca and thus the direction to face when lining up for prayer. This recess is the *mihrab*, or prayer niche.

Before *salat*, people take off their shoes. If they're not in a mosque, they unroll a prayer rug upon which to perform *salat*. Usually the prayer rug portrays the Grand Mosque of Mecca, Islam's holiest mosque. If one has no prayer rug, spreading out a newspaper will do.

While a Muslim can pray alone, Muslims prefer to perform *salat* in the presence of others Muslims. Muslims line up in orderly rows, while one person stands in front and serves as *imam* (that is, prayer leader). In accord with the general emphasis on male leadership in public arenas — a tradition which some Muslim women object to and say isn't grounded in the Qur'an — a woman can act as prayer leader for other women, but not for men.

Calling to prayer (adhan)

Each time of prayer is announced with the call to prayer, known as *adhan*. In the past, about 15 minutes before the designated time of prayer, the *muezzin* (the person who issues the call to prayer) would ascend the *minaret*, a tall tower that often adorns or adjoins a mosque as a steeple may adorn a church. From there, the call was recited.

While *muezzins* still exist, today the call is frequently sounded by a recording broadcast from loudspeakers located on the minaret or at the top of a multi-story building. Inside the mosque, the call is repeated in a variant form (the *iqama*), ending with the words, "the prayer is established" to indicate the actual start of the *salat* ritual.

Doing the first rak`a (bowing)

REMEMBER

Depending on which of the five prayer times is involved, the actual prayer ritual consists of two to four cycles of bowings *(rak`as)* — a sequence of prescribed movements and accompanying words. In the course of performing the five daily prayers, a worshipper completes a minimum of 17 *rak`as*. In a congregational *salat* led by an *imam* (prayer leader), much of what the individual worshippers say is spoken silently or in a very low voice. Although you may see minor variations in body position and what is said, each *rak`a* includes the following steps (preceded by each individual having explicitly avowed the intention to perform *salat*):

1. **Standing with feet slightly apart, the person raises their hands to head level, and with palms facing outward and forward says the *takbir,* an Arabic phrase meaning "God is greater," aloud. Moving their hands down to their sides, they pronounce the first Sura *(Fatiha)* and one other passage from the Qur'an.**

   This first position ends with another *takbir.*

2. **Bowing, with hands on the knees, the worshipper says three times: "Glory to God the Almighty."**

3. **Standing once again, they say, "God hears those who praise Him. O our lord, Praise be to you," ending with another *takbir.***

4. **The worshipper prostrates themself, their forehead touching the ground with both hands flat on the ground, and says, "Praised be my Lord, most high; praise be to Him" (three times), ending with a *takbir.***

   After years of doing *salat,* a person may acquire a visible mark on the forehead, which is regarded as an indication of piety.

5. **They sit up with their left foot and leg folded under them and their right leg straight back from knee to foot with toes touching floor and heel upright (it sounds much more complicated than it is).**

   Some Muslims pronounce a short petition for forgiveness of sins, and all utter another *takbir.*

6. **To complete the *rak`a*, the worshipper makes a second prostration and returns to a sitting position.**

Trying to describe the *salat* ritual without making it sound dry and artificial is like trying to describe the sequence of actions involved when you greet someone with a handshake. When do I extend my hand? Do I wait for the other person to extend their hand first? How do I clasp the other's hand? What words accompany all this? But you shake hands without having to think of the details, and this is also true for Muslims doing *salat*. They can complete a *rak`a* in a few minutes, without thinking about the details.

While the written description sounds somewhat rigid, you find some flexibility in practice. Children may be present and moving about. Some people arrive after the beginning of the first *rak`a* and catch up silently or repeat the missed *rak`a* at the end of *salat.*

TIP

To appreciate the *salat*, you must observe it. Many mosques in the United States and some other countries willingly open their services to non-Muslims, embracing you (literally!) cordially before and after and making their best efforts to help you feel comfortable. Call the mosque first to ask about attending. You'll probably be seated toward the rear (or with the women, if you're female) and be free to observe but not be expected to participate.

Adding additional rak`as and voluntary prayers

Remember that each of the five daily prayers involves two to four *rak`as*. Before the second and any subsequent *rak`as*, the worshipper stands up, pronounces a *takbir*, and begins the next cycle. At the end of the second and final *rak`as*, a formulaic greeting (the *tahiyya*) asks God's blessings on Muhammad. At the end of all the cycles of a *salat*, the worshipper sits back and recites the witnessing *(tashahhud)*, followed by invocation of blessing on Muhammad and Abraham. After a final prayer for peace, they turn their head to the right and then to the left, saying "peace be upon you" *(al-salamu `alaykum)*. According to popular belief, they are addressing not only the people on either side but also the angels who watch over them as they pray. This concludes the formal, obligatory *salat*.

Frequently, the worshipper then says several personal, individual prayers *(du`a)*, and then arises and says *al-salamu `alaykum* to the people near them. They may then perform an additional voluntary two *rak`as*.

An example of a voluntary prayer at the end of *salat* is:

> There is no God except God, the One. He has no partners. To Him belongs sovereignty and to Him belongs praise. He is all-powerful over everything. O God! None can deny that which you give and none can give that which you deny. The greatness of the great shall not prevail against you.

Of course, voluntary prayers are also used on many other occasions. Naturally, prayers attributed to Muhammad are popular, such as this one on going to bed:

> All praise belongs to God who provided rest to my body, restored my soul to me and allowed me to remember Him.

THE MOSQUE (MASJID)

Masjid, the Arabic word for mosque, means "place of prostration," emphasizing ritual prayer as the central worship activity. Any open area that's not ritually impure may be used as a place of prayer and referred to as a *masjid*.

The plan of a classical mosque derives from Muhammad's first house in Medina. On the east side of a large courtyard were rooms for Muhammad's wives. On the south side of the courtyard, two rows of pillars supported a roof providing shade from the hot Arabian sun. The flat roof, the pillars, the courtyard, and the roofed area oriented toward Mecca became the typical early mosque plan. Only later, after the conquest of Iran, did the domed structure enter Islamic architecture and come to be used for mosques.

A mosque has no pews or chairs (except perhaps at the rear for people with mobility issues). Other structures may be associated with a mosque or incorporated into the mosque itself, such as schools for young children, madrasas for higher training in Islamic studies, and hospices for travelers.

Mosques do vary. In some parts of Africa, the Friday service may be held in a large open area outside the mosque. In some Western countries, where Islam is relatively new, mosques may be converted church buildings or storefront structures with little on the outside to indicate they are mosques.

Third pillar: Purifying tax (Zakat)

Muslims believe that all things belong to God, and that humans only hold wealth in trust for Him. For that reason, they think wealth should be distributed throughout the community of believers, or *umma*, through a purifying tax (called a *zakat*). The usual payment is 2.5 percent of a person's assets. That means everything: grains; fruit; camels; cattle; sheep and goats; gold and silver; other assets and movable goods. The money is distributed to the poor, debtors, volunteers participating in a *jihad* (holy war), pilgrims, and the collectors of the tax. At one time, slaves seeking to buy their freedom got a handout.

The Koran explicitly requires *zakat* (Sura 9:60) and often places it alongside prayer when discussing a Muslim's duties. ("Perform the prayer and give the alms." — Sura 2:43, 110, 277) For those who believe in taking their wealth with them, the Qur'an minces no words: "The fires of hell will heat up the coins, and the greedy will be branded with them" (Sura 9:34–35).

REMEMBER

The *zakat* is designed to ensure that the wealthy help the poor, a practice that boosted Christianity in the eyes of pagans during its early years. Muhammad may have been motivated to add this rule because of the overt poverty he endured as a child. He was known to have been very kind toward orphans.

The Islamic state used to enforce *zakat*, but, today, it's an individual's choice unless a country demands strict adherence to religious law (called *shari'a*).

The Shi`ites emphasize this pillar by requiring an additional one-fifth tax (called *khums*) that must be paid for the benefit of orphans, the poor, travelers, and the *imams*.

TECHNICAL STUFF

Zakat is similar to voluntary *tithing* (the act of giving one-tenth of your income to the church) in both Judaism and Christianity. In the Church of Jesus Christ of Latter-day Saints, in contrast, tithing is a religious requirement.

Fourth pillar: Fasting (Sawm)

During the month of *Ramadan* (more on that later in this chapter in the section titled "Observing Muslim Holidays"), the ninth month in the Islamic calendar, Muslims fast between dawn and dusk (this act is called *sawm*). (Because Islam follows a lunar calendar, Ramadan moves around each year.) Muslims must abstain from food, liquid, and intimate contact during those hours of the day. Muslims fast to commemorate the descent of the Qur'an from the highest heaven to the lowest, from which it was then revealed to Muhammad over the next 22 years. Fasting is seen as a method of self-purification by cutting oneself off from worldly comforts.

The sick, elderly, travelers, and pregnant or nursing women are permitted to break the fast during Ramadan, provided they make up for it during an equal number of days later in the year. Children begin the ritual at puberty. The end of Ramadan is celebrated by the *Eid al-Fitr*, one of the major festivals on the Muslim calendar.

Westerners probably know the Islamic holiday of Ramadan more than any other.

Fifth pillar: Pilgrimage (Hajj)

REMEMBER

All Muslims are required to make one pilgrimage to Mecca in their lifetimes, called a *hajj*, provided they are physically and financially able to do so. Muhammad probably made this mandatory to gain support of Meccan merchants who were losing money because Islam didn't initially recognize the *Ka'ba*. That cut off visits by pagan pilgrims and undercut support for Islam. The required pilgrimages ended that concern.

Today, the requirement helps bring Muslims together and adds cohesion to the faith.

The pilgrimage lasts from the 8th to 12th of *Dhul-hijja*, which is the 12th and last month of the Muslim year, which means, like Ramadan, it doesn't correspond to a specific month in the solar calendar. Many pilgrims set out several months ahead of time in order to spend an extended time in the holy cities. Due to safe travel conditions and modern air transportation, more than two million people make *hajj* each year. Caring for the pilgrims — food, housing, guides, movement from place to place, even sanitation and toilet facilities — is a major logistical challenge for the Saudi government.

Like Ramadan, the end of the *hajj* is also celebrated with a festival, the *Eid al-Adha*, which is marked by all Muslims, whether or not they made the pilgrimage. This festival and the *Eid al-Fitr* at the end of Ramadan comprise the highlights of the Islamic year.

Consecrating oneself: Ihram

The pilgrims begin their *hajj* when they leave their normal mode of life and enter into a state of consecration *(ihram)*. Most pilgrims arrive at the Jeddah airport and enter into *ihram* there if they haven't already done so on the plane or at their departure airports. First, they perform the major purification *(ghusl)*, which involves a total washing of the body. Then, the pilgrims affirm the intention to perform *hajj*. Men put on two plain, white, seamless garments, one covering the body from the waist down and the other draped over the right shoulder and gathered at the waist. No specific dress is prescribed for women. They cover their hair but don't wear a veil, jewelry, or perfume. Because sewn and leather items aren't permitted, pilgrims wear plastic sandals and a plastic belt for money and documents. No longer can one tell by appearance who is rich and powerful and who is poor: all stand as equals before God. While in the state of consecration, Muslims aren't permitted to cut their hair or nails, or have sexual relations. At this time, pilgrims utter the prayer called the *talbiya*, which they repeat frequently over the following week: *labbayk allahumma labbayk* ("here I am, my God, here I am"). Tradition attributes this prayer to Abraham when he instituted the pilgrimage ritual.

Circling the Ka`ba: Tawaf and `umra

After purification and entrance into Mecca, the pilgrims proceed to circle seven times counter-clockwise around the *Ka`ba*. This circling is called the *tawaf* and it expresses the unity of God *(tawhid)*. All try to touch the Black Stone (see Book 6, Chapter 2) but most have to settle for making a gesture toward the stone. Lest it be thought that Muslims are worshipping the stone, a *hadith* reports that the caliph `Umar said, "I know that you're only a stone which doesn't have the power to do good or evil. If I hadn't seen the prophet kissing you, I wouldn't kiss you." Following the *tawaf*, pilgrims offer a personal prayer at a spot between the Black Stone and the door of the *Ka`ba.*

At the station of Abraham a few steps to the northeast, pilgrims perform a two-*rak`a salat.* Here, Abraham stood while building the *Ka`ba.* Next, pilgrims drink from the well of Zamzam. As his mother, Hagar, ran to and fro seeking water lest they both die of thirst, the infant Ishmael kicked his heel into the ground and water appeared, making a gurgling noise (sounding like *zam*). Pilgrims take small bottles of this water home. Today, pilgrims go down a flight of steps to a gallery where the sanitized water flows through a number of faucets. Finally, pilgrims walk and run *(sa'y)* seven times between the two small hills of Safa and Marwa, in memory of Hagar's search for water. Since the 1970s reconstruction of the mosque, this 900-plus-foot course is within the northeast wall of the mosque.

TECHNICAL STUFF

The activities mentioned so far, if performed outside of the *hajj* season, constitute the *`umra* (meaning "lesser pilgrimage"), which is an act of piety but not a fulfillment of the *hajj*. If not on *hajj*, at this point pilgrims terminate the state of consecration.

Standing at `Arafat: Wuquf

Before nightfall, the pilgrims depart for the village of Mina, about five miles from Mecca, where they spend the night. Some continue on and spend the night at the plain of `Arafat, 12 miles southwest of Mecca. The next day, the ninth of the month, they spend standing for all or a portion of the time between noon and sunset on the plain of `Arafat or the low "mount of mercy" from which Muhammad delivered his sermon on his farewell pilgrimage. A misting spray of water from sprinklers mounted atop tall poles helps reduce the temperature on the plain of `Arafat. The standing at `Arafat provides a foretaste of the Day of Judgment (see Book 6, Chapter 1), when some traditions say that Muslims who completed the *hajj* will appear in their *hajj* garments. This day is the peak of the pilgrimage experience.

Sacrificing: `Id al-adha

After sunset on the ninth day of the month, the overflowing or rush occurs. The masses of pilgrims hurry back toward Mina and Mecca, with the night being spent at Muzdalifah. The next day the pilgrims gather either 49 or 70 pebbles depending on the number of days the pilgrim stays (the pebbles should be no smaller than a chickpea or larger than a hazelnut) and depart to Mina. At Mina, they cast seven pebbles at the largest of three pillars. This recalls the incident when Abraham was called upon by God to sacrifice his son Ishmael. The birth of Isaac was a reward to Abraham for being willing to obey God's command to sacrifice Ishmael. (In the Bible, Genesis 22, it's the younger son Isaac who was to be sacrificed rather than Ishmael). Tradition reports that Satan three times called out to Ishmael, tempting him to opt out of being sacrificed. The casting of stones represents the rejection of the temptation of Satan. Details of the temptation vary in the traditions, some of which include also the temptation of Abraham and of Ishmael's mother, Hagar.

At this point or any time through the 12th of the month, the sacrifice of the *`id al-Adha*, the great *`id*, is performed at Mina. On the 10th of the month, Muslims around the world perform this same sacrifice. A goat, sheep, camel, or cow is sacrificed in memory of the ram provided to Abraham by God as a sacrifice in place of his son. The family head performs the sacrifice in the specified manner and shares the meat with neighbors and with the poor. How to handle and distribute all the excess meat resulting from the observance at Mina is a major logistical challenge for the Saudi government.

Just as Abraham was willing to sacrifice that which was most precious to Him, so every Muslim should be willing to sacrifice everything for God. Anyone who dies during the course of his *hajj* journey is a martyr who will go immediately to paradise.

The state of consecration comes to an end, symbolized by shaving the head (men only) or cutting a lock of hair. Pilgrims may remove their pilgrimage clothing and resume normal activities (except for sexual intercourse). They return to Mecca for the second circling of the *Ka`ba (tawaf al-ifada)*. If they didn't do the *tawaf* on arrival or did the *tawaf* without the running between Safa and Marwa, they do these now.

Ending the pilgrimage

The final three days of the *hajj*, the 11th, 12th, and 13th of *Dhul-hijja*, are called the *Days of Drying Meat.* Each day, those remaining cast seven pebbles at each of the three pillars at Mina. A modern two-story ramp accommodates the large numbers of people involved.

Pilgrims may end the pilgrimage on the 12th day. During this period, a new covering is put on the *Ka`ba*. Before final departure from Mecca, pilgrims usually make a third circling of the *Ka`ba (tawaf al-wada)*. meaning circling of farewell) and offer a farewell prayer:

> O Lord, do not make this my last visit to your house, and grant me the chance to return here again and again.

Observing Muslim Holidays

Muslims observe several holidays throughout the year with prayer, gatherings in the mosque, and occasional feasts. Each holiday is typically a solemn religious occasion, although, as you see below, there are exceptions. Different sects may have varied rituals or may not even celebrate some of the same holidays. Ramadan is considered the most important.

Muslims follow a lunar calendar. That's much shorter than a solar calendar, so holidays move around every year based on lunar cycles.

Ramadan: Remembering the revelation of the first Qur'an verses

Ramadan is the best-known Islamic holiday perhaps because of its unusual length and the novelty of a hefty fast. Devout Muslims fast for 30 days from sunup to sunset to thank God for giving them the Qur'an. Muslims use the last ten days of Ramadan for devotions and good deeds in an effort to draw closer to God.

The holiday comes with special foods, prayers, and readings from the Qur'an.

The 27th day of Ramadan is set aside as *Lailat-al-Qadr*, the day the archangel Gabriel introduced the first words of the Qur'an to Muhammad. Muhammad reportedly stayed awake all night. Some Muslims duplicate that feat, praying for forgiveness of any sin.

Hijra: Turning the page to a new year

The *Hijra* holiday commemorates Muhammad's exit from Mecca to the city of Yathrib (Medina) in 622 CE. This event, called the *Hijra*, marks the start of the Muslim calendar. Islamic years are numbered starting from the Hijra.

Ashurah: A day of many remembrances

The holiday of *Ashurah* recalls the martyrdom of *Imam* Husayn, the grandson of the Prophet in 663. The Shi`ites consider this day extremely important, and they still bemoan Husayn's death.

In addition, the day is also linked to an old holiday once followed by Jews in Medina. They would fast to remember their salvation from the Pharaoh in Egypt. Muslims multiplied the reasons behind the occasion by saying, on this day, Noah's Ark also came to rest on Mount Ararat, Abraham was born, and the *Ka'ba* was built.

Id Milad al-Nabi: Marking Muhammad's birth and death

The Muslim Christmas without the commercial hoopla, *Id Milad-al-Nabi* commemorates the birth of the Prophet and is celebrated on the 12th day of the month *Rabee-ul-Awwal,* the third month of the Muslim calendar. The day is not totally joyous because Muslims also mark Muhammad's death at the same time.

This holiday wasn't celebrated in earlier times and has not attained universal status in all Muslim countries. In addition, Muhammad's birth date is unknown.

Maulid, which means "birthday" and is spelled in various ways (such as *milad, mawlid, mulud, milad,* and *mevlut),* is an official holiday in most Muslim countries. The holiday lasts 12 days. Muslims whoop it up with carnivals and processions. Of course, time is also devoted to prayers and religious activities. There are even songs.

More conservative sects, such as the Wahhabis (see Book 6, Chapter 1), reject the idea of celebrating Muhammad's birthday.

Typical elements in the celebration of the *maulid*

Although details vary greatly, a typical *maulid* celebration may involve the following elements:

- A multi-day festival, culminating on the two evenings of the 11th and 12th of the month.
- A carnival-like atmosphere with tents, entertainment, and special sweets.

  In recent times, some governments have deemphasized the carnival atmosphere and promoted the festival as a time to take moral inspiration from Muhammad's life.
- Processions with lights, recitations, and songs.
- Qur'anic recitations, prayers, and poems about Muhammad.

Many countries have their own *maulid* customs. In Morocco, a child is considered lucky to be born during the *maulid* and thus may be named Mauludiyya. The *maulid* is also a good time to circumcise boys. People in some countries celebrate with a feast and give gifts to the poor.

The *maulud* poems

Maulud recitations are the distinctive feature of the *maulid* celebration. *Mauluds* are prose and especially poetic compositions celebrating the birth of Muhammad.

A *maulud* may be composed in a variety of literary genres, and a typical *maulud* contains the following elements:

- Opening invocation and praise of God.
- The creation of the "light of Muhammad."
- Miscellaneous information such as the ancestry of Muhammad.
- Announcement of the Muhammad's conception to his mother, Amina.
- An account of his birth and the miracles that occurred at that time.

Mauluds may include incidents from Muhammad's life, especially the ascension into heaven. Other poems in praise of Muhammad, such as al-Busiri's *Burda,* are frequently recited. The recitation conveys a blessing *(baraka)* upon both reciter and the hearer. *Maulud* recordings by professional singers are popular.

Id al-Adha: Honoring Abraham's dedication to God

The Festival of Sacrifice, *Id al-Adha,* recalls the biblical account of Abraham being asked to sacrifice his son Isaac. A sheep or cow gets it in the neck on this day, and much of the meat is donated to the poor. In some Muslim countries, this is a public holiday.

Lailat al-Baraa: Seeking and granting forgiveness

Borrowing from the Jewish Yom Kippur (see Book 4, Chapter 3), on this "the night of repentance," forgiveness is granted to those who repent.

15th of Sha'ban: Shaking things up

The 15th day of the eighth month, *Sha'ban,* is when the tree of paradise is shaken. According to tradition, each leaf of the tree bears the name of a living person. If the leaf bearing a person's name falls off during the shaking, Muslims believe, the person will die that year.

The holiday is marked with prayer and, in some countries, ceremonies that honor the dead.

GETTING TO KNOW SAINTS

Muslims revere saints, although the process of becoming a Muslim saint differs from the Christian canonization. A Catholic person thought to be a *saint*, or a devout person whose life can serve as an example to others, must meet certain criteria to merit that status, including the performance of miracles. However, in Islam, anyone revered as a saint instantly becomes one — alive or dead. Called a *Wali* (or "friend of God"), a saint can be very popular or completely ignored. Some countries that recently became Islamic cheerfully include pagan figures among Muslim saints.

Here are a few Muslim saints:

- **Ahmad Ibn Hanbal (780–855):** He was tortured by declaring the Qur'an was not created. His view won eventually, and he was honored as a saint in his lifetime.
- **Ahmad al-Badawi (1228–1297):** He founded a sect of the Sufis and was believed to have performed miracles.
- **Rabi'a al-'Adawiyya (c.717–801):** A mystic whom some followers called the second Mary, she taught her students to love God completely.

The day probably gained some distinction because it marks the anniversary of Muhammad's return to Mecca as a conqueror in 630 CE.

27th of Rajab: A heavenly holiday

On this day in 632 CE, Muhammad reportedly traveled to Jerusalem to ascend to heaven to greet Allah. Some sects believe he rose physically and then returned to earth. Others insist the visit was in spirit only. The day is marked with prayers and processions in many Muslim countries.

Carrying Out Common Rituals and Daily Practices

Muslims practice some familiar rituals. They circumcise their male children, though Muslim boys can be as old as 15 at the time of the ceremony. Some Muslims insist on circumcising girls, a practice that has been attacked in recent years as being mutilation. You can read more on this in Book 6, Chapter 5. Although there is no coming-of-age ritual, Muslims become adults by demonstrating an ability to read the Qur'an.

Getting hitched

Muslims are expected to marry. Having more than one wife *(polygamy)* is illegal in countries that ban it, but may be acceptable in some Muslim lands. The Qur'an talks about the issue specifically in what is known as the Noble Verse:

> And if you fear that you cannot act equitably towards orphans, then marry such women as seem good to you, two, three and four, but if you fear that you may not do justice to them, then (marry) only one — Sura 4:3.

Muslim women are also expected to provide a *dowry*, which is a gift from the bride's family to the husband.

REMEMBER

Love may not play a part in a marriage, which is often based on family relationships and economic considerations. A Muslim wedding is seen as a contract between the parties. As a result, there is no ceremony akin to a Jewish or Christian wedding. Instead, the man makes a formal offer that the woman accepts.

The actual ceremony involves a gathering of the bride and groom and their respective attorneys and two male witnesses. No religious prayers are said. Instead, the bride and groom may choose to recite passages from the *Fatihah*, the first seven verses from the Qur'an. These verses call for God's guidance and emphasize His power and mercy. The same verses are often included in traditional daily prayers.

After the brief ceremony is completed, the groom goes to a room where women in the bride's family are gathered. He offers gifts to the sisters (if any) and receives a blessing from the older women there. Men then gather in one place for a large meal; women in another. After dinner, the bride and groom are seated together for the first time. A single cloth *(dupatta)* is used to cover their heads as they say prayers. See Book 6, Chapter 5 for more details on Muslim weddings.

Other ways of keeping the faith

Other Muslim rituals include

- A sacrifice of sheep and goats when an infant is named in the first week after birth.
- Burial occurs on the day of death.
- Mourning lasts three days for friends. Widows are to mourn for four months and ten days.

» Dress is restricted. Some sects insist on veils for women, but the Qur'an only calls for loose coverings over the head and shoulders. Men are to wear tunics or loose-fitting gowns.

The rules are generally overlooked in Western lands, although arguments over security risks arose in France and the United States when Muslim women hid their faces behind veils on official photographs. Veils were eventually banned in France.

Muslim men may grow beards but are not required to. Men and women are required to remove pubic and underarm hair. No one is allowed to alter eyebrows. The idea is that the face was created that way and must be left alone.

Dietary requirements

Foods are limited for Muslims, akin to Jewish kosher laws (see more about those in Book 4, Chapter 3). The Qur'an stresses the need for a healthy body so the believer can worship Allah properly.

> O' Believers! Eat of the good and pure (lawful) that We have provided you with and be grateful to Allah, if you truly worship Him. — Sura 2:172

To accomplish that, a variety of foods are banned. Muslims can't eat the meat from a pig, animals that are found dead, or animals used in sacrifices by other religions. In addition, Muslim scholars outlined several more prohibitions:

» Animals killed by strangling.

» Animals killed by a violent blow. Muslims practice humane slaughtering techniques pioneered by Jews.

» Animals killed by a headlong fall or gored to death.

» Animals partially eaten by wild animals.

» Animals sacrificed in the name of idols.

Symbols and colors

Islam largely shuns icons, liturgy, and drama, as well as processions, festivals, and myths. As a result, the religion avoids symbols and symbolism, so Islam has no visual symbol like the Jewish star or the Christian cross.

A few symbols have, however, become unofficially associated with Islam:

- » The crescent moon, which appears on the flags of various countries, such as Turkey and Pakistan, is really not a religious icon, but was the insignia of the Ottoman Empire.
- » The single star is often joined with the moon (see Figure 4-1). Westerners saw the two paired so often in Middle Eastern countries that they simply assumed the crescent moon and star were symbols of Islam.
- » The Shi`ites have a symbol, a sword. They associate it with Caliph Ali, who was killed in battle.

On the other hand, colors have long been part of Islamic symbolism. They were associated with various dynasties as battle standards. Three colors — white for the Ummayads; black for the Abbasids; green for the Fatimids — have become traditional in Islamic countries, along with red.

Green receives a particularly high status because it was reportedly Muhammad's favorite color. He was supposed to have worn a green cloak and turban, and fought under a green banner. The Qur'an gives some credence to that claim, saying that the "inhabitants of paradise will wear green garments of fine silk" (Sura 18:31).

FIGURE 4-1: This symbol is often associated with Islam, but it's not an official emblem.

Introducing the Qur'an

REMEMBER

One of the characteristics of the scriptures of the three major Western monotheisms (Islam, Judaism, and Christianity) is that at the core of each is a scripture contained in a single book (in present form) that claims to be a revelation of God. All three claim that each of their books is or contains the direct word of God. In Islam, that book is the Qur'an, which Muslims believe God revealed to Muhammad in a series of revelations over a period of 22 years.

You can't understand Islam without coming to grips and spending time with the Qur'an. Yet a paradox faces non-Muslims. Muslims regard the Qur'an as a work of perfection both in its expression and in its content. Non-Muslims who know the Qur'an only in translation often agree with the British historian Thomas Carlyle who in 1841 described the Qur'an as "a confused jumble, crude, incondite; endless iterations, long-windedness, entanglement; most crude, incondite, insupportable stupidity in short." (And keep in mind that these are the words of a man who, compared to most Westerners, was sympathetic toward Muhammad and Islam.) Which view is correct? Read and decide for yourself.

The basics of the Qur'an

TIP

You can make much better sense of any book on Islam if you have handy a copy of the Qur'an to refer to as you read. The Qur'an is about four-fifths the length of the New Testament. Perhaps you won't read it all in one night, but it's certainly not too long to read in a week.

The Qur'an is divided into 114 primary units, each of which is a *sura*, like a chapter.

REMEMBER

Each sura is divided into verses. Sura 2, the longest sura, has 286 verses. Several suras (103, 108, 110) have only three verses. Like most non-Muslims, this book refers to a specific passage by sura and verse or *aya* number; for example, 24:35. (Note that *aya* means sign; Islam refers to the verses as signs because Muslims regard the Qur'an as God's greatest sign.) Listing the sura and verse helps anyone not well acquainted with the Qur'an find a specific passage. Muslims traditionally refer to the suras by name, such as the "opening" *(al-Fatiha)* for Sura 1 and the "cow" *(al-Baqara)* for Sura 2. Occasionally, names do relate to the dominant content of a sura, as in the case of Sura 12, the Joseph Sura. More often, the title is taken from a rare word or a word that occurs in the first couple of lines. Like musical symphonies, one can remember a sura more easily by name than by number.

For Islam, the Qur'an is the basic revelation or incarnation of God in the world. The Qur'an is God's spoken word in a literal sense *(kalam Allah)*. This goes considerably further than the view of some Christians that God dictated the words of the

Bible. The entire Qur'an is the first-person word of God. For Muslims, the prototype of the Qur'an, called the *mother of the book* (Sura 13:39), has existed eternally in heaven, and unlike the Bible, the Qur'an is a perfect replica of that book.

Hearing the Qur'an

REMEMBER

Because the Qur'an is a book, one may assume that the best approach is to read the book, but the word *Qur'an* means "the reading" or "the recitation." The corresponding verb occurs at least 80 times in the Qur'an and means to recite, proclaim, or read out loud. In what is often regarded as the call of Muhammad, Sura 96:1–5, Gabriel tells Muhammad to "recite." He doesn't tell Muhammad to read or to write. The verb "say" occurs in over 300 passages. In the Qur'an, various forms of the word Qur'an can refer to three things:

- » The entire holy book (this is the normal usage of the word)
- » An individual revelation contained in the Qur'an
- » A reciting of portions or the complete Qur'an

When Muhammad received a new revelation, he would need to convey it to his followers. Because according to Muslim tradition, some revelations were written down by scribes, one may think he would have a scribe make a copy of the written text and send that copy to Muslims living elsewhere. But instead, Muhammad sent "reciters" to convey the new revelation orally just as Muhammad had originally conveyed it to those who were with him. In reciting the Qur'an, the word of God is actualized. In the spoken word God is present, just as Christ is present in the consecrated bread and wine for many Christians (see more on that in Book 5, Chapter 4).

The newborn infant first hears the language of the Qur'an when the father whispers in their ear the *Shahadah* (testimony that God is the only God and Muhammad is His messenger). From that time on, the child hears the Qur'an frequently. When they learn to read, a primary purpose is so the child can recite the passages of the Qur'an needed for required prayer *(salat)*. In *salat*, the Muslim recites passages from the Qur'an in Arabic without the aid of a written text.

While Muslims can buy books with collections of prayers for devotional use, Islam has no official prayer book; instead, the Qur'an *is* Islam's prayer book. As one of the *hadiths* says, "In every *salat*, there is a recitation (of the Qur'an)."

As a child grows up, sounds of the Qur'an are everywhere. On the radio and on television, they hear readings from the Qur'an. A Muslim may gather with others before or after Friday noon prayer service to recite the Qur'an. In these groups, a Muslim has a copy of the Qur'an before them, but they still recite it out loud. When they take a bus to work or a taxi to visit friends, the driver is as likely to be playing a tape of Qur'anic readings as playing the latest popular songs.

Phrases from the Qur'an punctuate everyday speech, such as *insha'allah* ("if God wills"). Muslims recite specific suras or verses on particular occasions, including the following:

- The *Fatiha* (see the "Opening the Qur'an: The Fatiha" section later in this chapter) is recited on many occasions, such as at the conclusion of a wedding contract.
- Suras 113 and 114, as protection against evil.
- Sura 26 on the 15th of the month of *Sha`ban*, the night when destinies are determined by God for the coming year.
- The *basmala*, which is recited before meals and as an act of consecration before many other actions. The *basmala* is the phrase "In the name of God the Compassionate, the Caring" that opens every sura except Sura 9.
- Sura 112, Sura 2:255 (the throne verse), and Sura 24:35 (the light verse) on any number of occasions.

Gathering and Organizing the Qur'an

On the one hand, Muhammad received individual revelations throughout his life. On the other hand, the present Qur'an is an organized collection of many or all of those revelations. How does one get from the individual revelations to the Qur'an as an integrated book? When did this happen? By what principle were the suras compiled? Is there basically a single tradition as to the text of the Qur'an going back to Muhammad or were there variant traditions?

Putting the Qur'an into writing

The written text that lies behind all Qur'ans today was originally a consonantal text without vowels. The Arabic alphabet at that time had only 15 characters for 28 consonants. Later, special markings were added to distinguish letters, which appear similar or identical in Arabic. Due to the absence of written vowels and the possible confusion of consonants, no one can pick up and read a copy of the early written Qur'an unless they already knew the oral Qur'an. When in 1924, Egyptian scholars were preparing what became the standard printed edition of the Qur'an, they first consulted the living oral tradition. When vowels were later added to the text of the Qur'an, they were written with a different color of ink so the reader understood that the vowels weren't part of the Qur'an itself.

The early text that underlies all Qur'ans in use today was divided into lines but didn't indicate the verses *(aya)*. In most cases, stylistic considerations make clear where in the Arabic text a verse ends. However, in some cases, the division isn't entirely clear. The verse division of the 1924 Egyptian text is used in Arabic Qur'ans today. Traditional printed (or handwritten) texts indicate verse divisions with a *rosette*, a rose shaped icon between verses.

TIP

Some Western translations follow the verse division of a 19th century scholar named Flügel that differs in some cases by as much as seven verses from the Egyptian edition. If you're looking up a citation in an English translation of the Qur'an and can't find the indicated passage, read the seven preceding and following verses.

Organizing the Qur'an

How are the suras put together to form the Qur'an? After Sura 1, the longer suras come first. In general, the suras are arranged according to decreasing length. However, many exceptions to this rule occur. Here are two examples: by length (counting the number of lines), Sura 15 would be Sura 40 and Sura 40 would be Sura 22. So clearly length isn't all that was involved.

Twenty-nine suras are prefixed with what in English are called the "mysterious (or detached) letters" — from one to four letters of the Arabic alphabet that occur after the *basmala* (the phrase which begins with "in the name of God") but before the body of the sura. Muslims accept these as part of the original revelation. In some cases, suras with the same mysterious letters are grouped together. For example, the letters A (that is, *'alif*), L, and R stand at the start of Suras 10–15. This grouping may be one reason why some suras appear out of place when viewed in terms of length alone. What do the letters mean? No one agrees which is why they are called the mysterious letters.

Compiling the Qur'an

According to the traditional biography, Muhammad received his call to be a prophet in 610. On that occasion, the angel Gabriel transmitted to Muhammad the first revelation, usually regarded to be the opening verses of Sura 96. The Qur'an says, "We sent it down during a blessed night" (Sura 44:3). "Sent down" may refer to God's having sent down the entire Qur'an from the seventh heaven to the lowest heaven on one of the odd numbered nights of the last third of the month of Ramadan.

Throughout the remainder of his life, Muhammad continued to receive individual revelations. Only in the case of some of the short suras did a single revelation correspond to an entire sura. Instead, individual revelations were combined together to form the suras.

Some Muslims say that whenever Muhammad received a new revelation, he indicated where it should be placed (that is, in which sura) and what was the proper sequence of the suras. Although the Qur'an didn't exist as a single, physical book during the lifetime of Muhammad, according to this view, Muhammad had already determined the structure of the Qur'an. A typical English translation of the Qur'an is about 500 pages. Divide this over the 23 years from the call to the death of Muhammad, and you come up with approximately two pages a month or around 24 pages a year. Or take the approximately 6,200 verses and it amounts to a little less than a verse a day. Of course, revelations didn't come at such a regular pace and weren't all of the same length.

What follows is a summary of several traditions that relate the common Muslim view of how the individual revelations Muhammad received in his life were collected into a single, authoritative version of the Qur'an.

Within the first two years after Muhammad's death in 632, `Umar (the future second caliph) urged Abu Bakr (the first caliph), to collect the Qur'an out of fear that the reciters who preserved the Qur'an would all die in battle. Abu Bakr sent for Zayd ibn Thabit. Zayd sought out the preserved written versions of individual revelations — some written on stone, others on palm leaves, and others on bones. He also collected and wrote down portions of the Qur'an that were preserved only "in the hearts of men." Zayd gave the results of his work, which was on separate pages, to Abu Bakr, who passed them on to `Umar at his death. `Umar, in turn, gave them to his daughter Hafsa (a widow of Muhammad's) when he died. This is the first complete, written Qur'an, according to tradition. During the reign of `Uthman, the next (third) caliph, an army general named Hudhayfa came to `Uthman. He was concerned that different groups of the army had had different versions of the Qur'an. `Uthman sent for the pages of the Qur'an that were in Hafsa's possession. He ordered the same Zayd ibn Thabit to head a committee to organize the sheets into a book, resolving any differences in readings. `Uthman sent copies of this Qur'an to four of the major Muslim cities. All other written copies of the Qur'an (whole or partial), he ordered burned.

REMEMBER

What does the traditional account tell you?

» The story clearly has the purpose of legitimating the `Uthamanic version of the Qur'an, the version that is the basis for all Qur'ans used by Muslims today. Whether or not one accepts the historicity of the account of its origin, the text of the Qur'an used today is usually referred to as the `Uthman text or `Uthman version.

» The story indicates that even after Abu Bakr, different versions of the Qur'an were in use in the time of `Uthman.

» At Muhammad's death, the Qur'an didn't exist as a single manuscript.

» The text of the Qur'an was finalized in written form much more quickly than happened for the Biblical texts (for more on these, see Book 5, Chapter 2).

How complete is the present text of the Qur'an? While some Shi`ite Muslims believe the received Qur'anic text omitted some passages that speak about `Ali and his descendants, most Muslims agree that the present text of the Qur'an contains most of the revelations that Muhammad received during his lifetime. Tradition says the following principles guided the process of collection:

» The revelation was written down in the presence of Muhammad. In other words, no secondhand accounts were included.

» At least two witnesses heard Muhammad recite each specific revelation.

» All the revelations that Muhammad received were included. Nothing was omitted except for some passages that God explicitly nullified (see the section "The abrogated verses" later in this chapter).

The Style of the Qur'an

We now turn from the discussion of how the Qur'an came to exist in its present format to consideration of the style of the Qur'an. To a non-Muslim, the Qur'an often appears strange and difficult to get a handle on. A reader may wonder why Muslims praise its beauty so highly when a Western reader may find it boring and repetitive. How does it make its impact on the hearts and minds of Muslims? The effect of the Qur'an on a Muslim is due as much to how it presents its message as to the content of that message.

The idiom of the Qur'an

The language of the Qur'an isn't the normal Arabic of Muhammad's day. Some suggest the Qur'anic idiom derives from a kind of high literary idiom used and understood across Arabia at the time. Just as Shakespeare and the King James Bible had a formative influence on English, the Arabic of the Qur'an exercised a decisive influence on the development of Arabic.

The language of the Qur'an isn't normal prose or normal poetry. When one considers that some of Muhammad's contemporaries said he was a poet, a soothsayer, a madman, or a magician, it appears they were having trouble fitting the idiom of Qur'an into a recognized category of speech. Qur'anic language uses a form of rhymed and rhythmic prose.

In many translations of the Qur'an, without even reading the text, one can see that it's formatted like poetry. While lines don't have a fixed meter or set number of syllables, you can clearly see a pattern that's more like poetry than prose. Qur'anic language makes extensive use of assonance in which lines of a unit all end with the same sound.

TIP

Even though you may not understand it, if you want to sense something of the effect of the sound of the Qur'an on Muslims, listen to some suras being recited. Even better is to listen to the recitation as you follow along with a printed transliteration of the Arabic. Michael Sells' *Approaching the Qur'an: The Early Revelations* (White Cloud Press, 1989) includes transliterations of a number of short suras.

Recurring thematic elements in the Qur'an

In addition to analyzing the structure of words and sentences in the Qur'an, you can also look at the component elements that make up the various suras. Neil Robinson in his book, *Discovering the Qur'an, A Contemporary Approach to a Veiled Text* (Trinity Press International, 1997) speaks of six *registers* or modes of speech that make up the individual suras:

- Passages directed against pagan opponents in Mecca and subsequently against the "hypocrites" in Medina
- Signs testifying, for example, to the power of God to resurrect the dead
- Communications to Muhammad, including His call
- Signs that indicate the end of the world and the final judgment
- Material to establish the truth of the message and its messenger
- Narratives, such as accounts of earlier prophets who warned their people of impending destruction if they didn't change their ways

According to Robinson, blocks of material in these six modes of speech combine to construct entire suras. What appears on first reading as a series of unrelated units can now be understood as a coherent unity. Of course, Robinson's list of six modes of speech isn't the only way to analyze the recurring elements; for example, some additional common types of material include oaths, legislative passages, and parables.

Any number of other people have tried to organize the content of the Qur'an under certain themes. A. A. Islahi, a South Asian Qur'anic scholar, divides the Qur'an into seven sections, each with a different primary theme:

- Law
- Abrahamic religion (meaning, Judaism, Christianity, and Islam — all of which claim descent from the Biblical Abraham)
- The struggle between truth and deceit
- The proof of Muhammad's status as messenger
- The unity of God (the monotheistic emphasis that God is one, without children, parents, or spouse)
- The judgment
- Warnings to unbelievers

REMEMBER

Such arrangements of the Qur'an according to content can help the non-Muslim reader, but don't correspond to the structure of the Qur'an.

Interpreting the Qur'an

Islam has a long tradition of commenting on its scripture. In Islam, this is called *tafsir*, from a verb meaning "to explain." Interpretations began with Muhammad answering questions from his followers. For example, `A'isha (Muhammad's young wife) heard him say, "Whoever is called to account will be punished." `A'isha challenged Muhammad by quoting Sura 84:8, "His account will easily be settled," implying a less harsh judgment upon sinners.

The process of interpreting the Qur'an

A traditional commentary starts at Sura 1:1 and then works its way through the Qur'an verse by verse. The author quotes the full verse, breaks the verse into phrases, and then comments on each phrase. This produces a sense of what individual words and phrases mean but often no overall interpretation of the full text. The author explains any unclear words and points of grammar, notes the occasion of revelation if a relevant tradition exists, includes relevant comments about the passage from Muhammad or his companions or their successors, and uses other passages from the Qur'an to help explain the verse they are discussing. They may point out the legal or ritual implications of the passage or discuss pertinent philosophical and theological issues. The scholar may also make rhetorical observations. They won't explain the passage in the light of its historical setting or try to relate it to his own time. Al-Tabari's 39-volume commentary (tenth century) is one of the most important commentaries. Al-Tabari distinguishes between verses that everyone can understand, verses that only God can understand, and verses that the reader can understand only because they were explained by Muhammad.

Exoteric and esoteric interpretation

What we describe thus far in this section is exoteric interpretation *(zahir)*, which deals with the literal, "surface" meaning of the text. In the past, many Muslims have suggested that the text has additional levels of hidden or esoteric meaning. *Ta'wil* interpretation dealt with this deeper level of meaning. Although more literalistic Sunni scholars rejected *ta'wil*, other Sunni scholars recognized the legitimacy of such interpretation and said the Qur'an itself often signaled when a deeper meaning was the key to the text. Sufi interpreters downplayed the literal meaning in favor of an allegorical interpretation intended to illuminate the spiritual significance of the text. Shi`ite interpreters emphasized an interior meaning *(batin)* passed on from `Ali to the Shi`ite *imams* who, unlike Sunni interpreters, can provide new interpretations of the texts. To Sufis and Shi`ites, this interior meaning was often more significant than the exterior meaning of the text.

The abrogated verses

The concept of *abrogation (naskh)* says that God revealed some verses of the Qur'an that he later annulled (abrogated). Abrogation proved especially useful in dealing with two situations.

- Cases where two different verses from the Qur'an conflict with each other.
- Instances where Islamic law based on tradition and custom conflicts with statements in the Qur'an.

TECHNICAL STUFF

The Qur'anic basis for the concept of abrogation is three passages (Suras 2:106; 22:52; 16:106) in which *naskh* or a synonym is used to indicate a verse that was removed by God or replaced by another. Sura 22:52 is usually taken to refer to the Satanic verses episode in which the verse about the three goddesses was revealed to Muhammad by Satan instead of by God (Sura 53:19). God later annulled that revelation. From the eighth to the 11th centuries, scholars drew up lists of the abrogated and the abrogating verses. The earliest preserved treatise lists 42 abrogated verses, but this number expanded until a maximum of 238 abrogated passages were listed in one 11th-century book.

The most common form of abrogation is when God annulled the rule, but the verse itself remains in the Qur'an. Comparing three verses that speak of drinking wine illustrate how the concept of abrogation is applied. Sura 16:67 mentions wine along with food as a gift of God. Sura 2:219 says that both good and bad come from wine but the bad outweighs the good. Sura 4:43 warns believers not to come to prayer while drunk. Sura 5:90 says that wine along with gambling are works of Satan. Of course, this all depends on the assumption that the Qur'an is entirely self-consistent (it can't say one thing in one place and a contrary thing in another place) and on the correct dating of the passages.

IN THIS CHAPTER

» Marking major transition points in life

» Observing proper religious etiquette and custom

» Carving out a woman's ritual space in Islam

Chapter 5

Observing Other Religious Rituals and Customs

Scholars of religion often make a distinction between what some call the Great Tradition and the Little Tradition(s). *Great Tradition* is what the holy books of the religion teach and what official religious bodies have determined to be proper religious belief and practice. As a result, until recently, the Great Tradition was also religion as viewed by men, because most of these leadership positions were occupied by men.

In contrast, the *Little Tradition* is religion as lived in the lives of ordinary people. Little Tradition religion includes popular or folk religious beliefs and practices, many of which aren't authorized in the scriptures and which may be in conflict with the official Great Tradition version of the religion. The Little Tradition also often includes many religious practices of women and provides women an avenue for religious expression (and exercise of religious leadership) which Great Tradition religion may have denied them.

This chapters considers some of the Little Traditions of Islam.

TIP

Keep the following in mind as you read through this chapter:

- The extent to which these practices are observed and how they're observed varies widely from one Muslim culture to another, from one country to another, and from one age to another.
- Practices also vary according to education, social class, rural or urban setting, individual piety, and age.
- Describing what people actually do is more difficult than describing what official religious teachings say they "should" do. While official religion sets forth its beliefs and practices clearly, information isn't as easily available on the popular religion of the Little Tradition.
- Some Muslim theologians and legal scholars object to some of the practices associated with popular Islam because they believe such practices aren't supported by the Qur'an and the practice (tradition) of the first generation of Muslims. Movements have frequently arisen in Islam to purify the religion from practices of folk religion, some of which may have come from other religions or pre-exist Islam.

Marking Life's Transitions

Many religions, including Islam, claim to be a total way of life. When religion pervades all of life, most major transitions in life, such as birth, marriage, and death (often called *rites of passage*), have religious significance and are marked by religious rituals.

Being born

In some Islamic countries, as in other countries, pregnancy and the period between pregnancy and birth may be marked by celebrations, visits, and special foods. We start with what is the first main event in the life cycle: the birth of the child and associated rituals. Even this event, as with all the life cycle rituals, may be marked by additional rituals from the local culture that are not closely connected with Islam. For example, among the Yoruba tribe in Nigeria, many Muslim parents conduct an ancient naming ceremony designed to ensure the child a safe entry into the world, as well as a separate Islamic naming ceremony. Also in Islam, the naming and the other events are intended to welcome the new child into the Muslim community and ensure protection from any evils that may threaten the child at this first major life transition.

REMEMBER

At birth, the father speaks the first *(adhan) and* second *(iqama)* calls to prayer (see Book 6, Chapter 4) in the child's right and left ears. The father is encouraged to chew the meat of a date and put a little bit in the child's mouth because, as a number of traditions report (without explaining why), this is what Muhammad did when his children were born. Friends bring small gifts, and Sura 1, the *Fatiha* (see Book 6, Chapter 4), is recited in the presence of the infant.

Celebrations mark the birth. During these early days of the infant's life, the parents may take special action (such as good-luck charms or special spoken formulas) to ensure that evil *jinn* (see Book 6, Chapter 3) don't injure the child.

Receiving a name

The father chooses the child's name in consultation with the mother and other relatives. He may name the child at birth, but naming occurs normally when the infant is one week old. In the interval, the parents may call the child Muhammad or Fatima (the name of one of the daughters of Muhammad).

What will the father name the child? Compound names that indicate a close relation to God are popular — such as Abadallah (servant of God). Also highly recommended are any names linked to Muhammad and his family, including Muhammad (or any of the other names commonly used for Muhammad such as Ahmad) and `Ali (the husband of Fatima) for boys, and Fatima for girls. Shi`ite Muslims tend to favor names of the members of the 12 *imams'* families. Names not connected with Islam are permitted, but modern Islamist reform movements urge the use of Arabic names, which have specific Islamic meaning. As a result, Islamic names have become increasingly popular in non-Arabic countries such as Indonesia and the United States. In Arabic culture, a person usually receives a number of names — some acquired during their life — which are strung together and indicate important information about the person, which puts them in a social context (see the "Understanding Muslim names" sidebar).

All Muslims follow the basic naming custom of speaking the call to prayer in the infant's ear and reciting the *Fatiha*. Further details depend on the country, who is present for the ceremony (in addition to father, mother, and the infant), how the participants are dressed, and whether a feast or special meal is involved. For example, in Morocco, both mother and child wear special clothes, and their faces, hands, and feet are decorated with *henna* (reddish-brown cosmetic dye) designs.

Offering the sacrifice

The `*aqiqa* sacrifice, recalling Abraham's intended sacrifice of his son, often occurs along with the naming of the one-week-old child. Only the *Hanbalites*, followers of one of the four main Sunni schools of Islamic law, say this is a required ritual, but other branches of Islamic laws recommend it, especially for boys.

The sacrifice is two male sheep or goats for a boy and one for a girl — if the parents can afford to do so. Some of the animal is donated to the poor. In addition, wealthy parents may cut the child's hair, weigh it, and donate an equivalent amount of silver or other forms of cash or valuables to the poor or to a charitable foundation.

Circumcising (khitan)

Circumcision is not mentioned in the Qur'an but is almost universal among Muslim males, although only the Shafi`ite legal School mandates the practice for both sexes. Male circumcision is the removal of the foreskin from the penis. Male circumcision is based upon the belief shared with the Jews that Abraham, the common ancestor of Jews and Muslims, circumcised his sons (see Genesis 17 in the Christian Bible, which you can read more on in Book 5, Chapter 2). Circumcision also occurs in other cultures such as ancient Egypt. In Arabic, the rite is called purification *(tahara)*, pointing to one of its functions. Muslim scholars may also associate circumcision (male and female) with control (not elimination) of the passions of the lower self (called the *nafs*).

TECHNICAL STUFF

The age of circumcision for boys differs from birth to about age 15 depending upon the country. In some countries, it is done at the time of birth or in infancy, and functions in the larger context of rituals that accompany birth and infancy. Probably most common is circumcision around the age of six to seven, when the boy is about to begin to assume his religious responsibilities by participating in *salat* (Islamic prayer). In countries such as Java (part of Indonesia) and Yemen, circumcision is a coming-of-age (puberty) ritual when the child is between 10 and 12. In these cases, circumcision may be linked with the boy having completed recitation of the Qur'an in Qur'anic School. In still other countries, circumcision is done a couple of years later and functions as a preparation for marriage and full participation as an adult in the community. Sometimes, circumcision is a major celebration with special dress, foods, and processions. In some countries, several boys may share the same celebration of their circumcision. Among modernist Muslims, circumcision is more often a private, family occasion. Circumcision is recommended but not required for male converts to Islam.

For girls, circumcision has never been marked by major celebrations. Female circumcision (also called *clitoridectomy*) can vary from removal of a small portion of the prepuce of the clitoris to removal of the clitoris, the labia minora, and portions of the labia majora. Female circumcision is common in Upper Egypt, Sudan, Somalia, Ethiopia, West Africa, Southeast Asia, Southern Arabia, and parts of Indonesia. Where we have data, female circumcision in these areas (like male circumcision) seems to have predated the advent of Islam and thus doesn't originate due to Islamic influence.

Based on a tradition in which Muhammad advised against cutting a woman severely (in circumcision), some Muslim authorities discourage female circumcision entirely saying that Muhammad allowed but did not recommend the practice; others say the minimal form is recommended but not obligatory; some say it is required and still others say it's not permitted because mutilation of the body is against Islamic law. Even in the same country, one group may practice female circumcision and an adjacent group may not. A worldwide campaign has emerged against female genital mutilation.

Coming of age

One way of defining *coming of age* in Islam is to say that this is the point at which the child becomes responsible for performing the Five Pillars of Islam (see Book 6, Chapter 4). Generally at about this same time, the child is expected to observe the rules regulating contact and separation among the sexes. However, Islam does not have a universally accepted coming-of-age ritual comparable to the bar/bat mitzvah ceremony in Judaism (see Book 4, Chapter 3 for more on that). In some countries, circumcision (depending on the age at which circumcision is done) or ceremonies celebrating the completion of learning to recite the entire Qur'an function as coming-of-age ceremonies.

Getting hitched

As in the case of other rites of passage, much variation exists in how marriage is celebrated. The minimum requirements involving whom one can marry and the requirements for a marriage contract and a *dowry* (an agreed upon bridal gift from the husband to the bride) are followed by all Muslims so long as no conflict exists with local law. For example, Muslim men should not marry more than one wife in countries where polygamy is illegal. Beyond this minimum, as in the case of other rites of passage, much variation exists in terms of how a spouse is selected and regarding the various ceremonies that may begin with the contract and conclude with a wedding feast after consummation of the marriage.

Muslims are expected to marry, and the Qur'an and *hadiths* (traditions) encourage early marriage. The man and woman should be sexually mature and the man should be capable of supporting his wife financially. Practically speaking, a typical male would be in his late teens and the female the same age or several years younger, although earlier marriages occur. Marriage isn't based on romantic love but rather on considerations such as ancestry, property, how religious the proposed partner is, and benefits to both families. The couple may meet in the presence of a chaperon prior to signing the marriage contract, but this meeting isn't required. Although Muslim men may marry women of other people of the book (basically, Christians and Jews), Muslim women must marry Muslim men in order to ensure the children will be raised as Muslims. Islamic law also prohibits marrying close relatives.

In the eyes of the law

Marriage in Islam is a legal contract, not a religious sacrament. Legally, the marriage depends on a contract *(nika)* that includes the following:

- It is signed by the bride's father or guardian in the presence of two witnesses. This normally takes place before the actual wedding night.

  REMEMBER

  The bride's father or guardian acts for the woman in marriage negotiations. Differences exist among legal Schools as to whether the guardian may force his choice on the bride, but in Islamic countries today, the bride's father or guardian is required to act in the interests of the bride. Adult women have more say in choosing a husband than young women do. In the 20th century, some Muslim states set minimum ages for marriage (for example, 18 and 16 for the man and woman, respectively) and required registration of the marriage with the state.

- The groom's payment of a gift to the bride is based on Sura 4:4. Without this dowry, the marriage is invalid. The gift may be specified in the contract. While normally paid prior to the consummation of the marriage, the contract can allow for installment payments. The dowry remains the property of the wife to do with as she wishes, but in some cases she may be expected to buy furnishings for the home. The dowry may consist of money or goods. Tradition says that bridal gifts shouldn't be overly extravagant, although they should be comparable to what other brides of similar social status receive. Tradition reports Muhammad approving such things as a pair of sandals or a handful of flour in the case of a poor couple.

Here comes the bride: The ceremony

Islamic traditions agree that Muhammad commended holding a wedding celebration or feast, although this is not required by Islamic law. A celebration or feast is one way of fulfilling the requirement that a marriage take place in public. Beyond this, customs vary widely but at some point usually involve a party with singing, dancing, feasting, and perhaps Qur'anic recitations. Wedding celebrations (one or more) may be linked to signing of the contract, fetching of the bride to the groom's home, the night of the consummation of the wedding, and a wedding feast within two days after the wedding. However it is organized, this is a joyous occasion for the couple, the families, and the community. In these events, normal separation of men and women is observed.

Honeymoons are not a traditional Muslim custom and some say Muslims in Western countries should not adopt the honeymoon custom. Others, recognizing that wedding customs in Islam generally combine Islamic requirements with local custom see nothing wrong in a honeymoon.

TIP

A person invited to a marriage celebration is obligated to accept the invitation.

Taking many wives

You may have heard that Muslim men are allowed up to four wives. However, except among some traditional royalty, few Muslim men have more than one wife today. In parts of Africa where polygamy was traditional prior to Islam, it continued naturally under Islam.

Muhammad said that divorce is the most despised of the things that God nevertheless allows. No stigma attaches to marrying a divorced person, although tradition says it's better to choose a mate who is not divorced. Cases have existed in Muslim history of men abusing their rights of divorce. In the case where some Muslim men abuse their rights by marrying young girls, courts and legal reforms in a number of Muslim countries today endeavor to prevent such abuse.

Marriage as a coming-of-age passage

To some extent for men, but much more so for women, marriage is the equivalent to a coming-of-age ritual in many traditional Muslim societies. Women leave their home and often assume tasks such as managing the home and producing children.

In some countries, birth — even more than marriage or circumcision — marks the transition to adulthood for the mother. As in many pre-modern cultures, in some Muslim countries, special restrictions and purifications mark the integration of the new mother back into society. Special purifications may be required of the mother. Mother (and child) in some cases may undergo a period of seclusion — first to their room with no contacts outside the immediate family, then to the house, with broader contacts allowed during this period. Again, the details of seclusion and purification after birth vary and are not specified in traditional Islamic law.

Knocking on death's door

REMEMBER

Death, the event and its meaning, is an issue that all religions must guide its believers in how to handle it. While in other rites of passage, Islam has traditionally been willing to incorporate local customs or at least ignore them without objection, when it comes to the final transition — death — Islam is less willing to compromise with the practices of the local culture. Death in Islam is the point where it all comes together and determines the eternal destiny of the person. Death is natural, but still a momentous event. Beliefs and rituals for facing this transition should be dealt with in a strictly Islamic manner (see Book 6, Chapter 1 for more on Islamic beliefs about what happens at death). Therefore, greater uniformity exists in the rituals associated with death in Islam than in any other of the rites of passage.

Dying

When death is imminent, a Muslim is placed on his right side, the first testimony ("there is no God but Allah") is whispered in his ear, and Sura 36 is recited, including verse 12, which says, "We [God] give life to the dead and record that which they have forwarded and that which they have left behind," and also, "And the trumpet [announcing the Day of Judgment] will be blown, and men will slide forth out of their tombs to their Lord."

Preparing for burial

Because death is natural, no unnatural effort should be expended to make it appear as if death hasn't really occurred. Traditionally, corpses were not embalmed, although, as in other matters, here, too, Muslims follow local legal requirements. Because the body is literally to be resurrected, cremation isn't allowed. Relatives of the same sex as the deceased face the body toward Mecca and purify it three times with soap, water, and scents. These attendants completely wrap the body in white cloths (three for men; five for women). If the deceased had performed the pilgrimage to Mecca, their pilgrimage garments (see Book 6, Chapter 4) may be used for the wrapping. A special ritual prayer for the dead *(salat al-janazh)* is performed at a mosque, in a home, or, in the West, at a funeral home.

Burial

Burial occurs on the day of death, if possible. In a Muslim country, a procession winds its way through the streets, with four men carrying the bier. Strangers are encouraged to join the procession for a short distance. Sometimes women mourners who loudly cry out their sorrow are hired, although this practice is frowned on by legal scholars.

The grave is deep enough to protect from wild animals and to conceal odors. Coffins are permitted but not normally used unless legally required. A niche is carved out in one side of the grave, where the corpse is placed facing Mecca. If the first part of the *shahada* ("there is no God but God") wasn't said while the person was dying, it's spoken at this time. Someone may give a brief talk at the grave, and the mourners recite the *Fatiha*. The niche is sealed, the mourners toss three handfuls of dirt onto the grave, and the procession departs. They may stop and recite the *Fatiha* once again after 40 steps to aid the deceased who is already being cross-examined by the angels Munkar and Nakir (see Book 6, Chapter 1).

After burial

Islamic tradition recommends a simple grave marker with the name of the deceased and some verses from the Qur'an. This hasn't stopped very elaborate grave markers and mausoleums from being erected, however. Visiting the grave of the dead is recommended, especially on the fortieth day after death.

Mourning continues for three days for most friends and family, although widows observe mourning for four months and ten days.

Observing Everyday Customs

Religion as a way of life includes not only the mandatory ritual practices and the life cycle observances. Instead, any act, properly done, may have religious significance, including the most trivial and mundane actions. What non-believers may regard as manners, customs, or even superstitions also acquire religious meaning. Eating — both how to eat and what to eat — has religious significance in many cultures. What one wears may also have religious significance. You can recognize some Hasidic (mystical) Jews by their long, black coats and fur rim hats (more about this group in Book 4, Chapter 1). If you live in states such as Pennsylvania, Ohio, and Indiana, you instantly recognize the Amish by their fashion of dress that looks like it came out of rural America of 200 years ago. People recognize a picture of an Indian Yogi by the clothes he wears, and the turban worn by all male *Sikhs* (a South Asian religion) makes them instantly recognizable.

REMEMBER

Why do religious people observe these customs? The lead character in the musical, *Fiddler on the Roof* (a portrayal of life in a Jewish village in 19th-century eastern Europe) replies when asked the same question about the traditions of his village. The answer is simple and yet frustrating: tradition. They do it, because their fathers and mothers before them did it this way, as did their grandparents before them. Traditions help mark the boundary between members of the group and non-members. For Islam, an additional answer exists: the model of the prophet

Muhammad. When a Muslim tries to determine the proper way to behave, they look to see whether information exists as to what Muhammad did (or said).

This section introduces you to Muslim customs and manners, some of which are mandated by Islamic law (permitted and non-permitted foods, for example) and others of which are a matter of tradition.

Finding food for thought

REMEMBER

Most foods are permitted with the following three major restrictions:

- Sura 2:173 says,
  - He [God] has forbidden to you flesh from animals found dead [meaning they were not ritually killed], blood, pork, and any food offered to idols.

  Especially in China, where pork is crucial for Chinese cuisine, avoidance of all pork is a practice which sharply distinguishes Chinese Muslims from non-Muslim Chinese. Muslim, Jewish, and other scholars have tried to offer logical reasons for the avoidance of pork (for example, dangers to health from insufficiently cooked pork) but basically it comes down to matters of purity and the word of God. Many cultures have food taboos — dog, cat, and (generally) horse in America. Avoidance of certain foods is one way, according to anthropologists, of marking group (or religious) identity. Muslims are descendants of Abraham and simply took over the prohibition on pork from the Jewish tradition. Judaism has similar prohibitions, but in contrast to Jews, Muslims may eat shellfish.
- No drinking of alcoholic beverages.
- No consumption of blood or animals that were not properly slaughtered. The gullet, wind pipe, and arteries are quickly cut at the throat (while saying God's name) so that blood is drained quickly out of the animal's body.

REMEMBER

The process is much like *kosher* slaughtering in Judaism (see Book 4, Chapter 3). Muslims may eat kosher food when *halal* (permitted) food is unavailable, because kosher foods follow an even-stricter ritual standard than halal foods.

TIP

For Muslims in a non-Muslim country, such as the United States, being certain that processed foods haven't been contaminated with pork byproducts or alcohol is difficult. Some websites for Muslims provide detailed information about the status of various foods in America, including those at fast-food eateries.

Traditionally, Muslims eat with the right hand, with or without utensils, preceding the meal with the *basmala* ("in the name of God, the compassionate, the caring.") Muslims may eat at the homes of non-Muslims, assuming, of course, that the meal isn't pork roast with wine! Islamic legal scholars debate whether Muslims can eat or work in restaurants that serve alcohol.

Dressing the part

Muslims are expected to observe good hygiene, to be clean, and to dress modestly. Both sexes may wear perfumes, because pleasant smells are much appreciated in Islam. One shouldn't eat garlic before going out in public. As usual, much of this is based on traditions concerning what Muhammad wore or what he said about clothing. Sura 7:26 says, "We [God] have sent down on you clothes to cover your shame [nakedness] as well as to be an adornment to you" (see also 7:31), clearly stating the basic guideline of being attractively but modestly dressed (men and women). Traditional sayings of Muhammad warn against extravagant dress to simply impress others and specifically prohibit silk and gold for men while allowing them (in moderation) for women. Another saying of Muhammad is, "Cleanse yourself, for Islam is cleanliness." Of course, nothing in these requirements for proper dress and hygiene are unique to Islam, nor should they be because Islam would say this is proper human behavior and dress for all people.

TIP

Clothing styles are unique to each country, however, and Muslim men may wear purely Western clothing or a Western-style coat over a traditional tunic or gown. Here we describe what a typical, traditional Muslim man or woman would wear. Members of Islamist movements (as well as some Muslims in the West) adopt similar clothing to emphasize their identity as Muslims. Although you see men and women dressed as described in the following bullets in places like South Asia and West Africa, you see other men and women dressed in clothing that Westerners wouldn't immediately identify as Muslim dress.

Clothing for men and women differs, as follows:

- **Women:** Long skirt or loose-fitting trousers; long-sleeve, loose top that's unfitted at waist; head cover over the neck or shoulders. While some Islamic cultures say that Islam requires covering the women entirely from head to toe, including veiling the face, others disagree.
- **Men:** Long-sleeve tunic over baggy pants or a long, loose-fitting gown. They also wear a head cap, and keep a trimmed beard and mustache. In the Ottoman (Turkish) Empire, the head cap (called a *fez*) was shaped like a cylinder with a tassel. The Bedouin Arabic headgear *(kafia)* and turbans are other traditional head coverings.

AVOIDING THE EVIL EYE

Long before the advent of Islam, Arabs often attributed their misfortunes to someone having cast the *evil eye* upon them. As with witches in the West, old, unmarried women were particularly regarded as having the power of the evil eye. Spells and *amulets* (good-luck charms) helped avert the power of the evil eye, as well as mischief caused by *jinn* (evil spirits; see Book 6, Chapter 3). Another means (undoubtedly also pre-Islamic in origin) to counteract the effect of the evil eye was to stretch forth one's hand, palm forward, with the five fingers spread out. While such beliefs and practices are rather peripheral to Muslim theology and not found in the Qur'an, they continue in Islam, as folk practices do in many religions.

Minding your manners

A tradition attributed to Muhammad says, "Good breeding is a part of the faith." To be a Muslim is to act in a proper human manner, in contrast to the way that other creatures (in accord with their proper nature) conduct themselves. Thus Muslims have a whole category of literary works about proper manners and conduct.

REMEMBER

We offer several examples from such a modern manual, M. I. Al-Kaysi's *Morals and Manners in Islam: A Guide to Islamic Adab* (Islamic Book Trust, 2000):

- Be prompt to thank a person saying, "May God reward you well." According to a tradition, Muhammad said, "He who does not thank people does not thank God."
- Don't try to restrain a sneeze, which is a blessing from God. When a person sneezes, they should say, *al-hamdu lilah* ("Praise be to God").
- Mercy and kindness should characterize all aspects of the treatment of animals.
- In general, the right foot, side, and hand is favored in all positive actions such as eating, drinking, holding the Qur'an, shaking hands, putting on clothes, and putting on shoes. Remember this when interacting with Muslim acquaintances. This may seem discriminatory to lefties and probably has no logical explanation beyond the fact that in many cultures "right" is associated with positive and "left" with negative actions. It can as well be the reverse. The basic point seems to be to distinguish even by your bodily gestures which things are pure and which impure (remembering that impure does not mean "evil").

Looking at Women's Rituals

Women have traditionally been excluded from or restricted in their participation in the major religious rituals of Islam, including attending the mosque (some areas of the mosque may be shut off to women). In the United States, while separation of women from men is still the norm in the mosque, women play a crucial role in activities at the mosque. In addition, in the *hajj* (see Book 6, Chapter 4), women participate equally with men.

TECHNICAL STUFF

Because women don't participate to the same extent as men in "official Islam," many Muslim women have created their own substitutes. Women play a major role in various rites of passage, such as circumcision and marriage. More women than men visit saint tombs, where women are free to assert their own interests and desires. For example, a barren woman may visit a saint's shrine and pray to God to have a child. As part of that prayer, she makes a vow to return and praise God and Muhammad when her petition is granted. Here, vow refers to a formal promise made to God by the believer, but has nothing to do with more formal vows of chastity or poverty such as Roman Catholic and Buddhist monks and nuns take.

In parts of Egypt and the Sudan, women are prominent in *zar* ceremonies, which deal with causes and cures of mental and physical illness. *Zar* refers to both the possessed woman and the ceremony to cure her. Some Sufis (mystics) are women, such as the legendary medieval Sufi saint Rabi`a. In addition, key Sufi figures such as Ibn Arabi acknowledged their female teachers.

REMEMBER

While some traditionalist movements simply want to push women back into the shadows, other Islamist movements involve women (many of whom are college-educated professionals) actively in various ways.

7

Mormonism

Contents at a Glance

IN THIS CHAPTER

» Seeing life through Mormon eyes: The past, present, and future

» The Mormon view on God, Jesus, and the Holy Ghost

» Exploring how Mormons are different from other Christians

» Discovering Mormonism from its beginnings

» Finding out what it's like to be a Mormon

Chapter 1
A New World Religion

Buddhism, Judaism, Islam, Hinduism, traditional branches of Christianity — and Mormonism? If you ask some demographers and sociologists, the idea of Mormonism emerging as the newest major world religion isn't far-fetched. In the Christian sector, although Protestantism grew out of Catholicism (as outlined in Book 5, Chapter 5), Mormonism bills itself as a completely fresh start, with enough distinctive beliefs and practices to back up that claim.

Mormonism isn't the newest kid on the religious block, but its start during the 1820s seems relatively recent — in fact, compared to other world religions, Mormonism is a toddler, still maturing in terms of culture, identity, growth, government, and other aspects. This chapter gives an overview of what it means to be a Mormon.

Following the Mormon Worldview

The following equation best sums up how Mormons understand the universe and the purpose of life: As humans are, God used to be; as God is, humans may become.

REMEMBER

One main key to getting the gist of Mormonism is the belief that a person's existence doesn't begin with birth on this earth. Rather, Mormons believe that all people lived as spirits before coming here. For Mormons, this belief helps explain a whole lot about the conditions and purposes of this earthly life, which they view as God's test of his children. In addition, Mormons hold some unusual views about the afterlife, particularly regarding what human beings can become. (For more detailed information on the Mormon view of the afterlife, see Book 7, Chapter 2.)

Life before mortal life

If life doesn't start with conception and birth, when does it start? For Mormons, it never really started, because each person has an eternal essence that has always existed. However, Mormons believe that God created spiritual bodies to house each person's eternal essence, so he's the spiritual father of humankind. All human spirits were born before the earth was created.

Sitting at the knee of God and his wife, many spirit children expressed a desire to grow up and become like their Heavenly Parents. So God set up the *plan of salvation*, which involved creating an earth where his children may gain physical bodies and go through a challenging test of faith and obedience. Those who pass the test with flying colors get the chance to eventually start an eternal family like God's.

In *premortality*, as Mormons call this stage, two of the oldest spirit siblings made a big impression. The first spirit, named Jehovah, volunteered to help everyone overcome the sin and death they'd unavoidably encounter during the earthly test, and this brother was eventually born on earth as Jesus Christ. Mormons believe he's their Savior and strive to be like him. The other spirit, named Lucifer, rebelled against God's plan of salvation, convincing a bunch of siblings to follow him and start a war. God banished Lucifer and his followers to the earth without bodies, and Mormons believe that these spirits are still trying to win humans to their side and thwart God's plan.

Life on earth

Good news: In the Mormon view, everyone who's born on this earth chose to follow God's plan of salvation and come here. Even those who give in to evil during earthly life will still receive an eternal reward for making the correct choice during premortality. Mormons don't believe that humans are born carrying the stain of Adam's original sin, as Catholics and some Protestants do (see Book 5). But they do believe that each individual's circumstances in this life are at least partly influenced by what that person did in premortality.

One of the most difficult aspects of this mortal test is that humans can't remember what happened in premortality, so they must rediscover their divine origins through faith. However, God sent Jesus Christ not only to overcome sin and death but also to establish the gospel, which serves as a road map back to God. Two kinds of messengers help people understand and follow this gospel: prophets and the *Holy Ghost*, a spiritual being who speaks directly to the human spirit (for more on him, read on later in this chapter). By listening to these guides, people can figure out the puzzle of life. Unfortunately, the devil strives to fill the world with distractions and counterfeits.

WARNING

Another hard aspect of the earthly test is that God generally won't interfere with people's freedom to act, even when they do terrible things to each other or fail miserably. In addition, God allows accidents, natural disasters, illnesses, and other difficulties to challenge his children and prompt them to seek him out. For Mormons, it helps to remember that these temporary trials represent a mere blink of the eye on an eternal scale, and they exercise faith that God will comfort and protect those who ask for his help to endure suffering.

REMEMBER

During mortality, Mormons believe that everyone needs to participate in certain rituals in order to live with God in the afterlife and become like him. Someone holding God's priesthood authority, which Mormons believe currently comes only through the *LDS Church* (Latter-day Saints), must perform these rituals. If a person dies without receiving these ordinances, Mormons perform the rituals in temples on behalf of the deceased person, whose spirit then decides whether or not to accept. These ordinances are

- Baptism
- Confirmation, which includes receiving the gift of the Holy Ghost
- Priesthood ordination (for all worthy males)
- Washing and anointing
- Endowment
- Sealing, including celestial marriage for those wedded on earth

For more on many of these ordinances, see Book 7, Chapter 3.

TECHNICAL STUFF

Throughout this Book, we use the terms *Mormon, LDS,* and *Latter-day Saint* interchangeably to refer to the doctrine, teachings, practices, and members of The Church of Jesus Christ of Latter-day Saints.

Life after mortal life

Mormons believe that when humans die, they slough off their physical bodies and return to the spiritual state. Some go to spirit paradise, and some go to spirit prison. Mormons believe that the spirits in paradise visit the spirits in prison and teach them the gospel, and some choose to accept it and cross over into paradise. Whether they're in paradise or prison, the stopover in the spirit world is only temporary, because God has greater things in store.

Eventually, after God's spirit children have experienced their earthly tests and paid for their sins either by receiving the Savior's Atonement or suffering themselves, he'll resurrect everyone with perfect physical bodies that will last forever. Then he'll sort people into three heavenly kingdoms:

- **Telestial kingdom:** Those who live in sin, die without repenting, and never accept the Savior's Atonement go here, after suffering for their own sins in spirit prison.
- **Terrestrial kingdom:** Those who live good lives but don't embrace the full gospel will inherit this kingdom. Jesus pays for their sins.

  (Both the telestial kingdom and the terrestrial kingdom are glorious paradises, not hell or places of torture.)
- **Celestial kingdom:** This highest kingdom is reserved for those who live the full gospel and receive the proper ordinances. This kingdom is where God lives and where his children can become like him.

For more on the three heavenly kingdoms, see Book 7, Chapter 2.

The Head Honcho: God the Father

The Mormon God — usually referred to as *Heavenly Father* — is quite different from the God most Christians worship. In fact, Mormons reject the traditional concept of the *Trinity*, the idea that the Father, Son, and Holy Ghost are different forms of one entity whose ethereal substance fills the entire universe.

Rather, Mormons believe in a *godhead*, which is made up of God the Father, His Son, and the Holy Ghost, staffed by three individual beings — Mormons call them *personages* — who are one in mind and purpose:

- In the CEO position is God, a physically resurrected man who's achieved a glorified state of eternal *omnipotence* (meaning, he has all the power you could ever want and infinitely more). He's the literal father of human spirits and ruler of the universe.

» Second in command is God's son, Jesus Christ. He's a separate man whose spirit and physical body were literally procreated by God.

» Number three is a being whom Mormons commonly call the *Holy Ghost, Holy Spirit, Spirit of God,* or simply the *Spirit.* As a spiritual personage without a physical body, the Holy Ghost is able to directly communicate God's messages to the human spirit.

In addition, Mormons believe that God has a better half. He's eternally married to a glorified, deified woman who's known as *Heavenly Mother,* with whom he has spirit children. Most Mormons discuss their spiritual mother only rarely and briefly — but they do know that Heavenly Mother is like Heavenly Father in glory, perfection, compassion, wisdom, and holiness.

TIP

To Mormons, God is the same species as humans, but he's infinitely more advanced. To make a comparison, if humans are like newly hatched tadpoles, then God has already progressed through the frog stage and become a handsome prince. In the Mormon view, God isn't so much a *creator* as an *organizer* of raw materials.

Mormonism's founding prophet Joseph Smith taught

If men do not comprehend the character of God, they do not comprehend themselves.

More specifically, Joseph taught the following as life's great secret:

God himself was once as we are now, and is an exalted man, and sits enthroned in yonder heavens!

To Mormons, this means that God himself has gone through everything his human children have experienced, are now experiencing, and will yet experience. Nineteenth-century Mormon leaders taught that untold eons ago, God's eternal essence was born as a spirit to Heavenly Parents, just like human spirits would later be born to him. He received a physical, mortal body on an earthlike planet and passed his mortal test — evidently with flying colors. After his mortal body died and was resurrected, he advanced to his current position as supreme ruler of this universe. Of course, all this happened long ago and via a more advanced process than any human can comprehend. Modern-day LDS leaders are more reticent about God's origins than those 19th-century freewheelers, though they continue to emphasize that God has a glorified, resurrected physical body.

At some point after giving birth to their first spirit child (see the next section), God and his eternal wife had other spirit children as well — billions of them. To enable these children to start the cycle all over again by growing up and becoming like their own Heavenly Parents, God taught them the *plan of salvation*, which we describe in detail in Book 7, Chapter 2. All humans who pass through this earth are God's spirit children who agreed to undergo the most difficult phase of this plan: demonstrating their faith and obedience away from God's presence and thus determining their eternal status.

Second Mate: Christ the Son

Mormons view the New Testament as a mostly accurate account of Jesus's earthly ministry (for more on Mormon views regarding the Bible, see Book 7, Chapter 5). However, additional revelations to Mormon prophets have clarified aspects of what Jesus did before, during, and after his short mortal life, as well as what he's expected to do in the future.

First and best

In Mormon theology, the being who would become known as Jesus Christ was born first among all God's billions of spirit children, and he was by far the brightest, strongest, and most advanced of all God's children. In the premortal world, where human spirits dwelt with the Heavenly Parents and prepared for earthly birth, this eldest son took a primary leadership role and was known as *Jehovah*. Many people believe the names *Jehovah* and *the Lord* in the Old Testament refer to God the Father, but Mormons believe these names refer to the personage who would later be born as Jesus Christ.

God instituted the plan of salvation so that his spirit children can progress to become like him. In order for this plan to work, a savior was required to help everybody recover from the sin and death they'd encounter as part of the earthly test. Guess who volunteered? Jesus.

But also among God's oldest spirit children was another gifted and talented son, named Lucifer. Lucifer developed the worst ever case of sibling rivalry and rebelled against God and Jehovah/Jesus Christ, which got him and his followers kicked out of heaven. In the Mormon view, Jesus, the devil, and all humans everywhere are spiritual siblings.

Well before coming to earth to perform his saving mission, the Savior began serving as God's second in command. While God created the earth spiritually, the Savior (Jesus) took primary responsibility for the earth's physical creation. After mortals started wandering the planet with no memory of their premortal life, the Savior communicated with them through prophets and the Holy Ghost. On the rare occasion when God himself directly speaks or appears to a human, it's generally to introduce his Son.

Both mortal and divine

In the Mormon view, God fathered everybody's spirit, but the Savior's *physical* body was the only one literally procreated by God, in partnership with the mortal Mary. (We can discuss what some early Mormons believed about the logistics of that situation, but we won't go there.) Possessing both eternal and mortal DNA, Jesus was able to die and then be resurrected in glorified immortality, thus opening the way for everyone to eventually be resurrected.

Equally as importantly, Jesus paid the price for all the sins of humanity. In the Mormon view, whenever a moral law is broken, justice must be satisfied, and the Savior accomplished that for humankind on a spiritual, eternal level. Having paid this bill that mortals can't pay for themselves, he forgives the debt for all people who sincerely repent of their sins and strive to live his gospel. Although many Christians believe that Jesus extends his grace to anyone who simply asks, Mormon Christians believe the Savior picks up the slack as a person makes their best effort to be good.

REMEMBER

Together, the Savior's overcoming of death and sin is known as his *Atonement.* Mormons believe that the hardest, most significant phase of the Atonement occurred in the Garden of Gethsemane, during that long night when Jesus literally sweat drops of blood (as described in the Bible, Luke 22:44). Although crucifixion was a horrible way to die, numerous others died that same way. Consequently, Mormons don't place heavy religious significance on the sign of the cross. To Mormons, the most important aspects of the story are that Christ's sacrifice atoned for people's sins and that he lives today.

The Savior's post-crucifixion checklist

After his mortal body died on the cross, the Savior immediately got busy with the following tasks:

- **During the three days between Christ's death and resurrection, Mormons believe his spirit visited the realm of the dead.** Wanting to extend his atonement to every human who ever lived, he organized the righteous spirits to start preaching the gospel to those who died without hearing or accepting it. Until then, an impassable gulf had lain between the righteous and the wicked in the spirit world.

- **Jesus transformed his physical body into a perfect, glorified, immortal vessel for his eternal spirit.** At the time of his resurrection, all the righteous people who'd died before him got resurrected too, all the way back to Adam. Most of the righteous who died after him will wait until his *Second Coming* (the time when Jesus Christ will return to judge the world and bring about one thousand years of peace known as the "Millennium," more on that later in this chapter) to be resurrected. Mormons view the Savior's resurrection as the single most significant and miraculous event in human history.
- **As recorded in the New Testament, the resurrected Savior spent time teaching his apostles.** In addition, Mormons believe he visited the people living in the Western Hemisphere, part of the "other sheep" that the Bible's John 10:16 says he mentioned. Lasting several days, this visit is recounted as the centerpiece of the Book of Mormon, Joseph Smith's translation of the sacred account left behind by these people. He may have visited additional peoples around the world, who presumably have their own scriptures and sacred records about those encounters.
- **After the resurrected Savior ascended to heaven, he kept working behind the scenes among humans.** Mormons believe that, within a few decades after Christ left the earth, persecution and corruption ruined his church. For about 1,700 years, the Savior didn't reestablish an official church or prophet on the earth, although he continued blessing and inspiring worthy, faithful individuals, especially those who sought religious freedoms.
- **Finally, when conditions were right for the restoration of the true religion, God and Jesus appeared to Joseph Smith in 1820.** During the subsequent 24 years, Jesus restored his church, his gospel, and God's priesthood through the Prophet Joseph. Since then, Mormons believe the Savior has been actively leading the Church through whatever man is serving as the current prophet. One of the LDS Church's main purposes is to prepare people for Christ's eventual Second Coming.

As Mormons strive to develop a personal relationship with Heavenly Father, they recognize that Jesus Christ is the broker and the gatekeeper — in theological terms, the *mediator* — between God and humanity. The only way back to God is through him. Mormons feel deep gratitude and love for the Savior and pledge total allegiance to him. When they pray to the Father or do anything else of a religious nature, they do it in Christ's name. The Church is Christ's, the gospel is Christ's, and Christ administers God's priesthood among humans.

Although everything centers on Christ, Mormons view him as a means to an end, not an end in himself. Mormons are sometimes accused of blasphemy for believing that humans can become like God. However, from a Mormon perspective, the idea that the Savior accomplished his Atonement just so people can strum harps and sing praises for eternity seems almost blasphemous.

When he comes again

No one but God knows exactly when Jesus will return in glory to rule the earth for 1,000 years, but Mormons believe the time is fast approaching and people should prepare.

Signs of the times

Although the Church's restoration is one of the key signs that the Second Coming is near, Mormons believe they must still preach the gospel to all nations before Christ will return.

Unfortunately, many of the signs preceding the Second Coming don't sound like too much fun. The earth will go haywire with natural calamities, including earthquakes, disease, storms, and famine, and the wicked will run rampant. According to Mormon scripture, "All things shall be in commotion; and . . . fear shall come upon all people" (Doctrine and Covenants 88:91). Of course, the Lord has promised to comfort the righteous during these times of crisis, and many of them will survive to welcome him back.

It's a bird! It's a plane!

At a crucial point during *Armageddon*, the world's final catastrophic war, Mormons believe the Savior will descend out of the sky to assume control of the earth and accomplish the following tasks:

- **Levitate the good people:** As the Savior comes down from the heavens, he'll resurrect the righteous dead, who'll be airlifted up to meet him, along with those righteous people who are still living. Together with those who were already resurrected at the time of Jesus's own resurrection, these people will eventually inherit the *celestial kingdom,* where they'll live with God and potentially become like him.
- **Say goodbye to bad guys:** With the good people safe, he'll destroy the wicked mortals who are still living, imprison Satan, cleanse the earth with fire, and restore the earth to its Garden of Eden status, with no weeds or carnivores. All the wicked spirits from throughout history will stay in timeout in spirit prison.

» **Start his own show:** He'll establish a perfectly fair, just, and peaceful worldwide government — run by both Church members and nonmembers — and launch the 1,000-year period of earthly paradise known as the *Millennium.* After the Millennium begins, he'll resurrect the medium-good people from throughout history, those who lived decent lives but didn't fully embrace the gospel. These people will eventually inherit the *terrestrial kingdom.*

As great as the Millennium sounds, it has a catch at the end. Satan will be unleashed for one last time, and he'll succeed in turning away more people from God. The armies of the righteous will defeat the armies of evil for the final time, and God will forever cast out Satan and his followers into outer darkness. Then will come the final judgment, when all people receive their eternal reward in one of the three kingdoms of heaven.

God's Whisperer: The Holy Ghost

Mormons are unusual in their belief that God the Father has a physical body, like his Son Jesus Christ. The Holy Ghost, in contrast, is a spiritual being. In fact, Mormons often say *Holy Spirit* rather than *Holy Ghost*, using the two terms interchangeably. (*Ghost* was a term used in the 17th-century King James Version of the Bible to signify "spirit," and the name stuck.)

Mormons believe the Holy Ghost is a witness to truth, a comforter, and a sanctifier. The more pure and obedient that people are, the better they're able to feel the Holy Ghost's spiritual influence. Mormons strive to follow God's commandments so they can retain the companionship of the Holy Ghost as much as possible, and they draw upon his guidance when discerning right from wrong, evaluating spiritual teachings, and pressing on toward perfection. As the Spirit carries out the will of the Father, his influence can be felt everywhere in the world at the same time — in fact, Church leaders compare the Holy Ghost to the sun, which warms the entire earth and sheds light everywhere.

The Spirit who never got a body

The Holy Ghost is unique among the three personages in the Godhead because this member is the only one without a physical body. Church leaders have taught that the Holy Ghost has a *spiritual* body, which is presumably a more advanced, deified version of the spirit body that Mormons believe everyone had in the premortal life.

TECHNICAL STUFF

Mormon theology hasn't offered a definitive statement about the origins and identity of the Holy Ghost, focusing instead on this spirit personage's role in the Godhead and in people's lives. Some Mormons believe the Holy Ghost is one of God's spirit children who was called for this particular mission and will be the last spirit to be blessed with a physical body. Even more controversially, some Mormons would like to think the Holy Ghost is female, perhaps even Heavenly Mother herself. However, this is far from orthodox belief. As one Mormon apostle explained, God hasn't yet given revelation on the Spirit's origin or destiny, and debating it is "speculative and fruitless." In deference to current LDS Church usage, in this book we refer to the Holy Ghost with male pronouns.

Mormons believe that as a spirit, the Holy Ghost can communicate intimately with every person's spirit, though the person needs to strive to live righteously so as not to repel the Holy Spirit. No unclean thing can sustain the presence of God, and the Holy Ghost literally imparts God's presence to humans in a tangible way. With this idea in mind, Mormons who've been baptized and have received the gift of the Holy Ghost (see the next section) are careful to remain worthy of that gift.

The Holy Ghost's many roles

So what does the Holy Ghost do, exactly? While the Father organizes and sustains all things and the Son redeems mortality, the Holy Ghost kind of keeps the home fires burning. In fact, fire is one symbol of the Holy Ghost that frequently appears in scripture (see, for example, the apostles' experience with "tongues of fire" when they were baptized in the Spirit in the New Testament, recounted in Acts 2). The Holy Ghost performs several vital functions in the Godhead and in bringing people to Christ.

The witness of Christ

Have you ever noticed that in scripture, the Holy Spirit seems to show up just when Christ makes an appearance? When Jesus is baptized in the Bible's New Testament, for example, the Spirit descends — perhaps figuratively — in the form of a dove just as Heavenly Father announces the coming of Christ: "This is my beloved Son" (Matthew 3:16–17). In John 15:26, Jesus promises that the Holy Ghost will testify of him. In other words, the Holy Ghost is a witness of Christ, pointing people to Christ's glory and truth.

In Mormonism, the *law of witnesses* dictates that more than one righteous person will confirm a true spiritual principle. This idea seems to be true of the Godhead as well: The Spirit is an additional witness of Christ. In the Savior's baptismal story, for example, God announces Christ's identity while the Spirit rests on Jesus. The other members of the Godhead testify to Christ's divine nature.

The comforter

Shortly before Christ was crucified, he promised his disciples that he wouldn't leave them comfortless but would send a comforter to help them in their path (John 16). This promised helper was the Holy Ghost.

The Holy Ghost exists as a comforter for each person and also as an enabler of sorts: Mormons believe one of the primary ways God answers prayers is through other people, and the Spirit is the still, small voice of God that keeps members in tune with the needs of others. Sometimes Mormons feel a little tug to pray for someone or do something to help someone they know. This urge may be as simple as a phone call to a particular friend, only to find out the friend had a rotten day and needed a boost at just that moment.

The revealer of truth

In John 16, Jesus says that he has many other things to teach his disciples, but they aren't ready for those additional truths. Jesus assures them the Holy Ghost will be their new teacher after his departure, guiding them into all truth as directed by the Father. Mormons believe that human beings learn spiritual truths "precept upon precept, line upon line" — in other words, slowly but surely (Isaiah 28:10 in the Bible's Old Testament and 2 Nephi 28:30 in the Book of Mormon). People don't learn truth in a vacuum, because the Spirit is with them every step of the way, teaching them and helping them discern truth from error.

Mormons are a prayerful people, and they often bring things to God in prayer that other folks may consider trivial. They follow James 1:5, which says that if they lack wisdom, they should ask God, who gives to everyone liberally. With this idea in mind, Mormons pray for the answers to tough questions and for guidance in making all kinds of decisions, both major and minor. They believe the Holy Ghost often confirms the truth of something they've prayed about. Sometimes, they receive a tingling or warm sensation running through their bodies, or simply a peaceful sense of calm about a particular course of action. On the other hand, they believe they'll receive a "stupor of thought" if something isn't right.

The end of the Book of Mormon contains an oft-quoted passage about praying to know the truth and receiving spiritual confirmation. Widely shared by Mormon missionaries, the passage is called *Moroni's Promise*, because the Book of Mormon prophet Moroni pledged that people who ask God sincerely in the name of Jesus Christ can receive confirmation of the truth by the power of the Holy Ghost (Moroni 10:3–5). The scripture further guarantees that by the power of the Holy Ghost, people can know the truth of all things.

The sanctifier

The Holy Ghost plays an important role in helping members stay on the straight and narrow path. He *sanctifies*, or helps them become more holy. As we explain earlier in this section, the Holy Ghost is sometimes associated with fire, and fire is the ultimate refiner's tool. The Spirit's goal is to purify an individual.

REMEMBER

As we discuss in Book 7, Chapter 2, one of the most important principles of Mormon life is what they call *enduring to the end*. Having faith in Christ, repenting, and being baptized are all wonderful, but those actions don't help people much in the long run if they backslide or fall away from the faith. Enter the Holy Ghost — the Spirit helps members stay in tune with the will of Heavenly Father and his Son, Jesus Christ. He keeps members honest — who can say the Holy Ghost isn't responsible for those occasional prickings of conscience that help keep them on the right path?

TIP

Before you finish this chapter thinking everything about the Holy Ghost is warm and fuzzy, you should know one more thing: The Bible says that blaspheming the Holy Ghost is the one unpardonable sin (Matthew 12:31–32). This kind of blasphemy is one of the few things that absolutely guarantee someone a room reservation in Hotel Outer Darkness.

Figuring Out What Makes Mormonism Different

REMEMBER

Although Mormons share a lot in common with other Christian and non-Christian faiths, they hold several uncommon beliefs, especially when compared to Protestant Christianity. Here's a brief overview of some key points where Mormons differ from the norm:

- **Premortality:** No other mainstream Christian denomination agrees with Mormons that the essence of each human has always existed and that humans were born spiritually to Heavenly Parents before being born physically on earth. Although people who believe in reincarnation can easily relate with the concept of a life before this life, Mormons believe that everyone gets only one shot at mortality.
- **The Trinity:** Most Christians think of God as a universal spirit that manifests as Father, Son, and Holy Ghost. By contrast, Mormons see these deities as three separate, individual beings who are united in purpose.
- **God's nature:** Mormons believe that God the Father underwent a test much like this earthly one, which they argue doesn't deny his eternal nature because

all individuals have always existed, in one form or another. Today, God has a glorified body of flesh and bones, and he possesses all possible knowledge and power throughout the universe.

- **The Savior:** Mormons believe that Jesus Christ was God's firstborn spirit child, which means he's the oldest spiritual sibling of all humans. However, Jesus is God's only earthly child, which means that he's the only perfect mortal who ever lived.
- **The devil and hell:** Mormons believe that God didn't create evil but that each individual being has the ability to choose good or evil. The devil was God's first, most powerful spirit child to choose evil, and he tries to persuade others to do the same, but evil can still exist without him. As far as hell is concerned, Mormons believe that wicked people will suffer consequences for their sins, but only those who personally know God and still rebel against him will go to an eternal hell, which Mormons call *outer darkness.*
- **Adam and Eve:** In the Mormon view, Adam and Eve were heroes who consciously took the steps necessary to begin mortality. Mormons view mortality as an essential test for eternal progression. Without this physical experience in a fallen world, humans can't learn and grow enough to eventually become like God.
- **The Atonement:** Mormons believe that Jesus Christ paid for humankind's sins not just on the cross but also in the Garden of Gethsemane, where his pain was so great that he sweat blood. Christ pays the price of the sins of anyone who repents and obeys his gospel, but those who refuse will suffer for their sins. Mormons don't use the sign of the cross, as some Christians do, but they believe that Christ broke the bonds of death through his resurrection.
- **Salvation:** Mormons believe all humans will be resurrected and receive an eternal reward depending on individual worthiness. Although pretty much everyone will receive a measure of salvation in one of three eternal kingdoms, only those who at some point accept the Savior's complete gospel — the same one currently preached and practiced by the Mormons — will receive *full salvation,* which means returning to live with God.
- **Priesthood:** In the Mormon view, the *priesthood* is the authority to act in God's name for the salvation of his children, within the bounds of the LDS Church organization. Instead of ordaining professionals who've completed special training, the Church ordains all worthy and willing Mormon males from age 12 on up, via the laying on of hands by someone already holding the priesthood. Any adult priesthood holder can perform ordinances such as baptism and healing or be called to lead a congregation.
- **Ordinances:** Mormons believe each individual must receive certain physical ordinances in order to return to God's presence, and authorized priesthood holders must perform them. Mormons also hold the unusual belief that if a

person dies without receiving an essential ordinance, a living Mormon can perform it in a temple on the deceased person's behalf, and their spirit will decide whether or not to accept it.

» **Apostles and prophets:** Mormons believe that the Savior issues revelations to whatever prophet is currently leading the LDS Church. These revelations instruct how the leaders should administer the Church under current earthly conditions. In addition, Mormons believe that the Savior calls modern apostles to serve as his special witnesses, similar to the New Testament apostles.

» **Scriptures:** Most Christians believe the Bible is God's only authorized scripture. Although Mormons uphold the Bible and prayerfully study its teachings, they believe it contains some translation errors and omissions. In addition, they believe that other civilizations recorded scriptures equally as valid as the Bible, most notably the New World civilization that gave rise to the Book of Mormon. In fact, they believe that God is still revealing scriptures in this day and age.

» **God's only true church:** Mormons believe their own church is God's only "true and living" church currently on the face of the earth. Mormons respectfully acknowledge that many religions contain elements of God's eternal truths, but they believe that only the LDS Church possesses the full package of God's authorized priesthood, ordinances, and revelations.

Looking at Joseph Smith and Mormonism's Beginnings

To Mormons, the term *gospel* means the "good news" that Christ died to save humanity and also refers to a very practical package of tools and instructions that the Savior provides for getting humans back home to God. That package includes doctrines, commandments, ordinances, continually updated revelations, and the priesthood authority to act in God's name. Remember, Mormons believe that the Savior was God's first spirit child way back before the earth was formed, so he's been on deck to reveal his gospel to prophets from Adam onward.

In the Mormon view, the timeline goes like this: First the Savior gave his gospel to Adam, but Adam's descendants eventually lost it through disobedience and corruption. Then the Savior gave it to other prophets, such as Noah and Abraham, but their people gradually lost it, too. Finally, when the Savior was born on the earth to accomplish his mission of overcoming sin and death for all humankind, he reestablished his gospel. However, within a few decades after his resurrection, humans fumbled it away yet again.

During the 1,700-year religious dry spell that Mormons say started after the Savior's New Testament apostles died, he worked behind the scenes and prepared the earth to eventually receive his gospel again. In 1820 he began the process of restoring it for the final time. When a teenager named Joseph Smith knelt in prayer to ask God which church he should join, God the Father and his son Jesus Christ appeared to Joseph and told him that none of the existing churches were true. Within ten years, Joseph Smith launched the Savior's restored gospel in the form of what people now know as the Latter-day Saint religion.

Translating additional scriptures

After Joseph Smith's answer to prayer in 1820, which Mormons refer to as his *First Vision*, an angel began regularly appearing to prepare him for his prophetic calling. Finally, the time arrived for him to perform one of the most important steps in restoring the gospel: bringing forth additional scripture that helped restore correct principles and can serve as a witness and testament of the new faith.

As Mormons understand it, something very special happened in the New World between 600 BCE and 400 CE. At the beginning of this 1,000-year time period, God instructed a prophet named Lehi to leave Jerusalem with some other families and move to the Western Hemisphere. Over the centuries, this little tribe grew into to a major civilization that underwent continual cycles of faith and wickedness, prosperity and destruction. In his usual way, the Lord sent prophets to teach these people and call them to repentance.

Soon after the Savior's resurrection, he dropped by to spend a few days with about 2,500 of his followers in the Western Hemisphere, ministering to his "other sheep" (John 10:16). Before the Savior ascended to heaven, he called 12 additional apostles to carry out his work in this part of the world. Under apostolic leadership, the people managed to hold onto the gospel for another 400 years after the Savior's momentous visit. Eventually, however, their lack of faith led to their corruption and extermination, and that was the end of the Book of Mormon civilization.

The New World prophets and apostles kept records on metal plates. A prophet named Mormon made a shortened version of the people's spiritual history and his son Moroni buried it in a hillside. About 1,400 years later, Joseph Smith's family settled near this same hillside in upstate New York. With the help of God, who helpfully provided interpreting devices to go along with the metal plates, Joseph translated and published the ancient record, and today the LDS Church distributes millions of copies each year in over 100 languages. If the proof of Mormonism is in the pudding, then the Book of Mormon *is* the pudding. (For more about the Book of Mormon, see Book 7, Chapter 5.)

Establishing the Church

While translating the Book of Mormon, Joseph Smith and his helpers came across passages that prompted questions, such as how to properly baptize someone. The questions that Joseph asked Heavenly Father triggered the following key events:

- In 1829, John the Baptist appeared to Joseph and his chief scribe to restore the *Aaronic Priesthood,* the preparatory priesthood authority necessary to perform basic ordinances, including baptism.
- Soon after John the Baptist's visitation, the New Testament apostles Peter, James, and John appeared on earth to give Joseph the *Melchizedek Priesthood,* the full authority to act in God's name within the Church organization.
- In 1830, Joseph Smith officially organized the Church, which Mormons believe the Savior recognizes as his only "true and living" church.
- Until Joseph's assassination in 1844, he received numerous additional revelations, scriptures, and ordinances that helped fully establish the new religion.

COMING TO TERMS WITH THE M-WORD

As a prophet who lived somewhere in North or South America around 400 CE, Mormon was just one of dozens of important figures in LDS history. Nevertheless, he's the man whose name became the nickname for this whole religious movement. Unfortunately, The Church of Jesus Christ of Latter-day Saints is a tad frustrated with the nickname.

The prophet Mormon's claim to fame was compiling and abridging the ancient records that became the Book of Mormon, titled that way because of Mormon's central editorial role. After Joseph Smith translated and published the book, it didn't take long for detractors to start calling his followers *Mormonites,* because of their belief in the book. The Mormons got rid of the "ite" part of the nickname, and eventually the term stuck and lost most of its negative connotations. Still, *Mormon* is just a nickname. What would Mormons rather be called? Although the Church hasn't completely ruled out the terms *Mormon* and *Mormonism* at the cultural level, it asks the media to use the Church's full name on first reference in a story — in other words, The Church of Jesus Christ of Latter-day Saints — and then say "The Church of Jesus Christ" on each subsequent reference. However, that lingo hasn't exactly caught on, even at the daily Salt Lake newspaper owned by the Church.

Understanding the Priesthood

In the Mormon view, the *priesthood* is nothing less than God's power and authority. He can use the priesthood to create worlds, to keep the universe running smoothly, and to perform other godly tasks. In order to give his children — who someday will become godlike — an opportunity to learn the ropes of the family business. God grants priesthood power and authority to all worthy male members of Christ's church. This way, they can help carry out God's purposes on the earth and perform ordinances that hold eternal weight. Of course, a mortal's priesthood power compared to God's is like a candle compared to the sun, but the type of power is basically the same, and it can keep increasing eternally.

The Mormon priesthood is divided into two levels. The Aaronic Priesthood, also known as the preparatory priesthood, helps Mormon teens get ready to receive the higher Melchizedek Priesthood, which all worthy adult males can hold.

TIP

In Mormonism, the word priesthood usually refers to God's power and authority that he delegates to men, but sometimes people use the term to indicate male Mormons in general.

For boys: The Aaronic Priesthood

Named after Moses' brother Aaron (for more on Moses, see Book 4, Chapter 2), the Aaronic Priesthood mainly performs the Church's outward ordinances of repentance, such as baptizing people and administering the sacramental bread and water to congregations. In biblical times, adult descendants of Aaron administered this priesthood. In the modern Church, all worthy teenage boys do.

There are three ranks of the Aaronic Priesthood through which Mormon boys advance every two years. Each time a boy advances, he can continue performing the duties of the lower ranks. Before advancing in the priesthood, a boy discusses his worthiness in a private interview with his local congregational leader, who also holds an Aaronic Priesthood office.

When an adult male joins the Church, he's initially ordained to the Aaronic Priesthood, but he usually takes only a few months — rather than six years — to advance to the higher priesthood.

Step 1: Deacon

Turning 12 is a major milestone for a Mormon boy. He leaves the *Primary*, the Church's organization for children, and joins the *Young Men*, the program for boys ages 12 through 17. Even more significantly, if Church leaders deem him worthy, they make him part of the Aaronic Priesthood, starting with the office of deacon.

The main duty of a deacon is to pass the sacramental bread and water to the congregation during *sacrament meeting,* Mormonism's main weekly congregational worship service. In addition, deacons serve as messengers for priesthood leaders, help take care of the meetinghouse, and in heavily Mormon areas may go house to house collecting *fast offerings* from members. (Once a month, Mormons skip two meals and donate what they would've spent on the food — plus more, if they're able — to the poor and needy.)

Step 2: Teacher

At age 14, a Mormon boy can become a teacher in the Aaronic Priesthood. A teacher's main job is filling the sacramental trays with bread and water and setting them out to be blessed and passed. In addition, teachers can accompany adult priesthood holders on *home teaching* visits, which is the only teaching they typically do. (In Mormonism, the men visit each household in the congregation once a month — ideally — to see how the members are doing and to deliver a short gospel message.)

Step 3: Priest

At age 16, LDS boys can become priests. The main job of Mormon priests is to bless the sacramental bread and water, saying the prayer exactly right or repeating it until they do. (Don't worry; they can use a cheat sheet.) In addition, priests can perform baptisms, ordain other males to Aaronic Priesthood offices, and conduct meetings when an adult priesthood holder is absent.

The bishop

TECHNICAL STUFF

Okay, this section is a little confusing, so bear with us. The leader of a full-sized Mormon congregation, or *ward,* is called the *bishop* (his counterpart in a smaller congregation, or *branch,* is called a *branch president*). Why do we list that role here, under the Aaronic Priesthood? Because, technically, the office of bishop is part of the Aaronic Priesthood. The bishop directly oversees the boys who hold the Aaronic Priesthood, and he uses that priesthood to perform some of his duties, such as handling finances and helping the poor.

However, the bishop of a ward is also a high priest in the Melchizedek Priesthood (see the next section), which gives him authority to act as CEO of the ward and conduct its spiritual affairs. In addition to overseeing the efforts of all the volunteers who typically staff a ward, the bishop spends a lot of time interviewing individual members for a variety of reasons. Bishops act as judges in God's earthly kingdom, and Mormons believe they can receive revelation about how to run the ward, including discerning what individuals are really feeling.

For men: The Melchizedek Priesthood

Given to all worthy adult Mormon males, the *Melchizedek Priesthood* provides men with the power and authority to lead the Church and preside over their own families, including receiving revelations directly from God to help them carry out those stewardships. From the prophet on down, all men hold the same priesthood, but they have different offices and callings within that priesthood; the prophet is the only single man who can exercise or delegate all the keys of authority. Mormons believe God recognizes the actions of priesthood holders only when they're in complete harmony with the chain of command, so a priesthood holder can't go off and start his own church. (However, plenty of people have launched offshoots of Mormonism, all of which the LDS Church regards as illegitimate.)

Elders

During their 20s and 30s, nearly all Mormon men hold the Melchizedek Priesthood office of elder. This rank allows them to teach and administer in the Church, bestow the gift of the Holy Ghost, do missionary work, attend the temple, and perform a variety of blessings and other ordinances. Elders preside over meetings when no high priest is available.

High Priests

In order to hold a high-ranking leadership position, such as bishop or *stake president* (leader of a grouping of wards), a man is first ordained a high priest. A younger man can become a high priest if God has called him to a senior leadership position, but most high priests are middle-aged or retired. When a man approaches his 40s or 50s, he may become a high priest even if he's not called to a senior leadership position, probably just so he can stay with his peer group.

Patriarchs

Usually retirement-aged priesthood holders, patriarchs are fairly rare in the LDS Church, with many *stakes* (groups of wards) having only one. Typically during the teen years, a Mormon goes to a patriarch to receive a *patriarchal blessing.* This blessing tells the receiver which tribe of Israel they belong to and includes personal advice and revelations that Mormons consider important enough to transcribe and keep handy for lifelong reference. Adult converts to the Church can receive a patriarchal blessing, too.

Seventies and Apostles

The relatively few men who hold either of the two Melchizedek Priesthood offices of *seventy* and *apostle* typically serve the Church full time, and together they're also known as *General Authorities.* Usually based at Church headquarters in Salt

Lake City, Utah, they're assigned to oversee Church functions and departments and to rotate among positions governing the Church in large areas of the world.

Living Your Day-to-Day Life as a Mormon

Viewing this mortal life as a time of testing, Mormons see their faith as the textbook for an A+, and they strive to live the religion 24 hours a day, 7 days a week. In fact, one of the primary virtues in Mormonism is obedience to the commandments and counsel of the prophets, as well as to the spiritual promptings of the Holy Ghost. The religion provides standards that Mormons believe will help them become pure and righteous enough to reenter God's presence, with the Savior's crucial help to overcome sin and death.

Following is an overview of what daily life is like for Mormons all over the world. Not everyone lives up to all these standards, of course, but this is pretty much what practicing Mormons believe they ought to be trying to do:

- **They follow a disciplined routine.** Each day, most Mormons pray individually, pray as families, and spend time reading the scriptures. They may also devote time on one or more weekdays to fulfilling volunteer Church assignments, such as preparing a Sunday school lesson or helping clean the local meetinghouse (see Book 7, Chapter 3).
- **They embrace a G-rated lifestyle.** To avoid addictions and maintain spiritual purity, Mormons abstain from coffee, tea, tobacco, alcohol, and harmful drugs. In addition, they keep sex strictly within the bonds of heterosexual marriage and shun anything "unholy or impure," including immodest clothes, pornography, profanity, and gambling. Some Mormons even refrain from cola drinks and R-rated movies.
- **They seek a change of pace on Sunday.** On Sundays, Mormons spend the day resting and worshipping with their families, and they attend a three-hour block of classes and meetings at their local meetinghouse, which is open to the public. On the Sabbath, most Mormons avoid work, shopping, sports, and other worldly distractions.
- **They kiss Monday-night football goodbye.** Mormons devote Monday evenings to spending time and studying the gospel with their families.
- **They take part in rituals.** Mormons regularly attend the *temple,* a special building set aside for the faith's most sacred ordinances, such as celestial marriage. (See Book 7, Chapter 4 for more on Mormon temples.) Temples aren't open on Sunday or to the public, and most of the ordinances performed there are on behalf of the dead. Mormons who've gone through

the temple wear special undergarments each day to remind them of their covenants with God and to provide spiritual protection.

- **They occasionally sacrifice food and money.** Each month, Mormons fast for two meals (about 24 hours) to increase their spirituality, spending that time praying, reading the scriptures, attending church, and otherwise trying to get closer to God. They donate money saved from those meals — and more, if possible — to the Church's fund for helping the needy. In addition, Mormons tithe a full 10 percent of their income to the Church.

Considering Missionaries of All Shapes and Sizes

Upon hearing the word *Mormon*, many people instantly envision two clean-cut young men walking or bicycling through the neighborhood in dark suits, white shirts, ties, and the telltale black missionary badges. These junior gospel executives are the main means by which the LDS Church fulfills its sacred mandate to spread the doctrine of Christ throughout the earth. Largely because of this dynamic force of gospel representatives, the LDS Church has grown remarkably fast since World War II.

Getting the basics

At the age of 3, Mormon boys and girls begin singing a song at church titled, "I Hope They Call Me on a Mission." However, the song is really aimed mostly at the boys, who make up the majority of the total missionary force. Missionary service is practically encoded into the DNA of Mormon-born males, and it's considered a priesthood duty. Young women can serve missions, but Church leaders say they should feel no obligation to do so. On the other hand, Church leaders increasingly encourage retired Mormon couples to serve missions, if they don't have any dependent children and their health and finances allow it, because retirees provide maturity and wisdom that the youngsters can't match.

TECHNICAL STUFF

Citing the rigors and demands of missionary life, the Church has recently raised the bar on qualifications for missionary service, particularly for the boys. Increasingly, leaders are weeding out young people who sow their wild oats and then try to repent or who aren't prepared to succeed on a mission. The Church now expects missionaries to demonstrate real faith and a genuine desire to serve, instead of going to meet social expectations, to try to convert themselves to Mormonism, to please girlfriends who will marry only a returned missionary, or to get the new car their parents promised if they serve a mission. Those who are worthy to serve a mission but who suffer from physical or emotional problems often volunteer in local positions rather than in full-time, faraway missions. Not surprisingly, the number of full-time missionaries serving worldwide has dropped in recent years, although many people feel that today's missionaries are better qualified and more enthusiastic than ever before.

Boy wonders

For nearly a century, a mission has been Mormonism's rite of passage into adulthood for young men, almost like a two-year tithing on the first 20 years of life. Nearly all begin serving at age 18 or 19, after working or attending college for about a year following high school. A male can sign up for a mission as late as his mid-20s — but any later than that and he's expected to stay home and evangelize the single gals until he finds one who's willing to become his wife.

Notwithstanding the Church's raising of the bar, every qualified, able young man is still expected to serve, and the social pressure is enormous. Not going — or going but getting sent home early — can make a young man feel like a second-class Mormon for years afterward. Whether or not a missionary wins many converts, the experience is considered essential preparation for future Church service and leadership.

As the teen years progress, parents and youth advisors help Mormon boys prepare for their missions. This preparation includes both spiritual and practical elements. On the spiritual level, young men are expected to

- Gain an abiding faith in the Savior, Joseph Smith's prophetic mission, and the Church
- Read the entire Book of Mormon and study the Bible and other Mormon scriptures and manuals
- Develop a personal relationship with Heavenly Father through prayer
- Learn to recognize and follow the promptings of the Holy Ghost
- Keep themselves morally and ethically pure
- Share the gospel with their friends

In addition, the Church encourages teen boys to develop practical skills that will come in handy during their missions, such as how to

- Save and budget money
- Speak in public and teach individuals of all ages

» Work hard and get along with others

» Launder, mend, and iron their clothes

» Prepare nutritious meals and do basic housework

Girl power

In recent years, increasing numbers of young women have chosen to serve missions before getting married. These "sister missionaries" must wait until they're 19 to leave, but they don't have an upper age limit like the men do — even a 50-year-old woman can go on a mission if she's still single.

Although young men serve for two years and generally stick to finding prospective converts and teaching them, young women serve for 18 months and may receive special assignments, such as staffing a Church visitors' center or helping disadvantaged people improve their health and hygiene. However, female missionaries can also be extremely effective in their evangelizing, and the demand for sister missionaries exceeds supply in many parts of the world. Male missionaries typically baptize their own converts, but female missionaries can't, because Mormon women don't hold the priesthood. Instead, the male missionaries or a local priesthood holder does it for them.

Silver is golden

With today's prosperity and longevity, many Mormon couples find themselves with plenty of money and energy after they retire. After their children are grown, they can focus their efforts on helping the Church and its members. In particular, the Church has discovered that missionary couples provide a valuable leadership role in less-developed parts of the Church. Requests for couple missionaries have become more frequent and urgent in recent years, and it's becoming common for willing, able couples to serve multiple missions during their retirement.

Enlisting in God's Army

A few months before the desired departure time, a young Mormon man or woman begins filling out the missionary application, which requires medical and dental exams and worthiness interviews with local Church leaders. In applying to serve a mission, young missionaries don't get to choose where they'll go and what language they'll speak. What's more, they have to pay all their own expenses, except airfare to and from the mission field, which the Church covers.

Receiving the call

After the missionary's stake president sends the application to Church headquarters, it takes just a few weeks to process it. Because a missionary may be assigned anywhere in the world, anticipation runs high for receiving that all-important envelope from Salt Lake City. Before the missionary opens it, family and friends typically gather round, and many missionaries' hands tremble as they tear open the envelope.

Receiving a call to Wyoming when you were hoping to go to Hong Kong — or vice versa — can be a little challenging. However, Mormons believe that each mission call is divinely inspired, a hope encouraged by the fact that each letter is, by all appearances, signed by the prophet of the Church. Nevertheless, the number of calls issued each year undoubtedly results in some bureaucratic randomness. Reports say that top-level apostles review all the calls and correct any that don't feel right.

Some Mormons believe that a person's mission call was determined in the premortal life. Faith-promoting stories persist about the missionary who, while diligently knocking on doors, meets someone who seems instantly, uncannily familiar. The common explanation for such déjà vu is that in the premortal life, the missionary promised this person that during mortality, the missionary would find and teach him or her the truth. This widespread folk belief not only helps missionaries accept their callings, but also motivates them to work hard so they don't break their promise to find that special someone.

Following the rules

Succeeding as a missionary requires many strong qualities. A missionary must be patient, loving, persistent, and articulate. However, the Mormon missionary program seems to emphasize one virtue above all others: obedience. Over and over again, Church leaders tell missionaries that in order to effectively teach and convert people, they must follow the Holy Ghost's promptings, but they won't be able to feel the Holy Ghost unless they obey all the mission rules and regulations.

So what are the mission rules? Most of them are spelled out in a small, white booklet that missionaries are supposed to carry at all times. In addition, individual mission presidents make their own rules, which can sometimes seem arbitrary. Because the mission president can't be everywhere at once, missionaries supervise each other by means of an organized system of zones and districts.

Following is an overview of the most significant rules that missionaries must follow:

- **A missionary *always* stays with their companion.** For many people, this rule turns out to be the most difficult aspect of serving a mission. The only time a missionary can be alone is in the bathroom — and not for too long. This policy is mainly to protect missionaries from falling into sin or danger. In most missions, missionaries can occasionally swap companions for an afternoon or evening, but they're supposed to spend most of their time working with their assigned companion, even if they can barely stand each other. On the other hand, many become lifelong friends.
- **Missionaries follow a rigid daily schedule.** They arise at 6:30 a.m., spend an hour in personal gospel study, pass another hour studying with their companion, and then work all day and evening, with one-hour breaks for lunch and dinner. If they're assigned to speak a foreign language, they take additional study time for that. Lights must be out by 10:30 p.m. Frankly, many missionaries face a big challenge in not wasting time by idling in the apartment, going shopping or sightseeing, hanging out too long at members' homes, and so on.
- **To stay spiritually pure, missionaries don't watch TV or movies, read magazines or newspapers, or listen to secular music.** Some missions allow classical music and others permit inspirational Mormon pop music, while some limit missionaries strictly to Mormon Tabernacle Choir recordings. The only reading material allowed is the scriptures, the Church magazines, and a handful of approved Church-published books.
- **One day each week, missionaries take a preparation day, or P-day.** This time isn't really a day off, because missionaries still wake up at 6:30 a.m., do their studying, and get back to work after dinner. During P-day, missionaries shop for groceries, wash their clothes, clean their apartments, fix their bicycles, write letters home, and run personal errands. If they have any time left over, they can play mission-approved sports or visit nearby tourist attractions, but they can't leave their assigned areas without permission, and they always stay with their companion.
- **With few exceptions, missionaries always wear their formal proselytizing clothes outside the apartment.** Exceptions include playing sports on P-day and performing service projects that require grubby clothes; running personal errands, however, isn't an exception. In addition, they always wear their missionary badges as a reminder of their missionary calling — some even wear them on their T-shirts while playing basketball. They must address one another by the title of Elder or Sister and not use first names or nicknames. (Yes, it's ironic that teenaged boys go by "Elder," which is a priesthood title from the Bible.)

» **Missionaries write weekly letters to their mission president and to their parents, and they're allowed to phone home only twice a year, on Mother's Day and Christmas.** Missionaries can correspond with anybody who lives outside the mission, including loved ones waiting at home.

» **Missionaries don't date, flirt with, or even hug a member of the opposite sex.** Even in pairs, missionaries can't teach a member of the opposite sex without an additional chaperone present. If a missionary gets romantically involved with someone, the missionary is usually transferred far away, possibly even to another mission. If a missionary has sex, they are usually excommunicated and sent home, hopefully to repent and eventually get rebaptized.

Introducing the Eternal Family Unit

In the Mormon view, all human beings are the spirit children of Heavenly Parents and can grow up to become like them. So that humans can learn how to become parents, God commands them to form family units on this earth, which serve as miniature models of God's own eternal family organization. Mormons have faith that, through the gospel, their earthly families can eventually become like God's eternal family.

Upon hearing that Mormons believe families can be together forever, some people think the idea sounds more like hell than heaven, depending on the state of their own family relationships. Nevertheless, Mormons preach that people reach the highest level of heaven as families, not as individuals. Known for marrying younger, divorcing less often, and having more children than today's average couple, devout Mormons who are sealed to one another in the temple believe they can accomplish nothing greater than building a strong, successful family that will continue throughout eternity.

In addition, Mormons think that discovering their ancestors and taking certain steps to eternally bind together their extended families, all the way back to Adam and Eve, is extremely important. Also, Mormons believe that all humans can become part of God's eternal family by entering into covenants and getting adopted into the *house of Israel*, which is what God calls his covenant people.

Why families are so important

Mormons believe that the traditional nuclear family is part of God's plan and must remain the basic unit of society. In addition, they believe that the LDS Church's main role is to help families gain eternal blessings together, through Jesus Christ.

REMEMBER

In the Mormon view, all men and women are commanded to "multiply and replenish the earth" — in other words, have children. God wants all his spirit children to come to this earth, gain a physical body, and go through a test, and this can happen only if people make babies. However, Mormons insist that all children deserve to be born to a married husband and wife. Although the Church expresses compassion for those people who can't find a partner or bear children, it discourages self-imposed celibacy and has zero tolerance for sexual activity outside marriage.

WARNING

Because families are so central and important to their faith, Mormons believe the family is one of the devil's main targets. That's why Mormons get so alarmed about divorce, abortion, and gay marriage, which they view as sinful trends that move society away from traditional families. (Some observers find the Church's opposition to gay marriage ironic because its objections resemble those raised about polygamy in the 19th century, when the Church was on the other side of the table.) However, the Church seemingly softened its views toward gay marriage, going so far as to back safeguards in 2022 for same sex marriages in the United States so long as they don't infringe upon religious groups and their rights to believe how they choose. Yet, Church apostles put the focus on the fact that those safeguards also protected tax-exemption status and other freedoms for religious groups.

"Till never do you part": Eternal sealing

Mormons believe that love isn't enough to preserve relationships past death. Rather, an eternal *sealing* ordinance is necessary to join husbands, wives, and their children together forever.

Eternal sealings occur in a sacred building called a *temple*. After a Mormon couple is sealed, any children they have after that point are automatically sealed to them at birth. If a couple doesn't get sealed until after children are born, those children participate in a temple sealing ordinance with their parents. However, getting sealed doesn't guarantee that every family member will make it to the eternal reunion — the sin in an unrepentant person's life overrides the sealing ordinance for them.

For more on this, see Book 7 Chapter 4.

Raising up seed

Mormons aren't prohibited from using birth control, but they're still known for having large families.

Why do Mormons have so many kids? Beyond simply valuing family life and parenthood, several possible reasons exist.

- **To make sure they're not leaving anyone out:** Mormons believe that everybody's spirits lived together and formed relationships before coming to earth. Mormon parents sometimes have more children because they sense that another spirit who belongs in their family is still waiting to be born, although this widespread belief isn't official doctrine.
- **To give premortal spirits the opportunity of a lifetime:** Mormons want to give as many people as possible the opportunity to come to earth and be raised in a Mormon home, where they can learn the gospel and receive the necessary ordinances for salvation, such as baptism.
- **To extend their boundaries:** Mormons believe they'll progress together through eternity as families, and having lots of children is good preparation for that. In heaven, after an exalted couple — see Book 7, Chapter 2 for more about exaltation — produces a sufficient number of spirit children, these heavenly parents will eventually organize their own world over which they'll preside, like God the Father presides over this world. This belief has led evangelical Protestants and other Christians who oppose Mormonism to charge that Mormons believe in many gods, but Mormons point out that they never stop honoring and obeying their own Heavenly Father, even after becoming like him. He remains the only God to them throughout eternity.

IN THIS CHAPTER

- » Understanding humanity's origins
- » Fulfilling the purpose of this mortal life
- » Reaching the intermediate spirit world after death and going to an eternal heaven or hell

Chapter 2
The Mormon Plan of Salvation

When it comes to pondering existence, each human being invariably faces three fundamental questions: Where did I come from? Why am I here? What's on TV tonight? (Er, that last one should've been, Where am I going?)

As a religion, Mormonism prides itself on providing complete, satisfying answers to all three of these eternal questions, answers that together are known as the *plan of salvation*. Mormons are Christians, but their beliefs about humankind's origin, purpose, and destiny differ considerably from those of Catholic or Protestant Christians.

REMEMBER

In a nutshell, the Mormon plan of salvation takes humans through the following major phases of existence:

- » **Premortal life:** Before this physical earth was created, the eternal essences of all humans underwent spiritual birth and preparation in God's presence.
- » **Mortal probation:** Born into a physical body and with their premortal memories veiled, humans face trials and tests. All earth dwellers are at this stage.

» **Spirit world:** Depending on their earthly conduct and the desires of their hearts, spirits of the deceased wait in either paradise or prison for resurrection and the final judgment.

» **Three degrees of glory:** Except for a few really bad people, each human will spend eternity in one level of a multitiered heaven.

In this chapter, we discuss each of these phases in detail (see Figure 2-1 for a quick graphic summary).

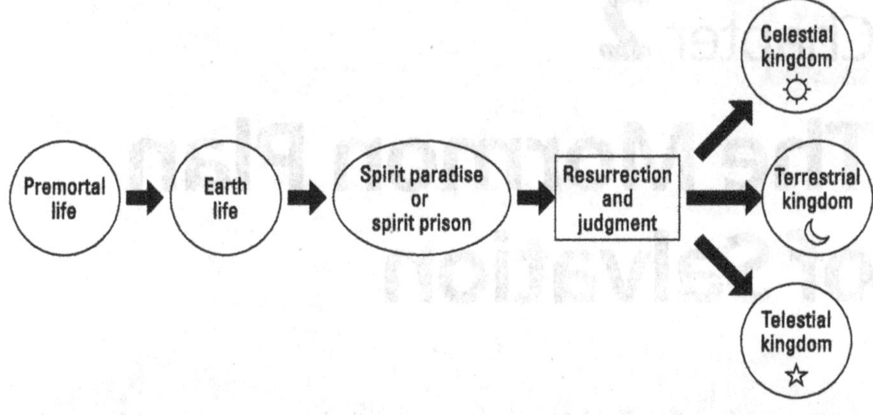

FIGURE 2-1: An overview of the Mormon plan of salvation.

Understanding Mormon Karma: The Premortal Life

Most religions make claims about the afterlife, but one of Mormonism's key concepts is the *before*-life. Mormons aren't the only ones who believe that humans are eternal beings, but Mormons are somewhat unusual — especially among other Christians — for believing that human eternity stretches in both directions, before and after mortality.

In Hinduism and Buddhism, a person's actions affect the nature of their next life, a process known as *karma* (more on those religions in Books 1 and 3, respectively). Mormons don't believe in reincarnation, but they do believe that a person's actions in the premortal life can affect the nature and circumstances of their earthly life. It's not uncommon for a Mormon, when faced with some earthly trial, to half-jokingly mutter, "What did I do in the premortal life to deserve this?"

From intelligence to spirit

Mormonism's founding prophet, Joseph Smith, taught that the essence of each human being has always existed, as opposed to being created. The Mormon term for an individual human essence is *intelligence*, but exactly what form an intelligence takes is a bit hazy. The important concept to understand, from the Mormon perspective, is that God didn't create our fundamental, individual identities out of nothing.

Instead, Mormons believe that, before this earth was formed, Heavenly Father and Heavenly Mother (see Book 7, Chapter 1) got together and procreated a spirit body to house each human intelligence. These spirit bodies resemble God's glorified physical body, but they don't yet have a physical presence. What God does for his spirit children is help them progress into increasingly advanced states of existence, potentially culminating in their becoming an eternal parent like him. After all, they carry his spiritual DNA.

But we're getting ahead of the story. Before the earth's creation, Mormon belief says that billions of spirit children lived in the presence of the Heavenly Parents across eons of premortal time — and, in fact, those spirits who haven't yet been born on the earth are still dwelling in their presence. In this premortal spiritual state, future humans developed their distinctive personalities, attributes, and talents and interacted socially with each other, preparing for the earthly test.

Why do the spirits want to come to earth? Just as an intelligence can progress only so far without a spirit body, a spirit can progress only so far without a physical body. Back before the earth was formed, the spirit children reached a point of maturity where they expressed the desire to gain a perfect, glorified physical body like God's and become like him. Without a physical body, they can't do many of the things God can do, including procreate other beings.

Mormons believe that in order to enable his spirit children to become like him, God offered them the plan of salvation, which would allow them to test-drive a physical body, prove how well they can exercise faith in God and follow his commandments, and strive to eventually return to God's presence. Through a mortal test like the one early Mormon leaders taught that God himself underwent innumerable eons ago, his children can start to learn the godly attributes of disciplining physical appetites, shaping the elements, and loving and serving their offspring.

In addition, they can gain godly wisdom by encountering the opposing forces of good and evil, pain and pleasure, sickness and health, age and youth, sin and virtue, time and eternity, and death and immortality. If they learned these lessons well enough, the potential payoff can be huge: Eventually they can become an eternal parent like God, perfect in love, justice, and mercy. Of course, they would still eternally respect and honor God as their father, even when having spirit children and creating planets of their own.

You've already passed the first test

Congratulations! As someone who lives here on earth, you've already passed the first test of choosing to follow God's plan of salvation. Due to what Mormons call the War in Heaven, it wasn't an easy choice to make. Allow us to explain.

As his spirit children considered the plan of salvation, God didn't hide the fact that the path would be fraught with danger, difficulty, and sacrifice. To facilitate effective testing conditions, he would place a veil over each spirit's memories of the premortal life. Each person would start over again as a baby and then age and die. God would allow evil to tempt people and chance to affect them for both good and bad. He would continue to absolutely respect human free will (Mormons call it *agency* or *free agency*), even when people chose to do terrible things to each other. In a kind of spiritual survival of the fittest — a process God would oversee with love and concern — only those who made enough progress in learning and obeying God's will would eventually be resurrected as heavenly parents; the rest would be resurrected to lesser degrees of glory, according to their efforts, desires, and faith.

REMEMBER

Because all earthly mortals would sin and become unworthy to reenter God's presence, a sinless redeemer would be necessary to pay the price of sin so that those who repented can become clean again. In addition, beings with mortal flesh would need a way to overcome their physical death. Mormons believe that during a great council in heaven before the earth was formed, two of God's spirit children volunteered to serve as redeemer of humankind:

- A high-ranking, widely influential spirit named Lucifer proposed to save everybody by forcing their obedience, and he would receive all the glory for himself. However, this plan didn't meet God's approval, because true progress is impossible without *agency* and *accountability* — in other words, the freedom to choose and the obligation to face the consequences.
- The firstborn of all the spirits, named Jehovah, offered to pay the price for everybody's sins, lead those who were willing to follow him back to God, and overcome death through resurrection. In addition, Jehovah promised to obey God's will and give all the glory to God. God chose him as the redeemer, and he was later born on earth as Jesus Christ.

Unfortunately, Lucifer was a sore loser. Declaring war on God and Jehovah, he persuaded a third of the spirit children to take his side. Perhaps these followers of Lucifer feared they'd fail if left to make their own choices on earth, and they wanted someone to guarantee success. Eventually, God cast Lucifer and his followers out of heaven, denying them the opportunity to ever receive a physical body. Lucifer became the devil (also known as Satan) and his followers became demons, and the spiritual war that started in premortality continues here on earth. Lucifer hasn't admitted defeat, and he still lusts for power and tries to thwart God's purposes by destroying human freedom through whatever means possible. (See this chapter's later section "Satan: A necessary evil" for more on Satan's role in Mormon theology.)

Premortality in the here and now

Premortality plays a central role in the Mormon religious imagination. However, the subject is also a troublesome area. Because the Latter-day Saints scriptures (LDS; see Book 7, Chapter 5) don't give many specifics about premortality, much of the Mormon outlook results from semiformal or even folk teachings. Perhaps more than any other Mormon belief, the idea of premortality has been shaped by sentimentalized pop culture, especially the influential Mormon musical *Saturday's Warrior*, performed live for hundreds of thousands during the 1970s and still widely viewed on video. Even worse, Mormon folk beliefs related to premortality have contributed to some harmful attitudes, particularly concerning racial matters.

TECHNICAL STUFF

Although Mormons are unique among Christians for believing in premortality, they've spotted many glimpses of the concept in both the Old and New Testaments of the Bible, especially the following passages: Job 38:4–7, Proverbs 8:22–31, Jeremiah 1:5, John 9:1–3, Acts 17:28, Ephesians 1:4–5, 2 Timothy 1:9, Titus 1:1–2, Hebrews 12:9, Jude 1:6, and Revelation 12:7–9.

The following sections show premortality's effects, both positive and negative, in the here and now.

Effect on earthly circumstances

Mormons tend to wonder and speculate about how premortality affects conditions in mortality. You can imagine the questions. Was someone born into a prosperous Mormon household because they fought valiantly on Jehovah's side, or was it because this person was a spiritual weakling who needed a head start on earth? Was a person born into the slums of Calcutta because they only barely supported Jehovah, or was it because they were a particularly gifted spirit who needed an extra challenging test? Although only God knows the reasons behind any particular individual's earthly situation, Mormons trust that premortality provides a comforting and reasonable explanation for the great variety of earthly circumstances, instead of attributing them to randomness.

REMEMBER

Although Mormons don't believe in predestination, they do believe in *foreordination*, which means that God chose spirits with certain skills and capacities to fulfill special purposes during mortality, such as becoming a prophet. However, being given a particular foreordination doesn't mean the person will necessarily succeed in fulfilling it. In the Mormon view, someone who did well in premortality can screw up on earth, and someone who lagged behind in premortality can catch up here.

On the other hand, Mormons commonly believe that some spirits were so valiant in the premortal life that they simply needed to receive a physical body without being morally tested, which helps account for childhood deaths and people born with mental limitations that make them unaccountable for their actions.

Effect on earthly attitudes

Following are some specific ways in which the Mormon belief in premortality affects earthly attitudes, for better or worse. Although widely prevalent, most of these beliefs aren't official Church doctrine.

- **Dreams and déjà vu:** Although humans have no conscious memories of premortality, some Mormons believe that the subconscious retains ideas, plans, goals, instructions, warnings, and other impressions and impulses from the premortal days. For some, this belief helps explain some dreams, sensations of déjà vu, and perhaps even premonitions that seem to hold spiritual meaning or significance.
- **Friendships and missionary work:** When a Mormon forms an unusually close bond with somebody and gets the feeling they've known each other forever, the Mormon will sometimes assume that the friendship began in the premortal life. Some Mormons believe they promised certain individuals that they'd find them on earth and convert them to Mormonism — in fact, many Mormon missionaries keep such a possibility in mind while knocking on endless doors. As missionaries contact people and try to teach them the gospel, they hope that spiritually sensitive people will recognize the plan of salvation from premortality.
- **The latter days:** As the Church's name indicates, Mormons believe that the period of earthly mortality is approaching its conclusion. Because this modern time is both the most advanced and most challenging era in the earth's history, with more temptations than ever before, Mormons believe that Heavenly Father reserved many of his brightest, strongest spirit children to be born in these latter days. Church leaders frequently repeat this message to the Church's teenage youth, which not only helps build spiritual egos but also gives Mormons a high standard to live up to — and yes, it can also increase guilt about shortcomings.

» **Marriage and family:** Some Mormons believe that during premortality, they formed spiritual bonds with their future earthly spouses, parents, and children. It's not unusual to find a Mormon couple who believes they're meant to be together because of promises made during premortality. Likewise, some Mormon parents conceive another child because they feel a spirit is missing from their family.

WARNING

In the past, early Church leaders claimed that people were born of supposedly inferior races if they performed inadequately during premortality. Today, the LDS Church no longer teaches these politically incorrect ideas, but some Church members may continue to hold these harmful beliefs.

Acing the Test of Mortality

With the successful completion of Phase One — premortality — all those spirits who chose to side with Jehovah in the War in Heaven proceed to Phase Two, which is mortal life, sometimes called *the second estate*. In Mormonism, everyone on earth is here because they chose to be, not by accident. That idea may give a spot of comfort when mortal life isn't a bed of roses.

Mormons regard mortality as a test. It offers the chance to come to know the Savior, Jesus Christ, and follow his teachings. Life's trials and triumphs can prepare humans to successfully return to their Heavenly Parents (see the section "The Afterlife: Eternal Progression," later in this chapter), provided they find and keep the faith and live worthily. If people want to be exalted through eternity, they have to go through this mortal life. There's no shortcut.

The basic principle of mortality is *agency*, or free will, and to understand that concept in Mormonism, you have to go way back. Back to a man, a woman, and a garden.

Adam and Eve: Heroes of humanity

In Catholic and Protestant Christianity (see Book 5), Adam and Eve (more on them in Book 5, Chapter 2) sort of get a bad rap. If they hadn't eaten the fruit and screwed up everything for everyone else, the thinking goes, everyone would be happily cavorting in Eden. But Mormons don't see it that way at all.

In the Mormon view, without Adam and Eve's heroic choice, no one but them would be on earth in the first place. Their decision to eat the forbidden fruit gave everyone the opportunity to experience a mortal life and have a crack at the celestial kingdom (see "Reaching the three degrees of glory . . . or outer darkness," later in this chapter). The Book of Mormon and the Pearl of Great Price (see Book 7, Chapter 5 for an explanation of these LDS scriptures) both agree that Adam and Eve's choice wasn't a mistake or some great cosmic tragedy, but a necessary decision. As the Book of Mormon puts it, "Adam fell that men might be; and men are, that they might have joy" (2 Nephi 2:25). In other words, their decision brought the world potential joy as well as pain — both essential parts of being human. God wouldn't create a fallen world or force his children to inhabit one, but he would let them choose for themselves whether to usher in mortal conditions and undergo such a test, and Adam and Eve paved the way.

In the garden, God gave Adam and Eve two seemingly contradictory commandments:

» Be fruitful and multiply, replenishing the earth — in other words, have kids.
» Don't eat from the tree of the knowledge of good and evil — in other words, don't usher in the mortal conditions necessary to have kids.

No, God didn't make a mistake by giving these apparently opposite pieces of instruction. It was a test of Adam and Eve's strength and determination. The decision to usher in mortality was so fraught with significance, difficulty, and danger that God had to make it crystal clear that they chose it for themselves and he didn't impose it upon them — in fact, he sternly warned them against it. Luckily, Adam and Eve passed this test with flying colors, due in no small part to Eve's particular understanding and vision. In so doing, they resolved two major problems for the human race:

» One problem was that Adam and Eve had to eat the fruit before they could be fruitful, so to speak. The Book of Mormon explains that they couldn't have any "seed" (translation: kids) in their state of innocence. So they needed to eat the fruit of mortality — the fruit from the tree of the knowledge of good and evil — in order to become parents, and thus become more like God. If the earth's first people hadn't been able to start procreating, that would've been bad news for all the billions of spirits stuck in the waiting room of premortality, chomping at the bit for their shot at the mortal test.
» A second problem with their situation in Eden (the place where they lived) was that Adam and Eve couldn't spiritually progress in their state of innocence. They were stuck, Peter Pan-like, in permanent immortality, which gave them nothing to lose or gain. In order to get the benefit of God's great plan of salvation, they had to prove themselves in mortality and die in order to return to God in heaven.

According to Mormons, Eve was the first to understand that she would have to disobey one commandment in order to obey the other. They consider her a heroine for making a difficult but correct moral choice, disobeying a lesser law and sacrificing her own peace and life of ease in the garden, where no one can age or die, in order to serve a higher law, enabling countless others to enter mortality and fulfill their earthly missions. By choosing death for herself, she gave the gift of life to all people, thus earning the name Eve, which means life, and the title "mother of all living." Mormons believe that God chose her for this mission in her premortal life and that she was one of the noble and great spirits mentioned in the Pearl of Great Price. In fact, modern LDS leaders have taught that Eve's premortal spirit even participated in the creation of the world.

REMEMBER

Although Mormons refer to this event as *the Fall*, they don't regard it as a failure, like some other denominations do. Catholics and some Protestants, for example, view the Fall as the moment that sin entered the world, and they believe that *original sin* — sin that is genetically passed from generation to generation at conception — is the direct result of the sin of Adam and Eve.

Mormons completely reject the idea of original sin; as the second Article of Faith states, Mormons believe that people "will be punished for their own sins, and not for Adam's transgression." Note the use of the word *transgression:* Adam and Eve *transgressed* because their actions literally went beyond a boundary that God had set for them. But Mormons believe their actions weren't *sinful*, because their choice paved the way for the plan of salvation.

Satan: A necessary evil

The Bible says that Eve made her choice in the garden following a proposal from a being who was, as Gollum in *The Lord of the Rings* may say, "very tricksy." Satan, disguised (perhaps figuratively) as a serpent, tried to trick Eve by telling her that the fruit would open her eyes and make her and Adam "as gods," knowing good from evil — all true, according to Mormons. But one of Satan's techniques is to mix the truth with lies so that people become confused. He also told Eve (in the Bible, Genesis 3:5) that she wouldn't die if she ate the fruit, which was a lie. She knew he was wrong but chose to partake anyway and embrace mortality.

So who is this guy? Satan, known in the premortal life as Lucifer, and his demonic followers hold an interesting place in Mormon theology. They make life on earth quite a bit harder. Motivated by selfishness and hate, they declared war on God and everything God represents, and yet God allows them to play an important role in the plan of salvation. Mormons believe these beings entice humans with evil, making mortality a tough road, so people must consciously choose good in order to grow and progress.

In the Mormon view, demons can do only what God permits them to do, even though they think they're rebelling against him. God allows them spiritual access to tempt humans because temptation puts pressure on humans to choose either good or evil, which is a main purpose of this earthly test. He allows these angels of evil to wreak havoc because that gives people a pressing need to seek out God. Eventually, Mormons believe, when the demons' usefulness in the plan of salvation has ended, God will permanently banish them to outer darkness, which we discuss at the end of this chapter.

TECHNICAL STUFF

Because each being is free to choose right or wrong, evil would exist without Satan, but he certainly fans the flames. He and his followers are miserable on account of their own choices and want everyone else to make the same mistakes, too. Mormons believe that one of the key ways demons work is by counterfeiting love, religion, happiness, family, spirituality, and many other facets of life. For example, human beings are wired to crave spiritual experiences, so demons try to counterfeit spiritual-seeming sensations through drugs and other means. Satan can guess at most people's weaknesses, but God won't let him tempt people beyond what they can bear, if they exercise sufficient resistance and faith (see 1 Corinthians 10:13).

Enduring to the end

Adam and Eve's choice in the garden was risky but absolutely necessary. It was the first earthly instance of human beings exercising their agency, or the freedom to make a choice between good and evil. As in the garden story, sometimes morally correct choices aren't always easy to discern; decisions don't come ready-made with a Hallmark ending. Of course, humans are going to make mistakes, but Christ's Atonement paved the way for everyone to receive forgiveness for all their sins if they truly repent.

REMEMBER

Mormons have a phrase for their stay-the-course philosophy: *enduring to the end.* This phrase is actually one of the main principles of the gospel: After faith, repentance, baptism, and receiving the Holy Ghost, all an individual must do to gain full salvation — in other words, return to live with God — is endure to the end in righteousness. These goals are easier said than done, however, because the journey is 24/7. Here are the basic expectations that Mormons consider to be part of hanging tough till the end:

- Exercise faith in the Savior, Jesus Christ.
- Repent and be baptized and confirmed. (More on these in Book 7, Chapter 3.)
- Do good works.
- Strive to keep the commandments and continually repent.

To bump salvation up a notch and achieve *exaltation*, which means becoming an eternal parent like God, enduring to the end includes making and keeping temple covenants, as discussed in Book 7, Chapter 4.

What's interesting about this enduring cycle is how it feeds upon itself: Doing good works, obeying the commandments, and studying the scriptures spring from faith and simultaneously make people more open to deepening that faith. To Mormons, faith in Christ *is* what saves, but faith isn't a one-time event that you can check off a list. Rather, faith is an ongoing journey that takes people through this life and the next. Faith is always growing, and obeying commandments and doing good deeds play an important part in nurturing and expanding faith. This whole process is what it means to endure to the end.

Sometimes it seems that mortal life is impossibly hard, and the paths people take are strewn with obstacles and suffering. Mormons believe that all life's ordeals and sufferings have the potential to bring people closer to God.

TECHNICAL STUFF

Mormons also believe that this mortal journey can yield great joy, even though trusting that all life's twists and turns will work together for good isn't always easy. One Book of Mormon prophet, Nephi, told people who had been baptized and were trying to stay on the right path to "press forward with a steadfastness in Christ, having a perfect brightness of hope, and a love of God and of all men" (2 Nephi 31:20). Mormons still cling to that advice more than 2,500 years later.

WHY DO BAD THINGS HAPPEN TO GOOD PEOPLE?

Every religion must answer the age-old question of why bad things happen in the world. Mormonism is different from traditional Christianity in its basic answer to that question. Traditional Christianity assumes that God is both entirely loving and entirely powerful, so it's very much an unresolved question why he doesn't intervene to save his children from things like famine, heartache, and untimely death. Mormonism also assumes that God is entirely loving but teaches that God limits his own power in order to grant human beings their agency and let them encounter hard realities that will help them grow in godly understanding.

Because free agency is such an important part of his plan of salvation, God won't typically intervene when people do bad things to each other, though Mormons believe he grieves deeply when his children hurt one another or themselves. In addition, God allows chance accidents and mishaps to occur. Mormons exercise faith that God will

(continued)

(continued)

protect them and help orchestrate their lives, but even faithful people can't always be sure whether God will intervene to limit, prevent, or reverse something bad. However, God always supports and comforts his children in their sufferings, when they turn to him and ask for his loving care. Of course, those who do harmful things to each other will eventually face the consequences.

To Mormons, it's a great comfort to know that God doesn't purposely smite them with difficult circumstances. Rather, he generally just allows people and events to take their natural courses in this fallen world, occasionally tweaking things when people exercise enough faith in accordance with his will. It's another great comfort that God gives his children the spiritual tools to endure and overcome hardships and traumas. Mormons don't feel they know all the answers about why suffering exists, but they trust in God's goodness and strive to exercise their agency righteously so they don't cause unnecessary suffering to themselves or others.

Exploring The Afterlife: Eternal Progression

The Mormon afterlife consists of two main phases. In the first phase, which human beings enter at the time of death, their disembodied spirits await resurrection. In the second phase, resurrected people dwell for eternity in one of several levels of heaven, as determined by the Lord's judgment of their worthiness.

A waiting room for spirits

Mormons aren't unusual for believing that when a human being dies, their eternal spirit leaves the body and goes to what Mormons term the *spirit world.* In this holding place, spirits temporarily await their resurrection and the final judgment, which won't occur until after all God's qualified spirit children have had a chance to get a body and experience mortality.

When the physical body dies, a person's spirit retains their personality, talents, habits, tastes, knowledge, attitudes, and so on. In the spirit world, people don't have tangible bodies but take a spiritual form that resembles their body in life. All spirits are in adult form, even if they died as mortal children, and the spirit body is perfect, with no defects or injuries. Mormon scriptures and prophets teach that the spirit world is divided into paradise for the righteous and prison for the wicked. In addition, prophets have taught that the spirit world is located right here on earth, but mortal eyes can't see it.

Free parking: Spirit paradise

For those people who repented of their sins and lived righteously during mortality, Mormons believe their spirits go to a place of paradise, where they can rest from worldly pains and problems. As in premortality, these spirits enjoy relationships with each other and create social organizations. They can continue learning and progressing, and they can help further God's purposes, particularly by serving as missionaries to those in spirit prison.

Can these spirits observe mortals and influence us? Some Mormon prophets have taught that they can, although most angelic messengers to earth are former mortal prophets who have been resurrected (and no, they don't have wings). Mormons believe that occult efforts to speak with the dead actually summon demons, who masquerade as dead spirits to confuse mortals. Another interesting question is whether unborn premortal spirits can mingle with deceased postmortal spirits. The concept isn't an official doctrine, but some Mormons believe it happens.

Do not pass go: Spirit prison

Mormons don't believe in the same concept of hell as most other Christians (outlined in Book 5) — in fact, Mormons don't even use the term *hell* very often. There are two places that Mormons think of when they imagine hell. We'll get to the second one, *outer darkness*, in just a moment. But first we discuss *spirit prison*, a temporary abode — although temporary may mean centuries or even millennia — where people's spirits go if they behaved wickedly on the earth, either because they didn't know or didn't accept the gospel message of Christ's Atonement. Mormon scriptures say that spirit prison is for all people who "died in their sins" and still need the opportunity to repent of them (D&C 138:32–35).

TECHNICAL STUFF

D&C stands for *Doctrine and Covenants*, which is a book of scripture containing revelations from God to Joseph Smith (more on him in Book 7, Chapter 1) and other prophets.

Although spirit prison isn't staffed by pitchfork-wielding horned demons, the place isn't warm, happy, and relaxing, and the devil can still influence people there. One Book of Mormon passage says there's a lot of "weeping, and wailing, and gnashing of teeth" in spirit prison, probably because people recognize the harmful consequences of their choices on earth. Good news, though: In spirit prison, the possibility of parole does exist, and someone's sentence there can be drastically cut short by a genuine change of heart and acceptance of Christ's gospel.

Mormons believe that an impassable gulf used to exist between paradise and prison. Jesus Christ bridged this gulf when his spirit visited the spirits in prison during the time between his death and resurrection (see 1 Peter 3:18–20 and

4:6 in the Bible). Ever since then, spirits from paradise have ministered to those in prison, teaching them the gospel and trying to convince them to accept Christ and repent.

For some spirits in prison, such as those who didn't get a fair chance to hear the gospel on the earth, learning the gospel and repenting may take a short time, and then they can cross over into paradise. Presumably, many people will become more eternally focused when they realize that their spirits have survived beyond death, and they'll accept the gospel and repent. For others, however, such as those who rejected the gospel or were grossly immoral on earth, repentance may be a long and painful process, far more difficult than it would've been during mortality. For the most stubborn spirits who never voluntarily accept the gospel and Christ as their Savior, they'll suffer for their own sins even as Christ already suffered on their behalf. However, even those souls eventually will be resurrected and assigned to the lowest degree of eternal glory; only a tiny percentage of people will spend eternity in outer darkness (see the next section).

Meanwhile, mortal Mormons continually perform crucial gospel ordinances, such as baptism, on behalf of dead people. If and when a dead person's spirit accepts the gospel in spirit prison, these ordinances allow them to potentially enjoy the gospel's full eternal benefits and, for those who qualify, eventually ascend to the highest tier of the celestial kingdom. Why can't a spirit perform its own ordinances? Because ordinances are physical and require a body.

Reaching the three degrees of glory . . . or outer darkness

One of the unusual features of LDS theology compared to other Christian denominations is that Mormons don't see heaven as a one-size-fits-all sort of place. Mormons believe that as in life, where some people are more spiritually oriented and Christlike than others, heaven will feature considerable diversity as far as who receives what eternal reward. For those who earn the highest blessings, those blessings carry great responsibilities and expectations.

TECHNICAL STUFF

For Mormons, the singular term "heaven" is a bit of a misnomer because the afterlife will feature not one but three distinct *kingdoms*, or heavens. Mormons believe that the biblical apostle Paul was referring to this distinction in 2 Corinthians 12:2, when he spoke of having been taken up into "the third heaven" in a vision. (see Book 5, Chapter 2 for more on Paul). In the Old Testament's original Hebrew, the word for *heaven* is always plural, and the Greek New Testament also often renders the term in plural form. So Mormons believe that the idea of a multitiered heaven is biblically based.

As is typical of the Mormon penchant for organization, each of the three kingdoms may have gradations within it. LDS leader James Talmage taught that because "innumerable degrees of merit" exist among all the people in the human race, it follows that God provides them with "an infinity of graded glories" in the afterlife.

Judging each person

After Christ returns and reigns on the earth for 1,000 years and all God's children — except the devil and his demons — have been resurrected, God's people and Satan will have one final battle. If you're one of those who likes to read the end of a good mystery first, here's a clue: God's people win. Then all people will face Judgment Day and find out where they'll cool their heels for eternity.

Mormons believe that the Savior and his apostles from different time periods will carry out the final judgment. LDS scriptures say that a perfect record of all human deeds and thoughts — frighteningly enough! — has been made in heaven, and that people will get to see that record on Judgment Day. Some imagine themselves viewing their best and worst moments on a giant screen. Maybe a sympathetic Jesus Christ will stand with them, holding their hand as they cringe at the moments when they screamed at their children or smile at the times they selflessly helped someone in need. Hopefully, the worst scenes will have wound up on the cutting room floor, forever forgotten because the person repented by asking the Savior's forgiveness and cleaning up their act.

Whatever the case, Mormon belief is clear on the idea that actions in this life are terribly important in determining what will happen to people in the life to come. Good deeds don't necessarily guarantee a place in heaven, but they're definitely not irrelevant, either. Mormons rely upon Christ's Atonement for salvation, but good works are an important measure of faithfulness and make people more able to receive God's grace and understand his goodness. Mormons believe that when Christ spoke of the kingdom of heaven in the New Testament, he regarded it as hard earned rather than easily understood or achieved. The kingdom of heaven, he said, is like the yeast that makes bread grow, or a pearl of great price that people may search for their entire lives, sacrificing everything in order to attain it (Matthew 13:33, 45–46). In other words, the covenant relationship with God established at baptism requires active human participation.

The challenging news about all this judgment business is that simply professing belief in Christ isn't enough; a person's actions must live up to the standard set by Christ's gospel. On the other hand, the good news is that Mormon theology doesn't send non-Christians to "hell" simply for not believing in Christ. In the Mormon view, the idea of a loving God sending whole cultures and peoples who never had the chance to hear of the Savior to eternal damnation makes no sense. Mormon theology teaches that good people of many different religious traditions will live in paradise forever; they may even dwell in the highest of the three kingdoms, if they accept the gospel in the spirit world and so qualify.

The following sections provide a rundown of the three basic kingdoms of the afterlife. Think of each of these kingdoms as layers of a wedding cake.

The bottom layer: Telestial kingdom

The lowest tier of the three-tiered heavenly wedding cake is the telestial kingdom, which is basically for the following kinds of people who died in their sins:

- Adulterers
- Liars
- Murderers
- Rapists
- Those who "received not the gospel of Christ, neither the testimony of Jesus," not even in the spirit world (D&C 76:82)
- Those who know all Justin Bieber's songs by heart

You may think that such obvious violators of God's laws would be consigned to everlasting torment, but the telestial kingdom is actually a lovely paradise. Remember that these people, not having accepted Christ's Atonement, suffer for their own sins while they're in spirit prison, and then Heavenly Father in his mercy allows them to head for the telestial kingdom after the great judgment. (Nice guy, that Heavenly Father.) Also, we should point out that Mormons believe there's no forgiveness in this life for criminal murderers; although liars, adulterers, and other serious sinners can choose to repent, murderers automatically go to the telestial kingdom.

So what's the telestial kingdom like? LDS leaders have taught that even this lowest degree of glory is so marvelous that humans can't possibly understand it. The Holy Ghost will minister to this kingdom's inhabitants, and Satan will have no power to tempt or torment them anymore. However, their eternal progress will be curtailed — and in that sense, the word *damnation* applies to them. In addition, they will live singly forever, with no family ties.

The middle layer: Terrestrial kingdom

This kingdom is even more glorious than the telestial, because terrestrial folks were basically decent and honorable during their time on the earth, although they didn't embrace the fullness of the gospel. The terrestrial kingdom will include the following kinds of souls:

- **Those who are confused about religion:** When it came to spiritual matters, they were "blinded by the craftiness of men" (D&C 76:75).
- **Lukewarm Mormons:** They were members of the LDS Church but "not valiant in the testimony of Jesus" (D&C 76:79).
- **Those who waited too long:** They rejected the gospel during their mortal lives but later received it in the spirit world (D&C 76:73–74). This idea doesn't apply to those who never *got* the chance to accept or reject the gospel during their earthly lives.

At this point, you may be wondering why good people won't automatically inherit the most glorious celestial kingdom. Fundamentally, such is the case because they weren't willing to do everything the gospel requires, including participate in sacred ordinances. As the Mormon prophet Brigham Young put it, if people aren't prepared for the celestial kingdom's eternal requirements, then putting them in that kingdom and making them stay there forever isn't kindness on God's part, because they would be uncomfortable there.

REMEMBER

For many people, even members of the Church, understanding the difference between the telestial and terrestrial kingdoms is tough, because both are paradises. Here's one key difference: Although the Holy Ghost will visit folks in the telestial kingdom, people in the terrestrial kingdom will also get to spend some time with Christ, whose Atonement will have paid the price of their sins. Church leaders compare the difference between these degrees of glory to the relative brightness of the stars (telestial) and the moon (terrestrial). However, like the telestial people, those in the terrestrial kingdom are limited in their eternal progression and live singly forever, without family relationships.

The top layer: Celestial kingdom

At the top of the three-tiered metaphorical wedding cake is the celestial kingdom. Imagine this kingdom standing high above the others on little pillars, because the difference between its glory and that of the terrestrial kingdom is like the difference in brightness between the sun and the moon.

GETTING IN ON THE GROUND FLOOR

REMEMBER

In the Mormon view, to cross the threshold into the celestial kingdom, where God himself lives, people have to

- Repent of their sins and accept Christ's Atonement
- Receive the saving ordinances of baptism and confirmation from an authorized priesthood holder
- Strive to keep God's commandments

In addition, God has promised that the following two kinds of people will receive celestial glory:

> All who have died without a knowledge of this gospel, who would have received it . . . with all their hearts (D&C 137:7–8)

> All children who die before they arrive at the years of accountability (D&C 137:10), which Mormons believe is age 8

RISING TO THE HIGHEST LEVEL

An entry-level spot living with God in the celestial kingdom is just the beginning. The celestial kingdom has degrees of glory within it, and Mormons strive to reach the pinnacle of celestial glory, where they can become eternal parents like God.

TIP

Picture a happy bride and groom on the very top of the wedding cake. This figurine is a good image to help people understand the highest tier of the celestial kingdom, because it takes two to get there — which makes sense, if they're going to become eternal parents. In Mormon belief, righteous husbands and wives who are sealed to one another for eternity in a holy temple can remain together forever in the celestial kingdom, and their children are also sealed to them. This pinnacle of success is known by several different names, including *exaltation* and *eternal life.* (For more on temples and celestial marriages, see Book 7, Chapter 4.)

Does that mean single people can't enter the highest level of the celestial kingdom? Well, although the highest level is reserved for married couples, LDS leaders assure righteous, unmarried Church members that they won't be denied any blessings in the hereafter. Some Mormons believe that these people may have the opportunity to marry in the afterlife.

People in the highest level of the celestial kingdom can potentially get it all, including

- » Unlimited access to God the Father, Christ the Son, and the Holy Ghost
- » The joy of being with their families for all eternity
- » A perfected body capable of producing spirit children
- » The right to continue in eternal progression, even to the point of divinity, although they'll always honor and respect Heavenly Father as their superior

But where much is given, much is also expected. The upper level of the celestial kingdom won't be an eternal resting place like many Christians imagine heaven. This heaven is Mormon, after all, so there's no rest for the righteous — and there's always work to be done! Ultimately, that work entails the parenting of spirit children, who will then start the whole mortality process themselves in some other yet-to-be-created world. (Presumably, raising kids in the celestial kingdom will be a lot easier and less messy than it is here on earth.)

If you're really, really, really bad: Outer darkness

Although Mormons believe that the vast majority of people will one day find themselves somewhere along the win-place-show spectrum of the three degrees of glory, that belief has one catch: outer darkness, which is one of the two "hells" of Mormon theology. (For more on the other, see the earlier section "Do not pass go: Spirit prison.") Because Mormons believe that even murderers, liars, and adulterers who died in their sins can inherit the telestial glory behind Door #3, it must follow that outer darkness is reserved for people who are worse than murderers. Those people include

- » The devil himself.
- » The one-third of spirits who chose to follow Satan in the War in Heaven (refer to the section "You've already passed the first test," earlier in this chapter). These spirits never received human bodies, so no one reading this book falls into this category.

- » The *sons of perdition* who knowingly and willfully turn against the gospel after fully comprehending and embracing it. This doesn't apply to people who never heard the gospel, or who heard it but didn't believe it was true, or who got baptized but then fell away, or who committed terrible sins. It's only for those who, during their lives, completely understood the gospel's truthfulness and received a spiritual witness from the Holy Ghost, but then deliberately chose to despise God and rebel against him. Mormons believe that when the Bible's New Testament speaks about blaspheming against the Holy Ghost as the "unpardonable sin," it refers to this extreme denial. Being a child of *perdition* — which means "loss" — is a one-way ticket to hell, and this time it's forever.

The best way to describe outer darkness is the complete absence of light and warmth. This place offers no forgiveness, no redemption, and no possibility of parole — in essence, outer darkness means permanent misery and perhaps even eventual dissolution. Thankfully, only a minuscule number of those who made it to mortality will inherit outer darkness, due to their fully realized hatred of God.

IN THIS CHAPTER

» Zoning in on the nuts and bolts of Mormon congregations

» Visiting a Mormon sacrament meeting and other special services

» Connecting with the larger stake

» Taking a quick tour of headquarters

Chapter 3

Welcome to the Meetinghouse and Headquarters!

When imagining Mormon life, many non-Mormons immediately picture an eye-popping Latter-day Saints (LDS) temple. And though these Magic Kingdom look-alike buildings house some of the most sacred rituals of the Mormon faith — see Book 7, Chapter 4 for the skinny on that — you need to spend some time in the meetinghouse of the local *ward*, or congregation, in order to understand the heart of what it means to be Mormon.

REMEMBER

The ward is the second-most-important unit of Mormon life and culture, after the nuclear family. In fact, wards are a lot like a family, with members addressing each other as Brother or Sister, followed by the surname — collectively, the men are called "brethren" and women "sisters." Led by a bishop, a ward usually encompasses all the Latter-day Saints within certain geographic boundaries.

Also in this chapter, we tell you what to expect if you find yourself a guest at a Mormon event, explore sacrament meetings, and dive into Mormon baptism, confirmation, funerals, and weddings. Then, we look at larger Mormon communities, called the *stake* (which is a grouping of several wards led by a stake president), and gatherings. Then we cover Church headquarters.

What's a Ward?

In plain English, a *ward* is simply a local Mormon congregation. Wards usually have about 300 to 350 members who meet for a three-hour block of time on Sundays. Often, the first part is *sacrament meeting*, during which everyone gathers in the chapel to partake of the sacramental bread and water and listen to *talks*, or short informal sermons, from other ward members. For adults and teens, this meeting is followed by 40 minutes of Sunday school classes and 50-minute meetings segregated by age and gender, with 10-minute breaks between each meeting; for the children, the Church provides a program called *Primary*. In some wards, this order of meetings is reversed, with sacrament meeting held last.

Unlike most other Christian denominations, The Church of Jesus Christ of Latter-day Saints is a geographically based organization. Ordinarily, the Church doesn't want members to choose the ward in which they want to participate; instead, the Church expects members to become involved with whatever ward encompasses the neighborhood or area where they live. Not only does this ideal avoid the phenomenon of church hopping, but Mormons also believe that part of the genius of the ward concept is that it puts all kinds of people into communion with each other — people who may not otherwise make a connection.

TECHNICAL STUFF

The geography of a ward can change when the congregation gets too large for every member to have an assignment, or *calling* (see "Getting to work: Every member has a job," later in this chapter), or otherwise becomes unwieldy. When a ward gets too large, the leaders may split it in half or create three wards out of two.

Specialty wards

Most wards are multigenerational and cater to all ages, including children. But the Church designs some wards to meet certain individual needs, including the following:

- **Singles wards:** Yep, this type of ward is the marriage market in its full gospel expression. (If you don't believe us, stream the 2002 screwball comedy *The Singles Ward*, which is a silly but entertaining glimpse of the Mormon dating scene.) Singles wards operate under the premise that young people and college students enjoy one another's company and learn the gospel best when they're serving as moral and spiritual examples for one another. When a member of a singles ward gets married, they leave that ward and become a member of the regular ward. Singles wards are most common in university towns and large cities. When a city has an especially large singles population, the singles are sometimes divided into under-30 and over-30 age groups.

(Singles don't have to attend these wards, by the way — they can just stick with their regular ward.)

» **Language wards:** Sometimes, the Church operates ethnic wards and branches (see the following section) in languages other than the one dominant in the nation where they're located. Numerous sign-language congregations for the deaf are in operation, too.

Wards in the making: Branches

Wards don't just spring up full-blown in an area shortly after the missionaries first set foot there to convert new members. In the beginning, only a few converts and the missionaries themselves may meet in members' homes or in a rented building. This would-be ward is called a *branch*, and it can consist of as few as two Mormon families if at least one priesthood holder is available to administer the Sunday *sacrament* (communion of bread and water; see the section "Knowing what to do when you're in the pew: Sacrament meetings"). The leader of a branch is called a *branch president*.

As branches grow in membership, they gradually add classes and programs until they become a fully functioning ward. When we say *ward* and *bishop* in this book, we generally mean branches and branch presidents, too.

Participating in the Ward

In contrast to the architectural appeal of LDS temples, most LDS meetinghouses appear, um, functional. Older wards were a bit fancier and sported different architectural styles, but newer ones are quite bland and usually very much the same architecturally.

Some visitors who come to church for the first time wonder aloud at the near-total absence of stained-glass windows, altars, candles, murals, and statues. A few older ward houses sport beautiful murals inside, but for the most part meetinghouse artwork is mass-produced. Various portraits and scenes from the scriptures and LDS Church history often adorn the buildings' halls and classrooms, but never the chapels themselves. You won't see any crucifixes; Mormons prefer to focus on the Savior's resurrection, not his death. Visitors who are used to a more visually stimulating atmosphere — all the "smells and bells," as Catholics may say (more on those in Book 5, Chapter 4) — are often a little disconcerted at the apparent starkness of Mormon ward buildings and services.

Looks can be deceiving, however, because the life that teems underneath the bland meetinghouse surface is something to behold. Participating in a ward community is a vital and exciting part of being Mormon, plain and simple.

GOVERNING THE CHURCH: GENERAL AUTHORITIES

Mormons believe that Jesus Christ directly governs their church, making his will known through revelation to 15 men who together function as the earthly heads of the Church. The most senior apostle (the highest priesthood office) — by date of apostleship, not date of birth — is set apart as the prophet (the one designated by God as his spokesperson and teacher) and president of the Church, and he selects two other apostles as his counselors to constitute the three-man First Presidency. The two counselors work closely with the president, and they're highly visible and respected leaders in the Church.

The remaining 12 leaders constitute the Quorum of the Twelve Apostles. Although the president is the only individual who holds all the Church's priesthood keys (meaning the authority to perform or delegate priesthood roles and ordinances) and the only one officially known as the prophet, the 15 men are all considered prophets, seers, and revelators who act as "special witnesses of the name of Christ in all the world" (Doctrine and Covenants 107:23). All 15 of these men generally govern together as an executive board, not taking any significant action without unanimity. Their average age is probably well over 70.

In addition, the Church calls men to serve as *seventies*, a New Testament term referring to the original number of such leaders (see Luke 10). Today's LDS Church has far more than just 70 seventies; organized into several quorums, they function under the apostles and are similar to vice-presidents in a corporation. Many seventies are middle aged rather than retirement aged, and although the president and apostles serve for life, seventies may eventually be given emeritus status or released.

Rounding out the Church's top government is the Presiding Bishopric (a bishopric is a three-man supervisory board, consisting of a bishop and two counselors). This bishopric leads the Aaronic Priesthood (see Book 7, Chapter 1) and oversees the faith's temporal concerns, such as building meetinghouses and collecting tithes. Together, the president, apostles, seventies, and Presiding Bishopric are known as *General Authorities*, because they preside over the whole Church. Often referred to informally as GAs, they're also known as the *Brethren*, with a capital B.

General Authorities receive no professional training specifically to lead the Church. Before being called as full-time GAs, most of these men establish successful careers in professions such as business, law, education, and medicine, which helps explain why the LDS Church feels so corporate in personality. Undoubtedly, all the General Authorities previously served the Church in many important, demanding volunteer leadership positions, which helped prepare them and bring them to the attention of Church headquarters. As General Authorities, they don't receive salaries, although the Church does provide a modest living allowance.

Getting to work: Every member has a job

In Mormonism, only General Authorities (see the nearby sidebar "Governing the Church: General Authorities") and mission presidents receive a living-expense allowance to facilitate their full-time church work. In addition, the Church has a few thousand full-time employees worldwide who work in administrative functions or teach in the Church Educational System (known as CES). Everyone else, including every person you see teaching or leading at the ward level, is a part-time volunteer who has accepted a calling.

Ward members have all kinds of callings: They may teach the *Sunbeams* (3- and 4-year-olds), keep the financial records, administer the sacrament, or plan activities for the youth. Others help people research their genealogy or direct the ward choir. Bishops and other high-level local leaders are also volunteers. Even the ward upkeep is generally the responsibility of members, who do the everyday cleaning themselves, while professionals attend to the heavy scrubbing.

Ward callings are extended by the bishop or one of his two counselors, who first pray collectively to God for guidance about where to assign various individuals. Some people stay in the same calling for years and years, while others receive temporary assignments (like being the youth summer camp director) or move around every couple of years. In less-populated wards, one person may hold two or more callings at the same time.

The LDS Church encourages members to accept whatever calling their bishop offers them and to regard it as coming directly from the Lord. However, in some circumstances, an individual may refuse a calling because of family issues, personal problems, or severe time constraints. Mormon adults are expected to consult with their spouses (especially if their spouse isn't a member) about a proposed calling from the bishop.

Knowing what to do when you're in the pew: Sacrament meetings

Mormon chapels are always open to visitors on Sundays, and stopping in is a great way to get a glimpse of Mormon life and practice. Here's a quick rundown of what to expect in a Mormon sacrament meeting (described earlier in this chapter in the section, "What's a Ward?").

What to wear

Although many churches and denominations have accepted the casual-dress movement, Mormon services are still pretty formal. Men typically wear a suit or jacket and a tie — if you dress like Mormon missionaries, you won't go wrong. In addition, men and boys often wear white shirts, especially if they're participating in rituals like passing the sacrament.

Women generally wear a dress, a suit, or a blouse and skirt; hemlines are conservative and below the knee. A few younger women are starting to wear dressy slacks to church, though such attire is still rarely seen in Utah, which has some of the most conservative dress standards anywhere in the LDS Church.

Where to sit

Seating in Mormon sacrament meetings is on a first-come, first-served basis. Visitors can sit anywhere they want except on the *stand*, an elevated area in front where the pulpit and organ are located. This part of the chapel is reserved for the day's speakers, the choir, and the *bishopric* (the bishop and his two counselors). Also, the front two rows of the chapel on the left or right side are reserved for the young men who pass the sacrament.

What about the kids?

Mormon services differ from those of many other Christian denominations in that children stay with their parents during the entire service. A nursery and classes are available for children during the remainder of the three-hour block, but sacrament meeting is for everyone, from Baby to Grandma and Grandpa. If you have children, bringing quiet games, coloring books, and simple snacks to entertain them during sacrament meeting is perfectly acceptable.

SPENDING A LITTLE TIME ALONE WITH GOD

Mormons pray directly to God the Father. They don't believe that having an intermediary (one who stands in between the person praying and God) is necessary. Therefore, they don't pray to Jesus Christ, Mary, or any saints (anyway, in Mormonism, the term saint applies to all members). Although Mormons sometimes don't feel like praying, they know that these times are when they especially need to pray, in order to maintain that close connection with their Heavenly Father. As Mormon missionaries teach, LDS-style prayer has four basic steps:

1. **Call on Heavenly Father.** The most common opening phrase is simply "Dear Heavenly Father," but variations are okay.
2. **Thank him for blessings.** Before getting into needs and desires, Mormons meditate on blessings and express gratitude for specific ones. Such blessings may include family members, good health, or the knowledge of the gospel. Many Latter-day Saints regularly thank God for the Atonement of Christ.
3. **Ask for blessings.** This part of the prayer is nearly always the longest. Mormons try to understand God's will and pray for it to come about. Here, Mormons may ask for strength to withstand temptation or meet new challenges; confess their sins to Heavenly Father and ask for forgiveness; remember loved ones who are ill or troubled; or pray about conflicts in the nation or the world.
4. **Close in the Savior's name.** Every Mormon prayer closes with this basic phrase: "In the name of Jesus Christ, amen." This practice stems from a verse in the Book of Mormon, where Jesus tells the Nephites to "always pray unto the Father in my name" (3 Nephi 18:19).

How the service proceeds

REMEMBER

With the exception of the monthly fast and testimony meeting (see the next section), most sacrament meetings follow the same basic order. They're predictable to a fault, which is good news if you're a visitor and don't yet know the score. Here's the rundown:

- **Announcements:** The meeting opens with the bishop or one of his counselors making announcements about upcoming activities and meetings in the ward and stake.
- **Opening hymn:** Hymn singing is important in Mormon services, which feature three or four hymns. The opening hymn is a time to get into the groove of preparing for worship; Mormons use this time to settle their hearts into a more reflective and spiritual mode. Many of the hymns in the LDS

hymnbook are recognizable, especially to visitors from a Protestant tradition; others are unique to Mormonism. Unlike most Protestants, however, Mormons usually remain seated while singing hymns. Visitors are always welcome to pick up a hymnbook and join in the singing.

- **Opening prayer:** Mormon meetings always begin and end with a prayer. Mormons bow their heads and fold their arms as they remain seated in the pews. One member of the ward comes to the front pulpit and offers a short invocation. In English-speaking wards, prayer language is formal, using "thee" and "thou" to address God; other languages may or may not follow similar customs. Every Mormon prayer ends with some variation of the phrase "In the name of Jesus Christ, amen." If you feel comfortable, you're welcome to join the congregation as they respond by saying "Amen" — however, that's the *only* time Mormon congregants say anything out loud. (For more on personal Mormon prayers, see the nearby sidebar "Spending a little time alone with God.")
- **Ward business:** At this point, the bishopric member conducting the meeting announces new callings that members have accepted, and the congregation *sustains* them on cue by raising their right hands in support. (Members also have the right to raise their hands in opposition to a calling, but most members go through their entire lives without ever seeing that happen.) Visitors don't vote in these proceedings. If any baby blessings or baptismal confirmations are scheduled to take place on a particular Sunday, they occur at this point in the program (we describe these events later in this chapter).
- **The sacrament:** Partaking of the *sacrament* (bread and water that members of the priesthood have blessed) is the main reason everyone gathers. After ward business, the congregation sings a special hymn to remind everyone of Christ's sacrifice and Atonement, which is what they celebrate by taking the sacrament. Then teenage boys who hold the Aaronic Priesthood (see Book 7, Chapter 1) bless the sacrament and pass it to the congregation (adult men can pass it too, if needed).

TECHNICAL STUFF

According to Mormons, the bread and water don't become the body and blood of Christ (a theological concept known as *transubstantiation*), as members of the Catholic faith believe they do. (More on that in Book 5, Chapter 4.) Rather, these elements are symbols that remind Mormons of the Savior's sacrifice and their own willingness to love and serve him. If you listen carefully to the words of the sacrament prayer — which is one of the few prayers in Mormonism that priesthood holders must recite absolutely the same every time — you'll hear the word "remember" a couple of times. Mormons believe that taking the sacrament of bread and water in a spirit of repentance helps them remember Christ's love, renew their baptismal covenants, and become more worthy of his Atonement.

TIP

If you decide to take the sacrament, take a little piece of bread and put it in your mouth before passing the tray along and then go ahead and chew; When the water is passed, take one of the little cups, chug it down, and drop the empty cup in the tray's waste receptacle before passing the tray to the next person. Mormons also give their kids the sacrament.

- **Talks:** The longest portion of a Mormon sacrament meeting consists of talks given by two to four members of the congregation, ranging anywhere from 2 to 30 minutes long. Laypeople give these short sermons, which are often pretty folksy; doctrine and scripture verses mingle freely with self-help advice, personal experiences, and anecdotes — not all of which may seem relevant to the topic at hand. Occasionally, the last speaker is a representative of the stake high council (see the section "Twice a year: Stake conference," later in this chapter), who addresses a topic assigned by the stake president. Before the last speaker, a hymn or special musical number may take place.
- **Closing hymn and closing prayer:** The congregation sings a final hymn, and after the closing prayer that follows, the organist or pianist usually plays postlude music as people get up and start chatting and moving to the foyer. This marks the end of the service.

WHO CAN PARTAKE OF THE SACRAMENT?

In the LDS Church, the only people who are forbidden from taking the sacrament are those members or former members who've been disciplined or excommunicated for serious sin. Obviously, if you're a first-time visitor, this doesn't apply to you. At the same time, partaking of the sacrament isn't a good idea if you know you have major, unresolved sins in your life or you don't believe in God and his Son, Jesus Christ. Otherwise, feel free to partake if you feel prompted by the Spirit to do so — in other words, if you have a good, warm feeling about it.

Mormons believe that they renew their baptismal covenants every time they partake of the sacrament, but those who haven't yet made any LDS baptismal covenants can still grow closer to God and Jesus Christ if they take the sacrament in the proper spirit.

The sacrament is the holiest part of what goes on in a Mormon service; now isn't the best time to take little Timmy to the potty. Latecomers who arrive during the sacrament's passing aren't seated until after it's finished.

Stepping up to the mike: Fast and testimony meeting

The first Sunday of each month is usually fast and testimony meeting, which differs from the ordinary pattern in two key ways. First, members come to the meeting having *fasted* (abstained from food and water) for two meals, or about 24 hours. Second, the meeting gives members the opportunity to "bear their testimonies" after the sacrament has been passed. In Mormon tradition, this phrase means that an individual offers a quick personal homily on some gospel truth. Everyone, including the smallest of the small fries, has the opportunity to take a turn at the microphone.

Although the other Sundays of the month feature assigned speakers who come prepared to address the congregation, testimonies are almost never prepared in advance. Members speak when they feel the Spirit move them. Testimonies give members a chance to express gratitude to the Lord for help in difficult times, bear witness of the Savior's love, explain why they believe the gospel, thank family and ward members for their love and support, and talk about struggles they may be facing.

Testimony meeting is fascinating because although a testimony has a certain basic formula ("I know the Church is true," "I know the Book of Mormon is true," and so on), the meeting is one of the most unscripted events in Mormon life. Some meetings are so full of people bursting to share their stories that there's not enough time to accommodate them all. Other meetings suffer awkward pauses between testimonies.

Holding ward conference

One weekend a year, each ward typically holds a *conference*, which stake representatives attend. The stake leaders of the Relief Society, Primary, Young Men, and Young Women organizations may meet with ward leaders on Saturday or just before church to assess how they're doing. During ward conference, sacrament meeting sometimes extends longer to allow more leaders a chance to speak, and the usual class schedule may be altered.

Getting dunked: Baptism

LDS baptisms generally take place in the local meetinghouse — unless someone is already dead, in which case Mormons can perform baptism on that person's behalf in a temple (see Book 7, Chapter 4). For Mormons, getting baptized signifies many important concepts:

- It marks the beginning of a person's official membership in the Church.
- It symbolically washes away sins, an effect that a person can renew each week by partaking of the sacrament (see the section "Knowing what to do when you're in the pew: Sacrament meetings," earlier in this chapter).
- It represents a covenant with God to keep his commandments, stand as his witness, and love and serve fellow Church members.
- It prepares a person to receive the constant companionship of the Holy Ghost (as we discuss in the section "Installing a direct line to God: Confirmation," later in this chapter).
- It obeys the example that Jesus set in the New Testament.
- It symbolizes being buried and then resurrected (being lowered into the water and then lifted out).
- It qualifies a person to receive salvation in the *celestial kingdom,* the highest level of heaven where God himself lives (see Book 7, Chapter 2).

Preparing for baptism

The earliest someone can receive Mormon baptism is at age 8, which Mormons view as the *age of accountability* — when a person is spiritually mature enough to discern right from wrong. (People with mental disabilities that prevent accountability don't need baptism — they're automatically saved. It's the same for children who die before age 8.) Mormons don't recognize baptisms performed in other religions, so anyone who wants to join the LDS Church must receive Mormon baptism.

Following are several ways in which baptismal candidates prepare for baptism. These steps don't necessarily happen in the order that we list them, and they often overlap. In fact, ideally a Latter-day Saint keeps cycling through these steps for the rest of their life.

- **Learn the gospel:** Children raised as Mormons learn the gospel by attending regular Sunday classes and being taught at home. People who've grown up outside the faith take a series of special lessons prior to baptism, usually from the local full-time missionaries. In addition, they study the scriptures and other sources on their own.
- **Exercise faith:** Preparing for baptism includes developing an abiding faith in Heavenly Father, Jesus Christ, the divine mission of the founding prophet Joseph Smith, and the truthfulness of the Book of Mormon, other scriptures, and the LDS Church itself. Faith begins with the desire to believe, and it grows

as a person experiences good results from studying, praying, repenting, and living the gospel.

- **Repent of sins:** Everyone makes mistakes due to ignorance, weakness, or disobedience. To gain freedom and forgiveness from sins through the Savior, a person feels remorse about their sins, asks the Savior's forgiveness in prayer, stops the sinful behavior, confesses and makes restitution to others as necessary, forgives others, and renews their commitment to keep the commandments.
- **Gain a testimony:** Mormons believe that real, lasting conversion comes through a personal experience with the Holy Ghost. As a person puts effort into learning the gospel, exercising faith, and repenting of sins, they can pray for confirmation that Mormonism is true. Usually in a private, prayerful moment, God's answer arrives through an unmistakable spiritual impression from the Holy Ghost, often accompanied by warmth, tingles, or other sensations.
- **Talk with a Church leader:** Before a person receives clearance for baptism, they undergo a private interview with a local priesthood leader to discuss their readiness. Even 8-year-old children meet with a leader. The leader asks questions to find out whether the person understands basic gospel principles, has developed sufficient faith, and is committed to living the gospel. Although the leader doesn't typically need to hear a confession of past sins, he makes sure the candidate isn't still committing significant sins, such as having sex outside of marriage. (For an overview of Mormon behavioral standards, see the temple-recommend questions that we summarize in Book 7, Chapter 4.)

Going through the baptism process

For 8-year-olds reared in the LDS Church, group baptismal services often take place once a month at a larger meetinghouse called a *stake center* (see the section "Participating in the Stake," later in this chapter). For converts, a ward often holds a special individual service. Baptisms can take place any day of the week, and they can occur in any suitable body of water, although meetinghouse fonts are preferred. Here's how the event typically plays out:

- Upon arrival at the meetinghouse, the baptismal candidate changes into plain, white clothing in a small dressing room adjacent to the baptismal font. Most congregations keep some baptismal clothes on hand, or the candidate can arrange to borrow some.
- Baptismal services generally take place either in the main chapel or in the auxiliary room where the font is actually located. White-clothed and shoeless, the baptismal candidate sits at the front with the baptizer, a priesthood holder

who's also dressed in white. The meeting begins and ends with a hymn and prayer, and assigned members give inspirational talks, usually on faith, repentance, baptism, and the gift of the Holy Ghost. At some point, a congregational leader usually offers words of advice and welcome.

- When it comes time for the actual baptism, the candidate and baptizer enter the font via steps descending from the dressing room.
- After the baptizer gets the candidate situated in the font, he raises his right arm, calls the person by their full name, utters a short, scripted baptismal prayer, and then lowers the person back into the water. Two witnesses standing at either side of the font make sure everything goes under — if even a big toe stays out, the baptizer does the ordinance over again. Most baptizers hold the candidate's wrist in such a way that the candidate can reach up and pinch shut their nose, and after the immersion, the baptizer pulls the candidate back up into the standing position.
- While the Church's newest member changes into regular Sunday-style clothes, the congregation sings hymns or watches a Church video.
- Confirmation and bestowal of the gift of the Holy Ghost (which we explain in the next section) can happen at the conclusion of the baptismal service or — especially for new adult converts — during sacrament meeting the following Sunday.

Installing a direct line to God: Confirmation

Any human being who's pure and sincere can feel the influence of the Holy Ghost on an extraordinary occasion, such as when praying to know whether a spiritual concept is true. However, Mormons believe that Church members can enjoy the constant companionship of the Holy Ghost if they're trying to live worthily. A priesthood holder bestows this gift during an ordinance commonly referred to as *confirmation*. The confirmation ceremony goes something like this:

- The recently baptized person sits in a chair. The priesthood holder who will act as voice places both hands on the person's head. Other invited priesthood holders can circle around and lay their hands on the new member's head.
- The priesthood holder calls the person by their full name, confirms them as a member of the Church, and confers the gift of the Holy Ghost, usually using the phrase "I say unto you, receive the Holy Ghost." These words don't have to be exact, as in the case of the baptismal and sacramental prayers.
- The priesthood holder blesses the person with some words of encouragement and advice as the Holy Ghost inspires him.

- Afterward, the person traditionally shakes hands with or hugs everyone in the circle.

REMEMBER

Mormons believe that receiving the gift of the Holy Ghost is essential to full salvation, because no one can make it back into God's presence without guidance and purification from the Holy Ghost. However, recognizing the Holy Ghost's promptings still takes effort. To invite his influence, members strive to obey the commandments and keep their thoughts and actions pure.

Welcoming a new lamb into the flock: Baby Blessings

A month or two after birth, new Mormon babies receive a blessing in front of the whole congregation during sacrament meeting. These blessings usually occur on *Fast Sunday*, which is almost always the first Sunday of the month. Here's what happens:

- The father and other invited priesthood holders stand together in a circle, which turns into an oval if too many men are present. (If the baby's father isn't a member or isn't in good standing with the Church, the family can ask another priesthood holder to perform the blessing.)
- The father holds the baby securely in both arms, and each man puts his left hand on the shoulder of the man in front of him and his right hand under the baby, helping gently bounce the baby to prevent crying (which doesn't always work). The baby usually wears something white.
- With the bishop or a boy holding a microphone near the father's mouth, the father calls on Heavenly Father in prayer, says the baby's full name, and then directly addresses the baby with advice and promises about its future. Typical utterances include telling the baby to always obey its parents and stay close to the Church and promising the baby that they will meet the right person to marry at the right time. If the baby's a boy, the blessing almost always includes a mention about serving a fulltime mission (see Book 7, Chapter 1).
- After the blessing, traditionally the father briefly holds up the baby for the congregation to admire. The mother stays seated in the congregation during the blessing, but she often says a few words later in the meeting, during the open-mike testimony-bearing time.

TECHNICAL STUFF

Although Mormons don't believe that a baby blessing is necessary for salvation, it does trigger the official listing of the baby as a *child of record* in the Church, and the parents receive a blessing certificate. Babies aren't yet technically members of the Church because they haven't been baptized, but they're counted in the Church's membership total.

Saying farewell, for now: Funerals

Usually held in the deceased person's home meetinghouse, Mormon funerals tend to be relatively upbeat, personalized affairs, celebrating the person's progress to the next step as much as mourning their departure. As always, the meeting begins and ends with a hymn and prayer, and it mainly consists of family members and friends giving talks and performing musical numbers. The talks tend toward specific personal remembrances of the deceased person, often sprinkled with humorous anecdotes. At least one talk primarily addresses how the Savior's resurrection opens the way for everybody to eventually be resurrected.

Adult Mormons who've been through the temple are buried in their temple clothes (for more on temples see Book 7, Chapter 4). After the funeral, a short graveside service usually takes place, during which a priesthood holder dedicates the gravesite as a place of shelter for the remains until the day of resurrection. Then a luncheon is usually served back at the meetinghouse, which frequently includes a certain cheesy potato casserole; many many Mormons refer to this dish as "funeral potatoes" no matter when it's served.

Mormons in other countries add a gospel spin to their own local customs. By the way, the Church discourages cremation unless the law requires it, as is the case in some countries.

Getting hitched: Weddings

Most Mormon weddings take place inside a temple, not a meetinghouse. When solemnized inside a temple, marriage lasts for eternity. When held in a meetinghouse, marriage lasts only until death.

TECHNICAL STUFF

Unlike a meetinghouse, which hosts Sunday worship, community events, and activities (like sports and youth groups) and that can be open to the public, temple admittance is typically reserved for baptized and confirmed Church members in good standing. Temples are also not open for Sunday worship, instead allowing individuals to attend their local gatherings.

If a couple isn't yet worthy of temple marriage — such as in the case of a shotgun wedding — the bishop can marry them civilly in the meetinghouse, in a ceremony much like that of other faiths. After the couple demonstrates repentance and worthiness for a suitable length of time, they can get eternally sealed together in the temple.

Meetinghouse weddings can occur on other occasions, too. If a woman is married to someone in the temple and becomes a widow, she can remarry "for time only" in a meetinghouse ceremony. (However, a widower can be married in the temple to both his first and second wives, if the second wife wasn't previously sealed to someone — a lingering echo of 19th-century plural marriage.) If a couple doesn't live near a temple, they can wed in a meetinghouse and get sealed later, when they're able to visit a temple. If a couple wants non-Mormon family members to witness the wedding, they can hold it in the meetinghouse and then wait a year to solemnize it in a temple, which only qualified Mormons can enter.

Taking a look at weekday meetings

Mormonism isn't just a Sunday religion, and if you drive by the parking lot of a local meetinghouse you may find it busy every night except Monday, which is family home evening (see Book 7, Chapter 1). The other weeknights are fair game for activities, meetings, book clubs, sports, holiday parties, wedding receptions, and the like.

Teens meet once a week for Young Men and Young Women activities, and teens and college-aged students may use the meetinghouse for their weekday religious classes called *seminary* and *institute*. Relief Society women gather monthly for a meeting called *Enrichment*. Enrichment meetings are meant to help sisters learn useful new skills (estate planning, food storage, self-defense, and so on) while sharing fun times, crafts, fellowship, and loads of sugary snacks.

Participating in the Stake

If a ward is the equivalent of a Catholic parish, then a *stake* is like a diocese (see Book 5, Chapter 4), a gathering of 5 to 12 adjacent wards that a stake president oversees. The word *stake* comes from the Old Testament prophet Isaiah's prophecies comparing the latter-day Church to a tent held fast by stakes (see Isaiah 33:20 and 54:2).

Each LDS stake usually has about 3,000 members. In heavily Mormon areas such as Utah, this quota is met in a matter of blocks. In other parts of the country and the world, traveling from one end of the stake to another can take several hours — a difficult consideration for unpaid stake leaders who regularly visit all the wards within their jurisdiction.

Unless they have a stake calling, such as stake high councilor or stake Relief Society president, most Mormons don't experience quite the same weekly connection with their stakes as they do with their wards. Their participation usually happens during the semiannual stake conference and in occasional stake activities.

Twice a year: Stake conference

Four Sundays each year, Mormons don't meet with their normal ward. They spend two of those Sundays every April and October watching *General Conference*, a Church-wide meeting. They spend the other two Sundays attending *stake conference*, a twice-yearly meeting that usually takes place at the *stake center*, a largish meetinghouse with overflow space to accommodate the crowds. (In addition, bigger regional meetings are sometimes held every few years, usually in a large, rented auditorium.)

Stake conferences usually feature several sessions within the same weekend. At the general two-hour session on Sunday, members of all ages hear from any General Authority who may be visiting, the stake president, and other male and female leaders and members. Members also listen to special music and hear about stake business, including the appointment and release of stake officers. Many stakes hold a Saturday evening session for adults, and special leadership training sessions help members with their callings in ward groups (Primary, Relief Society, Young Men, and Young Women). The sacrament isn't administered during stake conference.

Finding Grandpa's grandpa: Stake family history centers

Most stake centers in the United States, and many abroad, house a family history center where anybody, Mormon or not, can research their genealogy. Mormons are avid researchers into family history, and each stake family history center is a branch library of the largest Family History Library in the world, located in Salt Lake City, Utah. Some ward buildings also house small branch libraries. Mormons aren't the only ones who use these history centers — in fact, the majority of patrons are not LDS. They're often retired and are using the free resources to trace their family trees.

Touring Church Headquarters

In the heart of Salt Lake City, Utah, the LDS Church makes its headquarters on a sprawling campus of sturdy, staid buildings, many of them made of gray granite. From this headquarters, the *prophet* (the one man who serves as president and worldwide spiritual leader of the Church), the apostles, and other high-level leaders (the General Authorities), plus several thousand bureaucratic employees, run the affairs of Mormonism worldwide. In addition, some female leaders oversee the Church's programs for women, teenage girls, and children.

Temple Square, which makes up part of Church headquarters, is one of the most visited tourist destinations in the western United States. It is a walled city block dating back to 19th-century pioneer times. Headquarters, both at the downtown campus and at some significant sites around the city, is also made up of Church administration and office buildings, the Joseph Smith Memorial Building (which is a remodeled hotel that now houses offices, restaurants, and more), the Lion and Beehive Houses (originally built by Brigham Young to house his wives and children but that are now restored homes), the Family History Library, the Museum of Church History and Art, and more.

IN THIS CHAPTER

» Knowing the difference between temples and meetinghouses

» Summarizing what goes on inside a temple

» Getting ready for temple service

» Being initiated into the temple

» Becoming a forever family

Chapter 4

Sacred, Not Secret: Inside Mormon Temples

Like Charlie in the movie *Charlie and the Chocolate Factory*, Mormon children grow up wondering just what goes on inside a certain mysterious building. Ideally at least monthly, their parents dress in Sunday best, retrieve small suitcases from the closet, give last-minute instructions to the baby sitter, and disappear into the local temple for several hours. Although Mormon children learn the general purposes of temples, for all they know Oompa Loompas serenade those who go inside. Many non-Mormon observers are equally mystified about what goes on inside temples.

To Mormons, temples symbolize God's entire plan of salvation and provide a safe, private place for performing the faith's most sacred ordinances (for more details about the plan of salvation, see Book 7, Chapter 2). In this Internet age, the goings-on inside Mormon temples aren't secret to anyone who can use an online search engine. However, Mormons still revere temple work as too sacred to discuss in detail outside the temple itself. This chapter unfolds the Mormon temple experience in as much detail as practicing Mormons can reasonably discuss without breaking vows of sanctity. As Mormons often say, "It's sacred, not secret."

Distinguishing the Temple from the Meetinghouse

Although the Latter-day Saints (LDS) Church has built thousands of meetinghouses globally, so far the Church has erected only 335 temples worldwide. Many of these temples are magnificent multimillion-dollar whoppers, but many of the newer temples are much smaller than earlier temples, although still ornate.

TIP

Meetinghouses sport plain steeples, while temples are topped with a gold-leafed statue of the Angel Moroni, the Book-of-Mormon prophet who buried the golden plates and, as a resurrected angel, led Joseph Smith to them (for more on the Book of Mormon, check out Book 7, Chapter 5).

In short, the LDS Church puts more intricate detail and care into these temples than it does into meetinghouses because Mormons consider the temples to be the literal house of the Lord, a place of maximum beauty and reverence where they would feel comfortable hosting the resurrected Savior himself. Mormons use the meetinghouses, on the other hand, for day-to-day worship, instruction, and recreation.

The intricate detail and large size of Mormon temples aren't all that distinguish them from the more common meetinghouses, though. Here are a few of the major differences: meetinghouses are open on Sundays while temples aren't; visitors are welcome at meetinghouses but not temples; and children can only enter temples under certain extraordinary situations.

Understanding Why Mormons Go to the Temple: Temple Ordinances

Simply put, temples are where adults — and, to a limited degree, children and teens — perform a variety of eternally vital *ordinances*, or hands-on ceremonies, both for themselves and for people who've died. These ordinances are collectively known as *temple work.*

Appreciating the essential ordinances

To appreciate what goes on inside a temple, you first have to familiarize yourself with the basic Mormon ordinances considered necessary for full salvation and exaltation.

REMEMBER

In Mormonism, full *salvation* means returning to live with God, and *exaltation* means becoming an eternal parent like God (for more on these concepts, see Book 7, Chapter 2). In order to gain full salvation, a person needs to be baptized, be confirmed, and receive the gift of the Holy Ghost, which happens during confirmation. In order to qualify for exaltation, a person must receive four additional ordinances: priesthood ordination (if male), washing and anointing, the endowment, and celestial marriage.

Following is a more detailed overview of these six essential ordinances, in the order in which they occur. For living people, the first three ordinances occur in a meetinghouse, and the last three occur in a temple. On behalf of the deceased, Mormons perform all six ordinances inside a temple, which is why we include a summary of all six.

- **Baptism:** Full immersion to wash away sins and commence Church membership (see Book 7, Chapter 3).
- **Confirmation:** Laying on of hands to confirm Church membership and bestow the right to spiritual guidance by the Holy Ghost (see Book 7, Chapter 3).
- **Priesthood ordination for all worthy males:** Laying on of hands to confer priesthood power and authority (see Book 7, Chapter 1).
- **Washing and anointing:** A temple ordinance to provide spiritual cleansing and empowerment (see the section "Washing and anointing," later in this chapter).
- **Endowment:** A temple ordinance to teach the plan of salvation (see "Becoming endowed," later in this chapter).
- **Sealing:** A temple ordinance to bind spouses to each other and children to parents for eternity (flip ahead to "Sealing Families for Eternity," later in this chapter).

Why perform ordinances for the dead?

Before we discuss temple work for the dead, we must clarify one point: Mormons don't dig up decayed corpses and haul them into the temple Igor-style. Rather, genealogical researchers comb through records to extract names and essential data about people who've died all over the world — theoretically, anyone who's ever lived can appear on the list. Mormons who visit the temple perform ordinances as *proxies* (substitutes) on behalf of dead people, whose spirits choose whether or not to accept the ordinances.

Why do Mormons do this? Well, allow us to try to explain. Mormons believe that missionary spirits in the afterlife preach the gospel to all spirits who didn't receive a sufficient opportunity to hear the gospel while alive, thus allowing them to accept the gospel after death. (Head to Book 7, Chapter 2 for more about Mormon beliefs regarding the afterlife.) Mormons feel that during many historical eras, most notably in the Old World during the 1,700 or so years between the New Testament apostles and Joseph Smith, no one held God's true *priesthood authority* (the power to act in God's name). In the Mormon view, without the true priesthood the true church doesn't exist, and, as a result, they believe that billions of people died without receiving a fair chance to accept or reject the gospel. Since the time the LDS Church began in 1830, billions more have died before Mormon missionaries could reach them.

LDS theology says that disembodied spirits can't perform the physical ordinances that are essential for full salvation and exaltation. Consequently, earthly beings must do it for them. And because Mormons don't know who will accept the gospel and who will reject it in the afterlife, they aim to perform the necessary gospel ordinances for every person who ever lived so that those spirits potentially may be saved and exalted. After a living person has done temple work for a spirit, that spirit has the option of saying, "Thanks a lot, but no thanks," or of accepting the gospel message. If the spirits accept, they still await the final judgment before receiving their eternal reward (for more details, see Book 7, Chapter 2).

Beginning in childhood, Mormons are taught about the sacred obligation to perform temple ordinances for the dead, starting with their own ancestors. In fact, the Church teaches that temple work is urgent, because many departed spirits who've already accepted the gospel in the afterlife are anxiously waiting for somebody on earth to complete the ordinances on their behalf. In one commonly told story, a person performing baptisms for the dead reported seeing a queue of patiently waiting spirits. As the workers performed each spirit's baptism by proxy, that spirit disappeared from the line.

Yes, Mormons have undertaken a big job. Completing all the temple ordinances on behalf of one dead person requires several hours of combined labor, and Mormons have already completed the work for well over 100 million deceased people. In order to identify every human being who ever lived, Mormons spend considerable time and money on genealogical research. Having only just scratched the surface, the Church doesn't expect to complete this project until sometime during the 1,000-year Millennium that they believe will follow the Second Coming of Jesus Christ. (See Book 7, Chapter 1 for more details.)

REMEMBER

By providing the living with the opportunity to serve the dead in this manner, the temple helps draw together the entire family of God. Many have commented on the Christ-like nature of temple service: Just as mortals can never pay for their own sins and must rely on Jesus Christ, spirits can't perform their own ordinances and must rely on the disciples of Jesus Christ. In addition, the repeated visits to the temple help members better understand and remember the ordinances, particularly the lengthy, complex endowment.

A LITTLE TEMPLE HISTORY

Mormons believe that God always commands his people to build temples, from Old Testament times onward. Here's the lowdown on a few temples that are noteworthy because of their influence in the LDS Church:

- The early Mormons built their first temple in Kirtland, Ohio, in 1836. Many spiritual manifestations and heavenly visitations occurred in this temple. Persecution by local settlers led to its abandonment just a few years after its completion, but it still stands today and is owned by the Community of Christ, a denomination started by some Mormons who didn't go west after the murder of the prophet Joseph Smith.
- The Mormons completed an even grander temple in Nauvoo, Illinois, in 1846. Most of the ordinances and ceremonies that Mormons perform in today's temples originated during this Nauvoo period. Destroyed by arson and tornado soon after local persecution drove the Mormons from Nauvoo, this temple was rebuilt in 2002.
- In Utah, the Mormons completed three temples before finally finishing the flagship Salt Lake Temple in 1893, after 40 years of construction.
- During the first half of the 20th century, temples began to expand outside Utah, first appearing in Hawaii, Arizona, Idaho, and Alberta, Canada.
- The Church built its first temple outside the United States and Canada in Switzerland in 1955. By 1980, it had completed temples in New Zealand, England, Japan, and Brazil.
- Temples are now located in about 75 countries. By building a new generation of smaller temples, the Church can locate more temples closer to more people, which is a major development for Mormons living outside Utah.

Becoming Eligible for Temple Ordinances

REMEMBER

Entering the temple for your own ordinances requires careful planning and preparation on both the spiritual and practical levels. You have to be 18 or older, and you must have been a baptized Church member for at least a year (see Book 7, Chapter 3). In addition, you attend a special temple preparation class, buy or rent some special temple clothes, and allow local Church leaders to evaluate your personal worthiness.

However, before qualifying to perform their own temple ordinances, teenagers and converts who haven't yet reached their one-year baptismal anniversary can get their toes wet — figuratively and literally — by being baptized and receiving the gift of the Holy Ghost on behalf of dead people. Performing these two simple ordinances for the dead in the temple doesn't require as much preparation and provides a good warm-up for the full temple experience.

Getting a temple recommend

The Church is obligated to make sure that only sufficiently pure, worthy individuals (according to the standards set by Mormon prophets) enter the temple. The way the Church safeguards the temple's sanctity is by issuing a special card called a *temple recommend*, which a person must show at the front desk for entry into the temple.

To get a temple recommend for the first time, a member sits down in two private, confidential, one-on-one appointments with local church leaders and candidly answers pointed questions about personal righteousness. Initially, the *bishop* interviews the member, and within a few days the *stake president* interviews the member. (In Mormonism, a *ward*, like a parish, is a single congregation; a *stake* is like a diocese. A bishop oversees a ward, and a stake president oversees several adjacent congregations. See Book 7, Chapter 3.)

If you're simply performing baptisms for the dead, only your bishop interviews you, and the questions are simpler than those in the bulleted list that follows. In this case, the recommend you receive is called a *limited-use recommend*, because it allows you access only to the temple baptistry area.

REMEMBER

A temple-recommend interview usually takes about ten minutes, unless you want to discuss additional matters with the leader. The leader asks whether you obey Church standards in several areas, including the following (not necessarily listed in order of importance):

- Attendance of Church meetings
- Abstinence from coffee, tea, alcohol, tobacco, and harmful drugs
- Avoidance of any form of family-member abuse
- Avoidance of apostate beliefs and groups
- Belief in God, Jesus Christ, the Holy Ghost, and other points of Mormon doctrine
- Chastity outside of marriage and fidelity within marriage
- For divorced parents, payment of any court-ordered support
- Honesty
- Loyalty to general and local church leaders
- Payment of *tithe* (10 percent of all income)

Mormons renew their temple recommends every two years by going through the same two interviews, which in the case of renewals can be conducted by the bishop and stake president's counselors.

REMEMBER

Qualifying for a temple recommend gives members a practical, specific goal for religious discipline. While ever mindful of not being perfect, members take pride in staying current as literal card-carrying Mormons. If any serious sins come to light in a temple-recommend interview, the leader helps the member work out a plan for repentance and may possibly withhold the recommend for a time or initiate disciplinary action, which we talk about in the nearby sidebar "Facing the music."

Performing baptisms for the dead

Living Mormons don't receive their own baptism, confirmation, and priesthood ordination inside a temple — rather, temple-goers perform these ordinances only for the dead. However, living Mormons do receive their own washing and anointing, endowment, and celestial marriage inside the temple, in addition to performing these ordinances on behalf of the dead. We discuss baptism for the dead here because it's a good optional introduction to the temple for teens and new converts before they qualify to receive their own temple ordinances.

In the temple baptistry dressing room, baptismal proxies change into white baptismal clothing that they brought or the temple provided. After they're dressed, proxies gather at the temple baptismal font, which sits atop statues of 12 oxen that represent the 12 tribes of Israel (see Figure 4-1). After saying the brief baptismal prayer, a temple worker fully immerses the proxy on behalf of a dead person, repeating the process for several dead people in rapid succession.

FIGURE 4-1: Temple baptismal fonts are patterned after Old Testament fonts.

© John Wiley & Sons, Inc.

In addition, baptismal proxies can receive the gift of the Holy Ghost on behalf of deceased people. To complete this ordinance, which is generally known as *confirmation*, priesthood holders lay hands upon the proxy's head, confirm them as a member of the Church on behalf of a deceased person, and, most important, bestow the gift of the Holy Ghost.

TECHNICAL STUFF

Regarding baptism for the dead, much has been made of the Apostle Paul's comment in 1 Corinthians 15:29, which is the only biblical mention of the practice:

> Else what shall they do which are baptized for the dead, if the dead rise not at all? Why are they then baptized for the dead?

In other words, why would anyone bother getting baptized for the dead unless our souls continue living after death? Mormons emphasize this surviving fragment as proof that the practice has ancient validation, while opponents argue that Paul's comment means that he did not endorse baptisms for the dead as a Christian practice.

A preparation checklist

When Mormons turn 18 or reach their one-year baptismal anniversary, they can qualify for full temple privileges and receive their own temple ordinances. Most young men "go through the temple," in the common phrasing, a few weeks before leaving on a mission to preach the gospel full time, usually around the age of 19. Young women can now serve missions when they're 19 years old, too, but they can go through the temple before then if they so desire and qualify. For those who don't serve missions, a common time to go through the temple is prior to getting married in the temple.

The following checklist outlines the tasks that members complete before they arrive at the temple to receive their own ordinances. These items are roughly in chronological order:

- **Temple preparation class:** Most local congregations provide a temple preparation class for those anticipating going through the temple for their own ordinances. This class typically meets once a week for several weeks.
- **Temple recommend:** A *temple recommend,* a small card is needed to gain entry into the temple. We discuss the temple recommend in more detail in an earlier section, "Getting a temple recommend."
- **Temple clothing:** The Church encourages members to purchase their own set of white temple clothing, worn to symbolize purity and equality. However, some larger temples rent out temple clothing for a nominal fee. Temple clothing includes a basic white outfit and some ceremonial accessories.
  - The components of the basic outfit can be purchased at any store, including Church clothing distribution centers — as long as the items meet temple standards. Men wear a long-sleeved white shirt, white tie, white pants, white belt, and white socks and slippers. Women wear a plain white dress, white nylons, and white slippers.
  - The special ceremonial accessories can be purchased online or through one of the Church's clothing distribution centers by showing a temple recommend.
- **Temple garment:** As part of the temple ordinances, a Mormon dons a special garment that becomes their underwear style for the rest of mortality (see the section "Receiving the preparatory ordinances," later in this chapter). The first time through the temple, a Mormon brings a pair of new garments to wear home afterward, but doesn't try them on beforehand. Garments are sold only to temple-recommend holders through Church clothing distribution centers, and local leaders can answer any questions about buying and wearing them.
- **Special appointment:** Prior to attending the temple for the first time, a member should call the temple to make a special appointment and receive some additional preparatory instructions. (Appointments aren't necessary for subsequent temple visits, except at some small temples with limited hours of operation.) Keep in mind that all temples are closed on Sundays, to encourage

Sabbath meetinghouse attendance and home family worship. In addition, temples are closed on Monday evenings for family home evening, which we discuss in Book 7, Chapter 1.

» **Escort:** Oftentimes, Mormons invite some friends and family members to accompany them on their first temple visit, including one individual of the same gender who's officially designated as the escort.

GETTING A SNEAK PEEK DURING A TEMPLE OPEN HOUSE

The only time people can enter a temple without a temple recommend is during the open house held upon completion of a temple's construction or remodeling. Before the prophet or an apostle consecrates a temple for sacred use by saying a prayer of dedication, the building is open to the public for a short period of time, usually between a few days and a month. During this time, visitors of all faiths (or no faith) can tour the temple and learn a bit more about the worship services that occur there.

If you want to attend a temple open house, here are some things you should know:

- **You generally need a ticket.** The tickets are free, but they can go very quickly — for example, more than 250,000 people toured the rebuilt Nauvoo, Illinois, Temple; and most tickets were claimed several months in advance. Of course, if you don't have a ticket and there's room for you to join a tour, you're not going to be turned away.
- **Dress appropriately.** Visitors typically wear Sunday dress to show respect for the sacred nature of the temple.
- **It's movie time.** Before the tour, you usually watch a short film about Latter-day Saint beliefs, and you may walk through an informational exhibit as you wait in line.
- **Cover those kickers.** On the tour, you'll probably need to cover your shoes to avoid tracking dirt into the new temple and to show respect. Visitors usually receive little white booties to put over their street shoes as they walk through the temple.

Feel free to ask questions of your tour guide. However, please understand that Latter-day Saints consider the temple ordinances sacred and won't discuss them in much detail.

Receiving Your Own Temple Ordinances

Some Mormons compare receiving the temple ordinances to trying to catch the output of a fire hose in a teacup; you're faced with so much new information that it's hard to absorb much on your first time through. However, Church leaders encourage you to keep returning to perform the same ordinances on behalf of dead people so you can gradually digest the experience.

Receiving the preparatory ordinances

After checking your temple recommend at the front desk, where you leave behind any cameras or recorders, temple workers process your first-timer paperwork and then escort you to the dressing room. To maintain modesty, all patrons are assigned private changing booths.

When an adult receives their own temple ordinances, washing and anointing and the endowment take place during the same visit, and sealings often take place on another day. When people perform work for the dead, they can choose whether to do washings and anointings, the endowment, or sealings.

Washing and anointing

The temple ordinance process begins with ceremonial washing and anointing, which takes place in what's called the initiatory area, adjacent to the dressing room. Quite personal yet scrupulously modest, this ceremony involves some dabbing of water and olive oil on the body, accompanied by the pronouncing of blessings of purity, health, and eternal potential.

Donning the temple garment

The washing and anointing process concludes with putting on the white temple undergarment, which then becomes the member's underwear style for life. According to the official Church handbook of instructions,

The garment provides a constant reminder of the covenants made in a temple. When properly worn, it provides protection against temptation and evil. Wearing the garment is also an outward expression of an inward commitment to follow the Savior.

In addition to spiritual protection, many members feel that the garment can provide miraculous physical protection. Hearing stories about someone suffering a catastrophic accident but not sustaining injuries on areas covered by the garment isn't uncommon. For these and other reasons, many members report feeling uneasy while their garments are off. However, plenty of people suffer bodily injury and death while wearing garments, so they don't provide infallible protection.

In earlier times, the garment was a one-piece affair that reached to the ankles and wrists. Today's most-worn garment style comes in two pieces, with the bottom reaching to the knee and the top covering the shoulder and scooping down almost to the bottom of the breastbone. Garments are available in a variety of comfortable, lightweight fabrics, but wearing them still limits one's clothing style choices, especially in hot weather. Often visible through clothing, the distinctive neckline shape is affectionately known as the "celestial smile" and provides a good way to recognize fellow Mormons at first sight.

TEMPLE GARMENT WASH AND WEAR INSTRUCTIONS

One of the temple-recommend questions asks whether members properly wear and care for the garment. The Church gives some instructions and rules regarding garments, encouraging members to seek the guidance of the Holy Spirit in their personal habits and attitudes related to the garment. Following are several expectations for day-to-day life with garments:

- Mormons wear both pieces of the garment 24 hours a day, removing them only for such activities as showering, swimming, or sex, and putting them back on again as soon as reasonably possible. Some Latter-day Saints wear them during exercise, and some don't.
- Mormons don't wear clothing that reveals any portion of the garment, which rules out tank tops, shorts that rise above the knee, midriff-baring tops, and so on.
- Mormons aren't supposed to remove the garment top during yard work, roll up the garment legs to accommodate a favorite pair of shorts, or otherwise "cheat."
- Mormons avoid exposing the garment to non-Mormons. For some members, that means changing into regular underwear before visiting the doctor or the gym. Others, however, just try to be discreet.
- Mormons launder garments normally with other clothing. Some members try to avoid letting them touch the floor.
- Mormons are asked to keep garments in good repair. When a piece wears out, they destroy it before disposal.

Becoming endowed

Although most Mormon ordinances are short and simple, the endowment is a megaordinance that takes approximately two hours to complete. And that's relatively short — in the olden days, it took all day.

REMEMBER

The first endowment you receive is for yourself. For every endowment you attend after that, a temple worker gives you the name of a deceased person as you leave the dressing room.

Clothed in white, you sit quietly in a chapel until summoned for the next endowment session. Then you walk to a theater-style ordinance room, carrying the packet that holds some clothing accessories you'll don during the session. (In the new generation of smaller temples that don't have room for a chapel, you go straight to the ordinance room.)

REMEMBER

In a nutshell, the endowment dramatizes the entire plan of salvation, from the earth's creation to humankind's falling away from God and redemption through the Savior (for more about the plan of salvation, see Book 7, Chapter 2). After an overview of the creation stages — for long-time temple attendees who are prone to dozing, this can be a tricky stretch — the endowment film portrays the story of Adam and Eve, who represent everyone in the human dilemma. Temple workers stop the film at various points so participants can receive instructions, perform rituals, and make covenants, the details of which they don't discuss outside the temple.

Both symbolically and literally, the temple teaches members how to successfully pass the earthly test and reenter God's presence, where Mormons believe humans can eventually become eternal parents like God. According to the prophet Brigham Young, the gestures and phrases learned during the endowment

> *are necessary for you, after you have departed this life, to enable you to walk back to the presence of the Father, passing the angels who stand as sentinels.*

At the conclusion of the endowment, the projection screen rises, revealing a gauzy white curtain known as the *veil.* After passing through this veil, patrons enter the beautifully furnished *celestial room* — in Mormonism, the word *celestial* refers to the highest degree of heaven, where God the Father resides. This symbolic room provides comfortable chairs and couches for those who want to ponder and pray before returning to the dressing room.

REMEMBER

Mormons take their temple covenants extremely seriously. During the endowment, they make several promises, such as to be pure and obedient, follow the Savior's gospel, stay chaste, and serve the cause of righteousness to the best of their ability. In return, they're assured of God's promises regarding their eternal potential.

Sealing Families for Eternity

In the Mormon faith, the highest earthly ordinance is celestial marriage, also known as eternal marriage, temple marriage, or "getting sealed." This ordinance is necessary for exaltation, or becoming an eternal parent like God. Thanks to the sealing authority restored to Joseph Smith by the resurrected prophet Elijah and handed down since then from Mormon prophet to Mormon prophet, Mormons believe that marriages performed in the temple don't dissolve at death, but last forever.

In addition, Mormons believe that the sealing power eternally binds children to parents, linking each Mormon in a massive eternal family that can conceivably include each person's entire progeny and ancestry, all the way back to Adam and ultimately to God himself. Children who are physically born to a sealed couple are automatically sealed to them, which is known as being "born in the covenant." In all other cases, including adoption, the child is sealed to their parents during a special temple ceremony.

TECHNICAL STUFF

From the Mormon viewpoint, the Bible's most significant mention of the sealing power appears in Matthew 16:19, where the Savior says the following to Peter, the senior apostle:

> And I will give unto thee the keys of the kingdom of heaven: and whatsoever thou shalt bind on earth shall be bound in heaven: and whatsoever thou shalt loose on earth shall be loosed in heaven.

Mormons equate the word *bind* with *seal*. It's possible for sealings to be canceled or revoked — *loosed* — under certain circumstances, which we address in this chapter's later section "When the going gets tough: Sealing complexities."

Temple sealings for the living

Temple work for the dead includes performing sealings for all husbands, wives, and children who ever lived. In this section, however, we focus on two of Mormonism's most anticipated, celebrated events for the living: temple marriages and the sealing of children to parents.

Before a couple can get married in the temple, each must have received all the other essential ordinances. Couples who were married outside the temple can get sealed as early as a year after their civil marriage or a year after their convert baptism into Mormonism, and their children can be sealed to them at that time. Adopted children can be sealed after the adoption is final. In the United States and some other countries, temple sealings are recognized as legal marriages.

Kneeling on opposite sides of a cushiony altar and grasping hands, a couple is sealed together for eternity by one of the church's relatively few priesthood holders who hold the sealing power, given to him by the Church's prophet or an apostle. The brief ceremony is the same whether the couple is getting married for the first time or sealing their previous civil marriage. When children are being sealed, they gather around the altar to participate in a similar ceremony.

Eternal marriages and sealings of children to parents take place in special sealing rooms located near the endowment rooms. Sealings for living people differ from other temple ordinances in several ways:

- **The family can invite adult guests who hold temple recommends to enter the temple simply to witness the sealing.** These guests don't typically dress in white, but they do remove their shoes in a special waiting area.
- **Not only can children enter the temple to be sealed to their own parents, but they can also witness the sealing of a sibling.** These are the only occasions on which children under age 12 can enter the temple. Temple workers typically take care of the children in another room until they're needed.
- **Sealings for the living are generally preceded by a freestyle sermon.** The sealer, who is usually fairly advanced in years, typically offers some practical family advice combined with eternal perspective, oftentimes sprinkled with humor.

REMEMBER

Only adults who hold a current temple recommend can attend a temple marriage, which sometimes causes heartache for couples with family members who aren't Mormon. Most temples provide an outer lobby where underage family members and those without a recommend can wait. If a couple decides to get married outside the temple in order to accommodate family pressures, they must wait a full year before getting sealed in the temple.

If, for some reason, a Mormon couple can't get married in the temple, such as in the case of a shotgun wedding, a Mormon bishop can perform a regular "until death do you part" wedding in an LDS meetinghouse, although this is considered far from ideal, of course. If the couple demonstrates complete worthiness for at least a year, they can get sealed later and have any children sealed to them.

MY BIG FAT MORMON WEDDING

Whether a couple is getting married for their first time in the temple or eternalizing their previous civil marriage, Mormons celebrate the occasion in the following ways:

- The bride can wear a wedding dress in the temple. However, several style limitations and requirements apply, in order to make the dress suitable for the temple. The dress can't be sleeveless or backless, for example.
- Right after the ceremony, the couple usually kisses over the altar.
- The couple doesn't exchange rings as part of the sealing ceremony. However, they can step away from the altar and informally slip rings onto each other's fingers. Some Mormon couples have a public ring-exchange ceremony later, often as part of the wedding reception.
- Most, if not all, sealing rooms are furnished with large mirrors facing each other from opposite walls. At some point, the sealer typically invites the couple to gaze together into these endlessly reflecting mirrors and witness their image perpetuated into infinity.
- If they so desire, families can hold a reception or open house in the local LDS meetinghouse's *cultural hall*, a gymlike room used for sports, parties, and overflow seating.
- Mormons follow most other local marriage customs, from bridal showers to honeymoons. Cleaned-up versions of bachelor parties aren't unheard of, either.

When the going gets tough: Sealing complexities

Eternal sealings can bring up some complex family situations, and sometimes a person must exercise faith that Heavenly Father will eventually work out everything to everyone's satisfaction and fill in any gaps. The bottom line is that Mormonism abhors a sealing vacuum. It's always better for someone to be sealed than not to be sealed, even if the person to whom they are sealed doesn't seem ideal in the here and now.

Following are a few tricky situations about which the LDS Church offers some insight:

» **Death of a spouse:** The LDS Church stopped practicing earthly polygamy more than 100 years ago, but some hints of heavenly plural marriage remain. If a widower who was sealed to his first wife marries a new wife who isn't already sealed to a husband, the widower can be eternally sealed to both wives. However, a widow who was sealed to her deceased husband generally marries a new earthly husband only for the remainder of mortality. If she has any children with the new husband, the children are automatically sealed by virtue of the original sealing.

- **Divorced couple:** If a Mormon couple divorces — which, of course, the Church discourages — their sealing remains intact unless and until the wife finds someone else to be sealed with, at which time she can apply to cancel her sealing with her ex-husband. What's important is that she's not left without a sealing ordinance in place; if she doesn't ever find a new spouse, presumably God will somehow resolve the situation later. On the other hand, the man can receive clearance to be sealed to a new wife even if the sealing is still intact with his ex-wife, another lingering echo of patriarchal plural marriage.
- **Divorced parents:** From the standpoint of sons and daughters, what happens if their parents' sealing is canceled? The official Church handbook of instructions simply states:

  > Children who are born in the covenant or sealed to their parents remain so even if the sealing of the parents is later canceled or revoked.

  Again, the important principle is that the children don't lose their place in God's eternal family, and Mormons trust that any ambiguities will be resolved in heaven. By the way, if no prior sealings have taken place, a child can be sealed to a legal custodial parent and stepparent as long as the other legal parent gives permission.
- **Divorced couple, both passed away:** Interestingly, if a deceased couple was divorced before death and never sealed, their children may arrange for the parents to be sealed by proxy in the temple (see the previous section "Why perform ordinances for the dead?") so that the children can then be sealed to them. According to the Church handbook of instructions these sealings often provide the only way for children of such couples to be sealed to parents. Even if the parents don't accept the ordinances in the afterlife, the children still reap the full benefits of being sealed into God's eternal family.
- **Parents not Mormon:** Adult converts to Mormonism can perform temple work for their own parents after the parents die, eternalizing their parents' marriage and then getting sealed to their parents. Even if the parents don't accept the ordinances, Mormons believe that the convert will receive the full sealing benefits.
- **Spouse who leaves the Church:** If someone gets excommunicated from the Church or officially resigns by requesting removal of their name from Church records, that person's sealings are revoked. However, the spouse and children of that person don't lose their sealing blessings if they remain faithful.

» **Spouse who doesn't join the Church:** What if two members of another faith (or no faith) get married, and only one of them later converts to Mormonism? Because the non-Mormon spouse won't qualify to be sealed, what happens to the Mormon spouse's eternal prospects? If the quandary is never resolved during the couple's lifetime, the sealing can be performed posthumously in the hopes that the non-Mormon spouse will finally convert in the afterlife. Otherwise, the Mormon spouse simply trusts in Heavenly Father to eventually work things out to everyone's wishes and best advantage.

» **Never married:** For those who don't have the opportunity to marry during their earthly lifetime, through no choice or fault of their own, Mormons believe they can still qualify to receive all eternal blessings. Many believe that those who die single and worthy will be provided with an eternal spouse at a future time.

Occasional complexities notwithstanding, sealings imbue earthly family relationships with greater meaning and purpose. When you know you're building something that can last forever, you put more effort into it and value it more. Without a doubt, temples are one of the key ways in which Mormonism strengthens families.

IN THIS CHAPTER

» Knowing what Mormons believe about the Bible

» Getting to know the plot and themes of the Book of Mormon

» Bringing forth the Book of Mormon

» Noting key aspects of the Pearl of Great Price

» Looking into the Doctrine and Covenants

Chapter 5
The Bible, the Book of Mormon, and Other Scriptures

Mormons believe that both the Bible and the Book of Mormon are the word of God and that people need to study both books frequently and prayerfully. Mormons also hold up two other books, the Doctrine and Covenants and the Pearl of Great Price, as *scripture* (or sacred writings). Together, these four books of scripture are known as Mormonism's *standard works.*

Like the Bible (see Book 5, Chapter 2), the Book of Mormon is a collection of sacred texts written over the course of many centuries by many different people. Unlike the Bible, which was translated by hundreds of people (and continues being translated in new versions today), the Book of Mormon had only one modern-day translator, Joseph Smith.

However, when Mormons say *translate* in connection with Joseph Smith, they generally don't mean using human linguistic skills to turn a text originally written in another language into English. Rather, Joseph translated by receiving holy text from God via revelatory devices such as a seer stone or the Urim and Thummim, a prophetic instrument mentioned several times in the Bible. (We discuss this idea more in the section "Translating the golden plates" later in this chapter.)

Understanding the Bible: True, with a Few Tweaks

Mormons see their church as the restoration of the religion whose evolution is chronicled in the Old and New Testaments (see Book 4, Chapter 5 and Book 5, Chapter 2). So, of course the Bible is extremely important to Mormons, and they put a high emphasis on studying it and quoting from it. According to Mormonism's eighth Article of Faith, "We believe the Bible to be the word of God as far as it is translated correctly" (for more on the Articles of Faith, see the "Lining up the Articles of Faith" section later in this chapter). However, the ninth Article of Faith states that Mormons believe in continuing revelation — in other words, scripture is open to addition. The other three standard books of scripture work together with the Bible to establish Mormon belief and practice.

Thus saith the King James Version

Mormons recognize the *King James Version* (KJV), a certain translation of the Bible that is often cited for its use of words like "thee," "thou," and "ye," as their official Bible. They publish their own edition of the KJV, which stays true to the original text and is also jampacked with Latter-day Saints-specific supplements and reader aids.

TECHNICAL STUFF

Why do Mormons stick with the old-fashioned King James Version, even though so many more-accessible Bible versions are available? The main reason is that the KJV is the Bible version that founding prophet Joseph Smith used, as did most people in his time.

Joseph Smith's corrections to the Bible

With so many people having translated and rewritten the Bible over the centuries, Mormons believe that inaccuracies and omissions have crept into it. Even though Joseph Smith didn't possess the original Bible manuscripts, Mormons believe he could identify biblical trouble spots through God's inspiration. Joseph Smith received a divine commission to make a "new translation" of the King

James Version itself. (For Mormons the concept of *translation* carries a different meaning when applied to Joseph Smith: He prophetically received text from God, instead of using scholarly skills to rewrite original non-English text into English.) In carrying out this project, Joseph worked on more than 3,400 individual verses, sometimes tweaking just a few words and other times adding whole new chapters.

Getting Acquainted with the Book of Mormon

The Book of Mormon isn't just a simple batch of sermons or a book of prophetic sayings. The volume is a family saga that stretches over more than 1,000 years of history (roughly 600 BCE to 421 CE) and mixes visions, religious symbolism, and prophecies about the Messiah with records of migrations, civil wars, and the difficulties of governing a remote New World society.

TECHNICAL STUFF

This book is long — it has about 270,000 words — with a complex, involved story. It features 15 parts generally called *books*, and these parts are divided into chapters and verses, much like the Bible. The parts are in chronological order except for the 14th part, called the Book of Ether, which covers events that happened way before the rest of the Book of Mormon.

REMEMBER

The bulk of the Book of Mormon takes up the centuries-long civil war between the Nephites and their rebellious cousins, the Lamanites, a war of smoldering hatred that eventually spells doom for the Nephites. One of the key points to remember is that all the good guys die by the end of the book, mostly violently.

Lehi's journey to the New World

The Book of Mormon opens with the record of an Israelite man named Lehi who lived around 600 BCE. Lehi had a vision that foretold the destruction of Jerusalem (which actually happened around 587 BCE, when Babylonian invaders destroyed the temple there), so he started urging people to leave the city while they still had time. As you can imagine, most people didn't want to follow the counsel of this unknown man and began to threaten his life, so Lehi obeyed a directive from the Lord to gather his family together and escape. The family was fairly wealthy, and several family members were reluctant to leave their comfortable home and social position in Jerusalem. Lehi's oldest sons, Laman and Lemuel, openly rebelled.

The son who obeyed without quibbling was Nephi, a righteous young man who prayed to God for his own confirmation of the spiritual vision his father received.

He got that confirmation and more, so he threw himself into his father's work. After several unpleasant years of wandering in the wilderness (probably the Arabian Desert), Nephi and other members of the family constructed a boat to take them to the New World.

The journey by sea was no picnic. Laman and Lemuel resented the fact that Nephi, their younger brother, was their father's favorite and had taken to preaching at them a good deal. They tried to kill him several times, both en route and after arriving in the New World. (We don't know exactly where they lived, though some individual Mormons have identified Central America as a likely place.) Nephi was brokenhearted about his brothers' treachery, resulting in the "Psalm of Nephi," an achingly honest plea Nephi makes to God in 2 Nephi 4. Although he was sick about it, Nephi knew that he had to separate his followers from his wicked brothers and try to build a just society on his own.

The Nephites and the Lamanites

The majority of the Book of Mormon is taken up with the plots and perils of the *Nephites* (including the descendants of Nephi) and the *Lamanites* (including the descendants of Laman and Lemuel, who became like savages because of their wickedness). The Lamanites outnumber the Nephites throughout the Book of Mormon, causing some scholars to think that they successfully intermarried with natives already in the Americas.

Although good and evil may seem to be cut and dried in the Book of Mormon, with the Nephites always righteous and the Lamanites always sinful, the plot just isn't that simple. At numerous times, they switch roles. Dramatizing one of history's worst cases of *Groundhog Day*, the Book of Mormon tells about the same chain of events happening over and over again to the Nephites throughout the centuries:

- The Nephites love God and take care of their neighbors.
- Because of this righteousness, they prosper.
- They get obsessed with their own wealth, loving money and becoming corrupt and immoral.
- The Lord somehow humbles them, often by allowing the Lamanites to defeat them in battle or bring them into submission via slavery or heavy taxes.
- When the Nephites are humble again and repent of their sins, they resume doing what the Lord wants them to do: worship him and deal justly with one another.
- Sadly, before long, the whole pride-prosperity-greed-war-repentance cycle starts again with a vengeance.

Throughout Nephite history, numerous missionaries risk their lives to preach the gospel to their own people and to the Lamanites, with some success. At one point, the Lamanite king converts, and many of his people follow suit.

Having been saved from their sins, the Lamanite converts decide to bury their swords rather than risk murdering again. In battle, they fall face down before their fellow Lamanites who've come to kill them for adopting the Nephite religion. The result is a horrific massacre, but the sight of so many Lamanites going willingly to the slaughter makes such a deep spiritual impact that some of their countrymen also convert.

Despite occasional alliances or truces between the Nephites and Lamanites, no real or lasting peace exists between them until Christ comes.

The coming of Christ

The Book of Mormon is a very consciously Christ-centered book, featuring prophets hundreds of years before Jesus's birth who look forward to the event and declare Jesus Christ as the Messiah by name. (For more on Jesus, see Book 5, Chapter 1.) For example, 600 years before Christ came, Nephi wrote

> And we talk of Christ, we rejoice in Christ, we preach of Christ, we prophesy of Christ, and we write according to our prophecies, that our children may know to what source they may look for a remission of their sins — 2 Nephi 25:26.

In other words, Christ is the hero of the Book of Mormon, the one to whom all the people through the ages look for atonement for their sins.

The Book of Mormon teaches that Christ visited the Nephites after his resurrection and before he ascended into heaven, preaching among them, healing their sick, and calling 12 New World disciples (or apostles). These chapters are the climax of the Book of Mormon and feature some of the most beautiful passages of the text.

WARNING

Some anti-Mormons claim that the fact that Jesus's teachings in the Book of Mormon are so similar to those in the New Testament proves that Joseph Smith wrote the Book of Mormon himself, copying key passages from the Bible to supplement his own story. Mormons counter that it makes perfect sense that Christ's teachings in Jerusalem would be the same as those in the New World and elsewhere, because the core of the gospel is the same in all times and places. They see the Book of Mormon account as a second witness of these key teachings, fulfilling the Bible's promise that "in the mouth of two or three witnesses every word may be established" (Matthew 18:16).

Among the familiar teachings of Christ in the Book of Mormon, you'll find

- The Lord's Prayer ("Our Father, who art in heaven . . .")
- Teachings on faith, repentance, baptism, and the Holy Ghost
- The Beatitudes ("Blessed are the poor," and so on)
- Discussion of the last days and the restoration of Israel

Near the end of his visit to the Nephites, Christ promises 9 of his 12 disciples that they'll be with him in his kingdom immediately after they die. He allows the three other disciples, however, to remain on earth as long as they desire, establishing the gospel and helping God's people. As far as Mormons know, they're still ministering on the earth today. These fellows are called the *three Nephites*, and they occupy a delightful place in Mormon folklore. Through the years, Mormons have told stories around the campfire about possible sightings of one or more of the three Nephites, who've reportedly helped Mormons in danger, plowed fields when a person was too sick to do it, and even changed tires on cars when Mormons were headed off on missions of mercy. (We're a little skeptical about this last part, too.)

The end of the Nephites

After Christ's brief visit to the New World, the people put aside their old divisions, including the terms *Nephite* and *Lamanite*. Now sharing the same religion, they founded a church based on the principles Christ taught them. They shared everything, and no one was rich or poor. They healed the sick and worked mighty miracles. The Book of Mormon reports that during this peaceful time, crime and conflict didn't exist, and the people were united in love.

As in any tragedy worth its salt, the peace, love, and understanding couldn't possibly last. About 200 years after Christ's visit, this utopian society gave in to the same old story: The people prospered and then became full of pride. Class divisions between rich and poor again became a big problem. False religions arose, their leaders persecuted the Church, and the old lines between Nephite and Lamanite were redrawn in the sand. War became inevitable.

As the situation worsened, the Lamanites began to slaughter any Nephite who wouldn't deny Jesus the Christ. Most of the Nephites, in turn, became as wicked as the Lamanites or even more so. Seeing that their end was near, two faithful Nephite prophets named Mormon and his son Moroni set about creating a condensed *Reader's Digest* version of their people's records from Lehi on down, also adding some of their own words of wisdom. In addition, they included a historical summary of an earlier civilization called the *Jaredites*, some Israelites who'd journeyed to the New World hundreds of years before Lehi and his family.

REMEMBER

Mormon and Moroni engraved their abridgment onto golden tablets — which Mormons commonly call *plates* — and Moroni buried them in the ground for safekeeping, until that day some 1,400 years later when the time would be right to make them known to the world. Because Mormon did most of the editorial work on the book, it was named the Book of Mormon. Moroni did some of the writing and abridging too, but his reward was to serve as the angel who helped Joseph Smith discover the record.

Discovering How the Book of Mormon Came to Be

When Mormons give their testimonies at fast and testimony meeting on the first Sunday of the month (see Book 7, Chapter 3), they frequently mention that they know the Book of Mormon is true. What they generally mean by this claim isn't simply that the *teachings* of the book are true, but that it came into being the way Joseph Smith claimed: by a miracle.

In this section, you find out how the Book of Mormon appeared — it didn't exactly fall from the sky, but it was a pretty astonishing event.

An angel in the night

Joseph Smith had his first major spiritual experience when he was a young teen. This event, known as the *First Vision* to Mormons, was a direct answer to Joseph's prayer about which church to join. That incident opened the floodgates of Joseph's prophetic calling.

The second major event happened in September 1823, and again it was the direct result of prayer. Seventeen-year-old Joseph was praying for forgiveness of his sins (which apparently included *levity*, or lightheartedness) when a glorious being appeared in his room. The man was dressed in a loose white robe, and his feet didn't touch the floor. His whole body seemed to be luminous, almost glowing white. He called Joseph by name and said that he was named Moroni, sent from God to tell Joseph about the work he was called to do.

As you see in the earlier section "Getting Acquainted with the Book of Mormon," Moroni wasn't just a glow-in-the-dark angelic messenger but a resurrected inhabitant of the Americas who lived and breathed and helped edit the ancient record that became the Book of Mormon. Hovering there in Joseph's bedroom, Moroni discussed the book that he had buried in the ground some 1,400 years earlier and told Joseph how to find it. He also gave Joseph directions for using the *Urim and Thummim*, a biblical device that helped him translate this ancient record. In addition, Moroni instructed Joseph in biblical prophecy.

One of the most unusual features of this story — as if it weren't odd enough! — is that just after Moroni finished his little speech and zoomed back into heaven, leaving Joseph in bed to wonder about it all, the angel reappeared and proceeded to tell Joseph the same information again. And then he came a third time, repeating exactly the same stuff and adding a caution that Satan may try to tempt Joseph to get rich from the Book of Mormon plates, given the poverty of the Smith family.

The next day, Joseph found the golden plates buried on the hillside where Moroni had indicated, but the angel wouldn't let him remove them yet. Every September 23 for the next four years, Joseph went to the same spot for instruction. From Joseph's own account, Moroni seems to have been pretty severe with him, repeatedly lecturing him about not losing the plates and not making a profit from them. Finally, in September 1827, Joseph was allowed to take the plates and figure out how to translate them.

Translating the golden plates

Because word leaked out about the golden plates and many people wanted to see and handle them — something the Lord had forbidden except in special circumstances — Joseph temporarily moved to Pennsylvania with his new wife, Emma. There, with the assistance of several scribes, the translation went forth in earnest during 1829.

REMEMBER

Eyewitnesses to the translation process reported that, aided by a *seer stone* (a stone used to transmit revelations), Joseph dictated the Book of Mormon aloud while looking into his hat to block the light so he could see each character as it appeared. The plates themselves weren't even always necessary to the translation, as they were usually still covered by a cloth. Mormons believe that the Lord gave Joseph the translation by revelation, which explains why no one revised or rewrote this complicated narrative. When Joseph or his scribe needed a break, they resumed work precisely where they left off, because Joseph didn't need to look at the previous dictation to refresh his memory or remind himself where they were. He simply picked up where they stopped before the interruption. After the long wait to get the plates, the actual translation took only three months.

WARNING

With this 588-page book, Joseph made a remarkable achievement, one that Mormons believe couldn't have happened by natural means. The book displays remarkable self-consistency, especially considering that Joseph wasn't referring back to the English longhand dictation during the process. If the book were of his own creation, Mormons note, he would've had to remember hundreds of character and place names, master a dizzying timeline, be familiar with the history and geography of the ancient Middle East and Nephite lands, and be able to write in many different voices.

Contemplating what happened to the plates

According to Joseph Smith, shortly after the translation was finished, he gave the plates back to the angel Moroni. Skeptics see this claim as a convenient excuse for why the Latter-day Saints (LDS) Church can't produce the plates or submit them to scientific inquiry. Certainly, the skeptics have a good point. The plates are no longer available, so all we have is Joseph Smith's word on the matter.

Or is it? In the opening pages of every edition of the Book of Mormon, you see the testimony of 11 different witnesses who claimed that they saw the plates and believed Smith had translated them by the gift and power of God. Although several of the key witnesses later left the Church over personal or institutional disagreements, they never denied that Smith translated the Book of Mormon from the plates by divine inspiration.

Interestingly, Joseph translated only a portion of the plates, and not everything he translated got published. He couldn't access the majority of the plates because metal bands kept them locked tight, but Mormons believe that this sealed portion will one day be translated and published, if Moroni would be so kind as to return the plates. In addition, Joseph loaned the first 116 pages of his translation of the manuscript to the Book of Mormon's chief financer, Martin Harris, who lost them. This episode was one of Joseph's most difficult learning experiences as a prophet, and the Lord didn't allow him to retranslate those pages.

Reading The Pearl of Great Price: A Scriptural Hodgepodge

In addition to the Bible and the Book of Mormon, Mormons recognize two more books of scripture: the *Doctrine and Covenants* and *Pearl of Great Price.* If the Bible is the spiritual history of God's people in the Middle East until shortly after the time of Christ, and the Book of Mormon is the spiritual history of God's people living in the Western Hemisphere from about 600 BCE to 400 CE, then you can consider the Doctrine and Covenants to be the spiritual history of God's people —the Mormons —from about 1830 onward, though most of its revelations occurred in

America during the earliest days of the Church (see the next section for more on this book). And the Pearl of Great Price is a grab bag of scriptural odds and ends, both ancient and modern.

Diving into the Pearl of Great Price

Although the Pearl of Great Price contains much essential doctrine, it also sometimes seems like the stepchild among Mormon scriptures, for several reasons:

- At only about 60 pages, this text is considerably shorter than the other three Mormon standard works.
- The book is a jumble of several different eras and writing styles.
- It creates more than its fair share of ongoing controversy, especially with regard to some of the material's origins.
- This scripture is the only one of the four standard works that Church members don't study for a full year in the four-year teaching cycle, which goes through the Old and New Testaments, Book of Mormon, and Doctrine and Covenants. However, teachers touch upon aspects of the Pearl of Great Price in various classes.
- Its pages include three funky, Egyptian-looking facsimiles.

This book of scripture takes its name from a New Testament passage:

> A merchant man, seeking goodly pearls . . . when he had found one pearl of great price, went and sold all that he had, and bought it — Matthew 13:45–46

The Pearl of Great Price began as a collection of scripture published in England in 1851 by a Mormon apostle, but the Church didn't canonize it as a standard work until 1880. Over the decades, several components have been added or removed, such as in 1979, when Church authorities moved a couple of modern revelations into the Doctrine and Covenants, where all such other revelations were already collected (yes, scriptural change moves at glacial pace).

Revisiting Moses

As discussed earlier in this chapter, Mormonism's founding prophet Joseph Smith received a divine commission to make a new translation of the Bible's King James Version (KJV). Pondering Genesis, which Mormons believe Moses wrote, Joseph wrote an inspired expansion of certain sections, parts of which now appear as "Selections from the Book of Moses" in the Pearl of Great Price.

The eight-chapter book of Moses covers the following territory:

- **Details of a vision that Moses experienced but didn't discuss anywhere in his biblical writings:** During this vision, which happened after the burning bush incident but before the parting of the Red Sea episode, Moses is transported to "an exceedingly high mountain," where he meets the premortal Jesus Christ, who was then a spirit personage known as Jehovah, and learns more about the nature of God. In addition, Moses encounters Satan and learns more about the devil's goals, motivations, and methods.
- **A recounting of the earth's creation and Adam and Eve's experience, with more particulars than the Genesis account:** For instance, Mormons learn from these chapters that God first created everything spiritually before creating it physically. (When Mormons use the word *create,* they generally mean "form" or "organize," because they believe all spiritual and physical matter is eternal, not created.) In addition, these chapters touch on many aspects of God's plan of salvation and the uniquely positive Mormon outlook regarding the role of Adam and Eve.
- **New perspective on Adam's children and descendants:** Although Genesis only briefly mentions the prophet Enoch, the book of Moses provides several pages worth of Enoch's experiences and prophecies, which play an important role in Mormon doctrine, including what will happen in connection with the Savior's Second Coming. According to this section, Enoch led his people in such great righteousness that their entire city was taken up into heaven. This part also includes some additional chilling detail about Adam's bad seed, Cain.

Uncovering the writings of Abraham

In 1835, a traveling exhibit of Egyptian mummies and papyri passed through Kirtland, Ohio, where Joseph Smith was then living. After the Church purchased the papyri (in a package deal that included the mummies too), Joseph concluded that one papyrus contained writings of the Old Testament prophet Abraham, who lived about 2,000 years before Christ.

TECHNICAL STUFF

In the mid-1960s, a University of Utah professor discovered portions of Joseph Smith's Egyptian papyri in New York City's Metropolitan Museum of Art. Experts dated them as originating between 100 BCE and 100 CE, and translators found no resemblance to Joseph Smith's claimed translation. However, defenders point out that the papyri found in the museum may not have included the one containing Abraham's writings. Whatever the case, most Mormons continue exercising faith that divine revelation played a role in Joseph's translation of this document.

In the Pearl of Great Price, the five-chapter Book of Abraham covers the following territory:

- **The skinny on Abraham's origins and experiences:** The early chapters go into greater detail, including his ordination to the priesthood and his narrow escape from being sacrificed to pagan gods.
- **The Abrahamic covenant:** This covenant includes God's guarantee of a Promised Land, numberless descendants, priesthood authority, and eternal salvation. Mormons believe that anyone can enter into Abraham's covenant by joining the LDS Church, which Mormons view as the modern continuation of the same faith that Abraham practiced.
- **Details about sacred astronomy, an account of humankind's premortal existence, and a description of the earth's creation:** Abraham taught that the earth was formed from existing materials, not created out of nothing. (This scripture is one of the main reasons why Mormons reject the common Christian notion of creation out of nothing.) In addition, he calls the creative steps *times* rather than *days*, suggesting that the earth's creation took longer than six earthly days.
- **Three distinctively Egyptian images:** In 1842, Joseph Smith asked one of his followers to make woodcuts of some drawings from the papyri so he could print these images along with the translation. The pictures depict symbolic figures related to Abraham's experiences and his understanding of astronomy as discussed in the text, and it's not entirely clear to most Mormons why Joseph included these images. Still, during long meetings it's fun to puzzle over these *facsimiles*, as they're called.

Expanding Matthew

During Joseph Smith's prophetic revision — Mormons call it *retranslation* — of the KJV Bible, he made a particularly large number of changes to Matthew 24. This revised chapter now appears in the Pearl of Great Price as "Joseph Smith — Matthew." The original KJV chapter contains 1,050 words, but Joseph's version contains about 1,500 words.

In Matthew 24, the Savior gives several prophecies about two future times of trouble and destruction, including what would happen to Jerusalem soon after his death and what would happen before his Second Coming. As the KJV presents them, the chronology of these prophecies is hard to understand. Joseph's translation clarifies Jesus's distinction between the two time periods, which are separated by at least a couple thousand years.

Chronicling Joseph Smith

Although the first two sections in the Pearl of Great Price are from Old Testament times and the third section is from the New Testament era, the fourth section is an autobiographical account of Joseph Smith's early experiences as a prophet, which was first published in 1838. It covers events that occurred during the decade between 1820 and 1830. Titled "Joseph Smith — History," this part relates the following:

- **Religious upheaval:** In upstate New York during Joseph's boyhood, many churches were vying for members. Joseph writes that he felt it was vitally important to choose the right one.
- **Joseph's First Vision:** A Bible verse informed Joseph how to solve his dilemma: "If any of you lack wisdom, let him ask of God, that giveth to all men liberally, and upbraideth not; and it shall be given him" (James 1:5). In 1820, Joseph found a private grove of trees and knelt down to put James's promise to the test. Heavenly Father and Jesus Christ appeared to Joseph and told him not to join any of the existing churches.
- **The visitations of Moroni:** Over the next several years, Joseph was instructed several times by a resurrected being named Moroni, who in 421 CE buried the golden plates from which Joseph would translate the Book of Mormon.
- **More angelic visitors:** In 1829, after reading about baptism during the translation of the Book of Mormon, Joseph Smith and his scribe prayed to learn more. In response, the resurrected John the Baptist appeared to them, ordained them to the lower of Mormonism's two priesthoods, and instructed them to baptize each other. Soon after, the resurrected apostles Peter, James, and John ordained them to the higher priesthood. (See Book 7, Chapter 1 for more about the priesthood.)

Here, Joseph's Pearl of Great Price narration ends. Within another year or so, he published the Book of Mormon and formally organized what would subsequently become named The Church of Jesus Christ of Latter-day Saints. Further revelations and events dating from later in Joseph Smith's life are partially chronicled throughout the Doctrine and Covenants, described later in this chapter.

Lining up the Articles of Faith

In 1842, two years before his martyrdom (he was attacked and shot while in jail facing various charges, such as treason), Joseph Smith wrote a letter in response to some questions about Mormonism from a Chicago newspaper editor. Included in this letter were 13 statements of Mormon belief that later became canonized as Mormonism's Articles of Faith. This section occupies only two pages of the

Pearl of Great Price, and the individual articles are often the first scriptures that Mormon children memorize.

REMEMBER

Although the Articles of Faith touch on several important aspects of Mormonism, they aren't a comprehensive summary of Mormon beliefs. For instance, they don't say anything about humankind's premortal existence, the performance of gospel ordinances for the dead, eternal marriage, or humankind's potential to become like Heavenly Father. Rather, the Articles of Faith seem to function more as an introductory calling card to the faith, a way of establishing common ground with other Christians while also introducing some unique Mormon beliefs. These are the official statements of what Mormons believe:

1. We believe in God, the Eternal Father, and in His Son, Jesus Christ, and in the Holy Ghost.
2. We believe that men will be punished for their own sins, and not for Adam's transgression.
3. We believe that through the Atonement of Christ, all mankind may be saved, by obedience to the laws and ordinances of the Gospel.
4. We believe that the first principles and ordinances of the Gospel are: first, Faith in the Lord Jesus Christ; second, Repentance; third, Baptism by immersion for the remission of sins; fourth, Laying on of hands for the gift of the Holy Ghost.
5. We believe that a man must be called of God, by prophecy, and by the laying on of hands by those who are in authority, to preach the Gospel and administer in the ordinances thereof.
6. We believe in the same organization that existed in the Primitive Church, namely, apostles, prophets, pastors, teachers, evangelists, and so forth.
7. We believe in the gift of tongues, prophecy, revelation, visions, healing, interpretation of tongues, and so forth.
8. We believe the Bible to be the word of God as far as it is translated correctly; we also believe the Book of Mormon to be the word of God.
9. We believe all that God has revealed, all that He does now reveal, and we believe that He will yet reveal many great and important things pertaining to the Kingdom of God.
10. We believe in the literal gathering of Israel and in the restoration of the Ten Tribes; that Zion (the New Jerusalem) will be built upon this the American continent; that Christ will reign personally upon the earth; and, that the earth will be renewed and receive its paradisiacal glory.
11. We claim the privilege of worshiping Almighty God according to the dictates of our own conscience, and allow all men the same privilege, let them worship how, where, or what they may.

12. We believe in being subject to kings, presidents, rulers, and magistrates, in obeying, honoring, and sustaining the law.

13. We believe in being honest, true, chaste, benevolent, virtuous, and in doing good to all men; indeed, we may say that we follow the admonition of Paul — We believe all things, we hope all things, we have endured many things, and hope to be able to endure all things. If there is anything virtuous, lovely, or of good report or praiseworthy, we seek after these things.

Examining Modern-Day Revelations in the Doctrine and Covenants

As the ninth Article of Faith makes clear (see the previous section), Mormons don't see the canon as closed; they believe other scriptures are yet to come. Mormons trust that Heavenly Father is still revealing, and has yet to reveal, many "great and important things pertaining to the kingdom of God."

In this sense, Mormonism is a bit of a conundrum. On the one hand, Mormons claim to have fullness of truth, a restored gospel, and a Church organization established by Christ himself. On the other hand, they know that God hasn't yet spoken the last word on every subject, and they remain open to new revelations through the current prophet. At a minimum, Mormons realize that the Church's structure and programs continue to evolve to meet new needs and challenges.

In this section, we look at the Doctrine and Covenants, a canonized book of Mormon scripture that contains modern revelations, mostly from the 19th century.

God's revelations to Joseph Smith and others

Every president of the LDS Church is considered a *prophet*, *seer*, and *revelator*, which basically means that he has the spiritual authority to lead and guide the Church as God directs. Although any members of the Church can receive revelations pertaining to their own families, Church callings, and spiritual lives, Mormons believe that the prophet is the only one who can receive visions and revelations from God for the whole Church. Many of the Church's early revelations — and a handful of more recent prophetic statements — find their home in the Doctrine and Covenants, which Mormons affectionately call "the D&C."

Getting revelations

Almost all the revelations in the D&C came about because a prophet — usually Joseph Smith — had a question and prayed about it. The revelations are God's answers to specific questions, which is why so many of them open with the phrase "thus saith the Lord." For example, D&C 91 begins, "Verily, thus saith the Lord unto you concerning the Apocrypha." (The *Apocrypha* is the collection of ancient books that Catholics have as part of their biblical canon, but Protestants don't. Find out more in Book 5.) Joseph Smith was curious about the role of the Apocrypha when he retranslated portions of the Old Testament, so he asked God whether he should translate the Apocrypha, too. (Short answer: Translating it wasn't necessary, but it would be beneficial for study.)

The Mormon leader who received the most revelations, by far, is Joseph Smith, the religion's founder. Brigham Young has just one revelation in the entire D&C, and even that was basically how-to advice on organizing the Mormon pioneers for the trek west. The other prophets represented in the D&C include John Taylor, Wilford Woodruff, Joseph F. Smith (a son of Joseph's brother Hyrum), and Spencer W. Kimball. That leaves nine Mormon prophets who haven't added any revelations to the D&C, showing how rarely new scripture surfaces.

Tracing the evolution of the D&C

The D&C has gone through many different editions since the early 1830s, when the Church first published it under the title *A Book of Commandments*. Through the years, the Church has made changes to the collection's organization, removing some revelations, adding others, and combining others together. The book now contains 138 sections, plus a couple of official declarations (see "Wrapping up: Official declarations," later in this chapter).

The earliest editions contained the *Lectures on Faith*, unsigned discourses on faith that Sidney Rigdon or Joseph Smith may have written. Although Mormons still occasionally quote from these seven lectures, they haven't been part of the D&C since 1921.

How does the Church choose which revelations to include? The First Presidency and Quorum of the Twelve Apostles make this decision, with the consent of Church members who affirm it in General Conference. However, it's unusual nowadays for changes to be made to the D&C.

TIP

If you're new to Mormon culture, you may be surprised to find that Mormons don't use the same chapter and verse system for the D&C that they do for the other standard works. Each revelation is its own *section*, which is then subdivided into verses. So, a Mormon vegetarian may draw on section 89, verse 13 of the D&C to try to persuade a meat-eating Mormon that there's a scriptural precedent for abstaining from meat. Then the meat-eater would quote section 49, verse 19, which seems pretty clear that eating meat is okay.

Wrapping up: Official declarations

The closing pages of the Doctrine and Covenants feature two official declarations that represent a different mode of prophetic communication than the preceding 138 sections. Both of these declarations demonstrate that Mormonism is an evolving, dynamic religion in which belief in continuing revelation can cause 180-degree turns in direction, as the Spirit guides.

Making polygamy a no-no

The first of these official declarations is unusual in that it doesn't seem to come directly from the mouth of God. You may even consider it to be more of a press release than a revelation, because it begins with the bureaucratic statement, "Press dispatches having been sent for political purposes." Dated October 6, 1890, and read aloud to the members at General Conference, the statement basically bans the continued practice of plural marriage because of congressional laws forbidding it.

Now known as the *Woodruff Manifesto* because LDS President Wilford Woodruff wrote it, the document was widely circulated to smooth the Mormons' strained relations with the federal government and pave the way for Utah's statehood, which Congress finally approved in 1896.

Immediately after President Woodruff's declaration, a few members continued quietly entering plural marriage. President Woodruff warned in late 1891 that the Lord had shown him through a vision the trouble the Mormons would face if they didn't abandon polygamy. In 1904, the Church issued a clearer statement that absolutely prohibited new plural marriages and promised excommunication for anyone who disobeyed. That statement, or *Second Manifesto*, isn't in the D&C, but it's binding on all Latter-day Saints.

Extending the priesthood to all races

The other official declaration in the D&C is from June 1978, when the Church extended the priesthood to "all worthy male members" regardless of race. Before that time, the priesthood was denied to any man of African ancestry, a policy that offended many members and nonmembers alike.

Modern revelations not found in the D&C

Just because a prophetic teaching isn't contained in the four standard works of Mormonism doesn't mean that it doesn't carry the weight of scripture for most Mormons. In addition to the canonized revelations that appear in the D&C, recent prophets have made other statements that are widely regarded as modern additions to scripture. In fact, any time a prophet speaks in the capacity of his holy office, Mormons consider his words to be scripture.

Picturing the ideal family

In 1995, the *First Presidency* (the prophet and his two counselors) and Quorum of the Twelve Apostles released a statement that has since assumed the status of gospel. Its official name is "The Family: A Proclamation to the World," but most Latter-day Saints just call it the "Proclamation on the Family." We wouldn't be surprised to see it appear in future editions of LDS scriptures some years from now. In the meantime, the statement is springing up in kitschy, mass-market calligraphic editions that some members frame and display.

REMEMBER

Basically, the proclamation sets forth the Church's position on gender and family responsibilities more specifically than ever before, putting it all in theological perspective. Although the language is usually gentle, the message is clear: Mormons believe in traditional gender roles and the sacred nature of the nuclear family. The proclamation explains that

- **Gender is an eternal characteristic that follows a person before, during, and after mortal life.** In other words, our gender here on earth is the gender we've always been in the premortal world and always will be in the hereafter.
- **Marriage is between a man and a woman.** Not only does this proclamation rule out homosexual marriage, but it also slams the door on marriage between one man and several women, as some 19th-century Mormons practiced.
- **Children deserve to be raised in a home where parents honor their marriage vows completely.** The proclamation affirms that sex is a gift from God that people should enjoy only within the bonds of heterosexual marriage. What's more, the proclamation clarifies that sexual fidelity alone is not enough to guarantee a happy marriage; husbands and wives also need to practice forgiveness, compassion, and mutual respect. This part of the proclamation gently signals the Church's preference that children born to single mothers should generally be placed for adoption by a couple.
- **The primary duty of fathers is to preside over their families and provide for their material needs, while the first responsibility of mothers is to nurture their children.** Husband and wife are expected to honor one

another as equal partners in the fulfillment of these responsibilities. Although the proclamation doesn't pronounce dire punishments on women who work outside the home and even makes allowances for special circumstances, the general ideal is clear.

The proclamation closes with specific warnings against domestic abuse, adultery, and other moral failures, saying that people who engage in such behaviors will be held accountable before God. This proclamation is unusual in that it's worded as a warning to the whole world, not just Mormons.

Day-to-day wisdom from the prophet

In addition to the "Proclamation on the Family," any guidance that the General Authorities give during General Conference assumes the status of *de facto* scripture for Mormons. However, any Mormon who reads history knows that what some prophets (and other Church leaders) spoke in the past isn't necessarily Church doctrine today. The primary example of this situation is polygamy, of course; most 19th-century LDS leaders practiced it and preached glowing sermons about it from the pulpit. Obviously, though, Mormons don't feel this way today, and no prophet of the Church has sanctioned polygamy in over a century.

REMEMBER

So what happens when the teachings of LDS prophets seem to collide? The basic rule is that according to the doctrine of continuing revelation, the Lord continues to reveal more light and knowledge on various subjects as people are ready for it. In other words, a living prophet always trumps a dead prophet. Mormons expect that some Church programs will change as society evolves and the Lord offers new revelations.

Index

A

B

C

D

E

F

G

H

I

J

K

L

M

N

O

P

Q

R

S

T

U

V

W

X

Y

Z

About the Authors

Christopher Kimball Bigelow is the great-great-great-grandson of a Mormon apostle who had more than 40 wives. He served an LDS mission in Melbourne, Australia, and worked as an editor at the LDS Church's official *Ensign* magazine. A graduate of Emerson College and Brigham Young University, Bigelow cofounded and edited the Mormon literary magazine *Irreantum*.

David Blatner is a Seattle-based writer whose books have sold over a half-million copies and have been translated into 14 languages. He has presented seminars in North America, Australia, Asia, the Middle East, and Europe, and can be found online at 63p.com.

Stephan Bodian began practicing Zen meditation in 1969 and was ordained a monk in 1974 after studying Buddhism and other Asian religions at Columbia University. In addition to authoring several books, including *Meditation For Dummies*, and numerous magazine articles, Stephan was editor-in-chief of the magazine *Yoga Journal* for ten years.

Rev. Fr. Kenneth Brighenti, PhD, KGCO, served as a U.S. Naval Reserve Chaplain for ten years and, in 1988, was ordained a priest for the Diocese of Metuchen (New Jersey), where he served as pastor of St. Ann's Parish (Raritan, New Jersey) for more than eight years. Father Brighenti has co-authored many books, including *Saints For Dummies* and *Catholic Mass For Dummies*.

Gudrun Bühnemann earned her PhD in Buddhist and Classical Indian Studies from the University of Vienna in Austria in 1980. She later joined the University of Wisconsin – Madison, and authored and edited more than 15 scholarly books and numerous articles.

Warren Malcolm Clark (who goes by Malcolm) is Professor of Religion Emeritus at Butler University in Indianapolis, Indiana, where he taught for 30 years. Professor Clark's undergraduate degree is in American History from Harvard University, and he holds a Master of Divinity and PhD from Yale.

Rabbi Ted Falcon, PhD, one of the pioneers of Jewish spirituality within the Reform Jewish context, was ordained in 1968 from the Hebrew Union College – Jewish Institute of Religion, in Cincinnati, Ohio. He received a doctorate from the California School of Professional Psychology in 1975 and is a nationally recognized lecturer and teacher.

Rabbi Marc Gellman has written two volumes of modern Bible interpretations (midrashim) for children and is a past president of the New York Board of Rabbis. Rabbi Gellman holds an earned doctorate in Philosophy from Northwestern University. He is married to Betty Schulson and has two children, Mara and Max.

Monsignor Thomas Hartman has written books, including *The Matter of Life and Death: Surviving Loss and Finding Hope* and *Just a Moment: Life Matters with Father Tom.* Monsignor Hartman holds an earned Doctorate of Ministry degree from the Jesuit School of Theology at Berkeley, California.

Jonathan R. Herman received his PhD in Chinese Religion from Harvard University in 1992. He has since taught at Georgia State University in Atlanta, Harvard University, Boston College, Tufts University, the University of Vermont, and Lewis & Clark College, and he served for 12 years as an officer in the Society for the Study of Chinese Religions.

Jonathan Landaw attended Dartmouth College in New Hampshire, where he was exposed to and developed his lifelong interest in Buddhism. He later went on to attend graduate school at the University of California in Berkeley and then served in the Peace Corps. By 1972, Jon was studying Buddhism full-time and working as an English editor of the texts being produced by the Translation Bureau of His Holiness the Dalai Lama at the Library of Tibetan Works and Archives in Dharamsala, India.

William Paul Lazarus has taught at various institutions, including Daytona Beach Community College and Stetson University. A professional writer, he regularly speaks at churches and synagogues around Florida and had a successful radio show on 1340-AM, WROD, in Daytona Beach.

Jana Riess, PhD, is the author of *The Spiritual Traveler: Boston and New England* and *What Would Buffy Do? The Vampire Slayer as Spiritual Guide*. She holds degrees in religion from Wellesley College and Princeton Theological Seminary, and a PhD in American Religious History from Columbia University.

Dr. Amrutur Venkatachar Srinivasan is a popular writer and speaker and has published and presented numerous papers on a variety of cultural, social, and religious issues in the United States and India. He has taught courses on the classical literature of India at the University of Connecticut and Wesleyan University.

Annie Sullivan received her bachelor's degree from Indiana University and holds a master's degree in Creative Writing from Butler University. She is a co-author of *Catholicism All-In-One For Dummies, 2nd Edition*, and the author of several young adult fantasy books.

Mark Sullivan attended Columbia University, where he studied Comparative Literature and European Languages. He later attended the Juilliard School of Music for studies in composition. He has worked in book publishing in various roles, and his interests include languages, music, swimming, and travel.

Rev. Fr. John Trigilio, Jr., PhD, ThD, KGCO, is the former Director of Pastoral Formation and currently Formation Advisor, Spiritual Director, and Faculty Member at Mount St. Mary's Seminary, Emmitsburg, Maryland. He is a member of the Fellowship of Catholic Scholars and was ordained a priest for the Diocese of Harrisburg (Pennsylvania) in 1988.

Richard Wagner is the author of numerous books, including *Christian Prayer For Dummies*. Rich has served in church leadership and teaching roles for more than a dozen years. He graduated with a bachelor of arts degree from Taylor University and pursued graduate studies at The American University in Washington, D.C.

Publisher's Acknowledgments

Acquisitions Editor: Jennifer Yee

Compilation Editor: Annie Sullivan

Senior Managing Editor: Kristie Pyles

Cover Image: © leolintang/Getty Images